Media/Society

Sixth Edition

Sara Miller McCune founded SAGE Publishing in 1965 to support the dissemination of usable knowledge and educate a global community. SAGE publishes more than 1000 journals and over 800 new books each year, spanning a wide range of subject areas. Our growing selection of library products includes archives, data, case studies and video. SAGE remains majority owned by our founder and after her lifetime will become owned by a charitable trust that secures the company's continued independence.

Los Angeles | London | New Delhi | Singapore | Washington DC | Melbourne

Media/Society

Technology, Industries, Content, and Users

Sixth Edition

David Croteau
Virginia Commonwealth University

William Hoynes
Vassar College

Los Angeles | London | New Delhi
Singapore | Washington DC | Melbourne

FOR INFORMATION:

SAGE Publications, Inc.
2455 Teller Road
Thousand Oaks, California 91320
E-mail: order@sagepub.com

SAGE Publications Ltd.
1 Oliver's Yard
55 City Road
London EC1Y 1SP
United Kingdom

SAGE Publications India Pvt. Ltd.
B 1/I 1 Mohan Cooperative Industrial Area
Mathura Road, New Delhi 110 044
India

SAGE Publications Asia-Pacific Pte. Ltd.
3 Church Street
#10-04 Samsung Hub
Singapore 049483

Acquisitions Editor: Terri Accomazzo
Content Development Editor: Anna Villarruel
Editorial Assistant: Sarah Wilson
Production Editor: Tracy Buyan
Copy Editor: Pam Schroeder
Typesetter: C&M Digitals (P) Ltd.
Proofreader: Caryne Brown
Indexer: Judy Hunt
Cover Designer: Janet Kiesel
Marketing Manager: Staci Wittek

Printed in the United States of America

Library of Congress Cataloging-in-Publication Data

Names: Croteau, David, author. | Hoynes, William, author.

Title: Media/society : technology, industries, content, and users / David

Croteau, Virginia Commonwealth University, USA,
William Hoynes, Vassar College, USA.

Description: Sixth edition. | Thousand Oaks, California : SAGE, [2019] | Includes bibliographical references and index.

Identifiers: LCCN 2018017400 | ISBN 9781506315331 (pbk. : alk. paper)

Subjects: LCSH: Mass media—Social aspects—United States. | Mass media—Political aspects—United States.

Classification: LCC HN90.M3 C76 2019 | DDC 302.230973—dc23
LC record available at https://lccn.loc.gov/2018017400

This book is printed on acid-free paper.

SUSTAINABLE FORESTRY INITIATIVE

Certified Chain of Custody
Promoting Sustainable Forestry
www.sfiprogram.org
SFI-01268

SFI label applies to text stock

18 19 20 21 22 10 9 8 7 6 5 4 3 2 1

BRIEF CONTENTS

Preface   xv

Acknowledgments   xxi

PART I • **INTRODUCTION**   **1**

Chapter 1 • Media/Society in a Digital World   2

PART II • **TECHNOLOGY**   **23**

Chapter 2 • The Evolution of Media Technology   24

PART III • **INDUSTRY**   **61**

Chapter 3 • The Economics of the Media Industry   62

Chapter 4 • Political Influence on Media   107

Chapter 5 • Media Organizations and Professionals   151

PART IV • **CONTENT**   **189**

Chapter 6 • Media and Ideology   190

Chapter 7 • Social Inequality and Media Representation   225

PART V • **USERS**   **267**

Chapter 8 • Audiences and Creators   268

Chapter 9 • Media Influence   300

PART VI • **AFTERWORD**   **341**

Chapter 10 • Globalization and the Future of Media   342

References   373

Index   415

About the Authors   465

DETAILED CONTENTS

Preface   xv

Acknowledgments   xxi

PART I • INTRODUCTION   1

Chapter 1 • Media/Society in a Digital World   2

The Importance of Media   3

Models of Communication Media   7

    Interpersonal and "Mass" Communication   7

    Variable Boundaries and Active Users   8

    Communication Today: A First Look   9

A Sociology of Media   10

    The Sociological Perspective   11

    Structural Constraint and Human Agency   12

       Structure   12

       Agency   13

    Structure and Agency in the Media   13

       Relationships between the Media and Other Social Institutions   14

       Relationships within the Media Industry   14

       Relationships between the Media and the Public   15

A Model of Media and the Social World   16

Applying the Model: Civil Rights in Two Media Eras   18

    Mid-20th-Century Civil Rights Movement   18

    Black Lives Matter   20

Conclusion   21

Discussion Questions   22

PART II • TECHNOLOGY   23

Chapter 2 • The Evolution of Media Technology   24

The History of Media Technology   25

Technological Determinism and Social Constructionism   28

    Technological Determinism   28

    Media's Materiality   29

"Autonomous Technology" and "Technological Momentum"   30

Medium Theory   31

    McLuhan's Optimism   32

    Postman's Pessimism   33

Social Constructionism   35

From Print to the Internet   **36**

The Print Medium   36

The Telegraph   38

The Telephone   38

Sound Recording   42

Film and Video   45

Radio Broadcasting   46

Television   50

    Television and Daily Life   50

    Cable Television   52

The Internet   54

    Creating the Internet   54

    The Internet Grows Up   56

    Some Characteristics of the Internet Era   57

Conclusion   **59**

Discussion Questions   **60**

PART III • INDUSTRY   **61**

Chapter 3 • The Economics of the Media Industry   **62**

Media Companies in the Internet Era   **64**

Products   64

Platforms   65

Pipes   66

Changing Patterns of Ownership   **67**

Concentration of Ownership   67

    Products   68

    Platforms   72

    Pipes   73

Conglomeration and Integration   74

Strategy in a New Media Economy   78

The Power of Platforms: Facebook and Google as New Media Giants   79

    Users   80

    Media Content   80

    Advertising   81

    Telecommunications   82

Consequences of Conglomeration and Integration   **83**

Integration and Self-Promotion   83

The Impact of Conglomeration   84

The Effects of Concentration   85
    Media Control and Political Power   86
    Media Ownership and Content Diversity   90

Mass Media for Profit   92
    Prime-Time Profits   92
    Cheaper Programs for Smaller Audiences   94
    Controlling Content and Distribution   95
    Profit and the News Media   96

The Impact of Advertising   98
    The Advertising-Content Connection   98
    Advertising and the Press in the 19th Century   100
      The British Press   100
      The U.S. Press   102
    Advertising and the Contemporary News Media   103

Conclusion   105

Discussion Questions   106

Chapter 4 • Political Influence on Media   **107**

Media and Democracy   108

Free Speech to Free Markets: The Evolution of U.S. Regulatory Policy   109
    Regulate or Deregulate?   110
    The FCC's Variable Role   111

Regulation in International Perspective   113
    Regulation in Western Democracies   114
    Regulation in Developing Nations   115

Competing Interests and the Regulation Debate   116
    Industry Influence: Elections and Lobbying   117
    Citizen Action: The Case of Low-Power Radio   117
    Left and Right: Diversity versus Property Rights   120

Regulating Ownership   121
    Media Outlets   121
    Copyright and Intellectual Property   124

Regulating Content   126
    Accuracy: Advertising   126
    Diversity: The Fairness Doctrine   127
    Morality: Obscene Materials   129
    Self-Regulation: Censorship and Ratings   130
      Movie Censorship and the Ratings System   130
      Television Ratings   132
      Music Parental Advisory Labels and Video Games   132
    The "National Interest": Military Censorship   134

Regulating Access and Distribution   136
    Net Neutrality   136
      The Concept of Net Neutrality   137

The Policy Battle   137

The Implications   138

Vertical Integration: Movies, TV, and Streaming   139

The Hollywood Studio System   139

Television's Fyn-Syn Regulations   140

Netflix and the Streaming Wars   141

Social Media Platforms   142

What Are Platforms?   143

Social Media Regulation   144

Self-Policing   146

Informal Political, Social, and Economic Pressure   147

Conclusion   149

Discussion Questions   150

Chapter 5 • Media Organizations and Professionals   **151**

The Limits of Economic and Political Constraints   152

Working within Economic Constraints   152

Responding to Political Constraints   153

Decision Making for Profit: Imitation, Hits, and Stars   154

High Costs and Unpredictable Tastes   155

Art Imitating Art   155

Stars and the "Hit System"   156

Creating Hits and Producing Stars   158

Using Stars to Combat Uncertainty   159

Beyond Stars to a Universe of Products   160

The Organization of Media Work   161

Conventions   162

News Routines and Their Consequences   163

Technology and the New News Routines   166

Increased Economic Pressure   166

Expanded Volume and Diversified Sourcing   166

Increased Speed   167

Presentation and Engagement to Promote Traffic   168

Newsroom Automation   169

Objectivity   170

The Origins of Objectivity   171

Objectivity as Routine Practices and Their Political Consequences   172

Rejecting Objectivity: Alternative Journalism   173

Occupational Roles and Professional Socialization   175

Roles   175

Photography   176

Socialization of Photographers   177

Photographers' Work Roles and Organizational Goals   179

Editorial Decision Making   180

    The Work of the Book Editor   181

    Scholarly Publishing   183

Norms on the Internet, New Media, and New Organizations   185

Conclusion   188

Discussion Questions   188

PART IV • CONTENT   189

Chapter 6 • Media and Ideology   190

What Is Ideology?   191

  Ideology and the "Real" World   191

  Dominant Ideology versus Cultural Contradictions   192

  The "Culture War" Battles over Ideology   193

  Ideology as Normalization   194

Theoretical Roots of Ideological Analysis   196

  Early Marxist Origins   196

  Hegemony   197

News Media and the Limits of Debate   201

  Elites and Insiders   201

  Economic News as Ideological Construct   202

Movies, the Military, and Masculinity   204

  Action-Adventure Films   205

  Vietnam Films and Recent War Films   206

Television, Popularity, and Ideology   208

  Television and Reality   208

  Television and the Changing American Family   210

  Revising Tradition: The New Momism   212

Rap Music as Ideological Critique?   213

Advertising and Consumer Culture   216

  Selling Consumerism in the Early 20th Century   217

  Women's Magazines as Advertisements   218

Advertising and the Globalization of Culture   219

Internet Ideology   222

Conclusion   224

Discussion Questions   224

Chapter 7 • Social Inequality and Media Representation   225

Comparing Media Content and the "Real" World   226

The Significance of Content   228

Race, Ethnicity, and Media Content: Inclusion, Roles, and Control   231
    Racial and Ethnic Diversity in Media Content   232
    Growing Diversity and Abundance amid Audience Fragmentation   235
    Race, Ethnicity, and Media Roles   237
        Early Images of Race   238
        Slow Change and "Modern" Racism   239
        Race and Class   244
    Controlling Media Images of Race   244

Gender and Media Content   246
    Women: Presence and Control in the Media   247
    Changing Media Roles for Women . . . and Men   247
    The Case of Women's Sports   249

Class and the Media   251
    Class and Media Content   252
        Family-Based Situation Comedies   252
        Tabloid Talk Shows and Reality Television   254
        The Union Taboo   257
        News Media   258
        Advertising   259
    Explaining Class Images: "Some People Are More
    Valuable Than Others"   260

Sexual Orientation: Out of the Closet and into the Media   262

Conclusion   266

Discussion Questions   266

PART V • USERS   267

Chapter 8 • Audiences and Creators   268

The Active Audience: Balancing Agency and Structure   269
    Polysemy: Media's Multiple Meanings   270
    Interpretive Constraint: Encoding/Decoding and
    Social Structure   271

Decoding Meanings and Social Position   272
    Class and Nationwide News   272
    Gender, Class, and Television   273
    Race, News, and Meaning Making   274
    Resistance and Feminist Identity   275
    International Readings of American Television   276
    Making Meaning Online: Second Screens   278
    Social Position Online: Black Twitter   279

The Pleasures of Media: Celebrity Games   281

The Social Context of Media Use   283
    Romance Novels and the Act of Reading   283
    Watching Television with the Family   284

The Limits of Interpretation 285

From Active Audience to Resistant Actors 286

Interpretive Resistance and Feminist Politics 286

Culture Jamming 287

Content Creation and Distribution 288

Participatory Culture 289

Participation Online 290

Who Are the Content Creators? 293

Why Create? 294

Media Fans 295

Users as Gatekeepers and Distributors 296

Conclusion 298

Discussion Questions 299

Chapter 9 • Media Influence 300

Learning from Media Effects Research 301

Early Works: Establishing the Agenda 302

The Press and Democracy 302

Entertainment and Children 303

Mass Society and Media Influence 304

Mitigating Media Effects 305

Limited Effects and the Two-Step Flow of Influence 305

Active Audiences 306

Highlighting Media Influence 307

Agenda Setting and Framing 307

Framing: Second-Level Agenda Setting 308

New Agenda-Setting Players in the Internet Era 308

The Spiral of Silence 309

Learning from Media 311

Cultivation Theory 312

Mediatization 313

The Concept of Mediatization 314

The Mediatization of Society and Media Logic 315

The Mediatization of Politics 316

The Politics of Image 317

Political Actors 317

Setting the Stage 319

The Decline of Political Parties 320

Communication Professionals and "Post-Truth" Politics 321

Working with the News Media 321

Using the Internet 322

Social Movements 324

Citizen Alienation 326

The Internet's Uncertain Political Future 326

Digital Dilemmas: Online Media Influence   328
   Social Media Logic and Algorithmic Power   328
   The Crisis in Journalism   331
   Information Distortions: Misinformation and Echo Chambers   332
   Computational Propaganda: Trolls and Twitter Bots   334
   Hate and Censorship   336
   Managing our Social Selves   337
Conclusion   340
Discussion Questions   340

PART VI • AFTERWORD   341

Chapter 10 • Globalization and the Future of Media   342

What Is Globalization?   343
   Crossing Limits of Time and Space   344
   Crossing Cultural Boundaries   345
   The Promise and Reality of Media Globalization   346
The Global Media Industry   348
   Global Products, Centralized Ownership   348
   Traditional Media: Disney Worldwide   350
   The New Global Media Giants: Google and Facebook   352
Interpreting Global Media Content   355
   Cultural Imperialism and Its Limits   355
   Global Culture Clash?   357
   Hybrid Culture   358
Regulating Global Media   360
   The Politics of Information Flow   360
   Internet Governance   363
   Preserving Diversity   364
Global Media Users: Limits of the "Global Village"   366
The Ubiquity of Change and the Future of Media   369
Discussion Questions   371

References   373
Index   415
About the Authors   465

PREFACE

Aprés tant de bouleversements, de changements, il serait temps de s'apercevoir d'une chose. . . . Plus ça change—plus c'est la même chose.

After so many upheavals and changes, it would be time to notice one thing. . . .

The more it changes, the more it's the same thing.

—Alphonse Karr (1849: 305)

An epigram from 170 years ago serves as an apt reminder for us today: When it comes to media, everything has changed, yet much is the same.

The change is obvious. The rise of the internet, mobile communications, and social networks formed a "Triple Revolution" (Rainie and Wellman 2012) that enabled the transformation of the "media" (and much more) in our society. It's impossible not to notice the "crisis in journalism" (Curran 2011; McChesney 2007); the new television landscape (Robinson 2017); the redesigned music industry (Vonderau 2017); the expanding "connective media" of social platforms (van Dijck 2013); the intrusive commercial online surveillance (Turow 2011); the blurring between interpersonal and mass communication (Jenkins 2006); and the pervasive "culture of search" in the age of Google (Hillis, Petit, and Jarrett 2012), to name just a few.

Although change is obvious, persistence is easy to overlook. But with media, the more things change, the more they really do stay the same. Early techno-enthusiasts with their "digital optimism" (Turner 2010) suggested that the internet was so exceptional and transformative that everything we knew about media was obsolete. But the maturing internet has told a different—and more familiar—story. The new social networks spend a good deal of time reacting to the agendas set by the old mainstream media (Redden and Witschge, 2010). Internet access and social media space have come to be dominated by just a few giant corporations, leading to old-fashioned calls for "a rigorous discussion of the political economy of these social media monopolies" (Lovink 2013:11). The online posting of videos depicting beheadings by terrorist groups and the Russian use of Facebook and Twitter to interfere in the 2016 U.S. presidential election have reignited legal and popular debates about regulating these online spaces (Roberts 2017; Wu 2015). Teens tethered to smartphones are raising panicky public concern about the social impact of media use (Twenge 2017). And so it goes. Issues of media ownership and control, regulation, commercialization, and social impact—long among the staple topics of media studies—are as relevant today as ever.

We originally wrote *Media/Society* more than two decades ago in a very different media environment, before the "three revolutions" had fully developed. Although subsequent editions have addressed the ongoing changes in the media landscape, this sixth edition further integrates these changes throughout the book. Many of these changes are visible, including a retitling and reordering of chapters, the streamlining and reorganization of most chapters, and even a newly tweaked subtitle to better reflect the book's content and organization. In addition, this new edition features many less-visible changes, including updates to data, research findings, and examples, all of which help this edition better reflect our current media reality.

While reflecting the changing media landscape, we have been careful to retain the core framework, structure, and historical examples in *Media/Society*. These have made the book a favorite in mass communication, sociology, media studies, and political science courses addressing the media's role in society. The fascinating developments of the recent years raise fresh questions and issues for students of media. But they do not displace the sorts of questions that have always animated the study of media, including the following:

- How has the evolution of technology affected the media and how we use them?

- How does the business of media operate, and why does this matter?

- How do the professional norms, economic influences, and regulatory constraints that characterize media institutions influence what we see (or don't see) in our media?

- How well does media content reflect the range of realities in our society and our world?

- How are people today using the media and digital communications in their everyday lives?

- What influences do the media seem to be having on us and our society?

These sorts of questions were at the heart of *Media/Society* in its first edition, and they continue to animate this latest edition.

So, more specifically, what changes can you find in the sixth edition? Key changes— and some questions they raise—include the following:

- **A reordering of chapters.** More than ever, we need to understand how changes in digital technology have helped transform media. Therefore, we've expanded our discussion of media technology, deepened our historical overview, and moved it forward in the book. This helps better frame later discussions, which emphasize how social influences ultimately determine the ways technology is used.

- **A broader cast of characters.** Although creators of traditional media—print, radio, television, and film—remain essential, today's media also includes important players in the form of "platforms" (a term we investigate critically), search engines, and distributors. Facebook, Google, Twitter, Netflix—even Amazon and Apple—are among the actors to be reckoned with in the contemporary media environment, as are older—and now integrated—telecommunications firms like Comcast, AT&T, and Verizon. What role do these companies play in the media landscape? How do they make money? What are the ripple effects of their business models?

- **A reconsideration of content in an era of abundance.** Historically, media was characterized by scarcity. But finite airwaves, fixed airtime, and limited distribution have been supplanted by countless streaming options, deep on-demand catalogs, lower production costs, and diversifying producers. What is the significance of this abundance of content? How real is the new diversity?

- **A focus on the expanded role of users.** We've always acknowledged that audiences are active participants in the media process and have long noted the growth of user-generated content. This edition marks the full embrace of "users" as encompassing everything from consumption and interpretation of media to commenting on and creating media content. How do social media platforms that enable user participation change the media environment? How does users' digital labor provide the energy that fuels these platforms? How do users navigate their roles—audience, creator, consumer, citizen—in this complex environment?

- **A look at media as lived experience.** With smartphones to facilitate both access to traditional media and communication via social media, the ubiquity of media has reached unprecedented levels. Media no longer comprise products to consume but instead are fully integrated into a lifestyle where digital media and face-to-face interactions are interwoven. What do we know about the potential impact on users of this new way of living?

- **A deeper dive into recent issues.** Privacy, internet consolidation, the rising influence of algorithms, new monopolies, "fake news," propaganda, and invasive marketing are among the topics given a thorough introduction in various parts of the book. What are the cautionary red flags of today's media landscape? What issues remain to be grappled with?

- **A clarification of media.** There used to be a fairly clear distinction between interpersonal communication and "mass media." Now, though, the lines are blurred—or at least are variable. In response, Chapter 1 has an expanded introduction to simple media models that considers what "media" are and what constitutes "mass" media in our time.

- **A global perspective.** We've always included a look at media in a global context and the issues raised by globalization. We continue this tradition, sometimes integrating these discussions into a chapter and returning in more depth to them in the afterword on globalization and the future of media. The global media industry, regulation of media globally, social media use around the world, and so on, are all topics we explore.

- **Streamlined writing.** We've streamlined many sections of the book, trimming nonessential material and relaxing the language a bit to welcome students more easily.

If you are a longtime user of *Media/Society*, we hope you'll find the framework and focus of the text comfortably familiar, while the new content serves as a stimulating update and makeover. For new adopters, you've chosen a perfect time to come aboard as we take a fresh look at our contemporary media and consider the fascinating changes still to come.

In the end, we hope *Media/Society* continues to be a valuable tool to help students think critically about the media and their role in daily life. That critical framework is one that will always be relevant, whatever the future of media turns out to be.

DIGITAL RESOURCES

SAGE edge for Instructors supports your teaching by making it easy to integrate quality content and create a rich learning environment for students. Visit **http://edge.sagepub .com/croteau6e**.

- **Test banks** provide a diverse range of pre-written options as well as the opportunity to edit any question and/or insert your own personalized questions to effectively assess students' progress and understanding.

- Editable chapter-specific **PowerPoint® slides** offer complete flexibility for creating a multimedia presentation for your course.

- **Sample course syllabi** for semester and quarter courses provide suggested models for structuring your courses.

- Lively and stimulating **ideas for chapter and web activities** that can be used in class to reinforce active learning. The activities apply to individual or group projects.

- **Chapter-specific discussion questions** to help launch engaging classroom interaction while reinforcing important content

- EXCLUSIVE! Access to full-text **SAGE journal articles** that have been carefully selected to support and expand on the concepts presented in each chapter is included.

- **Multimedia content** includes third-party video, audio, and web resources that appeal to diverse learners.

- **Lecture notes** summarize key concepts by chapter to help you prepare for lectures and class discussions.

SAGE edge for Students provides a personalized approach to help students accomplish their coursework goals in an easy-to-use learning environment. Visit **http://edge.sagepub .com/croteau6e**.

- Mobile-friendly **eFlashcards** strengthen understanding of key terms and concepts.

- Mobile-friendly practice **quizzes** allow for independent assessment by students of their mastery of course material.

- **Multimedia content** includes third-party video, audio, and web resources that appeal to diverse learners.

- <u>EXCLUSIVE</u>! Access to full-text **SAGE journal articles** that have been carefully selected to support and expand on the concepts presented in each chapter is included.

ACKNOWLEDGMENTS

There are countless people who have helped make the six editions of this book possible. We are especially grateful to Udbhav Agarwal, Kassia Arbabi, Henry Bartlett, Johanna Buchignani, Matthew Dillard, Dave Gray, David Hurley, Marilyn Kennepohl, Caroline Lee, Kristin Monroe, Corrina Regnier, Mollie Sandberg, Jacinthe Sasson-Yenor, Heather Tomlins, and Kate Wood for their research assistance over the years. Thanks to Clayton Childress for his valuable suggestions during the early stages of preparing the fourth edition and to Stefania Milan for her contributions to the fourth edition. Thanks to the folks at Virginia Commonwealth University's Academic Learning Transformation Lab (ALT Lab), especially Tom Woodward, for provocative discussions about the promise—not just the perils—of the internet. Thank you to Pine Forge founder Steve Rutter for his assistance and encouragement on the first two editions of the book. We appreciate the support and assistance of the staff at SAGE as we prepared this new edition. We are grateful to the many SAGE and Pine Forge reviewers, who have provided very helpful comments on previous editions of *Media/Society*:

Terri L. Anderson, *University of California, Los Angeles*

Ronald Becker, *Miami University–Ohio*

Vince Carducci, *College for Creative Studies*

Victor P. Corona, *Polytechnic Institute of New York University*

Jiska Engelbert, *Erasmus University Rotterdam (The Netherlands)*

Paul Mason Fotsch, *New York University*

Donna L. Halper, *Lesley University*

John Hochheimer, *Southern Illinois University–Carbondale*

Aniko Imre, *University of Southern California*

Nick Jankowski, *University of Illinois at Chicago*

Dana Kaufman, *DePaul University*

Gholam Khiabany, *London Metropolitan University*

Osman Koroglu, *Fatih University*

Martin Lang, *Gustavus Adolphus College*

Linda Levitt, *Stephen F. Austin State University*

Eric Louw, *University of Queensland*

Michael H. McBride, *Texas State University–San Marcos*

Ryan Moore, *Florida Atlantic University*

Lisa M. Paulin, *North Carolina Central University*

Jeff Ritter, *La Roche College*

Gabriel Rossman, *University of California, Los Angeles*

Matthew Schneirov, *Duquesne University*

Fred Turner, *Stanford University*

Phyllis S. Zrzavy, *Franklin Pierce University*

And thank you to the reviewers of the current edition:

Jane Bloodworth Rowe, *Old Dominion University*

Stephen Hagan, *McKendree University*

Seong-Jae Min, *Pace University*

Ola Ogunyemi, *University of Lincoln, UK*

Abhijit Sen, *Winston-Salem State University*

We would also like to thank the students who have taken our media courses over the years. Their questions and concerns have kept us honest and provided wonderful fuel for thought.

Thanks to Ben and Nick Hoynes for providing their father with a continuing lesson about the complex role of the media. Finally, special thanks, as always, from David to Cecelia Kirkman and from Bill to Deirdre Burns—for everything.

INTRODUCTION

Chapter 1 serves as an introduction and overview of the book. We note the central role media play in our lives and present a model for understanding the media that helps organize the book. This framework highlights the push-pull relationships among elements of the media system—the industry, users, content, and technology—all of which are embedded in a larger social context. Understanding these elements and how they interact is crucial for tackling enduring questions about the media in any era.

PART I

1

MEDIA/SOCIETY IN A DIGITAL WORLD

In the 21st century, we routinely navigate through a dense media environment unprecedented in human history. Our everyday lives are saturated with words, pictures, videos, and sounds that we access through smartphones, tablets, laptops, televisions, streaming devices, radios, game consoles, MP3 players, newspapers, books, magazines, movie theaters, and more. Not only are we audiences for this vast sea of media content, but sometimes we also help circulate and even create some of it through our social media posts, photo shares, "likes," Tweets, texts, video uploads, online reviews, blog posts, and other efforts. Yet for most of us, all of this is utterly unremarkable. We're comfortable with media, so we often take them for granted. They are like the air we breathe, ever present yet rarely considered.

This book asks you to step back and seriously reflect on important questions about the media environment in which we live. It invites you to better understand your everyday media activities by placing them in a broader social, economic, and political context. In this book, we don't lecture about the "evils" of media, nor do we get caught up in the hype about the latest wonders of our digital age. Instead, we ask enduring questions about how the media work and why this matters:

- How have media technologies changed the way media operate?

- What can we learn about today's media by revisiting media from years past?

- How do companies like Google and Facebook shape what we see—and don't see?

- How are traditional media companies—in print, radio, television, film—still central to our media experiences?

- Why are some images and ideas so prevalent in the media, while others are marginalized?

- How do governments regulate media, and how does that affect media's operation?

- How does social inequality influence both what we see in the media and how we use media?

- How has the internet transformed politics and journalism?

- What is the significance of the ever-increasing globalization of media?

- What impact are media having on our society and on our world?

These questions and others like them are not simple to answer. Indeed, one of the arguments in this book is that popular answers to such questions often overlook the more complicated dynamics that characterize the media process. But these tough questions raise important issues with which we need to grapple if we are to understand the media and their important place in our society.

THE IMPORTANCE OF MEDIA

To realize the significance of media in our lives, we only need to notice all the media devices that surround us (see Figure 1.1):

- Radio is a nearly universal presence in U.S. households and automobiles, reaching more Americans in any given week than any other media platform (Nielsen 2017d).

- Television is in almost all homes, with 82 percent of TV households paying for programming—through cable (44%), satellite (30%), or a fiber-optic line from their phone company (8%)—and 13 percent relying on free, over-the-air

FIGURE 1.1 ■ U.S. Adoption Rates of Select Media, 2017

The importance of media in society and in our daily lives can be seen by the widespread adoption of many different media devices.

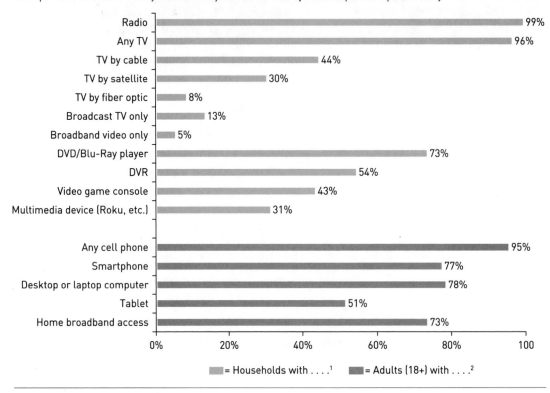

Sources: [1]Nielsen (2017e); [2]Pew Research Center (2017a; 2017b).

broadcast television. The remaining 5 percent of TV households forgo traditional broadcast or cable television and rely exclusively on a broadband internet connection for video content. Many TV households also have additional television-related electronic devices including DVD/Blu-Ray players (73%), DVRs (54%), video game consoles (43%), and multimedia streaming devices (31%) such as Apple TV, Roku, or Google Chromecast (Nielsen 2017e).

• Devices that can connect to the internet are available to most—although not all—Americans. About 95 percent of adults have a cell phone of some sort; 77 percent have a smartphone (Pew Research Center 2017b). More than three-quarters (78%) of U.S. adults have a desktop or laptop computer, and 51% have a tablet. Seventy-three percent of adults have broadband internet access at home (Pew Research Center 2017a). Teens, too, use media-related technology, sometimes at a higher rate than adults. For example, about nine out of 10 (88%)

U.S. teens ages 13 to 17 have some type of cell phone, and about three-quarters (73%) of them have access to a smartphone; 87 percent of them have access to a desktop or laptop computer (Pew Research Center 2015).

As users embrace new technology, they continually change the landscape of media equipment. For example, the proliferation of smartphones led to the decline of telephone landlines. More than nine out 10 U.S. households once had a landline; fewer than half now do (National Center for Health Statistics 2017). The growth of "connected televisions" (TVs with internet access) and video streaming services led to a rise in "cord-cutters," people who do not subscribe to traditional pay TV via cable, satellite, or fiber optics (Dawson 2017). Voice-activated "smart speakers," such as Amazon's Echo devices and Google Home, are mostly used now for music streaming and their digital assistants (Consumer Intelligence Research Partners 2017). Increasingly, though, such devices will likely be the household hub for the "internet of things" (IoT)—the network of internet-connected objects that enables machine-to-machine (M2M) communication—that will link media devices with each other and with non-media gadgets, altering the landscape again.

All of these media devices are an indicator of the enormous amount of time Americans spend watching, listening to, reading, or otherwise using various forms of media. For example, Nielsen (a firm that measures media audiences) estimates that, on average, Americans spend more than 7 hours a day watching television, including live TV (4:21), recorded programs (:34), and streaming via multimedia devices (2:19). Obviously, people are often doing other things while the TV is on—cooking meals, getting ready for work, and so on. Still, over the course of a year that amounts to more than 110 days of TV exposure! Those numbers vary by age; older Americans watch more than double the amount of television that young adults do (see Figure 1.2). (That's just one of the ways that media use varies by social grouping.) With vast exposure to media at all ages, it can be argued that the media are the dominant social institution in contemporary society, supplanting the influence of older institutions, such as schools, religion, and sometimes even the family.

With the pervasive presence of media throughout our lives, our media and our society are fused: media/society. If that seems an overstatement, then consider this simple thought experiment: Envision life *without* media. Imagine that you wake up tomorrow in a sort of parallel universe where everything is the same except that media do not exist: no smartphone, internet, or social media; no television or radio; no recorded music or video games; no books, magazines, or newspapers.

If the media disappeared, nothing else would be the same. Our entertainment would be different. We would not watch sports on TV, catch videos online, or go to a movie for fun. We would not listen to recorded music for relaxation. We would not use our phones to text or call friends. We would not post pictures or updates about ourselves—or look at others' posts—on Facebook, Twitter, Instagram, or other social media sites. Our understanding of politics and the world around us would be vastly different because we would not have websites, newspapers, radio, television, and books to explain what is happening in our world. Indeed, our world would be much "smaller" because we would know little beyond our direct experience and much "slower" because the pace of information reaching us would be greatly decreased. Even our perceptions

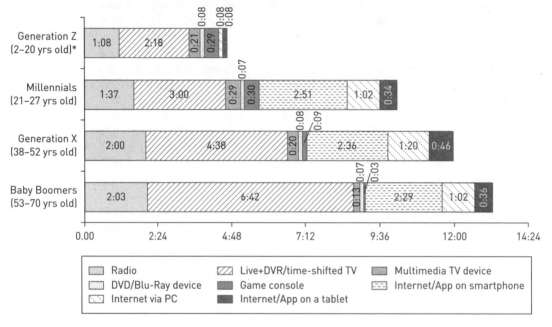

FIGURE 1.2   ■   Daily Time Spent with Select Media by Generation in Hours and Minutes, United States, 2017

Media use changes during the life cycle but is a significant factor at any age.

Legend:
- Radio
- DVD/Blu-Ray device
- Internet via PC
- Live+DVR/time-shifted TV
- Game console
- Internet/App on a tablet
- Multimedia TV device
- Internet/App on smartphone

*Generation Z does not include smartphone data due to privacy; radio data is for 12–20 years old only.

Source: Nielsen 2017e.

of ourselves would be different because we would not have social media posts, television characters, and advertising images to compare ourselves against. For example, we might not concern ourselves so much with the latest fashions and celebrities if ads and social media posts did not imply that we *should* be concerned with such things.

With no media, we would have a great deal of time on our hands, and like earlier generations, we would probably spend much of it interacting with other people face-to-face. We might entertain ourselves by playing musical instruments or games. We might attend meetings and lectures or discuss politics and current events to learn what was going on. We might take up hobbies or learn new skills to pass the time. Our social lives—how and with whom we interact—would change radically in the absence of media. We would likely develop more intense local relationships while losing touch with people who are physically farther away.

Of course, changes would reach well beyond our personal lives. The behavior of politicians, business executives, and leaders in other fields would change without media. Presidents wouldn't Tweet, campaign ads wouldn't exist, and government would operate differently. Without advertising, business would be fundamentally different. Education, religion, and every other social institution would also be different without media, as would social movements and citizens' organizations.

So, yes, our media and society *are* intertwined and fused together in ways that make it difficult to imagine their ever being separated. In studying media, we are examining a central feature of our society and our daily lives. But before we go any further in our discussion, let's consider a question that is not as simple as it seems: What are "the media"?

MODELS OF COMMUNICATION MEDIA

iStock.com/beer5020

We live in a media/ society. Media are so central to our daily lives that we often use more than one form at a time. Multitasking is common, and media devices— many of them portable—are deeply integrated into social life.

What are the media? Answering that seemingly simple question has gotten more complicated in recent years as media have evolved. But let's try to clarify some terms and their significance by reviewing some basic communication models (McQuail and Windahl 1993).

Interpersonal and "Mass" Communication

The word *media* is the plural of medium. It is derived from the Latin word *medius*, which means *middle*. Communication media are the different technological processes that facilitate communication between (and are in the middle of) the sender of a message and the receiver of that message (Figure 1.3). Print, telephony, radio, television broadcasting, cable television, film, and the internet are among the many types of media that exist.

This basic communication process applies to you talking on a cell phone to a friend. It also applies to, say, a radio station broadcasting a program to listeners. But there are crucial differences between these two types of communication. Your phone call is a one-to-one *interpersonal communication*; you are contacting a single person that is likely known to you. By contrast, radio is a one-to-many form of *mass communication*; a station uses airwaves to send a radio signal to an unknown and potentially mass audience (See Figure 1.4). Various mass media involve a known sender and generally anonymous receivers. For example, readers typically know the author of the book they are reading, but authors clearly cannot know who, exactly, is reading their book. When

---

FIGURE 1.3 ■ Basic Communication Media Model

All mediated communication involves a sender, message, medium, and receiver. The different technologies that make up the medium are what result in different communication experiences.

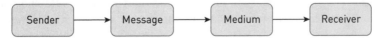

Sender → Message → Medium → Receiver

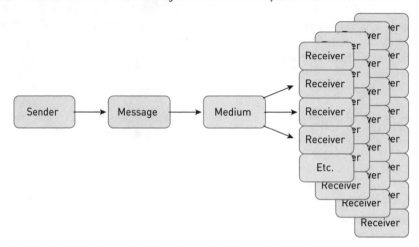

FIGURE 1.4   ■   Traditional Mass Media Model

Traditional "mass" media are characterized by a single sender and a potentially large and typically unknown set of receivers. Senders and receivers using such media traditionally have limited or no interaction.

we watch a television program or go to the movies, the names of the producer, director, and actors are prominently displayed, whereas the moviegoers and television audiences are unknown to the creators.

Furthermore, your phone conversation is likely to be highly interactive, featuring a back-and-forth dialogue; you are both a producer and receiver of messages. Unless it incorporates a different medium—as with call-in programs—a modern radio broadcast is not interactive; media personnel send a "message" out to an audience. These one-way communication channels create a clear distinction between producers and receivers of media content. With traditional mass media, the producers of most content are professionals in commercial companies, nonprofit media organizations, and governments, whereas members of the public are limited to being in the audience. Audiences have always been active in "reading" or interpreting mass media content (something we'll explore in more detail later in the book), but traditional mass media allow for only very limited interaction between receivers and the sender.

So the distinctions between interpersonal and traditional "mass" media are fairly clear. Personal communication tends to (a) be one-to-one, (b) involve a single known receiver, and (c) be very interactive. Traditional mass media tend to (a) be one-to-many, (b) involve a potentially large and unknown audience, and (c) feature limited, if any, interaction. But, today, such distinctions have eroded.

Variable Boundaries and Active Users

A few decades ago, our discussion of communications models would end with the distinction between interpersonal communication and mass media. However, the development of the internet blurred the lines between the two, enabling users to play different sorts or roles if they so choose. For example, you can use the internet to send an e-mail to someone you know—a regular one-to-one personal communication. But you can also post a public video on YouTube that could potentially go viral, reaching a mass audience. Or you could send a Tweet to a friend with a link to a newspaper story that alerts the journalist who wrote it by including her username—which could be retweeted by many other users, ultimately reaching a mass audience. It can all get a bit complicated!

So what is the internet: interpersonal communication or mass media? Clearly, it's both. The fact that the internet encompasses nearly all forms of communication is a big part of what made it a game-changer. As we will see later in the book, the variable boundaries between private interpersonal communication and public mass communication were an important change that produced a number of issues with which we are still grappling today.

In addition to blurring boundaries between private and public, the internet enabled people to be much more active, more easily, than they could with traditional media. Today, we can be *users* of media—the term we favor in this book—rather than merely receivers or audience members. With the internet, media users can be more active in the following:

- choosing *what* media content they will access from a range of choices that is broader than ever;

- deciding *when* they will use media rather than being dependent on scheduled broadcasts (e.g., via video-on-demand streaming, podcasts, music streaming);

- sharing, promoting, and distributing media content (e.g. Facebook "likes," reposting on Instagram, retweeting);

- responding to and commenting on media content (e.g. using a website's comments section; using hashtags and Twitter as a "second screen" while watching TV);

- creating their own media content (e.g., social media posts, uploaded photos and videos, product or Yelp reviews, blog posts, podcasts).

With this level of user activity, traditional mass communication models—showing merely "receivers" of a message—fail to capture the dynamic interplay that potentially exists between the media industry and nonprofessional media users. By adopting the term "user," we intend to encompass this full range of activities.

Communication Today: A First Look

So how can we summarize today's communication in a simple media model? In this book, we use the model in Figure 1.5, which we explain in more detail later in the chapter. For now, let's just note some of the elements that have changed from the traditional models:

FIGURE 1.5A   ■   Simplified Model of Media and the Social World

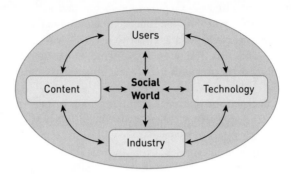

- The four primary elements of the model have changed:
  - ○ "Industry" replaces "sender" to flag the professional and usually commercial nature of media organizations responsible for most media content.
  - ○ The term "content" replaces "messages" to better reflect the wide range of media subjects as experienced by users.
  - ○ "Technology" replaces "medium" to isolate the material elements of media.
  - ○ "Users," who both actively consume content created by industry professionals and create their own content, replace "receivers."

- The entire model is embedded within a vital new element—the social world— which includes a variety of social forces and non-media actors that affect the communication process, such as cultural norms and government regulation.

- All of the arrows that indicate contact between elements in the model are double-headed, reflecting the potentially interactive nature of media.

- Finally, because users are more active than in the past, our contemporary media model is circular rather than linear. This suggests the endless feedback loops that occur among these components.

It is this more dynamic and sociological model of media that underlies this book.

The media world described by this model includes both "traditional" mass media *and* internet-based communication. For a time, observers distinguished between these two by referring to them as "old" and "new" media. However, they have blurred together in many ways as we will explore throughout this book. The internet, it turns out, is in many ways very similar to older media.

A SOCIOLOGY OF MEDIA

Sociologists are not the only ones who study media. Political scientists are sometimes interested in the media's role in politics. Literary scholars might examine the media as cultural texts. Some psychologists are interested in the effect of media on individual behavior. Most important, media studies and communication scholars explore a wide range of media issues that often emphasize how media institutions work.

The lines between the different approaches to the media are rarely clear. It is common to see references to sociological theories and concepts in the communication literature. In fact, some communications scholars were trained as sociologists before turning their attention exclusively to the media. In turn, sociologists draw on the work of media studies and communications scholars. But although they can overlap, there is a difference between these disciplines. The field of media or communications studies is defined by a particular substantive area of interest, whereas sociology is a perspective that is applied to a wide range of substantive areas, including the media. Not all sociologists study the media, and not all communications researchers use a sociological perspective.

Throughout this text, we will draw upon classic and contemporary media research that implicitly or explicitly employs a sociological perspective. A sociological perspective also informs our organization of this text, which emphasizes the interactions among the elements of our media model and the larger social world. Before we explore that specific model in more detail, let's consider the broader sociological perspective that informs it.

The Sociological Perspective

At its most basic level, a sociological perspective encourages us to see and understand the relationships between individuals and the broader social context in which they live (Croteau and Hoynes 2019). Collectively, people have created the social world, and in turn, they are influenced by it. For example, students make "individual" decisions about attending college. However, a sociological perspective reminds us that our society features an economy (in which higher education is required for many occupations), a dominant culture (in which formal education is highly valued), a government (which maintains public universities and offers funding for some—but not all—students), families (who often encourage children and spouses to attend college), and even the media (which often features positive portrayal of graduates and commercials for for-profit colleges). All of these social forces tend to encourage students to pursue a college degree. Thus, students do not make "individual" decisions about college in a vacuum; they are affected by the social context in which they live. A century ago, the percentage of young people "choosing" to go to college was much less than it is today; the social context of the time—including its greater race, class, and gender-based barriers—influenced individual actions in radically different ways.

More broadly, the individual is a product of social interaction to varying degrees. The language we use, the education we receive, and the norms and values we are taught are all part of a socialization process through which we develop and embrace a sense of self. We become who we are largely through our social relations with others.

Furthermore, our daily activities usually take place within the context of groups and institutions. Family, friendship circles, school, teams, work, community—these are the collective contexts in which we develop our roles and identities as daughters or sons, friends, students, athletes, employees, citizens, and so forth. Each role brings with it a set of expectations about our actions; being a "good" student, employee, or friend usually involves conforming to those expectations. In this way, too, sociology teaches us that, to understand people's actions, you must consider the larger social context in which they occur. That's because, although people collectively create the features of society—families, government, schools, and so on—those creations in turn influence how people act.

Our concern here is with media, not college attendance or the general socialization of individuals, but the principle is the same. To best understand media, we need to see it as a social institution comprising various elements that constantly interact. Furthermore, to understand this media system we need to put it in the larger context of the social world. This enables us to better see how media relate to other actors and social institutions as well as how media influence this larger social world. This push-pull interaction between elements of our model reflects sociology's broader interest in the role of structure and agency.

Structural Constraint and Human Agency

Sociologists often link discussions of interaction and social relations to the concepts of structure and agency. In this context, structure suggests constraint on human action, and agency indicates independent action. Combined, the push-pull interactions that result from structure and agency are essential to understanding social life, the media included.

Structure

Structure is not something physical. In the broadest sense, social structure describes any recurring pattern of social behavior. For example, we can talk about *family structure* as a pattern of behaviors associated with the culturally defined idea of family. The "traditional family" is actually a quite recent, historically specific phenomenon (Coontz 2016). During the post-World War II years in Western countries, the "traditional family" usually meant married, heterosexual couples with children. In such relationships, the expected role of the wife was to work at home raising children, especially in white, middle-class families. The expected role of the husband was to work for income to cover the household bills.

When sociologists speak of the change in family structure, they are referring to the changes in the pattern of expected family behavior. Traditional expectations that a family include two parents, that the parents be married, that they be heterosexual, that a woman work only in the home, and so forth, have changed dramatically. Single-parent families, blended families, two-income families, unmarried couples, child-free couples, and same-sex couples, to name a few, have supplemented the "traditional" family. The family structure—the pattern of behavior associated with families—has changed.

It's easy to see from today's perspective that the traditional family structure was an attractive one for some people. It enabled them to fit neatly into clearly defined roles that brought them significant rewards. Husbands and children were usually nurtured and cared for. Wives were spared the pressure of holding down a job outside the home, while often enjoying autonomy in the home. These are examples of how structures can be enabling; they help people achieve something. However, it is also easy to see that such a structure limited the options of many people. It constrained their behavior by encouraging or coercing them to conform to the accepted standards of family-related behavior. For example, wives were denied the opportunity to use their skills outside the home in paid employment, whereas husbands were denied the experience of participating significantly in raising children. These are examples of how structures can be restrictive or even coercive; they deter people from doing something.

A more immediate example of social structure is the complex pattern of institutions that make up the educational system in the United States, within which students, teachers, and administrators fulfill their expected roles. This structure can be enabling to students who successfully navigate through the system and eventually receive diplomas. Schooling often helps these students achieve a better life. However, as all students know, the educational structure can also be very constraining. Required courses, assignments, deadlines, and grades are all part of a structure that limits the actions of students and teachers. It is this constraint feature that is most important when considering structure.

Agency

When sociologists discuss structure, they often pair it with agency. Agency is intentional and undetermined human action. Human agency reproduces—or sometimes changes—social structure. The "traditional" family structure and the education system continue only as long as new generations of people accept the roles they are asked to fill within them. Most of the time, that's exactly what our actions do; they help reproduce existing social structures. But when enough people began to demand the right to choose from a wider set of possible family roles, including women having a career outside the home and same-sex couples being legally recognized, the "traditional" family structure began to change. With education, students have some leeway in what they study, how much time and energy they spend on schoolwork, and whether or not they even continue their studies. But, overall, their actions typically reinforce an existing model of education that has evolved only modestly in the last century. In both cases, while structure constrains agency, it is human agency that either alters or maintains social structures.

Structure and Agency in the Media

With respect to the media system, the tension between structure and agency is present on at least three levels. We can express these three levels of analysis as three pairs of questions about structural constraint and agency.

- **Relationships among institutions**. How do social structures, such as government and the economy, affect the media industry? How does the media industry influence other social structures?

- **Relationships within an institution**. How does the structure of the media industry affect media personnel and, indirectly, media content? How do media personnel influence media content and media organizations?

- **Relationships between an institution and the public**. How does the media industry influence the users of media? How do the choices and actions of media users affect the media industry?

One reason why media are often controversial is that different groups expect the media to play different—and often incompatible—roles. For users, the media can serve as the source of entertainment and information about the world beyond direct experience.

For advocates of various sorts—from politicians to social movement actors—media are important vehicles for transmitting messages they want others to hear. For media workers, the media industry offers jobs, with resulting income, prestige, and satisfaction, as well as a place for the development of a professional identity. For media owners, the media are a source of profit and, perhaps, a source of political power. For society at large, the media can be a way to transmit information and values (socialization) and can serve as a check on the abuse of political and economic power. By considering structure-agency dynamics, we can see the tensions between these sometimes divergent roles.

Relationships between the Media and Other Social Institutions

First, our broadest level of analysis is the tension between structure and agency produced by different institutions. We cannot adequately understand the media system without considering the social, economic, and political context in which it exists. Institutions outside the control of media personnel set certain legal and economic limits within which the media industry must operate. In turn, the media industry has agency in the sense of acting on its own and perhaps influencing other social institutions. A totalitarian regime, for example, is likely to exert extreme constraint on the press in that society. There would be little room for agency by the mainstream news media, although outlawed underground media may emerge to challenge the status quo. Labeling a society democratic, on the other hand, includes the suggestion that, at least in theory, the media are free of severe constraint by the government and thus have significant agency. Indeed, media in democratic societies can themselves exert a constraining influence over other institutions. However, media in democratic societies are often commercial ventures and so are subject to influence and limitations placed on them by corporate owners.

In the real world, there is always a mixture of structural constraint and independent agency. Media researchers, therefore, examine both how social structures external to the media affect the industry and how the media affect other social structures. This level of analysis includes questions such as these: Should the government enforce a policy of net neutrality? Have economic changes threatened the existence of journalism? How has the emergence of "fake news" in the media affected political campaigns? Does it matter who owns major media outlets?

Relationships within the Media Industry

Second, to understand the decisions made by journalists, writers, producers, filmmakers, media executives, and other media personnel, we must understand the context in which they labor. This means that we must be familiar with both the internal workings of mass media organizations and the processes of professional socialization. The sociological emphasis here is on social positions, roles, and practices, not on particular individuals. Relevant issues of concern include the structures of media institutions, those who wield power within them, what professional norms and expectations are associated with different positions, and so forth.

Within the media industry, the tension between structure and agency is related primarily to how much autonomy media personnel have in doing their work. The amount of autonomy will vary depending on the position an individual occupies. The questions raised include the following: To what extent do standard journalistic practices shape the process of news reporting or the content of the news? How do economic considerations enter into the decision-making process of Hollywood moviemaking? How "free" are musicians to create their music? How have independent bloggers influenced the norms and routines of commercial news media? In the language of sociology, structural considerations may significantly affect the individual agency of media personnel. At the same time, the collective agency of those who work in the media has the potential to alter the structures that constrain individual media professionals.

Relationships between the Media and the Public

A third kind of social relationship involves how media content and technology potentially influence users and, in turn, how media users can impact the media industry and the content it produces. Media users are not passive sponges that soak up the many messages they come across in the media. This would imply a one-way relationship with the media determining the thoughts and behaviors of users. Instead, as we noted, media users are often active on several fronts: choosing *what* media content they will use and *when* they will use it; promoting, redistributing, criticizing, or ignoring content; and even creating their own content. Media users also interpret media messages through their own social lenses; they are active "readers" of media content.

When we interpret the words of someone speaking with us face-to-face, we interactively construct the conversation. We can elicit more information from the speaker by asking a question of clarification or by using appropriate facial expressions to convey our reactions. We can comment on statements and thereby affect the course of the conversation. Such interaction between speakers helps promote mutual understanding about the messages being communicated.

Media content, however, usually does not allow for the intimate interaction of sender and receiver that characterizes interpersonal communication. We cannot ask a stand-up comedian on television to explain a joke. We either get it or we don't. It's unlikely that a question we pose on Twitter to our favorite musical artists will be answered. Media users, therefore, must rely on other resources to make sense of the messages in media content.

Relevant resources available to users might include knowledge and information gained from personal experience, other people, formal education, or other media content. These resources are neither randomly nor equally distributed. The interpretive skills that people bring with them to their viewing, listening, and reading are shaped by aspects of social structure, such as class, race, gender, and education. Thus, in constructing their own individual interpretations of the media, people constantly draw on collective resources and experiences that are shaped by social factors.

Active users are important, but the thousands of hours people spend with the media do have some influence on them. Users are not completely immune to the impact of media content and media technology. Here too, we have to explore the dynamic interplay between the power of social structure and the (always partial) autonomy of human activity. How powerful is media content in influencing how we think, feel, and even behave? For example, does racist internet content embolden people to be more overtly racist? How does media technology affect our social relationships? Do smartphones undermine or enhance face-to-face communication? How do the algorithms that drive search engine results affect how people use the internet? Ultimately, these are complex questions that do not lend themselves to easy answers involving all-encompassing media power or complete individual freedom. Instead, we need to pay attention to the push-pull relationships between structure and agency throughout the media system if we are to understand the role of media in the social world.

A MODEL OF MEDIA AND THE SOCIAL WORLD

How can we begin to make sense of the complex relationships we have identified? Let's return to Figure 1.5 and examine our simple graphic representation of these relations in more detail.

Four components, each represented by a separate box in the diagram, make up the core of our model. All four elements are simultaneously a part of the social world and surrounded by the social world (the shaded area). The graphic organization of these four elements is arbitrary; there is no "top" or "bottom" to the process; rather, it is a circular process. Double arrowheads represent the potential relationships among these components, although not all relationships will be relevant in all situations. We will first describe the elements represented by the four large boxes and then turn our attention to the unique status of the *social world* (represented by the shading), which is both in the center of the model and simultaneously surrounding it.

The box at the bottom of the model represents the *media industry*, by which we mean the entire organizational structure that makes up the media, including all media personnel. The media industry is affected by changes in *technology* (e.g., the invention of television) but is also instrumental in influencing the direction and application of technology (e.g., the use of computers for film animation). The media industry is the producer of the media *content*. For example, a book is written by an author, designed, typeset, printed (or formatted as an e-book), distributed by a publisher, and sold, either physically or electronically. However, the conventions of particular genres of media products also influence the creators of the content. The murder mystery genre, for example, requires the existence of a crime.

FIGURE 1.5B   ■   Simplified Model of Media and the Social World

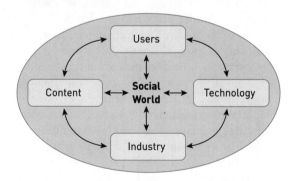

Users may be influenced by the media content they see (e.g., learning about an impending snowstorm from the weather report), but they must actively interpret and construct meaning from that content (e.g., deciding whether to trust the forecast and whether to act differently as a result). Sociologists call the process of actively creating meaning in this way the social construction of reality. This means that, although reality exists, we must negotiate the meaning of that reality. A student who sports a series of prominent tattoos is an objective reality. However, different people will interpret such body art in different ways. Is it a sign of conformity to a fad? A rebellious political statement? A playful snubbing of mainstream norms? A disgusting mutilation of the body? Or is it just an act of personal expression? The meaning of the tattoos must be constructed by those observing them. The same is true for the meaning of messages in media content. That is one reason why users—who must "read" and interpret media content—are such an important part of the media process.

As we have noted, users always had the capacity to respond to the media industry, for example, by writing a letter to a television network. But the internet has enabled much more active media users. In fact, "users" sometimes take on roles that used to be limited to the "industry," such as creating content to be widely distributed. Our simple model doesn't explicitly show this blurring of roles, but it is a dynamic we discuss throughout the book.

The direction and development of technology is affected by how the *users* choose to use it—or not to use it. Google Glass—a computer headset worn like a pair of glasses—generated curiosity when it was introduced in 2013, but users—as yet—have not embraced this particular type of wearable technology, forcing Google to withdraw the product. In turn, technology has a potential impact on the public. For example, movie viewing usually requires close attention because the medium communicates via both sound and images. This contrasts with radio, which does not demand our full attention. Unlike movies, which we must watch to fully follow, radio allows us to do other things while still attending to it, such as drive a car, run, cook dinner, or work. Each medium, therefore, tends to produce a different experience for the users. This is one effect of technology.

The middle—and broader context—of the model is the *social world*. This contains all the social elements not included in the four main boxes. Some of these elements are crucial for an understanding of the workings of the media and thus can be thought of as being at the center of the model. For example, the role of government and broader economic forces are non-media social factors that influence all the elements of our model.

Notice that the top and bottom elements of our model include human agents—real people—whereas the left and right boxes are human creations. People are the medium through which media content and technology affect each other. Similarly, the relationship between the media industry and most media users is mediated by content, technology, and other factors in the social world. Note, too, that any single component of the model simultaneously relates to other components. For example, media content is simultaneously influenced by the media industry that creates it and the users who access or ignore, interpret, share, and critique it as well as by and other aspects of the social world, such as government regulation.

Our simplified model is meant to identify some of the key components in the sociology of media and to clarify some of the relationships among these components. Like all models, it cannot fully account for the infinite complexities of the "real" social world.

However, applying the model to analyze the media can alert us to important questions and help us clarify the workings and social significance of mass media.

APPLYING THE MODEL: CIVIL RIGHTS IN TWO MEDIA ERAS

To illustrate briefly how the model can alert us to important real-life issues, let us consider the U.S. civil rights struggles of the 1950s and 1960s (Branch 1988; McAdam 1982; Morris 1984) and the ongoing Black Lives Matter (2018) movement that began in the mid-2010s (Ray, Brown, and Laybourn 2017). These movements existed in two different eras, and so their interactions with media varied significantly. We can think of these social movements as a part of the non-media social world insofar as they exist independent of our four components of the media model. For the moment, then, imagine each movement as being the element of the social world that occupies the center position in our model.

Mid-20th-Century Civil Rights Movement

In the mid-20th century, the civil rights movement launched a series of nonviolent direct-action campaigns to challenge the injustices of U.S. racial segregation. These campaigns, which were mostly in the South, sometimes were met with violence from segregationist counter-demonstrators and police. Often, these confrontations attracted media coverage, which helped raise awareness about racial injustice among mainstream, mostly white, Americans.

Our media model can be used to consider some of the push-pull dynamics involved in this effort. We'll work our way around the model components.

- **Industry-content.** The media industry created content featuring the civil rights movement; in turn, journalists were constrained by the genre norms of "news" coverage at the time. For example, reporters typically wrote stories about the movement to fit the journalistic convention of a balanced presentation of facts, including quotes from counter-demonstrators. Generally, they were not supposed to offer their opinion about the story at hand.

- **Content-users.** The media content about the civil rights movement affected many media users, who in turn, were interpreting the meaning of those messages. For example, some supporters in the North were moved by media accounts to make financial contributions to movement organizations in the South or even to volunteer for movement efforts. In contrast, others sympathized with the forces of segregation, often seeing civil rights activists—and the media organizations that covered them—as troublemakers. The media content had an impact, but media users could interpret the meaning and significance of the messages in quite distinct ways.

- **Users-technology.** Media users of the 1950s and 1960s relied on technology, especially print and recently introduced television, to access media content.

Meanwhile, technology may have indirectly influenced users, with the immediacy and impact of television pictures of police violence against demonstrators.

- **Technology-industry.** Technology was also helping change the media industry; the availability of lighter, handheld cameras allowed reporters more mobility to file "on-the-scene" stories that would not have been possible in an earlier era. Journalists often chose to use this technology to capture dramatic clashes during the demonstrations. Television footage of police using firehoses and unleashing dogs on civil rights demonstrators became iconic images that are well-known even today.

Now, let's move to the center of the model, where the movement itself was a part of the social world interacting with the media process.

- **Movement-industry.** The movement's tactics of escalating nonviolent confrontation made it more difficult for the media industry to ignore their cause. Segregation was not new, but now the movement's efforts drew the attention of national news organizations that had long defined civil disturbances as newsworthy. In the long term, the civil rights movement had additional impact on the media industry (and other social institutions) by helping reduce its discriminatory practices in hiring and promotion. The racial diversity that exists today in the media industry—even though limited—would not have come about without the influence of this social movement and the resulting changes in legislation and social norms. However, the media industry also had an impact on the civil rights movement. In this era, the only way a movement could reach a large and broad audience was through mainstream media coverage. Consequently, social movements often crafted strategies to try to attract such coverage, such as staging marches and demonstrations. By altering their behavior to fit media norms and routines, social movement activists were affected by the media industry even before the media produced any coverage of the group.

- **Movement-content.** Media content affected the civil rights movement as it tried to develop favorable media coverage and, in some cases, altered strategies that generated negative coverage. The movement did not affect media content directly but instead did so indirectly by trying to influence journalists covering them. In the long term, it also affected the industry as a whole and the content it produces. A media industry that employs more people of color in positions of power, for example, is more likely to be sensitive to race issues in its content.

- **Movement-users.** The civil rights movement was trying to get citizens—who were media users—to support their efforts. Thus they had an indirect influence on users through the content to which they were exposed. In the long term, the movement has also had a direct impact on media users because the presence of this movement has meant more social equality. At the same time, media users have sometimes acted in their role as citizens to support social movement efforts, illustrating the interaction between these two components of the model.

- **Movement-technology.** The technology of the 1950s that the civil rights movement relied on to communicate its messages seems ancient by today's standards, but it was an integral part of the ongoing organizing effort, both enabling and constraining what could be done. Because they had little or no access to television and radio, movement organizers relied on print for nearly all of their work. For example, if a leaflet announcing a meeting needed to be distributed, stencils might be cut for hand-cranked mimeograph machines often owned by African-American churches. African-American newsletters and magazines were a source of movement information. By today's standards, these sorts of print media were very slow in spreading news, but they enabled the movement to build systematically and expand their base. Once the movement began growing, it staged larger demonstrations that drew the attention of mainstream media, helping spread their message.

Even in this cursory summary, the usefulness of our model for investigating issues related to the media should be apparent. But what happens when the media environment changes? Do the kinds of dynamics described here still apply? Another brief case study can illustrate the enduring relevance of these dynamics.

Black Lives Matter

A half century after the peak of the civil rights movement, the Black Lives Matter (BLM) movement emerged as a response to police violence against African Americans and expanded to address broader issues of systemic racial injustice. A variety of decentralized efforts sought to draw attention to—and ultimately address—contemporary structural racism. Important changes in the media industry and technology meant that BLM operated very differently than the older movement. But the elements of our media model remain just as relevant in understanding these new dynamics. We won't repeat many of the features that BLM shares with the earlier civil rights movement. Instead, we'll note a few of the major differences that existed.

First, BLM took full advantage of new media technology, which transformed the role of some media users. BLM emerged from a Twitter hashtag, so from the very beginning it was activist-users who were creating media content that reached both their supporters—who often helped circulate this content—and the broader world of non-activist media users. (Opponents of BLM also used Twitter and other social media to spread their messages, often using the broader hashtag #TCOT—for Top Conservatives of Twitter.) As street demonstrations emerged, BLM activists often live-streamed events or posted video highlights to various social media platforms—video that sometimes went viral and was picked up by mainstream news outlets. Unlike previous generations of activists, BLM was less dependent on mainstream news media to get out its message. Traditional news coverage still mattered a great deal in helping shape mainstream media users' understanding of the movement, but the movement itself could use social media platforms to get out sometimes different and unfiltered content quite broadly. (At this writing, the main Black Lives Matter Twitter account [@Blklivesmatter] still has more than 290,000 followers.) This was done in real time, dramatically speeding up the process of growth for the movement.

Such rapid growth can be impressive but also problematic, thrusting the movement onto a national stage before a clear agenda, leadership roles, and organizational structures have fully developed (Sands 2017; Tufecki 2017).

Second, the media industry was vastly different in the 21st century from what it was in the mid-20th, affecting coverage of BLM. With the earlier civil rights movement, there were only three national television networks in the United States, each creating one nightly news broadcast that was seen by vast swaths of society. With BLM, the earlier rise of cable television and the internet had created highly fragmented news audiences spread across many different outlets. Many of these outlets offered breaking news and commentary 24 hours a day that often incorporated dramatic video of BLM events. These many channels hosted lengthy and often partisan discussion and debate about the merits of BLM. Meanwhile, conservative social media networks and talk radio programs rallied to disparage the movement, unrestrained by any of the balance norms of journalism.

So compared to the earlier civil rights movement, BLM's emergence in the digital age meant the following:

- New *technology* could be employed to gather and share *content*, often in real time.

- Some media *users* could play a more active role in creating and sharing this content; mainstream users, though, were divided into fragmented audiences seeing and reading very different types of coverage of the movement.

- The media *industry* was structured to produce more and quicker coverage across numerous outlets.

B Christopher / Alamy Stock Photo

Although the particulars of this movement had changed from the earlier one, the basic elements of our media model remain as relevant as ever in alerting us to important social dynamics. This illustrates the utility of a sociological approach to understanding how media interact with the social world, regardless of the historical era.

In part because they do not have regular access to the mainstream media, many social movements must adopt tactics that will attract attention and increase their chances of gaining media exposure. A common strategy is the public demonstration, featuring eye-catching signs, props, and chanting.

CONCLUSION

It is difficult to overestimate the importance of media in today's society. But it is hard to think analytically about a system that is so vast, pervasive, and complex. A sociological approach to the study of media encourages us to pay attention to key elements of the media process and to locate media in a larger social context. That's exactly what we do in the model of media and the social world presented in this chapter. This model is the underlying framework for the rest of the book, helping us identify questions we should ask when we study the media. The upcoming chapters focus on the push-pull relations among components of our model—technology, industry, content, and users—as well as the broader social world. Examining the relationships among these key elements is the first step toward developing a nuanced understanding of the role of media in our society.

Discussion Questions

1. What evidence is there that the media play a significant role in your life? (Do you have access to many of the devices mentioned in the chapter? Does your daily routine involve using media?)

2. How does the presence of media affect your life? How would it be different without access to media? What aspect of media would you miss the most? Why?

3. What is meant by the terms *structure* and *agency*? What is a media-related example that shows how the two concepts are connected to each other?

TECHNOLOGY

In Chapter 2, we survey how media technology has evolved from print up to the early internet. We highlight the distinctive features of each new technology and how they might have enabled significant social change. We also consider how social forces helped shape these technologies in often unexpected ways.

We begin with technology in large part because technological innovations have enabled the significant transformation of the media industry in recent years. With the digitization of media and the maturing of the internet, boundaries among different media forms have blurred, new media forms have emerged, and fresh questions about what this all means are plentiful. Ironically, one of the best ways to make sense of our rapidly changing media technologies is to look back at the evolution and impact of earlier technologies.

2

THE EVOLUTION OF
MEDIA TECHNOLOGY

From printed paper to digital screens, technology underlies all systems of mediated communication. To understand how media work, we need to consider these technologies and their significance. In this chapter, after briefly reviewing the history of media technology, we examine some of the scholarly approaches to understanding technology and then use some of these ideas to explore the evolution of media technologies from print up to the early internet. As we will see, technology matters in making each medium unique. However, each technology is influenced by a variety of social forces, including how the media industry elects to deploy it, whether and how users choose to adopt or adapt it and whether and how governments opt to regulate it. Together, all of these elements—which are components of the media model from Chapter 1—make up technology's story.

THE HISTORY OF MEDIA TECHNOLOGY

One way to tell the story of media is through the history of its technology (Brigs and Burke 2009; Kovarik 2016). For the vast bulk of human history, communication was conducted in the face-to-face, oral tradition. Then, centuries of one-of-a-kind creations followed, including artwork on cave walls, carvings in stone, impressions on clay tablets, and marks on bamboo or papyrus. Along the way, humans invented numbers and written language. But it was not until the invention of paper in China around the year 100 and printing, 500 years later, that communication using a medium began to be reproducible. By about 800, book printing began, using a single, carved wooden block to reproduce each page. For the first time, technology enabled the preservation and distribution of human thought to many others through the creation of duplicate copies. We had become a "world on paper" (Olson 1994).

FIGURE 2.1 ■ Time Line of Select Media Developments	
Year	**Media-Related Advancement**
100	Papermaking is developed in China
600	Printing using carved blocks of wood begins in China
800	First books are printed in China, using a single wood block for an entire page of text
1000	Movable clay type—with one piece of type for each character—used in China
1200	Movable metal type developed in Korea
1450	Modern, hand-operated printing press with movable type is developed in Germany
1600	First newspapers appear in Germany, France, and Belgium
1700	1702 London's *Daily Courant* becomes the first English-language daily newspaper
1800	1833 First low-cost "penny press" newspaper, the *New York Sun,* appears
	1837 Electric telegraph is patented
	1839 Early photographic camera for commercial sale is introduced
1850	1876 Telephone is patented
	1878 First practical sound recorder and player is patented
	1879 Electric light is patented
	1894 Motion pictures are invented and the first short films are shown to the public
	1895 Radio messages are first transmitted
1900	1920 Regularly scheduled radio broadcasting begins in Pittsburgh
	1927 *The Jazz Singer* is the first feature-length film with synchronized speech
	1928 Electronic television is first demonstrated
	1937 First digital computer is created from telephone parts
	1941 First commercial television is broadcast
	1946 Mainframe computer is invented
	1948 Early cable television captures and retransmits via wires local broadcast programs in areas with weak signals
	1949 Network television broadcasting begins in the United States

(Continued)

FIGURE 2.1   ■   (Continued)

1950   1957 First communications satellite, *Sputnik*, is launched by USSR

1961 Modern cable TV begins when a San Diego cable operator imports television broadcast signals from Los Angeles for distribution to subscribers

1969 First nodes of the internet created as part of a Pentagon program

1970 Videocassette recorder (VCR) appears; cheaper and popular by mid-decade

1971 Microprocessor, essential for computer advancement, is invented

1972 First video game console that connects to a TV is introduced

1975 •First microcomputer is marketed

  •Fiber-optics transmission begins

  •HBO is first to transmit programming to cable TV systems via satellite

1982 Audio compact disk (CD) is introduced

1990 World Wide Web (WWW) is released as simple user interface for a variety of data types

1994 •Commercial short message service (SMS), or "texting," begins in Finland

  •Cyber stations (radio stations on the internet) first appear

  •BellSouth introduces first multipurpose "smartphone"

1997 Digital video disks (DVD) are introduced

1998 •Digital TV broadcasting begins; in 2009 FCC makes digital signal mandatory

  •Rio becomes the first popular MP3 player

1999 •Netflix launches DVD-by-mail subscription service; adds streaming in 2007

  •Digital video recorders (DVR) are introduced

2000   2001 Satellite-based digital radio services grow with the launch of XM radio

2002 Friendster social networking site launched; Facebook (2004) follows

2003 Skype "over-the-top" internet telephone network is introduced

2004 •Flickr photo sharing site is launched

  •Podcasts become more popular when made easier to find and download

2005 YouTube video site is founded

2006 •First e-book reader is introduced

  •Twitter microblogging service is founded

2007 Hulu launched to stream commercial television programs and movies on demand

2008 Roku, digital media player set-top box, simplifies internet streaming television

2010   2010 •Apple's iPad helps spark revival in the dormant tablet computer market

  •Instagram appears, helping make photo sharing wildly popular

2011 Snapchat introduced, offering increased privacy via self-destructing messaging

2013 Google Glass is introduced, an early entry in the "wearable technology" field

2015 Sling popularizes live TV streaming; others follow

2016 Virtual reality enters the mainstream with Oculus Rift gear

2018 Smart speakers—voice-activated digital assistants that serve as hubs for home automation—gain in popularity with Amazon's Echo (2015), Google's Home (2016), and Apple's Homepod (2018)

Sources: Crowley and Heyer (1991); Jost (1994); *MIT Technology Review* (2002-2017); Rogers (1986); Shedden (2010); and media accounts.

Over time, the printing process was improved, but for 1,000 years print *was* media technology (see Figure 2.1). However, 19th-century industrialization drastically increased the pace of technological innovation, bringing the telegraph, camera, telephone, phonograph, radio, and motion pictures in rapid succession. The world of media technology became much more diverse, complicated, and rapidly evolving. In the 20th century, these media—along with television and the internet—were refined and developed into the commercial industries we know today, utterly transforming communication worldwide. Technology in the 21st century has enabled new social transformations by integrating digital multimedia platforms into all aspects of our lives and by making media-creating technology more accessible to ordinary users.

Given the inescapabilty of media and their significance in our lives, it's easy to forget that most forms of media technology simply didn't exist or were not widely available 100 years ago. Figure 2.2 shows adoption rates for select media technologies in the United States over the last century. Clearly, our media/society is a relatively recent development.

Figure 2.2 highlights another interesting fact about media: New technologies usually don't displace older technologies. Radio didn't destroy print; television didn't kill radio; and the internet has not put an end to television. Instead media technologies tend to accumulate, contributing to the pervasiveness of media in our lives today.

FIGURE 2.2 ■ U.S. Adoption Rates for Select Media Technology, 1920–2020

Much of the media technology we use today didn't exist a century ago. For the most part, older media have survived the introduction of newer media, resulting in a diverse and complex media environment.

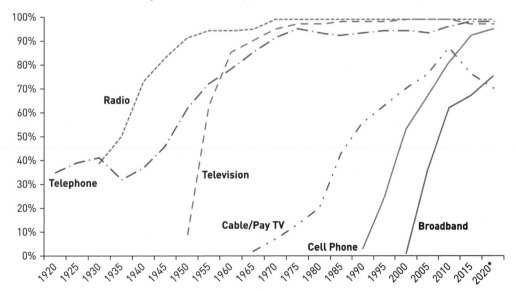

*2020 numbers are estimates. "Telephone" includes landlines and cell phones. "Cell Phone" and "Broadband" refer to percentage of adults with access; other categories are household adoption rates. "Cable/Pay TV" includes cable, satellite, and fiber-optic access.

Sources: Adapted from the U.S. Census Bureau (1999; 2012); Pew Research Center (2017a; 2017b); National Center for Health Statistics (2017); U.S. Energy Information Administration (2017).

How can we best understand this accumulating array of technology? How might it be affecting us? And why might this be important? Scholars have long debated such questions.

TECHNOLOGICAL DETERMINISM AND SOCIAL CONSTRUCTIONISM

There have been two general approaches to understanding the role of technology in society. The first, often referred to as "technological determinism," suggests that *technology* itself causes change, often in ways that people don't intend and are unaware of. The second, often referred to as "social constructionism" (or "social determinism" or "social constructivism") emphasizes that technology is made up of inanimate objects, and ultimately *people* decide how to use (or not use) technology. But even though debates about technology are often presented as a stark contrast between these two approaches, things are never quite so simple. In reality, nearly all scholars fall somewhere in between the extremes of pure technological determinism and social constructionism. We retain these well-known and usefully descriptive labels to identify general approaches to understanding technology. However, we consider them to be the opposite poles of a continuum rather than two mutually exclusive approaches. Technological determinists put more emphasis on the role of technology; social constructionists emphasize human agency. But nearly all scholars acknowledge a relationship between the social dimension of technology and their material components. The real debates are about the nature of this relationship and the degree to which technology or human action should be seen as determinant.

Technological Determinism

Technological determinism is an approach that identifies technology, or technological developments, as the central causal element in processes of social change. In other words, scholars who lean toward technological determinism emphasize the "overwhelming and inevitable" effects of technologies on users, organizations, and societies (Lievrouw and Livingstone 2006: 21). This applies to all forms of technology, most of which have nothing to do with media. From this perspective, technology produces change, albeit often through a series of intermediary steps. For example, the invention of the automobile might be said to lead to a reduction in food prices because the automobile "reduced the demand for horses, which reduced the demand for feed grain, which increased the land available for planting edible grains," making food less expensive (Fischer 1992: 8).

As we will see, critics argue that there is no human agency in this type of analysis. Pure technological determinism suggests that technological properties demand certain results and that actual people do not use technologies so much as people are used by them. In this view, society is transformed according to a technical, rather than a human, agenda. Critics contend this cannot be true. Technology is composed of inanimate objects; it is humans who cause things to happen by the choices they make and the actions they take.

However, this crude form of technological determinism is often an accusation leveled by critics more than a position advocated by scholars. In recent years, some scholars have adopted the language of "materiality" in arguing that the physical aspects of media technology matter but not in a simplistic way (Gillespie, Boczkowski, and Foot 2014). In using this language, they hope to distinguish their approach from both the simplistic caricature of technological determinism as well as social constructionism.

Lievrouw (2014: 25) cautions that "[m]ateriality itself is a complex, multidimensional idea, and open to a variety of interpretations, emphases, and disciplinary assumptions." There are many different meanings and uses of the term materiality, often making it difficult to pinpoint a single definition that would be acceptable to everyone using the term (Sterne 2014). Still, whether you call it a form of technological determinism or an emphasis on materiality, there is no doubt that the physical aspects of technology are of interest to contemporary scholars and to anyone who wants to understand the media.

Media's Materiality

It may seem odd to suggest that the inanimate objects making up technology can *cause* anything. But scholars who focus on the material influence of technology usually mean something more nuanced.

The obvious forms of materiality are the tangible objects and "things" that are involved in media communication—keyboards, screens, phones, paper, and the like. But materiality also includes things that we often forget have a physical foundation (Allen-Robertson 2015; Pinch 2008). Data are not objects, but they exist on hard drives and servers. If there was no material component to data, there would be no limit to the amount of data you could store on a computer hard drive. A change in materiality—the storage capacity of computers—has contributed to a change in how computers can be used. The internet is another example. Despite the popular metaphor, the internet is not an amorphous "cloud." Instead, data packets are transmitted along copper or fiber-optic cables to be displayed on our screens. As Blum (2012: 9–10) reminds us, the internet is made of pulses of light "produced by powerful lasers contained in steel boxes housed (predominantly) in unmarked buildings. The lasers exist. The boxes exist. The buildings exist. The Internet exists—it has a physical reality, an essential infrastructure." All of these material elements are necessary and help shape how we experience the internet.

More directly, all media technology has "material" elements that help determine how it can be used. Each medium has its own technological capabilities and limitations that affect the delivery of words, sound, pictures, and video (see Figure 2.3). For instance, a concert performed by one of your favorite musical artists could be broadcast live by a radio station; you would hear the sound but not be able to see the performers. A magazine could print a story about the concert and provide photographs to show you what the event looked like but only after the fact and without sound. A television program could deliver live sound and video, but any text delivery would be awkward, perhaps limited to a chyron at the bottom of the screen. The internet is unique in its ability to serve as a digital platform that enables all of these features—words, sound, pictures, and video—and do it live. In addition, those watching the streamed concert online could communicate with other music fans through instant messaging or Tweets, introducing a form of interactivity that is not possible with other media.

In this example, different technologies do not "cause" dissimilar concert coverage. However, because of their capacities and limitations, the various media technologies enable different ways of communicating the concert experience, both in the kinds of information they present and in the ways we access and experience them. Of course, the same is true for other types of media content as well. So this is one way technology

FIGURE 2.3   ■   Select Characteristics of Different Media

The technological capacities and limitations of each medium set the parameters for their use. However, the internet is, in effect, a generic platform that enables the delivery of all forms of media while adding unique, interactive capabilities.

	Text?	Sound?	Picture?	Video?	Live?	Interactive?[a]
Print	Yes	No	Yes	No	No	No
Radio	No[b]	Yes	No	No	Yes	No[c]
Film	No[b]	Yes	Yes	Yes	No	No
Television	No[b]	Yes	Yes	Yes	Yes	No
Sound recording	No[b]	Yes	No	No	No	No
Internet	Yes	Yes	Yes	Yes	Yes	Yes

Notes:

[a] We are using "interactive" here to mean a medium that enables easy, two-way communication between producer and user.

[b] Although digital radio, film, television (video), and sound recordings can show text on a screen, they are not primarily textual media.

[c] Two-way communication is possible using radio technology, but most modern radio sets do not allow for this.

matters; it offers opportunities and places limitations on what a medium can be used for and makes some types of media more suitable for some purposes than others. In this way, each medium can be said to influence its users.

"Autonomous Technology" and "Technological Momentum"

Technology matters in other ways, too. Scholars in science and technology studies (STS) have long noted that technology can "take on a life of its own," even though people create and use it. For example, Langdon Winner (1977: 15) used the term *autonomous technology* as "a general label for all conceptions and observations to the effect that technology is somehow out of control by human agency." Winner argued that political, economic, social, and cultural conditions shape the creation of technology and are embodied in technological artifacts and processes. However, Winner contended that technology is so vast and complex that it has unintended consequences that users and society as a whole often cannot control. He portrays technology as a potentially Frankenstein-like creation that can seem bewildering and unmanageable, especially in periods of rapid technological change. Today, the unknown implications of robotics equipped with increasingly sophisticated artificial intelligence and machine learning (where computers adapt without needing to be explicitly programmed by humans) is perhaps the most extreme and best-known example of potentially autonomous technology. In the world of media, the growing dependence on algorithms that humans create but often don't fully understand (which we discuss later) might also be seen as an example of "autonomous technology."

Similarly, Thomas Hughes's (1983) idea of *technological momentum* suggests that a technology's influence changes over time. When a technology is new, Hughes argues, humans have agency over the ways in which it is developed, deployed, and used. New technologies are still in flux and full of possibilities, as creators and users negotiate how the technology will be used. As time passes, though, a technology becomes established, routinized, and institutionalized, making it more difficult to contest or change. The analogy might be to a boulder at the top of a hill; the rock does not move without human initiative, but once it is pushed, it gains momentum that makes it extremely difficult to control or stop.

Once deployed and standardized, technology, too, is difficult to stop or divert. There are many reasons why this standardization of a technology might occur. Sometimes standardization or large-scale deployment facilitates use, making it difficult for alternatives to a well-known technology to succeed. Sometimes market forces, especially investment costs, make it impractical for alternative uses to flourish once an industry standard is established. Simple habit or inertia on the part of users also favors the retention of existing technologies. Whatever the reason, once a technology is established, a culture develops around it, and it gains a permanency that is difficult for people to alter. These ideas have new relevance today as the internet has matured and the early promise of wide-open innovation has given way to more established ways of operating, often heavily influenced by a few major corporate players.

Both concepts from Winner and Hughes are examples of ways to think about how technology can exert some autonomous influence over actors in society (a notion associated with technological determinism) while acknowledging the agency of humans in creating technology (an idea compatible with social constructionism). Understanding technology in such ways accepts the push-pull interaction between the material (nonhuman) and the social (human) as an essential dynamic of technological systems.

Medium Theory

Media scholars and commentators have long been concerned about technology's possible negative impact on society. As early as the 1920s, there was worry that newly introduced media technologies—film and broadcasting—might have some inherent power to influence susceptible audiences and thus were worthy of study. (We will explore some of these early studies in Chapter 8.) During the two world wars, for example, governments on both sides used radio and newsreel propaganda effectively, enhancing concerns about the impact to which these media technologies could be put. Later, television would be blamed for making people stupid, earning it nicknames such as the "idiot box" or the "boob tube." More recently, as we will see, the internet and smartphone technology have been criticized for possibly "ruining" an entire generation with their addictive properties. To varying degrees, all these critiques presented technology as at least the partial cause of a negative effect.

But such concern never constituted the bulk of media scholarship. "Autonomous technology" and "technological momentum," for example, are both ideas that come from science and technology studies, not media studies specifically. Historically, most media scholars have focused on media industries, the content they produce, and the users that consume it rather than on technology. (We examine all of these topics later in the book.) Most media scholars have long argued that technology was essentially "neutral." Its effects depended on the media industries that implemented it and on the "active" audiences who used media technology and interpreted media messages (Buckingham 1993; Williams 1974).

The notable exception to this is work known as "medium theory" or sometimes "media ecology" to emphasize media environments (Meyrowitz 1985; Scolari 2012; Strate 2017). Medium theorists see media as more than conduits for the transmission of messages; they argue that the very nature of the medium can be the key to its social impact. From this perspective, media technologies can be powerful social forces, affecting how we perceive and understand the world.

All medium theorists take seriously the potential impact of technology, but they differ in the degree to which they acknowledge the influence of social factors. Some analysts can be called technological determinists, whereas others more clearly emphasize the balanced interaction of various social forces with technological developments. They also differ in their assessment of the social changes prompted by new technologies. Some analysts have chronicled the dire effects of new technology, whereas others have optimistically embraced new developments.

McLuhan's Optimism

The best-known variant of medium theory was the so-called Toronto School. Initiated by political economist Harold Innis (1894–1952) and popularized by literary scholar Marshall McLuhan (1911–1980), this work was carried out mostly by literary and cultural critics rather than social scientists. Initially, Innis was interested in the effect of macro-level technologies on societies as a whole, such as the difference between cultures with oral versus written traditions. McLuhan, on the other hand, focused on the media's influence on how individuals perceived and thought about the world.

McLuhan can fairly be called both a technological determinist and an enthusiast for the cultural effects introduced into society by the prevailing electronic medium of his day, television. McLuhan (1964) argued that, if we are interested in understanding the influence of media, then we should focus our attention on the ways each new medium disrupts tradition and reshapes social life. The real message, for McLuhan, was not the formal content of media but the ways the media themselves extend our senses and alter our social world. McLuhan was quite insistent about this position, colorfully arguing that "the 'content' of a medium is like the juicy piece of meat carried by the burglar to distract the watchdog of the mind" (p. 32). What changes people, he argues, is not media content but the experience of the medium itself. Thus, McLuhan is best known for his succinct assertion that "the medium is the message" (McLuhan and Fiore 1967). If he were alive today, it's not hard to imagine McLuhan writing, for example, about how smartphones have altered our social interactions, regardless of what content we are accessing with them.

In an early work, *The Gutenberg Galaxy*, McLuhan (1962) focused on the shift from oral to print societies, exploring the social implications of the 15th-century invention of the modern printing press by Johannes Gutenberg. He argued that new media technologies rework the balance of our senses, isolating and highlighting certain senses at the expense of others. Print, from this perspective, intensified the visual—we use our eyes to read—and separated it from other senses, in particular, sound.

In another work, *Understanding Media: The Extensions of Man*, McLuhan (1964) turned to the shift from print to electronic media, especially television. In it, he argued that, by delivering both images and sound, electronic media could help reconnect the senses that had been fragmented by print's exclusive focus on the visual, thereby bringing us back to a kind of preprint state of harmony. Further, McLuhan argued, by allowing us to see images and hear sounds from distant places instantaneously, electronic media are a global extension of our senses. "[W]e have extended our central nervous system itself in a global embrace, abolishing both space and time" (p. 19), he wrote. This perspective led him to optimistic predictions of the development of a new "global village"—a term he popularized—based on the wonders of communication technology.

In McLuhan's technological determinism, each medium was seen to shape our senses in such a way that certain social outcomes would be almost inevitable. Because the dominant media of an era are all encompassing, McLuhan argued it is virtually impossible for people to see the ways technology influences them. Because McLuhan was generally an enthusiast for new technologies, this sort of stealth determinism did not alarm him. Instead, he saw electronic media as opening the door to new and more holistic ways of thinking.

Postman's Pessimism

Although McLuhan's vision of new technologies was an optimistic one, other analysts working in the tradition of technological determinism have cast a more skeptical eye on technology. For example, some critics—most notably Neil Postman (1931–2003)—argued that the rise of television was the central cause of the decline in the seriousness of public life. The underlying premise is that what we say is, in large part, the result of the form—or technology—we use to say it. According to this view, the substance of democracy—participation by an informed citizenry—was undermined by the rise of television. The properties of television encouraged, perhaps even dictated, particular ways of talking and thinking that were antithetical to serious debate and discussion. To envision an extreme version of this, we need only think of the rapid-fire sound bites and shouting matches that often characterize television programs about contemporary politics or the many "fluff" pieces that make their way onto "news" programs simply because they have engaging video. In the end, according to the title of Postman's best-known work, as a society infatuated with entertainment television that is no longer able to think seriously about social and political issues, we are *Amusing Ourselves to Death* (1985).

This kind of critique of the television age is often a nostalgic lament for the bygone days when print was the dominant form of media in American society. Following McLuhan, Postman (1985) argued that print-based societies changed how we think. But Postman saw literacy as encouraging rationality, seriousness, and coherence in both our ways of thinking and the content of public discourse. Reading creates a mind in which analytic thought, based on logic and clarity, is premium. Societies that rely on the printed word as the central means of both private and public communication, therefore, develop rational, serious populations, he argued. Postman identified 18th- and 19th-century America, which witnessed the birth and rise of U.S. democracy, as the most thoroughly print-based culture in history. Others have made similar arguments about the connection between print and rationality, suggesting that, for example, the development of the printing press played a key role in the rise of scientific thinking (Eisenstein 1979). Therefore, unlike McLuhan, Postman was concerned with the ways television challenges the rationality and coherence of print-based modes of thinking by holding up entertaining and trivial images that often work by generating emotional responses rather than by appealing to logic.

Postman's historical analysis connects the decline of serious substance in the media to the impact of even earlier technologies, in particular, the role of the telegraph and the photograph, in cultural change. By altering our sense of physical place—specifically, by making it possible to communicate with people who were physically distant—the telegraph, according to Postman, challenged the world defined by print in three fundamental ways. First, because they could get information from faraway places, newspapers were full of stories that were largely irrelevant to their readers. News no longer had to have any relationship to its audience, nor did information have to be functional in any way—it just had to be "new." Daily news consisted of new things, and novelty became more important than relevance. Second, because the telegraph made it easy to transmit so much information, little of which was relevant to the lives of readers, news no longer had any connection to action. People could not do anything about the things they read about in the paper. Information may have been abundant, but events were happening so far away and were so disconnected from people's lives that the news encouraged feelings of powerlessness. Third, in privileging speed and abundance of information, the telegraph sacrificed context. No longer did news have to be linked to any broader, historical framework. There was no need to connect one story to the next or one day's headlines to the next day's. The point was to keep the information flowing—to report the new things that happened—rather than to contextualize messages or events by linking them to prior messages or events. Quantity became more important than either quality or depth.

The photograph extended what Postman (1985) saw as a revolution in the ways we understand the world. Photos do not encourage logical argument or contextual knowledge. Instead, as Postman put it, "The point of photography is to isolate images from context, so as to make them visible in a different way" (p. 73). As the saying goes, a picture is worth 1,000 words. But Postman argued that, when we trade words for pictures, we lose something in the deal. The very meaning of information, of truth, is altered by a focus on the visual image of the photograph. Truth is no longer knowledge produced from logical thought, the kind of thinking that reading encourages. Instead, "seeing is believing."

If seeing is believing, then those who can skillfully manipulate what we see can also influence what we believe. A generation before Postman, historian Daniel Boorstin (1961) argued that the pervasiveness of visual images was changing the very meaning of "reality." Images have become so embedded in our consciousness, in this view, that it is becoming harder to discern the difference between image and reality. It is not that we are losing our ability to think; it is that image-oriented pseudo-events blur the distinction between image and reality. *Pseudo-events* are events planned for the express purpose of producing dramatic images that can be disseminated or reported. In effect, they are events that have no independent existence; they take place only to be publicized. Pseudo-events can include press conferences, televised debates between political candidates, and photo opportunities—all staged to produce dramatic images. Pseudo-events, however, are neither true nor false; they actually happen but only to produce dramatic images and sound bites. Appearance, not substance, is what matters. Indeed, pseudo-events may be more interesting than spontaneous happenings, a state of affairs that suggests that our definition of reality may be changing.

Postmodernist theorists suggested that contemporary society is increasingly characterized by this kind of "hyperreality," in which the boundary that used to separate reality from its representation has "imploded," leaving images with no real-world referents (Baudrillard 1988). One does not have to be a postmodernist, however, to see the significance of image making. Writing in the age of television—but still relevant today— Postman saw that, in a world dominated by visual media, fast-paced entertainment may have become the model for all of society.

There can be little doubt that critics such as Postman and Boorstin were correct about the significance of images and visual media in American society. However, the causal claims—that inherent properties of media technology are the key determining force—are much more difficult to accept. The problem with such technological determinism is that it ignores people, except perhaps as victims of an all-powerful medium. Even though it is rarely explicit, most critics of television write about *commercial television*, not simply television technology (Hoynes 1994). The claims that television, as a technology, must be about entertainment, attractive images, and rapid movement from one idea to the next are not some technological law of nature. They are the result of an industry—driven by people and market forces—in which the need to sell products and make profits has dominated (Croteau and Hoynes 2006). Similarly, today's internet has introduced a whole new level of endless engagement and entertainment, but these efforts are not inevitable; they are shaped by the commercial forces constantly seeking our attention (Wu 2016).

As should be clear now, there are a range of ideas that can loosely be grouped under the umbrella of technological determinism. What they have in common is a focus on the role technology plays in influencing individuals and society more broadly. This emphasis contrasts with the focus social constructionism brings to the role of human agency and social forces.

Social Constructionism

As the name suggests, social constructionism emphasizes the social construction of technology, focusing on the role of active human agents in ultimately determining how technology is developed and used. These analyses usually acknowledge that technology matters, but they theorize technology and social forces as interdependent and mutually influential. Social forces—such as cultural norms, economic pressures, and legal regulations—fundamentally shape the ways in which technologies are designed and developed. In addition, ordinary users influence how these technologies are ultimately used and, often, whether these technologies succeed or fail.

Social constructionism is part of the broader sociological perspective that sees all of social reality as socially constructed (Berger and Luckmann 1966). Specifically, social reality is produced in three steps:

1. People create society through ongoing processes of physical and mental activity.

2. Over time, these creations come to seem objectively real, separate from human activity.

3. People internalize the norms and values of their culture, thereby being influenced by their own creation.

So we are influenced by the things we create in part because we forget that we created them; they seem "normal," "natural," and perhaps inevitable to us. However, because we collectively create social reality, we can always change it.

This basic argument for the social construction of reality underlies the constructionist approach to media technology. Humans create technology, and even though it sometimes appears technology has a life of its own, in fact, we ultimately have the power to alter how we use it—a fundamental difference from technological determinism. This essential insight has long animated a range of work that highlights the social construction of technology, both in and outside of media (MacKenzie and Wajcman 1999; Bijker, Hughes, and Pinch 2012). Social constructionists in media studies proper include "British media studies" or the "Birmingham School" of cultural studies, developed around the work of Raymond Williams (1974), Stuart Hall (1980, 1997), Richard Hoggart (1957), and their colleagues at the Centre for Contemporary Cultural Studies at the University of Birmingham between the 1960s and its closure in 2002. Among other things, these researchers highlighted the important role of "active audiences" in interpreting and making use of media.

For example, Raymond Williams (1974: 9) opens a classic work by noting, "It is often said that television has altered our world." Williams then proceeds to dismantle this argument—which he says is technological determinism—by pointing out the interrelationship between technologies and the preexisting cultural values and practices in a society. Thus, he notes, television in the United States and the United Kingdom first emerged as two very different things because of the contrasting social values of the two societies. The more individualized values of U.S. society created a privately owned commercial television industry whose content was created to attract audiences to sell to the corporate advertisers who funded the medium. Meanwhile, comparatively collectivist British social values were embodied in the British Broadcsting Corporation (BBC), owned and funded by citizens, which focused on public service. In this way, technology did not inevitably lead to a single model for television; cultural values influenced variable development.

Social constructionists argue that users matter, too. For example, one variant of a constructionist approach, domestication theory, suggests that ordinary users "appropriate" technology of all sorts, bringing it into their homes and daily lives (Bakardjieva 2005, 2011; Silverstone and Hirsch 1992). In doing so they are consumers who both connect to the outside world of commerce while asserting their own identities through their consumption and use of technologies. Often, users end up changing technology by adapting it in novel ways, and these actions end up influencing the developers of future technologies.

FROM PRINT TO THE INTERNET

Having sketched out the differing ways technological determinists and social constructionists view technology, we move now to see how such dynamics played out during the emergence of various media technologies. In our overview, we attend to the material reality of technology (from the technological determinism end of the spectrum) but highlight examples of how human agency shaped technology (from social constructionism). As outlined in Chapter 1, our sociological approach embraces the tension between media technology and the people who create, regulate, and use it. It is part of the push-pull dynamic we intend to highlight throughout this book.

The Print Medium

The introduction of the printing press had a substantial impact on human history. Building on earlier technology, Johannes Gutenberg demonstrated a practicable way to print by converting a winepress into the first modern printing press with movable metal type in the mid-1400s. Although the technology had evolved, media content changed little at first. Reflecting the power of the Catholic Church in Europe at the time, the Bible was the book most often produced by early printers. Thus, as was true for later changes, social forces other than technology determined the direction of media development.

But printing technology also contributed to—or at least facilitated—social change that was unanticipated (Eisenstein 1979). Prior to printing, books and manuscripts were hand copied, making them expensive, rare, and available only to a small number of scholars, primarily clergy. Printing—and the corresponding growth in literacy—helped democratize learning by making books more affordable and widely available. The Protestant Reformation that began with Martin Luther in 1517 was fueled, in part, by the ability of literate believers to now read the Bible for themselves, sometimes calling into question the Catholic Church's interpretation and authority. Over time, printing accelerated the pace of innovation in philosophy, science, the arts, politics, and other fields by helping spread information and ideas throughout and across cultures. Rather than be dependent upon a mentor, it was now more possible for people to read and learn on their own, perhaps contributing to the rise of individualism in Western society, too. More broadly, print fundamentally changed how human societies operated. Oral traditions in storytelling and history were eventually supplanted by written texts. Arguably, as medium theorists contend, thinking changed as a result. Written texts required a disciplined approach to communication that favored linear sequencing of thoughts and reasoned arguments, which became a hallmark of Western philosophical and scientific thinking.

At the founding of the United States, print media—in the form of books, newspapers, and pamphlets—was still the only means for reaching a wide audience.

FIGURE 2.4 ■ Time (in Days) Required for News to Travel from New York to Select Cities, 1794–1841

In the era of print media, news could only travel as fast as people could physically carry it.

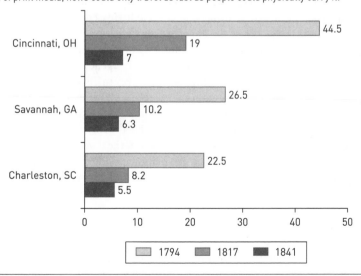

Source: Pred (1973).

However, distribution was limited and slow because of the need for physical delivery of print material (unlike later electronic media). Both routine and extraordinary information, from holiday greetings to news of the outbreak of war, traveled only as fast and as far as a horse, train, or ship could carry it: a slow speed difficult to imagine today. It routinely took four to eight weeks for information to travel from Europe to the United States. Even communication between distances that we now perceive to be quite short—from New York to Washington, for example—were slowed by the need for messages to travel physically between the two locations. As late as the 1840s, it still took several days for news to travel from one city to the next (see Figure 2.4). One consequence of this limitation is that most publications tended to remain local, resulting in a highly fragmented and isolated media landscape.

The Telegraph

Although it is not a mass medium, the telegraph was an advance in communications technology that had major implications for other media. The invention of the telegraph in the 1840s allowed for near instantaneous communication over long distances that were physically wired together. For the first time, there was a separation between physical transportation and long-distance communication. The telegraph did not reach a large audience, but it did speed up the spread of information through newspapers. Reporters could send news stories instantaneously over a long distance to newspapers that would then print and distribute the story locally. News not only spread faster and further this way, but wire services also began producing content that was used in multiple markets. These wire service stories helped unify—and critics would say homogenize—what had previously been a highly fragmented and localized news culture.

Print media had been highly decentralized, with local printers setting up shop in most communities. In contrast, the material nature of the telegraph—with single lines spread across thousands of miles—lent itself to more centralized control. In short order, companies competed until telegraph ownership became highly concentrated. By the 1870s, Western Union was the owner of the only nationwide telegraph network, and it carried Associated Press (AP) stories exclusively. Using this monopoly position, Western Union worked closely with the Republican Party to promote its agenda and candidates, arguably winning the election for President Rutherford B. Hayes in 1876. For example, Western Union provided Hayes with the telegrams of his rivals, allowing his campaign to be one step ahead of the opposition (Blondheim 1994; Wu 2011).

The telegraph foreshadowed several issues associated with emerging media technologies, including the increased speed of communication, the dangers of centralized control of technology, how control of technology can help shape which content is available, and how the integration of technology produced more unified—perhaps homogenized—content. All of these issues would reappear with later technologies.

The Telephone

The telephone is also not a mass medium, but it influenced other media in ways that are still felt today. In 1876, Alexander Graham Bell was issued a patent for the invention of the telephone, which opened the way for more widely accessible, personal, long-distance communication and later facilitated other media. But telephone techno-logy went through considerable evolution as users experimented with different ways of employing it, companies competed in how to deploy it, and the government eventually moved to regulate it—all of which shaped the evolution of the modern telephone (Fischer 1992; Wu 2011).

When the telephone was invented, Western Union hoped to use it merely to make its telegraph business more convenient. To send a long-distance telegraph message, cus-tomers would simply make a local phone call to the Western Union office. For a variety of reasons, including challenges to their patents, this never happened. Western Union agreed to drop out of the phone business as long as the newly created Bell Telephone Company agreed to stay out of the telegraph business. From that point on, Bell—later to become known as American Telephone and Telegraph (AT&T) became the dominant phone company. For two decades, it held the key patents that enabled it to operate as a monopoly, providing profitable service mainly to businesses and wealthy clientele in major cities. By 1893 about two-thirds of the nation's telephones were in businesses, while residential service was quite limited (Fischer 1992: 42)

In the mid-1890s, though, Bell's key patents expired, introducing a brief era of com-petition during which telephones were transformed from a luxury business service to a widespread and common utility. In just a few years, thousands of "Independents" sprang up, ranging from innovative businesses using the latest technology to very basic commu-nity operations operating as nonprofit cooperatives. About 3,000 of these were for-profit businesses, and by 1902 fully half of communities with a population of 4,000 or more had at least two competing, independent phone companies. In addition, another 6,000 shareholder-subscriber "mutuals" were created to provide low-cost community access (Fischer 1992: 43–44).

In some rural areas, where commercial service was unavailable or was too expensive, farmers even set up lines along existing barbed wire fences, providing unsophisticated but very low-cost phone service. These "farmer lines" had no privacy; they operated as a giant party line to which anyone in the community who was connected could listen. Users would sometimes organize telephone parties on a specific day and time, during which local musicians performed and storytellers entertained. Other time slots might be reserved for sharing the weather forecast and regional news. Using the technology in ways that were never intended, farmers were essentially "broadcasting" years before real radio broadcasting technology existed (Wu 2011).

Telephone competition was short-lived, however, coming to an end in 1913. The inde-pendents fought among themselves for small markets, often failing or being taken over by Bell—now a division of AT&T. Bell aggressively drove out local competition, some-times using the profits from its lucrative urban markets to engage in predatory pricing in smaller communities and rural areas. At the national level, AT&T also took over Western Union, gaining unmatched access to the "long lines" that connected cities. By moving to take over both local and national communications, AT&T consolidated its control over the entire industry.

As AT&T's monopoly status became clearer, government antitrust regulators began investigating. In the end, AT&T asked to be regulated in exchange for continuing to hold its monopoly. In the Kingsbury Commitment of 1913 it agreed to operate based on rates set by the government, to sell off Western Union, to stop acquiring any more

Independents, and to permit the remaining Independents to connect to its long-distance services. For the guaranteed revenue stream that came with such a monopoly, AT&T promised to make access to high-quality standardized phone service available to everyone. The company became a public utility and later officially became a "common carrier," equally open to all users without discrimination. (We explore the idea of "common carriage" and implications for today's internet in Chapter 4 on regulation.)

Often known as "Ma Bell" or simply "the phone company," the AT&T monopoly was a universal presence in American life until its breakup in 1982. The company had four divisions:

- Bell companies provided local telephone service.

- AT&T Long Lines connected local communities for long-distance service.

- Western Electric manufactured communications hardware.

- Bell Labs conducted research and development.

Government regulations protected the monopoly by forbidding competition. Consequently, AT&T controlled everything from the home phone (which was typically rented from AT&T, not owned by the resident or business) to the local and long-distance wires and all of the switching equipment in between.

Because telephone lines reached almost everywhere by the mid-20th century, they served as important information conduits for other media. Radio and television broadcast networks used phone lines to relay their programming across the country to be aired locally. Later, early dial-up modems and high-bandwidth Digital Subscriber Line (DSL) service used telephone wires to connect users to the internet, too.

With standardized equipment and centralized control, the quality of telephone service under the AT&T monopoly was generally quite good. Bell Labs also provided the government with valuable defense and security-related research. However, without competition, costs could be high, and innovation that did not serve the existing business model was often suppressed. For example, Bell Lab scientists discovered magnetic tape recording and created a prototype answering machine in the 1930s. However, the inventions were shelved because company officials feared the public would avoid using the telephone if they knew their conversations could be recorded. Magnetic tape recording in the form of the audiocassette became available only in 1962—first from foreign companies. Bell also discovered and put on hold early versions of fiber optics, mobile phones, DSL, fax machines, and speaker phones, among others (Wu 2011).

Over time, the political climate changed, and little by little, the AT&T monopoly was weakened. For example, building on a 1968 ruling, the Federal Communications Commission (FCC) mandated that what we now know as the standard phone jack—the RJ11—be used on all equipment. Previously an AT&T technician had to come to a home to attach a phone to the phone line; now a consumer could do it alone by simply plugging it in. This technological standard, enabling easy connection to a standard phone line, sparked innovative third-party products, such as fax machines, cheaper telephones, and later, the modem that allowed personal computers to talk to each other via phone lines. In 1971, the FCC barred AT&T from entering data processing or online services, creating rules to prevent AT&T from buying out new competitors. This enabled the growth of America Online (AOL), CompuServe, and other early innovative internet service providers (ISPs) (Wu 2011).

Most significantly, in 1982, a long-term antitrust suit was settled, and AT&T agreed to be broken up into eight separate "Baby Bell" entities that were required to accept connections from smaller competitors (see Figure 2.5). This breakup unleashed enormous competition and innovation. Most notably, expensive long-distance services—which had long subsidized local service in sparsely populated areas—were now open to competition, bringing costs down sharply. As media and legal scholar Tim Wu (2011: 162) notes,

> [T]he breakup of Bell laid the foundation for every important communications revolution since the 1980s onward. There was no way of knowing that thirty years on we would have an Internet, handheld computers, and social networking, but it is hard to imagine their coming when they did had the company that buried the answering machine remained intact.

FIGURE 2.5 ■ The Breakup and Reconsolidation of the Telephone Industry

Regulatory environments change, affecting the nature of communication technologies and industries. Long a state-sanctioned monopolgy, AT&T agreed to settle an antitrust lawsuit by being broken up into "Baby Bell" companies in 1982. Since then, though, the companies have signficantly reconsolidated and are major players in today's media industry.

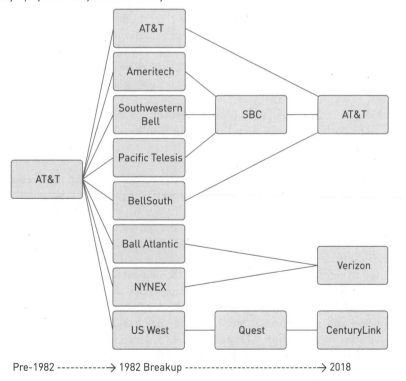

Pre-1982 ------------> 1982 Breakup -----------------------------> 2018

Source: Wu (2011).

But, again, this era of competition was short-lived. The pre-1982 AT&T has slowly reconsolidated over the past 35 years; the eight "Baby Bell" companies have become the "Big Three" telecom companies of today: AT&T, Verizon, and CenturyLink.

Telephone technology clearly changed the way we live. But the telephone's long and complicated history illustrates starkly how human agency ultimately determines the shape and direction of technological development and use. The regulatory environment, for example, fundamentally influenced the way telephone technology was created and deployed. Users, too, helped shape the way the technology was incorporated into daily life. In fact, in his classic social history of the telephone, sociologist Claude Fischer (1992) argues that we should not even ask what "impact" a technology has had on a particular society because this question implies from the outset that the technologies do something to us. Fischer contends,

> while a material change as fundamental as the telephone alters the conditions of daily life, it does not determine the basic character of that life. Instead, people turn new devices to various purposes, even ones that the producers could hardly have foreseen or desired. As much as people adapt their lives to the changed circumstances created by a new technology, they also adapt that technology to their lives. (Fischer 1992: 5)

Sound Recording

In 1878, Thomas Edison received a patent for the cylinder-based phonograph, which would lead to the first new mass medium since print. Edison referred to his invention as a "talking machine" and believed that "[t]he main utility of the phonograph [is] for the purpose of letter writing and other forms of dictation" to be used in conducting business correspondence (Katz 2012: 13). However, other developers and users had different ideas about how to use this technology.

Within a decade, phonograph records featuring musical recordings were introduced, and as other forms of sound recording later proliferated, music became the primary application of sound recording. At first, the standard phonograph record was the 78 rpm that could accommodate a three-minute recording on each side. In 1948, the long-playing (LP) 33 1/3-rpm record was launched and became the industry standard for more than 30 years. Magnetic tape became most popular in its easy-to-use cassette form, introduced in the 1960s, which enabled people to easily make their own recordings or assemble mix tapes for the first time. This technology made music more mobile, too, because tapes could be played in car stereos and on portable tape players such as Sony's Walkman, the precursor of the iPod. In the early 1980s, sound recording became digital, and the compact disk (CD) emerged as the dominant recording format. By the 1990s, compressed digital file formats, such as MP3, allowed music to be speedily distributed via the internet and stored on tiny MP3 players and smartphones. Since 2011, digital music has made up the majority of music sales, outselling CDs and vinyl LPs. However, sales of specific music recordings have been displaced by subscriptions to streaming audio services, such as Spotify, Pandora, and Apple Music, which have accounted for the majority of digital music revenue since 2016 (International Federation of the Phonographic Industry 2017a). Streaming enables users to listen without needing to purchase particular recordings while still being able to customize their experience by choosing from vast catalogs of recordings.

Through its various incarnations, the technology behind sound recording enabled significant social change for listeners and musicians alike. Recordings made musical performances—rather than just printed musical scores—permanent, altering how musicians performed and how audiences listened. Prior to recordings, music was experienced exclusively in live performances, often in group settings. Professional music could be heard only in public spaces such as concert halls, clubs, and the like. Recordings meant that such music was now available to hear—and replay at will—in the privacy of the home and was often experienced alone, making it a much more intimate listening experience. Solitary listening was so new and startling that users had to be educated about the experience. One article noted that if the reader found a friend listening to recorded music alone, they would be forgiven for thinking "such an activity would be evidence of an unwell mind, whether caused by mental instability or substance abuse" (Katz 2012: 16). Not to worry, though, the article continued, in the new age of recorded music, listening to music alone was perfectly normal behavior.

Because access to professionally created music was so limited before recordings were available, many amateurs played musical instruments and sang for family and friends. With recorded music now available, social gatherings didn't stop, but playing recorded music at such get-togethers became commonplace and sometimes controversial. Composer and conductor John Phillip Sousa gained fame from his early recordings of marching music (Eschner 2017). But he penned a wide-ranging essay in 1906 warning about recordings (and player pianos) as the "menace of mechanical music." Part of his concern involved the rights of copyright holders, but his apprehensions also included the worry that professionally recorded music would "substitute for human skill, intelligence and soul" that came from live performances. He was alarmed, too, that, with the rise of recorded music "it will be simply a question of time when the amateur disappears entirely" (Sousa 1906).

Recording technology helped change the music artists made, too. For example, one side of the early 10-inch 78 rpm record could only accommodate a three-minute recording, so musicians of all stripes changed how they wrote. Even classical composer Igor Stravinsky once reported, "I had arranged with a gramophone firm to make records of some of my music. This suggested the idea that I should compose something whose length should be determined by the capacity of the record" (Katz 2010: 3). The result was 1925's "Serenade for Piano," written in four movements of roughly three minutes each to fit conveniently on two records. By the 1950s, the 78-rpm record was replaced by LPs, which could accommodate recordings of more than 20 minutes on each side. However, the three-minute standard for a recording lived on because they could be conveniently sold as low-cost 45-rpm "singles." As a result, nearly every pop song of the 1950s, 1960s, and beyond was roughly three minutes in length.

New recording technology also changed the experience of musicians over the years. Prior to recordings, live performances were the essence of being a professional musician. As the recording industry grew, however, studio recordings became the primary source of income for popular musicians. (The same was true for the new breed of "session players:" highly skilled but largely unknown musicians who were hired to play on recordings.) By the mid-20th century, the most popular artists launched concert tours primarily as promotional vehicles for selling records. But elaborate studio recordings that used

Prior to the invention of sound recordings, listeners could experience music only in live public settings, which is one reason why so many communities had bandstands in their local parks. With the phonograph, music listening could become more private and individualized.

complicated production techniques, such as overdubbing many tracks of the same artist, enabled the creation of recordings that could never be played live. The Beatles, for example, famously stopped touring in part because the complex studio recordings they were making later in their career could not be performed on stage.

By the end of the century, though, new technology helped swing the pendulum back in the direction favoring live performance. On the one hand, the sales of recorded music were undermined by musical "piracy" (via easily downloadable digital recordings) and streaming services, which made the purchase of particular recordings largely unnecessary. Musicians, then, returned to relying on live performances to generate the bulk of their income. On the other hand, these live performances were sometimes now enhanced by new technologies. Synthesizers and sampling made the inclusion of complicated and prerecorded sounds in live performances easy. More controversially, lip-synching became common. Recorded music had long been used to mimic "live" performances.

As early as the 1940s, some artists lip-synched to their recordings in brief filmed "soundies"—the music videos of the day—which could be played on coin-operated film jukeboxes. On television in the latter half of the 20th century, popular teen dance programs such as *American Bandstand* and *Soul Train* featured musical acts lip-synching to their latest recordings. By the turn of the century, lip-synching to recorded music at "live" concerts became prevalent in the pop music industry as well. Well-known pop artists such as Beyoncé, Mariah Carey, Madonna, and Britney Spears all lip-synched on stage. The reasons for doing so varied: Vocals created in the studio through digital manipulation, most famously with Auto-Tune, could not be performed live; grueling touring schedules and outdoor performances in variable weather conditions stressed artists' vocal chords; and shows now often included athletic dance performances that made simultaneous singing difficult (Lubet 2017). Frequently, the result has been a mixture of live performance with prerecorded enhancements.

Sound recordings have affected how we live our daily lives and impacted how musicians work. However, the application and evolution of recording technology certainly did not proceed in the way its inventor had envisioned. Users made choices that significantly altered the trajectory of sound recordings away from simple dictation for business purposes to much broader applications. The music industry helped shape how we experience popular music. On the whole, recorded music also did not destroy amateur musicianship, as some had feared. To the contrary, millions of people were able to use sound recordings to help themselves learn how to play their own instruments. Many more experimented with new recording technologies, leading to new forms of music such as DJs "scratching" records in hip-hop performances and amateurs using a vast array of sampled sounds and digital audio workstations (DAWs) to program and play many types of music, especially electronic dance music (EDM).

Film and Video

Sound recordings enabled the permanent capture of what had previously been a fleeting auditory experience. Photography did the same for visual experiences. People could take photos of their loved ones to remember them in their absence. Historical events were captured for posterity. Soon, inventors created "moving pictures" through various devices that gave individual users the illusion of motion by peering into a box to see a series of photographs flicker past. Modern "movies" were born in 1895, when brothers Auguste and Louis Lumière first demonstrated their cinematograph, which used film to project moving pictures onto a screen to be viewed by a group audience. Film technology eventually evolved to include the use of synchronized sound, color film stock, and digital technologies that have largely replaced film.

In their first decade, "movies" were brief, and more than 80 percent of them were about topical subjects such as news, travel, documentaries of everyday life, and sports (Starr 2004). In time, filmmakers shifted from using film technology to produce simple animated photographs to creating increasingly elaborate fictional stories. The nature of this evolution varied greatly, though, based on the social context within which it occurred.

For example, in the 1910s, a New York City-based "Film Trust," a cartel of 10 companies, controlled the U.S. film industry. The Trust had every important patent on motion picture technology and therefore kept out competition while dictating how the industry operated. The Trust set a price per foot of film that distributors would pay producers, a weekly price that exhibitors paid for the use of patented technology in projectors and so on. Movies were, in effect, a commodity sold by the foot. The arrangement kept prices low to ensure a steady audience and guarantee a healthy profit. This monopoly, though, greatly restricted creativity. It blocked most film imports and limited U.S. moviemaking to short (less than 20 minutes), uncontroversial, uncomplicated films, featuring unknown and low-paid actors (Wu 2011).

Meanwhile in Europe, most notably France, there was no film cartel, and feature-length films starring well-known actors quickly became the norm. The model eventually made its way to the United States after a couple of renegade "independent" distributors—who refused to join the New York-based Film Trust—began importing foreign film stock and producing their own films. Sued hundreds of times by the Film Trust, the independent film producers fled New York and filmed in other locations, including Cuba. But Los Angeles proved the most convenient location for their work because they could quickly and easily cross the Mexican border to avoid court injunctions and subpoenas. Thus, renegade outlaw filmmakers founded what eventually became the Hollywood movie industry (Wu 2011). (Over time, the Hollywood studio system became a new monopoly and the courts would intervene, a story we explore in Chapter 4.)

Film production exploded with the rise of independents. In 1914, more than 4,200 new films were reviewed in the industry press. U.S. filmmaking prospered and catered to a wide and diverse set of market niches across racial, ethnic, and political spectrums. World War I decimated the European film industry, opening the way for the domination of the U.S. industry there, too (Wu 2011). Movies became a central element of American leisure. By 1930, an astonishing 65 percent of Americans were attending movies at least once a week. (That figure would drop by half with the introduction of television in the 1950s and then hover around 10% or less from the mid-1960s to today [Pautz 2002].)

By the late 1970s, technological innovations radically changed how users interacted with films. Videocassette recorders (VCRs) allowed people to purchase or rent movies to watch in their own homes, thereby privatizing the movie experience. Cheaper video cameras also enabled users to more easily film and show their own videos. In 1997, the digital video disk (DVD) was introduced, marking the shift of movies to digital formats. Digital cameras, smartphones, and related software made it easier still for the general public to record, edit, produce, and store their own videos, whereas websites such as YouTube and Vimeo offered platforms for the upload, storage, and exhibition of these amateur videos. With such sites and social media sharing, personal videos could now enter the public sphere. Meanwhile, a deep catalog of commercial films was increasingly available through internet-based video-on-demand and streaming services, such as those provided by Netflix, Hulu, and Amazon.

Film technology changed how audiences—and later amateur filmmakers—related to movies and videos. But the development and application of this technology was shaped by the social forces surrounding it. Industry collusion in the form of the U.S. Film Trust limited how the technology could be used, whereas European filmmaking evolved differently. The action of renegade independents changed the U.S. film industry. Much later, users changed the nature of videos by taking advantage of new technology to record and share videos online. From recording cat antics to documenting police shootings, smartphone videos and social media have added new complexity to the world of film/video creation and consumption.

Radio Broadcasting

Radio was developed over the first two decades of the 20th century. In contrast to a telegraph or telephone message sent via a wire to a particular person or destination, the unique feature of broadcast technology was that it used the electromagnetic spectrum to transmit audio signals that could be received by anyone with an inexpensive radio kit who was within range of the signal. Early amateur radio operators referred to this process as "broadcasting," taking the term from a farming technique in which seeds were "cast broadly"—that is, scattered widely—rather than planted in neat rows. For the first time, media producers no longer had to physically distribute their products (e.g., to newsstands, record stores, or movie theaters), nor did the public have to travel to these locations to have access to mass media. In addition, broadcasting introduced the possibility of live programming as well as "free" content. As sound recording had done earlier, radio broadcasting further enabled privatized and individualized media experiences, sometimes displacing social and public forms of entertainment.

Although early radio was essentially the same technology we know today, people knew radio by a different name and understood it as a very different form of communication than we do now. That's because the social forces that later shaped the direction of radio technology had not yet coalesced. Corporate consolidation of the radio industry had not yet occurred, the government had not yet regulated the use of the electromagnetic spectrum, and investors had not yet recognized the profitability of producing household radio receiving devices. What we now take for granted—a model of broadcasting music, news, and entertainment programming usually supported by advertising—took two decades to evolve (Douglas 1987; McChesney 1994; Schiffer 1991; Wu 2011).

For the first 10 years after its invention, people called radio the *wireless* because its creator, Guglielmo Marconi, promoted it as a telegraph without wires. For Marconi, the wireless was an improvement of an existing point-to-point, two-way communication technology; it had nothing to do with broadcasting. Marconi hoped his wireless could serve as a substitute, or an upgrade, for long-distance communication by large commercial interests that relied on the telegraph, particularly newspapers and steamships. Individuals were not seen as users, and receive-only devices—what we call radios today—were still far off. In fact, the uncertainty in the future of wireless can be seen in its eventual name changes. The wireless became *radiotelegraphy*; then, when it began to transmit voice instead of Morse code, it became *radiotelephony* and finally just *radio* (Douglas 1987).

Despite its inventor's intentions, amateur radio operators quickly began experimenting with the technology. As amateurs learned how to use the new technology and how to construct their own transmitters and receivers, a radio subculture emerged in which sending and receiving long-distance communications became a popular hobby. As listeners tuned in at night, seeking transmissions from sites hundreds of miles away, it was amateurs who planted the seeds of the broadcast model and made the act of listening a leisure activity.

Because the airwaves have limited space and demand for their use was growing, amateurs came into conflict with commercial interests and the government. Each of them wanted to use radio technology in a different way, and a struggle over the control, definition, and proper use of radio ensued. Corporate interests sought private control of the airwaves to use them for profit. The U.S. Navy sought government control of the airwaves to use them for military and security purposes, particularly during wartime. Amateur radio enthusiasts, mostly young men and boys in the years between 1906 and 1920, saw the airwaves as a form of public property to be used by citizens to communicate with one another.

Both the U.S. Navy and the Marconi Company supported government regulation of the airwaves to organize and set limits on electromagnetic spectrum use. Douglas (1987) explains they agreed that "the amateurs had to be purged from the most desirable portion of the broadcast spectrum. They had to be transformed from an active to a passive audience, allowed to listen but not to 'talk'" (p. 233). The result was the Radio Act of 1912, which regulated the use of the airwaves by requiring all transmitting stations to be licensed by the federal government, thereby curtailing access for amateurs. So even before the notion of broadcasting had taken hold, the institutional structure of broadcasting was in place: centralized, licensed senders and large numbers of individual listeners.

Despite these restrictions, amateurs continued to operate radios in even larger numbers. Some made use of the shortwave frequencies that the government allocated for them, a few were granted government licenses to use the airwaves, and many more continued to operate without licenses. In 1917, when the United States declared war on Germany in World War I, the government ordered all amateur radio operators to shut down and dismantle their equipment. The police closed down more than 800 operators in New York alone (Douglas 1987). At the same time, the Navy was in need of experienced radio operators, so it recruited amateurs who returned home after the war even more skilled in radio technology. By 1920, amateurs were experimenting with playing music and providing information over the air to other amateurs, who were encouraging their families and friends to listen along. Several amateur transmitters built up substantial audiences for their "programming," while the corporate radio industry continued to focus on point-to-point communication.

All of this changed when, in the hope of increasing sales of their radio equipment, a Pittsburgh department store ran a local newspaper advertisement for a musical program broadcast by amateur Frank Conrad. Shortly thereafter, Westinghouse, one of the major manufacturers of radio sets, began financing Conrad's station as a means of selling its radios. Radio manufacturers AT&T and General Electric, along with department stores, quickly jumped into the business of broadcasting by setting up stations to stimulate the sale of radio sets. They had realized that the market for the broadcast model of radio was much larger than for the point-to-point model, offering the possibility of greater profits.

Soon, owning a radio set and being able to listen to the programs became highly popular. In 1922, AT&T began selling access to the airwaves as Marconi had done for private communication. The commercial broadcast model, with programming financed by the sale of advertising, was established. Records are incomplete, but there were already more than 500 radio stations in 1923, and by the following year more than 2 million radio sets had been sold (Wu 2011: 35).

The emergence of radio advertising was an important part of the clampdown on amateurs. Wu (2011: 76–77) notes, "When revenues came from sale of radio sets, it was desirable to have as many people broadcasting as possible—nonprofits, churches, and other noncommercial entities. The more broadcasters, the more inducement for the consumer to buy a radio, and the more income for the industry." This revenue stream was limited, however; households needed only so many radios. In contrast, advertising was limitless, and "once advertisements were introduced, radio became a zero-sum game for the attention of listeners. Each station wanted the largest possible audience listening to *its* programming and *its* advertisements" In that scenario, amateur competition was a threat to profits and needed to be eliminated.

These developments were highly controversial and certainly were not inevitable. At first, even radio manufacturers worried about the emergence of radio advertising. The head of publicity for Westinghouse argued, "Direct advertising in radio broadcasting service [should] be absolutely prohibited" because "advertising would ruin the radio business, for nobody would stand for it." Then Secretary of Commerce—and later U.S. President—Herbert Hoover, said of radio in 1922, "It is inconceivable that we should allow so great a possibility for service, for news, for entertainment, for education, and for vital commercial purposes to be drowned in advertising chatter" (Wu 2011: 74). But in a few short years, that's exactly what occurred, and by 1931, Henry Lafount, the commissioner of the Federal Radio Commission (FRC, the precursor to the FCC) would write, "Commercialism is the heart of the broadcasting industry in the United States" (Wu 2011: 82).

Radio continued to evolve, of course. For example, because of its limited range, early radio had been an inherently local medium. That changed when AT&T used its exclusive access to long-distance phone lines to establish the first nationwide radio broadcast network. With this model, centralized programming was sent over the lines to be simultaneously broadcast in local markets. With a much larger audience and more advertising revenue, the company could afford to produce high-quality programs with nationally known talent against which local broadcasters could not compete. But AT&T's short-lived dominance was challenged on patent grounds by the Radio Corporation of America (RCA), which had been formed out of the American Marconi Company. Eventually, through a series of court and binding arbitration agreements, AT&T agreed to leave the radio business if RCA agreed not to challenge AT&T's long-distance operations. RCA gave its resulting network a new name: the National Broadcasting Corporation (NBC) (Wu 2011: 78).

The emerging group of major broadcasters encouraged the FRC to get rid of competing local stations to create "clear channels" for their large stations and networks, arguing that their better equipment and higher-quality programming better served the public. The FRC agreed, and the age of plentiful, small-scale local radio largely came to an end. Later, innovation was throttled for years when the FCC, at the behest of the radio giants who feared more competition, delayed the introduction of FM radio broadcasting, which enabled signals to be sent further, more clearly, and with less power. In these cases, too, a technology's application was shaped by the power of corporate and government players.

The route to radio broadcasting of music, news, and serials, all surrounded by ads, was not the straightforward result of some technological imperative. In fact, one of radio's great technological capacities—its ability to both send and receive messages—was largely abandoned in the final model, relegated to shortwave frequencies. By including factors beyond technology in our understanding of radio, we can see that what we often take for granted as radio's natural order of things is in fact the result of a com-

It took a number of years for the new medium of radio to evolve into what we know it as today. Beginning as the "wireless," radio was first conceived of as a telegraph without wires that could improve one-to-one communication. Amateur radio enthusiasts adopted the technology to send and receive long-distance messages as a hobby. Only later did radio become primarily a way to broadcast music, news, and talk.

plicated social process involving commercial interests, amateur users, and government regulators. Moreover, we can see that things could have turned out differently. Basic wireless technology might have been applied or further developed in a different direction, leading to different social consequences.

We don't need to rely on pure speculation to imagine these alternatives. In other countries, radio played a different role than in the United States. In some countries, radio served as a more distinct form of public service communication that was hoped would be beneficial, raising the standard of political discourse and cultivating more discerning musical taste. Sometimes such top-down communication was abused, as when Nazi propaganda minister Joseph Goebbels called radio "the spiritual weapon of the totalitarian state" and argued, "Above all, it is necessary to clearly centralize all radio activities" (Wu 2011: 303, 85). In other countries, listeners have much more widespread access to the airwaves, which are not used to sell products with the same zeal as in the United States. Instead, in several countries, including England, Australia, Argentina, and Uruguay, a portion of the airwaves has been earmarked for "community radio" (Gordon 2008; Hintz 2011; Rennie 2006).

The evolution of radio, and the variations in how it has been adopted, again illustrates the fact that we cannot understand a new medium simply by looking at its technological component because this ignores the social processes that ultimately shaped its use.

Television

As an over-the-air (OTA) broadcast medium, television combines the ability of film to record and display moving images and sound with the ability of radio to broadcast live. Until the 1930s, most television sets were mechanical devices that created an image by scanning a location using a spinning disk with holes in it. The image was transmitted to a user's receiver, which used another spinning disk to display the crude moving picture. Television became practical only in its electronic form, which used cathode ray tubes to produce a better-quality image by sweeping an electron beam across a phosphorescent screen.

The deployment of early television technology might have threatened the dominance of radio. However, after successfully eliminating amateur radio competition, the major radio companies effectively delayed and destroyed potential television competitors, too. NBC's owner, RCA, argued to the FCC in the 1930s that "[o]nly an experienced and responsible organization such as the Radio Corporation of America, should be granted licenses to broadcast material, for only such organizations can be depended upon to uphold high ideals of service" (Wu 2011: 144). The FCC agreed and sharply limited the television stations that could broadcast until the 1940s, effectively locking out any amateur or fledgling competition. This gave RCA time to catch up in developing—and in some cases stealing—new technology. It also scared away potential investors from competing technology ventures, driving inventors and innovators into bankruptcy. This left only the large radio corporations with enough capital to enter the electronic television field.

As a result, the few companies that dominated radio became the same players who dominated network television: NBC and ABC evolved from RCA's radio business, and CBS television was spun off from CBS radio. (A fourth, short-lived, Dumont network was owned by a manufacturer of television equipment.) As a result, there was almost no innovation in programming; early television was essentially radio with pictures. The three major networks simply began shifting their radio programs—and advertisers—to the new television medium.

Building on radio's success, manufacturers and broadcasters marketed television as another form of privatized entertainment that would bring the family together to enjoy public amusement without having to leave home. They succeeded wildly (harming movie box office revenue in the process). In the span of less than 10 years, between 1946 and 1955, television sets made their way into 65 percent of American households and were in 90 percent of households by 1960 (Spigel 1992). In relatively short order, television became a major part of American life. After a half century of analog broadcasting, manufacturers and broadcasters successfully lobbied the U.S. government to order all television stations to convert to digital signals in 2009. This marked yet another medium making the shift to the universal digital format. Digital programming could easily be transmitted over the air, via cable, via fiber optics, or through internet streaming to a wide range of devices, not just television sets.

Television and Daily Life

In its remarkable rise to prominence, the television industry both accommodated already existing family practices and tried to mold these practices (Spigel 1992). In this era, white

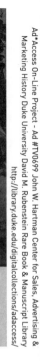

Atari Mania

Both early television and computer manufactures tried to sell new technologies as ways to enhance existing social relations. In time, both of them would enable significant change in the routines of daily life.

middle-class women were perceived as having a great deal of "free time" during the day for leisure or relaxation while also attending to housework. Therefore, producers directed most early television programming at women viewers, whom they considered to be the largest and most accessible audience. Although broadcasters had largely repackaged radio programs for television at first, they soon learned that the different technologies facilitated different sorts of audiences. Radio could provide entertainment while women worked because, as a purely aural medium, listening did not interfere with other activities. However, as a visual medium, it was more difficult to market television as something women could enjoy at the same time as they were doing housework. Leaders of the television industry were concerned that the new medium might not fit into women's lives and therefore might be underused or ignored altogether.

One 1952 effort to overcome this hurdle came from manufacturers who developed a TV-Stove, an appliance that allowed women to watch television while they cooked. By designing an apparatus that accommodated existing cultural practices and traditions, the television industry hoped to attract loyal viewers. The TV-Stove demonstrates that cultural practices can shape the development of media technology. It also shows how user preferences can be more powerful than technological innovation: The TV-Stove was a market failure.

Television broadcasters were more successful by designing the content of programming to accommodate the practices of 1950s middle-class women. Producers designed the "soap opera" (named after the soap manufacturers who often sponsored them) and the variety show as programming that would not interfere with women doing house-work. Soap operas contained little action but a great deal of verbal explanation and often repeated the same themes. Viewers could listen from an adjacent room or could miss episodes without losing track of plot developments. Variety shows moved from one act to the next, making it easy for viewers to enjoy them, even if they watched only parts of the program. This, too, was ideal for women working around the house.

The television industry also tried to reshape family routines to be compatible with television viewing. As Spigel (1992) puts it, "Not merely content to fit its pro-gramming into the viewer's rhythms of reception, the network aggressively sought to change those rhythms by making the activity of television viewing into a new daily habit" (p. 85). For example, promoters billed NBC's *Today Show* as the TV equivalent of the morning newspaper. In addition, the networks routinized their schedules, pre-viewed upcoming programs, and linked program times to the household activities of women and children, all of which encouraged viewers to adapt their daily routine to the television schedule.

In the end, broadcast television became the centerpiece of U.S. consumer culture, influencing and disrupting American traditions, practices, and buying habits. Still, tele-vision was not a predetermined entity; cultural practices shaped its early development and uses, just as the medium in turn influenced these practices.

Cable Television

Just like radio, broadcast—or OTA—television relies on the airwaves to send its signal. Due to limitations in bandwidth, the number of broadcast stations in any market is lim-ited, and the audience must be within range of the broadcast signal. Beginning in the late 1940s, amateur operators in remote areas where broadcast signals didn't reach properly began to put up huge antennas to catch the weak signal and resend TV content via wires to local paying customers. Known then as Community Antenna Television (CATV), this was the birth of cable television (Wu 2011).

The early cable markets were tiny, and because the practice merely expanded the audi-ence for existing programs, broadcasters were not particularly concerned. Over time, though, cable operations expanded. Cable companies moved into larger communities and eventually began to use microwave towers (which were the first practical alternative to phone lines for long-distance communication signals) to import programs from far away that would otherwise not be available over the air in the local market. Since the local audience now might be watching programs that originated elsewhere in the country, this threatened to undermine the broadcast business model. Broadcasters sued, claiming copyright infringement, but in 1968 the Supreme Court ruled in favor of cable operators. Broadcasters then turned to the FCC, which began using new regulations to bar cable from the largest markets and to otherwise strangle the industry. With cable expansion stopped, investment stopped.

By the end of the 1960s, though, the Nixon administration championed deregulating cable to open up the industry while avoiding monopoly concerns by keeping the owners of the wires separate from the producers of programming. Cable enthusiasts argued that it could help solve the problem of limited bandwidth. New channels could be devoted to public service and be a noncommercial alternative to advertiser-driven broadcasting.

In this vision, cable operators would be in control of a few of the channels, while the bulk of cable channels would be available for public interest programming or be made available for lease. Cable did expand, but it did so as a fully commercialized system with just a few local "public access" channels (Wu 2011).

Continuing the long-standing trend of privatizing public entertainment, in 1972 HBO launched its "Home Box Office" service, bringing commercial-free feature films and sporting events to television. It was among the first channels to rely primarily on subscribers paying a premium fee rather than on advertisers. In 1975, HBO innovated technologically when it began to use satellites to deliver its content rather than AT&T's long-distance lines or microwave towers. This caught the attention of Ted Turner, who, in 1976, created a "superstation" when he bounced the data from his Atlanta broadcast station off of satellites down to local cable operators across the country. Using a similar technological approach in 1980, he launched the Cable News Network (CNN). Over the next decade, many others followed suit as new cable networks such as ESPN, MTV, Bravo, Showtime, BET, Discovery Channel, and Weather Channel—along with many that have since failed—were created. Television, long known for its limited and homogenous programming from three major broadcast networks, was transformed by the spectacular growth of cable. Broadcast television networks (now often actually delivered via cable) would continue to be in the business of delivering large mainstream audiences to advertisers, but cable-only TV channels now could survive by "narrow-casting," delivering niche audiences to specialized advertisers, and by enticing these audiences to pay a premium for content they valued (Wu 2011).

Cable technology overcame the limited number of stations that could be accommodated in OTA broadcasting. As a result, television's business model—as well as its social impact—changed. As we've seen, early mass media—newspapers and local radio—were fragmented by locality because technological limits meant most content was created and distributed locally. Later, radio and television networks created a more unified, mainstream, national culture. For example, when Elvis Presley performed on *The Ed Sullivan Show*, his appearance drew an astounding 83 percent of American TV households. (In comparison, in recent years, even the highly rated Super Bowl has reached less than half of U.S. households.) American viewers shared a more common television culture in that time, but that programming was typically bland, designed so as not to offend viewers or potential advertisers, and wildly unrepresentative of the nation as a whole. People of color and others outside of the mainstream, white middle class were largely invisible in this content. Wu (2011: 214) calls the programming from this period "unprecedented cultural homogeneity" from networks that "were probably the most powerful and centralized information system in human history."

Cable changed that through an economic model that enabled the viewer to access a larger volume and variety of programming. However, content aimed at smaller and sometimes more adventurous audiences reintroduced cultural fragmentation. This time, though, fragmentation was based on interest, taste, and—with news and commentary—political orientation rather than locality. But cable was still homogenous in a key way: With few exceptions, its business model is unapologetically commercial, whether catering to advertisers or appealing to subscribers. Early cable enthusiasts, who saw cable as a public service alternative to the commercial broadcast networks, never saw their vision realized. Instead, cable grew into powerful local monopolies that, critics argued, offered high-priced packages bloated with many rarely viewed channels. Cable operators argued that this package model subsidized smaller niche stations that otherwise could not survive on their own. In recent years, cord-cutters, though, began voting with their feet as they abandoned cable in droves, relying more on streaming services for television and video entertainment (with the term "video" now often replacing "television"). One result has been an effort to unbundle cable with a variety of smaller, lower-cost options still emerging.

Whether delivered via broadcast, cable, or streaming technology, commercial television became the centerpiece of U.S. consumer culture, influencing and disrupting American traditions, practices, and buying habits. Still, as we have seen, television was not a predetermined entity; cultural practices shaped its early development and uses, just as the medium in turn influenced these practices.

The Internet

In many ways, today's media landscape is dominated by the internet. As with earlier technologies, the internet has enabled social change and, in turn, has been influenced by a variety of social forces. Because we will be exploring many of these internet-related dynamics throughout the book, we limit our discussion here to an overview of narrow technology issues that distinguish the internet from other forms of media.

Creating the Internet

The internet is a vast network of interconnected computer networks whose underlying technology was developed over a half century (Abbate 1999; Hafner and Lyon 1996; Naughton 2000).

In 1958, in the midst of the Cold War and in response to the Soviet Union launching the first space satellite, *Sputnik*, the U.S. government created the Advanced Research Projects Agency (ARPA) within the Department of Defense to develop forward-looking technology with military applications. Two years later, one of the program's leaders, J.C.R. Licklider, wrote, "The hope is that, in not too many years, human brains and computing machines will be coupled together very tightly, and that the resulting partnership will think as no human brain has ever thought and process data in a way not approached by the information-handling machines we know today" (Licklider 1960: 75).

By 1966, the group had launched ARPANET, a small network of government and university computers that pioneered the use of "packet switching" to break down messages into small data packets before sending them separately along different routes to be reassembled by the receiving computer (see Figure 2.6). Although this technology was seen as potentially enabling military communication to continue after a nuclear attack destroyed one or more nodes in the network, it instead became an essential element of the internet.

By 1968—a half century ago—Licklider and his colleague Robert W. Taylor were presciently writing, "In a few years, men will be able to communicate more effectively through a machine than face to face." They envisioned that "interactive communities of geographically separated people" would create "distributed intelligence," available to tackle any task. These "on-line communities" would be "communities not of common location, but of common interest . . . interconnected by telecommunications channels." They hoped that "life will be happier for the on-line individual because the people with

FIGURE 2.6 ■ Internet Packet Switching

The internet's technology enables messages sent from one computer to be broken up into tiny data packets that are routed through whatever optimal pathway is available and then reassembled at the receiving computer. This promotes speedy transmission by avoiding bottlenecks or breakdowns in the vast network. It also helped establish the internet as a highly decentralized medium that was not easy to block or shut down.

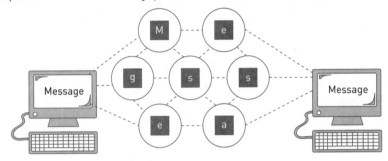

whom one interacts most strongly will be selected more by commonality of interests and goals than by accidents of proximity." They argued that access to such networks needed to be a right, not a privilege, so that everyone could benefit. They concluded, "[I]f the network idea should prove to do for education what a few have envisioned . . . surely the boon to humankind would be beyond measure" (Licklider and Taylor 1968).

ARPANET went online in 1969, at first linking just four universities. In the 1970s, researchers worked out the standard language and protocols that would be used by all computers wanting to connect to the network. By 1975, more than 50 university and government sites were networked, and the pace of growth increased. In 1983, ARPANET was split in two, resulting in MILNET, for military uses, and NSFNET—under the control of the National Science Foundation (NSF)—for civilian uses. Under NSF guidance, standardized communication protocols (Transmission Control Protocol/Internet Protocol [TCP/IP]) that regulate the size and flow rate of data packets were officially adopted, enabling any computer to connect to the growing internet. The NSF supported the national "backbone" of this network, free of charge.

Once the military uses of the internet were separated from civilian uses, government financial support came with relatively few strings attached. This enabled early developers to work without the pressures of commercial market forces while acting on their optimistic "technocratic belief in the progress of humans through technology" (Castells 2001: 61; Kahn and Kellner 2004). Within this context, a subculture of computer enthusiasts (sometimes known as hackers) promoted principles such as sharing, openness, decentralization, and free access to computers (Jordan 2008; Levy 2010). Their efforts were the foundation for later "open source" and "free software" movements.

In its early years, using the internet was generally limited to engineers, computer scientists, and others who possessed the necessary specialized computer skills. That changed when Tim Berners-Lee, a British scientist at the European Laboratory for Particle Physics (known as CERN) in Switzerland created a user-friendly network interface and freely released it into the public domain. Launched in 1991, this "World Wide Web" created the familiar "www" at the beginning of web addresses and used hypertext to enable "point-and-click" navigation, making it much easier for people to use the internet's growing archive of resources. (This also marked the beginning of the widespread but erroneous belief that the "web" and the internet were one and the same.)

Also in 1991, the U.S. Congress passed the High Performance Computing and Communication Act, authored by then-U.S. Senator Al Gore, to substantially expand the publicly funded infrastructure that was becoming popularly known as the "information superhighway." Shortly thereafter, the NSF issued an "Acceptable Use Policy" for NSFNET, confirming that its services were provided to "support open research and education." The research arms of commercial firms could also use it but only "when engaged in open scholarly communication and research" (NSF 1992).

But as the potential of the internet to reach the wider general public became increasingly clear, businesses began operating their own private networks, and investors sought to use the internet for commercial purposes rather that public ones. Back in 1988, the NSF had already begun discussions about commercial access to the internet and sponsored a series of conferences on "The Commercialization and Privatization of the Internet." As media scholar Robert McChesney (1999: 130) points out, "No one really had a firm sense . . . of what exactly, if anything, the privatization of the Internet would mean for individual users," and there was little public input into the process. Still, the transition happened quickly; by 1995, the NSF stopped funding NSFNET, and internet connectivity became the exclusive domain of private firms.

As the president of the Internet Society, a nonprofit group that helps maintain the technologies and applications that undergird the internet, noted, "The mechanics of the Internet are so widely distributed that for [the government] to try and exercise control is folly. Sure, they created the technology through their funding . . . but the baby has grown up and left home" (Quick 1998).

The Internet Grows Up

Some researchers within the military's ARPANET program had viewed themselves as nonconformists challenging the confining structures of the military establishment while promoting values of sharing and decentralization that became part of the internet's infrastructure. Similarly, as the internet became commercialized, some early internet-related companies were led by individuals influenced by the communitarian counterculture of the 1970s (Turner 2006). If an egalitarian, hippie lifestyle—supplied by products from the *Whole Earth Catalog*, fueled by the psychedelic drugs of the day, and aimed at cultivating personal freedom—turned out to be impractical, then perhaps new technologies offered a different route to liberation. The old, centralized, mainframe IBM computers of the corporate world came to symbolize the faceless establishment; the new, networked "personal" computers of Silicon Valley entrepreneurial start-ups represented the rebellious empowerment of the individual. A 1984 television commercial from Apple—with its bright, rainbow-striped fruit logo—embodied the sentiment, famously associating its new MacIntosh computer with an assault on an Orwellian "Big Brother" in a bleak, black-and-white world. This combination of zealous techno-utopianism (sometimes informed by the work of Marshall McLuhan), dressed in a countercultural "rebel" veneer, harnessed to maximize capitalist commercial success, proved to be a potent mixture that influences technological developments to this day. (The irony, of course, is that some of these once hip, rebellious, and disruptive technology companies became the established corporate giants of our age.)

As the internet "grew up," the excitement over the potential money to be made became frantic in the latter half of the 1990s, contributing to wild investment in new "dot-com" companies that drove the U.S. stock market to unprecedented levels. But consumers at the time were not interested in buying groceries (webvan.com), kitty litter (pets.com), or sporting goods (mvp.com) online. As a result, many much-hyped companies collapsed, and the dot-com "bubble" burst in 2000, sending the stock market plummeting.

But as the internet gained a greater foothold in society in the 2000s, more emphasis was placed on how this technology could enable users to customize, create, and share content rather than simply shop online. Web 2.0, one of the popular labels given to highlight this collection of interactive capacities, was a label that suggested a technological change from the earlier internet. New technologies, enthusiasts noted, enabled the rise of blogging, social-networking sites, content platforms such as YouTube, collaborative wikis such as Wikipedia, virtual game worlds such as World of Warcraft, and virtual worlds such as Second Life.

In fact, Web 2.0 did not reflect any substantial change in the technological capacity of the internet. Instead, Web 2.0 was a concept coined in 2004 to indicate a shift in how software developers and users utilized the existing medium (Scholz 2010). Part of this was marketing hype; in the wake of the dot-com bust, developers had to convince investors that there was something new and fundamentally different about Web 2.0 that made it a better and safer investment than the failed dot-com era. Just as the uses to which radio and television technology were put evolved over time, Web 2.0 highlighted and developed capabilities of the internet that had existed since its inception. This is another example of how changes that result from social forces have been popularly and erroneously understood as being the result of technological innovations.

The world of internet connectivity was enhanced by the growth of mobile devices, including laptops, tablets, and especially, smartphones. The ease with which users could now access these devices—and the internet—meant they could be easily integrated as an omnipresent element of daily life. The emerging innovations in wearable technologies and the "internet of things (IoT)" suggest this integration of internet with daily life will only increase in the coming years. (We explore some of the implications for users and society of this growth in Chapters 8 and 9.)

Some Characteristics of the Internet Era

As with other media technologies, the internet did not travel a straight line from introduction to mass adoption. Instead, as we have seen, the internet is the result of complex social processes, involving government funding, the culture of computer enthusiasts, commercial interests, and user preferences. But the technological infrastructure of today's internet—much of which remains invisible to users—has several unique features with significant social consequences.

First, the internet was designed and built to be an open, decentralized platform, accessible to anyone using its basic language and protocols. Unlike, say, cable television, it was not a private, commercial venture controlled by industry corporations. Instead, its creation was funded by research grants, it accommodated projects that were not commercially viable, and its pioneers encouraged a culture of public service. This enabled early internet pioneers to experiment and innovate at a rapid pace, tackling the enormous challenges they faced in creating a new medium. Some of the solutions they found for these challenges still shape how the internet operates today.

Second, the internet's structure was designed to give users considerable control over their experience; it is a nonspecialized platform made to accommodate whatever the user wants to do. This changes interpersonal communication by enabling user interactivity regardless of location. We can video chat with a friend across the globe or Tweet back and forth with people in different locations. As we saw in Chapter 1, this sometimes blurs the distinction between interpersonal and mass communication, supplementing the one-to-many model of traditional mass media with the possibility of a many-to-many network of communication. In addition, unlike with traditional broadcast media defined by a set program schedule, internet users decide what content to access and when. More important, people with relatively modest financial resources and basic technological literacy can use low-cost digital media tools to create and share original content. The requirements for such a task are still insurmountable hurdles for the world's impoverished and illiterate—and indeed the majority of the world's population—but the creation of widely sharable media content is within the grasp of more people than ever before in human history.

Third, the internet is the first medium to embody *digitization*—the shift from analog to digital media—and *convergence*—the blurring of boundaries among types of media. Analog media exist across largely unbridgeable material divides. The technologies underlying print on paper, sound pressed into the grooves of vinyl records, and images chemically developed on celluloid film, for example, each work in their own distinct ways. In contrast, digitization enables print, sound, images, and video to be recorded, copied, stored, and transmitted in a single universal language: the 1s and 0s of computer code. This common digital foundation is what enables your computer, television, or smartphone to access text, images, video, and sound and to "talk" with other digital devices. Such code can be easily copied and shared, making media content abundant. Digitization sets the stage for convergence, where previously distinct forms of media now blur. "Newspapers," for example, don't need paper, but they can post print stories with embedded videos and audio files on their websites. Over the past few decades, the growth of digital media, the rise of the internet, and the proliferation of mobile devices have combined to burst open the very meaning of media (Bolter and Grusin 2000; Lister et al. 2009).

Finally, the internet is a global system of communication whose governance structure transcends the regulatory reach of any single country. The result is vast gray areas of law and custom. For example, nation-states can impose regulations or even close off parts of the internet, but it is difficult to be totally effective in doing so. Intentionally designed to survive the shutdown of any particular node, the internet's decentralized structure offers many possible work-arounds for tech-savvy users. So who should have unfettered access to the internet? Who can regulate and control it in the face of cyber criminals and other nefarious users? As more and more of our world is connected to the internet and dependent upon it—not only individuals but energy grids, banks, schools, and the media—how can security be enhanced while maintaining the flexibility and openness of the internet? The sprawling reach of the internet raises many such questions and concerns, even while it still offers some of the hopes envisioned by its pioneers.

As Curran, Fenton, and Freedman (2016:1) note, "In the 1990s, leading experts, politicians, public officials, business leaders and journalists predicted that the internet would transform the world," by bringing prosperity, democratizing culture, rejuvenating political democracy, challenging autocrats, and promoting global understanding. Although falling far short of such idealistic predictions—and producing many unanticipated consequences—the internet has enabled a wide variety of economic, social, and political change, some of which we explore throughout this book.

CONCLUSION

Helsingborg, Sweden, is home to the Museum of Failure (2018). Among the many technology-based innovation failures featured there are the Divx Disc and the Teleguide, along with the better-known Google Glass, Apple Newton, and Sony Betamax. (You can learn about any one of those by simply searching for them on the internet, which is definitely *not* a failure.) In a sense the museum is a testament to one of the arguments of this chapter: The development and uses of a new technology are not inevitable. Their fate is determined by economic, political, and social forces. Technology matters, enabling the introduction of vast social change, but its development and application are the result of the people who create, deploy, regulate, and use them.

As we have seen, the last century has featured a series of disruptive innovations in communications technology, including the telegraph, telephone, radio, film, television, cable TV, and the internet. Media scholar Tim Wu (2011) argues that there is some similarity to the evolution of these new technologies. At first, he notes, the introduction of an innovation begins a period of idealistic experimentation. Often, the new technology is touted as providing significant altruistic or even utopian benefits for society. Inventor Nikola Tesla predicted that, with radio, "the entire earth will be converted into a huge brain, as it were, capable of response in every one of its parts." Pioneer film director D. W. Griffith declared that children would never again be asked to read history books because "children in the public schools will be taught practically everything by moving pictures" (quoted in Wu 2011). A study from the 1970s claimed cable television was bringing a revolution that was "nothing less" than that brought by movable type and "may conceivably be more" (Wu 2011: 6). And, as noted earlier, the internet has been touted as a transformative development in human history.

However, Wu continues, when the new technology threatens to displace or render obsolete older technologies and their reliable revenues, traditional technology companies seek to control it. They tame the experimental uses of the technology, standardizing it in a closed form that can be centrally controlled—and more efficiently tapped for profits—all in the name of a better user experience. The government is often enlisted to help by regulating against any new competition. Social and economic forces reassert themselves, and the field yields to the control of a few major corporate players. Over time, though, the novelty of the new technology wears off, users become familiar with its flaws and limitations, and dissatisfaction grows. Protected from real competition, the closed industry becomes stale and is ripe for challenges by new players promoting new technology.

Crucially, Wu makes clear that there is nothing inevitable about what he calls "The Cycle" of technological innovation. Instead, key players—including inventors, corporate executives, government regulars, and users—each make decisions and take actions that bring about the changes.

Arguably, the process continues today as debates swirl between public interest advocates and major media corporations concerning the direction the internet should take. As Wu observes, "It may be true, today, that the individual holds more power than at any time in the past century, and literally in the palm of his hand. Whether or not he can hold on to it is another matter" (p. 299).

Discussion Questions

1. Explain the differences between technological determinism and social constructionism.

2. What are some examples that show how human agency shapes the development and use of technology? What are some examples suggesting that technology may sometimes influence society?

3. In what ways have the use of electronic media, especially television and the internet, changed social life? What is different about how we live because of the presence of these media? What changes do you think might be coming in your lifetime?

4. What have been some of the most important advantages to the rise of the internet and the expanded use of mobile devices? What are some of the potential negative consequences of these changes?

INDUSTRY

Part III examines the social forces that influence the source of most media content: the media industry. In Chapter 3, we look at the economic forces that shape the industry and the consequences for media content. Chapter 4 turns to the political constraints on media, exploring various debates about government regulation. These two chapters focus on relationships *among* institutions. In Chapter 5, we turn our attention to social forces *within* the media industry itself, considering how the organization of the industry, its professional routines, and its organizational norms help shape media products.

The emphasis in Part III is on the broad structural constraints on media production; how these economic, political, and organizational forces shape decision making and influence media content; and how actors within the media industry interpret and respond to these constraints. This "production perspective" has been the principal lens through which much contemporary sociology has looked at media. As we will see, it has a great deal to offer for understanding processes of media production, distribution, and promotion.

However, as a production-oriented perspective tells us little about things such as how people use or interpret media products, it is important to remember that it is only part of our larger model of media and the social world. Issues of media content, the role of active users, and media influence will be addressed in Parts IV and V. Production, though, is an important piece of this larger media puzzle and an essential component of our exploration of the complex relationship between media and society.

3

THE ECONOMICS OF
THE MEDIA INDUSTRY

In June 2018, the Walt Disney Company announced an agreement to outbid rival Comcast and purchase most of 21st Century Fox, one of Disney's longtime rivals in the media and entertainment industry, for more than $71 billion. (At this writing the deal awaits regulatory approval.) In likely acquiring Fox, Disney will obtain the 20th Century Fox movie and television production company (including the rights to Fox's popular franchises such as *Avatar*, *X-Men*, *The Simpsons*, and *Modern Family*), several major domestic and international cable television networks (including

FX, National Geographic, and popular networks in India and Latin America), Fox's 22 regional sports networks, and 30 percent of Hulu, which will give Disney a majority share of the streaming service.

The Disney-Fox merger would be the second-largest media merger in history, combining the production, distribution, and promotional power of two of the most prominent global media companies. The merger means, for example, that the *X-Men* join Marvel's cinematic universe and that Disney owns the entire *Star Wars* film franchise. What does this merger suggest about the rapidly changing economic dynamics within media? Why did Disney buy Fox? What impact will an even bigger Disney have on contemporary culture and society? And what does this latest round of media mergers tell us about the role of media in our digital world?

This chapter helps answer these questions as we explore the economic dynamics within the media industries and their impact on media content. We focus on media ownership, the for-profit orientation of most media, the role of advertising, and how these economic dynamics are changing amid the kinds of technological developments we describe in Chapter 2. Whereas social media, much of which emphasizes commentary, photos, and video from people in our social networks, occupies a significant portion of daily media use, a great deal of the media content we consume is still produced by media companies, and most mass media in the United States and other Western democracies are for-profit businesses. Like all businesses, they are influenced by issues such as profitability, cost containment, and evolving ownership patterns. To fully understand the media, then, we must have some sense of the economic dimension of the media industry. (For a more in-depth treatment of the economic dynamics that shape the media industry, see Croteau and Hoynes 2006; for a focus on the global dimension of media, see Birkinbine, Gomez, and Wasko 2017.)

The types of questions we ask and the general orientation of this chapter build on the framework outlined in Chapter 1. We emphasize a sociological perspective that argues that social structures shape—and are in turn shaped by—human behavior. An emphasis on the push-pull tension between agency and structural constraint suggests that human activities and attitudes must be understood in relation to broader social forces. In this case, we cannot understand the media industry without understanding the forces that affect the industry. The individuals and groups that create the television and video we watch, the music we listen to, the websites we visit, the magazines and newspapers we read, the movies we attend, and the seemingly omnipresent advertisements we see, are not fully autonomous actors. They do not work in isolation from the social world. Instead, they work within the constraints of an existing organization, a broader media industry, and a larger social context.

A sociological perspective suggests that we cannot look at media products in a vacuum, either. Instead, we should see media products as the result of a social process of production that occurs within an institutional framework. Some researchers call this kind of institutional approach a "production perspective" (Crane 1992; Peterson and Anand 2004) because it emphasizes the media production process rather than either specific media products or the consumption of those products. The production perspective highlights the fact that most media products are the result of a complex production process shaped by a variety of social structural forces that operate on various levels, some affecting the industry as a whole and some affecting particular actors or groups of actors within the industry. Producers create media products under conditions that are always changing as economic, technological, political, and social changes occur in the broader society. Therefore, if we are to better understand media products, we must take into account the historically specific context in which people create them.

MEDIA COMPANIES IN THE INTERNET ERA

As we will explore further in Part V, in the digital media era audiences have become more active users, creating and posting their own content and commenting on postings by friends and family. Still, even amid such user activity, the importance of media companies has not diminished. Instead, as we will see, major media companies remain key players in our media experience. The difference is that now they include both traditional brand names like Disney as well as companies that were, until recently, more likely to be considered tech or phone companies.

Contemporary media companies perform three key tasks; they provide the following:

1. **Products**—the media content that we watch, read, and listen to, such as movies, original journalism, or music recordings.

2. **Platforms**—the sites and services that host, display, and find media content, such as Facebook, YouTube, and Google. In addition, streaming services—such as Netflix, Hulu, and Amazon for video content and Spotify, Apple Music, and Pandora for music—offer subscribers medium-specific platforms for accessing traditional mass media content.

3. **Pipes**—the conduits by which we access media content and platforms, such as wireless, cable, DSL, and fiber optics that are the arena of telephone (Verizon and AT&T), cable (Comcast and Charter Communications), and satellite companies (DirecTV, owned by AT&T, and Dish Network).

Although it is useful to disentangle these functions to better understand how the media industry works, in reality these elements overlap. In fact, one of the defining characteristics of contemporary media companies is that they are often involved in all three industry sectors: products, platforms, and pipes. The internet has changed how these companies operate in ways that we will explore later in the book, but they still dominate the media landscape.

Products

First, the products of media companies—their content—saturate our lives. Television and radio programs, print publications, and films, of course, all consist of such media products, and many of these traditional products are available via the internet along with internet-only creations. You can watch the opening monologue of a late-night TV show on YouTube, scan the *Los Angeles Times* leading news stories on its website, listen to your favorite band by streaming them online, or watch a movie on Hulu. Often, therefore, when we are talking about the internet, we are talking about content produced by traditional mass media companies now being accessed online.

Much of the internet's most-viewed content is created by traditional mass media companies. For example, most of the original reporting on news sites comes from traditional "legacy" news organizations, especially newspapers and television networks. Another example, at this writing, one of the most viewed titles on Google's YouTube site (with well over 3 billion views) is Wiz Khalifa's music video "See You Again." It was created for a song released by Atlantic Records as part of a soundtrack for the action movie *Furious 7*, distributed by Universal Pictures, which is owned by Comcast, the cable and broadcast TV giant. So even though this video is viewed on the internet, traditional media companies were ultimately responsible for its production, promotion, and distribution. We cannot understand how a YouTube video can amass 3 billion views without understanding its connection to these traditional mass media conglomerates.

How will traditional media companies continue to adapt as the internet continues to evolve? Thinking back to Disney's likely purchase of Fox, we can begin to see that this merger was driven, in large part, by Disney's effort to expand the online distribution of its vast media content by becoming majority owner of Hulu as well as launching its own Disney streaming services. This challenge of online distribution faces all of the major media content producers and has led to a streaming war discussed in the next chapter. How companies respond to the changing media environment is not yet clear; understanding the economic dynamics within the media industry helps us analyze ongoing developments.

Platforms

Second, to find content and to communicate on the internet, users rely heavily on media platforms owned and operated by companies like Facebook (which also owns Instagram, WhatsApp, and many others) and Google (which owns YouTube, Android, and many others). For the most part, these companies are not directly content creators. Instead, they deliver people to advertisers, in effect making users the product being sold. You may be creating the content that attracts your friends and family to Facebook, but Facebook is selling you and your friends to advertisers. This is a twist on an old reality: Most media have relied on attracting readers, viewers, and listeners to sell to advertisers. Commercial television, for example, is in the business of delivering audiences to advertisers; television programs are what attract and, when successful, hold viewers' attention, which is sold to advertisers seeking to promote products and services to those audiences. What's different today is that, on social media platforms, much of the content that serves to attract users is produced by users themselves rather than by media companies.

Sometimes, though, the lines blur between user platforms and media content companies. A significant amount of social media content is about traditional media, especially television. When the Nielsen rating service launched its Social Content Ratings during the 2016–2017 television season, it found nearly 3 billion social interactions on Facebook and Twitter were about television programs such as *The Walking Dead*, *Empire*, and *The Bachelor* (Nielsen 2017f). Nielsen differentiates between "owned activity"—social media content generated by official accounts associated with a program or network—and "organic activity"—content generated by the viewing audience (Nielsen 2017a). About two-thirds of social media content related to television is organic activity; one-third is owned. This varies by genre, though, with more than half of talk and news content being owned. So, often, the content social media users circulate, such as a news story, was originally created by a media company. When you post a link to an article you read in your favorite magazine, perhaps along with your own comments on the article, you are, in essence, helping distribute the content produced by the magazine. Indeed, in recent years, publishers have relied heavily on internet platforms to deliver readers for their content.

The lines between regular users and media companies blur in other ways, too. For example, at this writing, one of the YouTube channels with the most subscribers is that of PewDiePie, the alias of a sometimes-controversial Swedish-based video game reviewer and commenter, Felix Arvid Ulf Kjellberg. PewDiePie cultivated his more than 58 million subscribers largely outside the channels of traditional mass media. Beginning as a regular user, he eventually signed with a series of internet-based companies that host and promote multichannel YouTube sites. Traditional mass media companies long ago took notice of PewDiePie's huge subscriber base. In 2016, Time Warner bought Machinima, PewDiePie's first promoter, making it part of a traditional mass media conglomerate.

Even if you don't have aspirations to global internet fame and fortune, the internet is obviously historically unique with unparalleled opportunities for sharing your interests, creativity, and commentary with others on a variety of platforms. But will the internet continue to be an open medium for such experimentation in the coming years? Or will powerful mass media conglomerates and new digital giants simply dominate this medium as other media have in the past? That history is currently being written.

Pipes

Third, we rely on media companies to create and maintain the "pipes" that deliver our media experience. It's easy to overlook this part of the media system . . . until we lose the signal for our smartphone or our cable service goes out in the middle of a big game. In those sorts of moments, we are reminded of just how much we depend on this often-invisible infrastructure for our media and communications needs. Think for a minute about the infrastructure you rely upon to access media. Perhaps it is a cable company that brings high-speed coaxial cable lines into your home; these cables can carry enough data to provide access to live television and on-demand video services, telephone, and internet access. Alternately, the pipe may be a telephone line, which can provide phone service and DSL internet access, or more powerful fiber-optic lines that can handle phone, television, and internet service. Or perhaps you have a satellite connection or use your mobile device as the "pipe" into your home.

Regardless of the specific mechanism bringing media into your home, school, or workplace, the pipe metaphor alerts us to the power of the companies that own the systems that provide media access—and the influence they potentially have on both media producers and media users. Owning these pipes is incredibly valuable. Users rely on them for their everyday media activity, even if we only really notice the significance of these systems when they are on the fritz. And media producers rely on the network of pipes to distribute their content across various platforms. However, equal access to all parts of the internet has been repeatedly threatened in recent years as companies that provide the pipes seek new ways to increase revenue by charging some content producers for preferential "fast lane" treatment. Will the internet be an even playing field for all content in the coming years? Debates about "net neutrality" regulations—rules designed to prevent unequal treatment of content delivery—is one of the issues we will explore in Chapter 4.

CHANGING PATTERNS OF OWNERSHIP

Even as the media landscape changes, a long-standing question about the economic organization of media remains as pertinent as ever: Who owns the media? The assumption behind the question is that owners of the media influence the content and form of media products by their decisions to hire and fire certain personnel, to fund certain projects, to serve as a platform for certain content, and to develop or support certain technologies. In its least subtle version, such questions might imply a kind of conspiracy theory in which a small group of powerful owners uses the media to control the thoughts of the rest of us. With its Orwellian connotations of mind control, this extreme version of the ownership question is too simplistic and therefore not particularly illuminating. However, a substantial body of research has explored this topic in a more subtle—and helpful—way.

iStock.com/borntodeal

Most media we see and hear are owned by just a handful of major media corporations, including the Walt Disney Company.

Concentration of Ownership

One of the primary questions about media ownership is the degree to which ownership of major media is concentrated, that is, owned and operated by a small number of large firms. Beginning in 1983, journalism scholar Ben Bagdikian (1920–2016) chronicled the growing concentration of media ownership over two decades in a series of editions of his classic book, *The Media Monopoly*. By the publication of the last edition of the book in 2004, now *The New Media Monopoly*, Bagdikian argued that only five global firms dominated the U.S. media industry, operating like a cartel. He identified the five dominant companies as Time Warner, The Walt Disney Company, Viacom, News Corporation, and Bertelsmann, all multimedia entertainment conglomerates that produced and distributed newspapers, magazines, radio, television, books, and movies.

However, in the years since the 2004 publication of *The New Media Monopoly*, the media landscape has changed considerably. First, several of the traditional media giants Bagdikian identified have been transformed, and by 2018 only Disney and Bertelsmann remained intact. The other companies had become smaller, selling parts of their multimedia conglomerates to focus their businesses more narrowly:

- In 2006, Viacom split into two separate companies: Viacom, Inc., which owns a major movie studio (Paramount) and several prominent cable television channels (Comedy Central, Nickelodeon, MTV); and CBS Corp., which owns the CBS television network, a major television distribution company, and 29 local television stations.

- In 2013, Rupert Murdoch's News Corporation split into two companies: the smaller News Corp. that focused on newspapers (*Wall Street Journal*, *New York Post*) and book publishing (Harper Collins) and the new 21st Century Fox, with a movie studio (20th Century Fox), television network (Fox), and cable television channels (Fox News, FX). In 2018, as noted earlier, Disney announced plans to purchase most of 21st Century Fox.

- In 2014, Time Warner spun off its magazine division, the largest magazine publisher in the United States (with well-known titles such as *Time*, *People*, and *Sports Illustrated*) as a separate Time, Inc. In 2016, it sold Time Warner Cable, the second-largest cable television provider in the United States to Charter Communications (Spectrum). Later, in 2017, the phone and internet giant AT&T agreed to purchase the remaining assets of Time Warner; the agreement was challenged by the U.S. Justice Department, which cited antitrust concerns, but was approved by a federal judge in 2018.

As this history suggests, size alone does not guarantee success, and some of the media giants may have overreached in their efforts to acquire competitors.

The second major development during this period was the spectacular growth of new tech giants, especially Google and Facebook. Facebook was founded in 2004—the same year *The New Media Monopoly* was published—and although not traditional media companies, firms like Facebook and Google emerged as new media giants in their own right by dominating online advertising revenue. As we will see, the maturing internet had helped change the media landscape, enabling the growth of new competitors.

In the late 2010s, however, as the older media giants scrambled to compete in the new media landscape, they turned again to consolidation as a business strategy. Among the most significant developments were Disney's plan to buy Fox, AT&T's merger with Time Warner, and Verizon's 2017 purchase of Yahoo.

So even in the face of continuing change in the media industry, media ownership is highly concentrated heading into the 2020s. Within each sector of the media industry, a few large companies tower above their smaller competitors. Internet and telecommunications firms, especially, dominate their sectors, but to varying degrees, products, platforms, and pipes alike are led by a few firms.

Products

The major media companies own vast portfolios of products, spanning the range of media formats and delivery systems. Because most products carry a distinct name, rather than the label of the corporate owner, most media users are unaware that a large number of media outlets are actually owned by a single corporation. For example, in book publishing, Bertelsmann's Penguin Random House owns more than 85 publishing imprints, making it far and away the largest English-language book publisher in the world (see Figure 3.1).

FIGURE 3.1 ■ Book Imprints Owned by Penguin Random House, 2018

DK

DK

Alpha Books

Penguin Publishing Group

Avery

Berkley

Blue Rider Press

DAW

Dutton

Penguin Books

Penguin Classics

Plume

Portfolio

Putnam

Riverhead

Sentinel

Tarcher

Viking

Penguin Young Readers Group

Dial Books for Young Readers

Firebird

F. Warne & Co.

G.P. Putnam's Sons

Kathy Dawson Books

Nancy Paulsen Books

Penguin Workshop

Philomel Books

Puffin Books

Razorbill

Speak

Viking Children's Books

Random House

Alibi

Ballantine Books

Bantam Books

Del Rey

Delacorte Press

Dell

Flirt

Hydra

Loveswept

Lucas Books

Modern Library

Random House

Speigel & Grau

The Dial Press

Zinc Inc

Random House Children's Books

Alfred A. Knopf

Crown

Doubleday

Dragonfly Books

Ember

Golden Books

Laurel-Leaf Books

Random House Books for Children

Schwartz &Wade

Sylvan Learning

The Princeton Review

Wendy Lamb Books

Crown Publishing Group

Amphoto Books

Broadway Books

Clarkson Potter

Convergent Books

Crown Archetype

Crown Business

Crown Forum

Crown Trade

Currency

(Continued)

FIGURE 3.1   ■   (Continued)

Harmony Books	**Knopf Doubleday Publishing Group**
Hogarth	
Image Catholic Books	Anchor Books
Potter Craft	Black Lizard
Potter Style	Doubleday
Ten Speed Press	Everyman's Library
Three Rivers Press	Knopf
Tim Duggan Books	Nan A. Talese
WaterBrook Multnomah	Pantheon
Watson-Guptill	Schocken
	Vintage Books
	Vintage Español

Source: Company websites.

Movies. The global motion picture industry is dominated by seven companies that account for about 90 percent of box office receipts—Comcast's Universal Pictures, Viacom's Paramount Pictures, Time Warner's Warner Bros., Walt Disney Studios, Fox Entertainment Group's 20th Century Fox, Sony Pictures Entertainment, and Lionsgate. In 2016, Disney led the way with more than 26 percent of worldwide box office revenues, a total of more than $7 billion, with more than half of its ticket sale revenue (60%) coming from *outside* of North America. Disney had all top five films at the worldwide box office in 2016, including *Captain America: Civil War, Rogue One: A Star Wars Story,* and *Finding Dory,* each of which earned more than $1 billion. After it completes its likely acquisition of Fox, Disney will be, far and away, the dominant player in the movie industry, accounting for about 40 percent of domestic box office receipts. Warner Bros was a distant second at the global box office, with $4.7 billion in 2016 ticket sales, led by *Batman vs. Superman: Dawn of Justice* ($873 million). In addition, some of the leading "independent" film companies are actually owned by the industry giants—Focus Features (Comcast), Fox Searchlight (Fox Entertainment, soon to be Disney), Sony Pictures Classics (Sony), Paramount Vantage (Paramount), and New Line (Time Warner).

Recorded Music. Only three companies are responsible for the vast majority of U.S. music sales. Universal Music Group, Sony Music Entertainment, and Warner Music Group accounted for more than 68 percent of total global recorded music sales in 2016 (Music Business Worldwide 2017). Each of the big three controls a number of smaller labels and local subsidiaries (see Figure 3.2).

Book Publishing. The U.S. book market is dominated by the "Big Five" publishers—Penguin Random House (owned by Bertelsmann), HarperCollins (owned by News Corp.), Simon & Schuster (owned by CBS Corp.), Hachette Book Group, and Macmillan. Estimates in 2016 indicate that the Big Five account for about 80 percent

FIGURE 3.2 ■ Labels Owned by the "Big Three" Music Companies

Sony Music

Columbia Records
RCA Records
Epic Records
Arista Nashville
RCA Records Nashville
Columbia Nashville
Legacy Recordings
Sony Music Latin
Masterworks
RCA Inspiration
Provident Label Group
Essential Records
Reunion Records
Essential Worship
Beach Street Records

Warner Music Group

Asylum
Atlantic Records
Big Beat
Canvasback
East West
Elektra
Erato
FFRR
Fueled by Ramen
Nonesuch Records
Parlophone
Reprise Records
Rhino
Roadrunner Records
Sire Records
Warner Bros. Records
Warner Classics
Warner Music Nashville

Universal Music Group

Capitol Records
Virgin Records
Motown Records
Blue Note Records

Astralwerks
Harvest Records
Capitol Christian Music Group
Atom Factory
Deep Well Records
Decca
Def Jam Recordings
Deutsche Grammophon
EMI
222 Records
Aftermath Entertainment
Dreamville
Insomniac Records
Kidinakorner
Shady Records
Island Records
Polydor
Republic Records
Verve Records
Decca Gold
Decca Broadway
Universal Music Classics
ECM
Virgin Records
4th & Broadway
American Recordings
Brushfire Records
Casablanca Records
Cash Money Records
Lava Records
The Voice
Artium Recordings
Astralwerks Records
Sparrow Records
ForeFront Records
sixstepsrecords
Hillsong and Credential Recordings
Capitol Records Nashville
EMI Records Nashville
MCA Nashville
Mercury Nashville
Universal Music Latino

Source: Company websites.

of trade book sales in the United States. With electronic books gaining market share (via, e.g., Amazon and Apple's iBooks), some analysts believe that additional consolidation of the book industry is on the horizon (McIlroy 2016).

U.S. Magazines. Time Inc. towers above its competitors in the magazine sector. Its 19 major U.S. magazines (led by *People, Time,* and *Sports Illustrated*) have a print circulation of more than 30 million, with total revenue of more than $2.5 billion—about double the revenue of Hearst, its closest competitor (Spyglass Intelligence 2018). When online and mobile readers are included, the company estimates that almost half of U.S. adults read a Time, Inc. magazine. When Meredith Corp., the number four U.S. magazine publisher, completes its acquisition of Time, which was originally announced in 2017, the combined Meredith/Time will be an even more dominant force in the magazine industry.

Television Production. With the emergence of a variety of new television streaming viewing options, along with original programming on Netflix, Hulu, Amazon, and older premium services such as HBO and Showtime, the 2010s were widely regarded as a new "golden age" of television. In this context, competition to acquire quality programming is more intense than ever. While viewer options of where and what to watch have grown in recent years, television program production remains concentrated. According to industry analysts, the four largest television program producers accounted for about two-thirds of domestic revenue in 2017 (IBISWorld 2017). These major production companies—21st Century Fox, NBC Universal, Time Warner, and Disney—also own some of the most well-known broadcast and cable television networks (platforms) and, in some cases, own the cable and fiber-optic lines that deliver content into our homes (pipes).

Platforms

The platforms for the distribution of media have been changing, but they still remain heavily concentrated, with a small number of companies maintaining disproportionate market share in each industry segment.

Radio. In 2018, iHeartMedia (formerly Clear Channel Communications) has more than 850 radio stations in 150 different markets and is the dominant player in the U.S. radio industry. iHeartMedia's radio stations and online and mobile applications reach more than 250 million listeners in the United States each month (iHeartMedia 2018).

Music. In 2016, for the first time, revenue from streaming services generated more than half of all revenue in the U.S. music industry. According to the Recording Industry Association of America (RIAA 2017), 51 percent of music revenue came from streaming, 24 percent from digital downloads and ringtones, and 22 percent came from the sale of physical products (CDs and vinyl). The three leading streaming services accounted for more than 60 percent of the more than 160 million global streaming subscribers: Spotify 36 percent, Apple 17 percent, Amazon 10 percent (MIDIA Research 2017).

Television. Unlike other media sectors, television has become somewhat less concentrated over the past few decades in large part due to the variety of platforms that now exist. First, more broadcast networks appeared. FOX joined ABC, CBS, and NBC to expand the number of major broadcast networks to four back in 1986. Then, in 2006, Warner Bros. and CBS partnered to launch the CW Network after the two partners shut down their separate fledgling networks WB and UPN. Second, cable television channels proliferated, although most of the major cable channels are owned by a small number of major media companies:

- Time Warner (owned by AT&T) owns: CNN, HBO, TBS, TNT, Cartoon Network, truTV, Turner Classic Movies, and Cinemax.

- Disney owns: ABC, ESPN, Disney Channels Worldwide, ABC Family, and SOAPnet Networks and is part-owner of A&E, Lifetime Television, the History Channel, Vice Media, and other channels.

- Comcast owns: NBC, MSNBC, CNBC, Telemundo, Oxygen, USA Network, and Bravo, among others.

Still, cable offered new ways to exhibit programs.

Finally, streaming has radically changed the television landscape, opening it up to new competitors. Netflix, Hulu (owned jointly by the major television producers Disney, Fox, Time Warner, and Comcast), and Amazon, among others, stream a library of older television content and, increasingly, produce their own original programming, including popular shows such as Netflix's *Narcos*, Amazon's *The Tick*, and Hulu's *The Handmaid's Tale*. Other streaming services, like Sling (owned by the Dish Network) and DirecTV Now (owned by AT&T), focus on live television streaming. The growth of these streaming services, which allow us to watch "television" on a laptop, tablet, or mobile phone, has changed what the term "television" means. Streaming television services—sometimes with built-in DVR capacity—enable viewers to watch when they want. The original programming on such services largely ignores the traditional broadcast TV conventions of 22-week "seasons" that usually premiere in the fall. Instead, they employ variable release schedules throughout the year; rather than weekly episodes, they release a "season" of a program all at once, allowing viewers to binge watch; even the number of episodes in a season and the length of each episode are now variable. The flexibility of such a platform, along with the major investments made in original programming, are among the reasons why 2010s television is often said to have been in a "golden age" (Carr 2014).

Pipes

Building the infrastructure for the high-speed networks that carry media into our homes is so capital intensive that it is no surprise that this media sector is highly concentrated.

- The cable television industry, which also provides the infrastructure for more than 60 percent of U.S. broadband internet subscribers, is dominated by two companies: Comcast and Charter Communications (Spectrum).

- High-speed internet connections via phone lines is also an industry with a handful of major players, led by AT&T and Verizon.

- The satellite television/internet industry has two companies, Dish Network and AT&T's DirecTV, that are industry leaders in both market share and brand name recognition.

- Even the U.S. mobile network is a two-company industry, led by Verizon and AT&T, whose networks account for almost 70 percent of U.S. mobile subscriptions (Dano 2017).

Importantly, two of the companies that are the major owners of the digital media infrastructure—Comcast and AT&T—are also among the leading owners of media products and platforms, giving them some competitive advantages.

Conglomeration and Integration

Concentrated media ownership means that a small number of large corporations own a significant percentage of media production, platforms, and pipes. These large companies are conglomerates; they are made up of a number of different companies, all owned by the same corporate parent (see Figure 3.3). Much as in other industries, the largest media companies grow in size and reach as they purchase or merge with their competitors. With their substantial profits and high visibility, media—in both news and entertainment forms—are among the most attractive properties to both potential investors and buyers.

Media conglomerates are integrated firms. Economic analysts have long used the terms *horizontal integration* and *vertical integration* to describe two types of integration in any industry. In the media industry, vertical integration refers to the process by which one owner acquires all aspects of production and distribution of a single type of media product. For example, a movie company might integrate vertically by acquiring talent agencies to acquire scripts and sign actors, production studios to create films, and various venues to show the movies, such as theater chains, premium cable channels, broadcast television networks, and internet-based streaming services. The company could then better control the entire process of creating, producing, marketing, and distributing movies, giving it leverage in the marketplace. Similarly, a book publisher might integrate vertically by acquiring paper mills, printing facilities, book binderies, trucking firms, and internet booksellers (see Figure 3.4). To prevent unfair competitive practices, some regulations exist to prevent extreme vertical integration.

Horizontal integration refers to the process by which one company buys different kinds of media, concentrating ownership across differing media types rather than up and down through one industry. In horizontal integration, a media conglomerate might assemble a portfolio that spans across film, television, books, record labels, video games, and so on to promote one another's operations.

FIGURE 3.3 ■ Anatomy of a Media Conglomerate: The Walt Disney Company Corporate Holdings

Film	• Walt Disney Studios • Walt Disney Animation Studios • Pixar Animation Studios • Disneytoon Studios • Lucas Films • Marvel Studios • Disneynature • 20th Century Fox* • Fox Searchlight Pictures* • Fox 2000*
Television Networks	• ABC Television Network • Disney Channel • Disney Junior • Disney Channels Worldwide (120 entertainment channels available in 162 countries) • ESPN • ESPN 2 • ESPNU • ESPNews • ESPN Deportes • Freeform (formerly ABC Family) • A&E Network • Lifetime • Lifetime Movies • History Channel • Bio Channel • FX Networks* • National Geographic Channels* • Fox Sports Regional Networks* • Hulu
Television Production and Distribution	• ABC Entertainment • ABC Studios • ABC Signature Studios • ABC News • ABC Owned Television Stations Group (8 stations in major markets reaching 23% of U.S. households)Disney TV Animation

(Continued)

FIGURE 3.3   ■   (Continued)

	• Disney/ABC Home Entertainment and Television Distribution • 20th Century Fox Television* • FX Productions* • Fox 21 Television Studios*
Radio	• Radio Disney • ESPN Radio
Music	• Walt Disney Records • Hollywood Records • Disney Music Publishing
Publishing	• Disney Books • *ESPN The Magazine* • ESPN Books
Live Events	• Disney Books • Disney on Broadway • Disney on Ice • X Games
Disney Parks and Resorts	• 12 theme parks and 52 resorts in North America, Europe and Asia • Disney Cruise Line, Disney Vacation Club, and Adventures by Disney
Disney Stores	• 300+ stores (some licensed franchises) in North America, Europe, and China • ShopDisney.com

Sources: Disney and Fox Company websites.

Note: Items with an asterisk (*) are part of the acquisition of 21st Century Fox, still pending at this writing.

In a clear example of horizontal integration, Disney's Marvel Cinematic Universe produces new content that spans the whole range of Disney products: more than a dozen Avengers-themed films, including multiple Iron Man and Captain America movies; several television programs, including *Agents of S.H.I.E.L.D.*; a steady stream of Marvel comic books; film and television soundtracks released by Marvel Music; video games with the Marvel characters; live-action Marvel entertainment at Disney's theme parks; and a wide variety of Marvel-themed merchandise, including clothing, toys, and collectibles. The more recent Marvel films, such as *Guardians of the Galaxy Vol. 2* (2017) and *Black Panther* (2018) have taken advantage of newer promotional channels, such as blogs, smartphone apps, and social media sites, generating substantial promotional buzz even before the films were released.

FIGURE 3.4 ■ Vertical and Horizontal Integration in the Media Industry

Hypothetical Example of Vertical Integration:

MUSIC	BOOKS	FILM
Musicians	**Authors**	Actors
Talent agencies	**Literary agencies**	Talent agencies
Music labels	**Publishers**	Film studios
Sound recording manufacturers	**Paper mills and printers**	Film and DVD manufacturers
Internet streaming sites and/or digital sales	**Online e-book and print booksellers**	Premium cable, streaming services, and/or theaters

Hypothetical Example of Horizontal Integration:

MUSIC	BOOKS	FILM
Musicians	Authors	Actors
Talent agencies	Literary agencies	Talent agencies
Music labels	**Publishers**	**Film studios**
Sound recording (CD) manufacturers	Paper mills and printers	Film and DVD manufacturers
Internet streaming sites and/or digital sales	Online e-book and print booksellers	Premium cable, streaming services, and/or theaters

Note: Shaded, bold-faced companies are owned by the same corporation.

In another example, Disney turned its sports cable franchise ESPN into a multimedia cross-promotional vehicle, developing ESPN2, ESPN Classic, ESPNEWS, ESPN Deportes, ESPNU, espnW, the ESPN Radio Network, *ESPN: The Magazine*, FiveThirtyEight.com, the Watch ESPN streaming service, an ESPN mobile app, and ESPN Consumer Products, all working together to promote Disney's highly visible group of ESPN products. Such cross-media promotion can be a very powerful strategy. One experimental study found that a coordinated television and print ad campaign for a television program was far more effective than single-media campaigns; cross-media campaigns "resulted in higher attention from audiences, improved memory, greater perceived message credibility . . . and higher viewing intent compared to using repetitive single-source promotions" (Tang, Newton, and Wang 2007: 132). This kind of opportunity for cross-promotion is one of the driving forces behind the growth of horizontally integrated media companies.

Strategy in a New Media Economy

Several things can be learned from the conglomeration and integration of the media industry in the last couple of decades. First, traditional conglomeration by itself can fail in the new media economy; simply getting bigger is no guarantee of success. Second, despite setbacks, traditional media companies are highly resilient and are responding to the changing media landscape in a variety of ways—some of which involve new types of conglomeration and integration. Third, changes in technology—especially the maturation of the internet and the growth of wireless and mobile devices—have spurred innovative competitors that are not traditional media companies but that are now playing a central role in the new media economy.

The setbacks that led to the split of some major conglomerates, discussed earlier, have been followed by new efforts to reposition companies in the evolving media landscape. One recurring debate about how best to do this has been assessing the relative importance of owning products—information and entertainment—versus owning "pipes"—the infrastructure to deliver these products. In 1996, then-Microsoft CEO Bill Gates published an essay popularizing the phrase "content is king." In it he argued, "Content is where I expect much of the real money will be made on the Internet, just as it was in broadcasting." That's because "anyone with a PC and a modem can publish whatever content they can create" (Gates 1996). Thus enthusiasm for the early internet's potential helped fuel the idea that "content is king," suggesting the creation of a broad range of content through horizontal integration is the key to success. Companies such as Disney bet on their popular content as their primary path to success. However, there has always been a less glamorous argument that owning the pipes that deliver content—regardless of who creates it—is the key to steady industry success. In part, that's because content comes and goes with no guarantee of popularity. In part, it's because the maturation of the internet has shown that telecom and cable providers, such as Comcast and Verizon, control a key chokehold in the media system.

But the primary media strategy in the new media economy has not been content *or* pipes; it has been content *and* pipes—along with newer *platforms*. The media giants have been pursuing a strategy of vertical integration, building media companies that connect production and distribution. The evolution of Comcast and AT&T exemplifies one major change on the media landscape: Once traditional telecom companies are now integrated media companies. Comcast, the largest provider of cable and internet service in the United States (which means the largest network of pipes entering U.S. households) is now also the owner of content leader NBC Universal (film, television, and music) but failed to outbid Disney to buy 21st Century Fox. AT&T has long been a major owner of media pipes: DirecTV, the largest satellite television provider in the United States, high-speed fiber-optic internet connections in dozens of major metropolitan areas, and one of the two large national mobile networks in the United States. In buying Time Warner, AT&T is seeking valuable new content assets—including film, television, and music from Warner Bros, as well as HBO, Cinemax, and CNN. Owning Time Warner allows AT&T to leverage popular content assets in the competition for media consumers, whereas having guaranteed access to AT&T's pipes will ensure broad exposure for Time Warner content. For example, if you get your internet access through AT&T, you might also be offered a discount on, or higher-speed access to, HBO or perhaps access to early releases of new episodes of the latest hit series.

As telecom companies become media firms, traditional media firms are acquiring more pipes and platforms. In buying Fox, Disney is seeking new platforms to distribute its vast, and growing, collection of media products in the internet age; owning broadcast and cable networks such as ABC and ESPN is no longer enough. In addition to acquiring a controlling interest in Hulu when its merger with Fox is finalized, Disney plans to develop two new streaming services—one focused on entertainment and one on sports—to reduce its reliance on platforms owned by competitors.

The newest developments are a sign of how the economic dynamics in the media industry are changing as digitization and convergence have largely erased the boundaries among media sectors. In the contemporary media landscape in which users have seemingly unlimited media options, the major industry players have been scrambling to maintain and rebuild media companies that can be profitable amidst media abundance. That's why we continue to see consolidation in the media industry, with just a handful of major companies in media production, media platforms, and media pipes.

The Power of Platforms: Facebook and Google as New Media Giants

Early enthusiasts often believed that the internet would help decentralize media ownership by offering easy access for new competitors. The new companies came, but ironically, as the internet matured it consolidated even more than traditional media. As one analyst of media ownership concluded, "Generally, the more electronic and 'digital' a media subsector is, the more highly it seems to be concentrated." In fact, there has been "consolidation for the Internet itself as well as for many of its major applications. This pours cold water over the hope that the Internet will solve the media concentration problem" (Noam 2009: 5).

Such analysis reflects the reality created by the newest media giants: Google and Facebook. (Technically, Google is a part of the Alphabet holding company, but we use the better-known name throughout.) Google and Facebook (and other similar platforms like Twitter and Google-owned YouTube) are not traditional media companies. Neither hires journalists or other media producers, and therefore they don't produce media content. Until recently, their own executives preferred to call themselves technology companies. Industry analysts, however, now recognize just how powerful Facebook and Google's high-traffic platforms are within the media industry. Recently, the culture secretary in the United Kingdom has suggested that the UK officially change the legal status of Facebook and Google to recognize them as media companies (Ruddick 2017).

In fact, Google and Facebook *are* media companies because their platforms host a vast population of media users, have a powerful impact on media content, and take in a huge percentage of media advertising dollars. These companies have even ventured into areas traditionally controlled by telecommunications companies.

Users

More than just platforms for people to connect with friends and search the web, Facebook and Google are entry points to a wide range of media content. For example, the Pew Research Center (2017c) found that 45 percent of U.S. adults get news from Facebook and 18 percent of adults get news from Google's YouTube. Although more than three-quarters of adults under the age of 50 turn to these platforms for news, Pew notes that 2017 was the first time "more than half (55%) of Americans ages 50 or older report getting news on social media sites" (p. 2). And Facebook is now the "top source of political news for millennials" (Griffith 2017).

Google and Facebook deliver personalized content via proprietary algorithms to grow the size, engagement, and time commitment of users. Facebook offers a customized News Feed, mixing posts from friends and family along with mainstream media content and viral videos. Google is the go-to site for finding out just about anything, including the latest news via Google News search results. These sites also frequently tinker with ways to deliver video content to attract and hold users' attention. In 2016, Facebook signed contracts with 140 media companies and celebrities to create videos for its Facebook Live service (Perlberg and Seetharaman 2016), and Twitter experimented with live streaming NFL football games. In 2017, Facebook announced a "spotlight module" feature to showcase original video content through its mobile app (Alba 2017).

Media Content

Media producers have worked hard to connect to the massive number of users attracted to Facebook and Google. The simplest approach is to develop content specifically designed for Facebook and YouTube. To reach these users, media companies post a fresh stream of articles, videos, and other media on their company Facebook pages or YouTube channels, in the hopes that they will be noticed and shared. This is not a content-neutral activity. To reach audiences on social media, producers are creating content that fits the style of social media, particularly content that is mobile friendly and easy to share: short videos, top-10 lists, provocative celebrity photos, eye-catching slide shows, sensational headlines, and other attention-grabbing products. The omnipresence of such "click bait" all over the internet is the result of producers creating provocative content aimed at attracting the attention of social media users (Wu 2016).

Even traditional national news organizations in search of the large audiences on social media platforms are creating news that caters to the routines and expectations of social media users. A recent study of online journalism found that social media platforms have a significant influence on news content: "Publishers are making micro-adjustments on every story to achieve a better fit or better performance on each social outlet. This inevitably changes the presentation and tone of the journalism itself" (Bell and Owen 2017: 39). As a result, more and more news is now published directly on social media platforms rather than as links back to the news organization's home page. This kind of "native" social media news may get lots of clicks and eyeballs, but it changes the nature of the content because it is designed precisely to be clicked on and shared quickly before some competing content finds its way onto users' screens. Becoming "shareworthy" is a prominent goal for producers of all kinds of media content, including journalism (Trilling, Tolochko, and Burscher 2017).

Google has also directly entered the world of media content production. Google's YouTube Red is an ad-free subscription service, which it has used to launch original programs. It has invested millions in producing free, ad-supported, original programs available on various YouTube channels (Shaw and Bergen 2017).

Advertising

The media industry is, in large part, an advertising-funded business. Newspapers, magazines, radio, and television have long been organized as commercial industries whose primary source of revenue is advertising. After the broad failure of paywalls, online media have largely adopted a similar approach, providing content that is paid for by advertisers seeking the attention of users who can access the content for free. Advertising dollars chase attractive audiences—young and well-off users are typically the most desirable media targets—leading content producers to create or acquire media that are aimed at that target audience. Advertising, then, does more than just fund media; advertiser's preferences influence what media are produced and how they are distributed.

In 2016, online advertising overtook television as the world's largest advertising medium (Zenith 2017). Google and Facebook dominate this lucrative market (see Figure 3.5). In 2017, Google and Facebook together received more than 60 percent of all digital advertising spending in the United States (eMarketer 2017). This effectively makes digital advertising a "duopoly," dominated by just two companies, and makes control of online advertising more concentrated than any other media sector. More broadly, Google and Facebook account for about 20 percent of *all* advertising dollars—across all media worldwide. Dominance in the internet sector has catapulted these relative newcomers to the top of the list for all media advertising revenue. Google generated $79.4 billion in ad revenue in 2016, and Facebook earned $26.9 billion. Comcast was a distant third with $12.9 billion (Zenith 2017). This dominance is likely to continue. As the amount of money advertisers spend on digital media continues to grow, industry analysts note that virtually all of this growth—99 percent of the 2016 growth by one estimate—went to Google and Facebook (Ingram 2017). As a result, these two platforms are powerful media companies, bringing in users to sell to advertisers while influencing the nature of media content to attract users. Any successful company in the world of digital media will have to work, in some capacity, with these two new digital media giants.

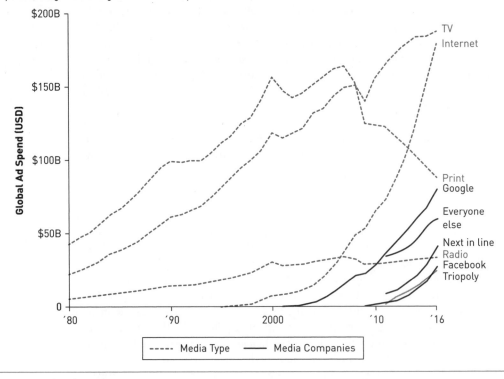

FIGURE 3.5 ■ Facebook/Google Ad Revenue Growth

The internet's share of overall advertising revenue has spiked in recent years, mostly at the expense of print ads. Among companies, Google is the largest individual recipient of ad dollars.

Source: Fischer (2017).

Note: "Next in line" is: Yahoo, Microsoft/LinkedIn, IAC, Verizon, Amazon, Pandora, Twitter, Yelp, Snapchat, Sina, and Sohu. 'Triopoly' is Alibaba, Baidu, and Tencent.

Telecommunications

While attracting users, selling ads, and creating content have transformed Google and Facebook media companies, both firms have also expanded into the domain of traditional telecommunications companies. Both companies invest heavily in internet infrastructure, including undersea cables to handle their data traffic. Both companies run projects to make their commercial services available more widely in developing countries. Facebook runs the nonprofit Open Compute Project, which assists in developing open-source hardware needed to run the internet, even laying some fiber-optic cable in Uganda as part of its test projects (Facebook 2018b). Facebook also offers Free Basics, an effort to "bring more people online" in developing areas where internet access is expensive. The program is a "walled garden" of limited basic services—including Facebook—that are available for free without data charges (Free Basics 2018). (We discuss the program and its critics later in the book.)

In turn, Google funds Project Loon, which uses high-atmosphere balloons to relay wireless internet service to remote locations (Google 2018e). The project successfully delivered basic internet access to 100,000 Puerto Ricans after Hurricane Maria devastated the island's cell-phone towers in 2017 (Statt 2017). Google Station works with providers to offer a unified system for logging into and paying for Wi-Fi in developing countries (Google 2018b). Google also has other limited-rollout projects in which it explores new opportunities for future expansion. It has created its own wireless telephone service, Project Fi, which resells existing network services, routing a

user's call to the best available service (Google 2018d). It offers extremely fast Google Fiber internet service in select locations, with plans to expand nationwide (Google 2018a).

Clearly, the companies once known for offering internet search capability and a place to post to friends and family have become the media giants of our era.

Project Loon, a balloon-based high-speed network, is one of many Google-funded projects aimed at building internet infrastructure. Both Google and Facebook have made substantial investments intended to make their services more widely available, particularly in developing countries.

CONSEQUENCES OF CONGLOMERATION AND INTEGRATION

Although the trends in media ownership may be of interest in themselves, our prime concern is with the relationship between ownership and the media product. What are the consequences of integration, conglomeration, and concentration of ownership?

Integration and Self-Promotion

The economic factors propelling both vertical and horizontal integration are clear: Owners perceive such arrangements as both efficient and profitable. The cultural consequences are more ambiguous. However, an institutional approach suggests that such ownership patterns are likely to affect the types of media products created. In particular, integrated media conglomerates seeking the benefits of "synergy" are likely to favor products that can best be exploited by other components of the conglomerate. (Synergy refers to the dynamic where components of a company work together to produce benefits that would be impossible for either of them to generate if they were separately owned.) For example, horizontal integration may well encourage the publication of books that can be made into movies and discourage the publication of those that cannot. Or it might encourage the creation of TV talent search programs because they can generate new musical acts who are contractually obligated to record for the company's music label, featured in the company's magazines, played on the company's radio stations, and showcased on their websites. More generally, promotion and marketing are likely to dominate the decision-making process within a horizontally integrated media industry.

Vertical integration becomes especially significant when the company that makes the product also controls its distribution. For example, as Netflix has vastly expanded its original programming, it has prominently featured these "Netflix Originals" while cutting dramatically the number of titles it carries from outside producers.

The possibilities for fully using horizontal and vertical integration are startling. In this era of integrated media conglomerates, media companies are capable of pursuing elaborate cross-media strategies in which company-owned media products can be packaged, sold, and promoted across the full range of media platforms. Feature films, their accompanying soundtracks and streaming/On-Demand/DVD/Blu-Ray releases, spin-off television programs, and books, along with magazine cover stories and plenty of licensed merchandise, can all be produced and distributed by different divisions of the same conglomerate—with each piece serving to promote the broader franchise. One consequence of integration, then, is an increase in media cross-promotion and, perhaps, a decrease in media products that are not suitable for cross-promotion. It also makes it more difficult for smaller media firms to compete with the major corporations that can use their vast and diverse holdings to saturate consumers during their promotional campaigns (often on social media platforms) and ensure prominent exposure on their various media outlets and platforms.

The Impact of Conglomeration

What has the growth of large multimedia firms over the past few decades meant for the news, television, radio, films, music, and books we receive? In other words, to what extent does conglomeration affect the media product? The loudest warnings about the impact of conglomeration have come from within the news industry, in part because some news media had traditionally been sheltered from the full pressure of profit making. For example, for much of television history, respectable television news divisions were understood to represent a necessary public service commitment that lent prestige to the major broadcast networks. They were not expected to turn a substantial profit. However, that changed with the takeover of news operations by major corporate conglomerates during the 1980s.

Ken Auletta's *Three Blind Mice* (1991) paints a vivid picture of the clash that ensued during that time, when new corporate owners took over the major television networks and their news divisions. For those who worked at NBC News, for example, the purchase of the network by General Electric led to conflicts about the meaning and role of television news. In most of these conflicts, the new corporate owners ultimately prevailed. As Auletta tells it, when General Electric took over as the new owners of NBC, they

> emphasized a "boundaryless" company, one without walls between News, Entertainment, Sales, and other divisions. . . . At NBC's annual management retreat in 1990, many of the 160 executives questioned why Sales or Entertainment couldn't have more input into news specials, or why News tended to keep its distance from the rest of the company, as if it were somehow special. (p. 564)

Then-General Electric chair Jack Welch even specified that *Today Show* weather reporter Willard Scott should mention GE lightbulbs on the program. According to former NBC news president Lawrence Grossman, "It was one of the perks of owning a network. . . . You get your lightbulbs mentioned on the air. . . . People want to please the owners" (Husseini 1994: 13).

Since that time, the network news programs have faced stiff competition from 24-hour cable news channels Fox, CNN, and MSNBC and a proliferation of online news. Similar to print journalism, broadcast news has seen advertisers shift their dollars to the internet. Yet despite these changes, they are expected to turn a profit by attracting audiences that owners expect and advertisers demand. One result has been an increased emphasis on entertainment and celebrities on the network news—what former CBS news anchor Dan Rather called "the Hollywoodization of the news" due to the growth of "stupid celebrity stories" (*Brill's Content* 1998: 117). The changes that were seen as a threat to serious broadcast news back in the 1980s and 1990s are now the norm in the industry, with the broadcast networks now routinely incorporating entertainment, celebrities, human interest, and other light fare into their broadcasts.

Conglomeration has affected print journalism as well, where the loss of advertisers and paid subscribers has hit especially hard. Some critics have long argued that corporate takeovers of print media put the emphasis on attracting and entertaining consumers rather than on informing citizens (Squires 1993). In this context, newspapers become increasingly colorful, focus attention on the lives of celebrities, and print sensationalistic stories about dramatic and bizarre happenings. One example is News Corp's Executive Chair Rupert Murdoch—best known as the owner of FOX News—who launched his career by buying up newspapers in Australia and England and converting them into tabloids that specialized in sex, scandal, and celebrities. This was epitomized by his purchase of Britain's *The Sun*, which became notorious—and popular—for its scandalous coverage, even adopting a "Page Three" feature—a daily photo of a topless or nude model (Braid 2004). The 2011 phone-hacking scandal in England, which led to the shutdown of Murdoch's British tabloid *News of the World*, showed how far profit-focused news organizations will go in search of a story. Hundreds, and perhaps thousands, of phones were hacked by reporters at the newspaper, who sought titillating information about crime victims, their families, and celebrities. In the report on the scandal commissioned by the British government, Lord Justice Leveson concluded that

> there has been a recklessness in prioritising sensational stories, almost irrespective of the harm that the stories may cause and the rights of those who would be affected (perhaps in a way that can never be remedied), all the while heedless of the public interest. (The Leveson Inquiry 2012: 10)

Finally, for today's multiplatform media companies, news becomes "content" that is increasingly expected to fit with and be usable by the other divisions of the company. Conglomeration, therefore, has led to increased bottom-line pressure, even in areas of the media that used to be partially insulated from such pressure.

THE EFFECTS OF CONCENTRATION

As with integration and conglomeration, a key concern with the concentration of media ownership has been its impact on the media product—especially the potential homogenization of media products. A broader concern, however, to which we first turn, is the relationship between media ownership and political power.

Media Control and Political Power

Can concentrated media ownership be translated into undue political influence? As we will discuss in Chapter 4, most people recognize the importance of such a question in examining the government's control of media in authoritarian nations. It is clear in such situations that state ownership and exclusive access are likely to affect media products. In the United States, most discussion about the First Amendment and free speech also focuses on the possibility of government censorship. This discussion is generally blind, however, to the impact of corporate ownership.

In addressing this concern, Bagdikian (2004) argued that the United States has a "private ministry of information," metaphorically referring to the type of government-led propaganda system that exists in authoritarian societies. In the case of the contemporary United States, however, private interests, not the government, largely control this information system. Bagdikian suggests that, when a small number of firms with similar interests dominate the media industry, it begins to function in a way similar to a state information system. Although the internet offers easy access to a wide variety of news and opinion, if one seeks them out, it is hard to question the underlying argument that those who own large media conglomerates still have at least the potential to wield a great deal of political power.

How might ownership of media translate into political power? It is possible that those building media empires could use their media outlets to promote a very specific political agenda. Furthermore, when media barons become candidates for major office, their media holdings can be invaluable political resources. Perhaps the starkest example of this in a Western democracy is the case of Silvio Berlusconi in Italy, who managed to use ownership of private media to gain public office—which then enabled him to influence public media.

Silvio Berlusconi, a media magnate and the dominant force in Italian broadcasting and publishing, was elected prime minister three times (1994, 2001, and 2008). For Berlusconi, ownership of television and radio clearly had great political value; he owned strategic assets that were unavailable to other political actors. In the 2001 electoral campaign, he was given four times the exposure of his rival candidate on the television networks that he owned. After winning that election, he went on to effectively control 90 percent of Italian television programming (*The Economist* 2001). That's because Italian prime ministers have the right to replace the boards of directors of the three public television channels, known as RAI, and thus can influence RAI's editorial choices. In subsequent election campaigns, Berlusconi not only had his own private television networks as a political resource, but he also influenced the public channels.

Berlusconi's domination of television was so great that, after the 2001 election and again in 2004, the European Federation of Journalists called for new regulations limiting media ownership. In 2004, both the European Parliament and the Council of Europe condemned the open conflict of interest between Berlusconi's role as prime minister and that of media magnate. The corrosive effect of this arrangement on Italian democracy was so serious that Freedom House, an independent watchdog group that produces annual rankings of freedom and democracy around the world, downgraded Italian freedom of the press from "free" to "partially free" (Freedom House 2004). Berlusconi resigned as prime minister in 2011 in the midst of a sex scandal. Still, he managed to stay in the public eye. In 2013, he lost a close election for a fourth term as prime minister, was then convicted of tax fraud, and was banned from running for public office for six years (Giuffrida 2017).

Although the U.S. media environment is quite different from Italy's largely because of the vast size of the U.S. media industry, private media ownership can be a huge political asset in the United States too. Media entrepreneur Michael Bloomberg amassed a fortune selling technology and media products to businesses. He drew on the widespread recognition of his brand-name line of Bloomberg business media products—and the enormous profits they have generated for him—in his successful campaign to become New York City mayor in 2001. In the process, he spent $69 million of his own money—more than $92 per vote. Bloomberg won reelection in 2005, then successfully had the term-limit law changed so he could run (and win) again in 2009. There has long been speculation that Bloomberg, one of the 10 wealthiest people in the United States as of 2017 (Forbes 2018), will one day launch a presidential bid.

In some cases, owners of media companies have direct control over media products and thus are able to exert political influence by promoting ideas that enhance their interests. For example, the Sinclair Broadcast Group, controlled by the conservative Sinclair family, owns almost 200 local television stations that reach about 40 percent of all U.S. households. The company requires its stations to run conservative, pro-Trump news segments, including lengthy political commentary by a former Trump campaign official. Sinclair ran 15 interviews with then-candidate Donald Trump in 2016, mostly on stations in swing states in the late stages of the campaign. Noting that the nation's largest owner of television stations broadcasts highly politicized news, former FCC Chair Michael Copps called Sinclair "probably the most dangerous company most people have never heard of" (Graves 2017).

Conservative media magnate Rupert Murdoch has also used a variety of his News Corporation's media holdings to advance his political and economic goals. In 1975, he had his Australian newspapers slant the news so blatantly in favor of his conservative choice for prime minister that Murdoch's own journalists went on strike in protest. His British papers played a crucial role in the 1979 election of British conservative Margaret Thatcher. In 1995, Murdoch financed the multimillion-dollar start-up of the high-profile conservative U.S. magazine *The Weekly Standard*. In 1996, Murdoch's News Corporation initiated a 24-hour news channel, Fox News Channel (founded by Rush Limbaugh's former executive producer and long-time Republican Party political consultant, Roger Ailes), which promotes a consistent conservative pro-Trump agenda (Ackerman 2001; Aday 2010; McDermott 2010). When Murdoch's News Corporation bought Dow Jones in 2007, it took over as owner of *The Wall Street Journal*, one of the most influential—and editorially conservative—newspapers in the country.

In 2017, Charles and David Koch, the billionaire brothers, who helped support the Tea Party movement and who provide major funding to the conservative movement more broadly, announced that they would invest in the Meredith Corporation's purchase of Time, Inc., the largest magazine publisher in the United States. In response to news of the Koch's investment, John Huey, former editor in chief of Time, Inc. highlighted the political value of owning major news: "It's difficult to believe the Kochs would pay a premium to buy into the print media model without the hope that they can harness *Time* and *Fortune* to further their agenda" (Snider 2017). Other billionaires have also recently invested in news, including Amazon owner Jeff Bezos's 2013 purchase of the *Washington Post* and casino magnate Sheldon Adelson's 2015 purchase of the *Las Vegas Review-Journal*.

However, some media outlets, especially news outlets, rely on a perception of objectivity or evenhandedness to maintain their legitimacy. Journalists often see themselves as members of a sort of fourth estate, complementing the executive, legislative, and judicial branches of government. Their job is to act as watchdogs over politicians (Louw 2010; Schultz 1998). As a result, with perhaps the exception of Fox News and Sinclair-owned stations, most major news media outlets will not consistently and blatantly promote a single political agenda. Instead, viewers are more likely to find such an approach on cable programs that focus on analysis and commentary or on the growing number of ideologically driven websites and blogs.

The process of using media to promote a political agenda is more complex than simply feeding people ideas and images that they passively accept. Owners can use media sites to disseminate a specific position on a controversial issue or to help legitimize particular institutions or behaviors. Just as important, owners can systematically exclude certain ideas from their media products. Although control of information or images can never be total, owners can tilt the scales in particular directions quite dramatically.

Ownership by major corporations of vast portfolios of media gives us reason to believe that a whole range of ideas and images—those that question fundamental social arrangements, under which media owners are doing quite well—will be visible primarily in less prominent media. This does not mean that all media images and information are uniform. It means that some ideas will be widely available, whereas others will be largely absent. For example, stories critical of gridlock in the federal government are frequent; in contrast, stories critical of capitalism as an economic system that can facilitate inequality are relatively rare. There is no way of proving the connection, but the media's focus on the shortcomings of the government, rather than of the private sector, seems consistent with the interests of the corporate media owners.

This process is most obvious in products that directly address contemporary social and political events, but it also happens in entertainment products. Consider, for example, the depiction of gays and lesbians on prime-time television. For most of U.S. television history, there were virtually no gay or lesbian characters. As gay rights advocates made advances in the 1980s and 1990s, gay and lesbian characters began appearing, although infrequently and in often superficial depictions. Also, gay characters faced constraints that heterosexual characters did not; for example, they typically did not kiss, even as popular television continued to become more explicit in depictions of heterosexual sex. It was not until 2004 that the first television drama series to revolve around a group of lesbian, gay, bisexual, and transgender characters appeared; *The L Word* ran from 2004 to 2009 on the premium cable channel Showtime. There is no conspiracy here. More likely, a small number of profit-making firms that rely on mass audiences and major advertisers simply avoided potential controversies that might threaten their bottom line.

As public opinion shifted and network executives and major advertisers began to define such images as more acceptable to mainstream audiences, LGBT characters have become much more commonplace and more diverse in recent years (GLAAD 2018). We return to these issues in Chapters 6 and 7, when we explore the content of mass media.

The political impact of concentrated corporate ownership, however, is both broader and subtler than the exclusion of certain ideas in favor of others. Herbert Schiller (1989) argues that "the corporate voice" has been generalized so successfully that most of us do not even think of it as a specifically corporate voice. That is, the corporate view has become "our" view, the "American" view, even though the interests of the corporate entities that own mass media are far from universal. One example of this is the entire media-generated discourse—in newspapers, television, radio, magazines, and the internet—about the American economy, in which corporate financial success provides the framework for virtually all evaluations of national economic well-being. The relationship between corporate financial health and citizen well-being, however, is rarely discussed explicitly—even in times of serious financial crisis. During the economic crises of 2008–2009, for example, the U.S. news media were remarkably unquestioning of the message from both government and the private sector that a massive and immediate bailout of banks, Wall Street firms, and other corporate interests was absolutely essential.

A concentrated media sphere can also undermine citizens' capacity to monitor their government's war-making powers. McChesney (2008: 98) argues that

> those in power, those who benefit from war and empire, see the press as arguably the most important front of war, because it is there that consent is manufactured, and dissent is marginalized. For a press system, a war is its moment of truth.

For example, the 2003 U.S.–led invasion of Iraq was justified by the alleged presence of weapons of mass destruction (WMD) in Iraq. The news media reported these WMD charges uncritically, relying on official sources and without in-depth investigation, effectively affirming the Bush administration's rationale for war. According to one study of U.S. news media coverage in the first three weeks of the Iraq war, pro-war U.S. sources outnumbered antiwar sources by 25 to 1, thus making it very difficult for citizens to access critical perspectives on the war (Rendall and Broughel 2003).

The internet offers the possibility for small producers to create professional-looking alternative media—from websites and blogs to mobile apps and streaming video. However, without a means to effectively promote such sites, and without the budget to pay for staff to continuously produce substantive new content that continues to draw users, most online alternative media are limited to relatively small, niche audiences. Television and the major daily newspapers—along with the social media content associated with these major media—are still the main sources of news for most of the population.

In the end, ownership of the means of information becomes part of larger patterns of inequality in contemporary societies, and large media conglomerates can use their capacity to shape media discourse and their substantial financial resources to influence public policy. In this sense, mass media institutions are no different from other social institutions; they are linked to the patterned inequality that exists throughout our society.

Media Ownership and Content Diversity

Does a change in the pattern of media ownership change the nature or range of media content? As this question suggests, macro-level patterns and specific media products need to be understood in relation to each other. The key is to explain the specific nature of the relations between broad institutional forces and the everyday world of mass media.

As media ownership became more concentrated, researchers became interested in the ways such ownership patterns influence the diversity of the media in terms of both form and content. *Media pluralism* refers to the degree to which there is diversity in media content readily available to audiences. This includes the presence of different and independent voices, an array of political views and opinions, and a variety of cultures (Doyle 2002). Media pluralism is a matter of both ownership (varied media suppliers) and output (varied content).

One widely adopted argument has been that media owned by a few will lead to products that lack diversity; that is, as ownership becomes increasingly concentrated, the content of media will become increasingly uniform. Bagdikian (2004) provides the best-known examination of the relationship between ownership concentration and diversity. His most important contribution is the way he draws connections across the various media, showing how companies that are giants in the music industry have similar positions in film, for example. The combination of ownership concentration and growing horizontal integration leads Bagdikian to conclude that the absence of competition in the media industry will lead inevitably to homogeneous media products that serve the interests of the increasingly small number of owners. Although Bagdikian's homogenization hypothesis seems plausible, historical research on the relationship between competition and diversity reveals a more complex situation.

In their analysis of the postwar music industry, Peterson and Berger (1975) argue that high market concentration leads to homogeneity, whereas a competitive market leads to diversity. They provide a historical analysis that demonstrates the relationship between market concentration and several measures of music diversity. The premise of their argument is that the late 1950s and 1960s produced a great deal of innovation and diversity in the popular music industry, representing a dramatic shift from the more homogeneous and standardized music available in the 1940s and early 1950s. The cause, they argue, was the opening of the popular music market to increased competition. Radio's shift from a national orientation to a focus on local markets helped spur this opening. Independent record companies entered the newly opened market and produced new and innovative styles of music, breaking the homogeneity-producing control of the major record companies. Peterson and Berger (1975) base their conclusion about the relationship between competition and diversity on analyses of both ownership trends within the music industry and *Billboard* magazine's singles chart from 1949 to 1972.

Peterson and Berger (1975) suggest two key components of musical diversity. First, they analyze the sheer number of different songs that made the top 10 list each year, arguing that an increase in number reflects an increase in diversity. Second, they analyze the number of new and established artists who made the top 10, from the premise that new artists are a reflection of diversity and established artists are a reflection of standardization. They found that the measures associated with increased diversity (number of songs and number of new artists) increased at times when market concentration (domination of the popular music industry by a small number of firms) decreased. They conclude that a loosening of market concentration through increased competition permits greater innovation and diversity in popular music. However, their data suggest that, in the 1970s, market concentration was again increasing. Thus, they foresaw a return to the *oligopoly* (control by a small number of firms) of the 1940s and predicted a renewed homogeneity within the popular music industry.

Sociologist Paul Lopes (1992) revisited the same question more than 15 years after Peterson and Berger (1975). Using a similar method of analysis—one that focused on the degree of concentration of the industry and the degree of diversity exhibited on the *Billboard* charts—Lopes found that the dynamics in the popular music industry had become more complex since the 1960s. In line with Peterson and Berger's (1975) prediction, market concentration increased substantially between 1969 and 1990, with the top four record companies controlling the vast majority of hit music. However, the accompanying decrease in diversity that Peterson and Berger predicted did not follow. Instead, the number of new artists and established artists fluctuated throughout the 1970s and 1980s, reaching roughly the same number in 1990 as in 1969. Although significant market concentration occurred during this period, Lopes found little evidence that musical diversity had suffered.

The explanation, according to Lopes (1992), is that the system of production within the music industry changed from what he characterizes as a "closed" system to an "open" system. The key change is in the ratio of record labels to record firms. As in other sectors of mass media, notably the book publishing industry, the major music firms own multiple record labels and maintain links with smaller, independent labels. Among the companies producing the top 100 albums, the ratio of labels to firms changed dramatically, from less than two labels per firm in 1969 to approximately four labels per firm by 1990.

Peterson and Berger (1975) suggested that a closed system of record production dominated the industry during the 1940s and early 1950s. In this system, major companies used a limited number of familiar channels to produce and distribute the music that dominated the charts. Lopes (1992), however, argues that the substantial increase in the number of labels per firm suggests new processes at work. In this open system, the major record companies control large-scale manufacturing, distribution, and publicity but draw on semiautonomous independent producers to maintain the vitality of the popular music market. This open system is the key to the continued diversity within the industry despite high market concentration. The open system allows for innovation and diversity, which helps the major companies maintain both their profitability and their control of the industry.

Sociologist Tim Dowd's (2004) research on the music industry echoes Lopes's findings, indicating that decentralized production is the key to musical diversity, even when only a few large companies dominate the music industry. And, despite the proliferation of independent labels and the rapid growth of streaming services that offer independent music, the major media companies continue to dominate music distribution. Although independently owned music labels accounted for 31.3 percent of global music sales in 2016, indie music's share of the download (27.5%) and streaming (28.3%) markets is smaller than the indie share of the shrinking CD/vinyl (38.2%) market (Music Business Worldwide 2017).

These studies of the popular music industry remind us that there is no single effect of concentrated ownership within media industries. Clearly, ownership and control within oligopolistic media industries matter. Controlling companies adopt strategies that determine, to a great degree, production and distribution systems within media industries. However, we need to explore the specific conditions under which concentration exists before we can make sense of the relationship between concentration and diversity. Still, as changes occur in the composition and tastes of the audience, the methods of distribution, the technologies of production, and the organization of media industries will likely respond in ways that enhance the bottom-line profitability of the major firms. Even when a small number of companies control media industries, increased diversity may prove to be an effective strategy in a profit-making industry.

MASS MEDIA FOR PROFIT

In a capitalist system, mass media organizations must focus on one underlying goal: the creation of products that will earn profits. This for-profit orientation provides the context within which media personnel make decisions. However, the focus on profits does not work in a uniform way across media industries or in different time periods. The above example of the popular music industry shows how the same industry responded to similar profit pressures in different ways under different conditions.

Prime-Time Profits

One of the most sensitive treatments of how profit requirements influence media production is Todd Gitlin's (2000) classic analysis of network television. In *Inside Prime Time*, Gitlin explores the decision-making processes at what were then the three major U.S. networks, suggesting that bottom-line profit pressures set the framework for programming decisions. The goal for network executives is steady profits. Executives achieve profits by broadcasting programs that will attract large audiences that will, in turn, lead to the sale of advertising time at premium rates. The problem is that there is no surefire formula for successful programming. Even the most sophisticated methods for predicting success are much better at determining which shows will not succeed than at identifying which programs will become hits.

One reason why this is the case is that failure is the norm in network television. Writers offer the networks thousands of ideas each year, but networks develop only a few hundred into scripts. Some of these scripts are made into pilots, of which a few dozen make it onto the schedule. Of those that make the schedule, networks renew only a handful. At each stage, executives and producers weed out another layer of programs. Only a small number of programs are ultimately successful in commercial terms. For example, of the 285 new prime-time scripted series ordered by the five major broadcast networks between 2009 and 2016, almost two-thirds (183; 64%) were not renewed for a second season (Porter 2016).

If failure is the norm in network television, how is the system profitable? In a situation similar to that in the music, film, and book industries, the big hits—as few as 10 percent of the products, depending on the particular industry—can provide profits large enough to make up for the vast number of programs that break even or lose money. Network television has an additional advantage: Even in the age of cable, satellite, and the internet, major advertisers still perceive the networks to be an effective medium for promoting products to a national market because their audiences are typically much larger than other media. For example, the top-rated scripted television program during the first week of January 2018 was CBS's *The Big Bang Theory*, with 16.2 million viewers (Porter 2018b). In contrast, the largest audience for a scripted program on cable that week was the History Channel's *The Curse of Oak Island*, with 3.3 million viewers, which would not have cracked the top 25 programs on network television that week (Porter 2018a). Measuring the audiences for streaming television series (which typically have no ads) is more complex because audiences do not watch episodes on a regular, weekly schedule. During the first week after release of the new season, when audiences are largest for streaming series, Netflix's original program *Marvel's The Defenders* had 6.1 million viewers in 2017, whereas *House of Cards* had 4.6 million viewers during the first week of its 2017 season (Levin 2017a).

As part of the all-encompassing search for steady profits, network programmers follow a logic of safety that revolves around minimizing the risk of losing money on programs. Risky programs are those that seem unlikely to attract a mass audience or, even worse, a large advertiser. However, as we have seen, ratings hits are rare.

One consequence of the profit-driven logic of safety is the general tendency to avoid controversy in broad mainstream media, even when it might bring high ratings. The logic of safety, however, has much broader consequences than the avoidance of controversial programs. Network executives are never sure what audiences will watch or why some programs succeed and others fail. Therefore, Gitlin (2000) suggests that the corollary to the logic of safety is the notion that "nothing succeeds like success." As a result, network television constantly imitates itself, creating copies and spin-offs that can reach bizarre proportions.

Hit 1970s programs such as *The Mary Tyler Moore Show* (*Rhoda*, *Phyllis*, *Lou Grant*) and *All in the Family* (*The Jeffersons*, *Maude*, *Good Times*, *Gloria*, *Archie's Place*) produced multiple spin-offs and new programs for the stars. In the 1980s, *Cheers* led to both the short-lived sitcom *The Tortellis* and the hit program *Frasier*. The 1990s was awash in gritty police dramas—from *NYPD Blue* and *Homicide* to *Law & Order* and its various spin-offs, *Special Victims Unit*, *Criminal Intent*, *Trial By Jury*, and *Law & Order: LA*. The success of the urban 20-somethings of *Friends* spawned a rash of imitators trying to cash in on the concept, from the 2004 spin-off bust *Joey* to popular programs such as *The Big Bang Theory*, *How I Met Your Mother*, and *2 Broke Girls*.

In the 2000s, crime scene investigators were among the most popular television characters, led by those on the hit programs *CSI*, *CSI: Miami*, and *CSI: New York*, along with *NCIS* and *NCIS: Los Angeles*. Since 2000, broadcast and cable networks filled the airwaves with a steady stream of "reality" programs, including household-based programs like *The Real World* and *Big Brother*, dating shows such as *The Bachelorette* and *Are You the One?*, workplace contests such as *America's Next Top Model* and *Deadliest Catch*, skills contests such as *Project Runway* and *Top Chef*, and self-improvement programs like *Extreme Makeover* and *The Biggest Loser*. Talent shows flourished as well, including *American Idol*, *The Voice*, *America's Got Talent*, and *Dancing with the Stars*. Perhaps the most well-known genre of reality program is the season-long adventure contest, most notably the 35 seasons of *Survivor*, starting in 2000 with *Survivor: Pulau Tiga*. *Survivor* has been a ratings success for more than a decade, ranking among the top 10 programs from 2000 to 2005 and remaining among the 30 most highly rated programs through the 2017 season with *Survivor: Heroes vs. Healers vs. Hustlers*. The program spawned a wide array of competition shows—from *The Amazing Race* and *Gold Rush* to *The Profit* and *Shark Tank*—all trying to capitalize on a new twist on reality-based contest programs.

Whether it is courtroom law programs, crime investigation shows, 20-something sitcoms, prime-time game shows, or reality programs, each network tries to exploit what appears to be the prevailing trend. Without any other accepted method for making programming decisions and with profit demands moving from an annual to a quarterly or weekly basis, programmers choose shows that resemble the latest hit on another network. Increasingly, they also look abroad for program ideas or export homegrown fare for foreign audiences. *Big Brother*, *America's Got Talent*, *Dancing with the Stars*, *Who Wants to Be a Millionaire?*, and many other programs have all been reproduced in slightly different versions, modified for local tastes, to be distributed in different countries.

Cheaper Programs for Smaller Audiences

Over the last couple of decades, network television has had to deal with declining audiences and a corresponding decline in advertising revenue. At the same time, the cost of producing quality programming has increased. To compensate for these two trends, the networks have turned to programs that are less expensive to produce, filling their schedules with programming that does not feature big budget production or expensive actors.

The decline in network advertising revenue was due to the loss of audience share. Broadcast network television ratings are much lower than they were in previous decades. The emergence and growth of cable and satellite television, as well as online viewing platforms such as Netflix, Amazon, and Hulu, have eroded the traditional network audience dramatically. Whereas 90 percent of active television sets were tuned to the three major networks during prime time in the 1970s, by 2017, fewer than 30 percent of sets were tuned to prime-time offerings on the now four major networks—ABC, CBS, NBC, and Fox—and given the growing range of television viewing options, including streaming, premium services, and YouTube, the measure of audience "share" is no longer a key metric. Although the broadcast networks still play an important role in the U.S. television market, the audience size for their programs is small in comparison to that of the 1970s or 1980s. Not only have TV viewers turned to cable, but many former viewers now go online for news and entertainment, resulting in fewer television viewers overall. But network executives can no longer draw audiences that match those for hit programs from previous generations, such as *M*A*S*H*, *Dallas*, or *The Cosby Show*. In fact, the television business has changed so much that the ratings for even the most popular programs in the 2010s, such as perennial hits like CBS's *NCIS* or Fox's *The Simpsons*, would probably have led to quick cancellation two decades ago.

The cost of producing network television dramas and sitcoms escalated because several factors combined to allow suppliers to charge higher rates for their programs. To begin with, the existence of more channels and more competition for viewers led to more demand for program content. Next, to stand out amid the competition, networks had relied on giving their programs an often-expensive look or casting high-profile celebrities. Finally, there was more leverage for actors and directors who had other options in the multichannel universe. By the 2010s, cable and streaming television had lured away talent and created some of the best-known, high-quality drama series, such as HBO's *Game of Thrones* and *Westworld*, AMC's *Mad Men* and *Breaking Bad*, Showtime's *Ray Donovan* and *Homeland*, Amazon's *Transparent* and *Bosch*, Netflix's *The Crown* and *Narcos*, and Hulu's *Chance* and *The Handmaid's Tale*.

With lowered expectations regarding audience size, stiffer competition from new platforms, and tighter budgets with which to work, television networks turned to low-cost programming that could be produced in-house. As we've seen, in the 2010s, that means the network schedule is full of game shows, talent contests, animated programs, and reality programs, all of which fit with the current economic dynamics of broadcast television. Both developments followed a similar logic; these programs attract what historically would have been small audiences, but because they are so inexpensive to produce, they can still be profitable for the networks.

Controlling Content and Distribution

In 2016, a full 92 percent of adult TV viewing minutes were spent watching a television screen rather than a computer, tablet, or mobile device (Nielsen 2017b). Still, the range of options for television and video viewing—both what and how to watch—continues to proliferate. You can watch a vast array of national and local broadcast and cable network programming through your cable or satellite provider. You can "timeshift" your viewing to fit your schedule, by watching programs that you have recorded on your DVR, watching on-demand television, or going online to watch the same programs on your laptop, tablet, or phone. You can stream directly from a network's website; access content via subscriptions to Netflix, Hulu, and Amazon Prime; or download a program through the iTunes store. A huge amount of video content, including recognizable television programs and original content, is available on YouTube, or you can find just about anything online on websites that stream copyright-protected content without permission.

This proliferation of viewing options poses challenges to the television industry. First, competition for viewers is becoming increasingly intense. We have already seen that audiences for any individual program are far smaller than in the network television era, and advertising revenue, although still the financial bedrock of television, is now divided within a growing pool of channels. Second, determining audience size has become increasingly complex, as viewers watch on the many different platforms, often at different times. Declining prime-time ratings, in part, represent a shift away from traditional viewing to on-demand and online viewing rather than simply indicating a smaller overall viewership. Accurately determining ratings that include these new viewing habits is crucial because ratings are the measures that determine advertising rates.

Third, the most prominent new television viewing platforms are based, in large part, on subscriber fees, so they need to attract and hold viewers who pay a monthly or annual membership fee.

In response to these changing economic dynamics, major players in the television industry are seeking new ways to control both programming and distribution channels. This is what makes both Comcast and Disney such formidable media conglomerates. Comcast is among the largest global media companies, with 2016 revenues of more than $80 billion. Comcast is built around its linkage of programming and distribution. Comcast controls more of the wires coming into U.S. homes—for cable television, high-speed internet, and digital phone services—than any other media company. This makes the company the nation's largest cable television provider and largest broadband internet service provider—two key channels for distribution of video content. Comcast also owns 28 local television stations that reach 36 percent of U.S. households and owns part of the streaming service Hulu. In addition, Comcast owns a large portfolio of television networks that are a major source of programming, including NBC, Telemundo, USA Network, Bravo, E!, CNBC, Syfy, MSNBC, Oxygen, and The Weather Channel as well as one of the major Hollywood studios, Universal Pictures, and a major producer of television programming, Universal Television. By controlling both a large amount of television and film content and distribution channels that reach into most U.S. households, Comcast has the resources to manage the uncertainty of the new media environment. It can also present hurdles to competitors, for example, by setting up tiered usage plans that charge more to customers who download large amounts of data—such as Netflix viewers.

As we have already seen, Disney's plan to buy Fox is part of a similar approach to linking ownership of media content with control of media distribution channels. Newer players in the television world are, similarly, seeking to control both content and distribution. Netflix helped pioneer streaming television, originally offering its subscribers access to a huge library of recent and classic television series. Its service is so popular that Netflix users represented more than 35 percent of all downstream traffic on North American fixed networks in 2017, with streaming services accounting for more than 70 percent of all traffic (Sandvine 2016). Over time, though, Netflix changed, entering the content business by producing original programming that is available only to Netflix members, while slashing its library of content from other producers. Other streaming television services, including Amazon, Hulu, and YouTube Red, moved ahead with new original programming, aiming to offer potential subscribers a specific reason to sign up. Apple is expected to enter the streaming business, investing $1 billion in 2018 in original programming to be streamed through an expanded Apple Music platform (Mickle 2017).

Profit and the News Media

How do such profit pressures influence the content of news media? News outlets, like any other company, have two ways to enhance their profits: They can either cut costs or increase revenues. In today's highly competitive news industry, both of these approaches are evident. To cut costs, news outlets rely on several or all of the following strategies:

- Decrease the number of journalists.

- Use journalistic and production staff on multiple company-owned news outlets.

- Cut back on long-term investigative reporting that produces a small number of stories.

- Use a larger percentage of wire-service-reports and videos from online sources.

- At television stations, use video public relations (PR) segments (reports that have been prepared and provided free of charge by PR firms) in newscasts.

- Rely on a small number of elites (who are easy and inexpensive to reach) as regular news sources.

- Focus the news on preplanned official events (which are easy and inexpensive to cover) instead of less routine happenings.

- Focus coverage on a limited number of institutions in a handful of big cities.

All these methods allow news organizations to lower the cost of gathering and producing the news.

In recent years, the number of daily newspapers shrank from 1,457 in 2004 to 1,331 in 2014 (Pew Research Center 2016). In addition, the number of newspaper jobs dropped by more than half from 2001 to 2016 (Bureau of Labor Statistics 2017). (See Figure 3.6.) Although these cost-cutting efforts save money, they are likely to make news coverage oriented more toward elites and government who provide easy-to-use information, with

FIGURE 3.6 ■ Newspaper Employment, 2001–2016

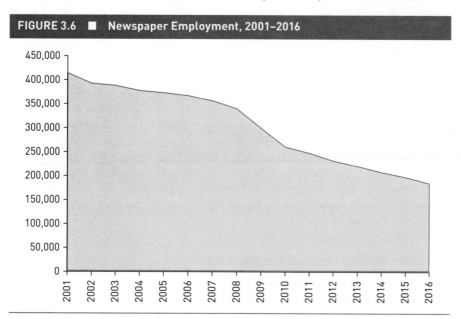

Source: Bureau of Labor Statistics (2017).

less coverage of events or perspectives outside the official world, which requires a bigger investment of resources.

One dramatic result of cost cutting at the network news divisions was the closure of foreign bureaus throughout the 1990s and, more generally, the scaling back of television news coverage of international affairs. In the wake of the September 11, 2001, attacks, the news media's cutbacks in global news gathering and international reporting left them generally ill prepared to help Americans understand the context for the unfolding events and the attitudes outside of the United States (McChesney 2008).

At the same time, news organizations try to increase revenues by maximizing their audience and advertiser bases. The most straightforward approach for audience maximization is to create a light, entertainment-oriented news product that makes watching or reading the news fun and exciting. This helps explain why so much of our daily news focuses on the lives of celebrities and on titillating or dramatic weather or crime stories.

Online, news organizations have wavered between making their content available for free to erecting paywalls that require subscriptions for access. One common strategy has been the return of partial paywalls—offering access to a limited number of articles for free while generating revenue from loyal readers.

Profit pressures have intensified in the 2010s as a result of increased competition in the overall media sector and the demand by corporate owners for substantial returns on their investments. The result is that news editors, increasingly trained in the world of business instead of news reporting, focus more on marketing and packaging the news. Profit pressures have different consequences for different media outlets. Still, the combination of cost-cutting and audience-enhancing demands is one of the key reasons why some set of news outlets, all responding to a comparable set of profit pressures, produce news that looks so similar, whereas others, particularly Fox News, seek to create distinct ideological identities to build and hold a loyal audience.

THE IMPACT OF ADVERTISING

As we have seen, profit requirements provide incentives for the operators of media outlets to keep costs down and to create a product that will bring in sufficient revenue. We must weigh one additional factor: the specific source of revenue. For most media, the key source of revenue is advertising. As a result, it should be no surprise that the magazines we read often seem more focused on the full-page glossy ads than on the articles that are buried between ad pages or that television commercials frequently seem more clever and interesting than the programs they surround. Advertising is, after all, what pays the bills for most print, broadcast, and online media.

The Advertising-Content Connection

Because advertisers are doing the most important buying, the principal products being sold are the audiences, not the newspapers, magazines, or programs produced by media organizations. Advertisers are not interested in media content, except as a kind of bait to lure audiences and expose them to ads. As the phrase goes, media are in the business of "delivering audiences to advertisers." Our attention is on what is being bought and sold, and competition for that attention has intensified as technologies, such as the remote control, video on demand, and DVRs, make it easier to avoid ads. Advertisers' perception that public attention is hard to attract leads to a continual search for new ways to reach consumers. And this is why Facebook and Google have become so valuable to advertisers; they collect troves of data about our online (and offline) activities and can offer increasingly more precisely targeted audiences for advertisers.

One result of this ongoing search has been the growth of advertising in realms of media that had previously been largely ad free. Take movies, for example. Movie theaters have always run ads for their snack bars along with previews of coming attractions, a form of industry advertising. Now many theaters run advertisements for local or regional merchants and service providers before the coming attractions. Initially advertising free, many DVD and Blu-Ray discs now contain ads and previews before the movie begins, some of which are locked so viewers cannot skip them.

Advertisements do not stop when the movie begins. Product placement within movies—whereby a character sips from a can of a well-known brand of soft drink or flies on a prominent airline—is a big business and a subtler way to promote products. The use of products on screen or the mention of brand names by star actors can bring in big money, helping offset the rising costs of film production and marketing. For example, Ray Ban sunglasses got prominent screen time in the 2016 films *X-Men Apocalypse* and *Ride Along 2*. According to brand tracker Concave (2017) Dell Computers received the most product placement visibility in 2016 films, a full hour of screen time in such films as *Captain America: Civil War*, *Sully*, and *Jason Bourne*.

In recent years, product placement has become increasingly sophisticated. Advertisers now think strategically about how best to build their products into the story line of a movie, television series, or video game, constructing a seemingly natural and recurring product placement that may be hard to recognize. For example, chefs on cooking shows use and talk about various brand-name cooking products; the judges on *American Idol* drink prominently displayed cans of Coca-Cola, and Papa John's pizza appears prominently in the 2016 *Ghostbusters* remake.

Similarly, video game developers are crafting new, innovative forms of in-game advertising to more fully integrate products into the video game environment. Whereas billboards advertising real-world products have long appeared in a wide range of video games—on the ski slopes, on the walls of race tracks, in the urban environment—games feature more and more brand-name products for game players to drive, wear, and consume. As product placement opportunities continue to grow, advertisers now speak of "branded entertainment," such as *The Lego Movie* and its spinoffs, in which the brand is the center of the media product.

One trend linking products with media content involves complex partnerships that advertisers call "brand integration." In some of these partnerships, companies contribute products or props that keep film production costs down, whereas other cases involve joint marketing campaigns to promote both a film and the brand-name products. For example, in a 2016 episode of ABC's long running comedy *Modern Family*, one of the principal characters, Phil Dunphy, reflects on his career in real estate, proudly explaining what it means to be a Realtor. The episode was developed in partnership with the National Association of

Advertisements are the routine backdrop to many video games, including sports simulations such as this one. Advertisers like such placements because users cannot avoid the ads while playing the game.

Reators (NAR) as a brand integration promotion. The actor, Ty Burrell, still in character as Dunphy, also appeared in a series of television ads for NAR, offering humorous "Phil's-Osophies" on real estate.

From the standpoint of advertisers, television and film product placement and brand integration are smart investments, largely because they aren't easy to avoid. However, sophisticated approaches to branded integration may be effective precisely because the sales pitch appears less intrusive. With products integrated into the storyline—as they are in the episode of *Modern Family*—the brands themselves become integral characters in the film or television experience. Increasingly, media producers consider potential brand integration partnerships from the earliest stages of project development, as they assess what ideas are financially viable and how they can most effectively market new content in an increasingly cluttered media landscape (Clifford 2010).

Advertisements also make their way, through various media, into unlikely places, such as the high school classroom and the doctor's office. Whittle Communications pioneered the art of producing media products, with ample room for advertisements, that reach captive audiences and ensure that other media are not available to compete for consumer attention. One example was the creation of several advertiser-friendly magazines for distribution to participating doctors. Doctors' offices received the magazines for free in exchange for an agreement to carry Whittle publications exclusively.

Similarly, Microsoft targeted kids in classrooms with its student-oriented products and its school initiatives. Programs like the Service & Technology Academic Resource Team (START), launched in 2010, support student leadership in the classroom while at the same time familiarizing the students with Microsoft products. The company's recurrent donations of computers and software to impoverished schools in the United States and abroad provides Microsoft with positive publicity while promoting brand loyalty among new computer users. In these cases, doctors and educators exchange the attention of those they serve—patients and students—for free media products.

Advertising and the Press in the 19th Century

Advertising is a central force in the workings of contemporary mass media, providing the bulk of the revenue for newspapers, magazines, television, and radio. In addition, as we have seen, advertising needs can generate new media products and appear in forms of media that once existed without ads. But what influence does the introduction of advertising have on the content of these media? One well-documented historical example is the impact of advertising on the British and American press in the 1800s.

The British Press

James Curran's (1977) historical account of the British press provides an important institutional analysis of the relationship between news and advertising. Traditionally, historians have argued that British newspapers gradually won their freedom from government and party control as they shifted to a financial structure that relied on advertising. In this view, newspapers achieved a kind of economic independence, permitting the press to take up its contemporary role as the fourth estate. Curran, however, argues that the simple equation of advertising with press freedom neglects the substantial influence this new economic structure had on the radical, working-class press in England. His approach is a textbook example of how the production perspective provides new insight into the workings of mass media systems by asking questions that researchers would otherwise not explore and by examining relationships that researchers had previously neglected.

During the first half of the 19th century, according to Curran (1977), a radical, working-class press thrived in England, breaking circulation records. At the same time, efforts by the government to control the press—through libel laws and press taxes—were largely ineffective. Rather than being constrained by government action, the British working-class press was undermined by the changing economics of the newspaper business, whereby the less politically inclined, middle-class papers turned to advertisers, instead of readers, as a central source of revenue.

Curran (1977) argues that the growth of advertising changed the playing field and led to the decline of the British radical press. Advertising made circulation figures (the number of readers) less important than the patronage of advertisers. Radical papers did not receive the support of advertisers, even though they had large numbers of readers. More mainstream papers, meanwhile, were able to make profits with a substantially smaller readership base. Advertisers' political interests were dramatically different from the ideas espoused by the radical press. In essence, the working-class press presented a political critique of industrial capitalism, while potential advertisers were generally beneficiaries of that same system. Given a choice of which newspaper to support, advertisers elected not to support their political opponents.

In addition, advertisers had economic reasons for avoiding the radical press. Radical newspapers appealed largely to a working-class audience, and even though the papers were widely read, advertisers did not perceive the readers to be a valuable market. To advertisers, reaching smaller numbers of upper- or middle-class readers seemed to be a better sales strategy than reaching large numbers of working-class readers who did not have the necessary resources to buy many of the advertised goods and services.

Advertising changed the meaning of economic viability within the newspaper industry. With new resources coming in, the advertiser-supported papers were able to produce papers with more pages, containing both news and ads. This pushed up the cost of producing a competitive newspaper. At the same time, with advertising revenue as a base, the cover price of papers dropped dramatically, making it difficult for papers without advertising to compete.

The consequences of the rise of advertising were grave for the radical press and tell us a good deal about the broader impact of advertising on the news. Without advertising support, several high-circulation, working-class papers ceased publishing because they could be underpriced by competitors that also had the resources to produce and distribute a more attractive product. One important consequence of advertising, then, was the end of a national radical press in Britain. Owners transformed those papers that did survive in one of two ways. Some publications became small-circulation papers, much like our alternative press today. These papers did not even try to compete with the national press. Other papers moved away from their working-class audience by focusing on items of interest to upper- and middle-class audiences. By losing their radical political commitments, these newspapers were better able to attract advertisers. Either way, from the standpoint of the working class and its radical supporters, the shift to an advertising-based press did not represent progress toward press freedom. Instead, the introduction of advertising and the subsequent decline of the radical press resulted in newspapers that provided a more limited view of events than they had before.

The U.S. Press

The move toward advertising-supported newspapers also had a significant impact on the content of the U.S. press. Until the late 1800s, U.S. newspapers had been largely funded and controlled by political parties, politicians, and partisan organizations. Then, the news shifted from a partisan, politically based press to a commercially based press. A principal consequence of this shift was a change in the definition of a newspaper's very purpose. As advertising became the key to success, news moved from the realm of politics and persuasion to the realm of business (Baldasty 1992). This was no small change. Newspapers were no longer partisan, and they no longer perceived their readers as voters or citizens. On the contrary, newspapers made an effort to avoid partisanship as much as possible and instead looked upon their readers as consumers. There is, in fact, good reason to believe that the historical roots of what we now refer to as "objectivity" in journalism lie in this process of commercialization, whereby the news industry developed a new, nonpartisan framework for reporting news.

The move toward a commercial press in the United States shaped news content in two significant ways (Baldasty 1992). News purveyors began to avoid controversy, preferring instead a blander product that would be likely to attract (and not offend) large numbers of readers as well as advertisers interested in reaching those readers. This shift went beyond a nonpartisan style or voice. As advertisers' desires became intertwined with news values, political news itself—even that without any intentional partisanship—became problematic because of its inherent focus on difficult, sometimes unpleasant issues. As a result, newspapers shifted their focus away from substantive political news.

As news increasingly shied away from political issues, it turned to a variety of features—including sports, fashion, recipes, and entertainment—that existed largely to support the accompanying ads. Then, as today, such items may have been of substantial interest to readers, but they became part of the daily newspaper because these new forms of news would be both advertiser friendly and entertaining.

Commercialization led to one additional consequence of lasting significance. Newspapers became advocates for their newfound economic patrons. According to Baldasty (1992), "Early nineteenth-century newspaper editors were unabashed *advocates for political parties.* Late-nineteenth-century newspaper editors were advocates as well, *advocates for business,* for their advertisers" (p. 141). Our contemporary sensibilities suggest that news should be independent of political control. However, independence from direct political influence was achieved only by introducing a new business influence. The financial role of advertising shaped daily practices within the news industry and transformed the meaning of news for both producers and consumers.

Advertising and the Contemporary News Media

Advertising continues to exert a powerful influence on the news media (Jackson 2014). Advertisers are the dominant source of revenue for print, broadcast, and online news media; journalists, editors, and producers are well aware of who pays the bills. At the same time, most journalists do not set out to intentionally produce news that is advertiser friendly. The dynamics are not so simple as either routine intervention by advertisers to protect their interests (although this does happen) or daily compliance with advertiser agendas by reporters. Rather than directly determining news content, advertising is a force that provides both incentives and constraints that influence the news in a generally predictable way.

At the most general level, news usually depicts advertisers' products and their broad interests in a favorable light. Reporters and editors may not perceive themselves as defending their advertisers' interests, but there is no doubt that they are fully aware of the economic role of their major advertisers. As a result, the dominant influence in this regard is probably more akin to self-censorship, perhaps unconscious, on the part of journalists. Self-censorship refers to the ways reporters doubt themselves, tone down their work, omit small items, or drop entire stories to avoid pressure, eliminate any perception of bias, or advance their careers.

A 2000 survey by the Pew Research Center for the People and the Press found that 41 percent of journalists had engaged in self-censorship—purposely avoiding newsworthy stories or softening the tone of their stories (Kohut 2000). Concern persists among media analysts about self-censorship resulting from advertisers' powerful role as the primary revenue stream for news. For example, BuzzFeed deleted (and later reinstated) an article by beauty editor Arabelle Sicardi criticizing an ad campaign by the soap brand Dove, a company that is one of BuzzFeed's advertising partners. In response, media scholar Victor Pickard noted that the Dove episode highlights "how the increasingly cozy relationship between advertisers and news organizations can encourage less obvious forms of self-censorship." Pickard makes it clear that self-censorship is likely to be common in the digital media environment: "As the distinctions between advertising and news operations continue to blur, we can expect more of these controversies in the future" (quoted in Colhoun 2015).

Even though many critics express outrage at such a scenario, this kind of response by journalists should not be surprising. Professionals are not isolated from the social world around them, nor can they be entirely unmindful of their economic patrons. Lawyers serve their clients' interests; academics are often aware of tenure decisions and funding priorities when they are choosing their research projects; doctors respond to the financial situations of hospitals and insurance companies. Journalists are no different.

Of course, the ways journalists respond to advertiser interests are complex. Rarely is one particular advertiser important enough that journalists need to avoid any hint of criticism, and media outlets can often replace unhappy sponsors with new ones. There are other ways to protect advertisers; for example, network news producers will pull ads from an oil company on the evening that a large oil spill is in the news. More generally, though, news organizations and broadcasters need to pay attention to the interests of the entire class of advertisers, not individual sponsors. In practical terms, news personnel will tend to avoid content that is too critical of the system of consumer capitalism because this system is at the core of the interests of advertisers as a collective. Sometimes the problem for advertisers is not news content, but the news anchors. After revelations of sexual harassment settlements by Fox News personality Bill O'Reilly in 2017, more than half of the advertisers for *The O'Reilly Factor* stopped buying ads on the program. Without advertiser support—total advertising time dropped from 15 minutes before the revelations to only 7 minutes one week later (see Figure 3.7)—the show went off the air in just 10 days (Russell 2017).

Some types of news reporting are more vulnerable to influence than others. In local newspapers, especially since classified ad revenue shifted from newspapers to online spaces, real estate, dining, and automotive coverage are notorious for their reverence of local advertisers. There are clear economic reasons for this. Local real estate agencies, restaurants, and local automobile dealers generally fill the bulk of these sections with their ads, often perceiving that they virtually own the pages. With other advertisers unlikely to pick up the slack, reporters writing in these three areas have little freedom to deviate from traditional, light, industry-pleasing coverage.

This dynamic works in a more affirmative way in a variety of news settings. Editors and producers create new sections in newspapers and new features on radio and television to attract new advertisers. Coverage of music, computers, food, health, and fashion, for example, is prominent in our news because it attracts advertising revenue from companies that sell products in these industries. Lifestyle coverage is an advertiser's dream because much of it focuses on a variety of forms of consumption. Entertainment-oriented coverage meets advertisers' agendas in an additional way. News should, at the very least, maintain a tone that contributes to—and certainly does not undermine—a "buying mood" (Baker 1994). If news content is consistently negative or upsetting, audiences are

FIGURE 3.7 ■ Advertisers Leave *The O'Reilly Factor*

- 34 ads
- 30 advertisers
▸ 14 minutes, 25 seconds of ad time

▸ 7 minutes of ad time
- 10 ads
- 10 advertisers

March 31, 2017   April 1, 2017   April 11, 2017

Publication of *New York Times*   Final Show
article detailing payments to
five women to settle sexual
harassment allegations

Source: Russell (2017).

not likely to be in an appropriate frame of mind to respond to the ads that accompany it. When news is in some way negative, as it often is, there is generally an attempt to brighten the picture and reassure the audience. One example is the convention of television news to end a broadcast with an upbeat story.

Finally, because news outlets need to court advertisers for financial support, there is an incentive to produce news that will appeal to an audience the advertisers want to reach: those who are well-off. As competition for sponsors increases, news outlets face increased pressure to deliver an upscale audience. One result of this pressure is that there is rarely news about the poor, except when they commit crimes, violate basic social norms, or become objects of charity. In essence, editors and producers generally restrict news about the poor to stories about how the poor affect the middle and upper classes. Much of the style and fashion coverage is geared toward people with high incomes. Of course, not all news is successful at reaching an upscale audience. Still, news outlets that we can most easily identify as upscale—the *New York Times*, PBS's *NewsHour*, the *Wall Street Journal*, the *Washington Post*—are also perceived by industry observers to be the best news in the business.

In the end, advertising does not directly determine news, but news cannot be entirely independent of advertising. Both historical and contemporary analysis indicates that the language we use to talk about news—discussions of objectivity, the meaning of "quality" or "prestige" journalism, the very categories that are defined as news—is derived, in part, from the central role of advertising in the news industry.

CONCLUSION

This chapter has examined the ways in which economic versions of the production perspective help us understand the media industry. Such an approach is essential, but a focus on the economics of media is a limited lens from which to view the relationship between mass media and society.

One line of argument suggests that the approach outlined in this chapter has a tendency to present an overdetermined view of the mass media; that is, it overemphasizes the ways in which economic forces determine the nature of media products. *Determine* is the key word here, for this critique suggests that the economics of the production process cannot fully define the specific nature of mass media. According to this argument, the production process involves too many additional intervening variables. Media production is directed by human beings who make judgments and interpretations at every stage. As a result, there is more variability within media than some production-oriented critics imply, and the institutional constraints on production are not all-encompassing. We accept the basic contours of this criticism but see no need to discard the insights gained from the production perspective. We cannot ignore, nor should we overstate, the impact of economic forces on media production and distribution.

The economic dimension of the media industry is certainly a critical component for analysis. However, as the next two chapters will show, more than economics is involved in understanding the contours of the media industry. We must also consider political and organizational factors.

Discussion Questions

1. What is the difference between products, platforms, and pipes? How do these three concepts help explain economic dynamics in the media industry?

2. What is the significance of ownership concentration within the media industry (film, television, music, publishing, internet platforms) in a digital era?

3. How has ownership of internet platforms followed a similar path to that of traditional media?

4. How do profit pressures influence the news media? Do you think nonprofit journalism is, or can be, significantly different from for-profit journalism?

5. How responsive, if at all, are you to advertising strategies such as product placement and brand integration? What does this suggest about the effectiveness of, and potential resistance to, various forms of digital advertising?

POLITICAL INFLUENCE ON MEDIA

This chapter considers the influence of political forces on the media and explores questions about the appropriate role of government in regulating media. (Later, in Chapter 9, we will look at the media's influence on society, including politics.) Our concern is not with the details of media legislation but rather with the general dynamics that characterize the relationship between government and media. We also address the more informal political pressure brought to bear on the media by media advocacy groups, public interest organizations, religious groups, and media critics.

MEDIA AND DEMOCRACY

The nonprofit watchdog group Reporters Without Borders listed three democratic countries—Norway, Sweden, and Finland—at the top of its 2017 annual Press Freedom Index, and three countries with authoritarian governments—Turkmenistan, Eritrea, and North Korea—at the bottom of the list. (The United States ranked 43rd of the 180 countries in the report.) The Index was constructed from several criteria, including the amount of violence against journalists, the nature of legislation governing media, and the degree of economic pressures on the media (Reporters Without Borders 2017).

Reporters Without Borders Secretary-General Christophe Deloire has noted that the Index "does not take direct account of the kind of political system but it is clear that democracies provide better protection for the freedom to produce and circulate accurate news and information than countries where human rights are flouted." But being in a democracy does not mean the media are totally unconstrained. Deloire continued, "In dictatorships, news providers and their families are exposed to ruthless reprisals, while in democracies news providers have to cope with the media's economic crises and conflicts of interest" (Reporters Without Borders 2013). These various types of pressure on the media differ widely, but they all have an effect.

As the Index rankings suggest, to better understand media—news and entertainment media alike—we need to consider the political environment in which they operate. Government in all nations serves as an organizing structure that can, to varying degrees, constrain or promote the free activity (or agency) of the media. This is the tension between structure and agency as it applies to media and the political world. State regulation of media can include policies aimed at influencing the ownership structure of media, the content being produced, and the technological infrastructure used to access and distribute content.

In totalitarian systems, the structural constraint of the state largely dominates the potential agency of the media. Sometimes state-owned news agencies, broadcast media, and film studios can act as propaganda arms of the state, promoting a narrow set of government-sanctioned images and messages. Even if media outlets are not state-owned, autocratic governments often impose both formal and informal ground rules for what can and can't be said in the media. Indirect mechanisms supporting state interests can be used as well. For example, authoritarian regimes hire sympathetic bloggers and tweeters to spread their messages, while using censorship and surveillance technologies to monitor potential political threats. In extreme cases, journalists can be imprisoned or killed for challenging state polices.

Democratic societies, on the other hand, pride themselves on protecting freedom of the press and freedom of expression. That's why it was so startling when President Trump referred to the *New York Times* and other mainstream media outlets as "the enemy of the American people," gave "awards" for "fake news," and routinely made disparaging remarks about the press (Flegenheimer and Grynbaum 2018; Grynbaum 2017). Such attacks are more commonly seen in autocratic societies. Critics—including some in his own party—argued that Trump's words were giving cover to repressive leaders abroad (Sullivan 2018). The Committee to Protect Journalists (2017) reported a rise in attacks on journalists by repressive leaders and suggested that, "President Donald Trump's nationalistic rhetoric, fixation on Islamic extremism, and insistence on labeling critical media 'fake news' serves to reinforce the framework of accusations and legal charges that allow such leaders to pre-side over the jailing of journalists."

Unlike repressive states, democratic societies are usually characterized by a more diverse mix of public and privately owned media outlets offering a variety of arts, news, information, and entertainment. The media in such societies are still subject to government regulation, but they are usually given much greater latitude to operate independently. However, in some democratic societies, the media are still largely controlled by a relatively small group of powerful interests—commercial corporations. In those cases, it is corporate domination of media rather than government control that is of most concern, and governments can use anti-trust laws to break up concentrated media ownership if it is deemed to be a threat to the public interest.

But democratic societies still regulate their media. The nature and extent of such regulations is a topic of ongoing debate.

> **Donald J. Trump** ✔
> @realDonaldTrump
> Follow ⌄
>
> The FAKE NEWS media (failing @nytimes, @NBCNews, @ABC, @CBS, @CNN) is not my enemy, it is the enemy of the American People!
>
> 1:48 PM - 17 Feb 2017

Twitter/@realDonaldTrump

As candidate and president, Donald Trump routinely attacked mainstream media outlets, calling journalists "scum," "sleaze," "corrupt," and "dishonest." His remarks went far beyond those of previous presidents who sometimes complained about unfavorable coverage but supported the democratic principle of a free press.

FREE SPEECH TO FREE MARKETS: THE EVOLUTION OF U.S. REGULATORY POLICY

In the United States, debates about media regulation go back to the founding of the country. Most Americans are familiar with the First Amendment to the U.S. Constitution, which guarantees, among other things, freedom of the press. The amendment in its entirety reads as follows: "Congress shall make no law respecting an establishment of religion, or prohibiting the free exercise thereof; or abridging the freedom of speech, or of the press; or the right of the people peaceably to assemble, and to petition the government for a redress of grievances."

Because the amendment begins with "Congress shall make no law," this "first freedom" suggests that the government should take a hands-off approach toward the media. The framers of the Constitution knew all too well how European governments had persecuted authors, printers, and publishers. Throughout Europe, governments limited the rights of printers through tactics such as requiring licenses, heavily taxing newsprint, censorship, and aggressively prosecuting libel (Eisenstein 1968). The U.S. legal and legislative system took a different route. It protected the freedom of the press in several key ways. First, it treated the licensing of the press as a case of illegal "prior restraint." Second, it developed a tradition of opposing special taxes on the press. Third, it greatly restricted criminal libel suits. (In 2018, President Trump called the laws governing libel suits a "sham" and pledged to make it easier to sue news organizations and publishers [Grynbaum 2018].) This was the hands-off dimension of public policy embodied in the First Amendment.

But we do not have to go any further than the U.S. Constitution to see another dimension of the government's relationship with the media. Section 8 of Article I lists the powers of Congress, among which is the power "to promote the progress of science and useful arts, by securing for limited times to authors and inventors the exclusive right to their respective writings and discoveries." Here the Constitution explicitly gives Congress the right to intervene in the communications marketplace to defend the interests of authors and inventors. By protecting the incentivizing rewards authors and inventors receive for investing time, effort, and resources in creating new things, Congress promotes innovation in science and the arts and advances the public interest.

Thus, in various ways, the relationship between government and media in U.S. society involves balancing the protection of free expression by *limiting* government intervention with the protection of the public interest by *using* government intervention. In many ways, these competing demands have been at the heart of the long-standing debates about government regulation of the media.

Regulate or Deregulate?

With modern media, policy debates are largely about the balance between using the government to regulate versus allowing the "free market" to determine the fate of media through unregulated competition among privately owned companies. Supporters of deregulation generally assert that the "free market" system is adequate for accommodating the needs of both media producers and media consumers. They argue that consumers have the ultimate power to choose to tune into or buy media products and that there is no need for government interference in the form of media regulation. The marketplace serves as a quasi-democratic forum in which consumers, not government agencies, get to decide the fate of media. Furthermore, the absence of regulation empowers companies to experiment and innovate to meet changing consumer needs.

In its pure form, the deregulation approach is a negative prescription for policy. That is, deregulation advocates suggest what they are *against* (regulation), not what they *favor*. They clearly support the "free market" process, but there is little or no discussion about the undemocratic nature of a marketplace where more dollars mean more influence and where people are viewed as consumers rather than citizens. Nor is there much discussion of the outcome of this market process beyond the idea that media products would reflect changing market tastes. But what if an unregulated market results in monopoly control of a medium by a corporate giant, undermining the benefits of market competition? Should the government step in to regulate ownership? Or what if explicit sex, graphic violence, and endless trivia are what is popular—and profitable—in the marketplace? Should the government involve itself in the regulation of such content? And should the government support efforts to better meet the needs of a democracy for news and information that may not be profitable? These are among the dilemmas raised by the deregulation position.

In contrast to the deregulation approach, support for media regulation is usually based on a desired outcome. The most common standard for assessing this outcome is the "public interest," a generalized concern for the well-being of the citizenry as a whole rather than individual private interests. This standard reaches beyond merely market concerns to include the overall health of a democratic society. In the modern era, the idea that media should serve the public interest was first explicitly articulated in the earliest days of radio broadcasting, when the government tied serving the public interest to the granting of licenses because broadcast media were using publicly owned airwaves. But what is the "public interest" and who decides? These are among the central dilemmas raised by the pro-regulation position. (For a more detailed comparison of the "free market" versus "public interest" models, see Croteau and Hoynes 2006.)

The FCC's Variable Role

Many debates regarding media regulation involve the Federal Communications Commission (FCC), the independent U.S. government agency established in 1934. Comprising five commissioners, appointed by the president and confirmed by the Senate for five-year terms, the FCC regulates U.S. interstate and international communications by radio, television, wire, satellite, and cable, including the internet. The FCC is also responsible for the issuance of licenses, the setting of some charges, and the enforcement of communication rules (Zarkin and Zarkin 2006).

The FCCs role has shifted over the years, as its appointees have reflected the political climate of different periods. In the broadest sense, the FCC's role has evolved through three distinct eras: (1) pre-World War II, (2) World War II until the 1980s, and (3) the 1980s to today (van Cuilenburg and McQuail 2003). Prior to World War II, media policy was newly emerging and ad hoc in nature. As we saw in Chapter 2, for example, the United States had government-regulated private monopolies in the telegraph and telephone industries, whereas radio broadcasting moved from an unregulated to a regulated medium.

During the second era, after World War II until the 1980s, the notion of protecting the public interest by regulating for public service and social responsibility gained ground. As we'll see in the next section of this chapter, this was especially true in Europe, where much of broadcasting was financed with public funds and so was more closely aligned with the public interest. European media producers generally retained editorial independence but were accountable to elected officials for maintaining diverse content in terms of political orientation, cultural tastes, and minority communities served.

In the United States, even though private ownership of media was the norm, a variety of reform initiatives and legal rulings around World War II solidified the idea that the media were a special resource for a democratic society. Consequently, they had social responsibilities and should be regulated for the public good (Pickard 2015):

- In 1943, concerned about monopolistic ownership of the media, an FCC ruling led NBC to sell off a radio network that became the American Broadcasting Company (ABC).

- In 1945, in an antitrust ruling against the Associated Press, the Supreme Court affirmed the duty of the government to promote media that includes "diverse and antagonistic voices."

- In 1946, in response to public concern about the crass commercialization of the media, the FCC issued the "Blue Book" report that laid out the public service responsibilities of broadcasters, including providing programming that was local, discussed public issues of the day, included public service programs that could not be sustained by advertisers, and excluded "excess" advertising.

- In 1947, the "Hutchins" Commission on Freedom of the Press—formed at the request of Henry Luce, the influential publisher of *Time* and *Life* magazines— published a report that laid out recommendations for the role of government, the press, and the public in a modern democracy. It accepted the idea that the press "must be accountable to society for meeting the public need and maintaining the rights of citizens and the almost forgotten rights of speakers who have no press" (Commission on Freedom of the Press 1947: 18).

- In 1949, the FCC implemented the Fairness Doctrine, which required broadcasters to cover public issues and to include a variety of views that fairly represented opposing viewpoints.

Communication scholar Victor Pickard (2015: 4) notes that all of these efforts "prioritized the collective rights of the public's 'freedom to read, see, and hear' over the individual rights of media producers and owners. And, as important, they all assumed a proactive role for government to guarantee these rights affirmatively." Even though the implementation of these initiatives varied considerably, with some never enforced, they still created a foundation upon which public interest advocates could build their case for socially responsible media. As a result, the climate of post-World War II America was permeated by a broad understanding that the government had a role to play in regulating media to protect the public interest—and that privately owned media had a public service duty.

Up until the 1980s, FCC policy makers generally expressed agreement with the importance of serving the "public interest," and they shared some common ground in understanding the term (Krugman and Reid 1980). For example, policymakers commonly believed that the FCC served the public interest by attempting to balance the interests of various groups, suggesting that there is no single public interest. They also stressed that the government cannot write media regulation in stone for all eternity because technological and economic changes are constantly occurring. Finally, they believed that regulation that promotes diversity in programming and services is in the public interest.

All of that began to change in the 1980s when conservative forces—embodied in the election of President Ronald Reagan—advocated deregulation across all industries, including the media. Parts of the media industry were never happy with the efforts to hold them accountable to public interest standards, and now they increasingly found political allies in key positions of power. The Reagan-appointed chair of the FCC, Mark Fowler, even wrote that "broadcasters as community trustees should be replaced by a view of broadcasters as marketplace participants." The FCC's role, he argued was simply to "rely on the broadcasters' ability to determine the wants of their audiences through the normal mechanisms of the marketplace. The public's interest, then, defines the public interest" (Fowler and Brenner 1982: 209–210). The idea that media was simply another commodity in the marketplace, rather than a resource for a democratic society, was perhaps best summed up in Fowler's notorious quip that "television is just another appliance—it's a toaster with pictures" (Mueller 1981).

From the 1980s onward, "free market" advocates largely succeeded in dismantling public interest regulation. This included everything from abolishing the Fairness Doctrine in 1987, to making broadcast license renewals virtually automatic without review, to even eliminating requirements that broadcasters file program logs with the FCC so citizen groups—and the FCC itself—could monitor what was being broadcast. Without basic accountability, critics argued, children's television became markedly more violent and commercialized, as with the introduction of children's programs based on toys—essentially half-hour commercials. More generally, advertising increased on all programming, and the pressures on broadcast journalism to make a profit grew dramatically. The FCC abolished rules that limited how quickly stations could be sold, paving the way for massive mergers in the media industry that helped convert broadcast journalism—once considered the public responsibility of media companies—into profit-making ventures just like entertainment programming.

Anti-regulation advocates usually argued for "promoting competition, removing artificial barriers to entry, [and] preventing any one firm from controlling price or eliminating its competitors" (Fowler and Brenner 1982: 210). Such an approach laid the foundation for breaking up the telephone monopoly, discussed in Chapter 2. But in broadcasting and other media, the argument was that new technologies—including cable and the early internet—had introduced substantial new competition, so old restrictions on ownership were unnecessary. Digital convergence meant companies were competing across media so older policies that made sharp distinctions between technologies and between forms of media no longer made sense. As a result of these beliefs, ownership regulations were severely relaxed, and single companies were allowed to become larger integrated media conglomerates, as we discussed in Chapter 3. However, in some cases, what were portrayed as opportunities for new competition instead became opportunities for growing concentration of ownership.

While the era of deregulation continues today, new regulatory challenges remain unresolved. The FCC and other regulatory bodies have struggled to keep up with technological changes and figure out how best to respond. The contentious debate about net neutrality—which we discuss later—is one example of the new regulatory issues. Developments such as the Russian intervention in the 2016 U.S. presidential election, mounting concerns about the impact of social media use, and the growing power of new technology companies have spotlighted new areas of concern. But in the absence of a consensus over policy goals, the general inclination toward deregulation typically continues to win the day.

REGULATION IN INTERNATIONAL PERSPECTIVE

All governments develop media regulations because they understand the media's political and social importance. Of course, the method by which governments try to achieve such control varies. In the book's final chapter, we explore some of the media's global dynamics, including some of the unique regulatory issues raised by global media. Here, we only make some brief observations to contrast efforts of other countries with the U.S. approach.

As noted, some nations have taken direct authoritarian control of media through state ownership of broadcast outlets, bans on opposition media, and constraints on internet access. But most nations engage in media regulation that is nonauthoritarian in nature, combining government policies with market forces. These policies vary significantly based, in part, on the development level of the country. Wealthy Western democracies and developing nations have had differing regulatory concerns, both of which contrast with the U.S. experience.

Regulation in Western Democracies

The role of the U.S. government in regulating the media has always been much more limited than in many other Western democratic nations (Starr 2004). For example, the early days of radio in the United States were characterized by free market commercialism that produced considerable chaos. In contrast, European nations adopted an approach that involved government operation of the media as a technique to avoid signal interference. The result was a system that (1) emphasized public service, (2) was national in character, (3) was politicized, and (4) was noncommercial (McQuail, de Mateo, and Tapper 1992).

In many countries, this approach meant adopting a state monopoly system. The British Broadcasting Corporation (BBC), established in 1922, was the first such system. Within four years, Italy, Sweden, Ireland, Finland, and Denmark had copied the BBC model. Over time, more nations developed similar arrangements, and many variations developed. Most monopolies, for example, were nationwide. But in countries such as Belgium, where both Flemish and French were widely spoken, each linguistic group had a separate public broadcasting service. Also, countries with state systems have mostly adopted approaches that couple state-run with privately owned media.

In the post-World War II era, in most European countries, the purely commercial marketplace was not the dominant media approach. Although there was no single model, governments typically controlled the organization and financing of broadcast services, investing substantially in supporting the production of both news and entertainment. This made the government a central force in broadcasting even while producers outside the state-run system often created the actual programming. The point of government involvement was to ensure that broadcasting could deliver quality programming that served the public interest. As in the United States, the interpretation of "public interest" was debated in Europe. However, people generally considered the purpose of public service broadcasting to be to provide citizens with a diverse range of high-quality entertainment, information, and education, some of which might not be profitable (Donders 2011; Hills 1991).

Government media, however benignly run, present difficulties. In some countries, controversy regarding the political content of programs plagued public service broadcasting. In part because of such debates, in part because of changes in technology, and in part because of shifts in the political winds, European broadcasting, like its U.S. counterpart, has undergone dramatic changes since the 1980s. Governments significantly reduced regulations concerning the structure and financing of broadcasting, opening the way to more competition between public broadcasters and commercial stations. In some countries, such as Italy, the pressure to liberalize airwaves came from private companies and business leaders, who saw the profit potential inherent in television and radio stations and challenged the state by operating illegal stations, forcing the regulators to reconsider the state monopoly principle (Ginsborg 2005; Hibberd 2008). Thus regulators introduced advertising into many public stations (although not the BBC, which inside the UK remains advertising free) and added new commercial stations. The results were increases in advertising, increases in imported programming (which is often cheaper to air than original, domestically produced programming), and the consolidation of media companies into ever larger corporate conglomerates that bought up formerly independent producers (Hills 1991).

Ironically, deregulation in structure and finance was followed by increased regulation of media content. Free market competition led to more violent and sexually explicit programs as a way to attract audiences and to crasser commercialization to maximize profits. In response, governments introduced limits on programming and regulated the amount and frequency of advertising. For example, France, Great Britain, and Sweden (along with Canada and Australia) have restrictions against broadcasting violent programs during children's hours, with broadcasters subject to stiff fines for violations. In some European countries, governments required that news, public affairs, religious, and children's programming run for 30 minutes before a commercial break (Hirsch and Petersen 1992). Also, countries in the European Union limit the amount of advertising on commercial stations to 12 minutes an hour (20%). In 2016, at the behest of broadcasters facing competition from online streaming services, the European Commission began the process of relaxing the rules by retaining an *overall* daily limit on ads to 20 percent of airtime, while giving broadcasters flexibility in *when* they would air those ads (European Union 2017). Even relaxed rules go further than in the United States, where there are no such regulations at all. In 2017, U.S. broadcast networks aired more than 14 and half minutes of commercials each hour, whereas cable channels featured over 16 minutes an hour (Nielsen 2017c).

The rise of the internet posed new challenges and generated new responses from European nations. Here, too, European nations have been more proactive than the United States in regulating the internet in an attempt to protect citizen privacy, crack down on online hate speech, and pursue anti-monopoly cases against online giants like Google. We will consider examples of these efforts later in the chapter.

Regulation in Developing Nations

Regulation in developing countries has raised different issues from those in wealthier nations. In earlier years, the media industries in developing countries were typically smaller and less robust than their counterparts in wealthier nations, and so developing countries also tend to have more state-owned media (Djankov, McLiesch, Nenova, and Shleifer 2003). Well-financed Western media companies could provide developing countries with relatively low-cost media content, thereby undermining the development of private indigenous media industries. For example, Western wire services and major Western media outlets were often the source of news and information in such countries. Because revenues from international markets were sometimes a "bonus" for already profitable global conglomerates, Western firms could license their entertainment products for broadcast and exhibition in developing countries at low rates. This filled the airwaves and movie theaters of developing countries with Western-created media content. Such experiences raised concerns that local cultures could be eradicated in the face of a flood of foreign imports, a process sometimes referred as "cultural imperialism." Thus some media regulation has involved the protection and promotion of fledgling indigenous media industries—both public and private—in the face of competition by global media giants. One simple mechanism has been requirements that broadcasters air a certain percentage of domestically created programming, carving out space for indigenous programming in the sea of international content.

In more recent years, internet use has exploded in developing countries, especially via smartphones and wireless broadband (Panday 2017). The voice and video services on internet-based platforms such as Skype and Facebook give users much lower-cost alternatives to the texting and voice services of traditional telecommunication companies. Similarly, online streaming services offer an alternative to traditional broadcast or cable media. These internet-based apps and services—often referred to as "over-the-top" or OTT services—have largely been unregulated, unlike their traditional counterparts that are often taxed, licensed, and subject to regulations. Now, though, governments in developing countries such as India, Thailand, and Indonesia are moving to create new regulations, such as requiring companies offering such services to have local offices and employees, mandating that they work with local network providers and use local IP addresses and payment services. In some cases, service providers would be required to pay bandwidth fees and be subjected to "throttling"—slowing down of traffic on their service—if they fail to comply with regulations. Some of these efforts aim to protect local traditional telecommunication companies from global competition, similar to how local content requirements aim to protect local media producers. Others seem thinly veiled efforts to censor internet usage by making sure traffic can be monitored and controlled, if necessary. Either way, they hint at some of the challenges raised by regulating a global internet.

COMPETING INTERESTS AND THE REGULATION DEBATE

So far, we have presented the regulation debate mostly in its simplest form—a free market deregulatory approach versus government regulation in the public interest. But in reality, the debate is more complicated. Despite simple rhetoric calling for "deregulation," virtually everyone involved with the media *wants* government regulation. This includes liberal and conservative politicians, industry executives, and public interest advocates. What these groups disagree about is *what kind* of government regulation should exist.

For example, almost all calls for deregulating media are, in practice, calls for *selective* deregulation, leaving in place many of the laws and policies that benefit the media industry. Indeed, the media industry could not exist in its present form without active government regulation and control through broadcast licensing, copyright enforcement, and other provisions. In addition, different parts of the media industry favor regulations that protect them from competitors in other parts of the industry. In this way, the industry does not necessarily speak with one voice. But all media companies actively support *some* regulations, namely, those that benefit either the industry as a whole or their portion of it.

Meanwhile, supporters of press freedoms and increased media diversity often call for regulations that protect the interests of the public against the influence of the powerful media industry. The media industry usually cites the merits of deregulation when it is faced with such constraints. So, as we will see, the history of regulatory debates is not about *whether or not* the government should play a role in regulating the media. Instead, it is about *how* and *to what extent* government should act.

Industry Influence: Elections and Lobbying

Regulation debates reflect competing interests (Freedman 2008). Regulatory decisions create winners and losers, so it is important to ask, "Who benefits from such regulation?" as well as "Who is constrained?" This can explain a great deal about regulation debates. The media and telecommunications industry promotes its interests through a well-organized and powerful political arm that finances political candidates and lobbies elected officials (see Table 4.1). It is safe to assume that such efforts are aimed at promoting legislation in which the industry has an interest and at derailing efforts it deems threatening. And, of course, the media industry controls the biggest soapbox in society. One FCC official pointed out that one reason broadcasters are such a powerful Washington lobbying group is because they control the air time given to members of Congress on local stations (Hickey 1995). Politicians courting favorable media coverage for reelection are likely to be highly conscious of legislation that can affect the media industry.

On the other hand, in addition to electing officials who reflect their views, ordinary citizens can try to influence regulatory debates through their own advocacy groups and social movement organizations or by giving feedback to elected officials or the FCC when regulatory debates arise. Often, these struggles go back and forth for a long period of time as new regulations are introduced, a backlash ensues, and changes are implemented, only to be challenged. As we will see, many of the debates regarding specific forms of regulation have been going on for decades and continue to this day. A good example of such struggles is the campaign to permit low-power radio.

Citizen Action: The Case of Low-Power Radio

It was 6:30 A.M., says Doug Brewer (a.k.a. Craven Moorehead), when government agents burst into his Tampa Bay, Florida, home. The agents wore flak jackets and had their guns drawn. They made Brewer and his family lie on the floor while they searched the house. A police helicopter circled the neighborhood, and other officers with submachine guns stood outside. When they found what they had come for, the agents handcuffed Brewer to a chair while they removed thousands of dollars' worth of contraband (Nesbitt 1998; Shiver 1998).

Brewer was not a drug dealer. He was a "radio pirate" whose unlicensed microstation—"Tampa's Party Pirate"—broadcast "biker rock" music. The agents entering his home on that morning in November of 1997 included FCC officials who were enforcing federal regulations prohibiting unlicensed radio broadcasting. The raid was part of an FCC crackdown on "radio piracy." The contraband they confiscated was electronic broadcasting equipment.

If Brewer had produced a magazine or a website, he would have been protected by the Constitution's First Amendment. But government and the courts treat broadcast media differently because they use the public airwaves to reach an audience. There is a limited spectrum of available electromagnetic frequencies, and the government regulates who can use certain frequencies. (A radio station's call number—e.g., 98.6 or 101—refers to the frequency at which the station broadcasts.) The government does this by issuing licenses, which "pirate" broadcasters do not have, to stations that seek to broadcast at certain frequencies.

TABLE 4.1   ■   Spending on Elections and Lobbying by Select Media-Related Industry Sector

The various sectors of the media and communications industry try to influence government policy by spending tens of millions of dollars a year on lobbying efforts and campaign contributions.

	Elections (2016)	Lobbying (2017)	Total
Electronics Manufacturing and Equipment (e.g., Apple, Intel, Oracle, Dell, Cisco, IBM)	$90,338,592	$107,914,723	$198,253,315
TV, Movies, and Music (e.g., Disney, National Assoc. of Broadcasters)	$84,045,507	$45,651,093	$129,696,600
Computer Software (e.g., Adobe, Microsoft, Entertainment Software Assoc.)	$48,667,672	$34,443,959	$83,111,631
Telecom Services (e.g., Comcast, Cox, Cellular Telecom. Industry Assoc.)	$26,037,716	$61,733,551	$87,771,267
Internet (e.g., Alphabet/Google, Facebook, Amazon, Verizon)	$33,785,894	$50,016,850	$83,802,744
Printing and Publishing (e.g., NewsCorp, RELX Group, Assoc. of American Publishers)	$70,251,000	$7,865,443	$78,116,443
Books, Magazines, and Newspapers (e.g., Thomson Reuters, Magazine Publishers of America)	$67,770,685	$6,681,443	$74,452,128
Telephone Utilities (e.g., AT&T, Verizon, CenturyLink, U.S. Telecom Assoc.)	$15,714,959	$26,260,925	$41,975,884
Commercial TV and Radio Stations (e.g., National Assoc. of Broadcasters, Hubbard, Sinclair)	$9,313,054	$21,571,125	$30,884,179
TV Production (e.g., Bad Robot Prod., Liberty Media, Fuzzy Door Prod.)	$23,846,092	$200,000	$24,046,092
Motion Picture Production and Distribution (e.g., Sony, Time Warner, Motion Picture Assoc. of America)	$20,811,499	$3,060,000	$23,871,499
Recorded Music and Music Production (e.g., Vivendi, Recording Industry Assoc. of America)	$6,122,152	$9,957,403	$16,079,555
Cable, Satellite, and TV Production (e.g., 21st Century Fox, Time Warner)	$2,879,530	$3,928,843	$6,808,373
Total	$499,584,352	$379,285,358	$878,869,710

Source: Federal Election Commission data and lobbying disclosure reports summarized by the Center for Responsive Politics (www.opensecrets.org). Accessed January 11, 2018.

Notes: Election spending includes contributions from industry individuals, political action committees (PACs), and soft/outside money in 2016. Lobbying spending is from 2017 records through December 8. Individual companies are merely listed as examples of businesses in that industry sector; some companies operate in more than one sector.

The argument for broadcast licenses is practical: An unlicensed radio signal can interfere with the signal of another station that is legally licensed to use the same, or a nearby, frequency. Or it may interfere with other wireless services—such as cellular phones, pagers, police walkie-talkies, digital television signals, or even air traffic control communication—all of which use the airwaves as well. The absence of government regulation of the airwaves might lead to chaos as multiple stations drowned each other out at the same frequencies and personal communications devices were interrupted. The result would be akin to a street and highway system with no lanes, signs, stoplights, or speed limits. In fact, fear of this sort of chaos in the early days of radio contributed to regulation and the practice of requiring broadcast licenses. The government, therefore, says it uses licensing requirements to protect the "public interest."

But unlicensed "pirate" operators—who generally prefer the more neutral term *microbroadcaster*—told a different story. They suggested it was commercial media corporations that were really behind the effort to keep them off the air, just as early commercial broadcasters helped push amateur radio enthusiasts off desirable spectrum space a century ago. They pointed out that low-power stations were just that—low-power—and posed virtually no interference threat to other stations. In addition, microbroadcasters went to great lengths to ensure that their signals didn't interfere with other broadcasts or communications. Even so, their efforts were illegal at the time because the FCC simply did not grant licenses to small microstations, leaving radio to be dominated by larger, mostly commercial, interests. If the FCC is so concerned about chaos on the airwaves, radio activists asked, then why didn't it simply allocate a section of the broadcast spectrum for microstations and then issue licenses?

That idea ran into stiff opposition from commercial broadcasters. The National Association of Broadcasters (NAB), the industry's lobbying group, used the fear of widespread signal interference to oppose the creation of a new category of low-power FM radio stations. The NAB even distributed a CD to members of Congress supposedly documenting what such interference would sound like. However, the FCC's own engineers said the audio simulation was fraudulent, and the FCC's then-chair William E. Kennard accused the NAB of a "systematic campaign of misinformation and scare tactics" (Labaton 2000: C1). Later, an independent study commissioned by the FCC confirmed that low-power radio posed no significant interference issues (FCC 2004).

With the industry's primary argument exposed as bogus, community radio activists finally achieved some limited success in 2000 when the FCC agreed to begin licensing low-power stations. At first, existing broadcasters, including both the NAB and National Public Radio (NPR), successfully lobbied Congress to make licensing so restrictive as to limit the number of such stations to just a few dozen instead of the thousands originally proposed. But community radio advocates continued to pressure for more. Finally, the Local Community Radio Act was signed into law in January 2011, giving the FCC a mandate to expand the broadcast spectrum allotted to community radio stations, marking a major victory for low-power radio advocates.

By early 2018, about 2,500 new stations had been, or were in the process of being, licensed. Over a third of those were held by religious organizations, whereas the remaining microstations served a wide variety of community needs. The stations, almost always run by amateur volunteers, have a reach of about three and a half miles depending on surrounding terrain and so are often focused on very local concerns. They broadcast everything from local news and high school sports to eclectic musical playlists that often

Citizen activists work on a wide range of media-related issues. Here, advocates of "net neutrality" regulation protest in front of the Time-Warner building in New York City. As of December 2017, Time-Warner and other media companies successfully lobbied the FCC to repeal the regulations.

highlight local bands. Some stations serve local ethnic communities by broadcasting in their native language. What they all share is an interest in providing radio content that cannot be found on mainstream commercial stations. As Rebecca Webb, the founder of a microstation in Portland, Oregon, put it, "The fact that we have gathered ourselves up by our bootstraps and created a community radio station is in direct response to the ownership concentration of large media companies" (Johnson 2018).

The long road from "pirate radio" to legal microbroadcasting shows that policy is a product of political activity and that competing interests are at stake in such media policymaking. These will be recurring issues as we explore various policy debates.

Left and Right: Diversity versus Property Rights

In the everyday political world, calls for media regulation come from both liberals and conservatives. However, the intended target of the regulation differs based on political orientation. The sides do not always line up neatly, but conservatives and liberals generally tend to approach the topic of regulation differently.

Liberals and the left usually see the government's role in media regulation as one of protecting the public against the domination of the private sector. (Conservatives see this as government meddling in the free market.) As we will see, this view manifests itself in liberal support for regulating ownership of media outlets, with the aim of protecting the public interest against monopolistic corporate practices. Inherent in this approach is the belief that the marketplace is not adequately self-regulating and that commercial interests can acquire undue power and influence.

Liberals and the left tend to support regulation that encourages diversity in media content, such as the Fairness Doctrine. Finally, liberals also back government financing for public media because such outlets can sometimes support important programming that may not be commercially viable. In the United States, such funding is quite modest—$445 million in 2016, that is, about 0.01 percent of the federal budget or $1.38 per American (Bump 2017). The largest source of public funding for non-commercial media is that allotted by Congress to the nonprofit Corporation for Public Broadcasting (CPB 2018). In turn, CPB uses this money to fund about 15 percent of the budget for Public Broadcasting Service (PBS) and National Public Radio (NPR); the remainder of their funding comes from corporate and foundation sponsors and viewer/listener fundraising (NPR 2018; PBS 2018).

Conservatives and the right tend to respond to such arguments with staunch support for property rights and the free market system. (Liberals see this as protecting corporate interests at the expense of the public interest.) When it comes to regulating ownership and control of media, conservatives tend to advocate a laissez-faire approach by government. They caution against the dangers of bureaucratic government intervention and the tyranny of "politically correct" calls for diversity. They are often enthusiasts for the ability of the profit motive to produce positive media outcomes for all. Conservatives generally see the marketplace as the great equalizer, a place where ideas and products stand or fall based on the extent of their popularity. They often portray ideas like the Fairness Doctrine or public broadcasting as illegitimate attempts by those outside the American mainstream to gain access to the media.

Although conservatives abhor the idea of limiting, restricting, or regulating private property rights, they are often quite comfortable with restricting the content of media products, especially in the name of morality. A free market system for the media tends to lead to things such as graphic violence and misogynistic pornography; media images of sex and violence are popular and profitable (Dines 2010). However, nearly all observers agree that some restrictions on the content of media are necessary, especially to protect children and minors. In fact, it is conservatives who have often led the call to regulate material they deem unfit for minors. So while conservatives oppose government regulation that requires additional content for the sake of diversity, they are generally comfortable with regulations that restrict or prohibit the dissemination of material they deem unsuitable. The result, as we will see, has been both voluntary and mandatory regulation of media content.

Following this broad overview of the contest over media regulation, we turn now to some examples of media regulation and the sorts of debates they have generated. We group the issues into three broad categories: the regulation of (1) ownership, (2) content, and (3) access and distribution.

REGULATING OWNERSHIP

In this section, we review examples of the debates over regulating media ownership and technology in the United States (Doyle 2002; Freedman 2008; Noam 2009, 2016). We do not attempt to provide any sort of comprehensive review; rather, our goal is to show how debates about the relationship between politics and the media represent one kind of tension between agency and structure in the social world.

Media Outlets

When early government officials crafted the First Amendment, media ownership was largely a local, decentralized affair. As a result, the First Amendment closely links "freedom of speech or of the press" because, in colonial times, the two were very similar. Individual printers or shops employing just a couple of people created the media products of the day. The written word, therefore, was largely an extension of the spoken word. In this context, the issue of ownership was of little concern. The equipment needed to operate a press was relatively straightforward and affordable for purchase or lease to those with modest capital. In theory, there was no limit on the potential number of different presses.

Over time, however, communication media have changed in significant ways. First, *media technology* evolved in ways that have encouraged centralization and larger-scale operations. Beginning as early as the telegraph, some forms of media technology were most efficiently used when centrally controlled. Western Union's "long lines" connected communities across the country, which meant a single owner was now influencing the flow of information on an unprecedented scale. Telephone lines, radio and television broadcast networks, and cable services all shared similar features.

Second, *ownership patterns* changed. With more centralized technology and larger-scale production, the amount of investment capital necessary to produce and promote major state-of-the-art media products grew. As the wry saying goes, freedom of the press exists only for those who can afford to own one; in the era of large-scale media production and distribution, most competitive media ownership is affordable only for those with substantial capital. Although the internet is often touted as creating an even playing field that allows small players to compete, in reality the start-up costs for major media websites now routinely run into the millions of dollars. As we saw in the previous chapter, most sectors of the media industry moved away long ago from the days of small, independent, local publishers to the era of centralized corporate conglomerates that often have global reach.

Finally, far-reaching technologies owned by large-scale corporate actors dramatically expanded the *potential influence* of media producers in society. They could now reach hundreds of millions of people through networked systems that blanketed the country and crisscrossed the globe. This ability transformed the nature of media and, as a result, ownership issues became more of a regulatory concern.

As these developments emerged, regulators had to grapple with how best to respond. One approach was to treat each medium differently, based on its unique characteristics. In general, the rules have historically differed among types of communication media:

- **Print** media are essentially unregulated.

- **Broadcast** media are regulated because they use the public airwaves, and the limited electromagnetic spectrum space creates scarcity by restricting the number of free broadcast stations that can operate in any market

- **Common carriers** are monopolies or near monopolies that are regulated to provide equal access to their services because users have no practical alternative. Basic utilities, including telephone companies, have long been classified as common carriers. In recent years, as we will discuss later, there has been an ongoing "net neutrality" debate about whether or not internet service providers (ISPs) should be classified as common carriers.

These distinctions matter in the regulation of media ownership. For example, the FCC has long regulated the number of broadcast radio and television stations a single company can own. The aim was to limit the potential monopolistic power of a media conglomerate and to encourage diverse media ownership. However, deregulation advocates argued that with digital convergence—which enabled competition among producers who had previously been in separate media—and the internet—which lowered the hurdles to entry for new competitors—the media landscape was more competitive than ever. As a result, changes introduced in the 1996 Telecommunications Act eased restrictions on television and radio station ownership, leading to more concentrated ownership patterns (Aufderheide 1999). (See Figure 4.1.) For example, less than two years after the elimination of limits on radio ownership in 1996, there was a 12 percent decline in the number of radio station owners, even while the total number of stations increased by 3 percent. The FCC acknowledged that the regulatory changes had led to "consolidations of radio ownership [that] have reshaped the radio industry" (FCC 1998).

FIGURE 4.1 ■ Examples of Ownership Regulation and Deregulation

FCC regulations on media ownership were relaxed significantly as part of the 1996 Telecommunication Act. Another round of deregulation took place in 2017 that eliminated some cross-ownership regulations. Overall, the trend has been to allow larger media conglomerates to operate. Critics are concerned about the increased power of media conglomerates. Deregulation advocates argue these changes reflect more realistically the competitive media landscape brought about by convergence and the internet.

Sector	Before 1996 Telecommunication Act	After the 1996 Telecommunication Act
National TV	One company may own: • 12 stations • reaching up to 25% of U.S. TV households	One company may own: • stations reaching 35% of U.S. TV households
Local TV	One company may own: • one station in a market	One company may own: • two stations in a market with at least 8 other independently owned stations there
National Radio	One company may own: • 20 AM and 20 FM stations	Rule eliminated
Local Radio	One company may own: • 2 AM and 2 FM stations in a market • with 25% audience share or less	One company may own: • up to 8 stations (with no more than 5 FM or 5 AM), depending on market size
Sector	Before 2017 Changes	After 2017 changes
Local TV	One company may own: • two stations in a market if there are at least 8 other independently owned stations there	Rule eliminated
Radio/Television Cross-Ownership	One company may own: • 2 TV stations and 1 radio station in most markets	Rule eliminated
Newspaper/Broadcast Cross-Ownership	One company may NOT own: • a full-power broadcast station (AM, FM, or TV) and a daily newspaper in the same market	Rule eliminated

Sources: Aufderheide (1999); Federal Communications Commission (2017).

The FCC also restricted certain types of cross-ownership. Common ownership of a television broadcast station and a cable system in a single market is prohibited, for example. Also, a single company could not own both a daily newspaper and a broadcast outlet (radio or TV) in a single city—except in the 20 largest markets, where there were at least eight independent media outlets. The aim was to prevent monopolistic control of media in a local market. But this rule, too, was eliminated in 2017.

Media companies regularly work to have ownership limits relaxed, and they have plenty of opportunity to succeed: The 1996 Telecommunications Act requires that, every four years, the FCC reviews all of its broadcast ownership rules with an eye toward eliminating or modifying any that are no longer in the public interest due to increased media competition. Some observers have seen an unprecedented threat emerging from the consolidation of media ownership into fewer and fewer hands. As far back as 1995, Reuven Frank, former president of NBC News, suggested that

> it is daily becoming more obvious that the biggest threat to a free press and the circulation of ideas is the steady absorption of newspapers, television networks and other vehicles of information into enormous corporations that know how to turn knowledge into profit—but are not equally committed to inquiry or debate or to the First Amendment. (quoted in Shales 1995: C1)

In the decades since that statement, the trend toward less regulation and more concentrated ownership has continued.

One clear way in which government can intervene in the media industry, then, is by regulating ownership of media outlets. By preventing monopoly ownership of media, the government attempts to act in the public interest because control of media information by a few companies may well be detrimental to the free flow of ideas. Through such regulations, the government prevents media giants from acquiring control of the media market.

Copyright and Intellectual Property

Rap music fans know Public Enemy's 1990 album, *Fear of a Black Planet*, as an early classic in the genre. The album epitomized the group's "wall of noise" approach that layered sound fragments cut from other recordings into a new and unique composition. Although Public Enemy's use of nearly a hundred samples on the album was extreme, frequent sampling was a common practice during the "golden age of hip-hop" in the late 1980s. But that age was over in 1991 when a U.S. District Court ruled in *Grand Upright Music Ltd. v. Warner Bros. Records Inc.* that artists were breaking copyright laws if they sampled sounds from other people's work without first obtaining permission from the copyright owners. The ruling changed music forever because bands could not afford to pay the permissions fees for so many different samples. Instead, contemporary recordings that use the technique typically sample only a few sounds to keep costs down.

In 2010, Benjamin Franzen directed a documentary film about music sampling and copyright law. In it, he used more than 400 unlicensed music samples. But despite the title of his film, he and his collaborators were not *Copyright Criminals*. That's because their work is protected under the "fair use" provision of copyright law that allows creators to quote from copyrighted works without permission for the purposes of education, commentary, criticism, and other transformative uses (McLeod 2010). Ironically, the film is available for sale in a copyrighted DVD version.

The case of music sampling and the "fair use" exemptions illustrate the complicated world of copyright laws that have developed since the copyright clause of the Constitution and the original 1790 Copyright Act. Those laws protect the sale and distribution of this book. If you flip to the beginning of this book, you will find a copyright page that includes the publication date of the book, the name and address of the publisher, and a statement of copyright. This copyright statement reads, "All rights reserved. No part of this book may be reproduced or utilized in any form or by any means, electronic or mechanical, including photocopying, recording, or by any information storage and retrieval system, without permission in writing from the publisher." This statement, enforced by government laws and regulations, makes it illegal for someone to simply copy and sell this book without permission from the publisher. Such regulations exist to protect both the publisher, who collects income from the sale of books, and the authors, who receive royalty payments from publishers for each new copy of the book that is sold. Because they have invested the time and money necessary to create the book you are holding, the law says that they should control the right to sell, distribute, and profit from such sales. If the copyright laws didn't exist, there would be no way for publishers and authors to earn a return on their investment.

Over the years, the government and the courts have extended copyright laws to include a wide variety of visual, sound, and computer software products under the rubric of *intellectual property rights*. It is illegal to copy and sell music CDs, digital music files such as MP3s, movies, and computer software. Likewise, it is illegal to use a copyrighted photograph in a commercial publication. We had to acquire permission to use all the photographs you see in this book. The media industry may not want government regulation in some matters, but in this case, it certainly *does* want government intervention. The government's protection of copyright is crucial to the continued functioning of the media industry. Without government enforcement of copyright laws, the for-profit media industry would be unable to survive.

Copyright laws were originally intended to provide incentives for people to invest the time, effort, and resources necessary to produce new creations, while ensuring the public benefited from these efforts. In the original 1790 Copyright Act, authors were given exclusive rights to their work for 14 years, renewable one time if they were still alive, for a maximum of 28 years. After that, copyrighted works became part of the public domain, freely available for anyone's use. However, media companies have since successfully lobbied Congress to repeatedly extend the period covered by copyright. The "Copyright Term Extension Act" of 1998 is sometimes known as the "Mickey Mouse Protection Act" because of Disney's key role in lobbying for its passage. It extended copyright to cover an individual creator's lifetime plus 70 years or, in the case of corporate authorship, 120 years after creation or 95 years after publication, whichever is shorter. Advocates argue this allows creators to pass on the benefits of lucrative work to their heirs or profit reasonably from their creation. Critics argue this undermines the entire purpose of copyright

www.fbi.gov

The FBI's anti-piracy warning label can be used to accompany copyrighted content, including films, audio recordings, electronic media, software, books, and photographs. The language that accompanies the warning notes that "[t]he unauthorized reproduction or distribution of a copyrighted work is . . . punishable by up to five years in prison and a fine of $250,000."

FIGURE 4.2   ■   Creative Commons Copyright Alternatives

Creators who use a Creative Commons copyright can choose different license options, placing varying degrees of restrictions on the use of their work.

 **Attribution by**

 **Share Alike sa**

 **Non-Commercial nc**

 **No Derivative Works nd**

You let others copy, distribute, display, and perform your copyrighted work — and derivative works based upon it — but only if they give credit the way you request.	You allow others to distribute derivative works only under a license identical to the license that governs your work.	You let others copy, distribute, display, and perform your work — and derivative works based upon it — but for non-commercial purposes only.	You let others copy, distribute, display, and perform only verbatim copies of your work, not derivative works based upon it.

Source: Creative Commons (2018).

law to both incentivize creativity and also support a robust public domain while enriching media corporations that are often the holders of copyright.

In recent years, creators seeking to enrich the public domain have developed alternative approaches to copyright, such as Creative Commons licenses. Creative Commons is a nonprofit organization that offers free legal tools to protect the use of creative work while maximizing the amount of material that is available for free and legal sharing, use, repurposing, and remixing (Creative Commons 2018). Unlike traditional copyright, Creative Commons licenses allow creators to give users specific rights to use their work while giving the creators the option of having "some rights reserved" (Lessig 2005). (See Figure 4.2.)

REGULATING CONTENT

While the regulation of ownership raises fundamental questions about the relationship between government and media, a different set of issues is raised with respect to the regulation of media content itself. However, the basic dynamic of structure and agency remains. We consider a few examples.

Accuracy: Advertising

Perhaps the most widely accepted regulation of media content is the regulation against fraudulent or deceptive advertising by a variety of difference agencies:

- The Federal Trade Commission (FTC) monitors ad industry practices and enforces truth-in-advertising laws across all media. It handles most cases of deceptive or fraudulent advertising, paying special attention to products that can have health consequences, such as over-the-counter drugs.

- The Food and Drug Administration (FDA) regulates advertising of prescription drugs.

- The Transportation Department oversees airline advertising, preventing hidden fees by requiring that any price advertised is the "full fare" that the customer would pay.

- The Treasury Department's Bureau of Alcohol, Tobacco, and Firearms (ATF) regulates most tobacco and alcohol advertising.

- The FCC is responsible for overseeing children's television ads.

Such regulations aim to ensure that advertising is truthful and transparent and that the products being promoted are safe.

The agencies' efforts protect the public against fraudulent or deceptive advertising. Segments of the advertising industry have a reputation for hucksterism that involves, at best, the distortion of fact and, at worst, wild claims that echo turn-of-the-century patent medicine advertising. But misleading ads can be more subtle as well. On the internet, consumers can be deceived in covert ways. For example, about 15 percent of all customer reviews on sites like Yelp! and Amazon are fake, with many of them paid for by advertising and public relations (PR) firms (Weinberg 2016). Other companies provide free products to bloggers in exchange for a favorable mention in a post. Since 2009, though, anyone paid in cash or with free products to provide an online endorsement of a product must disclose this arrangement to readers; otherwise it is considered deceptive advertising. Although difficult to enforce, the FTC periodically cracks down in highly visible cases, including charging one PR firm with having their employees post video game reviews at the iTunes store while posing as satisfied customers (Sachdev 2010).

Advertising regulation is also intended to promote safety, especially when the ads are targeted at minors. For example, the ATF regulates advertising for products such as alcohol and tobacco. Cigarettes cannot be advertised on television, and tobacco company ads are banned at televised sporting events. Also, the FDA requires that ads for prescription drugs disclose potential side effects.

Although the government regulates advertising, it also helps the advertising industry in a variety of ways. Most advertising is a tax-deductible business expense, saving businesses millions of dollars annually and helping support the advertising industry. The Department of Agriculture provides subsidies for advertising particular commodities. Postage rates subsidize magazines and newspapers that are filled with advertisements. Each election cycle brings a windfall of political advertising to television and radio stations. Finally, the government is a direct purchaser of advertising, spending more than $945 million on advertiser services in 2010, including $545 million on military recruiting advertisements (Kosar 2012).

So in this area, too, fundamental issues of constraint and agency emerge as government seeks to protect the public from misleading sales pitches, and advertisers, in turn, seek to protect the benefits they receive from government.

Diversity: The Fairness Doctrine

Although media have tremendous potential to inform citizens about events and issues, they also have unparalleled potential for abuse by political partisans and commercial interests. The government once attempted to protect against abusive media domination with the Fairness Doctrine, an example of media content regulation in the public interest (Aufderheide 1990; Cronauer 1994; Simmons 1978).

In 1949, based on the idea that the airwaves were a scarce resource owned by the public, the FCC adopted a policy that broadcast licensees "devote a reasonable percentage of their broadcasting time to the discussion of public issues of interest in the community served by their stations" and, second, "that such programs be designed so that the public has a reasonable opportunity to hear different opposing positions on the public issues of interest and importance in the community" (13 FCC 1246 [1949] in Kahn 1978: 230). Although the specific dimensions of the Fairness Doctrine evolved over time, the two basic provisions—requiring broadcasters both to cover public issues and to provide opportunity for the presentation of contrasting points of view—remained intact. These criteria were considered a public service obligation and could be used in reviewing a station's application for license renewal.

The goal of the doctrine was to promote serious coverage of public issues and to ensure diversity by preventing any single viewpoint from dominating coverage. The Fairness Doctrine never suppressed views, but it sometimes required additional speech to ensure vigorous debate and dissent. FCC involvement in any Fairness Doctrine case came only after someone filed a complaint. Over time, competing actors tried to use and, in some cases, abuse the Fairness Doctrine. The Kennedy, Johnson, and Nixon administrations, for example, harassed unsympathetic journalists by filing complaints under the Fairness Doctrine (Simmons 1978). But in many more cases, the doctrine enabled the airing of opposing views that the public would not otherwise have heard, thus fulfilling its intended purpose.

When the broadcast industry challenged the legality of the Fairness Doctrine in 1969, the Supreme Court unanimously upheld the policy based on the scarcity of broadcast frequencies. Two decades later, though, cable had arrived, bringing new media outlets that didn't rely on the airwaves. As part of the Reagan-era push for broad deregulation, the FCC voted in 1987 to no longer enforce the Fairness Doctrine.

In the ensuing years, various attempts to revive the Doctrine occurred. In 2007, a study jointly issued by liberal/progressive media groups revealed that more than 90 percent of the political talk radio programming on the stations owned by the top five commercial companies was conservative leaning (Center for American Progress and Free Press 2007). The authors cited two related factors for this development. First, as we saw earlier, limits on radio station ownership had been eliminated in 1996, resulting in large, centrally owned radio networks that often aired cheap-to-produce, nationally syndicated programming. Second, the repeal of the Fairness Doctrine meant this programming could now feature just one viewpoint. Although they didn't call for the Fairness Doctrine's return per se, the authors did hope to encourage more diverse program content through the following:

- Restoring local and national limits on the ownership of commercial radio stations

- Ensuring greater local accountability over radio licensing

- Requiring commercial owners who fail to abide by enforceable public interest obligations to pay a fee to support public broadcasting

The effort not only failed; it helped spark a backlash from conservatives and the radio industry that led to the formal repeal of the Fairness Doctrine in 2011, which had been unenforced for a quarter century but was still on the books.

The saga of the Fairness Doctrine harkens back to a day when liberals hoped for mainstream democratic media that featured serious coverage and robust debate of current affairs. In fact, much of mainstream broadcast and cable media has evolved into more iso-lated pockets of programming with distinctly ideological slants: Fox News and talk radio for conservatives, MSNBC for liberals, and so on. The internet, too, facilitates content with a single viewpoint aimed at niche audiences rather than content with diverse views aimed at a general audience. As we will see in Chapter 9, such developments continue to raise serious concerns about the media's impact on democracy.

Morality: Obscene Materials

The United States has a long history of regulating sexually explicit material on moral grounds. As early as 1711, the "government of Massachusetts prohibited publication of 'wicked, profane, impure, filthy and obscene material'" (Clark 1991: 977). The debates that have ensued ever since often focus on the definition of obscenity.

Legally, obscene material is different from both pornography (sexually arousing material) and indecent material (material morally unfit for general distribution or broadcast). Pornography and indecent material are legal, although the government may regulate their broadcast or distribution. The government outlaws only obscene material. (The major exception is that the government also outlaws sexually explicit materials involving children, regardless of whether it judges such material to be obscene.) A 1973 Supreme Court decision set the standard for determining what is to be considered obscene—and thus beyond First Amendment protection. Material is deemed obscene if it fails a three-prong test that asks

> (1) whether the average person, applying contemporary community standards, would find that the work, taken as a whole, appeals to prurient interest; (2) whether the work depicts or describes, in a patently offensive way, sexual conduct specifically defined by applicable state law; and (3) whether the work, taken as a whole, lacks serious literary, artistic, political or scientific value. (in Clark 1991: 981)

The courts have used this definition to limit the production and distribution of printed materials, films, and computer-based material.

Various laws regulate materials that are sexually explicit but not obscene. For example, merchants cannot legally sell pornographic magazines and videos to minors. Laws also restrict what broadcasters can air radio and television. Because children are likely to be tuned in, the FCC prohibits the broadcast of indecent material between 6:00 a.m. and 10:00 p.m. The idea in this situation is to protect children from being exposed to material that may be too mature for them (FCC 2017). Periodic attempts have been made to remove all indecent programming from the airwaves, but the courts have generally supported the position that the First Amendment protects indecent material.

The internet raised new questions about whether and how to limit sexually graphic material. Minors with access to a computer can easily obtain sexually explicit materials from online sites, which would be illegal for them to acquire in their print or video versions.

They can also take part in online discussion groups that involve sexually explicit material. Should the government ban such online material because it is available to minors? Should public libraries offering internet terminals install filtering software to prevent access to objectionable sites? Such questions continue to be debated.

Producers of sexually explicit material argue that the internet should be treated like print media and thus remain unregulated. Internet producers do not use the public airwaves and are not distributing or broadcasting the material; minors must take the initiative to access sexually explicit online sites. In addition, internet filter software is available if parents want to restrict their children's access to some types of internet sites and protect them from predators. Opponents argue that the internet should be treated more like a broadcast medium and thus that its content should be subject to government regulation. Accessing an internet site, they argue, is no different from tuning in to a particular television channel.

An initial pro-regulatory position was supported by the enactment of the Communications Decency Act (CDA)—a part of the 1996 Telecommunications Act—that outlawed the transmission of sexually explicit and other indecent material on the internet. However, before the year was up, free speech activists had sued, and the courts ruled the CDA to be unconstitutional. The 1998 Child Online Protection Act (COPA 1998), also popularly referred to as CDA II, was narrower than the original CDA in that it was limited to creating criminal penalties for any commercial distribution of material deemed "harmful to minors." After years of court battles, though, that law was also struck down in 2009.

One of the problems with COPA was that it relied on the "community standards" clause of the legal obscenity definition to determine which material was inappropriate. Because material on the internet may originate in one place but be accessible worldwide, which community is supposed to set the standard? The notion of a self-contained community implicit in the Supreme Court's 1973 obscenity decision is not applicable to the internet. Today, pornographic materials—some of which would likely meet legal obscenity standards—are readily available online from sites both in and out of the United States, raising new challenges for regulation of any sort.

Self-Regulation: Censorship and Ratings

One way content is monitored is by industry self-regulation rather than formal government involvement. The rating and warning systems devised for different media fall into this category (Gentile 2009; Gentile and Murray 2014). These ratings typically alert parents to content that may not be appropriate for children.

Movie Censorship and the Ratings System

One well-known example of self-regulation is that used for the motion picture industry. Before 1934, Hollywood films could be surprisingly frank for their time. For example, women were sometimes portrayed as sexually forthright, as in 1933's *I'm No Angel*, when a character played by Mae West—one of the most famous actresses of the day—quips suggestively, "Is that a gun in your pocket are you just happy to see me?" (in Wu 2011: 118).

That changed dramatically when a group of Catholic activists calling themselves The Legion of Decency lobbied the president of the Motion Picture Producers and Distributors of America (MPDA), William Hays, to adopt a strict code regulating movie content (Wu 2011). Concerned about a possible loss of profits at the box office if the Catholic group protested and about possible government regulation in response to the group's concerns, Hays agreed to implement the code. From 1934 up to the 1960s, the "Hays Code," as it came to be known, enabled the Legion of Decency and the MPDA (later renamed the Motion Picture Association of America [MPAA]) to work together to censor films without any government involvement.

Sometimes tinged with anti-Semitism, the Legion of Decency blamed "Hollywood Jews" for undermining morality in America. The code they created resulted in sanitized films. For example, dance could not be sexually suggestive, and married couples could not be shown in anything other than twin beds. But its most important impact was in dictating an entire approach to moviemaking that uncritically reaffirmed prevailing norms and values. Crime could occur in a movie, for example, but justice needed to prevail, and the audience could not be asked to sympathize with a criminal. The result was that Hollywood films in the 1930s, 1940s, and 1950s were largely simplistic morality tales that wrapped up in "Hollywood endings"—neat and unambiguous conclusions that reinforced respect for authority, confirmed that all was right with society, and excluded anything remotely critical of dominant social institutions, including marriage, government, the justice system, and religion.

Such comprehensive self-censorship was possible only because movie industry ownership was so centralized—a classic example of the dangers of a media industry monopoly. The Hollywood "studio system" featured single companies that owned both production studios (with writers, directors, and actors often under exclusive, long-term contracts) and the theater chains where films were exhibited. That centralized control began to erode in 1948, when the Supreme Court ruled that the Hollywood studio system was an illegal restraint of trade, and over the next few years, theater and studio ownership were separated. (We discuss additional details of this case below.)

Free now to show whatever films they wanted, some theaters began importing foreign films that were more cerebral and openly erotic than the sanitized, simplistic American movies. After seeing the popularity of these films, U.S. studios began to change in the 1960s, producing more complicated, countercultural, and challenging films. Some of these movies were controversial because of their sexuality, violence, explicit language, and mature themes. Such controversy led to public concern and calls for new controls. Congress seemed poised to require a rating system. To ward off government regulation, the MPAA in 1968 collaborated with theater owners and film distributors to develop a rating system that filmmakers would adopt voluntarily. An anonymous panel of citizens representing a national cross section of parents would implement the new system by a process of majority vote.

For years, the rating system used G to indicate material appropriate for general audiences, PG to suggest parental guidance because some material might not be suitable for young children, PG-13 to caution that some material might be inappropriate for preteenagers, R to restrict access to adults or to those under 17 accompanied by a parent or guardian, and X to indicate a film intended only for adults.

This system presented some problems. First, theaters were notoriously lax in enforcing the supposedly restricted access of R-rated films and the FTC even found that 80 percent of the R-rated movies it studied were being marketed to children under the age of 17. In 64 percent of the cases, the industry's own marketing plans explicitly stated that the target audience included children under 17 (FTC 2000).

In addition, the public came to associate the X rating with hard-core pornography, even though some films—like the 1969 Academy Award winner for best picture, *Midnight Cowboy*—received the rating because of its adult themes. The X rating could mean the kiss of death for a mainstream film because many newspapers would not carry advertising for X-rated films, and many theater owners refused to show such films. The MPAA had failed to acquire trademark protection for their rating system, and pornographers exacerbated the confusion in the public's mind by informally adopting the rating of XXX—unrelated to the MPAA's ratings—as a selling point in their advertising. Finally, in 1990, the MPAA replaced the X rating with a new NC-17 rating, indicating that theater owners would not admit children under the age of 17 (see Figure 4.3). It also made sure to acquire a trademark for this new system. The development pleased artists and producers, who hoped it would lead to the possibility of more viable adult-oriented films. Some religious and conservative groups, though, denounced the move as an attempt to acquire mainstream legitimacy for sexually explicit material.

Television Ratings

Movie ratings are an example where possible government regulation was enough to spark industry self-regulation. TV ratings are an example where government-imposed requirements were coupled with industry self-regulation, this time taking advantage of new technology. The Telecommunications Act of 1996 required development of a rating system for television programming along with the establishment of standards for blocking programming based on those ratings. In 1997, the NAB, the National Cable Television Association (NCTA), and the MPAA collaborated in producing the ratings system. It designated programs aimed at a general audience as either TVG (general audience), TVPG (parental guidance suggested), TV14 (unsuitable for children under 14), or TVMA (intended for mature audiences). In addition, children's programming was divided into TVY (suitable for all children) or TVY7 (intended for children 7 and above). (The system exempted news, sports, and unedited motion pictures on premium cable channels.)

Parents' groups complained that these broad ratings were too vague, so in 1998, additional ratings were added to create the current "age-plus-content" system. These guidelines add the designation FV (fantasy violence) in the TVY7 category and S (sexual situations), V (violence), L (coarse language), and D (suggestive dialogue) in the remaining categories. In addition, since 2000, the FCC has required that all new television sets must be equipped with the V-chip, capable of blocking programming based on the ratings system. This rating system has also been voluntarily adopted by most television streaming services—including Netflix, Hulu, and Amazon—and video vendors like Google Play and the iTunes Store.

Music Parental Advisory Labels and Video Games

The labeling of music lyrics is yet another example of industry self-regulation (RIAA 2018). Responding to the increasingly graphic sexual language in popular music lyrics, a

FIGURE 4.3 ■ Content Ratings and Warnings

The film rating system is an example of industry self-regulation. Established by the Motion Picture Association of America (MPAA), the ratings are meant primarily to help parents decide whether or not a film is appropriate for their family. Television also uses similar ratings (see tvguidelines.org).

THE FILM RATING SYSTEM

EMPOWERING FAMILIES TO MAKE INFORMED MOVIE CHOICES

GENERAL AUDIENCES

Nothing that would offend parents for viewing by children.

PARENTAL GUIDANCE SUGGESTED

Parents urged to give "parental guidance." May contain some material parents might not like for their young children.

PARENTS STRONGLY CAUTIONED

Parents are urged to be cautious. Some material may be inappropriate for pre-teenagers.

RESTRICTED

Contains some adult material. Parents are urged to learn more about the film before taking their young children with them.

NO ONE 17 AND UNDER ADMITTED

NC-17

Clearly adult. Children are not admitted.

FILMRATINGS.COM

Source: Motion Picture Association of America (2018).

group of Washington, DC, parents formed the Parents' Music Resource Center (PMRC) in 1985. These weren't just any parents, however. Their founding ranks included the spouses of six U.S. representatives and 10 U.S. senators (most notably, Tipper Gore, wife of then-Senator Al Gore). After organizing a well-publicized congressional hearing—dubbed by the media the "Porn Rock" hearings—the PMRC persuaded the recording industry to adopt a system of voluntary parental-warning labels.

At first, each record company designed its own labels, but in 1990, the companies adopted a standardized label that read "Parental Advisory: Explicit Lyrics." The label is affixed to CDs, and the advisory logo is used by most online music stores. In recent years, about 5 percent of releases have carried the advisory logo. The warnings' impact is amplified by the refusal of some retailers—most notably Walmart—to carry CDs that have the advisory (Fox 2006). Many artists agree to record "clean" versions of their songs that remove objectionable lyrics, so they can be sold without the advisory label.

In 1994, in response to government pressure, the video game industry set up its own body, the Entertainment Software Rating Board, to assign ratings to video games. This voluntary rating system followed in the tradition of films and television. Video game ratings, though, were widely ignored, and California later enacted legislation preventing juveniles from renting or purchasing violent video games. However, in 2011 the Supreme Court struck down the legislation, ruling that video games are a form of art protected by the First Amendment.

The "National Interest": Military Censorship

What constitutes the "national interest" is a debatable topic, but governments sometimes regulate media to protect or advance what they define as the national interest—the goals and ambitions of a nation. One important case of such regulation involves direct and indirect military censorship.

During the Civil War, Union generals regularly read Southern newspapers to gain information about troop strength and movement. Ever since then, a tension has existed between the media's right to provide information to the public and the government's need to protect sensitive information during times of war.

The nature of this tension has varied at different points in history. During World War II, for example, the media voluntarily complied with military restrictions on information and in many ways helped promote the Allied war effort. A dramatic change in this cordial relationship occurred during the Vietnam War. After the media followed the military's lead in the early years of the war, they later began reporting more independently in ways that military leaders sometimes thought was irresponsible. From the media's perspective, the military's publicity apparatus lost credibility with the press and a significant portion of the U.S. public. Well-publicized incidents of the Pentagon lying to the press and the public contributed to a highly skeptical tone in the media. As the war in Vietnam dragged on, the press corps so distrusted the information being provided by the Pentagon that they dubbed the afternoon military press briefings the "Five O'clock Follies." The Vietnam War was also the first to be given extensive television coverage. While the government repeatedly claimed that victory was near, network television images of dying American soldiers and dissenting American demonstrators revealed a different reality.

The decision by the *New York Times* and *Washington Post* to publish the "Pentagon Papers" solidified this antagonistic relationship. The Pentagon Papers was the name given to a secretly commissioned Pentagon report—leaked to the press—that reviewed the history of the U.S. role in the region. Among other things, the report documented that, contrary to government assertions, the United States had played an active role in the 1963 overthrow and assassination of the South Vietnamese president and that years of massive U.S. bombing campaigns had not been effective in deterring the enemy. In fact, the report showed that American presidents and Pentagon officials had repeatedly lied to Congress and the public about the U.S. role in the region.

The experience in Vietnam led the military to take the offensive on two separate fronts. First, it developed a massive PR machine to project a more positive image of the military. Ironically, part of this effort involved hiring press personnel (at officer status) to provide expertise on how to handle the media. Second, the military began developing a strategy for controlling the dissemination of information through the media to the public. The central element of this strategy was the press pool (see Cheney 1992 and critical views in Bennett and Paletz 1994; Denton 1993; Jeffords and Rabinovitz 1994; Mowlana, Gerbner, and Schiller 1992; Taylor 1992).

Tested in the invasions of Panama and Grenada and fully implemented during the 1990–1991 Persian Gulf War, the press pool system controlled the information that journalists would report during a conflict by choosing which media personnel would be included in the press pool, controlling their means of transportation in the field, and permitting access only to predetermined locations. Military press personnel even monitored interviews with soldiers and screened media dispatches before publication. As a result of the restrictions, much information about the war that might have been controversial—such as the high civilian death toll or the fact that the U.S. military used huge bulldozers to bury Iraqi troops alive in their trenches—did not reach the public until well after the end of the war. President George H. W. Bush even prohibited pictures of the flag-draped coffins of U.S. soldiers being unloaded from planes that had returned to the United States. (This ban was lifted in 2009 by President Barack Obama.) Journalists bristled at these new restrictions, but the major media complied, sometimes posting a notice on the front page of their newspapers stating that U.S. military censors had approved all information about the war. Many critics thought the military had gone too far in restricting the press, but the Pentagon argued it needed to limit access to protect journalists, and the majority of the public supported the restrictions.

Public support for press restrictions continued as George W. Bush launched a "war on terror" in the wake of the September 11, 2001, attacks on the World Trade Center and the Pentagon. In this case, however, the Pentagon simply banned press personnel from covering the fighting, citing the need for secrecy for special operations forces. The press was given limited access to U.S. military personnel on aircraft carriers and in other staging areas, but they were prevented from accompanying troops in battle zones. Once again, the Pentagon largely succeeded in providing a sanitized version of the war and in avoiding the full coverage that characterized the Vietnam era.

During the 2003 invasion of Iraq, the U.S. military sought a more cooperative relationship with journalists. The centerpiece of the military's media management approach in the Iraq War (as well as the ongoing war in Afghanistan) was a program of embedding reporters with troops in the field under the Pentagon's ground rules. Rather than formally reviewing and censoring news coverage, the embedded reporter program gave journalists access to the front lines. Embedded reporters traveled and lived with a military unit for weeks or months, sharing regular meals and conversation with the troops that they relied upon for protection (Cortell, Eisinger, and Althaus 2009). Reporters agreed to get consent from individual soldiers to include their names or hometowns in their reports and to exclude from their stories any information on strategic issues, such as troop movements, specific locations, or future combat plans.

Pentagon officials saw the embed program as an opportunity to shape public perception of the war by emphasizing the stories and experiences of U.S. soldiers. Critics have argued that embedded reporters lose their independence, becoming too reliant on military sources with whom they come to identify and thus framing news reports from the perspective of U.S. soldiers rather than neutral observers (Goodman and Goodman 2004). Subsequent research on the content of news coverage of the Iraq War found that embeds were far less likely than "unilaterals"—reporters who were not affiliated with the U.S. or British military—to produce stories about the reconstruction of Iraq or civilian casualties and presented far fewer images of wounded or dead Iraqis in their reporting. And, just as the Pentagon had hoped, embedded reporters were much more likely than unilaterals to focus their stories on U.S. troops, including quotes from and pictures of U.S soldiers (Aday, Livingston, and Hebert 2005).

In recent years, the internet has been used to challenge the control of information by the military (Hindman and Thomas 2016). For example, in 2010, WikiLeaks released a classified video showing a 2007 U.S. airstrike in Baghdad, Iraq, in which U.S. troops killed two Reuters employees whose cameras were mistaken for weapons. The video had been leaked by U.S. Army Private Bradley (now Chelsea) Manning, along with more than a quarter million diplomatic cables. WikiLeaks later released more than 90,000 of the documents Manning had leaked, providing considerable insight into the workings of the U.S. government and its diplomatic corps (*The Guardian* 2010).

The basic tension between an active press and a constraining military has centered on how much information the military has a right to control and how much the media has a right to reveal. The press typically has no problem with restricting information that might directly endanger U.S. troops. History shows, though, that the government has sometimes invoked "national security" when restricting the media in an effort to hide embarrassing or controversial information from the public. As a result, debates about the role of government restrictions and the responsibilities of a free press—even in times of conflict—will certainly continue.

REGULATING ACCESS AND DISTRIBUTION

Another category of regulations is those that limit—or protect—media access and distribution. A few examples are described here.

Net Neutrality

In 2000, America Online, an early dial-up internet service provider (ISP), merged with Time Warner, one of the largest traditional media conglomerates. A key idea behind the blockbuster move was that AOL could deliver its internet users to a "walled garden" of mostly Time Warner content, providing benefits for both companies. The idea failed miserably, and the companies formally split up just eight years later. It turned out that internet users did not want to be confined or steered to content chosen by their ISP; they wanted to have easy access to the entire internet (Wu 2011).

The Concept of Net Neutrality

The idea that ISPs should simply offer access to the internet and be "neutral" in their handling of internet traffic became known as "net neutrality." For the most part, net neutrality existed long before the term was coined. The internet was designed as a neutral platform upon which all sorts of data types could travel. Hobbyists and independent start-ups could create and post content right alongside major corporate players, available on an equal basis to anyone with internet access. Search engines gave the users power (although not complete control) to find whatever content they were looking for; the ISP merely provided access.

But as the AOL Time Warner example shows, there was always interest in creating a different sort of internet experience that would presumably be more profitable for ISPs. To prevent such efforts and to protect the open internet, public interest advocates began calling for the establishment of formal "net neutrality" regulations that would require ISPs to treat all internet traffic equally. They would not be able to limit or favor access to particular sites or speed up or slow down traffic from particular sites. The idea turned out to be controversial (Coldewey 2017; Free Press 2018; Madrigal and Lafrance 2014; Public Knowledge 2018; Reardon 2015; Wu 2017).

The Policy Battle

ISPs argued net neutrality was a solution in search of a problem. The marketplace, they assured the FCC, would take care of consumers without the need for government regulation. ISPs like Verizon and Comcast opposed net neutrality, whereas a wide variety of internet producers and tech giants who relied on an open web, like Google and Facebook, mostly supported it. The public overwhelmingly supported net neutrality regulation.

In 2010, the FCC issued an Open Internet Order that fell far short of true net neutrality because, among other things, it allowed cable and phone companies to charge for access to data-heavy websites and exempted wireless service providers. For the first time, this industry-friendly "compromise" created a two-tier internet where wireless service providers could discriminate against any site they chose (Karr 2010; Stelter 2010).

Despite the order's limited reach, Verizon and other ISPs launched a legal challenge, and in 2014 they won their case on a question of technical classification that had been around ever since internet, cable TV, and telephone service converged in the 1990s. With the lines between those technologies largely erased, should broadband internet service be considered a cable service, a telecommunication service, or an information service? Each legal designation brought with it different types of regulation. Now the court's ruling turned on this classification question, which affirmed that the FCC had the right to regulate internet access, but it could not do so without reclassifying the internet as a "common carrier" *telecommunication* service rather than the existing *information* service.

In the wake of the ruling, more debate and compromise proposals followed, with the FCC proposing an alternative that would allow "fast" and "slow" internet lanes. A public outcry ensued, including a highly visible online "Internet Slowdown Day" in September of 2014 in which a variety of public interest groups and internet producers urged opposition to the watered-down FCC proposals. Finally in 2015, on a 3–2 Democratic majority partisan vote, the FCC reclassified broadband providers as "common carriers" and issued an Open Internet Order that banned paid "fast lanes," blocking, and "throttling" slowdowns on both wired and wireless services. ISPs challenged the order in court, but this time they lost.

The victory, though, was short-lived. With the inauguration of President Donald Trump in 2017, the new FCC majority tilted to the Republicans, and the new FCC chair announced plans to eliminate net neutrality regulations. Despite yet another public outcry and an online Day of Action, the FCC, in another 3–2 partisan vote, eliminated the Open Internet Order that mandated net neutrality. As of this writing in early 2018, legal challenges are pending, but net neutrality is no longer the law of the land.

The Implications

In the absence of net neutrality regulations, some ISPs have wanted a different, more profitable, internet system that favors some content providers over others, especially when delivering access to mobile devices. Although there are many hypothetical ways ISPs could gain advantages from doing this, there are existing practices that already violate the net neutrality principle, including the following:

- **Pay-for-play "zero-rating."** AT&T's "Sponsored Data" program and the "FreeBee Data" program from Verizon Wireless are arrangements that give preferential treatment to content providers who pay a fee to have their content "zero-rated"—that is, exempted from the data limits on users' plans (Brodkin 2016). For example, if you are a video streaming service, by paying a fee to one of these ISPs, users can stream unlimited videos from your site without using up their data allotments; if you don't pay, users eat up their available data every time they access your site. Such arrangements favor larger, more established content providers who can afford these fees while making it harder for new or smaller providers to be competitive. In early 2017, the FCC (2017) found that such plans violated net neutrality principles, but in the absence of net neutrality regulations, they are now legal.

- **Tiered access**. A different model can be found in Europe where sometimes "zero-rated" sites are paid for by the consumer directly, through tiered services that resemble cable packages. In one example, Portugal telecommunications service provider, MEO (2018), offered a basic plan with "free" access to their own generic services. To get access to better-known sites and services, users had to pay additional fees for each package such as "email and cloud" services (e.g., Gmail and iCloud); "messaging" (e.g., iMessage, WhatsApp, Skype, and Facetime); "social" (e.g., Facebook, Twitter, Pinterest, Snapchat, and Instagram); "music" (Spotify, Pandora, SoundCloud, and TuneIn.); and "video" (e.g., YouTube, Netflix, and Periscope). In such cases, not only is internet access tiered by price, but the ISP chooses which sites and services to include in their packages.

- **Unfair competition.** There are a number of other examples of ISPs using their technology to give themselves an unfair advantage (Karr 2017). For example, from 2007–2009, AT&T— then the exclusive carrier of the iPhone in the United States—had Apple block iPhone access to Skype and other internet-based phone products that competed with some of AT&T's services. In 2013–2014, service slowdowns—known as "throttling"— from some data-heavy sites like Netflix were found to have been caused deliberately by major broadband providers by limiting the data transfer capacity at key interconnection points.

ISPs can violate the principle of net neutraliy in a variety of ways. In one example, pictured here, European-based Vodafone partitions internet access by charging mobile broadband users separate fees to get unlimited "zero-rating" access to social media, music streaming, maps, or video.

ISPs, though, continue to argue that net neutrality is an unnecessary regulation that interferes with innovation in the marketplace. As a result, the battle over net neutrality is ongoing.

Vertical Integration: Movies, TV, and Streaming

We saw in Chapter 3 that vertical integration occurs when one owner acquires all aspects of production and distribution of a single type of media product. Such arrangements can lead to unfair competitive practices, have prompted regulatory intervention in the past, and are still a concern today.

The Hollywood Studio System

The biggest and best-known example of vertical integration involved the Hollywood "studio system" that emerged in the late 1910s through 1948 (Wu 2011). Fleeing the monopolistic domination of the early New York-based Film Trust (discussed in Chapter 2), early independent movie producers set up shop in southern California. They succeeded in reaching new urban ethnic audiences of the day and soon attracted major financing that enabled higher-quality productions that reached broader audiences. When the courts ordered the trust dissolved in 1915 due to its monopolistic practices, the movie industry became a competitive one.

Ironically, the growing Hollywood studios, led by Paramount, soon developed their own monopolistic practices. They had already inked star actors and writers to long-term contracts that shackled them to a single studio; now they combined film production with distribution, insisting that theaters pay for "block booking" deals up to a year in length.

Under "block booking," if a theater wanted to show major movies featuring star actors of the day, it also had to pay and exhibit the studios' less desirable films. Sometimes theaters had to sign such contracts before the films had even been produced. Theater owners tried resisting by collectively financing their own production efforts, but the major studios responded by buying up a critical mass of more than 1,000 theaters nationwide. Each studio's theaters would only show films produced by the studio-owner. This was the fully integrated "studio system," controlling creative talent, production, distribution, and exhibition.

Such an arrangement was in violation of the Sherman Antitrust Act. In 1921, the FTC began investigating Paramount for antitrust practices, but studios resisted, and the system remained in place until it was finally broken up by the Supreme Court in 1948, when the court ordered the studios to sell off their theater chains. A watered-down version of the "studio system" comprising a few major studios with creative talent under long-term contract continued to exist through the 1960s, but after the Supreme Court ruling, it never again included theater exhibition.

Television's Fyn-Syn Regulations

The lessons of the Hollywood studio case informed the FCC's much less-known regulation of broadcast television programming. Although the medium was different, the concern again was preventing monopolistic practices by separating ownership of content from ownership of exhibition, thereby preventing vertical integration.

Through much of television history, the TV networks generally did not own the programs they broadcast. They merely bought the rights to broadcast programs produced by others. The "fin-syn" (financial interest and syndication) rules, established in 1970, limited the ability of the three major TV networks (ABC, CBS, and NBC) to acquire financial interests or syndication rights in television programming (Crawford 1993; Flint 1993; Freeman 1994a, 1994b; Jessell 1993). (In syndication, a producer sells the rights to rebroadcast a program.) The fear was that the three networks—which shared an oligopoly in television broadcasting in 1970—could also dominate programming industry-wide if they were able to own and control the creation and syndication of programming. Regulators theorized that they could encourage the emergence of a more competitive marketplace of program producers by forcing the networks to buy programming from independent producers.

For more than two decades, the fin-syn rules were the law of the land. During that period, though, the landscape of American television broadcasting changed dramatically. Finally, in 1993, a U.S. district court ruled that networks were not subject to many of the FCC's fin-syn regulations because competing cable stations and the emergence of new networks and independent stations precluded them from monopolizing production and syndication. Again, changes in technology were a factor in changing how government regulates media.

The changed FCC rules meant that, among other things, networks could now acquire financial interests in and syndication rights to all network programming. This encouraged vertical integration and shifted power from studios and independent producers to television networks (Bielby and Bielby 2003). Before the changes, network production was limited to a maximum of 20 percent of a network's prime-time programming. One year after the changes in regulation, the "Big 3" networks either produced in-house or had financial interests in about half of all prime-time programming. By the 2007–2008 season, for example, in-house production accounted for two-thirds of prime-time programs on the four major networks. The major studios that own networks—Disney (ABC), Universal (NBC), 20th Century Fox (Fox), and Warner Brothers (CW)—produced about 90 percent of the series on the major networks (Kunz 2009). Independent producers were largely left out of this closed system of production. But the new rules were a very lucrative opportunity for networks to generate more revenue, at no additional cost, by licensing long-running programs they produced to appear in reruns on other stations. For example, NBC generated $130 million by selling syndication rights to its popular comedy *The Office* (Dempsey and Adalian 2007).

The fin-syn debates, in all their inside details, illustrate some of the basic tensions that exist in the media industry. The unbridled growth of major media conglomerates potentially threatens small media producers. In turn, major conglomerates argue that monopolistic control is no longer possible because we live in a diverse media world with many options. The question for policymakers is whether the government needs to use any regulatory constraint to control the actions of the large media corporations.

Netflix and the Streaming Wars

The issue of potential monopolistic practices reappeared when Netflix emerged as the market leader in streaming services, reaching more than 100 million subscribers in 2017 (Koblin 2017; Spangler 2017a). Once simply a distributor of others' content via DVDs by mail and, later, by streaming, Netflix began investing its massive subscription revenues into producing original content with the release of *House of Cards* in 2013. It went on to produce dozens of original series, spending $8 billion on original programming in 2018 alone—much more than rival streaming services. A full quarter of Netflix spending on content was dedicated to original programs—including 80 films released in 2018—with the aim of making such original content half of its available catalog by 2019.

With Netflix prioritizing original programs, the number of titles by outside producers dropped by 50 percent between 2012 and 2016 (Feldman 2016). Netflix's efforts prompted moves by competing streaming services aimed at attracting or retaining subscribers. The parent companies of streaming rival Hulu—including 21st Century Fox, Comcast, Disney, and Time Warner—signaled that their content would no longer be available to Netflix but would instead stream exclusively on Hulu. Disney even announced a 2019 launch of its own streaming service, focusing on its own productions. Consumers interested in seeing their favorite content—regardless of who produced it—were now faced with the expensive prospect of having to subscribe to multiple streaming services.

At this writing, the outcome of the streaming wars is still uncertain. Will Netflix subscribers miss having access to content from a variety of producers and begin abandoning the service? Or will Netflix be able to exploit its market dominance in distribution to continue financing exclusive hit shows that viewers are willing to pay for? Will the struggling cable industry intervene, perhaps negotiating to provide bundled streaming service from multiple providers, much like traditional cable television packages? Will regulators see a reason to intervene to limit vertical integration again? None of the answers to such questions are yet clear.

Netflix

Once just a streaming (and DVD distribution) service, Netflix has integrated vertically, becoming a major producer of original content. It planned to make "Netflix Originals" fully half of its catalog by 2019.

However they turn out, the streaming wars once again raise questions about the impact of vertical integration in the media industry, echoing the studio system and fin-syn debates. These debates are yet another illustration of the tension between structure and agency. Government intervention protects media producers' copyright interests but also potentially limits how these producers can operate. They illustrate some of the ways that market forces can be subverted when the power of ownership is concentrated in a few hands. They also suggest that, in some cases, regulations can help to protect smaller producers and media users as well. Once again, regulations constrain some and benefit others.

Social Media Platforms

Every January, Facebook CEO Mark Zuckerberg announces a New Year's project for himself, such as learning Mandarin, reading a book every two weeks, or taking a tour of the United States to meet someone from every state. In 2018, though, he announced something rather different: He would focus on trying to fix some of Facebook's many problems, acknowledging that "we currently make too many errors enforcing our policies and preventing misuse of our tools." Facebook would focus, he wrote, on "protecting our community from abuse and hate, defending against interference by nation states, [and] making sure that time spent on Facebook is time well spent" (Zuckerberg 2018).

The announcement came after a year of growing public backlash against Facebook and other social media platforms. The public learned that Russian interference in the 2016 U.S. presidential election involved spreading false and inflammatory advertising and messages via online platforms such as Facebook, Twitter, and Google. At the same time, incidents of online racist and misogynistic hatred, as well as the online promotion of terrorism, gained prominence on YouTube and social media sites. Finally, popular concerns about the negative impact of extensive smartphone and social media use by young people grabbed the headlines. (These are all topics we explore in Chapter 9.)

Any one of these issues could easily spark the interest of media regulators; together they were a potential tsunami heading straight for Facebook and other media and tech companies. During congressional hearings about Russian election interference, one Democratic senator bluntly cautioned executives from Facebook, Google, and Twitter, "You've created these platforms, and now they are being misused. And you have to be the ones to do something about it, or we will" (Timberg, Shaban, and Dwoskin 2017). "We take what happened on Facebook very seriously," admitted Facebook's lead attorney, Colin Stretch. "The foreign interference we saw was reprehensible" (Pierson 2017).

Such acknowledgements were new. Facebook, Twitter, Google, YouTube, and other online companies had earlier refused to take responsibility for how their sites were used. After misinformation was spread during the 2016 election, Twitter executives had proclaimed, "We, as a company, should not be the arbiter of truth" (Crowell 2017), and Zuckerberg had scoffed, "The idea that fake news on Facebook . . . influenced the election in any way I think is a pretty crazy idea" (Sullivan 2016). But just a few months later, Zuckerberg was apologizing in a Yom Kippur (the Jewish Day of Atonement) post, "For the ways my work was used to divide people rather than bring us together, I ask forgiveness and I will work to do better" (Zuckerberg 2017). Zuckerberg's New Year's announcement was another step in the turnaround and a not-so-subtle message that Facebook now took these issues seriously and intended to address them. It was squarely in the tradition of media companies hoping to stave off government regulation by taking actions to police themselves.

What Are Platforms?

Traditional print, broadcast, and cable media operate as gatekeepers and are responsible for deciding who and what to publish or air. The internet enables ordinary users to bypass gatekeepers and publish content on their own websites and blogs. Social media platforms are somewhere in the middle; they usually don't generate original content, relying instead on user-generated material from amateurs and professionals, but they (along with search engines) operate with various algorithms that filter content and steer users toward "recommended" material.

These companies have long argued that, because they didn't create the content, they are not media companies; they are merely technology "platforms" that host the work of others. Mark Zuckerberg once stated flatly, "We're a technology company. We're not a media company" (CNN 2016). One key reason for this position is that the 1995 Communications Decency Act protects computer service providers from liability for the content they carry if it is not produced by them (Electronic Frontier Foundation 2018). The provision was created before Facebook, Twitter, and YouTube existed and was meant to protect ISPs and web hosting services but could now be applied to social media platforms.

But social media platforms and search engines are different. Facebook's News Feed has operated much like a traditional print newspaper's front page, steering users to certain news of the day. Over 60 percent of Americans get news from social media sites, including two-thirds of Facebook users (Gottfried and Shearer 2016). Meanwhile, trending hashtags on Twitter flag breaking news for users, and Google search results steer users toward certain stories and media outlets. And the algorithms behind these services are not neutral; they intentionally steer particular users toward content they are likely to find most engaging, enticing them to return to the site again and again. As we will explore in Chapter 9, various users found ways to exploit these algorithms to steer their deceptive messages to receptive audiences, often out of sight of most users.

The 2017–2018 period seemed to be a turning point of sorts as public understanding grew of how these sites operate in ways that mimic media companies. As one business journalist put it in a column of the same name, "Facebook and the rest of Big Tech are now Big Media, and it's time we start treating them that way" (Kovach 2017). Even the pronouncements of tech executives evolved. At the end of

2016, Zuckerberg signaled the coming shift, now acknowledging that "Facebook is a new kind of platform. It's not a traditional technology company. It's not a traditional media company" (Constine 2016). The backlash against Facebook for its role in the Russian interference in the 2016 election included a #DeleteFacebook campaign that helped reduce its stock price by more than 15 percent. When Zuckerberg was called to testify in 2018 Congressional hearings, his position had shifted again. "I agree that we're responsible for the content," he now said. "But we don't produce the content" (Roose and Kang 2018).

So what are social media platforms, and should they be regulated? Those are questions that are yet to be fully resolved.

Social Media Regulation

Some steps toward regulating social media platforms and other internet companies have already taken place, especially regarding copyright enforcement. Courts in the United States and abroad have long held platform providers responsible for copyrighted content illegally posted on their sites. For example, by using specialized software to search each other's hard drives, early peer-to-peer (P2P) platforms allowed users to share digital files—including copyrighted music, movies, and games. These platforms hoped to avoid enforcement of copyright laws because the illegally shared copyrighted material did not reside on their central servers. This logic, though, failed to convince the courts. In 2001 a federal court shut down one of the earliest successful P2P sites, the Napster music-sharing site, ruling that file sharing was an infringement of copyright laws. (Naptser later reemerged as a legal music streaming site.)

Although P2P sites were different from today's social media platforms, the precedent was set. For example, YouTube explicitly prevents users from posting copyright-protected content. Its "Content ID" system works by automatically checking uploaded content against a massive database of copyrighted material submitted by the copyright holders. If new user material matches an item in the database, YouTube responds in the way the copyright holder has asked—either by giving them their share of ad revenue generated from the content or by taking down the video (YouTube 2018).

The most significant regulation of internet companies has come from the European Union, which passed the General Data Protection Regulation (GDPR) in 2016. The regulation took effect in 2018 and applies to all companies doing business in Europe, including global giants Google and Facebook. Companies that fail to comply could face fines of up to 4 percent of their global revenue, potentially hundreds of millions of dollars for some firms. Aimed at protecting user privacy and reducing the risk of data breaches, the regulation establishes some basic rights and responsibilities for users and firms collecting data (European Union 2016; Trunomi 2018).

- **Right to Access.** Users have the right to receive an electronic copy of all personal data a company may have on them, along with an explanation of where and for what purpose the company is using the data.

- **Right to be Forgotten.** Users have the right to have their personal data erased and prevented from being distributed. Users' requests must meet conditions to qualify for erasure, including "the data no longer being relevant to original purposes for processing, or a data subjects withdrawing consent." In addition, companies can weigh the users' rights against "the public interest in the availability of the data" when considering such requests.

- **Privacy by Design.** Companies are required to incorporate data protection into their system designs from the beginning—not as an afterthought. This includes mechanisms to minimize the amount of time data are held and processed as well as limiting the access employees have to these data.

- **Data Protection Officers.** Companies are required to disclose their data processing and data protection activities through a designated data protection officer that reports directly to highest level of management.

- **Breach Notification.** Upon learning of a data breach, companies have 72 hours to notify affected users.

Some observers believe this could be a model for future regulation in the United States. A variety of other legal and regulatory actions have been taken against internet firms:

- In 1998, the Justice Department filed an antitrust lawsuit against Microsoft for engaging in illegal anticompetitive practices in bundling its internet browser (Explorer) with its monopoly operating system (Windows) and pressuring computer manufacturers to include this package on their computers. The suit was settled with relatively minor changes in Microsoft practices (Auletta 2001). However, in 2004, the European Commission—the executive body of the European Union—similarly found that Microsoft had abused its dominant position in the operating system software market by its bundling of the Windows Media Player with Windows, ordering Microsoft to release a version of Windows without its Media Player, so consumers would have a choice. It fined Microsoft US $655 million, and when Microsoft repeatedly failed to comply, it fined the company again, for $370 million in 2006 and $1.18 billion in 2008 (European Commission 2010).

- In 2017, the European Union fined Google US $2.7 billion (which Google appealed) for manipulating search results in a way that favored its own "shopping" comparison services. The finding indicated that Google had "abused its dominant position" in the search market (Vincent 2017).

- In the wake of Russian interference in the 2016 election, the Federal Election Commission (FEC) began requiring that online political ads include a disclaimer stating who paid for and authorized the ad. Political ads endorsing or opposing a candidate in traditional media already had this requirement. Internet companies like Facebook and Google had successfully resisted this regulation, arguing that online ads were often too small to have room for the information. In a compromise, the FEC's new regulations narrowly applied to ads large enough to have an image or video (Glaser 2017).

Such diverse actions signal the growing concern regulators have about the influence that major internet and technology firms have on how the internet operates.

Self-Policing

In the face of possible regulation, there has been a flurry of self-policing by the social media platforms themselves. In 2018, Facebook announced a change in the newsfeed algorithm to prioritize content shared by friends and family over publisher content and viral videos (Isaac 2018). It vowed to show users all the ads that a particular Facebook page buys, so ads would receive more widespread scrutiny. Facebook also announced steps aimed at reducing the spread of fake election-related information. It shut down thousands of fake accounts, began requiring an authentication process for political advertisers, and started labeling political ads and listing who paid for them (Nicas 2018). Twitter, too, said it would add a special marker indicating a political ad, along with a dashboard feature to show who bought an ad and provide information on how long it has run and who was targeted.

Such actions were triggered by the Russian interference scandal. But issues of online hate and child safety have also led to changes. In 2017, several major advertisers stopped advertising on YouTube after they discovered their ads were appearing next to videos of children in various stages of undress that were generating comments from pedophiles. Shortly thereafter, YouTube began more actively policing its videos, taking down more than 150,000 videos featuring children that had been targeted by sexual predators in the comments section. They disabled comments on more than 625,000 videos, terminating the accounts of hundreds of users, and removed ads from nearly 2 million videos and more than 50,000 channels that it said were "masquerading as family-friendly content" (Spangler 2017b).

In 2017, the European Commission—the European Union's legislative body—issued new guidelines for social media platforms "to increase the proactive prevention, detection and removal of illegal content inciting hatred, violence and terrorism online" (European Commission 2017). In essence, the guidelines require social media companies to provide the necessary resources and staff to adequately monitor content on their site and remove illegal content. Recommendations include clearly identifying a point of contact for law enforcement when illegal content is discovered, using qualified third-party "trusted flaggers" to monitor potentially illegal posts, and investing in better technologies to automatically detect potentially illegal posts and speech. Although somewhat symbolic, the guidelines put social media sites on notice that they can expect further regulation—and potentially huge fines—if they do not take more responsibility for the content that is posted on their sites (Kastrenakes 2017).

As the internet has taken center stage in today's media, concerns about abuse by giant internet firms and other actors have followed. The nature of these concerns and the responses being developed are somewhat different than with earlier media debates. However, the broad questions they raise about the role of media in society—and the role of regulators in protecting the public interest—remain remarkably similar to those that have come before.

INFORMAL POLITICAL, SOCIAL, AND ECONOMIC PRESSURE

This chapter has focused on formal government regulation and informal government pressure on the media. However, it is important to remember the political role played by other actors in either directly influencing the media or prompting the government to act in relation to the media. This active role of nongovernment players is also a type of political influence on the media.

The most obvious players in the debates over the media are media critics and media-related think tanks that produce much of the information that forms the basis of popular media criticism. Some of these critics are academics who specialize in studying the media. Others are affiliated with privately funded think tanks that produce analyses and policy recommendations relating to the media. Such critics span the political spectrum, and knowing a little about their funding sources can provide insight into their perspectives on the issues at hand.

More important than media critics are the citizen activists from across the political spectrum who write, educate, lobby, and agitate about the media. These groups need not focus exclusively on media issues. For example, among their many varied activities, religious groups sometimes pressure the media on moral grounds. In some cases, they have organized boycotts of advertisers that sponsor certain controversial programs or of stores that carry controversial books and magazines. There are hundreds of local, regional, and national organizations that are exclusively devoted to media-related issues, ranging from violence in Hollywood films or political diversity in the news to children's television or public access to the internet. These groups, too, span a wide spectrum of political orientation (see Figure 4.4).

In the United States, citizens' groups have legal status when it comes to renewing broadcast licenses. In the early years of broadcasting, the government allowed only those with an economic stake in the outcome to significantly participate in FCC proceedings regarding radio and television licenses. This changed in the mid-1960s when the Office of Communication of the United Church of Christ won a court case allowing it to challenge the granting of a television license to a station in Jackson, MS. The Church of Christ contended that the station discriminated against black viewers. The U.S. Court of Appeals for the District of Columbia Circuit ruled that responsible community organizations, including civic associations, professional groups, unions, churches, and educational institutions, have a right to contest license renewals. Although ensuing challenges rarely succeeded, activists discovered that some broadcasters were willing to negotiate with community groups to avoid challenges to their license renewals (Longley, Terry, and Krasnow 1983). They also recognized that such challenges could sometimes spark public debate about the nature of the media.

In 2003, when the FCC, in response to a request from media firms that wanted media ownership rules abolished, tried to lift the remaining barriers against media consolidation, public interest groups organized to defend the policies that limit the size and reach of the major media companies. The Philadelphia-based Prometheus Radio Project sued

FIGURE 4.4 ■ Examples of Media Advocacy Organizations

A variety of organizations educate and advocate on media-related issues. Their sites often include extensive information on a broad array of media topics.

About-Face. Combats negative and distorted images of women. *about-face.org*

Accuracy in Media. Conservative/right media criticism. *aim.org*

Adbusters/Media Foundation. Liberal/left activism aimed at advertising and consumer culture. *adbusters.org*

Alliance for Community Media. Works to broaden access to electronic media. *allcommunitymedia.org*

Campaign for Commercial-Free Childhood. "Works to reclaim childhood from corporate marketers" and limit the impact of commercialism. *commercialfreechildhood.org*

Center for Democracy and Technology. A nonprofit public policy organization that focuses on "public policies that will keep the Internet open, innovative, and free." *cdt.org*

Center for Digital Democracy. Promotes open broadband networks, free universal internet access, and diverse ownership of new media outlets. *democraticmedia.org*

Center for Media and Public Affairs. Conservative/right studies media. *cmpa.com*

Center for Media Democracy. Focuses on the public relations (PR) industry, "exposing corporate spin and government propaganda." *prwatch.org*

Center for Media Literacy. Resources "to help citizens, especially the young, develop critical thinking and media production skills." *medialit.org*

Commercial Alert. Helps people defend themselves against harmful, immoral, or intrusive advertising and marketing and the excesses of commercialism. *commercialalert.org*

Committee to Protect Journalists. Monitors restrictions on press freedom worldwide. *cpj.org*

Commonsense Media. Provides information, advice, and tools to help make media and technology a positive force in kids' lives. *commonsensemedia.org*

Electronic Frontier Foundation. Works to protect free speech, privacy, innovation, and consumer rights on the Internet. *eff.org*

Fairness & Accuracy In Reporting. Liberal/left media watch group. *fair.org*

Fight for the Future. Creates civic campaigns that empower people to demand internet and technology policies that serve the public good. *fightforthefuture.org*

Free Press. Promotes media reform, independent media ownership, and universal access to communication. *freepress.net*

GLAAD. Monitors and works directly with media to ensure that the stories of LGBT community are heard. *glaad.org*

Media Action Network for Asian Americans. Works for accurate, balanced, and sensitive Asian American images. *manaa.org*

Media Alliance. Media resource and advocacy center for media workers, nonprofit organizations, and social justice activists. *media-alliance.org*

Media Research Center. Conservative/right group that aims to "expose and neutralize the propaganda arm of the Left: the national news media." *mrc.org*

Parents Television Council. Conservative group advocating more family-friendly programming. *parentstv.org*

Progressive Media Project. Helps diverse communities who have been shut out of the mainstream media get op-eds published. *progressive.org/op-eds*

Prometheus Radio Project. Helps grassroots organizations to build community radio stations and advocates more low-power radio. *prometheusradio.org*

Note: More educational and advocacy groups can be found on the website for this book, http://edge.sagepub.com/croteau6e.

the FCC in federal court. In the 2004 case, *Prometheus Radio Project v. FCC,* the court ruled in favor of Prometheus, deeming the FCC's *diversity index* (a measure to weigh media cross-ownership) inconsistent.

The regulatory debates about net neutrality have generated an outpouring of public reaction and comments. In 2017, when the FCC announced it was considering scrapping net neutrality rules (which it subsequently did), more than 21 million comments were submitted electronically—more than all previous public comments across all government agencies combined. Although public opposition to the changes was clear, millions of the comments were subsequently shown to be falsified in some way, using temporary email addresses, fake names, or comments generated by bots, leading to a widespread call for revising the public comment system (Hitlin, Olmstead, Toor 2017; Laposky 2017a)

The action repertoire of citizen groups is diverse. Some, which have access and accept the institution as legitimate, adopt a cooperative attitude, such as lobbying the FCC to promote reform from the inside. When citizen groups have no access or do not consider the institution as legitimate, they can be confrontational, such as protesting the NAB for its opposition to low-power broadcast licenses, discussed earlier in this chapter. Public shaming through Twitter hashtag campaigns has also brought pressure on some media companies. Finally, rather than trying to change mainstream media, some groups promote reform from the grassroots, creating alternative media (Downing 2001; Lievrouw 2011; Milan and Hintz 2010). In practice, such strategies have translated into groups that have studied their local media and issued reports; testified before Congress on media matters; advised parents on teaching their children "media literacy" skills; organized consumers to communicate their concerns to media outlets; protested the FCC or major media headquarters using direct action and civil disobedience tactics; or developed alternative media.

Although various forms of activism have ebbed and flowed in response to changing media issues, citizen group pressures from both liberals and conservatives have been a constant in the media debate. They can constitute important, informal political pressure on the media industry.

CONCLUSION

Government regulation is important because it sets the ground rules within which media must operate. As this survey of regulatory types makes clear, forces outside the media have had significant impact on the development and direction of the media industry. When we consider the role of media in the social world, we must take into account the influence of these outside forces. The purpose, form, and content of media are all socially determined, as are the rules that regulate them. As a consequence, they vary over time and across cultures. The particular form our media system takes at any time is the result of a series of social processes reflecting competing interests.

Media organizations operate within a context that is shaped by economic and political forces at least partially beyond their control, but the production of media is not simply dictated by these structural constraints. Media professionals develop strategies for navigating through these economic and political forces, and media outlets have their own sets of norms and rules. In Chapter 5, we examine these media organizations and professionals.

Discussion Questions

1. Deregulation advocates generally suggest what they are *against* (regulation) but not what they *favor*. What are some of the potential problems with this position?

2. Advocates of regulation generally argue that government must intervene on behalf of the "public interest" to counter the influence of powerful media conglomerates. What are some of the potential problems with this position? How would you define the "public interest" in this context?

3. In what situations do you think the government has the right to regulate media content? Explain why you believe what you do.

4. Social media platforms are not public spaces; they are owned by commercial corporations. Do you think such companies should be responsible for the content posted on these sites? What difficulties are raised by such a requirement?

Bloomberg/Getty Images

5

MEDIA ORGANIZATIONS
AND PROFESSIONALS

Chapters 3 and 4 highlighted the ways in which economic and political forces constrain the media industry. However, we must keep in mind that action does not follow inevitably and directly from structural constraint. At most, broad structural constraints will influence behavior by making some choices more attractive, some more risky, and some almost unthinkable. Despite working within certain constraints, professionals who help create media products make a series of choices about what to make and how to produce and distribute the final result. People—Hollywood directors, network television executives, book editors, news reporters, podcast producers, and so on—are not simply mindless cogs in a media machine. They do not churn out products precisely in accord with what our understanding of social structure tells us they should.

Our task, then, is to make sense of the dynamic tension between the forces of structure, which shape but do not determine behavior, and the actions of human beings, who make choices but are not fully autonomous. To adapt an often cited comment by Marx, media professionals make their own products, but they do not make them just as they please; they do not make them under circumstances chosen by themselves but under circumstances directly found, given, and transmitted from the past.

This chapter focuses on the structure–agency dynamic within media organizations. We explore how professionals create media products, the ways in which media work is organized, the norms and practices of several media professions, the social and personal networks that media professionals cultivate, and the ways the organizational structure of media outlets shape the methods of media work.

THE LIMITS OF ECONOMIC AND POLITICAL CONSTRAINTS

As we have seen in earlier chapters, economic and political forces can be powerful constraints. As we examine next, media personnel actively respond to these constraints when making decisions, often limiting their impact.

Working within Economic Constraints

Let's briefly return to our discussion in Chapter 3 of the commercial logic of prime-time broadcast television. Recall that profit demands shape programming decisions in network television. Profits result from high ratings and desirable audience demographics, which lead to strong advertising sales. Network executives, facing severe pressure to schedule programs that will attract large audiences, select programs that are safe, trying not to offend any significant constituency. It is the commercial logic of network television then that leads to the fact that programs on different networks look so much alike. Similarly, the economic dynamics associated with premium cable channels and streaming services—both of which rely on subscribers and are less dependent on advertisers—help explain the growth of high-quality television programs in the 2010s that is sometimes referred to as TV's new "golden age."

In Chapter 3, we emphasized the constraining power of the commercial organization of network television. However, Gitlin's (2000) classic study provides a nuanced analysis of the tension between these economic constraints and the agency of network programmers, producers, and writers. The people who actually create and select television programs work in an environment in which the decisions they make carry real costs. If you write too many scripts that are considered to be commercially unviable, your future as a television writer may be in jeopardy. Likewise, if you choose unorthodox programs for your network's prime-time lineup, and they are ratings flops, you will be looking for a new job in short order. The economics of prime-time television, then, may shape the decision-making environment, but decisions are still made at various stages by various players. And because audience tastes are both dynamic and unpredictable, these decisions cannot use any one simple formula to determine which programs will be profitable and which will not. As a result, people who work in the world of television must try to interpret both the current mood of the audience and the appeal of particular programs if they are to create and select shows that will meet profit requirements.

Here the structure–agency dynamic is quite clear: Economic forces identify the goals and shape the terrain of the decision-making process, but human actors must assess both program and audience in their effort to deliver the "correct" product. The fact that the vast majority of programs do not succeed tells us that this is not easy terrain to master. Despite the difficulty of the field, however, players within the television world still try to navigate it safely; along the way, they adopt certain rules or conventions to smooth out and routinize the decision-making process. Imitation, for example, has been routinized in the television world. One basic rule of thumb is to create programs that look like those that are currently popular. Throughout this chapter, we will look at the conventions that media professionals adopt because they provide an insightful window on production processes within media industries.

Responding to Political Constraints

Political forces, particularly government regulations, also play a significant role in shaping the environment within which media organizations operate. Even here, where federal laws require or prohibit specific actions, the constraints of government regulation do not determine what media organizations will do. Sometimes media organizations comply with government regulations, but sometimes the media preempt, ignore, reinterpret, or challenge regulations.

Compliance is the easiest strategy for media organizations because it avoids conflict with regulators, thereby enabling them to shape the actions of media organizations. As we saw in the previous chapter, since Vietnam, the Pentagon has been quite adept at influencing the content of news reports using various strategies. During the 1991 Persian Gulf War, the government regulated access to information through a press pool system and required journalists to submit their battle coverage stories for approval by military censors. During the Iraq War that began in 2003, the government took a different approach, cultivating favorable coverage by embedding reporters with troops with whom they built relationships. In both cases, the Pentagon was largely successful in achieving press compliance. The popular belief in supporting troops during war, coupled with widespread public skepticism about the media, likely made press criticism of Pentagon restrictions difficult.

A second strategy used by the media in dealing with government regulation is preemption. Media industries can preempt external regulation by engaging in a public form of self-regulation. This is the strategy that the film, television, music, and video gaming industries used in their voluntary adoption of age-appropriate content ratings and warning labels for their products to stave off more direct government regulation.

A third often-used strategy is rooted in the fact that government regulations are almost always subject to interpretation, giving media organizations the power to read regulations in ways that match their broader agendas. In a classic example, the 1990 Children's Television Act required stations to include educational television in their

Saturday morning lineups but left a good deal of room for interpretation of the meaning of "educational" programming. As a result, broadcasters were willing to define almost anything as educational, including old cartoons such as *The Flintstones* and *The Jetsons*. While regulations were on the books, broadcasters found innovative ways to respond, demonstrating that regulation is, at best, only a partial constraint.

Fourth, media industries can simply ignore regulations. Passing laws is one thing, but enforcing regulations is another. The FCC historically has been reluctant to be a firm enforcer, in large part because of the complexities of its relationship to the U.S. Congress and to the media industries it is supposed to regulate. Sometimes FCC board members have been former industry lawyers with little incentive to alienate industry colleagues with whom they will be working again in the future. As a result, communications regulations can often simply be ignored with few consequences.

Finally, if they have the resources, media organizations can challenge regulations to try to alter them or rescind them altogether. Media organizations can adopt legal strategies, challenging the constitutionality of specific regulations, or they can use political strategies, lobbying potentially supportive politicians and threatening opponents in an effort to win new legislation more to the liking of the industry. The FCC's 2017 vote to loosen television station ownership rules, a policy change that would permit the Sinclair Broadcast Group to purchase the Tribune Company and thereby own local stations reaching more than 70 percent of the U.S. population, is one example where this tactic was successful.

Ultimately, just as economic forces do not fully determine the actions of media professionals, media organizations are not passively compliant in the face of political constraints. In both cases, media personnel are active agents, making decisions and pursuing strategies within particular economic and political frameworks. Their actions sustain, and sometimes help change, the basic structural constraints, but they are not determined by them.

So far, we have focused our attention primarily on the broad environment within which media producers and consumers exist. We now move more directly into the world of those who produce media to examine the processes involved in their decision making and how their work is organized.

DECISION MAKING FOR PROFIT: IMITATION, HITS, AND STARS

The broader political and economic environment sets the stage for the work of media personnel. In the United States and other democratic societies, political pressures on most types of media workers are modest, notwithstanding a steady stream of inflammatory tweets from President Trump directed at the news media. Generally speaking, commercial mainstream media workers within these societies face enormous economic pressures to make decisions that will translate into profits for company owners. Although the details of these decision-making processes are different across media industries, individuals working in media fields almost all have to contend with two basic problems: the high cost of producing media and the unpredictability of audience tastes.

High Costs and Unpredictable Tastes

Deciding to turn a manuscript into a book or a pitch into a movie is a difficult and risky financial decision. The up-front cost of creating and promoting media is usually quite high, and there is no guarantee that this investment will be recouped. A television studio must make a substantial investment to create a pilot before they know if anybody will be interested in watching their new TV show. A book manuscript has to be written, edited, and published before the publishing house knows if enough people are willing to spend money to read it. Even media products that are relatively inexpensive to create—such as a basic music recording—must then be packaged and promoted if they stand any chance of finding a broad mainstream audience. Such promotion is expensive.

The high cost of creating and promoting media products is accompanied by a second problem: the unpredictability of audience tastes. We tend to assume that "good" media have an intrinsic value that makes them so popular. We think best-selling songs sell so well because they are the catchiest or that a best-selling novelist achieves fortune and fame because his or her writing is the most interesting and engaging. But research suggests that success is more complex than we often assume.

For example, Salganik, Dodds, and Watts (2006) created multiple music websites on which more than 14,000 participants were allowed to listen to and download songs from the same unknown bands. If songs have an inherent quality that makes them widely popular, then the same songs should become popular on each website. Instead, the researchers found that songs that were highly rated by the earlier listeners on a particular site would go on to become increasingly popular on that site—but not necessarily on the other sites. The study showed that listener decisions about what was good and worth downloading were influenced by the judgments of earlier visitors to the site. Those early judgments were more important than any intrinsic value in the individual songs.

In a subsequent analysis of *Billboard*'s Hot 100 charts from 1958 to 2016, Askin and Mauskapf (2017) found that popular songs exhibit "optimal differentiation"; that is, they must be familiar to audiences without being too typical. Managing to be both fresh and familiar at the same time is no easy task, especially because audiences compare new songs to other contemporaneous new songs, so musicians must always negotiate uncertainty about the evolving musical context. As a result, Askin and Mauskapf note that their "findings speak to the inherent difficulty—and folly—in practicing 'hit song science'" (p. 932) and point out just how hard it is, even in an age of big data, to reverse-engineer popular songs.

Because popularity is not based simply on the intrinsic quality of a media product, predicting success can be extremely difficult. However, media producers don't just give up. Instead, they rely on a different set of techniques to try to predict and create popular hits, including imitating success and relying on stars.

Art Imitating Art

Perhaps the most common strategy mainstream commercial media companies use to increase the odds of success is to imitate products that have already been successful, offering a new twist on a popular formula. Variations on this strategy include copying the sound of current hit bands, remaking hit movies, making sequels to previous film hits, and signing producers of recent hits. The underlying assumption in these cases is that hits and their makers beget more hits.

We saw in Chapter 3 how the commercial dynamic of network television helps create the conditions for rampant imitation on the small screen. We can see this dynamic in other media industries. The commercial success of New Edition and New Kids on the Block in the 1980s and Backstreet Boys, Boyz II Men, and NSYNC in the 1990s prompted the big music labels to look for other "boy bands" that might ride the same wave. A stream of imitators saturated the market. Heavily promoted on the Disney Channel, the Jonas Brothers achieved success in the 2000s, and K-Pop boy bands, led by BTS and EXO, rode a new wave of boy band success in the 2010s.

In book publishing, authors of popular mass-market books, such as Stephen King, Anne Rice, Nora Roberts, Patricia Cornwell, and James Patterson, are paid huge sums of money for the rights to their future works. Virtually every hit movie seems to produce a sequel, and when a new hit television program emerges, each network rushes to develop its own version—or extension—of the latest hit. For example, following the success of *The Osbournes* and *The Anna Nicole Show* in 2002, television producers developed a remarkable number of new "reality" programs over the next ten years that focused on the lives of marginal and former celebrities, from *Celebrity Rehab with Dr. Drew* to *Married to Jonas*. The cable channel VH1 even organized most of its prime-time programming schedule from 2005 to 2010 around its "celebreality" series of shows.

Even when using formulas for hits, however, there is no guarantee for popularity or economic success. Many products that were supposed to be popular failed to meet expectations. Witness, for example, the failure of the 2017 fantasy film *The Dark Tower*, a film that appeared to have all the ingredients of success and seemed likely to be the first installment in a lucrative film franchise. Based on a popular eight-book series by Stephen King and starring Matthew McConaughey and Idris Elba, the film was panned by critics and performed poorly at the box office. In his review of *The Dark Tower*, film critic David Edelstein (2017) explained that the film "has the bad fortune to seem like the distillation of everything derivative and dull-witted in the sci-fi–fantasy genre that has a stranglehold on our current pop culture." Similarly, the 2017 film *Baywatch*, an adaptation of one of the most-watched television programs of all time, with stars Dwayne "The Rock" Johnson and Zac Efron, was a box office bust. Even though the film shared a name and setting with the wildly popular television program, *Baywatch* was unable to duplicate *21 Jump Street*'s huge success in moving from television to the big screen. Thus, imitation does not guarantee economic success; but as a kind of informal operating assumption, it is one way for media organizations to try to maximize the likelihood of success.

Stars and the "Hit System"

Another strategic asset in the media industry's pursuit of success is fame or stardom. Stardom is such an important resource that the media industry relies on marketing research firms to measure it. The best known of these measures is the "Q Score" (Q for *quotient*), developed by Marketing Evaluations, Inc. (qscores.com), which indicates the familiarity and appeal of anything from a Hollywood actor to a fast-food chain. The more people know about and like something, the higher its Q Score. In 2016, for example, the performers with the highest Q Scores were well-known, longtime film favorites Tom Hanks, Johnny Depp, and Samuel L. Jackson, along with the British musician Adele, who was also named Billboard's Artist of the Year in 2016.

In its initial stages, fame is fleeting. The public's attention shifts often, and minor celebrities come and go frequently. But this initial attention can take on a "snowball" quality for some; a modest incident of notoriety is parlayed into more fame that, in turn, grows cumulatively (Cowan 2000). Only a small percentage of celebrities who obtain some initial fame are able to build that notoriety into major stardom. However, once major stardom has been achieved, fame tends to endure and is relatively stable (van de Rijt, Shor, Ward, and Skiena 2013). This small group of major stars is crucial to the hit system.

In a media-saturated society, popular and well-liked stars can seem almost omnipresent because a large celebrity-producing apparatus promotes them incessantly. We can see them on TV talk shows advertising their latest projects, we know about their personal lives through magazines and gossip blogs, and we can follow their daily musings on Twitter and keep up with what they are doing and wearing on Instagram.

The principal reason why stars are so visible and seem to dominate our media is that they are the physical embodiment of hits. Just as producers imitate already successful movies, television programs, and books in an effort to produce new successes, producers seek out stars and promote them heavily to increase the odds of successful projects. The presence of stars is a significant inducement in the public's selection of films to attend, television programs to view, music to buy, magazines to read, and so on. In turn, stars can draw higher salaries because the odds of producers recouping those expenses are greater than they would be with a relatively unknown artist. Therefore, it is in the interest of aspiring stars to maximize their exposure to the public—to become well-known and well-liked—as this translates into financial clout in signing new project deals. At the same time, it is in the interest of the producers to ensure that the stars they use remain in the public limelight, attracting attention to their projects. The result is a popular media system infused with star power.

Stars increase the chances of producing hits. Publishers want best sellers; record labels are looking for Top 40 songs and platinum albums; movie studios seek blockbuster films. But most movies, songs, and books lose money. That makes hits all the more important because they more than compensate for the losses incurred by other projects. In short, the hit system is the underlying operating principle of most major media companies. And if hits are the goal, then producers see a star who can attract audiences as one of the keys to success. Stars with a major social media presence are particularly valuable because their visibility is a key resource in promoting potential new hits.

This star principle is so widely adopted as a basic norm of the media world that we see its manifestation in unlikely places. Broadcast journalism, with its heavy promotion of program hosts, such as Anderson Cooper, Megyn Kelly, and Lester Holt, vies for the news audience by selling the appeal of big names. These anchors and a handful of other network reporters are full-fledged celebrities who make appearances on talk shows, are the subjects of high-stakes bidding wars, and have programs created for the purpose of giving them even more exposure. The college textbook industry also adopts the star system, seeking well-known professors as authors of high-volume introductory texts, even when unknown coauthors do most of the writing. Given a market that is dominated by a small number of standard-bearing texts—the equivalent of the hit song or blockbuster film—it is no surprise that textbook publishers seek the prestige and visibility that come with academic stars.

Because acquiring already existing stars is both expensive and difficult, most media organizations will try to create their own. One popular approach in recent years has been through talent search shows like Fox's *American Idol* and *So You Think You Can Dance*, and NBC's *The Voice* and *America's Got Talent*. The vast majority of the shows' contestants quickly return to obscurity, but a few survive to create hits and become stars, including *American Idol*'s Kelly Clarkson and Carrie Underwood and *The Voice*'s Cassadee Pope.

Creating Hits and Producing Stars

We might think that all new media products have equal chances to be hits and that their main players have equal chances at stardom—especially in the age of social media. After all, audiences are the only true judges; they make hits and stars. This view suggests that hits succeed and stars rise to the top because audiences love them, but this is a misleading view.

All media products do not have the same chance for hit status, nor do all media personalities have the same chance at stardom. Hits and stars are rare, and the resources to produce them are limited. So before audiences ever get to see them, media organizations make advance decisions about which products and people have the best chance of success. It is virtually impossible to be a star if the firm that produces and distributes your work has already decided that you do not have what it takes to be a huge hit. On the other hand, you have a chance—although no guarantee—of stardom if media executives deem you are a possessor of star quality. Thus, media executives, rather than audiences, make the initial judgments crucial for achieving success.

Films that are seen as potential hits, for example, are slotted for heavy promotion. This might include online movie trailers, frequent television commercials, talk show appearances by the stars-to-be, cross-promotional campaigns with fast-food restaurants and other outlets, an active social media presence aimed at key audience segments, and release of the film to theaters all over the country. Movies not seen as potential hits will receive much less promotion and will be released to a much smaller number of theaters, virtually guaranteeing they will not reach hit status. The next time you browse Netflix, Hulu, or Amazon Video, take note of the large number of films that you have never heard of; many come and go from the theaters so fast, with so little advertising, that only true film enthusiasts know they exist. Some never even make it to the theater but instead are released directly to DVD and on-demand services. As a result, only those films that the movie studios identify as potential hits will ever get the visibility to have a chance to become blockbusters. For example, the Weinstein Company bumped James Gray's acclaimed film *The Immigrant* from a 2013 holiday season release to spring 2014, and it never showed in more than 150 theaters. Although critics loved it and the film featured stars Joaquin Phoenix and Marion Cotillard, the studio made a pre-release decision that *The Immigrant* was a film with narrow appeal, a self-fulfilling prophecy that limits such films to a modest audience—and virtually no chance of becoming a hit.

The same dynamic is at work in the music industry. Acts are split into potential earning divisions, with some being classified as big time and others as possessing only minor or specialized appeal (Frith 1981). The first hurdle for musicians, then, is to get through the initial classification process, which occurs before the first album is even released. Those who are identified as potential big timers will have much more opportunity, and many more resources, than those who are categorized as minor players. Such support, though, comes at a cost; artists who receive heavy promotional support must typically conform to standardized formulas that have been identified for "success." A band with a hit record is likely to be pressured by their label to produce something very similar for their next record rather than branching out to embrace new sounds or styles.

We can see a similar process in the book industry, where publicity and marketing resources are concentrated on the most likely best sellers, whereas mid-list authors frequently see their books disappear relatively unnoticed. Publishers decide how to package a book, how many copies to print, what to price the book, how to promote it, whether or not to invest in an audio version, and where to distribute it based on advance judgments of sales capability. These judgments are often made before the final draft is completed. Likewise, the key decision for television programs, once they are selected for the prime-time lineup, is where they will be scheduled. Will the program be slated to pick up the tailwind of an already successful show or be dropped into a Friday night time slot where ratings are low and fewer viewers are at home? What will be showing on the other networks during that time slot? Some time slots are more favorable than others, and programs that are predicted unlikely to attract top-level ratings are generally scheduled in a way that practically guarantees they will fail to find an audience and be canceled in short order.

Using Stars to Combat Uncertainty

Media organizations are attempting to produce popular and profitable hits, and they see stars as one key way to do this. In a media world in which uncertainty is a constant, executives seek rules to make their decisions less arbitrary. The deep commitment to stars and to the importance of reputation more generally is one of the principal ways that the fluidity and ambiguity of the media industry are brought under control.

Moviemaking, for example, is a very uncertain business. Without any method for ensuring commercial success and with so many players involved in the production and distribution of a film, the presence of a star helps reduce the perception of risk. Stars make people more comfortable with the risks they are taking, even if they are not demonstrably less risky. The presence of a star, in essence, rationalizes the entire process by providing an agreed-on currency for assessing potential projects. The star system is a useful coping mechanism in such an uncertain industry (Prindle 1993).

The dynamic in television is similar. Programmers rely on producers of prior hits as a strategy for legitimizing their decisions (Bielby and Bielby 1994). As in the film industry, network programmers operate in a situation in which hits are hard to come by and even harder to predict. Programmers have to satisfy various constituencies—advertisers, local station managers, and network executives—and they have to demonstrate that their programming decisions are not arbitrary. In this case, reputation—the result of the prior production of a hit—is the key currency. The various players within the television industry agree that past hit production is a legitimate criterion for selecting programs.

A major star like Johnny Depp playing a well-known role from a classic hit should have added up to success. However, it's never certain that employing stars can reduce risk; 2013's *The Lone Ranger* was a massive failure at the box office.

They even try to sell viewers on this notion when promotional commercials emphasize that a new series is brought to you by the producers of a previous hit.

However, the *stars = hits = success* formula is not as accurate a description of media products as industry common sense would suggest. For example, pretend you were the head of a movie studio during the 2010s and wanted to rely on the star power of Jennifer Lawrence to sell a new dramatic film. You could look at the four *Hunger Games* films (U.S. box office ranging from $282 to $425 million) released between 2012 and 2015 or Lawrence's three *X-Men* films released between 2011 and 2016 (U.S. box office from $146 to $234 million) and feel reasonably safe moving forward with your new movie. Then again, you could also look at *Joy* (U.S. box office: $56 million) in 2015 or *Mother!* ($18 million) in 2017 and have substantial reasons for concern. What's the best decision to make when you know that a drama starring Jennifer Lawrence might make anywhere between $18 million and $425 million in the theaters? Of course, there are other sources of revenue for major motion pictures—in particular, international theaters, DVD sales, and on-demand and streaming rights—and some genres of films that do not turn a profit at the domestic box office tend to find substantial revenue elsewhere. These factors, however, create a whole additional set of variables to manage and consider.

Television networks regularly try to attract and keep celebrities on the small screen, but building a program around a star personality is also no guarantee of success. Perhaps you want to create a spin-off with a character from a wildly popular show, as was the case with the *Cheers* spin-off *Frasier* (episode run: 264) but also the case with the *Sex and the City* spin-off *The Carrie Diaries* (episode run: 26). You could also try to lure a less popular movie star into a role on TV, like Kiefer Sutherland in *24* (episode run: 192) or Jerry O'Connell in a show by the creators of *Ugly Betty* and *The Office*, as was the case with *Do Not Disturb* (episode run: 2). These examples suggest that the stars = hits = success formula is far from reliable. But the organization of production in the film and television industries and the ambiguities of these creative businesses help explain why the hit–star relationship continues to shape decision making—even in the face of conflicting evidence.

Beyond Stars to a Universe of Products

Compared to Pixar Animation's other wildly popular films, the 2006 children's movie *Cars* received the worst reviews and was among the company's poorest performers at the box office. But that didn't stop a sequel, *Cars 2*, from being released in 2011, or a third installment, *Cars 3*, from appearing in 2017. That's because *Cars* was a huge merchandising hit, generating nearly $10 billion in product sales over five years. Its anthropomorphic automobiles—sold as toys and emblazoned on an endless variety of products—were so successful that *Cars 2* was developed to do the same, only this time with planes, trains, and boats, too. In fact, *Cars 2* spawned more than 300 toys and countless other merchandising products from children's clothes and backpacks to bedding and SpaghettiOs. Coupled with video games, a 12-acre Cars Land attraction at the Disney theme park in California, and TV programs, *Cars* was developed to be a massive commercial franchise, not just a movie. To maximize the appeal abroad of both the film and its spin-off products, the lead character, Lightning McQueen, competes in a World Grand Prix in Japan, France, England, and Italy (Chmielewski and Keegan 2011). Despite poor box office performance from the first two *Cars* movies, *Cars 3* promised to continue to drive *Cars*-themed merchandise sales and to promote the Cars Land attraction at Disney's California Adventure Park.

Cars represents the emergence of a type of media product that is not limited to a single form. Henry Jenkins defines *convergence culture* as a "flow of content across multiple media platforms, the cooperation between multiple media industries, and the migratory behavior of media audiences who will go almost anywhere in search of the kinds of entertainment experiences they want" (Jenkins 2006: 2–3). Whereas, in the past, media organizations tended to rely only on the power of a good story (say, a novel or a single movie) or the power of a celebrity (say, a hit novelist or blockbuster star), they now work to create entire fictional universes that can be extended and sold across a range of media platforms—films, television shows, video games, comic books, websites, and more.

For example, think of the eight hit movies in the *Star Wars* film franchise (with the final installment of the nine-film sequence due in 2019). Although these movies have all been huge economic successes, they make up only a small portion of the media content that constitutes the vast universe of *Star Wars* products. To truly grasp the impact of *Star Wars*, we must also consider the six different animated *Star Wars* television programs, the dozens of *Star Wars* licensed apps and games, hundreds of serialized *Star Wars* novels and comic books, multiple lines of *Star Wars* toys, apparel and shoes, Halloween costumes, and so on. We can see similar developments in Marvel's expansion of its multiple-platform cinematic universe of superheroes. Of course, developing an entire universe of fictional characters that are compelling enough for viewers to follow across multiple media platforms is no small feat, but if a media organization is able to do so, it provides good security against the largely unpredictable success or failure of a specific media product.

Media professionals are not only constrained by continued uncertainty in the quest for producing hits or by finding a multi-platform fictional universe that will connect over time with consumers out in the marketplace. Media workers must also navigate through the long-standing roles and conventions that exist within the media industries themselves. Although they have some agency in choosing which media to bring to market, they face the structural constraints of their industry traditions, to which we now turn.

THE ORGANIZATION OF MEDIA WORK

In a classic study, sociologist Howard Becker (1982) observes that "producing art requires elaborate cooperation among specialized personnel" (p. 28). We can make the same statement about the production of media content. Whether we are talking about films, books, music, radio, magazines, newspapers, or television, the production and distribution of the message become the work of many people. When released by a major media company, even the most apparently individualistic media presentation—a solo album by a singer–songwriter—still requires many other actors, including the music producer, the representatives of the music label, the designer of the album cover, the publicists who promote the music, and so on. One line of research, therefore, has been studying the organization of media work, examining how media workers collaborate to produce media products.

Conventions

Becker (1982) asks an important question about the many people who do media work: "How do they arrive at the terms on which they cooperate?" Some researchers have argued that the behavior of media personnel is shaped by the "needs" of an organization (Epstein 1973). In other words, maintaining the existence of the organization points different individuals within that organization in the same direction. In its strongest application, this approach is usually too constraining to account for the independent action of media personnel. Another way we might account for the collaboration of media workers is to suggest that they must negotiate the terms of their cooperation before each new endeavor. This approach emphasizes the capacity for independent action, but it ignores the constraints under which media personnel labor.

In contrast to these approaches and consistent with what sociologists who study occupations have found, Becker (1982) focuses on the tension between structure and agency. He tells us that "people who cooperate to produce a work of art usually do not decide things afresh. Instead, they rely on earlier agreements now become customary, agreements that have become part of the conventional ways of doing things" (p. 29).

A *convention* is a practice or technique that is widely used in a field. It is much easier to identify something as conventional than it is to explain the source and meaning of the convention. All of us could likely identify some of the conventions that govern news reporting, pop music, or advertising. For example, the sound of Top 40 music rarely surprises us because it follows broad conventions regarding what instruments are used, the length of the song, the verse/chorus structure, and so on. We could ask how radio programmers learn to follow these conventions and how they know which songs will fit their stations. The answer is that radio programmers see themselves as middlemen between record producers and listeners, develop an understanding of the genres their stations represent, and establish a set of repertoires for action to ensure that both listeners and record companies feel supported and understood. Without these conventions, radio programmers couldn't do their jobs (Ahlkvist and Faulkner 2002).

Hollywood agents must also learn to casually perform the social conventions of their industry to be taken seriously as players. These conventions include hosting meetings in and around Beverly Hills in modernist buildings; coming off as confident, casual, and hip; and giving creative gifts with a personal touch (Zafirau 2008). Industry conventions also take forms that are more easily recognizable to consumers. You don't need to be a graphic designer to know that magazine covers have the publication's name in large letters at the top and will almost always feature a large, dominating graphic or that an evening news broadcast will take place in a studio with a broadcaster behind a desk. Even late-night comedy news programs like *The Daily Show* and *Late Night with Seth Meyers* follow these conventions. If Trevor Noah told jokes about the day's politics while standing up, we might assume *The Daily Show* was just another late-night comedy show and not actually a comedic re-creation of a news broadcast. When media products break from convention, they appear striking and innovative primarily because both producers and audiences are accustomed to conventional forms.

One recent study of television interview programs found distinct conventions at celebrity talk shows in comparison to those at news programs (Loeb 2015). Whereas news interviewers take a stance of detachment, celebrity talk show interviews typically personalize their interviews, talking about themselves and sharing their experiences in the midst of the interview. In addition, news interviews often take an adversarial tone, with interviewers asking tough questions; in contrast, celebrity talk show interviews are friendly and flattering. Audiences are familiar with these conventions, so they don't expect Ellen DeGeneres to ask questions the same way Rachel Maddow does. When the worlds of celebrity talk and news converge, interview conventions may become unstable. For example, in the early months of the 2016 presidential campaign, then-candidate Donald Trump, best known for his television program *The Apprentice*, was typically treated like a celebrity during his regular appearances on Fox News programs, where he often called in by phone for friendly and personal conversations with program hosts.

Conventions are not arbitrary, even though they may often seem to be. They are the result of the routinization of work by media professionals and partially a consequence of professional education and job training. To understand media content on the basis of its conventions, we need to consider where conventions originate, how they are followed in the work process, and how they lead to the production of media that we perceive as conventional.

News Routines and Their Consequences

News production is one type of media work that has been studied extensively, not only for its reliance on conventions but also for the distinctive dynamics associated with the field that illustrate the interaction of structure and agency. A series of classic studies from the 1970s and 1980s laid the groundwork for our understanding of news production that is still applicable today (Epstein 1973; Fishman 1980; Gans 2004; Sigal 1973; Tuchman 1978; and, for a review, see Cottle 2007). This work has since been supplemented by more recent studies that examine some changes in newsrooms, including those brought on by technological innovation and economic pressures (see Powers 2011 for a review). Together, they illustrate some of the dynamics involved in the organization of media work.

These studies help us consider a simple question: What is news? At first, the answer seems self-evident: News is information about recent important events beyond our direct experience. But how do we know what makes an event important? How do we know what information about an important event is relevant? We leave it to professional journalists to handle these questions. As a result, we rely on journalists to act as "gatekeepers" (White 1950)—to make judgments about what is or is not important, or *newsworthy*—and to provide us with factual accounts about these newsworthy events. Ultimately, if we are to understand what news really is, we need to understand how journalists form their judgments and construct their accounts. In other words, we need to examine the day-to-day work of the professional journalist because this is where news is defined and news stories are written.

Let's look at the process from the perspective of people within a news organization. A news staff must generate content for a website, broadcast, or newspaper regardless of what did or did not happen that day. This means that editors and reporters must find news. At the same time, literally thousands of things are happening: People eat meals, walk their dogs, buy and sell goods, commit crimes, announce new policies, argue court cases, participate in sporting contests, lie on the beach, fight wars, campaign for elected office, and so on. The list is virtually endless. News outlets, however, cannot report on all the things that happen; only some happenings are defined as important enough to be news. For reporters, the difficulty is determining which events are newsworthy and gathering enough information to cover these newsworthy events.

On the face of it, news reporting may seem to be an impossible job. How can journalists know which events to report and which to ignore? They cannot go to dozens of different events before deciding which one to cover; they would never meet their deadlines. How do reporters find out about relevant happenings in the first place?

Two classic sociological studies (Fishman 1980; Tuchman 1978) argue that we can find answers to these questions in the routine practices of journalism. Because news organizations cannot constantly reinvent the wheel, the processes of news gathering and news reporting must be rationalized. In other words, news organizations must be able to anticipate where news will happen—before it happens—and structure their reporters' assignments accordingly. Within news organizations, reporters follow routines that tell them where to look for news and how to gather it efficiently. When the same basic routines are adopted as professional norms, as they are in contemporary American journalism, different news outlets will make similar judgments about newsworthiness. This state of affairs makes it difficult to see that any judgments are being made at all.

What are these journalistic routines? Tuchman (1978) adopts the metaphor of the "news net" to explain the standard practice for gathering news. News organizations cast a net—made up of wire services, full-time reporters, and stringers—to catch newsworthy happenings. The net, however, does not catch everything; like all nets, it is full of holes and catches only the "big fish." This serves as an initial filter, sorting out those happenings that do not meet the standard criteria for news.

The organization of news gathering shows which criteria determine how the news net is constructed. News organizations will have staff or bureaus in places they define as important. For example, news outlets typically have bureaus in Washington, DC, and London, England, but not Houston, Texas, or Nairobi, Kenya. As a result, happenings in and around these predefined important places are more likely to become news, whereas happenings outside of these areas are more likely to be ignored.

News organizations also establish "beats" at prominent organizations where news can be expected to occur. In practice, this means that a series of official locations—police stations, courthouses, city halls, state houses, Capitol Hill, the White House—become sites where reporters are stationed. Each day, the reporter on the city hall beat will be responsible for providing one or more stories about the happenings there. It is likely that the city government will have a media relations staff who will be more than happy to provide the beat reporter with daily doses of news in the form of press releases, public announcements, press conferences, and so forth. Finally, areas such as sports, business, and the arts are topical beats that are expected to produce news each day, so reporters establish relationships with key players in these areas to guarantee a regular supply of news.

Beats are central to how reporters "detect" events, but each beat covers so much potential territory that reporters have to develop strategies for detecting the newsworthy events. Fishman (1980) uses the example of a local paper's "justice" beat, which included, among other things, "three law enforcement agencies: city police, county sheriffs, and an FBI office; four penal institutions . . . two juvenile facilities; two entire court systems; an extensive drug subculture" (p. 33). With such a vast terrain to cover, Fishman notes, reporters develop complex work routines that he calls "rounds."

The round structures the workday and defines what events the reporter will be exposed to in the first place. In essence, the round is a process by which beat reporters develop schedules for visiting locations and talking to sources that are likely to produce news. Such work routines are built around the bureaucratic organization of the institutions that make up the beat. For example, a justice reporter will build a work routine around the schedules of the courthouse, police department, and district attorney's office to be on hand for meetings, press conferences, and prescheduled events and to gain access to official records. The reporter may also check in on a regular basis—perhaps hourly—with a range of sites to see if anything is "happening." For example, a beat reporter might call each prison, juvenile facility, law enforcement agency, and courthouse to make sure that important events do not go undetected.

The definition of what is a relevant beat and whether what happens there deserves coverage is not universal. Rather, it changes according to a given media outlet's target audience and, more generally, its mission. For example, TMZ, a celebrity gossip-based website and television program owned by Time Warner, covers "news" that traditional news outlets typically do not consider to be newsworthy. TMZ stands for Thirty Mile Zone, and their beat encompasses the 30-mile radius around the intersection of West Beverly and North La Cienega in Los Angeles, in which all of the major U.S. production studios are headquartered. Sometimes tipped off by celebrities and their publicists seeking media attention, reporters and celebrity photographers prowl luxury stores, restaurants, and other locations seeking candid pictures and brief interviews with stars. The result is very different from a daily newspaper, but the process involved in creating the content is similar.

Because reporters on deadline must produce a news story for their employers, we should not be surprised that news work is routinized in this way. How else could reporters gather news in an efficient, consistent manner while meeting the needs of their news organizations? The problem, however, is that we rarely talk about the news in these terms, nor do we take note of the consequences.

For example, when we consider news beats, we can see that, before anything even happens on a given day, news organizations have already made decisions about where they intend to look for news. The flip side, of course, is also true: The routine practices associated with news gathering virtually ensure that certain happenings will be excluded from the news. News from Africa and South America, for example, is notoriously scarce in the U.S. media in large part because reporters are less likely to be assigned there. The example of news beats shows that, rather than being an inherent characteristic of events, newsworthiness is typically constructed each day by professional journalists and news organizations.

Another consequence of routine journalistic practices is a reliance on official sources to feed journalists a steady diet of information to use in their stories. This dependence upon official sources for "news" means that these sources have routine access to media coverage, whereas outsiders or critics have a more difficult time gaining entrée to the news. The result is that news tends to reflect the views and opinions of those already in power.

Finally, routine journalistic practices result in an emphasis on events at the expense of processes. Reporters look out for what is new in the world around them (the event) and often have few resources (time, money, and expertise) to spotlight the long-term developments that may have been at the origin of the event. As a consequence, news coverage is often fleeting, shining a momentary spotlight on some event and then moving on to a new and unrelated event. This focus on events at the expense of processes likely has an impact on whether and how people understand complicated issues, such as wars, financial crises, crime trends, and budget decisions.

Technology and the New News Routines

Since the classic studies of newsrooms were done, journalists have altered their routines significantly as a result of industry changes and new technology. As Powers (2011: 12) summarizes, "Compared to the time of the classic studies, today there exist more outlets, more formats, more interactions across both, and more uncertainty over who and what counts as a journalist and as journalism, respectively." Many of the basic insights about the social construction of news remain valid today, but the specifics of how this process works have changed as the structural context within which journalists' work has changed.

Increased Economic Pressure

The growth of media conglomerates described in Chapter 3 has meant increased economic pressure on news organizations, with dubious consequences for the quality of news (Klinenberg 2007; McChesney 1999, 2004). With the rise of the internet, newspaper revenue from classified and display advertising, as well as subscriptions, plummeted. In both print and broadcast journalism, such economic pressures led to massive downsizing and increased competition for jobs, less secure employment, and management demands that journalists be more efficient and productive in their work as news organizations seek to cut costs (Deuze 2007; Majoribanks 2000). At the same time, increased pressures to attract audiences to sell to advertisers have meant that ratings and readership numbers (easily measured on news websites) have grown in importance. Taking the audience into account is a growing part of determining what does or does not become news, resulting in more content that is entertaining or oriented toward broad "lifestyle" topics (Boczkowski 2010).

Expanded Volume and Diversified Sourcing

The expansion of news to cable and the internet has dramatically altered the volume of news-related material that is available. Instead of a need to whittle down content to fit the space available in a daily newspaper or half-hour television news broadcast, news organizations today must produce an almost endless supply of "content" to fill 24-hour cable news channels and websites that have no limits. This need to fill a vastly expanded news hole—coupled with the downsizing of actual news staffs—led to the growth of cable news talk programming, featuring pundits, commentators, and advocates. It has also led to the expansion of what are treated as legitimate news sources. One study of content from the *New York Times* and the *Washington Post* found that traditional news organizations increasingly use blogs as source material, especially in covering politics. In turn, the study found that blogs depend heavily upon traditional news outlets as sources, thereby creating a "news source cycle" (Messner and DiStaso 2008).

Technological innovations have also changed sourcing. For example, Twitter is now a part of many journalists' daily routines, as they tweet regularly and keep an eye on their Twitter feed throughout the day (Barnard 2016). Sources can be cultivated and information can be gathered this way. One notable example is NPR reporter Andy Carvin (2013), who relied upon Twitter to build a network of sources to report remotely about developments on the ground from the uprisings in Tunisia and Egypt during the 2011 Arab Spring.

The internet also enables information to circulate before journalists can confirm it or provide context. With smartphones and social media, non-journalists can capture and disseminate their pictures and video with commentary, meaning that traditional news outlets no longer have a monopoly on coverage of breaking news stories. You might learn about a train derailment or political demonstration on Twitter or Facebook before you get any news from mainstream news organizations. News organizations now routinely use user-generated images and other social media content in their reporting.

Increased Speed

The era of newspapers, newsmagazines, and broadcast evening news—the subject of the classic newsroom studies—was characterized by a daily news cycle with a single deadline. In the era of 24-hour cable news and news websites, this predictable news cycle has been replaced by an unending and erratic "news cyclone" (Klinenberg 2005) in which journalists must constantly rewrite and update news stories. The need to constantly update websites has meant the time frame for making decisions about news is tightly compressed, compared to earlier times. Journalists often complain this leads to more stress and less time to make informed news judgments. Usher (2014) cites media critic Dean Starkman, who compared the work of online journalism to running on a hamster wheel producing, as Usher notes, journalism "where speed is more important than fact checking, and quantity is more important than quality" (p. 12).

Ever since the rise of CNN, newsrooms constantly monitor 24-hour cable news organizations to follow what stories are being covered. Newspapers preview the next day's content on their websites, and editors and reporters at competing news organizations scrutinize these sites closely. If one outlet covers a story, others are likely to follow quickly. This has contributed to further homogenization of mainstream news. Imitation of other news outlets means journalists don't have to consider newsworthiness as closely (Boczkowski 2009, 2010). If a competing news outlet is covering a story, then it is automatically deemed newsworthy.

In fact, some news stories are simply rewritten versions of news from other outlets. As Philips (2010: 96) notes, "There is now a widespread practice across the news media, of reporters being asked to rewrite stories appearing elsewhere, in some cases without a single additional telephone call, and to lift quotes and case histories without any attribution." As a consequence of such practices, news from different outlets tends to be more similar today than it was in the past, even though there are many more outlets available today (Boczkowski 2010; Schudson 2011).

All of this emphasis on speed has produced a counterdevelopment, sometimes called "explainer journalism," that seeks to look beyond the breaking news headlines and provide background and context for understanding issues of the day. Such efforts can be found at sites devoted primarily to explainer journalism, such as Vox and FiveThirtyEight as well as within features at mainstream news organizations, such as the *New York Times*'s "The Upshot" and *The Guardian*'s "Explainers." These have been made possible by the flexibility of the internet, which does not have the space or time constraints of print or television news, as well as data analysis and data visualization tools that are sometimes incorporated into such coverage.

Presentation and Engagement to Promote Traffic

Journalism is now often a multimedia enterprise, incorporating print, video, and graphics, changing how journalists tell their stories (Boczkowski 2004). Such presentation is aimed at

promoting engagement. In her study of how news is made inside a contemporary newsroom, media scholar Nikki Usher (2014) shows how the values of immediacy, interactivity, and participation are challenging traditional work practices among journalists. For example, news organizations' long-standing commitment to immediacy has escalated to a kind of hyper-immediacy in the internet age. Journalists constantly produce updated stories to post online as they seek to engage audiences by reporting each new bit of information they learn, whereas editors seek a steady stream of fresh content so they can continue to drive web traffic to their site.

Technology has changed the look and substance of the contemporary newspaper newsroom, as with *The Wall Street Journal*'s, pictured here. Flanked by always-on television screens, journalists at newspapers create web content that is constantly updated and produce a steady stream of text, audio, and video reports as a routine part of their work.

Embracing this intense level of immediacy means that news stories may come and go from a news site very quickly; if a story does not produce visitors, comments, and shares, then it is likely to lose its prominent display among the top stories, only to be displaced by newer content, perhaps just a few hours later. At the same time, Usher finds a growing commitment to producing interactive journalism that compellingly engages users and keeps them on the page longer. This means web designers, computer programmers, digital photography experts, and video editors, among others, are becoming key players in the news production process, upsetting the traditional status hierarchy at news organizations. Staff with the skills to produce interactive content, even if they have little or no background in journalism, are at the center of news work, thereby changing what it means to do journalism today.

Whether classic studies or contemporary updates, a sociology of news work gives us insight into the making of news by demonstrating the significance of the ways in which journalists respond to the demands of news organizations. The standard practices for gathering news, the shared definition of where news is likely to happen, and the increasing likelihood that cash-strapped news organizations imitate other outlets help explain why so much of our daily news across so many news outlets looks so similar and focuses on the activities of official institutions. The news we get is the result of professional routines, which generally focus on the activities of legitimate, bureaucratic institutions.

Newsroom Automation

New digital tools are helping change reporters' work routines. It's not yet clear how much change will occur because we don't know how these technologies will evolve or whether journalists and their employers will embrace or reject these new tools. But change is happening. For example, news organizations are experimenting with automating the work of reporters by adopting artificial intelligence (AI) tools as powerful labor-saving devices. As newsrooms struggle financially in an environment where so much free content is available online, such automation holds out the possibility of allowing news organizations to produce more stories with fewer reporters.

News companies are employing AI—robots—to do everything from background research to writing news stories. For example, the *Washington Post*'s AI robot Heliograf wrote 850 news stories in its first year of operation, producing stories on the 2016 Rio Olympics, local high school sports, and 2016 congressional elections (Moses 2017). In another case, a grant from Google is funding an initiative by the Press Association in England to develop Reporters And Data And Robots (RADAR)—that will write thousands of local news stories each month, including auto-generating graphics to accompany the stories (Gregory 2017).

News-writing robots use data-gathering algorithms and preprogrammed news templates to collect, synthesize, and present information in a news story format. The robots' AI allows them to learn from experience what makes a desirable news story. So, for example, news robots can track which stories get the most clicks, create the most social media buzz, or generate the most positive comments, and adjust the algorithm to maximize the preferred outcomes. Although most robot-reported stories are short and data rich, the algorithms are effective enough that it can be difficult to determine whether a story was written by a human reporter or an AI robot.

Many in the news business are optimistic about the potential uses of news robots. One reporter, describing Heliograf, explained: "Instead of targeting a big audience with a small number of labor-intensive human-written stories, Heliograf can target many small audiences with a huge number of automated stories about niche or local topics" (Keohane 2017). To illustrate the value of a tool like Heliograf—and similar newsroom AI tools such as Buzzbot, Wibbitz, and Wordsmith—Keohane contrasts the *Post*'s coverage of elections four years apart: "In November 2012, it took four employees 25 hours to compile and post just a fraction of the election results manually. In November 2016, Heliograf created more than 500 articles, with little human intervention" (Keohane 2017).

Producing local content for small audiences can sound attractive, especially to people who find that most news doesn't really cover their communities. Small audiences, however, are only a small step from an audience of one; news algorithms make it possible to imagine fully personalized journalism. This wouldn't just mean a news feed that select stories of interest to each individual but, instead, a news feed that *produces* stories for each individual. Such extreme personalization may only exacerbate existing political polarization that makes it increasingly difficult to distinguish between news stories that are verifiably true and those that only seem true because they appeal to our preconceived beliefs and fears. According to the CEO of the nonprofit Global Editors Network, algorithmic journalism will open new journalistic possibilities but also pose serious challenges: "What is certain is that mass misinformation will be powered and facilitated by AI. If engineers create automated news today, they will also create automated fake news tomorrow" (Pecquerie 2018).

Because part of the motivation to implement algorithmic reporting is to enhance efficiency and cut labor costs, then we should expect more robots take on the work of at least some subset of newsroom employees. Some journalists are likely to find this a chilling prospect. Citizens, too, might be concerned about what it will mean to rely on robot reporters to keep us informed.

One vision that might allay some of these concerns involves adopting new algorithmic tools to work *with* journalists rather than replace them. Labeled "augmented journalism" (Marconi, Siegman, and Machine Journalist 2017) or "algorithm-assisted journalism" (Lecompte 2015), this form of journalism will have a different workflow than previous generations of journalists experienced but will still require human reporters. The most optimistic vision for augmented journalism suggests that AI can do many of the menial tasks that journalists now do, freeing up people to spend time on more complex forms of reporting. In addition, AI tools can help journalists analyze vast amounts of data, including statistics, photographs, video, and all kinds of documents. In an age of augmented journalism, newsrooms can rely upon algorithms to regularly query databases to make reporters aware of potentially newsworthy happenings or trends. The *Los Angeles Times*, for example, has an algorithm, Quakebot, that writes reports on every earthquake over a predetermined magnitude and another algorithm that tracks every homicide in the city (Lecompte 2015). Summarizing how AI is likely to disrupt the flow of work in the newsroom, Marconi, Siegman, and an AI "machine journalist" that helped write their report (2017), note, "Reporters may spend less time transcribing and manually poring over datasets and instead spend that time making calls and pursuing leads derived from an AI analysis."

There are complex ethical matters associated with the growth of augmented journalism. News organizations will face questions about journalistic transparency (Renner 2017). Do citizens have a right to know when they are reading an algorithm-produced news story? Even more challenging, should news organizations communicate the underlying principles that inform the programming of news-writing algorithms so that readers know the computational basis of news judgment? Journalists and media scholars alike will be paying careful attention to how the work of journalism changes, and the consequences of such change, as AI becomes increasingly integrated into newsroom routines.

Objectivity

We have seen that the specific definitions of *news* and *newsworthiness* are, in large measure, the result of the ways reporters organize their work. However, there is more to be learned by exploring the profession of journalism. Consider the concept of *objectivity*. Most contemporary evaluations of the performance of the American mainstream news media begin or end with claims about their adherence (or lack thereof) to the standard of objectivity and related notions of impartiality, balance, and fairness. Politicians and other public figures routinely criticize the press for its supposed lack of objectivity, charging journalists with taking sides, being too opinionated, or having a routine bias. Even popular discussions of news media often focus on the question of objectivity. The central position of objectivity in American journalism is something we take for granted. We all seem to "know" that the news is supposed to be objective; the problem is that the news often does not live up to this widely shared expectation.

But where did the value of objectivity come from? Why are we so concerned with it? How does the ideal of objectivity affect the daily practice of journalism? Michael Schudson's (1978) important study, *Discovering the News*, treats the ideal of objectivity as something to be explained rather than something to be taken for granted. It is a perfect example of how studying professional norms and practices can help us better understand the media.

The Origins of Objectivity

What do we mean by *objectivity*? Schudson (1978) provides a useful definition: "The belief in objectivity is a faith in 'facts,' a distrust of 'values,' and a commitment to their segregation" (p. 6). Objectivity is a doctrine that perceives the separation of fact and value as a messy business that requires the use of a method, or set of practices, to ensure their separation. This method is objective journalism. According to Schudson, the concept of objective journalism is a relatively recent development. Only in the years after World War I did objectivity become the dominant value in American journalism.

Prior to World War I, reporters did not subscribe to a belief in what we now term *objectivity*. The AP—one of the first wire services—tried to present news in a way that would be acceptable to many different papers, and the *New York Times* used an "information" model of reporting to attract an elite audience. But journalists did not think about the separation of facts and values, nor did they believe that facts themselves were at all problematic. Rather, to journalists before World War I, the facts spoke for themselves. The goal of fact-based journalism was simply to uncover these facts, and doing so did not require a method of objective reporting. The task was straightforward: Find and report the truth. In this era, journalists were confident of their ability to identify the relevant facts and to report them accurately.

This faith in facts held by American journalists was thrown into doubt in the 1920s. Many American reporters had participated in wartime propaganda efforts during World War I. The success of such efforts made them uncomfortable with any simple understanding of "facts." Having seen how easily facts could be manipulated, journalists became more cynical. They began to mistrust facts, realizing that facts could be made to serve illusion as well as the truth.

At the same time, the field of PR emerged, and professional publicists became early "spin doctors." They fed information to reporters, carefully controlling access to their powerful clients, and they staged events such as the press conference or photo opportunity expressly for the media. With PR professionals spinning the facts, dispensing information strategically, and shaping a good deal of news content through the use of official handouts or press releases, journalists' emerging cynicism became even more pronounced.

The recognition that information could be manipulated and the rise of a profession—PR—expressly dedicated to the shaping of public attitudes left journalists with a crisis of confidence about their own ability to report the "facts" in a neutral way. In Schudson's

(1978) account, objectivity emerged as a "scientific" solution to this crisis of confidence—in other words, "a method designed for a world in which even facts could not be trusted" (p. 122). By training would-be reporters in the "scientific" method of objectivity, journalists transformed their fact-based craft into a profession with a particular method. Objectivity, therefore, can be seen as a set of practices or conventions that the professional journalist is trained to follow.

What practices make up this method? W. Lance Bennett (2009), synthesizing the research on the professional norms of journalism, identifies six key practices: (1) maintaining political neutrality; (2) observing prevailing standards of decency and good taste; (3) using documentary reporting practices, which rely on physical evidence; (4) using standardized formats to package the news; (5) training reporters as generalists instead of specialists; and (6) using editorial review to enforce these methods. The practical implication of belief in the ideal of objectivity is adherence to these basic practices.

Objectivity as Routine Practices and Their Political Consequences

The day-to-day routine practices of journalism, more than some abstract conception of objectivity, are key to understanding the news media. News accounts have a tendency to look similar because reporters all follow the same basic routines. They talk to the same people, use the same formats, observe the same basic dos and don'ts, and watch one another closely to make sure that they are not out of step with the rest of the profession. If we understand objectivity to be a set of routine journalistic practices, we can see why all news coverage is pretty much the same. Journalists adhere to the same methods and monitor each other's work so they produce similar news. In fact, if news differed substantially from outlet to outlet, questions would be raised about the method of objective reporting, likely signaling a new crisis for the profession.

However, following a common set of practices does not ensure the achievement of the ideal of objectivity, that is, the separation of values from facts. Indeed, it can be argued that adherence to the practices associated with objectivity directly benefits particular political interests.

As we have seen, things that happen in and around established institutions, especially official agencies, are defined as news. Happenings outside of these boundaries are likely never to be detected by professional journalists. Even if they are detected, they are not likely to be defined as newsworthy by the established definitions of importance. This is one of the principal reasons why so much news is about the world of officialdom, even when such stories are often routine and predictable. Journalists and news organizations rely on and build their work around the routine and predictability of these established institutions. Newsworthiness, then, is socially constructed. It is not a property inherent in events but is instead something that is attached to happenings by journalists. Once we realize this, the traditional ways we talk about news begin to seem inappropriate. In particular, the metaphor of news as a "mirror"—a simple reflection of events—no longer works. Even a mirror cannot reflect the whole world. It must be facing a particular direction, including some subjects in its reflection and excluding others. Thus, the image propagated by the media is far from complete. At most, it reflects only a small part of society.

In addition, the objects being reflected in the media are not passive. Instead, people holding different interests, wielding different amounts of power, and enjoying different relationships to those producing the news actively attempt to influence the content of the news. Thus, the resulting images often reflect the relative power of actors in our society rather than some "objective" reality.

News, therefore, is the product of a social process through which media personnel make decisions about what is newsworthy and what is not, about who is important and who is not, and about what views are to be included and what views can be dismissed. None of these decisions can be entirely objective. The ideal of objectivity—separating values from facts—is ultimately unobtainable, although some would argue it is a valuable goal. Furthermore, the practices associated with objectivity are tilted in one direction; they give those in power enormous visibility in the media, whereas those outside the centers of power are largely ignored. The reliance on "appropriate," available, and preferably authoritative sources means journalists talk mostly to government and corporate officials and end up reproducing their view of the world. Thus, "objective" journalism, by highlighting the views and activities of officials, can be seen on balance to favor those in power.

Rejecting Objectivity: Alternative Journalism

As we have seen, objectivity as a standard of U.S. journalism is a fairly recent phenomenon. When the nation's founders protected the freedom of the press, they were referring to publishers of what were mostly highly partisan pamphlets and periodicals. Through the 19th century, newspapers were often affiliated with political parties, openly arguing from a particular perspective rather than trying to retain a neutral stance on the issues. Although "objective" journalism has displaced this older tradition, "advocacy" or "alternative" journalism has survived and can be found in many forms today.

Atton and Hamilton (2008) argue that alternative media "seek to challenge objectivity and impartiality from both an ethical and a political standpoint." They challenge the very notion that "it is possible in the first place to separate facts from values and that it is morally and politically preferable to do" (Atton and Hamilton 2008: 84). Alternative journalists not only reject the idea of not getting involved in the story; they seek to play an active role in advancing their causes.

Alternative journalism projects span a wide range of media, including newspapers, magazines, websites, radio programs, and television shows. In recent years, the internet has made alternative journalism more easily accessible and more visible while enabling its unprecedented global expansion (Lievrouw 2011).

There is a broad range of work that might be called alternative journalism. Some of it is in the progressive muckraking tradition—fact-based reporting aimed at exposing a social ill or wrongdoing that is being ignored by mainstream media—that dates back to the 19th century. For example, founded in 1976, the nonprofit magazine (and now website) *Mother Jones* is named after an early labor movement leader and bills itself as "a reader-supported nonprofit news organization [that] . . . does independent and investigative reporting on everything from politics and climate change to education and food" (Motherjones.com 2018). It has won numerous awards for its investigative reporting as well as the American Society of Magazine Editors' Magazine of the Year Award in 2017.

Other efforts are aimed at broadening the range of perspectives available in the news. *Democracy Now!* is "a daily, global, independent news hour." As its website notes, the program's reporting includes breaking daily news headlines and in-depth interviews with people on the front lines of the world's most pressing issues. On *Democracy Now!*, you'll hear a diversity of voices speaking for themselves, providing a unique and sometimes provocative perspective on global events. (Democracynow.org 2018)

Some efforts take advantage of the internet to build international links. For example, the global network Indymedia offers what it bills as "a network of collectively run media outlets for the creation of radical, accurate, and passionate tellings of the truth" (Indymedia.org 2018). Indymedia activists do not aim at being objective; they take sides, presenting a typically left or progressive view on issues of the day.

Conservative activists have also created their own media forms that blend news and opinion. Breitbart News has become the most high-profile online destination for extreme right news and commentary. Created in 2005 by conservative activist Andrew Breitbart (who died in 2012), Breitbart.com garnered international attention when its chief executive, Steve Bannon, left Breitbart to run Donald Trump's 2016 presidential campaign. Bannon would subsequently become President Trump's chief strategist, leave the White House to return to Breitbart a few months later, and ultimately lose his job at Breitbart in the wake of a conflict with the Trump family. Breitbart's association with the Trump campaign and its aggressively conservative attitude made it a prominent site for political news in far right circles. In addition, websites like Townhall—a commercially owned operation—assemble what it describes as "political commentary and analysis from over 100 leading columnists and opinion leaders, research from 100 partner organizations, conservative talk-radio and a community of millions of grassroots conservatives. Townhall.com is designed to amplify those conservative voices in America's political debates" (Townhall.com 2018). The site links to hundreds of conservative bloggers.

At their best, efforts that—through well-reasoned, fact-based reporting—broaden the range of perspectives or tackle issues overlooked by mainstream commercial media can make a substantial contribution to keeping people informed and engaged, even when they clearly approach the issues from a particular political viewpoint. But at their worst, some partisan media—whether bitter cable talk shows on mainstream media or alternative websites—can also contribute to political polarization and the propagation of falsehoods. If people immerse themselves only in media that confirm their preexisting beliefs and play to their prejudices, it is unlikely that they will understand the arguments of opponents, be able to productively discuss issues with people who hold different opinions, or find the kind of common ground necessary for a healthy functioning democracy. Instead, relying solely on such media may contribute to the entrenched and bitterly divisive politics of recent years.

As we have seen, news media production is the result of a series of conventions and routines that enable professionals collectively to do their jobs and meet the demands of the organizations for which they work. These conventions incorporate fundamental professional norms (e.g., objectivity) and basic organizational goals (e.g., gathering news). Routine media practices shape, to a great degree, the final media products.

We have also seen that technological changes can alter these routines and that some media reject some of these conventions—most notably the idea of objectivity—to create new forms of reporting and opinion.

OCCUPATIONAL ROLES AND PROFESSIONAL SOCIALIZATION

Journalists are not the only media professionals who follow routine practices. Analyzing work practices and professional norms can help us understand other media as well. Let's turn to two additional examples—photographers and book editors—and place them in the context of roles.

Roles

The concept of *role* has a long history in sociological theory and research. It has helped clarify the relationship between society and individuals and the relationship between the forces of structure and agency. We also use the term in everyday conversation: We know that actors play specific roles, we might refer to a member of a basketball team as a role player, and on learning of a recent dispute at the local bar, we might ask our friends what role they played in the squabble. Sociologically, roles can be thought of as the bundles of expectations that are associated with different social positions. For example, students know the basic requirements of their role: attend class, complete assignments, show a certain measure of respect for teachers, and so on. We rarely think about the specific content of roles because we have largely internalized them. In fact, roles become part of our sense of self. You would say, "I am a student," not "I play the role of a student."

However, sometimes the socially constructed nature of roles becomes apparent, for example, when role expectations are obviously breached. Take the classroom as an example. If a student were to fall into a deep sleep in class, begin snoring loudly, and perhaps even slide onto the carpeted floor to get a bit more comfortable, others in the class would feel a bit uneasy because the snoring student had rather blatantly violated a key component of the student role. Students are expected not only to attend class but to show some interest—even if feigned—in what goes on there. These kinds of situations clarify role norms; seeing what we shouldn't be doing reaffirms what we should be doing.

Another time when we become aware of roles is when we have to learn a new one. Think about starting a new job that involves a kind of work you have never done. During the first few days, the bundle of expectations associated with this new role—whether it be waitress, teacher, or stockbroker—is likely to be a bit unclear, even confusing. Eventually, though, you must learn the ropes to be successful in your new job. You do this by following instructions, watching others do the work, and getting feedback on your own efforts.

The process by which we learn the basic ground rules of a role is called *socialization*. Every media occupation that we will encounter in this book—journalist, photographer, writer, filmmaker, musician, and so on—requires a kind of socialization into that role. We tend to think of this kind of work as *creative*, done by people who have a special talent. However, we need to keep in mind that even these creative media jobs are performed by people who must fulfill the expectations of their role and must fit into the expectations of the organizations with which they work.

On one hand, the concept of role highlights the significance of external social controls. Specific roles, we might say, serve as a social control mechanism by clarifying what is expected of us. Because other members of a social group also know the norms of the role, the expectations are enforced by our interaction with others. We generally do not consider role expectations oppressive because the social control is not simply imposed on us. We internalize, to varying degrees, the components of the role, often so thoroughly that we hardly acknowledge any social control. The role concept, then, explains how individual behavior is both patterned by and influenced by broader social forces.

This is, however, only half of the story. Roles are not rigid; they do not dictate specific behaviors. On the contrary, individuals often have a good deal of room for negotiation within the framework of the roles they occupy. Parents, for example, can relate to their children in a variety of ways—as friend, strict disciplinarian, or hands-off monitor—without violating the norms of the parent role. However, there are limits. Certain actions will be widely perceived as violating basic norms, and some actions may even lead to the removal of children from the home, an effective termination of the parent role.

Roles also are not static. The parent example illustrates the dynamic nature of roles. What is expected of parents today is different from what was expected 50 years ago. Nor are roles permanent. Changing social conditions both create and eliminate the need for particular roles. In the following sections, we explore how roles and socialization apply to media professionals and how changing social conditions have affected these roles.

Photography

We see photographs everywhere, and to most people they are not much of a mystery. Our phone cameras allow us to easily capture pictures of everyday activities of all kinds. We can take pictures of a friend sleeping in the library, the meal we just prepared, or a selfie in a snowstorm. And, with just a few clicks, we can share photos with friends and family on social media. We can use simple photo editing software to modify a photo or use Photoshop for more elaborate manipulations. So what separates those of us who take photos from someone who is a professional photographer?

The easiest answer is to note that photographers get paid for their pictures, but many of us know people whose amateur photographs rival anything that is published, making this distinction a mere technicality. Another answer to this question is talent. Professional photographers have a vision for their pictures that the rest of us typically lack. There is undoubtedly something to this distinction, but we would be hard-pressed to put it to practical use. Who should define this talent or vision? How do we decide who is worthy of the status of photographer and who is just a weekend picture taker?

Instead, it is more useful to think about photographers as people who take on the role of photographer and behave according to the norms of that role. Indeed, Battani (1999) demonstrates how a specific occupational role of the photographer emerged in the mid-19th century, as early photographers sought to institutionalize their emerging field as a legitimate profession. To enhance their reputations, attract wealthy customers for portraits, and build favorable relationships with the suppliers of photographic materials, the early photographers worked to promote "an image of their studios and practices as places of refined culture" (p. 622).

Of course, there are different types of photography and, therefore, different versions of this role. For example, the photojournalist and the advertising photographer may use similar basic equipment, but each has a different role—with different sets of tasks, expectations, and norms. Rosenblum's (1978) classic study *Photographers at Work* shows that role expectations and organizational demands are central to explaining the different styles of photography in newspapers and advertising as well as the different conceptions of creativity held by photographers in the two settings.

News photos and advertising photos draw on distinct stylistic conventions that make the images quite different from each other in ways that are readily apparent even to the untrained eye. Photo images selling jeans or perfume in *Vanity Fair*, for example, are usually easily distinguishable from a front-page photo illustrating the lead story in the *New York Times*. If the photo styles and their associated conventions are different, the sources of these differences can be found in the socialization of photographers, their work roles, and the organizational goals the pictures need to meet.

Socialization of Photographers

Socialization refers to the process by which people learn the expectations of a particular role. It is likely that young news and ad photographers begin with similar sets of skills. Each knows the basic technical requirements of taking pictures. Socialization allows the beginner to move beyond the technical aspects of the work and learn how to conceptually see images in ways that are distinct to the professional photojournalist or the ad photographer. This distinct vision must be learned for each photographer to produce suitable pictures. One underlying assumption here is that ways of seeing images are socially constructed. Photojournalists and ad photographers must learn to see images in ways that are in line with their professional and organizational roles.

Entry-level photographers have to learn and internalize the basic norms of the organizations they work for and, at the same time, learn the culture of their profession. A beginning photojournalist for a newspaper learns the kind of news that the paper and its website feature and, more important, becomes acquainted with the picture selection process at that news organization. Of the many photos the journalist takes on assignment, only one of these shots may make it into the paper, and only a few of them are likely to be featured on the newspaper's website. The photo editor is the person responsible for selecting which pictures to use. Part of the process of socialization, then, is learning the norms of the selection process to be able to produce the kinds of pictures that the photo editor will select.

One of the fundamental professional norms of photojournalism is that pictures should document happenings, not transform them. Although pictures inevitably provide selective snapshots of complex phenomena, the commitment to unobtrusiveness is central to the ideology of photojournalism. News photographers, then, have to learn techniques to stay out of the way yet still get good pictures.

Because the events that photographers cover are almost all either prescheduled (e.g., press conferences, parades, sporting events) or fit into standard story formats (e.g., fires, accidents, crimes), photographers learn that they will be successful if they can anticipate what they will see to plan the kinds of shots they will take. This anticipation allows photographers to locate themselves in strategic spots, use the appropriate lenses, focus on the setting or people who are central to the event, and produce the kinds of pictures that will be acceptable to their editors. Thus, the socialization of the photojournalist involves learning how to anticipate action and plan shots in advance.

Both of these photos show people eating. Which is from the news and which is the sort used in an advertisement? The obvious differences illustrate the different levels of control that news and ad photographers have over their pictures.

Advertising photographers, on the other hand, must learn a set of organizational and professional norms that are different from those of photojournalism. One difference is that, rather than remain unobtrusive, advertising photographers learn to leave nothing to chance; every aspect of each photo is the responsibility of the photographer. Every last detail in an ad photo is staged: lighting, setting, hairstyles, clothing, jewelry, items in the background, props. The ad photographer must learn how to exert precise control and develop the technical skills required to accomplish it.

Advertising photographers learn that ad photography is a collective process; managing relationships with art directors and representatives of the advertiser is a key part of the job. The ad photographer learns that success requires not only vision or skill in creating compelling images but also the ability to negotiate with—even please—those who have creative control over the advertisements. In practice, this means that photographers learn that there is little room for individualists who perceive themselves as pure artists. The profession requires that ad photographers see their role as just one part of a collective process driven by the logic of commerce.

Photographers' Work Roles and Organizational Goals

The division of labor within newsrooms shapes the kinds of pictures that photojournalists take. Professional photojournalism typically involves various people in coordinated activities: the person who decides on the assignment, the photographer, the photo editor who selects the pictures, the printer, the editor who decides which stories to run, and the web designers who create and update the paper's site. News organizations are highly developed bureaucracies that rely on clearly defined rules and classification systems. This kind of organization leads photographers to take standard pictures, the kinds of photos that we would be likely to be recognized as news photos. The key is the system of classification in which events are grouped into types: the disaster, the war, the political campaign, the legislative debate, the community conflict. In producing news coverage, news organizations impose a standard script—including images—on these basic types of stories. Photographers are expected to produce images that fit the standard scripts. When images that do not fit the script are routinely weeded out by the photo editors, photographers soon learn not to take these kinds of pictures in the first place.

Role expectations also provide the framework for definitions of creativity. Editors expect photographers to have good news judgment, to be willing to use initiative to get good pictures, and to produce pictures that can tell various aspects of the story. Moreover, photographers are expected to regularly provide the kind of standard pictures that can accompany standardized stories, which both editors and readers come to expect. This expectation does not leave much room for the independent creativity of the photojournalist. The subject matter is assigned, and the organizational norms suggest the kinds of pictures that are appropriate. As a result, photojournalists generally see themselves not as creative artists but as reporters who take pictures.

Ad photographers, in contrast, take on the role of merchants as they must sell their services to an ad agency and an advertiser, follow the lead of the art director, and produce pictures that are generally pre-scripted. Thus, much ad photography is reduced to technical work. The photographer must have the knowledge and skills to effectively carry out the wishes of those making the creative decisions. Much of the day-to-day work of the ad photographer involves creating scripted images and adding small variations—in angle or lighting, for example—so that art directors have several different versions of the picture from which to choose.

For the vast majority of ad photographers, creativity is not in the conception of the images but in the ability to capture the desired image. They often achieve this by devising solutions to technical problems in the photographic process. Creativity in ad photography, then, is being innovative enough to figure out how to get the image the art director wants when standard techniques do not work. The creativity of ad photography is not in the vision but in a kind of technical mastery (Rosenblum 1978). In the digital age, this technical mastery increasingly involves the skillful use of software to manipulate images to meet client needs.

Photographers, then, are not all the same. They work in different kinds of organizations that place different demands on them. They are socialized into different professional roles and take different kinds of pictures. Organizational and professional norms provide the context for understanding the pictures photographers take, the daily routines in the workplace, and the ways photographers evaluate their own work. One of the central lessons to be learned from our focus on photographers is that authority relations within the workplace can tell us a good deal about the kind of work that media professionals do. Photographers, in both news and advertising, have specific superiors whom they must satisfy by producing appropriate pictures. Most of the time, they carry out the creative wishes of others rather than conceptualizing on their own. With a growing number of photographers working as freelancers or project-specific contractors, rather than as full-time staff, the ability to recognize organizational expectations and be able to supply photos that fit organizational needs has become an increasingly significant factor in shaping photographers' career trajectories.

What about media professionals who are higher in the organizational hierarchy? What norms or social forces affect how they organize their work? A look at the work of book editors will help us answer these questions.

Editorial Decision Making

Book publishing is a dynamic, multifaceted industry. Books are published on a wide range of subjects, packaged in various formats, sold in many different settings, and bought by many types of readers. In addition, there are several different kinds of publishing companies, from large commercial houses that sign prominent authors to seven-figure advance-payment contracts to small presses that publish scholarly monographs.

In all publishing firms, the key decision is which manuscripts to publish. Regardless of whether the house is aiming for the best-seller list, with sales in the millions, or for adoption by college professors as a classroom text, where success might mean only a few thousand copies sold, all publishers have to sift through many submissions and proposals and select the few that will become books. These selection processes take place in other media industries as well. Record labels sign a small number of musicians, Hollywood studios produce a limited number of films, and the television networks add only a handful of new programs to their prime-time schedules each year. In each of these industries, decision makers need to make a large number of choices for projects about which they have only partial knowledge. These decisions, of course, have substantial consequences—they dictate the books, music, films, and television programs that will be available.

Different industries and the various sectors within each industry have different rules that govern the decision-making process. The search for steady profits by commercial media companies makes evaluations of the potential for economic success a central feature of the decision-making process. Those in decision-making roles need to develop strategies for evaluating the potential profitability of a particular movie or book.

The Work of the Book Editor

In most publishing houses, the people who solicit, evaluate, and sign manuscripts are called acquisitions editors. It is their job to get high-quality books for the press, to weed out titles that do not fit, and to work with authors to produce books that will meet organizational goals. Acquisitions editors have varying degrees of autonomy and different editorial mandates at different presses, but they are ordinarily the principal filter through which the decision to publish is made.

One classic study of publishing (Coser, Kadushin, and Powell 1982) found that a key factor in whether a manuscript is published is the channel that brings a potential author to a publisher's attention. Abstract measures of the quality or significance of a book manuscript are far less important—at least in determining whether a book is published—than the way the manuscript comes in the door. There are different "lines" of authors (perhaps a better image is piles of manuscripts) awaiting the eyes of editors. These different piles are organized according to how they were received. The longest, and by far least successful, line is made up of authors who send their unsolicited manuscript to a publishing house, hoping that it will be impressive enough to be accepted for publication. Unfortunately for aspiring authors, there is very little likelihood that this route will pay off. One large publisher estimated that only one out of 15,000 unsolicited manuscripts is published each year (Anand, Barnett, and Carpenter 2004).

Other avenues are more likely to lead to publication. Unsolicited manuscripts that are addressed to the appropriate editor by name are more likely to be considered seriously than those not directed at an individual. More important, personal contacts are what really facilitate the publication of a book. Manuscripts that come through informal networks—other authors, friends, or professional meetings—go into a much smaller pile that is taken more seriously. And authors who are represented by agents are placed in the most favorable pile. Prospective authors who hope to find a literary agent to represent them will find that agents are very selective about whom they decide to represent. Sociologist Clayton Childress notes that literary agents are powerful gatekeepers on the road to publication; he reports that the founder of a large literary management firm estimated that "for every unsolicited author query that eventually leads to representation, over eleven thousand are rejected" (2017: 70).

Manuscript "piles" are not likely to exist in any concrete form, but the metaphor suggests that publishing houses organize work, even if unconsciously, along these lines. Organizationally, this system operates like a kind of obstacle course with different entry points. Depending on where each manuscript starts the course, it will face different hurdles, opportunities, time frames, and perhaps even personnel until it completes the course or is rejected. The specific nature of the obstacle course depends on the particularities of the organization of the publishing house.

Although the basic factors influencing acquisition editors discussed by Coser and colleagues (1982) still hold true, more recent studies have found additional dynamics at play in today's publishing industry. For example, acquisition editors often feel increasing pressure to sign only books with blockbuster potential. Likewise, they struggle with reading submissions as more of their time is dedicated to the marketing and publicity of books, and specialized marketing and publicity staff have an increasing say in which books are published (Greco, Rodriguez, and Wharton 2007). Publishing houses often resort to working with authors who have their own ability to get their names out and cross-promote their books—through popular blogs they write, shows they host or appear on, or newspapers and magazines to which they regularly contribute. More than ever before, authors are expected to have an active online presence to be able to promote their new book through Twitter, Facebook, and other social media platforms.

With an increased emphasis on potential blockbuster books—and the lucrative movie rights often associated with them—the growth of famous authors who command a loyal readership, and the rise of "super-agents" who are advocates for their author/clients, the balance of power in this portion of the publishing industry has shifted in recent years away from the publishing houses to the celebrity authors and their agents. In his study of the trade book industry in the United States and Britain, John Thompson (2010) notes that these new super-agents

> thought of themselves less as intermediaries, mediating between author and publisher, and more as dedicated advocates of their client's interests. They conceived of their task primarily in legal and financial terms, and they displaced the centrality of the publisher by asserting control over the rights of their client's work and deciding which rights to allocate to which publisher and on what terms. In their eyes, the publisher was not the central player in the field but simply a means to get what they wanted to achieve on their clients' behalf, which was to get their work in to the marketplace as effectively and successfully as possible. (p. 66)

Thompson stresses that this portion of the publishing world is unique and does not represent the vast number of smaller publishers who handle the work of authors without powerful agents.

With some 300,000 titles published by U.S. houses each year, editors and publicity staff feel great strain in competing for the public's attention—and new competition has appeared as self-publishing has exploded in recent years. Although firm numbers are difficult to determine, some estimates are that more than 725,000 new titles are now self-published each year in the United States (Bowker 2016). Most of these self-published books have tiny sales figures, but some have had moderate success, and a few have become best sellers. The massive best-selling erotic romance novel, *Fifty Shades of Grey*, for example, began as a self-published title before being bought by a traditional publisher. Publishing houses have taken notice, and some have even responded by launching their own self-publishing brands, such as Simon & Schuster's Archway Publishing.

With so many books published, there are far too many new books available for any one bookstore to place on its shelves. Just as publishers follow a set of conventions as they determine which books to publish, brick-and-mortar bookstores adopt their own conventions to help them decide which books to sell. Advance reviews and publishers' catalog descriptions help booksellers make selection decisions. As on the front pages of newspapers, publishers put their most promising books toward the front of the catalog and dedicate more space to their displays. In addition to these catalogs, according to Miller (2006), the buyers for booksellers (those who decide which books a bookstore will carry) consider past sales of the author's previous work; the current popularity of the book's genre; the publisher's promotional budget and plans; whether the author will be touring or making any media appearances; the sales rep's or editor's enthusiasm and recommendations; the ease of ordering and receiving from the book's supplier; the terms at which the book is being made available (discount, shipping costs, payment, and return policies); the book's list price, production quality, and cover design; the book's topicality; the buyer's understanding of local tastes and habits; and the buyer's personal tastes. Miller argues that both independent bookstores and the chains employ routine conventions to sift through the vast array of potential books, but the independents give much more weight to local interest in their decisions.

Online sellers like Amazon don't have to worry as much about which books to stock as their store exists only in virtual space, with physical books stocked in relatively inexpensive, unadorned warehouses. Although this gives them an advantage over physical bookstores that have to pay high prices for rent in foot-trafficked areas and that have to contend with not having an in-store copy of a book that a reader may want, online sellers face additional difficulties in allowing users to browse their selections. In response to this problem, online sellers use pictures of book covers on their websites, show similar and recommended books on the webpage of a book that a user has searched, and provide options like the "Look Inside!" feature on Amazon to try to give buyers the experience of browsing in a physical bookstore (Weedon 2007). The steady, but no longer growing, popularity of e-books, and improved devices that make e-reading more comfortable, give online retailers the additional competitive advantage of being able to provide books instantly—without the cost of storing and shipping a physical product. E-books made up about 24 percent of book sales in 2015 (Milliot 2016).

Scholarly Publishing

Walter Powell (1985) studied the operating procedures that govern the process of manuscript selection in two scholarly publishing houses. Scholarly publishing is a segment of the book industry that is not so clearly oriented to profitability. As a general rule, books need to be able to sell enough copies to pay for the costs of production and meet the house's criteria for scholarly quality. However, editors do not have to focus their attention on signing best sellers. As a result, acquisitions editors at scholarly publishing houses have a more ambiguous goal than their counterparts at the large commercial houses, where sales potential is the dominant goal.

As is the case at commercial houses, scholarly editors follow a set of routines, governed by standard operating assumptions, which help them make decisions about what to publish. The volume of manuscripts is so high that it is impossible to attend to each project. Manuscripts from unknown authors who have never had contact with the publishing house do not receive much editorial attention and are, therefore, unlikely to be published. Manuscripts from an author with previous connections to the house or those solicited by an editor receive much more thorough and quicker attention. In addition, editors make use of prominent academics who serve as series editors to help attract new authors or evaluate manuscripts. In this way, editors can farm out evaluations to a stable, trusted group of scholars who may be more expert in the particular field. Most scholarly houses also use outside reviewers—people the editor selects to anonymously assess the quality of the manuscript. Editors use all of these practices to manage their workloads in ways that are consistent with their editorial goals and their obligations to their authors, colleagues, and friends. All of this suggests a good deal of autonomy for editors; they can draw upon series editors when they choose to, send manuscripts to an outside reviewer who is likely to be supportive (or not), and give closer attention to projects that involve scholars they already know.

In his study, Powell (1985) first accepted editors' explanations that they had wide discretion in acquiring books. However, he later noticed several things that made him skeptical: Editors had a clear sense of which authors deserved priority service and which could be put off for long periods; editors never proposed atypical books, demonstrating their sense of boundaries; and there was a high turnover rate among editors yet stability in the kinds of decisions that were made. In addition, Powell found that his observation at the houses had made him an expert in predicting which manuscripts would be signed and which would be rejected. In essence, he had learned the informal rules so well that the decision-making process was no longer a mystery.

Scholarly publishing is similar to photography. Through a process of socialization, acquisitions editors learn the values and preferences of their publishing houses. This socialization process is one of the mechanisms by which organizations assert a kind of unobtrusive control. The key to the socialization of editors is learning about the types of books the press publishes. As part of their socialization, editors learn about the history and traditions of the house; they may already be familiar with the prominent books and authors that the house has published. In short, successful editors must understand the house's "list"—its currently available books, including new releases and the backlist of older titles. New books must complement other titles. Editors understand this constraint and adopt it as a norm in their own editorial decisions. In this way, choices about new books are shaped in important ways by the types of books that a house has previously published. In addition, most outside reviewers are authors who have published with the house, thus reinforcing a similar set of norms for each new year's crop of books.

Powell (1985) attributes his finding that editors rarely had their selections rejected by their superiors to their internalization of the basic norms of the publishing house. Editors do not have their projects rejected because they have already weeded out those that do not fit. The manuscripts that they send on for approval by superiors fit with the house list. This is what makes them good editors. They enjoy a good deal of autonomy in their work because they do not think too independently while doing it.

A focus on the practices that editors use to organize their work and on the organizational premises that guide these decisions shows the dynamic relationship between human agency and structural constraint in media production. Although organizational premises—structure—may make change more difficult, small changes in routine practices may help alter these premises, leading to the publication of new types of books. The backlist is the concrete embodiment of the relationship between agency and structure.

It represents the accumulation of decisions made by prior editors, a tradition that shapes current decisions. But those current decisions will alter the backlist and, in turn, affect the framework for future decisions. In this example, we see both the stability and the potential dynamism of the socialization process.

NORMS ON THE INTERNET, NEW MEDIA, AND NEW ORGANIZATIONS

The three occupations we have explored—journalism, photography, and editorial work—are well-established professions with lengthy traditions. But what about newer forms of media and online interaction? How does work in these media differ from—and in what ways does it resemble—the occupations and organizations found in traditional media?

The highly decentralized nature of the internet makes it tempting for us to think that social activity online is totally autonomous, free from the kinds of conventions that guide the production of traditional media forms. But although the internet, and especially social media, permits new forms of interaction, anyone who has spent time online is likely to have a sense of norms that govern behavior there. These norms and conventions are generated by both the creators of websites and social media platforms and the users who contribute to them.

The creators of many internet sites are part of larger media organizations and are governed by the occupational norms and standards that predominate in their fields. For example, professional web developer associations promote norms and conventions regarding user-friendly web design, universal access standards, and other issues. These groups operate much like other traditional media professionals. Those who have constructed and are expanding the networks that connect us to one another—through discussion groups, instant messaging, microblogging, photo sharing, social networking sites, e-mail, and websites—both draw on and create conventions that help structure our interaction within these networks.

For example, a search engine such as Google operates within a set of conventions that were created—and sometimes change—based on its design. The rankings of search results are produced by Google's algorithm for the number and importance of pages that link to each site, thereby steering users toward the sites with more links to them. As Vaidhyanathan (2011: 14) notes, "Through its power to determine which sites get noticed, and thus trafficked, Google has molded certain standards into the web." For example, Google downplays the importance of porn sites to reduce the likelihood of unintentionally stumbling across such sites when posing ambiguous search terms. Placing the word *define:* before a word in a Google search produces definitions of that word. *Time* plus a name of a city produces the local time there. These and many other features of a site are the structural conventions produced by its creators. Every form of media has similar conventions, such as Twitter's once-famous 140-character limit or Facebook's use of *friends*, *likes*, and *pokes*.

However, as noted earlier, one of the defining characteristics of the internet as a medium is that *users* are often the source of content, a topic we explore in Chapter 8. These users are not professionals, nor is content creation their occupation. As a result, different and more informal mechanisms have developed to teach the conventions of the medium—and of specific online venues—and guide appropriate behavior. You probably know, for example, that it isn't wise to post your vacation photos on your LinkedIn profile because they are not relevant (and may even be counterproductive) for job networking. Similarly, you probably won't post your résumé or recommendations from coworkers on your Facebook page. In both cases, you know the norms guiding what's appropriate to include in different social media arenas. Sometimes norms are policed more formally. For example, Glassdoor, the popular job review site, has a team of 26 content moderators in an Ohio office, each of whom reads 80 to 100 job reviews an hour. When moderators identify reviews that violate Glassdoor's community guidelines (which are posted on the site), the reviews are rejected (Widdicombe 2018).

Over time, we developed language that helps users understand online technology. This language also imposes a kind of logic onto online media by formalizing conventional ways of perceiving, and even behaving on, the internet. Terms used to describe online behaviors—such as *trolling*, *spamming*, *ghosting*, and *lurking*—characterize some of the ways our virtual behavior is both predictable and patterned. Some social media terms, such as *newbie/noob* and *moderator*, even explicitly describe particular online roles with accompanying expectations.

Another example of a common set of conventions involves "emojis" to simulate the inflection of face-to-face talk. We use emojis to express emotion, to strengthen a message, and to express humor, usually in informal communication and in a positive context rather than in a negative one (Derks, Bos, and von Grumbkow 2008). We know that emojis are not appropriate in formal communications. Another online linguistic convention is the use of acronyms and slang in chat conversations. Such terms can seem perplexing at first until a user is socialized into learning their meaning. Examples range from the once-common LOL (Laughing Out Loud) to the less obvious (CD9; "Code 9, parents near"). Many acronyms are fleeting, falling in and out of favor. BRB (Be Right Back), for example, used to be common, but as people began staying online continuously via their smartphones, it no longer made sense; they weren't going anywhere.

Often the norms that develop on new media platforms closely emulate the conventions that already exist in traditional media. But new media forms also require new conventions. In one early study of conventions on the internet, McLaughlin, Osborne, and Smith (1995) explored the "standards of conduct" in online discussion groups, then known as newsgroups. In effect, they examined the expectations associated with the role of the online conversation participant. In particular, they argued that there are specific types of "reproachable" network behavior, that is, actions that violate the basic norms of the internet, commonly referred to as "netiquette."

What are the behaviors that elicited reproaches from other early online users? One involved the incorrect use of the technological apparatus and was generally associated with novices who had not mastered the format. An example is a user who accidentally posts a message to an entire newsgroup that was intended only for a single recipient. A second norm was not to write messages in capital letters (which is equivalent to SHOUTING). A third was the violation of a basic network convention, such as failing to include your electronic signature with your message or neglecting to include a previous message about which you are commenting ("quoting"). Users who behaved in these reproachable ways were likely to be admonished online by fellow users who were committed to the orderly functioning of the group. Such admonishment may be, at least initially, gentle and intended to be educational in nature. But admonishment could become rather venomous, referred to as "flaming." Many violators likely learned from their mistakes, sought help with the technology, and learned the conventions. Those who persisted in their reproachable behavior could be threatened with loss of access to the group, and repeat offenders were ultimately expelled.

Online norms are powerful shapers of virtual behavior. Perhaps that is why the vast majority of newsgroup subscribers were perpetual lurkers, reading messages but not posting their own. One widely held group norm, in fact, was to follow a group for some time before posting a message. This allowed newcomers to become socialized into the ways of the group, to learn about the group's history and traditions, and to see the kinds of issues that are generally on the group's agenda. Additional practices helped socialize new members of newsgroups. For example, upon subscribing, members received an electronic how-to manual for participation in the group, which included both technical advice on the workings of the system and instructions on appropriate conduct. Archives of previous group discussions were often available, and new group members were encouraged to read through them. In addition, a file of frequently asked questions (FAQs) was sent to new members so that they would not clutter up the network with the same questions.

Why do such standards of conduct develop in the first place? One answer is that they provide a foundation for the maintenance of the identity of the newsgroup. This identity is passed along to new members through socialization into the norms of the electronic community and is enforced when new members are admonished for not adhering to the ground rules. Where do these standards come from? Many are practical responses to the needs of the medium. For example, regular users are aware that certain conventions, such as using an appropriate subject line on a posting, enable users to follow threads over time or search and find them later on. Those who use subject lines inappropriately or leave the line blank make participation in the virtual community both more confusing and more time-consuming.

Technological conventions may seem trivial, and notes of reproach for violations may seem nasty, but the requirement of maintaining some kind of order in cyberspace is their driving force. Perhaps most important, McLaughlin and her colleagues (1995) argue that there are underlying social roots to online conventions. These conventions reinforce and protect the collective identities of the electronic communities and can be used to ward off newcomers who pose a threat to these identities or to the stability of the group. Like other producers of media, users of the internet are part of a social world in which tradition, organizational history, group identity, and the routinization of daily activities help shape the norms and practices that pattern even our virtual behavior.

The lessons from these early internet newsgroups apply to more recent media platforms. New users on social media sites must also learn norms of appropriate conduct—including where to post, when to retweet, whom to share with—from some combination of official site policies (such as Glassdoor's community guidelines) and the socialization that occurs during initial participation on the site. Just about all social media sites—such as Facebook, Snapchat, and Twitter—have their own official policies on acceptable behavior: Facebook's Statement of Rights and Responsibilities, Snapchat's Community Guidelines, and the Twitter Rules. These policies define appropriate (and inappropriate) uses of these social media services, specifying rules on, for example, privacy, copyright, spam, pornography, and hate speech. These policies establish a framework for conduct on social media sites and provide guidelines for how to respond to those who violate established policies. However, such official policies are only a starting point. Regular users of social media are socialized into the conventions of these online spaces and are familiar with a wide range of norms that go beyond official policies, including the informal dos and don'ts of posting on friends' Facebook walls or how to respond (or not) to Facebook friend requests.

CONCLUSION

This chapter has rounded out our discussion of media production by showing how professional norms, institutional premises, and organizational structures shape the day-to-day work of media producers—whether professionals or amateurs. We have seen that human agents—reporters, photographers, book editors, and internet users—are active participants in the construction and reconstruction of production routines. These routines serve as conventions that help organize the collective work of media production.

Routines and conventions are shaped by economic, political, and organizational forces, as well as technological constraints, in each sector of the media industry. Conventions can change, although this change is likely to be slow. Ultimately, conventions become a form of structural constraint, producing guidelines for action and decision making by future media professionals.

Studying the media industry helps us understand the media messages that are part of our lives. In Part IV, we turn to the content of media, focusing on questions of inequality and ideology.

Discussion Questions

1. How do media producers respond to economic and political constraints? In what ways do these constraints shape media work? To what degree do media professionals have autonomy in the face of these constraints? Use examples to illustrate your analysis.

2. What are "conventions," and how does this concept help us understand the work of media professionals? Why do media professionals make use of conventions? Use examples to illustrate your discussion.

3. What is the relationship between news routines and the organization of news gathering? Why do reporters and news organizations develop such news routines?

4. Explain how social media have developed conventions similar to those of more traditional media. What might this suggest about the "newness" of social media and the continuity found across different forms of media?

CONTENT

Media Representations of the Social World

Part III emphasized processes of production within the media industry. However, outside of the media content we create as users, most of us never actually see these processes taking place. What we are exposed to—what we watch, read, listen to, and click through—are media content, the movies, music, television shows, websites, and print publications that result from this production process. These media content are the most common way that most of us experience mass-produced media.

In Part IV, we turn our attention to media content, exploring the ways in which media represent the social world. Chapter 6 introduces the question of ideology, exploring the values, beliefs, and norms that media content routinely display. The chapter looks at the underlying perspectives in the images that confront us every day as well as the potential contradictions and ambiguities that are built into media texts. Chapter 7 examines how media portray central social inequalities in contemporary society, focusing on issues of race, class, gender, and sexual orientation. The chapter looks at how various groups are depicted in media content, how such depictions have changed over time, and how these representations relate to social reality.

Screen Gems/Getty Images

6

MEDIA AND IDEOLOGY

Most media scholars believe that media texts articulate coherent, if shifting, ways of seeing the world. These texts help define our world and provide models for appropriate behavior and attitudes. How, for example, do media products depict the "appropriate" roles of men and women, parents and children, patients and doctors, or bosses and workers? What defines success, and how is it achieved? What qualifies as criminal activity, and what are the sources of crime and social disorder? What are the underlying messages in media content, and whose interests do these messages serve? These are, fundamentally, questions about media and ideology.

Most ideological analyses of media products focus on the content of the messages—the stories they tell about the past and the present—rather than the effects of such stories. In this chapter, then, we focus primarily on media messages. In Part V, we will turn to the relationship between media messages and media users.

WHAT IS IDEOLOGY?

An ideology is basically a system of meaning that helps define and explain the world and that makes value judgments about that world. Ideology is related to concepts such as *worldview*, *belief system*, and *values*, but it is broader than those terms. It refers not only to the beliefs held about the world but also to the basic ways in which the world is defined. Ideology, then, is not just about politics; it has a broader and more fundamental connotation.

Ideology and the "Real" World

Ideologies do not necessarily reflect reality accurately; in fact, they can often present a distorted version of the world. In everyday language, it can be an insult to charge someone with being ideological precisely because this label suggests rigidly adhering to one's beliefs in the face of overwhelming contradictory evidence. When Marxists speak of *ideology*, they often mean belief systems that help justify the actions of those in power by distorting and misrepresenting reality.

As we will explore in the next chapter, media scholars are often interested in assessing how media content compares to the "real" world. But analysts of ideology generally perceive the definition of the *real* as, itself, an ideological construction. Which aspects of whose "reality" do we define as the most real? Those that are the most visible? The most common? The most powerful? Instead of assessing images and making some judgment about levels of realness, ideological analysis asks what these messages tell us about ourselves and our society.

We can often be unaware of the ideological position of contemporary media because it reflects our own taken-for-granted views of the world. It is easier to recognize ideological content of media images by looking at older media. Old movies or television programs, for example, can seem unusual to us because they present an understanding of society that is at odds with our contemporary assumptions. For example, most U.S. television programs made in the 1950s and early 1960s featured almost entirely white casts; African Americans and other racial and ethnic minorities were virtually nonexistent. These same programs typically assumed that sharply defined, divergent, and unequal gender roles were appropriate and desirable, usually with men as breadwinners and women as stay-at-home moms. Old Western movies of the era typically took for granted the right of European Americans to conquer the land of native peoples, who were often portrayed as violent savages rather than as indigenous people trying to defend against invaders.

In discussing ideology, the primary question about such images is not whether they were realistic reflections of society; they clearly were not. (At best they were distorted and selective representations of a narrow slice of white middle-class life; at worst they were highly prejudicial stereotypes that are offensive to today's sensibilities.) Instead, an examination of ideology is concerned with what messages these images send about the nature of the world, how it operates, and how it should be. Media portrayals from this period reflect an ideology—beliefs about who is and isn't worthy of inclusion, what roles are appropriate for different groups, and what is just. The images in today's television and movies often suggest a different ideology from the one portrayed in this earlier era.

In our digital era of media abundance, with so much content produced and distributed from varying perspectives, it may seem relatively easy to spot ideological content in media products with which we disagree. Conservative viewers, for example, often claim that mainstream journalism reflects a liberal bias; many viewers who are moderate or liberal see Fox News as a purveyor of a consistently conservative version of the news. Scholars of media ideology challenge us to dig beneath the surface and look beyond our own political preferences. If it is easier to see ideology in media that seem disagreeable or unfamiliar, it can be particularly helpful to look at media that seem comfortable and familiar from a fresh perspective. At its best, ideological analysis offers us a new lens through which to analyze media content.

When scholars examine media products to uncover their ideologies, they are interested in the underlying images of society they provide. Therefore, they tend to be interested in the recurring patterns that are found in the media rather than in a specific example of media content—things depicted in a single newspaper, website, movie, or hit song. For ideological analysis, the key is the fit between the images and words in a specific media text and broader ways of thinking about, or even defining, social and cultural issues.

Dominant Ideology versus Cultural Contradictions

One key debate regarding the ideology of media is between those who argue that media promote the worldview of the powerful—the "dominant ideology"—and those who argue that media texts include more contradictory messages, both expressing the dominant ideology and at least partially challenging worldviews.

We prefer to think of media texts as sites where cultural contests over meaning are waged rather than as providers of some univocal articulation of ideology. In other words, different ideological perspectives, representing different interests with unequal power, engage in a kind of struggle within media. But it is not an even battlefield. Some ideas will have the advantage—because, for example, they are perceived as popular or they build on familiar media images—and others will be barely visible or difficult to communicate in certain forms because they are unfamiliar.

For example, a political analyst who says, "We need a strong military to fight terrorism," is tapping into a popular sentiment in the United States, which requires no explanation; it is a widely taken-for-granted assumption about the world—an ideological position. Another analyst who says, "Perhaps the presence of our troops around the world is one factor provoking terrorism," is likely to generate puzzled looks or even anger. Such an argument will require much more explanation to be understood because it runs counter to the dominant ideology in the United States—although it would be much more familiar in some other societies.

Different actors try to use media to communicate their interpretation of the world to a broader audience. But there is no guarantee that audiences will understand or interpret the meaning of this content in any uniform way—a topic we explore more fully in Chapter 8. For example, the 2017 film *Get Out* is a horror comedy hybrid film about a young African-American man's visit to the country home of his white girlfriend's wealthy family. The film is full of surprises—no spoilers here—as it offers a satirical critique of racial politics in the United States. Written and directed by comedian Jordan Peele, *Get Out* was a box office success and earned four academy award nominations. What is the ideological content of such a movie? The film received near universally positive reviews, with a Rotten Tomatoes score of 99% positive reviews. For example, in her rave review of *Get Out, New York Times* film critic Manohla Dargis (2017) points to the film's ability to challenge viewers: "[O]ur monsters, Mr. Peele reminds us, are at times as familiar as the neighborhood watch; one person's fiction, after all, is another's true-life horror story." In contrast, *National Review's* Armond White (2017) was among the few critics who found the film problematic, calling the film "lightweight" and arguing that filmmaker Jordan Peele "exploits racial discomfort, irresponsibly playing racial grief and racist relief off against each other." Clearly, the meaning and significance of this single media product were interpreted very differently by different critics.

In addition, broader trends in media content—and their ideological significance—are often the focus of controversy and debate. For example, some Christian conservatives and Islamic fundamentalists find themselves in agreement when they point to the U.S. media as a prime example of a decadent and sinful society, whereas most Americans take the presence of sex, violence, and consumerism in the media as a simple fact of life. Time and time again, the media are simultaneously criticized by some for the messages they supposedly send while being applauded by others. These media battles often become quite fierce, with some voices calling for outright censorship, others defending free speech, and still others worrying about the consequences of cultural struggles that seem to illustrate an intensifying political polarization with no possibility of compromise.

The "Culture War" Battles over Ideology

For those engaged in the promotion of particular ideas, including diverse groups such as politicians, corporations, citizen activists, and religious groups, media are among the primary contemporary battlegrounds. Media, in fact, are at the center of what James Davison Hunter (1991; Hartman 2015; Hunter and Wolfe 2006) has called the "culture wars" in contemporary American society, in which fundamental issues of morality are being fought. Hunter stresses the ways in which media—advertising, news, letters to the editor, and opinion commentary—provide the principal forms of public discourse by which cultural warfare is waged. The morality of abortion, homosexuality, immigration, or capital punishment is debated, often in very polarized terms, in media, as cultural conservatives and cultural progressives alike use various media technologies to promote their positions—including traditional newspaper columns and television advertisements as well as the full range of social media activity from blogs and Tweets to YouTube videos and Facebook posts.

One of the principal reasons why media images often become so controversial is that they are believed to promote ideas that are objectionable. In short, few critics are concerned about media texts that promote perspectives they support. Ideological analysis, then, often goes hand in hand with political advocacy as critics use their detection of distorted messages to make their own ideological points. As a result, exploring the ideologies of media can be very tricky.

The most sophisticated ideological analysis examines the stories media tell as well as the potential contradictions within media texts, that is, the places where alternative perspectives might reside or where ideological conflict is built into the text. Ideological analysis, therefore, is not simply reduced to political criticism, whereby the critic loudly denounces the "wrong" ideas in the media. Nor, in our view, is analysis particularly useful if it focuses on the ideology of one specific media text without making links to broader sets of media images. It may be interesting to ruminate over the underlying ideology of a popular movie such as *American Sniper*. (Is it a glorification of the military or a story about the traumatic consequences of war?) However, this inquiry will move from party conversation to serious analysis only if we think more carefully about the patterns of images in media texts rather than analyzing one film in isolation. At its best, ideological analysis provides a window onto the broader ideological debates going on in society. It allows us to see what kinds of ideas circulate through media texts, how they are constructed, how they change over time, and the ways they are being challenged.

Ideology as Normalization

In a September 2015 *Rolling Stone* article, journalist Paul Solotaroff (2015) reported on his time following then-candidate Donald Trump on the campaign trail: observing Trump at campaign events and talking with him in his Trump Tower office and on his campaign airplane. Solotaroff described Trump watching Fox News on the plane after a rally in front of an enthusiastic New Hampshire crowd, making critical comments about his Republican primary opponents. When Carly Fiorina appeared on screen, Trump exclaimed, "Look at that face! Would anyone vote for that? Can you imagine that, the face of our next president?! I mean, she's a woman, and I'm not s'posedta say bad things, but really, folks, come on. Are we serious?" This was just one in a continuing stream of comments by candidate and later President Trump, often posted on his Twitter account and regularly reported in the media, that judge women (often negatively) based on their appearance. Defenders of the president may think he is being playful or sarcastic or that he is just being honest, saying what others think and are afraid to say. However, the regular appearance on the news and in social media of judgmental comments about prominent women's appearances—political leaders, corporate executives, journalists, celebrities, athletes—can have a powerful, if subtle, impact.

What are the stakes in the battles over the ideology of media? As the Trump example highlights, media texts can be seen as key sites where basic social norms are articulated. The media give us pictures of social interaction and social institutions that, by their sheer repetition, on a daily basis, can play important roles in shaping broad social definitions. In essence, the accumulation of media images suggests what is "normal" (e.g., women must be preoccupied with their appearance if they want to be successful) and what is "deviant." This articulation is accomplished, in large part, by the fact that traditional popular media, particularly television and mass advertising, have a tendency to display a remarkably narrow range of behaviors and lifestyles, marginalizing or neglecting people who are different from the mediated norm. However, when difference is highlighted by, for example, television talk shows that include people who are largely invisible in most media—trans activists, squatters, or strippers—the media can paint difference as part of a spectacle of the bizarre.

The key in understanding such messages is to see the overall pattern rather than any single story. For example, the 2015 Global Media Monitoring Project (GMMP 2015) found that only 10 percent of newspaper, television, and radio news stories have a woman as the central focus, and most news stories reinforce traditional gender stereotypes. In fact, only 4 percent of news stories in the 2015 monitoring report challenged traditional gender stereotypes. In her Foreword to the 2015 GMMP report, Margaret Gallagher makes a compelling case for the significance of monitoring media content:

> The media are powerful not simply as cultural or commercial institutions that select and represent social and political reality. Even more important is the symbolic power of the media—their ability to shape what is perceived as normal, and which social divisions are accepted or taken for granted. This symbolic power means that the media may legitimise existing social and political relations, including unequal gender relations. (p. 1)

Despite the likelihood of their having very different political stances, those who are concerned about media depictions of, say, same-sex marriage have the same underlying concern as those who criticize the prominence of stereotypical gender images. In both cases, the fear is that media images normalize specific social relations, making certain ways of behaving seem unexceptional. If media texts can normalize behaviors, they can also set limits on the range of acceptable ideas. The ideological work lies in the patterns within media texts. Ideas and attitudes that are routinely included in media become part of the legitimate public debate about issues. Ideas that are excluded from the popular media or appear in the media only to be ridiculed have little legitimacy. They are outside the range of acceptable ideas. Therefore, the ideological influence of media can be seen in the absences and exclusions just as much as in the content of the messages.

Media professionals generally have little patience with the argument that the media are purveyors of ideology. Instead of seeing media as places where behaviors are normalized and boundaries are created, those in the industry tend to argue that the images they produce and distribute simply reflect the norms and ideas of the public. This is not ideology but simply a mirror that reflects the basic consensus about how things are.

To be sure, ideologies do not usually appear in media texts because writers and producers consciously want to impose their value systems on audiences. Rather, they are the result of the intersection of a variety of structural forces, including the producers' ideas of who the target audience is and what viewers would like to see, industry culture, genre conventions, the producers' own knowledge of human relationships, and more general cultural standards in a given social context (Levine 2001). In fact, as we saw in Chapter 3, most media are commercially organized to attract audiences for profit, so there is good reason to believe that popularity will be more important to media producers than a commitment to any specific ideology beyond the promotion of consumerism. So our investigation of the ideology of media does not mean that producers are consciously trying to sell certain ways of thinking and being. Ideology is produced not only by committed ideologues. As we will see, we can find ideology in our everyday lives, in our definition of common sense, and in the construction of a consensus.

THEORETICAL ROOTS
OF IDEOLOGICAL ANALYSIS

The analysis of ideology can be traced back to the works of Karl Marx and, especially, to 20th-century European Marxism. The analysis has evolved over time, maintaining some elements of its Marxist origin while developing more complexity and nuance. In what follows, we take a look at the evolution of ideological analysis, starting with its Marxist origins. This work is relevant insofar as it helps uncover a specific view of how society functions—that privilege and power are connected to one's position in the economy and class structure.

Early Marxist Origins

For early Marxists, the discussion of ideology was connected to the concept of "false consciousness." Ideology was seen as a powerful mechanism of social control whereby members of the ruling class imposed their worldview, which represented their interests, on members of subordinate classes. In such a system, the subordinate classes who accepted the basic ideology of the ruling class were said to have false consciousness because their worldview served the interests of others. For Marx and early Marxists, social revolution depended on the working class breaking free of the ideas of the ruling class—moving beyond their false consciousness—and developing a "revolutionary" consciousness that represented their material interests as workers. This new way of thinking would then stand in opposition to the ruling ideology, which promoted the economic interests of the capitalist class. (Later, scholars looked beyond the economy and the class structure to analyze how privilege and power are distributed according to other identity factors, such as race, gender, and sexual identity.)

In this context, ideology was understood to involve having ideas that were "false" because they did not match one's objective class interests. One of the ways capitalists ruled industrial society was by imposing on the working class a worldview that served the interests of capitalists yet pretended to describe the experiences of all humankind. For example, owners often used a divide-and-conquer strategy in stoking conflict among workers by promoting resentment and hatred toward racial minorities and recent immigrants. In the United States, white workers often came to believe that their biggest problem was minorities or immigrants taking away their jobs. As long as this belief was dominant, employers knew that internal divisions among workers would prevent effective organizing for better pay and working conditions. For workers, holding such beliefs actually worked against their own economic interests.

Ideology, then, was about mystification, the masking of interests, and the conflation of the particular and the universal. Moreover, ideology could be understood in straightforward economic-class terms. Capitalists had a class interest in the accumulation of capital through the exploitation of labor. Their ideology, which celebrated individualism and the free market, was a result of their economic interests. Workers had a class interest in fundamentally changing the conditions of their work and restructuring the social relations of production; this could be accomplished by a social revolution—a collective response and a regulation of markets. Any system of ideas that did not recognize these economic realities, according to an early school of Marxism, was the result of the ideological power of capitalists. Ideological analysis, from this perspective, meant identifying the ways working people's ideas failed to reflect their class interests; in essence, it was about pointing out how consciousness was "false" and in need of correction.

The critique of ideology has evolved a great deal from its connections to the concept of false consciousness, but it still maintains some of the basic outlines of the early Marxist model. Ideological analysis is still concerned about questions of power and the ways in which systems of meaning—ideologies—are part of the process of wielding power. And ideological analysis continues to focus on the question of domination and the ways certain groups fight to have their specific interests accepted as the general interests of a society. But the contemporary study of ideology is more theoretically sophisticated, paying attention to the ongoing nature of ideological struggles and to how people negotiate with, and even oppose, the ideologies of the powerful. Ideas are not simply false, and the connection between ideas and economic interest is not necessarily straightforward. In fact, much of the contemporary study of ideology has moved away from a focus on economic-class relations toward a more dynamic conceptualization of the terrain of culture.

Hegemony

The key theoretical concept that animates much of the contemporary study of the ideology of media is *hegemony*. Drawn from the work of Antonio Gramsci (1928/1971), an Italian Marxist who wrote in the 1920s and 1930s, the notion of hegemony connects questions of culture, power, and ideology. Gramsci argued that ruling groups can maintain their power through force, consent, or a combination of the two. Ruling by way of force requires the use of institutions such as the military and the police in an effort to physically coerce—or threaten coercion—so that people will remain obedient. There is no shortage of historical examples of societies in which the use of force and the threat of even more severe forms of coercion have been the principal strategy of ruling. The military dictatorship is the most obvious example.

Gramsci (1971) noted, however, that power can be wielded at the level of culture or ideology, not just through the use of force. In liberal democratic societies, such as the United States, force is not the primary means by which the powerful rule. Certainly there are important examples of the use of force—turn-of-the-century efforts to crush the labor movement, the internment of Japanese Americans during World War II, the incarceration of members of the Communist Party in the 1950s, the violence directed at the Black Panther Party in the 1960s, the detention of hundreds of Muslim men after 9/11. But these examples stand out because the use of physical force is not the routine strategy for maintaining social order. Instead, Gramsci's work suggests that power is wielded in a different arena—that of culture in the realm of everyday life—where people essentially agree to current social arrangements.

Consent, then, is the key to understanding Gramsci's use of hegemony, which is exercised through a kind of cultural leadership. Consent is something that is won; ruling groups in a society actively seek to have their worldview accepted by all members of society as the universal way of thinking. Institutions such as schools, religion, and the media help the powerful exercise this cultural leadership because they are the sites where we produce and reproduce ways of thinking about society.

Hegemony, though, is not simply about ideological domination, whereby the ideas of one group are imposed on another. Instead, the process is far subtler. Hegemony operates at the level of common sense in the assumptions we make about social life and on the terrain of things that we accept as "natural" or "the way things are." After all, what is common sense except for those things we think are so obvious that we need not critically evaluate them? Common sense is the way we describe things that "everybody knows," or at least should know, because such knowledge represents deeply held cultural beliefs. In fact, when we employ the rhetoric of common sense, it is usually to dismiss alternative approaches that go against our basic assumptions about how things work. Gramsci (1971) reminds us that one of the most effective ways of ruling is through the shaping of commonsense assumptions. What we take for granted exists in a realm that is uncontested, where there is neither need nor room for questioning assumptions (Gamson, Croteau, Hoynes, and Sasson 1992).

Hegemony theorists remind us that commonsense assumptions, the taken for granted, are social constructions. They imply a particular understanding of the social world, and such visions have consequences. It is common sense, for example, that "you can't fight city hall" or that women are better nurturers than men or that "moderate" positions are more reasonable than "extreme" positions. When people adopt common-sense assumptions—as they do with a wide range of ideas—they are also accepting a certain set of beliefs, or ideology, about social relations.

A similar dynamic applies to what we think of as "natural." Nature is something that we define in opposition to culture because nature is perceived to be beyond human control. We generally think that the "natural" is not a social construction; nature is more enduring and stable than the creations of human societies. Thus, if social structures and social relationships are defined as natural, they take on a kind of permanency and legitimacy that elevates them to the realm of the uncontested. Think about the social relationships we call "natural" (or "unnatural"). Is it natural that some people are rich and some are poor, that people will not care about politics, or that people of different racial and ethnic backgrounds will prefer to live with their own groups? If these conditions are simply natural, then there is little reason to be concerned about economic inequality, political apathy, or residential segregation because they are not social problems but the natural order of things.

Let's look at some more controversial claims about the natural. One of the principal underpinnings of racist ideology is the belief that one race is naturally superior to others. Sexism rests on the assumption that men and women, by nature, are suited to different and unequal tasks. And contemporary discussions of sexuality are filled with claims about the "natural" status of heterosexual relationships and the "unnatural" status of gay and lesbian relationships. These examples illustrate how claims about nature work in the service of ideology. If such claims are widely accepted—if they are seen as the outcome of nature instead of culture—then there may be legitimate reason for racial inequality, sexual discrimination, and the demonization of lesbian gay, bisexual, and transgender (LGBT) people as these relationships are the result of the natural order of things. What we think of as natural and normal, then, is a central part of the terrain of hegemony.

Hegemony, however, is neither permanent nor unalterable. Gramsci (1971) understood it as a process that was always in the making. To effectively wield power through consent, ideological work through cultural leadership is an ongoing necessity. The terrain of common sense and the natural must be continually reinforced because people's actual experiences will lead them to question dominant ideological assumptions. People are active agents, and modern society is full of contradictions; therefore, hegemony can never be complete or final. Some people will not accept the basic hegemonic worldview, some people may resist it, and changing historical conditions will make certain aspects of hegemonic ideology untenable. Ultimately, Gramsci saw hegemony as a daily struggle about our underlying conceptions of the world, a struggle always subject to revision and opposition. Rulers who try to maintain their power by defining the assumptions on which the society rests work to bring stability and legitimacy and to incorporate potentially opposing forces into the basic ideological framework. In a striking example, images of rebellion from the 1960s have become incorporated into our democratic story and now are used to sell cars and clothing.

Sociologist Stuart Hall, the leading voice of British cultural studies, provided a sophisticated analysis of how media institutions fit into this conception of hegemony. He argued that media are one of the principal sites where the cultural leadership, the work of hegemony, is exercised. Media are involved in what Hall called "the politics of signification," in which the media produce images of the world that give events particular meanings. Media images do not simply reflect the world, they *re-present* it; instead of reproducing the "reality" of the world "out there," the media engage in practices that define reality. As Hall (1982) put it, "Representation is a very different notion from that of reflection. It implies the active work of selecting and presenting, of structuring and shaping; not merely the transmitting of an already-existing meaning, but the more active labour of *making things mean*" (p. 64).

Media representations are intertwined with questions of power and ideology because the process of giving meaning to events suggests that, potentially, there are multiple definitions of reality. For example, a workers' strike can be represented in several competing ways. The personal stories of the workers or an interview with a union leader can give a positive picture of the strikers. Reports highlighting statements from the company's management may shed negative light on the strike. A story that focuses on the inconvenience caused to the general public can make the issues involved in the conflict seem irrelevant. In *Prime Time Activism*, media sociologist Charlotte Ryan (1991) recalled her early activity as a union organizer in a public hospital. Every evening, after leaving the picket line, union activists would run home to watch the news on television to see how their efforts had been represented on the local news: Was the workers' or the company's perspective emphasized? How were the workers on strike represented?

Media have, as Hall (1982) said, "the power to signify events in a particular way." The question, then, is, "What are the patterns by which events are represented?" This is fundamentally a question about ideology because it suggests that media are places where certain ideas are circulated as the truth, effectively marginalizing or dismissing competing truth claims. Many scholars argue that media generally adopt the dominant assumptions and draw on the commonsensical views of the world that everyone knows. As a result, media representations, while not fully closed, have the tendency to reproduce the basic stories and values that are the underpinnings of this hegemony. For example, according to sociologist Austin Johnson (2016), even as transgender people have become more visible in popular media, their experiences have been depicted through a "transnormative" lens. Analyzing a group of documentary films about trans lives, Johnson finds that the films emphasize a medical model for explaining transgender identity. Johnson describes transnormativity as "a hegemonic ideology that structures transgender experience, identification, and narratives into a hierarchy of legitimacy" (p. 466) that is rooted in a medical explanation. Johnson argues that the media circulation of this transnormative ideology is consequential as it squeezes out alternative understandings of transgender experience, particularly those that are not rooted in a medical model. Ultimately, the ideology of transgender life presented in contemporary media participates in broader cultural conflicts about gender conformity and sexual identity, offering a particular perspective on, for example, the continuing debate about access to public bathrooms.

Media are, without doubt, not simple agents of the powerful—such as political leaders, major corporate actors, or cultural and religious authorities. As we will explore further in Chapter 8, the ideas of the powerful are not simply imposed on readers or viewers. Media are cultural sites where the ideas of the powerful are circulated and where they can be contested. Social change activists and social movements, for example, regularly seek to challenge the ideas of the powerful in the media (Andrews and Caren 2010; Lievrouw, 2011; Ryan 1991). As we move from a theoretical discussion of media, ideology, and hegemony to specific cases that illustrate the ideology of media products, we will see the complex ways in which media products are a part of larger ideological debates.

The U.S. media's assumptions about the world are discernible when we consider the perspectives used in foreign media. For example, the English-language version of Qatar-based *Al Jazeera* (available in the United States, http://english.aljazeera.net) hosts a regular investigative unit that aims to "reveal secrets and expose truths surrounded by silence," a documentary series *People and Power* that "looks at the use and abuse of power," and a regular program *Empire*, that "reports on and debates global powers on behalf of an international citizen." Such programs often present an approach distinctly different from popular U.S. news media.

NEWS MEDIA AND THE LIMITS OF DEBATE

For decades, Americans have debated the politics of the news media, with criticisms of the news coming with equal vigor from both sides of the political spectrum. The underlying assumption in this debate is that news media are, in fact, ideological; the selection of issues, stories, and sources is inescapably value laden. Although media outlets fend off attacks from the political right that they are too liberal and attacks from the left that they are too conservative, journalists find themselves precisely where they want to be: in the middle. This middle ground serves as a haven for reporters, a place that is perceived as being without ideology. After all, if ideological criticism comes from both sides, then the news must not be ideological at all. Attacks from both sides make the center a defensible place.

Because we generally associate ideology with ideas that are perceived to be extreme, those in the middle are viewed as pragmatic rather than as ideological. And as ideology is something to be avoided, the journalistic middle ground becomes safe. There is good reason for journalists to want to occupy this territory. It insulates them from criticism and gives the news legitimacy with a wide range of readers and viewers who see themselves as occupying some version of a middle ground.

However, the notion that the news reflects the "consensus" is itself ideological because news does the active work of defining that consensus. Once that consensus is defined, the claim that reporting is a mere reflection of an already existing consensus is blind to the ways such definitions work to solidify it. We might say the same thing about the journalistic center. The news does not so much occupy the middle ground as define what the middle ground is. In the process, news reporting effectively defends the legitimacy of this worldview, which is oriented to the reproduction of current social arrangements. In short, the middle ground is ideological precisely because it is a cultural site where commonsense assumptions are produced, reproduced, and circulated.

Elites and Insiders

A large body of scholarly literature has explored the ways in which news media produce ideological visions of the nation and the world. One of the principal findings of this research is that news focuses on powerful people and institutions and generally reflects established interests. Whether this makes news "liberal" or "conservative" is another matter; some claim "the establishment" is liberal, whereas others argue that it is conservative. In either case, our reading of the research literature suggests that news reaffirms the basic social order and the values and assumptions it is based on.

In his classic work *Deciding What's News,* sociologist Herbert Gans (2004) found that two of the most prominent enduring values in the news are *social order* and *national leadership.* This focus on order and leadership gives the news a view of society that is both moderate and supportive of the established hierarchy. As Gans notes,

> [W]ith some oversimplification, it would be fair to say that the news supports the social order of public, business and professional, upper-middle-class, middle-aged, and white male sectors of society. . . . In short, when all other things are equal, the news pays most attention to and upholds the actions of elite individuals and elite institutions. (p. 61)

With its focus on elites, news presents images of the world that are significantly lacking in diversity. This has substantial consequences for the way the news depicts the political world. Politics, according to most major news media, is not about broad questions of power—who wields it, in what arenas, under what circumstances, with what consequences—nor is it a forum for wide-ranging debate and controversy about current events. Instead, politics is framed as an insider's debate, with only a privileged few invited to the table.

The "insider" nature of political news means that a small group of analysts are regular commentators and news sources, regardless of the wisdom of their previous commentary or of their prior actions when they occupied positions of power. To be—or to have been—an insider, with access to powerful circles, makes one a de facto "expert" as far as the news is concerned. As a result, individuals are qualified to comment on and analyze current events to the extent to which they are or have been insiders. The "debates" we see in the news, therefore, are often among insiders who share a common commitment to traditional politics to the exclusion of those outside the constructed consensus.

The range of insiders invited to discuss issues is often so narrow that a host of unaddressed assumptions are implicit in their approach. For example, debating the effectiveness of U.S. drone attacks in Pakistan, Yemen, and Somalia in 2018 ignores a variety of assumptions about the consequences of this kind of military action in the first place. Debating President Trump's 2017 attempt to repeal the Affordable Care Act versus Democratic efforts to protect "Obamacare" neglects other possible alternatives, such as a single-payer system. The result is that contrasting perspectives in the news frequently represent the differences—generally quite narrow—between establishment insiders. This approach to the news does little to inform the public of positions outside this limited range of opinion. More important, it implicitly denies that other positions should be taken seriously. Ultimately, one principal way the news is ideological is in drawing boundaries between what is acceptable—the conventional ideas of insiders—and what is not.

Economic News as Ideological Construct

News coverage of economic issues is remarkable in the way it reproduces a profoundly ideological view of the world. Most news coverage of the economy is by and about the business community (Croteau and Hoynes 1994). Although individuals can play a range of roles in economic life—worker, consumer, citizen, or investor—economic news focuses overwhelmingly on the activities and interests of investors. One of the most striking examples of this phenomenon is the fact that virtually every newspaper has a Business section, whereas almost none has a Consumer or Labor section. As a result, economic news is largely business news, and business news is directed at corporate actors and investors.

In this kind of news, the ups and downs of the stock market are often the centerpiece, serving as an indicator of the economic health of the country. But, in fact, about half of American households own no stock whatsoever (Wolff 2017), and more than 80 percent of stocks in the United States are owned by just the wealthiest 10 percent of households (Cohen 2018). By equating economic health with the fortunes of investors, news tips its ideological hand. Such definitions fail to recognize that different groups of people can have different economic interests. Although a rise in the stock market is depicted as positive economic news for the country as a whole, there are clearly losers even when the market soars. For example, a rise in corporate profitability may be the result of an increase in productivity, which in turn may be accompanied by extensive layoffs. When business news programs cover corporate layoffs, stories often focus on the implications of such layoffs for stock performance. Or, as we have seen in the last few years, soaring stock prices can be fueled by growing consumer debt. Focusing primarily on the health of companies that sell goods and services neglects the long-term effects of this growing debt burden on ordinary Americans.

The government bailout and recession that followed the economic crisis of 2008 is another striking example of the top-down view and preoccupation with investors that dominates economic news reporting. In a comprehensive study of media coverage from February to August 2009, the Project for Excellence in Journalism (PEJ 2009: 1) found that

> the gravest economic crisis since the Great Depression has been covered in the media largely from the top down, told primarily from the perspective of the Obama Administration and big business, and reflected the voices and ideas of people in institutions more than those of everyday Americans.

The study found that corporate voices were the most common source in news stories, appearing in about 40 percent of the coverage, whereas representatives of labor unions were "virtually shut out of the coverage entirely" (p. 8), appearing in just 2 percent of the stories. Further, the study found that when the interests of investors were threatened—as indicated by stock market declines—the media dramatically increased its economic coverage. Once that threat to investors had receded and the stock market rose, economic coverage—as a percentage of the "news hole" or amount of time and space devoted to news—declined accordingly (see Figure 6.1). Meanwhile, though, millions of ordinary Americans faced continuing economic uncertainty and unemployment.

The U.S. media were not alone in presenting narrow economic coverage during the economic crisis. One study of British news outlets concluded that, despite the massive meltdown of the global capitalist economy, "the range of stories and the form of reporting presented a fairly homogeneous array of messages which, with only a few exceptions, promoted or at least did not question the dominant free-market ideology" (Robertson 2010).

Let's hypothetically turn the tables on this traditional way of viewing economic news. What if coverage of the economy focused predominantly on the experiences and interests of workers, evaluating economic health from the standpoint of working conditions and highlighting the economic analysis of labor union officials? It would likely be labeled "anti-business" or "pro-labor" and be targeted by critics for its "biased" reporting. It would, in short, be identified as providing a fundamentally ideological view of the economy. It is striking, however, that the news media's emphasis on the corporate and investor perspective is generally accepted as the appropriate way to cover the economy. Indeed, the dominance of the business worldview in economic news coverage is so complete that it seems natural. We take it for granted, assuming that the economy equals corporate America and that economic health is equivalent to investor satisfaction. No conscious effort at manipulation is being made here, but it is a clear example of the ways media products draw on and reproduce a hegemonic ideology.

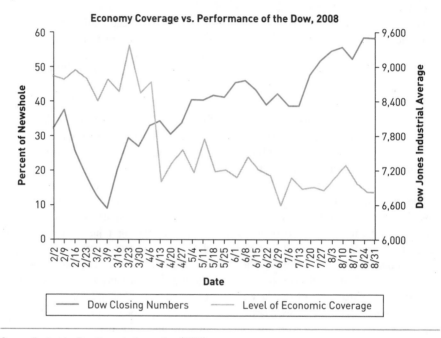

FIGURE 6.1   ■   Economic Coverage and the Threat to Investors

The media's economic coverage tends to highlight a top-down, investor perspective, neglecting ordinary working Americans. The economic crisis of 2008 threatened investors by producing a plunge in the stock market and elevated levels of economic coverage in the media. After government bailouts of Wall Street firms led to rising stock prices and the threat to investors was reduced, the media's coverage of the economic crisis declined dramatically, despite the fact that ordinary Americans saw little or no improvement in their economic fortunes at that time.

Source: Project for Excellence in Journalism (2009).

MOVIES, THE MILITARY, AND MASCULINITY

One of the difficulties of ideological analysis of media products is that there is no singular media. The term *media*, we should reiterate, is plural, signifying the multiple organizations and technologies that make up our media environment. As a result, we have to be careful when we make generalizations about the ideological content of media in large part because we are usually talking about a specific medium and perhaps even specific media texts. Another challenge for ideological analysis is that media texts are produced in specific historical contexts, responding to and helping frame the cultural currents of the day. Mass-mediated images are not static; they change in form and content in ways that are observable. Ideological analysis, therefore, needs to pay attention to the shifts in media images—sometimes subtle and sometimes quite dramatic—to allow for the dynamic nature of media.

If the study of media and ideology needs to be both historically specific and wary of over-generalizing from single texts, what analytic strategies have proved useful? One of the most common approaches is to focus on specific types or genres of media, such as the television sitcom, the Hollywood horror film, or the romance novel. Because texts within the same genre adopt the same basic conventions, analysts can examine the underlying themes and ideas embedded within these conventional formats without worrying that any contradictions they might uncover are the result of the distinct modes of storytelling of different genres. The result is that most scholarly studies of media ideology are both quite specific about their subject matter and narrow in their claims, focusing on issues such as the messages about gender in television cooking shows (Matwick & Matwick 2015), meanings of global political conflict in popular film (De Lissovoy, Ramaprasad, Cedillo, and Cook 2017), or ideas about militarism in video games (Robinson 2016).

In addition, scholarly studies of media texts generally either focus on a specific historical period—for example, foreign policy news in the Reagan era (Herman and Chomsky 2002)—or provide comparisons of one genre of media across several time periods—for example, best-selling books from the 1940s through the 1970s (Long 1985). These analyses provide, on one hand, an understanding of how a specific medium displays a particular worldview or ideological conflict and, on the other hand, an understanding of how such stories about society change over time in different historical contexts.

Two film genres in a particular historical period—action-adventure and military/war films from the 1980s and early 1990s—are worth exploring for their underlying ideological orientation because of their popularity. With action-adventure movies, such as *Raiders of the Lost Ark* and *Romancing the Stone*, and military movies, such as *Rambo* and *Top Gun*, attracting large audiences—and inspiring sequels and seemingly endless imitators—scholars have used an ideological framework to understand the underlying messages in these films. What are these movies about, and why were they so attractive to American audiences of this period? In other words, what are the ideologies of these films, and how do these ways of seeing the world fit within broader ideological currents? These questions help both interpret the films and locate their meanings in a social context.

Action-Adventure Films

Action-adventure films were among the most popular movies of the 1980s. Many of the most popular films in the genre produced sequels or later remakes, so they are likely familiar to audiences today. The four Indiana Jones films, starring Harrison Ford, are the archetype of this genre, in which the male hero performs remarkable feats that require bravery and skill throughout a fast-paced 90-minute struggle with an evil villain. The hero ultimately emerges triumphant after several close calls, defeating the villain, saving the day, and usually winning the affection of the female lead. One version of this genre places the hero in faraway, exotic lands, making the villains and the action more unpredictable. But the basic story line can be found in films set in the United States, such as *Die Hard*, *Speed*, *Rush Hour*, and *Mission: Impossible.* On one level, these kinds of movies can be thrilling, suspenseful (even though we know, deep down, that the hero will triumph), and even romantic as we watch the hero overcome new challenges and seemingly impossible odds on the road to an exciting and satisfying finish. However, if we dig below the surface of the action, we can explore the kinds of stories these movies tell and how the stories resonate with our contemporary social dilemmas.

Gina Marchetti (1989) argued that the key to the ideology of this genre is the typical construction of the main characters, the hero and the villain, which leads to specific stories about the nature of good and evil, strength and weakness, and courage and cowardice.

One underlying theme of the action-adventure genre is the drawing of rigid lines between "us" and "them," with the villain representing the dangers of difference. There are, of course, many different versions of the central determinant of the in-group and the out-group. Nationality and ethnicity are frequent boundary markers, with white Americans (Michael Douglas, Bruce Willis) defeating dangerous foreigners. In other versions, civilized people triumph over the "primitive" (*Indiana Jones and the Temple of Doom*), or representatives of law and order defeat the deranged (*Speed*).

Ultimately, the hero effectively eliminates the danger represented by "the other"—the difference embodied by the villain—usually by killing the villain in a sensational, climactic scene. Metaphorically speaking, social order is restored by the reassertion of the boundaries between what is acceptable and what is not, with the unacceptable doomed to a well-deserved death. The films go beyond xenophobic demonization of difference, however, by demonstrating the terms on which people who are different can become part of mainstream society. The hero's local accomplices—such as Indiana Jones's child sidekick, Short Round, in *Temple of Doom*—demonstrate that it is possible to be incorporated into mainstream society. This is the flip side of the violent death of the villain: The difference represented by the friend or buddy can be tamed and made acceptable (Marchetti 1989). Difference, then, must be either destroyed or domesticated by integrating the other into the hierarchical social relations of contemporary society, where the newly tamed other will likely reside near the bottom of the hierarchy. Ultimately, the action-adventure genre, with its focus on the personal triumph of the hero, is a tale about the power of the rugged male individual, a mythic figure in the ideology of the American Dream.

Vietnam Films and Recent War Films

One particular 1980s version of the action-adventure genre was the return-to-Vietnam film, symbolized most clearly by the hit movie *Rambo*. In these films—which also include the *Missing in Action* trilogy and *Uncommon Valor*—the hero, a Vietnam veteran, returns to Vietnam a decade after the war to rescue American prisoners of war that the U.S. government has long since abandoned. In the process, the Vietnamese are demonized as brutal enemies who deserve the deaths that the heroes—most notably Sylvester Stallone and Chuck Norris—inflict on the captors as they liberate the prisoners.

The ideological work of these films is not very subtle, and given that they were popular during the presidency of conservative Ronald Reagan, their ideological resonance should not be surprising. In essence, these films provide a mediated refighting of the war, in which Americans are both the good guys and the victors. The films serve as a kind of redemption for a country unable to accept defeat in Vietnam and still struggling with the shame of loss. If the United States did not win the Vietnam War on the battlefield, the movies allow its citizens to return in the world of film fantasy to alter the end of the story. In these stories, there is no longer shame or defeat but instead pride, triumph, and a reaffirmation of national strength. This outlook was, to be sure, part of the appeal of Ronald Reagan, whose campaign for president in 1980 called for a return to a sense of national pride, strength, and purpose that would move the nation beyond "the Vietnam syndrome."

The back-to-Vietnam films were, perhaps most fundamentally, part of the ideological project to overcome the Vietnam syndrome by providing a substitute victory. Susan Jeffords (1989) has argued that these films are about more than our national pride and the reinterpretation of defeat in Vietnam. She makes a persuasive case that the return-to-Vietnam films are part of a larger process of "remasculinization" of American society, another key component of the ideology of the Reagan years, in which a masculinity defined by its toughness is reasserted in the face of the twin threats of the defeat in Vietnam and the growth of feminism.

These Vietnam films are, to Jeffords (1989), fundamentally about the definition of American "manhood" at a time when the traditional tough image had been challenged by the social movements of the 1960s and the defeat in Southeast Asia. The Sylvester Stallone and Chuck Norris characters—Rambo and Braddock—return to Vietnam to recapture their strength and power, all the while resisting and chastising the government for being too weak (read: "feminine") to undertake such courageous missions. The return is as much about returning to a mythical past in which a strong America ruled the world and strong American men ruled their households as it is about rescuing prisoners of war. Rambo and Braddock symbolize the desires of, and provide a mediated and ideologically specific solution for, American men struggling with the changing social landscape of the 1980s.

Such popular media images are not simply innocent fantasies for our viewing entertainment. If we read these films in ideological

Wikimedia Commons/Chief Mass Communication Specialist Kathryn Whittenberger, U.S. Navy

terms, both the film texts themselves and their popularity tell us something about American culture and society in the 1980s. The masculine/military films of the time both reflected the fears and desires of American men and helped reproduce a new brand of toughness that became prevalent in the 1990s. The films were part of a political culture that created the conditions for the popular 1989 invasion of Panama and the even more popular 1991 war in the Persian Gulf, where TV news images did not differ much from those in the 1986 hit film *Top Gun*. Americans did overcome the Vietnam syndrome in the late 1980s, as symbolized by the willingness of the population to support military action in Panama, Iraq, and later in the "war against terrorism." Part of the ideological work necessary for that transformation was performed by popular Hollywood films.

By the 2000s, though, real-world events challenged the simple Hollywood vision of war. The vulnerability of the United States to a powerfully symbolic terrorist attack on 9/11, the failure to find weapons of mass destruction during the invasion and protracted occupation of Iraq, the emergence of the Islamic State of Iraq and Syria (ISIS), and the continuing war in Afghanistan, in its 17th year at the time of this writing and "at best a grinding stalemate," according to award-winning journalist Steve Coll (Gross 2018), were reflected in a new generation of war movies. Some films, such as *Three Kings* (1999) and *Syriana* (2005), still privileged the perspectives of the American characters and, despite a potentially critical lens, ultimately defined as "abnormal, unacceptable, or impossible" alternative visions of U.S. foreign policy (Fritsch-El Alaoui 2009/2010: 131). The Academy Award–winning film *The Hurt Locker* (2008) glorified the work of explosive ordnance disposal (EOD) teams in a way that simply updated the war films from the

Promoting a brand of tough masculinity common in war films, the 2012 film *Act of Valor* featured plenty of military helicopters, amphibious assault ships, drones, and other taxpayer-financed equipment and personnel, including active duty Navy SEALS. That's because the very ideas for the film, which depicted an elite Naval Special Warfare team's attack on a terrorist compound, originated with the Pentagon as a recruitment project.

1980s and 1990s. But other films, such as *Jarhead* (2005) and *Stop-Loss* (2008), focused on the growing cynicism and despair of U.S. soldiers caught in the seemingly endless cycle of war. In one unique approach, Clint Eastwood's World War II drama *Flags of Our Fathers* (2006) exposed the mythology behind the iconic raising of the U.S. flag at Iwo Jima, whereas his accompanying *Letters from Iwo Jima* (2007) presented the horrors of that battle from a Japanese perspective. In a more recent set of films about contemporary wars, *Eye in the Sky* (2015) explores the ethics of drone warfare, *Billy Lynn's Long Halftime Walk* (2016) suggests that popular stories of soldierly heroism don't capture the reality of the Iraq War, and *Thank You for Your Service* (2017) emphasizes the sustained impact of war on the lives of soldiers after they return home. These recent war films suggest a broader range of approaches than has been common in the past.

TELEVISION, POPULARITY, AND IDEOLOGY

Although certain genres of popular films have been the subject of ideological analysis, it would be fair to say that the whole range of television programming has been studied for its ideological content. In fact, ideological analysis of media is sometimes reduced to the study of television, just as claims about "the media" are often claims about televised images. That's because television has been the dominant form of media. For the moment, this continues to be true even as new forms of online media grow in popularity and even as television viewing habits are changing with DVRs and the streaming of TV programs to computers and mobile devices. In 2018, a top-rated network television program could still be viewed by about 15 million people, and more than 100 million people in the United States watched the 2018 Super Bowl on television. From presidential elections to championship sporting events, from natural disasters to mass shootings, ideas and images still circulate most widely through television.

Television is more than just the most popular medium in terms of audience size. It also regularly comments on popular media. In fact, an astounding number of television programs have been, at least in part, about the media (see Figure 6.2). In addition, talk shows and entertainment-oriented programs focus on the lives of media celebrities and the ins and outs of the television, film, and music worlds. With popular media as the subject and setting for so much programming, television is a virtual running commentary on the media world. Television is often so self-referential—or at least media centered—that the programs assume that viewers are deeply engaged with the culture of media, and the humor often requires knowledge of the specific media reference. Our exposure to television and its self-referential "winking" about popular culture have made most of us rather skilled viewers who catch the references and know what they are all about.

Television and Reality

If television is as central to our mediated culture as a broad range of scholars maintain, then the underlying ideas that television programs disseminate are of substantial social significance. What stories does television tell us about contemporary society? How does television define key social categories, depict major institutions, or portray different types of people? What is "normal" in the world of television, and what is "deviant"?

FIGURE 6.2 ■ Select Television Programs about the Media

Program	Network (Dates)	Featured Media Setting or Occupation
The Dick Van Dyke Show	CBS (1961–1966)	Writer for a comedy/variety TV show
The Partridge Family	ABC (1970–1974)	Musicians
The Mary Tyler Moore Show	CBS (1970–1977)	Local TV station
Lou Grant	CBS (1977–1982)	Major newspaper office
WKRP in Cincinnati	CBS (1978–1982)	Radio station
Family Ties	NBC (1982–1989)	Public television station
Murphy Brown	CBS (1988–1998)	Network newsmagazine
Home Improvement	ABC (1991–1999)	Home improvement TV show
The Larry Sanders Show	HBO (1992–1998)	Late-night talk show
Mad about You	NBC (1992–1999)	Documentary film maker
Frasier	NBC (1993–2004)	Radio call-in program
News Radio	NBC (1995–1999)	All-news radio station
Everybody Loves Raymond	CBS (1996–2005)	Newspaper sports writer
Just Shoot Me	NBC (1997–2003)	Fashion magazine
Sports Night	ABC (1998–2000)	Sports news TV show
Curb Your Enthusiasm	HBO (2000–2011, 2017)	TV writer
Entourage	HBO (2004–2011)	Hollywood film star
Extras	HBO (2005–2007)	Movie industry
How I Met Your Mother	NBC (2005–2014)	TV reporter
Ugly Betty	ABC (2006–2010)	Fashion magazine
30 Rock	NBC (2006–2013)	Sketch comedy program
Flight of the Conchords	HBO (2007–2009)	Musicians
Mad Men	AMC (2007–2015)	Advertising agency
The Newsroom	HBO (2012–2014)	Cable news station
Good Girls Revolt	Amazon (2015–2016)	News magazine
Catastrophe	Amazon (2015–2018)	Advertising executive
Great News	NBC (2017–2018)	Television news
Ten Days in the Valley	ABC (2017–2018)	Television producer
The Mayor	ABC (2017–2018)	Aspiring rapper

Source: Project for Excellence in Journalism (2009).

One reason why television is often considered to be so ideologically charged is that it relies, almost exclusively, on conventional, "realist" forms of image construction that mask the workings of the camera. As a result, the family sitcom invites us to drop in at the home of our electronic neighbors, and the courtroom drama allows us to sit in on a trial. Most of us do not consciously mistake such families and courtrooms for "real life"; we would not confuse these televised images with our real neighbors, for example. Still, part of the allure of television is that it seems real; we routinely suspend disbelief while we are watching. The pleasures of television are a result of our ability to temporarily ignore our knowledge that there is no *NCIS* forensic scientist named Abby Sciuto, there is no Olivia Pope & Associates crisis communications firm, and Westworld does not exist.

The ideological work of television, then, lies in the ways it defines and orders its pictures of "reality"—in its claims to reflect the humor and hardships of family life, the dangers of police work, the fun and confusion of 20-something single life, or the drama of the courtroom. This reality is created and packaged by writers and producers with the goal of attracting a loyal audience. The images are not simple reflections of an unproblematic reality but representations of a world that is not as orderly as a 30- or 60-minute program.

In striving for popularity, the television producers have often adopted the strategy of least objectionable programming, whereby programs are intended to avoid controversy and remain politically bland. This approach is, itself, ideological; blandness favors certain images and stories and pushes others to the margins or off the air entirely. This is one reason why, for example, television programs typically avoid dealing with topics like abortion or religious beliefs—both of which could be seen as controversial.

It is difficult, however, to make broad generalizations about the ideology of television programming beyond the observation that network executives want popularity without controversy. This formula for programs reaffirms the dominant norms of contemporary society. For a more nuanced understanding of how television programs are ideological and how they respond to the often volatile social and political world, we need to look more carefully at a particular genre of programming. Ella Taylor's (1989) study of the changing image of the family on prime-time television from the 1950s through the 1980s provides a clear example of the ideological twists and turns of network television.

Television and the Changing American Family

Beginning in the 1950s and 1960s, domestic life as represented by programs such as *Leave It to Beaver*, *Ozzie and Harriet*, and *Father Knows Best*, along with zanier fare such as *Bewitched* and *I Dream of Jeannie*, was predominantly white, middle class, happy, and secure. Network television presented the suburban family as the core of the modern, postscarcity society—a kind of suburban utopia where social problems were easily solved (or nonexistent); consensus ruled; and signs of racial, ethnic, or class differences or conflict were difficult to find. Taylor (1989) suggests that if, indeed, such families existed, they were precisely the people whom network advertisers sought. Still, this image of the postwar family—and the not-so-subtle suggestion that this was what a "normal" family looked like—was a particular story masked as a universal one. Certainly, these families were not typical American families, no matter how often they were served up as such.

The television family did not remain static, however; changing social conditions and new marketing strategies in the television industry helped create competing domestic images. The biggest change came in the 1970s with what Taylor (1989) calls the "turn to relevance," when the television family became a site where contemporary social and political issues were explored. The program that epitomized the new breed was Norman Lear's *All in the Family*, which was expected to flop yet became one of the most popular and profitable shows of the decade. The program revolved around the ongoing tension among a cast of diverse characters in their Queens, New York, home. These included Archie Bunker, a stereotypical white, working-class bigot; his strong but decidedly unliberated wife, Edith; their feminist daughter, Gloria; and her husband, Michael, a sociology graduate student with leftist political views. From week to week, Archie and Michael argued over race relations, the proper role of women in society, American foreign policy, and even what kind of food to eat. Throughout the political debates, the main characters traded insults and vented their anger at each other, while Archie waxed nostalgic over the good old days of the 1950s and Gloria and Michael looked nervously at their futures. Programs such as *The Jeffersons* and *Maude*, both *All in the Family* spin-offs, as well as *Sanford and Son* and *Good Times*—among the most popular programs of the mid-1970s—may have been less acerbic than *All in the Family*, but they were all a far cry from the previous generation of conflict-free, white, middle-class family images.

By the middle of the 1970s, the image of the family was neither all white nor all middle class, and domestic life was no longer a utopia; instead, the family was depicted as a source of conflict and struggle as well as comfort and love. In short, social problems made their way into the television family. Taylor (1989) argues that the key to this change was the networks' desire, particularly at CBS, to target young, urban, highly educated viewers—an audience that was highly coveted by advertisers. The new image of the family, self-consciously "relevant" instead of bland and nostalgic, was perceived to be attractive to the youthful consumers who had lived through the social turbulence of the 1960s. But television's ideological change was slow and in many respects subtle. Nostalgic programs that presented the ideal middle-class family were also popular in the 1970s—*Happy Days* is a classic example.

At the same time that the television family was losing its blissful image in the 1970s, a new version of family appeared in the world of work. In programs such as *M*A*S*H*, *The Mary Tyler Moore Show*, *Taxi*, and *Barney Miller*, the setting was not the home; instead, the programs revolved around the relationships among coworkers that Taylor (1989) calls a "work-family." In these programs, the workplace became a place where people found support, community, and loyalty and served as an often warm and fuzzy kind of family for people who were much more connected to their work than to their home lives. Taylor argues that the image of the work-family was popular precisely because of broad cultural anxiety about the changing boundaries between private life and public life in the 1970s, particularly for young professionals seeking prestige and success. Work-families, in essence, provided a picture of a safe haven from domestic conflicts in both the world of television and the experiences of viewers.

Given the growing rationalization of the American workplace in the 1970s, when more men and women came to work in large, bureaucratic organizations, finding images of the family in the workplace is surprising. Taylor (1989) argues that the popularity of the work-family programs tells us a great deal about the social role of television:

If we understand the television narrative as a commentary on, and resolution of, our troubles rather than a reflection of the real conditions of our lives, it becomes possible to read the television work-family as a critique of the alienating modern corporate world and an affirmation of the possibility of community and cooperation amid the loose and fragmentary ties of association. (p. 153)

Of course, the neat and orderly resolution of social dilemmas is precisely the area in which television is ideological. In this case, network television presented images of domestic conflict but resolved them in the workplace through a professional, career-oriented ideology that reassured us that, despite change, everything would be OK. In the end, even as it incorporated conflict and relevance into its field of vision, television still gave viewers satisfying families and happy endings that affirmed the basic outlines of the American Dream.

The last few decades have presented television viewers with conflicting visions of family life. In the 1990s, popular programs included everything from the nostalgic

Bob D'Amico/Getty Images

Wonder Years and the idyllic *Cosby Show* to the cynical *Married with Children* and the sober *Grace under Fire*. In the 2000s, the dysfunctional animated families of *The Simpsons* and *Family Guy*, the secret-filled lives of well-off suburbanites in *Desperate Housewives*, and the sober, two-career family of *Friday Night Lights* were among the programs that vied for viewer attention. Programs with a variety of family structures became common, including *Gilmore Girls* (single mother), *Two and a Half Men* (single father), *Modern Family* (same-sex parents, multiethnic parents), *The Fosters* (multiethnic, blended family), and *This Is Us* (multiracial, adoptive family). Single-parent families, two-career families, same-sex parents, and blended families are all part of the universe of television families today.

Television's early days featured "traditional," white, two-parent, heterosexual families exclusively, while today's programs feature a wider variety of families. The popular long-running program *Modern Family* features several family types, including a same-sex couple who adopted a child—something that would have been unthinkable on U.S. television in an earlier era.

The ever-changing family images show that television programs and the ideology they circulate are far from static. In the midst of cultural conflict over the meaning of family today, network television images are, themselves, part of the ongoing ideological contest to shape the definition of a proper family.

Revising Tradition: The New Momism

Amid the newly diverse images of American families that now populate the media, some traditional ideas remain prominent. In particular, the perfect mother who featured notably in 1950s television has been resurrected, revised, and distributed across media platforms in what Douglas and Michaels (2004) call the "new momism." Ads, movies, and magazines show mothers changing diapers, taking care of their children, and looking after the house, but now they also show mothers going to the gym, pursuing careers, and looking sexy. Usually media show "perfect" mothers, such as when glossy magazines celebrate celebrity moms, highlighting both their accomplishments and their splendid bodies while distributing advice on how to be a "good" mother. Douglas and Michaels (2004) argued that the "new momism" involves a "set of ideas, norms, and practices, most frequently and powerfully represented in the media, that seem on the surface to celebrate motherhood, but which in reality promulgate standards of perfection that are beyond our reach" (pp. 4–5). According to Douglas and Michaels, this "new momism," grounded in the feminist belief that women have autonomy and can make choices about their lives, actually contradicts feminism by implying that the only enlightened choice for a woman is to become a mother.

More broadly, argued Douglas and Michaels, motherhood has been under the media spotlight across media platforms. An ideology of motherhood that romanticizes and commercializes the figure of mothers can be found in magazines such as *Parents* and *Working Mother*, television shows like *Mom* and *Odd Mom Out*, talk radio programs like *Dr. Laura*, as well as advertising images and news segments. These media images perform classic ideological functions by setting standards of perfection and prescribing what a "good mother" should do. In addition, media representations of mothers instill a sense of threat in contemporary mothers: Being compared to "perfect" models, many are likely to end up feeling inadequate and constantly under surveillance. According to Douglas and Michaels, this media obsession with motherhood is fueled by specific media dynamics, most notably the interest of producers and advertisers in reaching a target audience of working women.

This orientation has extended onto the internet as well. For example, early "Mommy blogs" served as a space for mothers to discuss the challenges and dilemmas of motherhood. With names like "Rage against the Minivan," these sites often fostered supportive communities who shared their own experiences affirming, as one writer put it, "I've been there. It's awful. You will survive." Over time, though, advertisers identified the most popular of these blogs and began sponsoring their content. Sites that built a following confessing to the underside of parenthood became places with perfectly staged photos loaded with product placements. As one person involved in blogging put it, "Companies don't want to align themselves with the difficulties of motherhood. They want to align themselves with people who are winning." The idealized, commercialized, "perfect" mother was now online (Bailey 2018).

RAP MUSIC AS IDEOLOGICAL CRITIQUE?

We have seen that media can be analyzed in ideological terms, but media products are not ideologically uniform. They are both contradictory and subject to change. In short, there is no single ideology embedded within media texts. Even so, most media can be seen as sites where facets of the dominant version of the American story—an ideology that essentially sustains the current social order of our capitalist and democratic society— are displayed, reworked, and sometimes contested. At the same time, conventional norms and mainstream values are generally reaffirmed, even if in slightly modified form, by those media texts—news, popular films, and network television—that seek large audiences. Thus, hegemony is constructed, perhaps challenged, and reasserted on a daily basis through the products of our media. But is it possible for widely circulating mass media texts to be oppositional or counterhegemonic? Can media provide challenges to the dominant ways of understanding the social world?

Tricia Rose (1994), in her classic study of the meanings of early rap music (and a follow-up in *The Hip Hop Wars* [2008]), argued that rap should be understood as a mediated critique of the underlying ideology of mainstream American society.

Rap presents an alternative interpretation—a different story—of the ways power and authority are structured in contemporary society. Robin D. G. Kelley (1994) argues that some rap lyrics are "intended to convey a sense of social realism" that "loosely resembles a sort of street ethnography of racist institutions and social practices, but told more often than not in the first person" (p. 190).

Much of early rap music was a critique of institutions such as the criminal justice system, the police, and the educational system, all of which are reinterpreted as sites that both exhibit and reproduce racial inequality. These alternative interpretations are not always explicit; often they are subtle, requiring a form of insider knowledge to fully understand what they are about. Rose (1994) suggested that rap

> uses cloaked speech and disguised cultural codes to comment on and challenge aspects of current power inequalities. . . . Often rendering a nagging critique of various manifestations of power via jokes, stories, gestures, and song, rap's social commentary enacts ideological insubordination. (p. 100)

Although public attention once focused on the anger of "gangsta rap," Rose (1994) pointed out that a much larger body of rap music acts in subtle and indirect ways to refuse dominant ideological assumptions about black youth, urban life, and racial inequality by articulating opposing interpretations of current social relations.

Rap's ideological displacement of the conventional story with new stories is rooted in the inequalities of the social world. Rose (1994) argued that rap's stories—its ways of understanding society in alternative, even oppositional ways—come from the life experiences of black urban youth. In essence, rap presents an ideological critique from below; it is a musical form that criticizes social institutions from the perspective of those who have comparatively little power in contemporary society.

At the same time, rap is full of ideological contradictions. Although some politically radical male rappers critique the institutions of society as being racist, the lyrics and imagery of their music are often sexist and homophobic. They often depict women in degrading ways, including references to violence against women. So even as they are challenging the dominant ideology about race, some black male rappers generally accept and reinforce traditional ideological assumptions about gender roles and sexuality. The discourses within rap music, then, are not unambiguously oppositional in ideological terms.

Rose (1994) noted, however, that the alternative interpretations of social reality in rap lyrics, although partial and contradictory, only partly explain why rap can be understood as a form of ideological critique. Rap music, even that not expressly political in its lyrical content, is part of a broader struggle over the meaning of, and access to, public space. In short, the dominant discourse about rap—one frequently encountered in news media coverage of the rap scene—is connected to a broader discourse about the "spatial control of black people." In the case of rap, the focus is on ways in which the culture of rap, particularly the gathering of large groups of black youth at concerts, is a threat to social order. Rose contended that the very existence of public rap events, at which black youth make claims to their right to occupy public space, is part of an ideological struggle in which the rap community refuses to accept the dominant interpretation of its "threat" to society. It is in such large gatherings, already politicized by the kind of resistance implied by the use of public space, that new forms of expression and new ideas have the potential to emerge. This fight for public space is at the center of what Rose calls rap's "hidden politics."

Rap, of course, is much more than a form of political expression, however contradictory, that circulates within the black community. It is also a highly profitable commercial industry. In fact, rap's commercial success is due, in large part, to the fact that the music is popular among white suburban youth. Whites actually buy more rap and hip-hop music than blacks. This complicates the ideology of rap, making it difficult to simply accept the argument that rap can be "counterhegemonic," a form of resistance to dominant ideological constructions. Such media messages are unlikely to be attractive to upper-middle-class white suburbanites or corporate record companies. Central to Rose's (1994) argument is that the ideology of rap is often masked and is most accessible to those who know the black urban culture that forms its roots. Therefore, black youth may interpret the meaning of rap in ways very different from white youth, even though both may enjoy the music. As we will explore in Part IV, there is good reason to believe that the meanings of rap are multiple and contested. Even so, we are still stuck with the dilemma posed by commercialization.

Is it possible for corporate-produced commercial media products to be fundamentally oppositional in ideological terms? Even rap music—with its critique of the police, schools, and mainstream media—is part of the corporate sector and, as such, is subject to the rules that govern the culture industry. In particular, this means that rap is a commercial product that is packaged and marketed to be sold to demographically specific sets of buyers. To the extent that the music does not sell, it will not be available in the mass market for very long; the musical packages and marketing strategies that do work will lure record companies into strategies of imitation until profits dry up. In short, rap is as much a commercial commodity as it is an intervention in ideological contests.

As it did with the commercialized images of rebellion from the 1960s—Janis Joplin's tongue-in-cheek prayer for a Mercedes was used in ads for Mercedes-Benz cars and an image of John Lennon and Yoko Ono helped market Apple computers—the culture industry is capable of incorporating potentially oppositional forms of expression into the mainstream by turning them into commercial products subject to the rules of the market. By becoming a prominent commercial product that is now routinely used in national advertising campaigns, rap may have lost a good deal of its critical impact. Rap music is now about selling records and products as much as it is a forum for potentially oppositional expression. Still, incorporation into the marketplace is not likely to entirely empty a cultural form, such as rap, of its potential to provide ideological critique, particularly if that critique is disguised in the ways Rose (1994) suggests.

Furthermore, the adoption and adaptation of rap—and the broader hip-hop culture of which it's a part—to reflect local circumstances worldwide has often revived rap's more critical ideological edge (Morgan and Bennett 2011). One example is the work of Tunisian rapper Hamada Ben Amor, known by his MC name, El Général, whose work had long been banned by his government. Just before the Arab Spring uprisings in 2010, El Général released a song on YouTube called "Rais Lebled" ("Head of State") that chronicled the complaints against the repressive government and became what *TIME* magazine called "the rap anthem of the Mideast Revolution." The song and a subsequent one that praised the growing protest movement in Tunisia brought the wrath of the Tunisian government, which arrested El Général, only to release him a week later after political protestors rallied to his cause. After the Tunisian government was overthrown, El Général was invited to perform his anthem live for thousands of young demonstrators.

Ultimately, the example of rap music at home and abroad demonstrates the workings of hegemony. Mass media texts are contradictory; they can be oppositional, presenting ideological alternatives, even as they reproduce specific dominant ideological assumptions. But maintaining even this limited form of critique is difficult. Commercialization is part of the process through which the ideological struggle is waged; even critical media products have a tendency to be (at least partially) incorporated into mass commercial products that accept the boundaries of mainstream definitions of social reality. This is, of course, an ongoing process, and incorporation is never total. But the media industry has proved to be remarkably resilient and innovative—it seems that virtually any form of expression can be tamed enough to be sold to a mass market. But the growth of platforms like YouTube and SoundCloud as sites for music distribution suggests that, under the right circumstances, rap music can now be distributed in a way that bypasses the taming influences of the commercial marketplace to play a role in vibrant movements for political change.

ADVERTISING AND CONSUMER CULTURE

Each day, we are bombarded with advertisements in our homes and cars, at workplaces, online, and on the street. As businesses seek new places to advertise their goods and services, ads can be found just about everywhere. Buses and subways have long been prime advertising spaces, catching the eyes of riders and passersby alike. Airlines sometimes sell ad space on the outsides of planes. Television and radio have long been chock-full of ads. When you log onto the internet, you find that colorful advertisements are a central part of the online experience: pop-up windows and banner ads on online news sites, ads surrounding "free" blogging platforms and websites, sponsored Tweets, printable coupons, and ads woven into Google and Facebook pages. Ads surround sporting events, both on television and in sports arenas. They arrive in the mail and via smartphone. We wear advertising logos on our clothes and hum advertising jingles in the shower. In short, ads are so deeply embedded in our environment that we are likely to see, hear, and even smell them (in the form of magazine perfume ads) without thinking twice.

What kinds of stories do advertisements tell about ourselves and our society? Certainly, on one level, ads are specific to their product or service. They tell us that, if we drink a particular brand of beer, we will meet attractive women; if we wear the right makeup, we will meet handsome men; if we purchase a certain automobile, we will gain prestige; if we use specific cleansers, we will save time; and if we wear certain clothes, we will find adventure. Ads may also tell us that a particular item will save us money, that a specific service will make us healthier, or that a new product will make a great gift for a loved one. There is a wide range of specific messages in these ads, suggesting connections between products and lifestyles and between services and states of mind and presenting a host of information about prices, availability, and the like. We are not simply passive participants in all of this. We recognize advertising conventions and don't expect the connections depicted in ads—cosmetics and love, suits and success, for example—to be taken literally.

Despite the diversity of advertising messages and their frequent use of irony and humor, there is an underlying commonality to almost all advertisements: They are fundamentally about selling. They address their audiences as consumers and celebrate and take for granted the consumer–capitalist organization of society. This perspective is, of course, decidedly ideological. Ads tell us that happiness and satisfaction can be purchased, that each of us is first and foremost an individual consumption unit, and that market relations of buying and selling are the appropriate—perhaps the only—form of social relations outside the intimacy of the family. Sometimes even the intimacy of the family is seemingly up for sale. One recent commercial implied that families could create lasting memories by baking at home with Pillsbury products. Advertising presumes and promotes a culture of consumption, normalizing middle- or even upper-middle-class lifestyles and making buying power a measure of both virtue and freedom.

In the process, advertising elevates certain values—specifically, those associated with acquiring wealth and consuming goods—to an almost religious status. Moreover, advertising promotes a worldview that stresses the individual and the realm of private life, ignoring collective values and the terrain of the public world (Schudson 1984). The values that advertising celebrates do not come out of thin air, but this does not make them any less ideological. Whether or not ads are successful at selling particular products—some ad campaigns succeed, and others fail—the underlying message in advertising, which permeates our media culture, is the importance of the values of consumerism.

iStock.com/emyu

Advertisements occupy increasingly large amounts of public space. This photo of Times Square in New York City shows a striking example of ads towering over an urban setting. Ads also populate our daily landscape in less dramatic forms. In addition to television, social media, and billboard ads, shoes, taxi cabs, grocery bags, coffee cups, and many other sites all carry ads. Where have you seen advertisements today?

Selling Consumerism in the Early 20th Century

Stuart Ewen (1976) explored the historical roots of what we now call consumer culture, tracing the role of early 20th-century advertising in its creation. Turn-of-the-century capitalists, captains of industry, saw mass advertising as a means of shaping the consciousness of the American population in a way that would give legitimacy and stability to the rapidly industrializing society. The key to this new consciousness was the creation of a new way of life based on the pleasures of consumption. Mass advertising emerged in the 1920s, when leaders of the business community began to see the need for a coordinated ideological effort to complement their control of the workplace. Advertising would become the centerpiece of a program to sell not only products but also a new, American way of life in which consumption erased differences, integrated immigrants into the mainstream of American life, and made buying the equivalent of voting as a form of commitment to the democratic process.

From the start, then, advertising was more about creating consumers than selling individual products. If a mass production economy was to be profitable and if those who worked for long hours under difficult conditions in the factory were to be pacified, new needs and habits had to be stimulated. This was the job of advertising. Its early practitioners built on people's insecurities about their lives and their appearances to shape desires for new consumer products. Solutions to personal problems were to be found in the world of consumption, an early version of the currently prevalent attitude that views a day of shopping as a way to cheer up oneself. Ads suggested that new products, such as mouthwash, hand lotion, and deodorant, would protect people from embarrassment and give them tickets to the modern world. Old habits and folkways—the traditions that recent immigrants brought to the United States—were to be discarded in favor of the new "American way," participation in a consumer society.

Ads sold consumerism as a gateway to social integration in 20th-century America and as an ideology that would smooth over social conflicts—especially class conflict—and serve as a form of social cement.

One way advertising tried to sell a cross-class ideology of consumerism was through its focus on the realm of consumption and its neglect of production. The industrial workplace might be unsatisfying, even degrading, but advertising offered a world that was far removed from the drudgery of work, emphasizing the wonders of the consumer lifestyle. It was, after all, that lifestyle and associated worldview that ads were selling, regardless of whether people had the means to really live it. As Ewen (1976) put it, although the ideology of consumerism

> served to stimulate consumption among those who had the wherewithal and desire to consume, it also tried to provide a conception of the good life for those who did not. . . . In the broader context of a burgeoning commercial culture, the foremost political imperative was *what to dream.* (p. 108)

So-called women's magazines are loaded with advertisements and editorial content, nearly all of which promote an ideology that celebrates consumption associated with beauty, fitness, attracting men, and the "good life."

Such dreams could be realized only by consuming goods, and even this was only a temporary realization, requiring continuous consumption in search of the lifestyle promoted by advertising. Our culture of consumption, then, is intimately connected to advertising, which helped create it and continues, in new forms, to sustain consumerism as a central part of contemporary American ideology.

Women's Magazines as Advertisements

The "women's magazine" is one medium that is particularly advertising oriented and consistently promotes the ideology of consumerism. Its emphasis on ads—which often seem to make up the bulk of the content—has led one critic to label this genre the "women's advertising magazine" (McCracken 1993). Publications such as *Vogue*, *Glamour*, *Redbook*, *Cosmopolitan*, and *Elle* include page after page of glossy ads featuring products targeted specifically at women.

More generally, the magazines promote the consumer lifestyle by showing how beauty, sexuality, career success, culinary skill, and social status can be bought in the consumer marketplace. Social problems, from the standpoint of consumer ideology, are redefined as personal problems that can be solved by purchasing the appropriate product. Women's magazines, in addressing a specific social group, identify women as a consumption category with special product needs. The magazines link an identity as a woman with a set of specific consumer behaviors, making the latter the prerequisite for the former. To be a "woman," then, is to know what to buy; the ad content in women's magazines both displays the specific products and celebrates the pleasures and needs of consumption.

But there is more to women's magazines than just the ads, even though a common reading strategy is to casually leaf through the pages, glancing at the ads and headlines. Ellen McCracken (1993) argues that the editorial content—the nonadvertising articles— is itself a form of "covert advertising" that promotes the same kind of consumer-oriented ideology. The most visible ad is the cover of the magazine. The standard image of the ideal woman on the cover suggests that purchase of the magazine will provide clues to how and what to buy to become the ideal woman. In addition, covers are often reproduced inside the magazine along with information about the products displayed, suggesting that the image depicted is one that can be purchased.

Even the "editorial advice" provided by women's magazines is a form of covert advertisement, selling the consumer ideology. Beauty advice, for example, routinely suggests the consumption of various forms of makeup as a way to achieve beauty. Such advice often identifies brand names that are most effective—brands frequently promoted in ads in the same magazine. The regular makeover feature, in which an "average" woman is turned into a glamorous model look-alike, is, in essence, an endorsement of the beauty products advertised elsewhere in the magazine. Advice, then, really concerns appropriate consumption habits. Just as early ads identified newfound needs, the women's magazine suggests what women need. In the end, women's magazines use both direct and covert advertising to sell magazines and promote an ideology that celebrates the consumption of gender-specific products as a means to identity formation and personal satisfaction—the dream of the "good life."

ADVERTISING AND THE GLOBALIZATION OF CULTURE

The dreams that advertisements sell within the United States are also exported all around the globe. American-made ads for American brands—from Coca-Cola to Nike—circulate through the growing global media culture. More generally, American media products, from television programming to Hollywood films, are consumed by a vast international audience. Both the ads and the programming serve as a kind of international promotional vehicle for the American way of life by focusing on the material abundance and consumer opportunities available in the United States.

Although different products use different sales pitches and the entertainment media explore a range of themes set in various locations, most American media—especially those that are exported—share an underlying frame of reference that defines America by its combination of consumer capitalism and political freedom. Because media are owned and operated by profit-making companies, it should not be surprising that the cornucopia of images converges in the promotion of the benefits of a consumer society. Given the growing accessibility of international audiences, American-based companies see the global market as one of the keys to 21st-century success.

If advertisements and exported entertainment promote the American way of life, what exactly are they selling? After all, it is difficult to reduce the United States, a diverse and fragmented culture, to simple, unambiguous themes. The images on global display, like much domestic advertising, are about dreams. America is portrayed as a kind of dreamland where individuals can fulfill (or buy?) their desires. The images of the dreamland do not require a rigid uniformity because central to the ideology on display are the notions of individuality and freedom, which merge into the concept of *consumer choice*. Dreams are fulfilled by individual consumers who make choices about what to buy: Coke or Pepsi; Calvin Klein, Tommy Hilfiger, or The Gap; Nike or Under Armour; iPhone or Galaxy; Avis or Hertz. The route to happiness in this electronic dreamworld is consuming the "right" product. Think about how happy the diners are in McDonald's commercials or how peaceful the world is in the Ralph Lauren magazine ads.

The world portrayed in television programs, such as *Modern Family* or *Big Little Lies*, similarly displays images of attractive people living comfortable lives surrounded by contemporary consumer goods. Both advertisements and entertainment media promote a commitment to the latest styles—for example, in clothes, cars, leisure activities, and food—that requires not just consumption but continuous consumption to keep up with stylistic changes. The focus on style is directed particularly at youth, who are increasingly the most coveted market and who are particularly avid media users. The international advertising, television, and music scenes have helped generate an emerging cross-national, global youth culture in which teens and young adults in different countries adopt similar styles in clothes and appearance and select the same brands; consume the same soda, cigarettes, and fast food; and listen to and play the same kinds of music. The international teen market may cross national boundaries, but with the help of American media products, youth style is based to a great degree on American images and consumer goods.

American media products may be the most prominent in global circulation, but they are not the only media images out there. Various European and Japanese companies also produce media and advertising for an international market, often in concert with U.S.–based companies. Herbert Schiller (1992), one of the early critics of the export of American media, argued that globally circulating media images all promote a similar ideology, regardless of their national origin. Although the use of media as a tool for marketing lifestyles may have had its origins in the United States, it has become a global phenomenon. Although global media images may display national cultural differences as part of the sales pitch, they highlight difference as part of the promotion of the value of consuming and acquiring things. Ironically, cultural differences in global media images—such as multicultural images in American media—attract audiences for the promotion of a consumerist ideology that most fundamentally aims to bring different cultures together into an increasingly homogeneous, international consumer culture. If "we are the world," as the 1980s hit song for famine relief asserted, it is because we all buy, or dream about buying, the same things.

Culture has become increasingly global, with media images circulating across national boundaries. At the same time, U.S. media images display more difference than they did a generation ago. But what messages do U.S. media images present about the status of Americans and the status of foreigners in this global culture? This question fundamentally addresses ideology.

In his study of advertising images of foreigners, William O'Barr (1994) argued that the ideological analysis of ads requires us to look at what he calls the "secondary discourses" within the advertisements. As opposed to the primary discourse, which concerns the specific qualities of the advertised product, secondary discourses are those ideas about social relationships that are embedded within the ads. The ideology of advertising images, from this perspective, is to be found in the ways the images convey messages about social life at the same time they try to promote a specific product.

Context, setting, characteristics of the principal actors, and the interaction between actors within the ad are central to these secondary discourses.

In contemporary print ads, according to O'Barr (1994), there are three main categories of ads that feature images of foreigners: travel ads, product endorsements, and international business ads. The foreigners within travel ads are depicted as the "other"—different from the "us" that the ad is targeting—and the ads suggest that these others are available for the entertainment of American tourists. Implicit both within the images of local people dancing, painting, and smiling with American tourists and within the ad copy that invites tourists as "honored guests" or offers to "open both our homes and hearts" to visitors is a message that foreign lands are in the business of serving American visitors. Such images, by offering satisfaction from local people who aim to please, suggest that the needs and desires of Americans are the key to this potential relationship. The pattern in travel ads is unambiguous; the American tourist dominates the relationship with foreign cultures, particularly when the ads promote travel to Third World countries.

Product advertisements that draw on images of foreigners make connections between the advertised commodity and associations we have with foreign lands. O'Barr (1994) suggested images that, for example, link lingerie to Africa through the use of black models in apparently "primitive" clothing or that connect perfume to China or India by associating the product with Chinese art and characters or the Taj Mahal tell us stories about these foreign societies. The irony is that the products—in this case the lingerie or perfume—have nothing to do with societies in Africa, China, or India; the images of "others" are used to promote products made and used in the West.

Why, then, do ads draw on such images? O'Barr (1994) argued that the images of foreign lands are intended to suggest that the products are exotic or romantic. In so doing, they suggest that Africans, Chinese, or Indians are different from Americans, often depicting them as more primitive and, particularly, more sexual. These associations are intended to make the products attractive while simultaneously reaffirming that foreigners are fundamentally different.

Images of foreigners in ads for travel and products highlight difference, depicting an "other" who is subordinate to, but a source of pleasure for, American tourists and consumers. The ideology underlying these images about the place of the United States in the contemporary global order differs little from the messages in earlier ad images of foreigners. But the globalization of the economy has produced a new ad image of the foreigner: the potential business partner.

When the issue is international business, ad images no longer suggest difference, which might be an obstacle to conducting business. Instead, images of foreigners in international business ads emphasize that Americans and foreigners share a perspective and have a common set of goals. Foreign businesspeople are depicted not as "others"—as an exotic or threatening "them"—but as people just like us. These ads are directed at a much more limited audience—international businesspeople—than are the travel or product ads. Business ads, however, do suggest that there is an alternative to the depiction of foreigners as others, even if it is now limited to the global corporate community.

The most widely circulating images of "otherness" in advertising convey messages about foreigners from a distinctly American point of view and suggest that there are fundamental differences between "us" and "them"; that we have power in our relationships with "them"; and that "they" are available to stimulate, entertain, and serve "us." Media in a global culture may provide more images of foreign people and lands—and international business ads suggest that new kinds of images are emerging—but the underlying message in advertisements about who we are and who they are draws on age-old assumptions about the relationship between powerful Americans and subordinate foreigners.

INTERNET IDEOLOGY

Ideology, as we have noted, is most powerful when it operates at a taken-for-granted level, that is, when things seem obvious and uncontested. In some ways, the internet and related digital technologies have their own ideology. That is, they tend to encourage a way of being that seems commonsensical and "natural," when, in fact, it is the product of a particular set of social and power relations.

In the fall of 1968, *The Whole Earth Catalog* published its first edition, which included a manifesto by Stewart Brand (1969) touting the coming age of new technologies:

> We are as gods and might as well get good at it. So far, remotely done power and glory—as via government, big business, formal education, church—has succeeded to the point where gross defects obscure actual gains. In response to this dilemma and to these gains a realm of intimate, personal power is developing—power of the individual to conduct his own education, find his own inspiration, shape his own environment, and share his adventure with whoever is interested.

In this early incarnation, new technologies were envisioned as empowering individuals to exist outside of the control of society's dominant institutions. We noted in Chapter 2 that early internet innovators were influenced by this sort of countercultural belief—that social institutions, especially government, were oppressive and that solutions would come from individualism supported by new technologies.

Fast-forward a half century, and the fruition of this belief system can be seen in the internet. The focus on individual self-empowerment that began as a countercultural value became fused with Silicon Valley capitalism. It morphed into an approach combining libertarianism and neoliberalism—an ideology supporting the deregulation of industry, the defunding and privatization of public services, and the undermining of labor unions that serve as a bulwark against capitalist exploitation. The internet enabled free-trade and the free flow of capital (although *not* of humans), destabilizing economies and limiting the ability of national governments to control their own economies. In determining economic outcomes (made difficult with the free flow of global capital) to regulating speech on privately owned digital platforms (where the First Amendment doesn't apply), governments—the collective expression of the public will—are often not in control; private corporations are.

As the legitimacy of governments to seriously address major social problems has been undermined, and as other social institutions have been challenged, technology and the associated information society has been hailed by many as a savior, amounting to a "techno-redemptive ideology" (Mattelhart 2003: 152). Representing individual freedom and what another critic calls "technological solutionism" (Morozov 2013), the internet is presented as a neutral "platform" for communication and self-expression; digital technologies and "big data" are touted as the source of solutions for everything ranging from personal troubles to global crises.

Carrying a few too many pounds? Strap on a data-gathering sports watch to monitor your movement and vital statistics. Poor love life? Sign up for an online dating service. Failing students in school? Introduce more computers and educational software. Traffic congestion driving you crazy? Don't worry, driverless cars and virtual traffic lights will make commuting effortless. Oppressive government still got you down? Use Twitter to launch a protest and a social revolution. Worried about the value of the dollar? Invest in cryptocurrencies unaffiliated with any government and largely shielded from monitoring. The list of ways that new technologies—almost always connected to internet cloud services—are supposed to solve our personal and social ills is seemingly endless.

For many people, the internet has come to represent a way of life. It is about instantaneous and continuous connection: to others, to information, to entertainment, to the marketplace. As a node in a networked society, we participate in internet life in a way that reaffirms its particular mode of operation and makes it seem more inevitable and ordinary. As Katharine Sarikakis and Daya K. Thussu (2006) put it, "Thus, like all ideology, the main aim of Internet ideology would appear to normalize a particular set of ideas, a distinctive worldview predicated on the almost mythical power of new information and communications technologies" (p. 3).

Critical observers, though, have challenged the "ordinary," "normal," "inevitable" nature of the internet. They argue that a dangerous internet ideology serves as cover for corporate manipulation that enriches a few elites while duping the rest of us. Sometimes these cautionary analyses come from people who once lived in the belly of the beast, so to speak: Silicon Valley insiders who have become disillusioned with the direction that digital technologies have taken (Morozov 2011, 2013; Lanier 2013).

Jared Lanier, a computer scientist best known for his virtual reality research, argues that wealth accumulation has come to be concentrated in a few oligopolies that use algorithms to dominate the internet and the broader economy. These "Siren Servers," as he calls them, tempt users by offering free or low-cost goods and services. Our e-mail service, our video platforms, our social media connections, our music streaming are offered to us for free, obscuring the commercial dynamics that underlie their production. Of course, these services are advertiser supported; we are the product being sold to advertisers. But unlike earlier advertiser-supported media, by participating in this "free" online environment, we willingly give up an enormous amount of personal data about what we do, where we do it, and with whom. Indeed our internet digital trail gives data miners a very good idea of who we are and what we are thinking at any given time. Data that is voluntarily handed over becomes a source of wealth for the companies that control and sell it. It also becomes a source of insight about how to better manipulate users. So the hidden price of the "free" internet economy is the need to surrender massive amounts of personal data via constant monitoring of our online activities.

At the same time we are expected to voluntarily work to create content that will attract more people to view more ads. That is the basis for social media and other platforms that rely on user-generated content. This development requires the normalization of extreme self-disclosure and self-promotion, coupled with the minimization of concern about privacy, all of which serves the purpose of social media platforms that depend upon free user labor to create content to engage more users.

So, in the end, we have growing oligopolistic corporations—Facebook, Google, Amazon, and the like—who mine our data, feed us our news and entertainment, and deeply affect our understanding of the world through the use of algorithms that shape our online experiences. But rather than conjure up images from dystopian science-fiction novels about an oppressive "Big Brother," this condition seems to us perfectly normal, ordinary, and in our best interest. That is the power of ideology.

CONCLUSION

This chapter has looked at the content of media by adopting an ideological approach. We have reviewed the underlying theoretical frameworks of ideological analysis and examined several specific cases to detect ideology at work in media. As our examples suggest, there is no singular ideology that is promoted by popular media. Researchers who study the ideology of media are interested in the underlying stories about society that the media tell, the range of values that the media legitimize, and the kinds of behaviors that are deemed "normal." Most popular media promote, often in subtle and even contradictory ways, perspectives that support our basic social arrangements and endorse the legitimacy of social institutions, marginalizing attitudes and behaviors that are considered to be out of the "mainstream."

Media images can and sometimes do challenge mainstream ideology by providing a critique of contemporary social organization and norms, but commercialization makes it difficult for media to maintain a critical voice. The competition for popularity, wider distribution, and profitability tends to dull the critical edges of media imagery, pushing media back toward more mainstream (and marketable) ideologies. There are, to be sure, media that consistently promote alternative ideological perspectives. Local weekly newspapers, journals of opinion, public access television, alternative media sites, and independent films are often quite self-conscious about providing perspectives that differ from the dominant popular media. These alternatives, however, remain on the margins of the media scene, reaching small audiences and lacking the capital to mount a serious challenge to the dominant media.

In this chapter, we have explored the ideology of various media texts, examining the underlying perspectives within the images that confront us every day. As we examine media content, we need to look even more specifically at the ways that media represent the social world. In Chapter 7, we turn our attention to the relationship between media images and social inequality.

Discussion Questions

1. What is ideology and how are media images central to the contemporary "culture wars" in the United States? Use examples to illustrate your analysis.

2. How and why is the concept "hegemony" significant for ideological analysis of media? How does it differ from analyses of "false consciousness"? Where does the concept suggest we look for evidence of ideology at work?

3. How have television images played a role in the long-standing cultural conflict about the definition of the family? What is the relationship between changes in images of the family and changes in family structure?

4. Can rap music be seen as a critique of mainstream norms and values, even when popular rap songs are used as advertising jingles? Why or why not?

SOCIAL INEQUALITY
AND MEDIA REPRESENTATION

The examination of media content traditionally has been the most common type of media analysis, perhaps because of the easy accessibility of media products. The production process takes place in the relative remoteness of movie lots, recording studios, and editors' offices. In contrast, media products surround us and are within easy reach of the researcher.

Whatever the reason, there is an enormous volume of research and commentary on the nature of media content. Rather than try to review this vast literature, we have organized this chapter on media content around the single theme of representation. We explore the question, "How do media representations of the social world compare to the external 'real' world?" As we will discuss, this is not the only possible line of investigation related to media content. However, given our sociological interest in the relationship between the media and the social world, it is a central one.

Furthermore, our discussion focuses on the issue of social inequality. We argue that the creators of media content often reproduce the inequalities that exist in society based on race, class, gender, and sexual orientation. This is not to say that the media have acted as a mirror, passively reflecting the inequalities of society. Rather, white middle- and upper-class men have historically controlled the media industry, and media content has largely reflected their perspectives on the world. Therefore, the inequalities in the social world have affected the organization of the media industry that produces media content.

In turn, activists have challenged the media to broaden their narrow perspectives. Some have developed alternative media and told their own stories through words and pictures. Over the years, progressive social change movements have succeeded in altering some facets of social inequality in society at large. This human agency has created changes in the social world, which in turn, have affected the organization of the media industry. Increasingly diverse contemporary media content reflects these changes to varying degrees.

Finally, changes in media technology have facilitated changes in content. With more media outlets, content has shifted from being scarce to being abundant. This abundance can accommodate more content diversity.

COMPARING MEDIA CONTENT AND THE "REAL" WORLD

Content analyses of media products have repeatedly shown them to be quite different from key measurable characteristics of the social world. This gap between the "real" world and media representations of the social world is the subject of this chapter.

"How do media representations of the social world compare to the external 'real' world?" is an important question because we conventionally organize media according to how closely they represent reality. We talk, for example, about fiction versus nonfiction, news or public affairs versus entertainment, documentaries versus feature films, "reality" programs, and so on. The impact of media, as we will see in Part IV, can actually become more significant if media products diverge dramatically from the real world. We tend to become more concerned, for example, when media content lacks diversity or overemphasizes violence, sex, or other limited aspects of the real world.

The question of how media representations of the social world compare to the external "real" world also raises several issues. First, the literature in media and cultural studies reminds us that representations are not reality, even if media readers or audiences may sometimes be tempted to judge them as such (Hall, Evans, and Nixon 2013). Representations—even those that attempt to reproduce reality, such as the documentary film—are the result of processes of selection that invariably mean that certain aspects of reality are highlighted and others neglected. Even though we often use the "realness" of the images as a basis for evaluating whether we like or dislike particular representations, all representations *re-present* the social world in ways that are both incomplete and narrow.

Second, the media usually do not try to reflect the "real" world. Most of us would like news programs, history books, and documentary films to represent happenings in the social world as fairly and accurately as possible. (After examining the production process, we now know how difficult it is to achieve this, if only because of limited time and resources.) But by its very nature, a science-fiction film, for example, will diverge significantly from contemporary social life. Without that gap between reality and media image, the genre would cease to exist.

We cannot push this point too far, however, because even fantasy products such as science-fiction films hold the potential for teaching us something about our society. Often, this is the attraction of the genre. When Captain Kirk and Lieutenant Uhura of *Star Trek* kissed on prime-time television in the 1960s, it was the first interracial kiss on a U.S. television series. This media content, although clearly embedded in a fantasy science fiction about the future, just as surely was making a statement about race relations in contemporary America. Social commentary continued in later *Star Trek* spin-offs when producers cast an African American as the commander of *Deep Space Nine* (1993), a woman as captain of *Voyager* (1995), and a gay couple on *Star Trek: Discovery* (2018). More recently, the growing genre of Afrofuturism (Womack 2013) goes a step further, depicting future or alternative worlds grounded in African culture rather than just a black character or story line in a predominantly white world. For example, a major 2018 Hollywood production, *Black Panther*, presented a combination superhero, political leader, and religious figure returning to a mythical African nation that has been shielded from colonialist exploitation, allowing it to use its resources to become the most technologically advanced country on Earth. All of these productions were science fiction, yet clearly they were commenting on social conditions at the time of their creation.

The point is that there is potential social significance in all media products—even those that are clearly make-believe fantasies. Creators of media products are often aware of this fact and use entertainment media to comment on the real social world. In turn, readers and audiences develop at least some sense of the social world through their exposure to both entertainment media and news media. It behooves us, therefore, to attend to what these media messages might be. That includes looking at media forms—including science fiction, soap operas, music videos, and romance novels—that clearly do not claim to accurately reflect society.

A third issue raised by the question of how media representations of the social world compare to the "real" world concerns the troublesome term *real*. In an age in which sociologists teach about the social construction of reality and postmodernists challenge the very existence of a knowable reality, the concept of a "real" world may seem like a quaint artifact from the past. We generally agree with the social constructionist perspective, which suggests that no representation of reality can ever be totally "true" or "real" because it must inevitably frame an issue and choose to include and exclude certain

Marvel Studios, LLC

Although the original Black Panther comic book character pre-dates the 1960s civil rights group, its title character was the first African American protagonist in either the Marvel or DC universes. Superhero, political leader, and religious figure rolled into one, Black Panther reappeared in the 2018 Hollywood film of the same name. Part of the growing Afrofuturism genre, *Black Panther* is an example of how even fantasy and science fiction content can comment on the "real" world.

components of a multifaceted reality. However, some social facts seem solid enough to be used as a measure of reality. To give a simple example, we have a pretty good idea of the age distribution in the United States, and in recent years about 23 percent of the U.S. population has been younger than age 18 (U.S. Census Bureau 2018). Imagine that television situation comedies became inundated with children who made up, say, half of all characters. We could then reliably state that, compared to the real world, such programs featured twice as many children. Such a claim is possible only because we have a reasonably accurate way of measuring age distribution in the population as a whole.

The legitimacy of the question becomes much more dubious, however, with other examples. Is media content more liberal than society at large, as some contend? That depends on how you go about defining *liberal* and how you attempt to measure it in both the media and the "real" world. Such a concept is much more ambiguous than age, and therefore, we have to be careful about claims of "bias" leveled at the media. In the end, we can make some useful comparisons between the content of media and society, but our limited ability to measure the social world necessarily limits such claims.

Finally, the question of how media representations of the social world compare to the "real" world seems to imply that the media *should* reflect society. This premise is not agreed on. For many people, media are an escape from the realities of daily life. Therefore, how "real" media products are is irrelevant to many people.

However, it is not necessary to believe that the media should accurately reflect society to compare media representations with the social world. Gaps between media content and social reality raise interesting questions that warrant our attention.

THE SIGNIFICANCE OF CONTENT

Although this chapter focuses on the content of media, it is important to realize that many researchers study media content to make inferences about other social processes (Berelson 1952; Holsti 1969; Neuendorf 2017). In other words, they study media content to assess the significance of that content. There are at least five ways in which researchers can assess the significance of media content. They involve linking content (1) to producers, (2) to audience interests, (3) to society in general, (4) to audience effects, or (5) to content independent of context.

To illustrate, let's return to our hypothetical example about children and situation comedies. If researchers found that child characters appeared on situation comedies twice as often as children do in the real world, then several lines of interpretation would be possible. Each of these different approaches tries to explain the source and significance of media content.

Content as Reflection of Producers. First, it would be possible to infer that this child-centered content reflected the intent of the program writers and producers. This line of interpretation—linking content to producers—encourages us to investigate the social characteristics of situation-comedy writers and producers. We might find that such creative personnel are disproportionately 40-somethings with children of their own who draw on their own family lives for story inspiration. As a result, a disproportionate percentage of programs feature children. Or perhaps corporate advertisers have expressed strong interest in sponsoring child-related programs, influencing producers to create more such programs. Determining this connection would require research that moved beyond media content and studied media personnel—or in the case of user-generated content, users—and the production process more generally (exactly the kind of research we examined in Part II). Content analysis would alert us to this issue but by itself could not provide an adequate explanation for the heavy population of children on such programs.

Content as Reflection of Audience Preference. Second, we might infer that perhaps the high number of child characters reflects the audience for situation comedies. This does not necessarily suggest that children constitute a large percentage of the audience. It may simply mean, for example, that many viewers are parents who enjoy watching the antics of young children on situation comedies. Here the implication is that media personnel are merely responding to the interests of their likely audience, not to their own interests or to the influence of the production process. This approach suggests that content is a reflection of audience preference. The idea that media producers are only "giving the people what they want" also implies that people want what they get. To test such claims, researchers must explore more than media content. They must move into the area of audience research.

Content as Reflection of Society in General. Third, some researchers investigate media content as a gauge of social norms, values, and the interests of society in general—not just the audience. Some analysts might suggest that child-dominated situation comedies reflect a high level of social concern for children. They might reflect the fact that we live in a child-centered society where people value children highly. The difficulty in firmly making such sweeping assessments should be clear. To support such claims, research would need to extend well beyond the boundaries of media content.

Content as an Influence on Audiences. Fourth, researchers sometimes examine media content for potential effects on audiences. Perhaps the preponderance of children on television will encourage couples to have children or to have more children—or to avoid having children! Here, too, the researcher would have to link content analysis with research on audience interpretations—a topic examined in Part IV. The influence of media is so diffuse, however, that a direct link is usually very difficult to establish. The emphasis in this case—in contrast to the first three—is not on content as a reflection of the production process, audiences, or society. Instead, it is on content as a social influence on audiences.

Content as Self-Enclosed Text. Finally, a substantial body of work addresses media content on its own terms. That is, it makes no attempt to link content to producers, audiences, or society but instead examines media as a self-enclosed text whose meaning is to be "decoded." For example, in the 2007 thriller *The Brave One*, Jodie Foster plays a New York City radio host whose fiancé is murdered while they are walking through Central Park. In response, Foster's character takes the law into her own hands and kills several people who have committed crimes. One analysis of this film suggested it was a metaphor for the trauma faced by the United States in the wake of the 9/11 attacks, concluding that the film

> is constituted by and constitutive of cultural trauma. Its confrontation with personal trauma functions as a trope for not only recoding the vigilante film but also figuring the nation as posttraumatic. While [*The Brave One*] posits the damaging effects of traumatic loss, it does so in order to mitigate such harms; and, while this film insists that its female hero walk in a man's shoes, it does so while carefully mapping the boundaries of gendered and national identity. (King 2010: 128)

This tradition has many variations associated more with the structuralism and semiology found in literary and film studies and linguistics than with the content analysis found in the social sciences. However, researchers sometimes combine this approach with studies of production and audience reception under the rubric of cultural studies. It is often difficult or impossible to assess the validity of the claims of such analyses because no standard methods exist in this field. Still, such work can be useful for those whose concerns lie with issues such as the relationship between elements of a text or the language, grammar, and vocabulary of image production.

Having sketched out the different ways in which researchers assess the significance of media content, we now turn to the content itself. As you will note, it is impossible to examine content without touching on the role of producers, audiences, or larger social norms. However, we will focus primarily on media content per se. We will also limit our discussion to a few basic characteristics—race, class, gender, and sexual orientation—that are illustrative of a sociological approach to content analysis and that relate to our theme of inequality.

RACE, ETHNICITY, AND MEDIA CONTENT: INCLUSION, ROLES, AND CONTROL

Sociologists and anthropologists recognize that *race* is a socially constructed concept whose meaning has evolved over time and varies across cultures (Smedley and Smedley 2012). There is no biologically valid difference in the genetic makeup of different races. In fact, different blood types might be more biologically significant than different racial classifications. However, racial distinctions have powerful social meaning with profound real-world consequences. Social scientists chart the development and implications of these socially constructed distinctions, especially as they influence discriminatory structures and practices. *Ethnicity*, which refers to shared cultural heritage that often derives from a common ancestry and homeland, is also a cultural creation.

Given their significance in social life, it is not surprising that there has been much interest in content analysis that examines how media messages address race and ethnicity (Dávila and Rivero 2014; Dines, Humez, Yousman, and Yousman 2018; Lind 2017; Luther, Lepre, Clark 2018; Rodman 2014; Squires 2009). Historically, mainstream U.S. media have taken "whites" to be the norm against which all other racial groups are measured. The taken-for-granted nature of "whiteness" means that it need not be explicitly identified. For example, we generally do not talk about "white culture," "the white community," "the white vote," and so forth. We do, however, often hear reference to "black culture," "the Latino community," and so on. The absence of a racial signifier in this country usually signifies "whiteness." The pervasiveness of white perspectives in media is perhaps its most powerful characteristic.

With whiteness as the unspoken backdrop, the study of race and ethnicity in the U.S. media tends to focus on the portrayal of minorities. To understand how racial difference is portrayed in the mass media, we must recall the earlier roots of racial stereotyping in American culture. Throughout much of U.S. mass media history, blacks, Native Americans, Asians, Latinos, and other racial and ethnic minorities have been, at best, of little consideration to the media industry. Because such minorities comprised a relatively small part of the population, mainstream media did not see them as an important segment of the mass audience (something that began to change in recent years). When it came to media content, racial minorities were either ignored or stereotyped in roles such as the Black Mammy, the Indian Maiden, the Latin Lover, or the sinister Asian Warlord. Such stereotypical images were the product of white media producers and bore little resemblance to the realities of the different racial and ethnic groups (Wilson, Gutierrez, and Chao 2013). In recent years, significant changes have occurred, but a more subtle range of stereotypes sometimes remains.

When we consider how racial and ethnic differences have been portrayed in the media, three crucial issues emerge. First is the simple issue of *inclusion*. Do media producers include the images, voices, and cultures of different racial and ethnic groups in media content? The second issue of concern is the nature of media *roles*. When producers do include members of racial and ethnic minorities in media content, how do they portray them? Here the history of racial and ethnic stereotypes takes center stage. Finally, the *control* of production is crucial. Do people from different racial and ethnic groups

© Bettmann/CORBIS

From 1968 to 1971, Diahann Carroll portrayed the title character on the sitcom *Julia*. A widowed single mother (her husband was killed in Vietnam), Julia was a nurse and lived a middle-class life. Criticized at the time for being apolitical and distant from the concerns of poor and working-class African Americans, Julia was also one of the earliest non-stereotypical roles for a black woman on network television.

have control over the creation and production of media images that feature different groups? This last issue is more about the production process and the nature of the media industry than about media content in itself. However, the history of media suggests that content very often reflects the views of those in control.

Racial and Ethnic Diversity in Media Content

A sample of some research findings on racial and ethnic inclusion in the modern media will help provide historical context and alert us to the changes that have occurred over time. In general, the inclusion of different racial and ethnic groups in the media has changed dramatically, with the media becoming much more diverse today than it was in the past. However, the progress has been uneven and incomplete.

Film. In early Hollywood films of the 1920s and 1930s, blacks were largely absent or were relegated to two roles: entertainer or servant. Not until after World War II did more African Americans begin appearing on the screen, and even then, there were a limited number of available roles (Bogle 2016; Cripps 1993). Since then, the gradual trend has clearly been toward more racial diversity in films, and in recent years, black roles have been roughly proportional to the black population in the United States. For example, whereas blacks made up 13.3 percent of the U.S. population in 2016, African-American actors made up an almost identical percentage (13.6%) of speaking or named roles in the 100 top-grossing U.S. box office films of 2016. Asians were underrepresented, though, accounting for 3.1 percent of speaking roles compared to 5.7 percent of the population. The Latinx community (who can be of any race) was underrepresented significantly, holding just 3.4 percent of roles in 2016 films, even though they were 17.8 percent of the population. Collectively, minority racial/ethnic groups made up 38.7 percent of the population but only 29.2 percent of roles (Smith, Choueiti, and Pieper 2017; U.S. Census Bureau 2018).

Television. On television through the 1940s and 1950s, the presence of blacks was limited largely to their traditional, stereotypical roles as entertainers and comedians, with virtually no serious dramatic roles. Instead, comedies and variety shows were the only regular forum for black talent (Dates 1993). In the 1960s and 1970s, this began to change as television programs featured more blacks and, to a lesser extent, other racial and ethnic groups. By the 1969–1970 season, half of all dramatic television programs had a black character. Surveys conducted from this period through the early 1980s show that, whereas roughly 11 percent of the population was black at that time, 6 percent to 9 percent of all television characters were black (Seggar, Hafen, and Hannonen-Gladden 1981). During the 1990s, African-American representation on television increased and was nearly proportional to their presence in the population as a whole (Greenberg and Brand 1994). However, this period also reflected significant racial segregation on television; one study sampling television programs from 1997 to 2006 found many shows still had all-or nearly all-white casts (Signorielli 2009).

Few other racial or ethnic groups were regularly portrayed on early prime-time TV. In the 1970s, only two situation comedies, *Chico and the Man* and the short-lived *Viva Valdez*, centered on Latino characters. The 1980s saw a few major roles for Latino characters on programs such as *Miami Vice* and *L.A. Law*, but Latinx underrepresentation continued through the 1990s and beyond (Mastro and Behm-Morawtiz 2005). Asian characters, too, were few and far between. It was only in 1994 that an Asian family was used as the premise for a situation comedy, *All-American Girl* (Wilson et al. 2013).

Kenya Barris, creator of ABC's sitcom *black-ish*, recalled that, when growing up, "I saw *Friends* and *Seinfeld* and thought, 'What part of New York is this?'" (Bauder, Elber, and Moore 2015). Both long-standing hits were almost exclusively white. In recent years, though, racial and ethnic diversity has become a staple of many prime-time television programs, with barriers being regularly broken. In the 2010s, Fox's sitcom *The Mindy Project* starred a South Asian American actress—a first for network TV; ABC's political drama *Scandal* starred an African-American woman—the first black female lead in a network series in nearly 40 years. Barris's *black-ish*, along with *Empire*, *Fresh Off the Boat*, and a host of other recent hits have continued the trend. Since the 2016–2017 season, African Americans and Asians have been represented at or above their rate in the U.S. population but Latinx characters remain significantly underrepresented (GLAAD 2018). (See Figure 7.1.) Although varied in methodology and precise results, other studies have also documented the growing diversity on television (Chin et al. 2017; Smith et al. 2016). As one watchdog group summarized in its annual diversity study, "It seems that the broadcast networks are finally making serious strides towards more racially diverse representations as most have steadily increased in the past few years after long periods of little variation" (GLAAD 2018: 14).

Advertising. Early studies of advertising repeatedly found underrepresentation of people of color, but more recent research shows significantly increased diversity. For example, in the fashion field, one study of *Cosmopolitan*, *Glamour*, and *Vogue* in the late 1980s found that only 2.4 percent of ads featured black women (Jackson and Ervin 1991). However, advertisements are now far more diverse. One study of models in a 2004 sample of major magazines found that 19.2 percent were black, 14.5 percent Hispanic, and 7.2 percent Asian (Peterson 2007). One industry review of nearly 800 fashion magazine covers across 49 international fashion publications found a steady and significant improvement in the inclusion of people of color on their covers: from 17.4 percent in 2014 to 32.5 percent in 2017 (Tai 2017).

The percentage of regularly recurring characters who are racial and ethnic minorities on prime-time scripted
broadcast series has increased significantly in recent years. Since the 2016–2017 season, African Americans
and Asians have been represented at or above their rate in the U.S. population but Latinx characters remain
significantly underrepresented. In the 2017–2018 season, a full 40 percent of broadcast characters were
people of color. (In 2016, the U.S. population was 61.3% white [non-Hispanic], 13.3% black, 5.7% Asian, 17.8%
Hispanic [of any race] [U.S. Census Bureau 2018].)

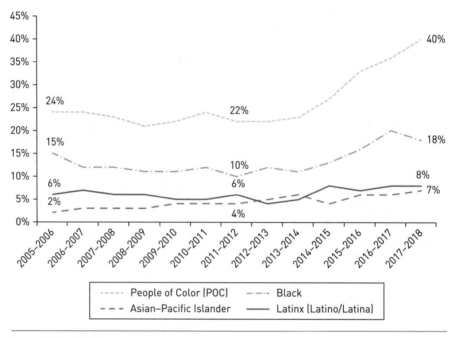

Source: GLAAD (2018).

Note: Latinx (Latino/a) can be of any race.

Video Games. As video games became an increasingly large component of the media
landscape, research on representations within gaming worlds emerged (Dill, Gentile,
Richter, and Dill 2005; Nakamura 2009). One effort to describe the demographic
landscape of the video game universe was a "virtual census" of all the characters in
the 150 most popular games on Xbox, Playstation, and Nintendo platforms in 2005
(Williams, Martins, Consalvo, and Ivory 2009). The "census" found some overrepre-
sentation of whites (80.1% in games versus 75.1% in the U.S. population at the time)
and Asian/Pacific Islanders (5% vs. 4%), along with underrepresentation of blacks
(10.7% vs. 12.3%) and, especially, Hispanics (2.7% vs. 12.5%). Native Americans
were accurately represented at just less than 1 percent. The racial and ethnic makeup
of primary game characters was less diverse, though, with whites accounting for

85 percent of the primary roles, whereas blacks constituted fewer than 10 percent and Asians fewer than 2 percent. None of the games had Hispanics or Native Americans as a primary character; they were present solely as secondary characters (Williams et al. 2009). Increasingly, video games have enabled users to choose among several racial and ethnic categories when creating their avatars. The "South Park: The Fractured but Whole" game even provocatively turned such capabilities into a social commentary; the harder the difficulty level you choose for the game, the darker your character's skin becomes (Yin-Poole 2017).

Growing Diversity and Abundance amid Audience Fragmentation

Not that long ago, any review of inclusiveness in media representation was relatively simple to write: It was dreadful. White men dominated across all media; underrepresentation of racial and ethnic minorities (and, as we will see, women) was considerable. Today, that story is more complicated. Although uneven and incomplete, media have become significantly more diverse, as our cursory overview suggests. Indeed, minority racial and ethnic groups are sometimes even *overrepresented* in some media content. Trends can change, but for the moment we seem poised for continued growing inclusiveness in media content. But why? We can better understand what is likely to be going on with these changes by taking a sociological approach that draws from our media model in Chapter 1.

First, most mainstream media are commercial ventures that pay close attention to user trends. Racial and ethnic diversity has increased in the population as a whole, and inclusive content is more likely to attract these diverse audiences to sell to advertisers. In this way, increased diversity is a moneymaking proposition. And it will only continue as the nation's media users continue to diversify. By 2040, the U.S. population is projected to be about 72 percent white (51 percent white, non-Hispanic), 13 percent black, 8 percent Asian, and 6 percent multiracial, as well as 24 percent Hispanic (of any race) (U.S. Census Bureau 2014).

Second, activists from both inside and outside of the industry have worked tirelessly to change media practices. Watchdog groups have long advocated change. Various annual diversity reports on media content and personnel have become common (some of which we cite in this chapter). Individual and collective efforts to promote more diverse hiring in key positions have been undertaken within different media sectors. Symbolic protests targeting major awards programs, such as #OscarsSoWhite and #GrammysSoMale, call attention to continuing underrepresentation of women and people of color and invite users to express their support for more diverse representation. Lesser known groups, like "Blacks in Gaming" form online communities to network and share ideas to promote change.

Third, this trend has been facilitated by the growth in media outlets—especially cable television and streaming services—and the resulting abundance of media content (see Figure 7.2). In the late 1980s, for example, the new Fox network created a significant number of programs aimed at black audiences because the other networks were largely ignoring this market niche; new competition led to creating new programs aimed at neglected audiences. Back then, broadcast media were still dealing with issues of scarcity (bandwidth, prime-time schedule slots, etc.), but more cable channels and streaming

FIGURE 7.2 ■ Scripted Television Series, 2002–2017

The growth in cable and streaming has created an abundance of content, offering opportunities for more diverse programs.

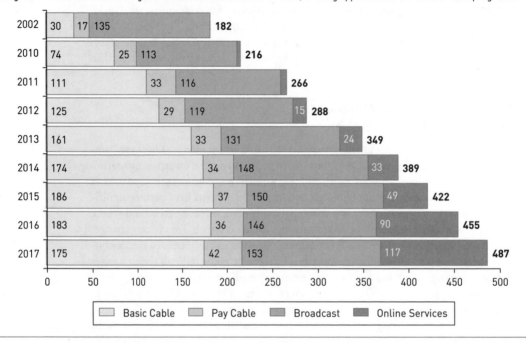

Source: **FX Research in Schneider (2018).**

options—not subject to such limitations—have resulted in a major increase in television programming. More than 500 scripted television series were expected to be produced in 2018; this represents a 150% increase over just eight years earlier (Schneider 2018).

Although the growth in abundance likely facilitates growing diversity, ironically, it may undermine the impact of that diversity. With more choices, audiences are fragmenting, and many Americans are not seeing the growing diversity in media content. Instead, television programming can be quite segregated. For example, during the 2017 season, none of the top five most-popular scripted series among African-American viewers were among the top five of white viewers (Levin 2017b). (See Figure 7.3.)

As we will see later in the book, the segmentation of media audiences has stirred concern that the media are losing their role as a common socializing agent. Media companies compete for advertising dollars by developing products that are targeted at the narrow, demographically specific audiences advertisers want to reach. Television commercials for automobiles and other products, for example, are designed to appeal to segments of the audience based on the race and ethnicity of the people in them (Maheshwari 2017). As targeting becomes more sophisticated, audiences increasingly pay attention to media

| FIGURE 7.3 ■ Top Prime-Time TV Programs among Racial/Ethnic Groups, 2017* |

U.S. television audiences are often segregated. There is very little overlap between the top five programs among black viewers and those of other racial and ethnic groups.

Program (Network)	White	African American	Asian American	Hispanic
NCIS (CBS)	1st			
This Is Us (NBC)	2nd		4th	4th
The Big Bang Theory (CBS)	3rd		5th	
America's Got Talent (NBC)	4th		1st	2nd
The Walking Dead (AMC)	5th		3rd	1st
Empire (Fox)		1st		5th
Star (Fox)		2nd		
Love & Hip Hop Atlanta (VH1)		3rd		
The Haves and Have-Nots (OWN)		4th		
How to Get Away with Murder (ABC)		5th		
World of Dance (NBC)			2nd	3rd
*Numbers cover the January to June season.				

Source: Levin (2017b).

products that are designed specifically for their demographic, or lifestyle group, and ignore media designed for others. Turow (1997) warned two decades ago that this process "may accelerate an erosion of the tolerance and mutual dependence between diverse groups that enable a society to work" (p. 7).

Race, Ethnicity, and Media Roles

Growth in the simple inclusion of people of color is an encouraging development. But what is the nature and quality of the roles being developed? For much of U.S. history, most white-produced images of other racial groups have been unambiguously racist. As early as the late 1700s, the "comic Negro" stereotype of "Sambo" appeared in novels and plays. On the stage, Dates and Barlow (1993) note, this racist character "was cast in a familiar mold: always singing nonsense songs and dancing around the stage. His dress was gaudy, his manners pretentious, his speech riddled with malapropisms, and he was played by white actors in blackface" (p. 6). Such images in popular culture are the precursor of racist stereotypes in later mass media.

Early Images of Race

Racist stereotypes were peppered throughout popular culture in the 19th century. In the novel *The Spy,* James Fenimore Cooper introduced the stereotypical image of the loyal, devoted, and content house slave who doubled as comic relief because of his superstitious beliefs and fear of ghosts. This image reappeared in many later books and films. Whites in blackface performed racist stage acts, portraying blacks as clownish buffoons. In the 1830s, a white actor named Thomas Dartmouth Rice copied a song-and-dance routine he saw performed on a street corner by a young slave boy. Rice used burnt cork to blacken his face, dressed in tattered clothes, and popularized the Jump Jim Crow routine. Early minstrel shows consisted of whites in blackface copying black music and dance traditions. Native Americans, too, were ridiculed in stage performances. One popular play was titled *The Original, Aboriginal, Erratic, Operatic, Semi-Civilized and Demi-Savage Extravaganza of Pocahontas* (Wilson et al. 2013). Popular songs, sung on the stage and printed in sheet music, also featured many racist stereotypes. Even well-intentioned works, such as Harriet Beecher Stowe's antislavery novel, *Uncle Tom's Cabin,* perpetuated a "positive" stereotype of blacks as gentle, suffering victims with childlike innocence.

The end of slavery brought different but equally racist images. The "contented slave was taken over by the faithful servant: the female side of this stereotype became the domestic mammy caricature, while the male side matured into elderly Uncle Toms" (Dates and Barlow 1993: 11). The folksy character of Uncle Remus, speaking in stereotypical black dialect, became the prototypical apologist for postbellum plantation life. Free black men began appearing as angry, brutal, and beast-like characters in novels. When D. W. Griffith's 1915 film glorifying the Ku Klux Klan, *Birth of a Nation,* featured similar characters, it was an indication that producers would fill the new film medium, as well, with racist images.

By 1920, the United States had fought in World War I "to make the world safe for democracy," according to President Wilson. However, early U.S. films were routinely presenting racist images of white supremacy. Blacks were viciously attacked in films such as *The Wooing and Wedding of a Coon* (1905) and *The Nigger* (1915). The Mexican government banned films such as 1914's *The Greaser's Revenge*, which portrayed Mexicans as bandits, rapists, and murderers. Movies portrayed Asians as a threat to American values, as in the film *The Yellow Menace* (1916). Early films openly advocated white supremacy over American Indians, as in the 1916 film *The Aryan* (Wilson et al. 2013).

As the film industry matured and grew in the pre-World War II years, it continued to use stereotypically racist images, albeit in less crude forms. Clichéd portrayals of Native Americans filled the popular Western film genre. Movie directors transferred the faithful black servant image to the silver screen, leading to the first Oscar for a black actor when Hattie McDaniel won the award for her portrayal of "Mammy," Scarlett O'Hara's slave in *Gone with the Wind.* Hollywood responded to complaints—and to declining distribution sales in Mexico and Latin America—by largely replacing

Photo 12/Alamy Stock Photo

Early films often portrayed Asians as an exotic threat. Here the white actor Boris Karloff plays an Asian evil criminal menace, Dr. Fu Manchu, in the 1932 film, *The Mask of Fu Manchu*. Based on earlier novels and short stories, a series of Fu Manchu movies were made, all of which featured the title character as a diabolical killer bent on vengeful murder of whites. In *AsianWeek*, Fu Manchu was chosen as the "most infamous yellow face film performance" ever for representing "pure evil, the very embodiment of the 'yellow peril' menace" (Chung 2007).

the earlier "greaser" image with the exotic "Latin lover" stereotype. Asians were either violent villains, in the mold of Dr. Fu Manchu, or funny and clever, as in the enormously popular Charlie Chan film series.

Slow Change and "Modern" Racism

It is out of this long legacy of racist imagery that the modern media's portrayals of racial minorities emerge. Media images have changed over the years. Since World War II, and especially since the 1960s, the trend has been toward more inclusiveness and growing sensitivity in media of all types. The civil rights struggle for racial equality influenced Hollywood, and discrimination against blacks became the theme of a number of prominent movies in the late 1950s and 1960s, including *The Defiant Ones* (1958), *To Kill a Mockingbird* (1962), *Black Like Me* (1964), *In the Heat of the Night* (1967), and *Guess Who's Coming to Dinner* (1967). In 1964, Sidney Poitier became the first black actor to win the Academy Award for Best Actor. The more militant black power struggles in the late 1960s and early 1970s were accompanied by the rise of "black exploitation" films with nearly all-black casts, such as *Shaft* (1971) and *Foxy Brown* (1974). The 1980s and 1990s witnessed the huge success of some black performers, and directors cast these stars in a wide variety of roles, from comic to dramatic. A milestone was reached in 2001 when the Academy Awards for Best Actress and Actor went to two African Americans: Halle Berry and Denzel Washington. Still, when all 20 Oscar-nominated actors in the best leading and supporting actors category were white in 2016—for the second year in a row—an #OscarsSoWhite protest and boycott brought attention to the issue and calls for diversifying the industry (Kirst 2016). The nominees were much more diverse in the two years immediately following.

Meanwhile, white reassessment of the domination of Native-American Indians surfaced in a series of movies. The 1970 film *Little Big Man* suggested that, as General Custer had engaged in years of atrocities against American Indians, he got what he deserved at the Battle of the Little Big Horn. Films in the 1990s began to create a different stereotype: the idealized Indian. *Dances with Wolves* (1990) and *Geronimo* (1993), for example, extended the theme of white guilt and Indian dignity. Film portrayals of other racial groups followed this general trend toward a new set of roles for people of color (Wilson et al. 2013).

Although mainstream media have generally grown more sensitive to stereotypes, controversial racial and ethnic images continue to emerge. In recent decades, even before the 2001 9/11 attacks, stereotypes of Arabs have taken center stage. For example, *The Siege*, a 1998 film depicting an epidemic of Arab terrorism in New York City, and *Rules of Engagement*, a 2000 film about the killing of demonstrators outside the U.S. embassy in Yemen, sparked protests from Arab-American groups, such as the Council on American-Islamic Relations (CAIR), who believed both films perpetuated stereotypes of violent, fanatical Arabs. (Ironically, both films starred African-American actors, Denzel Washington in the first and Samuel L. Jackson in the second.) In fact, the media's stereotypical depictions of Arabs and Arab Americans have long been the subject of scrutiny (Fuller 1995; Lind and Danowski 1998). In the wake of 9/11, even more attention was brought to the negative coverage of Arab Americans in the news (Nacos and Torres-Reyna 2007) and the stereotypical images of Arabs and Arab Americans that populate entertainment media such as Hollywood films (Shaheen 2008, 2014). For more than 35 years, Jack Shaheen studied images of Arabs in Hollywood movies. He found that film stereotypes of Arabs got worse, not better, noting that, compared to the past,

> today's reel Arabs are much more bombastic, brutal, and belligerent, much more rich, ruthless, and raunchy. They are portrayed as the civilized world's enemy, fanatic demons threatening people across the planet. Oily sheikhs finance nuclear wars; Islamic radicals kill innocent civilians; bearded, scruffy "terrorists," men and women, toss their American captives inside caves and filthy, dark rooms and torture them. (Shaheen 2014: 4)

However, the responses of other underrepresented groups to media stereotypes gave Shaheen (2014) some hope of improving the situation for Arab Americans. "For decades many racial and ethnic groups, gays and lesbians, and others suffered from the sting of reel prejudicial portraits," he writes. But eventually, "people worked together, until finally they managed to become filmmakers themselves, producing, directing, and appearing in courageous movies that elevated their humanity" (p. 5).

Increasingly, stereotypical imagery has been challenged by organizations that monitor and respond to such content (see Figure 7.4). Asian-American organizations, for example, have decried the relative absence of Asian-American characters on television. This was especially visible on programs such as *Party of Five* or *Suddenly Susan*, which were set in San Francisco—a city where more than one-third of the population is Asian American—but which rarely or never featured Asian-American characters. A study of television programs during the 2015–2016 season concluded that Asian Americans and Pacific Islanders (AAPI) were still "Tokens on the Small Screen" (Chin et al. 2017). The study included first-run prime-time broadcast, basic cable, and premium-cable scripted programs as well as original scripted programs from streaming services. AAPI characters were underrepresented (4.3% on TV vs. 5.9% in the U.S. population). Nearly two-thirds (64%) of the programs had no regular AAPI characters at all, and more than two-thirds (68%) of the programs that had an AAPI character featured only one—the epitome of a "token." Even with shows set in cities with high AAPI populations, underrepresentation was common: 70 percent of shows set in New York City (13% AAPI population) had no AAPI regulars, as did 53 percent of shows set in Los Angeles County (14% AAPI population). When they did appear, AAPI characters were less likely than others to be fully drawn out with familial or romantic relationships and common stereotypes such as "forever foreigner, yellow peril, model minority, emasculated men, exoticized women, sidekicks to White characters" (p. 2) continue. However, some shows were singled out for exemplary and multifaceted representations of AAPI characters, including *The Night Of* (HBO), *The Walking Dead* (AMC), *Master of None* (Netflix), and *Fresh Off the Boat* (ABC).

Blatantly racist images of people of color are now rare in the mainstream U.S. media. Certainly, it is still possible, without much effort, to find examples of stereotypical racial images in film, television, novels, and other media, but the clear trend has been away from such unabashed stereotyping. However, the legacy of racism may well manifest itself in more subtle but perhaps equally powerful ways, including what researchers refer to as "modern racism" (McConahay 1986) or "color-blind racism" (Bonilla-Silva 2014).

For example, in a classic study of local Chicago news coverage of blacks and whites, Robert Entman (1992) distinguished between two forms of racism. *Traditional racism* involves open bigotry usually based on beliefs about the biological inferiority of blacks. *Modern racism* is much more complex, eschewing old-fashioned racist images. As a result, according to Entman, "stereotypes are now more subtle, and stereotyped thinking is reinforced at levels likely to remain below conscious awareness" (p. 345).

Entman documented how news media contribute to modern racism in his study. He found that the local news prominently covered the activities of politically active African Americans. We could easily see the *exclusion* of such activities as racially problematic, but here, Entman (1992) said that the form of their *inclusion* is what makes it racist. Entman found that "black activists often appeared pleading the interests of the black community, while white leaders were much more frequently depicted as representing the entire community" (p. 355). Thus, Entman argued, viewers may get the impression that blacks are pursuing a politics of "special interests" rather than one of public interest. The cycle of racial stereotypes is difficult to break. Political marginalization, as a result of years of racism, may spur black leaders to agitate on

FIGURE 7.4 ■ Fighting Media Stereotypes

Numerous organizations fight stereotyping by the media, including the Media Action Network for Asian Americans (MANAA). The following is excerpted from their open memo to Hollywood on "Restrictive Portrayals of Asians in the Media and How to Balance Them" in which they state:

"Despite the good intentions of individual producers and filmmakers . . . Hollywood typically restricts its portrayals of Asians to a limited range of clichéd stock characters. And this has affected how Asian Americans are perceived and treated in the broader society. . . . Below is a list of restrictive Asian portrayals that are constantly repeated in the mainstream media. . . . Each description is followed by a 'Stereotype-Buster' that can combat the inaccuracies of such portrayals. . . . [The goal of this effort is] to help Hollywood prosper by embracing a more inclusive vision of the human community."

Stereotype	Stereotype-Buster
"Asian Americans as foreigners who cannot be assimilated."	"Portraying Asians as an integral part of the United States. More portrayals of acculturated Asian Americans speaking without foreign accents."
"Asian cultures as inherently predatory."	"Asians as positive contributors to American society."
"Asian Americans restricted to clichéd occupations."	"Asian Americans in diverse, mainstream occupations: doctors, lawyers, therapists, educators, U.S. soldiers, etc."
"Asians relegated to supporting roles in projects with Asian or Asian American content."	"More Asian and Asian American lead roles."
"Asian male sexuality as negative or non-existent."	"More Asian men as positive romantic leads."
"Asian women as 'China dolls'."	"Asian women as self-confident and self-respecting, pleasing themselves as well as their loved ones."
"Asian women as 'dragon ladies'."	"Whenever villains are Asian, it's important that their villainy not be attributed to their ethnicity."
"Asians who prove how good they are by sacrificing their lives."	"Positive Asian characters who are still alive at the end of the story."
"Asian Americans as the 'model minority'."	"The audience empathizing with an Asian character's flaws and foibles."
"Asianness as an 'explanation' for the magical or supernatural."	"Asian cultures as no more or less magical than other cultures."
"Lead Asian roles labeled 'Amerasian' or 'Eurasian' solely to accommodate white actors."	"Until the proverbial playing field is truly level, Asian roles—especially lead roles—should be reserved for Asian actors."

Source: Adapted from Media Action Network for Asian Americans (2018), http://www.manaa.org/asian_stereotypes.html.

behalf of the "black community." The news media duly cover this activism. Such coverage unintentionally conveys a message that blacks are seeking special treatment, thus fostering white resentment and perpetuating the political marginalization of African Americans. (Interestingly, a similar dynamic played out online in recent years. The #BlackLivesMatter effort, protesting police violence toward black people and systemic racism, was interpreted by many white people as somehow seeking special status for black people, resulting in a counter effort, #AllLivesMatter, that downplayed the unique circumstances faced by African Americans [Carney 2016].)

Entman (1992) also criticized the regular use of black newscasters, who are generally "unemotional, friendly but businesslike" (p. 357), as a coanchor with a white newscaster. Although this practice may be seen as a positive development, Entman suggests that "[s]howing attractive, articulate Blacks in such a prestigious public role implies that Blacks are not inherently inferior or socially undesirable—and that racism is no longer a serious impediment to black progress" (p. 358). Entman's analysis suggests that we have to understand race and the media in a holistic fashion. Racially diverse news anchors really do not indicate much progress if, at the same time, the content of news remains racially skewed. Real change will come when all aspects of the media—including media content—more accurately reflect the racial diversity of society. To achieve this, Entman (1992) suggests that we must pay closer attention to how the process of media production influences the content of the media. Entman believes that the production norms of news are linked with the perpetuation of stereotypical images. To create dramatic stories, for example, reporters will often choose sound bites from black leaders that are emotional and suggestive of conflict. Such dramatic quotes, although sometimes misleading, follow media conventions for "good television." The unintended result is that such norms and practices contribute to stereotypical images of African Americans.

These stereotypical images are often subtle, as Entman and Rojecki (2000) found in their survey of various forms of media. On local television news, for example, crime stories tended to overrepresent both black perpetrators and white victims. Compared to whites, blacks were more likely to be shown in mug shots and were twice as likely to be shown under the physical custody of police. Thus, the authors contend, blacks tend to be portrayed in ways that make them more threatening and less sympathetic than whites.

Much of the news coverage of Hurricane Katrina in New Orleans in 2005 took a similar approach. By depicting African Americans as either helpless victims or looters, in contrast to depictions of whites as rescuers and protectors, news media undermined their compassionate tone by reinforcing negative stereotypes. One study of new photographs in Katrina coverage in the most widely circulating daily newspapers in the United States concludes that photojournalism of events in New Orleans built upon and reproduced the kind of modern racism that Entman and others have described: "The overwhelming representation of White military and social service personnel 'saving' the African-American 'refugees' may be one of the most significant themes in images of people in the coverage" (Kahle, Yu, and Whiteside 2007: 86). A variety of more recent work has suggested some improvement in the nature of local news coverage but has also documented that many of the dynamics found in earlier work continue (Campbell, LeDuff, Jenkins, and Brown 2012; Dixon 2015).

Finally, a small but growing body of research on racial representation in online media tends to find that such an environment is not substantially different in other media (Josey et al. 2009; Melican and Dixon 2008; Lind 2017; Noble and Tynes 2016). Perhaps not surprisingly, given that they are created by the same industry, research shows online content from traditional media companies, such as those at news sites, tends to closely mirror earlier findings regarding television and print news. As we will see in Chapter 8, user-generated content, too, can contribute to stereotypical imagery online, as with the circulation of viral videos with racist overtones (Gray 2015).

Race and Class

Entman's (1992) study hints at—but does not explore—the intervening issue of class in the portrayal of African Americans. He is, in effect, contrasting black anchors who exude upper-middle-class manners and confidence with the poor and working-class blacks featured in many news accounts. To understand contemporary media images of different racial and ethnic groups, therefore, it is important to consider their class (and, as we will see, their gender). There is no longer any single image of African Americans in the mainstream media.

The intervention of class in the portrayal of blacks on television has resulted in a bifurcated set of images (Gray 1989, 2004). On one hand, middle-class blacks have long been mainstream in prime-time entertainment programs. Epitomized by *The Cosby Show* of the 1980s and seen in more recent programs such as *black-ish*, these programs portray African-American families who have succeeded in attaining a piece of the traditional American Dream. On the other hand, news coverage and documentaries about blacks tend to focus on poor African Americans in the so-called underclass, mired in drugs, crime, and violence. One implicit message in these contrasting images may be that, because some blacks have clearly succeeded, the failure of other blacks is their own fault.

In their conclusion to a sweeping review of black images in television, radio, music, films, advertising, and PR, Dates and Barlow (1993) suggest that the tension between white-produced images of blacks and black cultural resistance "has become increasingly entangled in more complex social conflicts and concerns. In effect, the primacy of the 'color line' is being challenged by generational, gender, and class differences" (p. 527). We have moved well beyond the point where we can say that a single set of media images represents African Americans—or any other racial or ethnic group.

Controlling Media Images of Race

The absence or stereotyping of different racial groups in the media highlights a fact often taken for granted: Affluent white men have historically controlled the mainstream mass media, often perpetuating racist stereotypes in the content they produced. For example, in their overview of U.S. press history Gonzalez and Torres (2011: 2) contend that white-controlled "newspapers, radio, and television played a pivotal role in perpetuating racists' views among the general population. They did so by routinely portraying non-white minorities as threats to a white society and by reinforcing racial ignorance, group hatred, and discriminatory government policies." They note

Those stereotypes that achieved the most currency [in the general population] tended to mirror the worldview of media owners and editors and their top writers. Exploiting racial fears became not only a reliable way to increase newspaper sales and broadcast ratings, but also served as a tool by which powerful groups in society could stir up public support for projects of territorial and imperial expansion, or by which to weaken opposition among the lower classes to unpopular government policies. (p. 4)

But although whites have often propagated racist images, historically, African Americans and other minorities have responded by producing a culture of resistance. From the slave chronicles of Frederick Douglass to the poetry of Langston Hughes, from the blues of Bessie Smith to the progressive hip-hop of Kendrick Lamar, from the diverse work of Paul Robeson to the social commentary of actor/writer/director Jordan Peele—to name just a few of the better-known personalities—black activists and artists have worked both inside and outside of the mainstream to advance a counterculture that opposes the racist stereotypes being propagated in white-owned media and culture. *Freedom's Journal* was the first African-American newspaper in the United States. Its editors wrote in the first 1827 edition, "We wish to plead our own cause. Too long have others spoken for us. Too long has the publick been deceived by misrepresentations" (in Rhodes 1993: 186).

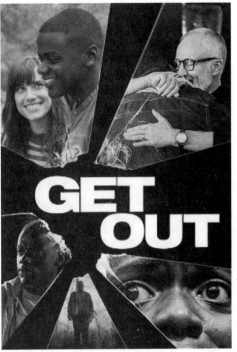

Blumhouse Productions, Monkeypaw Productions, QC Entertainment; distributed by Universal Pictures

Using the conventions of the thriller/horror genre, *Get Out* (2017) writer and director Jordan Peele offered a sophisticated commentary on contemporary race relations by taking aim at liberals who are inadvertently racist. The popular film was an example of increasingly nuanced representations of race, even in mainstream Hollywood movies.

These sentiments also underlie efforts by other racial groups to create alternatives to mainstream media. In journalism, for example, the first Latino paper, *El Misisipi*, was published in 1808 (by a white publisher) in New Orleans. The first Native-American newspaper, *Cherokee Phoenix*, was published in 1828. What was probably the first Asian-American newspaper, *The Golden Hills' News*, first appeared in San Francisco around 1851. All three publications were bilingual, and ever since, bilingual publications have served Latino, Asian, and Native-American communities in many areas (Wilson et al. 2013).

People of color, as well as women and people promoting the interests of the working class and poor, have had to confront a basic dilemma: They have had to choose between developing alternative media and struggling to change mainstream media from within. (As we will see in Chapter 8, social media can offer another option, enabling networked users within a like-minded community to critically comment on mainstream content.) The first strategy—developing alternative media—has the advantages of being feasible with more limited financial resources and of promising control for the producers. The internet has enabled the creation of a vast array of websites that provide news, entertainment, and political discussion specifically aimed at different racial and ethnic groups. However, this approach usually means sacrificing the chance of reaching a mass and broad audience in favor of a smaller, narrower one, in part because media operations working on a shoestring budget cannot hope to match the slick, seductive production quality and staffing levels of the mainstream media.

The second strategy—changing the mainstream media from within—offers an opposite set of advantages and challenges. Mainstream success can result in access to major financial resources that allow a product to reach millions of people. However, Oprah and Russel Simmons notwithstanding, ownership and control of mainstream media are still predominantly in the hands of wealthy white men. Although some people of color and some women have worked their way into positions of authority and influence, they are still vastly underrepresented.

The example of newspapers illustrates this limited influence. In 1978, the American Society of News Editors (ASNE) pledged to create newsrooms that reflected the nation's diversity by the year 2000. When they failed, they reaffirmed the goal but set a new deadline of 2025 (Ho 2017). They still have a long way to go. The 2017 ASNE Newsroom Diversity Survey examined 661 news organizations and found that, in a country with about 39 percent minorities, the overall workforce in newsrooms was only 16.5 percent minorities, including 5.6 percent black, 5.6 percent Hispanic, and 4.5 percent Asian or Pacific Islander. Leadership positions were even less diverse, with only 13.4 percent minority. The 63 online-only news sites in the survey were more diverse (24.3%) than the 598 newspapers (16.3%). Although falling short of equal representation, these numbers are a significant improvement over just a few years ago. The percentage of racial and ethnic minorities in the ASNE's surveys was only 4.2 percent in 1978 and just 12.4 percent as recently as 2012 (ASNE 2017). One way minority journalists have worked for change in their field is by organizing a variety of associations that often collaborate on efforts to promote diversity in the newsroom. These include the National Association of Hispanic Journalists, the Asian American Journalists Association, the National Association of Black Journalists, and the Native American Journalists Association.

Minority underrepresentation exists in other media fields as well. For the top 100 movies each year from 2007 to 2017, only 5.2 percent of the directors were black, whereas 3.2 percent were Asian (Smith, Choueiti, and Pieper 2018a). The 2016 Hollywood Writers Report found that minorities were just 7 percent of film writers and 13 percent of television writers (Hunt 2016). People of color were overrepresented in some parts of popular music, though. Of the 600 songs appearing on the Billboard Hot 100 end of year charts from 2012 through 2017, 42 percent of the artists were from racial or ethnic minorities; this reached 51.9 percent by 2017 (Smith, Choueiti, and Pieper (2018b).

GENDER AND MEDIA CONTENT

In some ways, the media's history of portraying women parallels its history of portraying people of color. Women were often marginalized in all types of media. Simple, blatantly stereotypical images dominated the earlier years of mass media. As media audiences and the media industry felt the influence of movements struggling for women's rights, these stereotypical images gave way to a wider diversity of images and roles for women. Here too, then, we see a history of injustice, inequality, and change.

Women: Presence and Control in the Media

Family and heterosexual relationships are central to the plots of many films, music videos, and television programs, ensuring that women (unlike people of color) are regularly included in these media. However, reviews of the extensive literature on gender and the media reveal an inequality in the frequency of appearance of women and men. Prime-time television, for example, has long featured more portrayals of men than women, and men appear more often in lead roles (Fejes 1992; Greenberg and Worrell 2007; Scharrer 2012; Signorielli 2009). Essentially unchanged for over a decade, in the 2017–2018 season on scripted prime-time broadcast, cable, and first-run streaming programs, men were still a majority of recurring characters—57 percent, compared to women's 43 percent (GLAAD 2018). Similarly, characters in animated television programs and in video games are disproportionately male (Klein and Shiffman 2009; Robinson, Callister, Clark, and Phillips 2009).

Although women are regularly included in the media, control of the creation and production of media images is much more likely to be in male hands. In the top 250 domestic grossing films in 2017, women were just 11 percent of directors, 11 percent of writers, 19 percent of executive producers, 16 percent of editors, and 4 percent of cinematographers (Lauzen 2018). Of the directors associated with the top 100 movies of each year between 2007 and 2017, only 4.3 percent were women; roughly 22 male directors for every female director (Smith et al. 2018a). Overall, the 2016 Hollywood Writers Report found that women were 16.9 percent of film writers and 28.7 percent of television writers (Hunt 2016). Women were dramatically underrepresented in popular music, too. Of the 600 songs appearing on the Billboard Hot 100 end-of-year charts from 2012 through 2017, 16.8 percent of the artists were women, 12.3 percent of the songwriters were women, and only 2 percent of the producers were women (Smith et al. 2018b). (See Figure 7.5.) Women make up 33.1 percent of radio and TV news directors and 44.2 percent of all radio and TV news staffers (Women's Media Center 2017). Women made up 38.9 percent of newsroom employees at newspapers and 47.8 percent at online news sites in 2017; they were 38.9 percent of the leadership positions in those newsrooms (ASNE 2017).

Indeed, the dynamics relating to gender are similar to those found in the discussion of race and ethnicity. Women are generally not in positions of control and, perhaps as a result, are less likely than men to be prominently featured in media products. Summarizing the status of women and minorities in television—in words that apply to other media forms as well—sociologist Darnell Hunt (2013:1) concludes that "despite a few pockets of promise—much more work must be done on the television diversity front before the corps of writers telling our stories looks significantly more like us as a nation."

Changing Media Roles for Women . . . and Men

The media images of women and men reflect and reproduce a whole set of stereotypical but changing gender roles. On prime-time television, men are more likely than women to be cast as main characters, and men typically speak more than women. In addition, we are likely to see women focused on family, friends, and romance, whereas men are more likely to be portrayed in work-related activities (Lauzen, Dozier, and Horan 2008). Men are also more likely than women to be portrayed as having high-status jobs—in traditionally male occupations—and are less likely to be shown in the home (Glascock 2001). Female

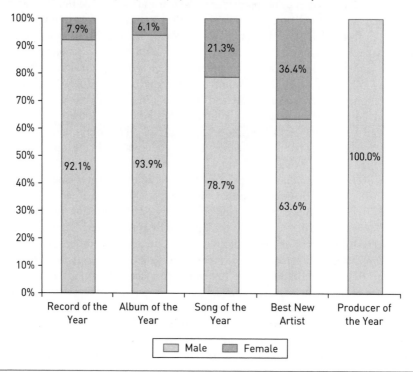

FIGURE 7.5 ■ Gender Inequality in Grammy Nominations, 2013–2018

In 2018, the #GrammysSoMale campaign flagged the underrepresentation of women in the music industry's most prestigious award nominationts. Underrepresentation of women has existed for years and reflects long-standing inequality in employment within the music industry.

Source: Smith et al. (2018b).

Note: "Record" and "Album of the Year" are awarded to the performer and production team; "Song of the Year" is awarded only to the composer.

television characters are, on average, younger than male characters; and middle-aged male characters are more likely than their female counterparts to "play leadership roles, wield occupational power, and have goals" (Lauzen and Dozier 2005: 253).

A recent content analysis of prime-time television found that "[w]hen women are depicted, some troubling gender stereotypes have persisted, whereas others appear to be declining" (Sink and Mastro 2017: 16). In particular, male characters still appear more dominant through more verbal and physical aggression and bullying, whereas women were both more sexualized and family oriented than men. However, surprisingly, men were more objectified—that is, seen as a sex object or sexually degraded—than women, a trend noted in other studies as well (Gianatasio 2013; Rohlinger 2002). In addition, male and female characters did not differ in terms of intelligence, articulacy, or motivation.

Despite some changes, the relative stability in the portrait of gendered roles can be seen in the fact that a summary written 25 years ago remains a generally accurate overall assessment: Fejes (1992) concluded then that "men, as portrayed on adult television, do not deviate much from the traditional patriarchal notion of men and masculinity" (p. 12). They are generally portrayed in the media as powerful and successful. They "occupy high-status positions, initiate action and act from the basis of rational mind as opposed to emotions, are found more in the world of things as opposed to family and relationships, and organize their lives around problem solving" (p. 12).

Women's roles have often reflected similar stereotypes about femininity. Over the years, the dominant roles for women have been as mother, homemaker, or sexual object. The media industry, though, responded to feminists organizing for social change. As with racial stereotypes, the industry has muted the blatant simplicity of stereotypical gender images in more recent years. There is certainly a wider palette of roles and media images of women today than there was a few decades ago. However, the inequality that women still face in society as a whole is clearly reflected in the unequal treatment women receive in the media. As Sink and Mastro (2017: 18) conclude in their study of television,

> Certainly, shows like *Madam Secretary*, *Scandal*, and *How to Get Away with Murder* are notable for featuring powerful female leads; unfortunately, these examples seem to represent the exception and not the norm in primetime programming. Instead, young, submissive, and sexually provocative women appear to commonly populate the TV landscape.

Some of the unequal treatment that women receive, such as that in sexist advertising and degrading pornography, is straightforward and easy to spot, as are some of the stereotypical roles writers still create for women on television situation comedies and dramas. However, like racist stereotypes, sexist stereotypes have often taken subtler forms, as in the coverage of women's sports.

The Case of Women's Sports

For more than a quarter century, researchers have studied both the quantity of coverage women's sports receive as well as the quality and nature of that coverage. They have found some encouraging changes and troubling continuities.

Early studies found little coverage of women's sports, and the coverage that did exist was blatantly sexist. Tuggle (1997) found that ESPN's *Sports Center* and CNN's *Sports Tonight* devoted less than 5 percent of their coverage to women's sports, concluding that "in nearly every measurable way, the two programs portrayed women's sports as less important than men's athletic competition."

Studies conducted in the 1970s and 1980s found that, on the rare occasions when women athletes were covered on television, they "were likely to be overtly trivialized, infantilized, and sexualized" (Messner, Duncan, and Jensen 1993: 123). Schell (1999) noted women were often portrayed as "sexual objects available for male consumption rather than as competitive athletes." Musto, Cooky, and Messner (2017) summarize their findings from the 1990s, noting, "Commentators routinely discussed women athletes in overtly sexist and denigrating ways. Commentators snickered with sexual innuendo when showing bikini-clad women spectators at a men's baseball game or leering at conventionally beautiful professional women athletes."

Some of the sexism was more subtle. When Messner and his associates (1993) studied television coverage of the 1989 men's and women's National Collegiate Athletic Association (NCAA) basketball tournaments and various matches in the 1989 U.S. Open tennis tournament, they found the commentary framed women's and men's sports differently. Gender was constantly "marked" in women's basketball coverage, as in "NCAA Women's National Championship Game" or "women's basketball." In contrast, television coverage referred to men's competition in a universal way, without mentioning gender at all: "The Final Four," "The NCAA National Championship Game," and so on. The naming of athletes also differed by gender. Commentators covering tennis matches referred to female athletes by first name seven times as often as they did male athletes. In basketball, the ratio was about two to one. Messner and his associates reminded readers that "dominants generally have license to refer to subordinates (younger people, employees, lower-class people, ethnic minorities, women, etc.) by their first names" (p. 128). Finally, an array of differences appeared in the language used to describe athletes. Male coaches "yelled," whereas female coaches "screamed." Whereas an excellent shot by a female player was "lucky," excellent play from a male player showed that he was "imposing his will all over this court."

By the 2000s, Messner and Cooky (2010) found the quantity of women's coverage had not improved; less than 2 percent of local television sports coverage focused on women's sports; similarly, ESPN's *Sports Center* devoted less than 2 percent of its coverage to women's sports. They concluded that "the gap between TV news and highlights shows' coverage of women's and men's sports has not narrowed, it has widened" (p. 22). Kian, Mondello, and Vincent (2009) noted that,

> despite the vast increase in the number of women and girls who actively participate or once played organized sports, research has consistently shown sport media generally provide far more coverage of men's sports than women's sports. This holds true in nearly all levels of competition and in the vast majority of sports. (p. 447)

While quantity remained scarce, the nature and quality of the coverage shifted. Messner and Cooky (2010) examined ESPN's *SportsCenter* as well as television sports news on the local network affiliates in Los Angeles. They found that stories that trivialize women's sports and sexualize female athletes were now rare. Disparaging portrayals and sexualized humor, which aim to make women's sports attractive to male viewers, had largely disappeared. Instead, a new focus emerged on women athletes as family members, emphasizing their roles as mothers, wives, or girlfriends—another strategy for attracting male audiences. As Musto et al. (2017) later observed, this contrasted sharply with coverage of men:

> over the 25-year span of our study coverage of male athletes, rarely—if ever—did they include discussions of men as fathers, husbands, or boyfriends. Despite recognizing women's athletic accomplishments, this frame continued to marginalize women by emphasizing their adherence to the conventionally heterofeminine roles of wives, mothers, or girlfriends. (p. 580)

Andy Lyons / Staff / Getty Images

Research shows that women's sports receive less coverage than men's sports and that the nature of that coverage often has been stereotypically sexist—although less blatantly so in recent years.

In the 2010s, coverage evolved again (Cooky, Messner, and Musto 2015; Cooky and Messner 2018). Musto et al. (2017) note that recent coverage has been characterized by its "lackluster, matter-of-fact manner. Rather than being insulting or ambivalent, most women's sports coverage lacked the action-packed, humorous language, lavish compliments, and dominant descriptors routinely found in men's sports commentary" (p. 590). This limited and inferior coverage, they argue, represents new and more subtle forms of sexism. Just as overt racism has given way to more subtle "color-blind racism," overt sexism has been replaced with what they call "gender bland" sexism. Rather than being "blind" to gender differences, this "gender bland" situation acknowledges the segregation of women and men's sports and "makes women's athletic accomplishments appear lackluster compared to men's through the inferior coverage given them. "This 'bland' language normalizes a hierarchy between men's and women's sports while simultaneously avoiding charges of overt sexism. . . . [and therefore] reinforces gender boundaries and hierarchies, presenting a fictitious view of inherent male superiority in a way that is subtler and more difficult to detect than before" (p. 578).

CLASS AND THE MEDIA

The election of Donald Trump as president produced a good deal of discussion about the "forgotten" working class—always white in this narrative. Much of that analysis and commentary was based on inaccurate premises that don't match the reality of a

U.S. working class that is actually more racially diverse than the rest of the population and that is based in service jobs, not manufacturing (Rowell 2017). However, this discussion did stumble across one reality: The U.S. media often pay little attention to the working class—of any race.

Interestingly, researchers have not given a great deal of attention to class in media content either. There are far fewer studies about class in media content than about either race or gender. Yet as sociologist Diana Kendall (2011) notes, "Even a cursory look at the media reveals that class clearly permeates media content. Regardless of whether journalists and scriptwriters or entertainment writers consciously acknowledge the importance of framing class in their analysis of everyday live, it continually imbues the millions of articles and television shows written and produced each year" (p. 3). It is useful, therefore, to examine both the class distribution of people in the media and the roles given to characters of different class status. It is also important to keep in mind the unique relationship between issues of class and the media industry.

Class and Media Content

Overwhelmingly, the American society portrayed in the media is wealthier than it is in the real world. Although there are various ways of measuring social class that lead to somewhat different estimates, about two-thirds of adult Americans do not have a four-year college degree—one indicator of working-class status (U.S. Census Bureau 2017a). Also, most Americans work in service, clerical, or production jobs (rarely depicted in the media), and nearly half self-identify as working class (Hout 2007). Media, however, portray the social world as one overwhelmingly populated by the middle class—especially middle-class professionals.

Family-Based Situation Comedies

One well-documented area of class imagery is the family-based sitcom. Butsch (2003) examined 315 family-based situation comedies that aired from 1946 to 2000. Because programs based in a workplace—such as police shows—would dictate the occupation of the main characters, he intentionally excluded these. The focus of domestic-based situation comedies is home life away from work, enabling creators of such programs to give their characters a wide range of potential occupations. Butsch found that only 14 percent of such programs featured blue-collar, clerical, or service workers as heads of the household. More than two-thirds (68%) of home-based situation comedies featured middle-class families. And the adults in these television families weren't your run-of-the-mill professionals, either. The elite professions were vastly overrepresented. Doctors outnumbered nurses nine to one, professors outnumbered schoolteachers four to one, and lawyers outnumbered less glamorous accountants 10 to one. All these high-paying jobs for television characters meant lots of disposable income, and families in these situation comedies overwhelmingly lived in beautiful, middle-class homes equipped with all the amenities.

There are exceptions, notable precisely because there have been so few over the decades:

- Ralph in *The Honeymooners* (1955–1956) was a bus driver.
- Archie Bunker from *All in the Family* (1971–1979) was a bigoted dock worker.

- *Good Times* (1974–1979) featured a working-poor family headed by Florida, a maid, and her husband, James, who fought unemployment, sometimes working two low-paying jobs when he could find them.

- Al Bundy, the father in the highly dysfunctional family on *Married with Children* (1987–1997), was a shoe salesman.

- The main character in *Roseanne* (1988–1997; 2018) held various jobs, including a factory worker, waitress, and shampooer in a beauty salon, whereas her husband struggled as a construction worker and mechanic.

- Harriet Winslow, the mother on *Family Matters* (1989–1997), worked various jobs in a department store while her husband, Carl, was a police officer.

- Doug Heffernan in *King of Queens* (1998–2007) was a deliveryman, and his wife was a secretary.

- *The George Lopez Show* (2002–2007) revolved around a low-level manufacturing plant manager and his working-class family.

- *The Middle* (2009-current) featured a father who was a quarry foreman and a mother who worked a series of service jobs.

Interestingly, such working-class programs often highlighted their characters' aspirations for middle-class life through the launching of small businesses. For example, Archie Bunker became a bar owner in the later program, *Archie's Place* (1979–1983), and both parents on *Roseanne* opened up businesses, an unsuccessful motorcycle shop and a diner.

There is an exception to the relative scarcity of working-class characters on sitcoms: animated programs. Ever since Fred in *The Flintstones* was written as a rock quarry "crane" operator, prime-time animated comedies have highlighted working-class characters: Peter Griffin of *Family Guy* was a blue-collar worker; Cleveland Brown in *The Cleveland Show* was a cable installer; *King of the Hill* featured a propane salesman; and Homer in the long-running program *The Simpsons* was a woefully underqualified technician in a nuclear power plant. The prominence of the working class in cartoon portrayals contrasts sharply with its scarcity in live-action programs.

In contrast to the relatively few portrayals of working-class families, there are a large number of domestic-based situation comedies in which the head of the household had a middle-class job. The list of lawyers, doctors, architects, advertising executives, journalists, and businesspeople on such programs is a long one. Butsch (2003) argues that the predominance of middle-class characters in these television situation comedies conveys a subtle but significant message. The few working-class characters who do populate some programs are the deviant exception to the norm, and therefore, it must be their own fault that they are less economically successful.

The message that people in the working class are responsible for their fate is a quintessential middle-class idea that ignores the structural conditions that shape social class. It is also an idea reinforced by another tendency identified by Butsch (2003). In contrast to most middle-class television families, the father in working-class families is usually ridiculed as an incompetent, although sometimes lovable, buffoon. Ralph Kramden, Fred Flintstone, Cleveland Brown, Peter Griffin, Doug Heffernan, Al Bundy, and Homer

Simpson are perhaps the most obvious cases. All, to varying degrees, were simpletons who pursued foolish get-rich schemes and wound up in trouble because they simply weren't very smart. Each of these shows portrayed the female main character as more levelheaded and in control. Often, these programs even portrayed the children of working-class men as smarter and more competent than their fathers. In fact, Butsch (2005) argues that television representations of working-class men have followed this relatively standard script for five decades:

> While there have been variations and exceptions, the stock character of the ineffectual, even buffoonish, working-class man has persisted as the dominant image. In the prime-time tapestry he is contrasted with consistently competent working-class wives and children and manly middle-class fathers—a composite image in which working-class men are demasculinized and their class status justified. (p. 133)

Butsch (2003) acknowledges that this kind of program sometimes also ridiculed middle-class fathers but not nearly as often as working-class fathers. Instead, the long-standing norm in comedies with middle-class families—from *Father Knows Best* and *Leave It to Beaver* to *Bewitched* and the *Brady Bunch* to the *Cosby Show* and *The Wonder Years*—is for middle-class fathers to be competent at their jobs and often to be wise and capable parents. The implication, argues Butsch, is that working-class families struggle because of incompetence and lack of intelligence, while middle-class families succeed because of competence and intelligence. Such images help reinforce the idea that class-based inequality is just and functional. Various other studies over the years have also found that middle-class TV fathers are portrayed as more competent than working-class fathers (Cantor 1990; Pehlke, Hennon, Radina, and Kuvalanka 2009). One small study of father-child interactions in sitcoms during the 2000s found that, compared to portrayals of working-class fathers, portrayals of middle-class sitcom fathers were more positive, featuring somewhat more involvement, more friendly and fun interactions, and fewer negative interactions (Troilo 2017).

Perhaps the distorted image of class on television contributes to the feeling of exclusion so often described in the news media after Trump's election. Commenting on "TV's callous neglect of working-class America," freelance writer Noel Murray (2017) notes,

> when our highest-profile comedies and dramas have no interest in—or perhaps even no understanding of—what really goes on in low-rent office parks, supermarkets, fast food restaurants, un-gated subdivisions, and apartment complexes, then a large chunk of the populace can feel like their voices are going unrepresented in the mainstream media. They've become forgotten, invisible . . . implicitly told that they're uninteresting, or even alien.

Tabloid Talk Shows and Reality Television

Daytime television talk shows and reality television are two other media genres where class issues are evident. In very distinct ways, each tends to help reinforce myths about class.

Adam Rose / Contributor / Getty Images

Ron Tom / Contributor / Getty Images

The class status of television characters is communicated to viewers in various ways, one of which is the set used to represent home life. When *Roseanne* was revived briefly in 2018, it kept its iconic working-class set with worn furniture, cheap wall hangings, and household clutter. In contrast, though *black-ish* was applauded for its racial diversity, it reproduced the usual upper-middle-class household found on many sitcoms. The set featured an expensive-looking elegant dining room, a gourmet kitchen, massive closets, and tasteful artwork.

Daytime talk shows featuring ordinary citizens first began appearing in the United States in the 1970s but reached their peak of popularity in the 1980s and 1990s. Early daytime talk show pioneer Phil Donahue often featured serious discussion about contested issues such as abortion, women's rights, and new cultural trends. Defenders of daytime talk shows saw them as providing a unique space for the inclusion of voices that were otherwise ignored. In his study of these programs, Gamson (1998) notes

> Talk shows, defenders claim, give voice to common folks and visibility to invisible folks. . . . Indeed, Donahue and others assert, the talk show genre was and is a "revolutionary" one. "It's called democracy," Donahue argues, "but [before my program] there were no shows that—every day, let just folks stand up and say what-for. I'm proud of the democracy of the show." (p. 14)

Such democratization had it benefits. Gamson (1998) credits these talk shows with increasing the visibility of LGBT people in American households. However, especially as the genre evolved over time, the format and structure of these programs presented a wildly distorted take on "common folks." They highlighted tawdry subjects, encouraged conflict, and orchestrated bizarre spectacles, becoming known as "tabloid talk shows" or "trash TV."

As a consequence, one of the only television forums where working-class and poor people were routinely spotlighted ended up perpetuating the myth that such people were undisciplined, violent, lazy, sex-crazed, and generally dysfunctional. Sensationalistic talk shows, such as those hosted by Jerry Springer and Maury Povich, often highlighted particularly extreme lifestyles of people from poor or working-class backgrounds. Sought out precisely for their wild behaviors—and often coached by producers to exaggerate such antics to create dramatic and entertaining television—guests were treated as freak shows to entertain audiences.

Although daytime talk shows continue the class spectacle today, their popularity has been supplanted by more recent "reality television" (RT) programs. Media studies scholar June Deery's (2015) analysis of RT programs in the United States and Britain finds a mixed treatment of class, in part depending on the type of reality show. She notes, sometimes "class is muted or evaded just as it is in other programming, in others it is unusually conspicuous and becomes a topic of conversation among participants and viewers" (p. 128). Although class is secondary in many programs, it is front and center in others. For example, in home "makeover" programs, affluent class values dominate: "No one goes into a middle-class home and makes it over into something working-class: Formica must be replaced by granite and plastic by steel," Deery observes. Sometimes, though, these makeover programs implicitly celebrate working class—and usually male-centered—skills, such as elaborate car restorations on *Pimp My Ride*.

Deery writes that there has been a particularly worrying side to reality television in recent years as "stereotypes and even caricatures have been trotted out to create easy comedy, mockery, or disgust," including "rednecks" and "guidos" in the United States and "chavs" in the UK (p. 131). Program producers sometimes exploit working-class and poor people as cheap labor, explicitly seeking contestants they think exhibit stereotypical class attributes to heighten the tension and drama of competitive reality programs. Deery argues that reality television has "become a reliable way to make working-class identities productive for middle-class media producers and audiences, whether it be the good and deserving poor who need rescue (makeovers) or the badly behaved poor who are proud of their recalcitrance (numerous docusoaps)" (p. 143). She contends,

> Working-class characters are simply a cheaply mined resource, more easily lured by modest financial incentives and apparently less concerned about social embarrassment than those holding a superior status. In a kind of economic draft, many voluntarily participate even in humiliation perhaps [as one RT producer suggested] because they feel socially marginalized and seek public attention. (p. 134)

The Union Taboo

A focus on individualism, as opposed to collective action, is another key feature of media content. If media rarely show working-class folks, they are even less likely to show working people in labor unions, despite the fact that more than 14 million Americans currently belong to a union (Bureau of Labor Statistics 2018). When unions are featured, it is usually in a negative light.

In one classic study, Puette (1992) examined the image of labor unions in Hollywood movies, television dramas, TV news, and editorial cartoons and argued that there are some basic "lenses" that color and distort media portrayals of organized labor and its leaders. Among these media images are the stereotypes that unions protect and encourage unproductive, lazy, and insubordinate workers; that unions undermine America's ability to compete internationally; that union leaders, because they do not come from the educated or cultured (privileged) classes, are more likely to be corrupted by power than are business or political leaders; and that unions are no longer necessary. Certainly, unions are far from perfect organizations, and they are fair game for media criticism. However, with very few exceptions, Puette's analysis points to a systematic and relentless disparagement of the most visible effort at collective empowerment by working Americans.

A decade later Martin (2003) added to the study of media coverage of unions, examining the reasons why the coverage is so poor. His analysis focuses on the idea that media outlets relate to their audiences almost exclusively as consumers rather than as workers. By focusing on consumer issues, commercial media manage to sidestep the actual questions involved in labor disputes. For example, the news media spend more time highlighting travel delays for passengers than they do on why airline employees have gone on strike. News media conventions also rely on simply reporting "both sides" of the story, rarely informing viewers or readers about the veracity of the conflicting claims. Such coverage is uninformative and tends to portray labor disputes as bickering that is of little relevance to the audience.

The idea of a positive—or at least balanced—portrayal of a labor union is so rare on U.S. television that, when one does occur, it becomes notable. When the police drama *The Bridge* first appeared on CBS, the *Los Angeles Times* television critic noted that the program would appear foreign to viewers not because it was set in Canada but because of its major story line. "Americans will know they're viewing an import the moment the uber narrative makes itself clear. 'The Bridge' is about a street cop attempting to rid the force of corruption through . . . wait for it . . . its union" (McNamara 2010). In addition to a rare positive portrayal of a union, the program also highlighted class issues. The show's title refers to a bridge that separates a wealthy Toronto neighborhood from a poor one. The program was canceled after just three episodes aired in the United States but was renewed for another season in more union-friendly Canada.

The situation has not improved. Recent studies show that media continue to paint union members as overpaid, greedy, and undeserving (Brimeyer, Silva, and Byrne 2016; Kane and Newman 2017).

News Media

Class enters directly into news media content as well. News tends to highlight issues of concern to middle- and upper-class readers and viewers. Take the example of stock market reports. Only about half of American families own any stock at all—directly or indirectly (such as through mutual funds, pensions, or retirement accounts). In fact, more than 80 percent of the nation's stocks (whether owned directly or indirectly) are owned by just the wealthiest 10 percent of the nation's families (Wolff 2017). Thus, the vast majority of the public is unlikely to be interested in stock reports. Most Americans do not even understand stock listings and reports. Yet stock market reports are a prominent feature of news programs and newspapers. Now think for a moment. When was the last time you saw a news story explaining how to apply for welfare benefits, or an extension on unemployment insurance, or reviewing the legal rights of workers to form a union or to learn about health and safety hazards in the workplace? Even suggesting such stories might seem odd because it contradicts our taken-for-granted notion of what news is "supposed" to be.

On the whole, the news reflects a middle- and upper-class view of the world. In this world, newspaper business pages flourish, but labor reporters are almost an extinct breed. News may address "regular" people as consumers, but it almost never addresses them as workers. Even consumer-oriented stories are scarce because they have the potential to offend advertisers. For example, the *San Jose Mercury News* once published an innocuous feature story advising consumers on how to buy a new car. A group of 47 local auto dealers retaliated by canceling 52 pages of advertising in the paper's weekly "Drive" section—a loss of $1 million for the paper. Although pressure from local car dealers is infamous in the newspaper industry, this time the paper went to the Federal Trade Commission (FTC), which ruled that the auto dealers had illegally conspired. The dealers reached an agreement with the FTC and agreed not to boycott the newspaper in the future (Chiuy 1995). This episode is a dramatic illustration of how advertisers can influence media content—directly or indirectly. Advertisers do not want media content to interfere with the "buying mood" of the public.

The people who populate news and public affairs programs also represent a skewed sample of American life. "Hard news" usually features people in positions of power, especially politicians, professionals, and corporate executives. We might argue that, for many journalists, the very working definition of news is what those in power say and do. As we saw in Chapter 5, the organizational structure of journalism also favors coverage of the wealthy and powerful. The industry organizes its news beats around powerful political institutions, such as the city hall, the state house, and federal offices. People with substantial resources and influence can also command attention from the media by supplying journalists with packaged information, such as press releases, press conferences, and pseudo-events. The only regular features on working-class and poor people are likely to come from the reporter on the crime beat.

Unlike straight news broadcasts, public affairs programs offer a great deal of flexibility in the list of guests who are invited by producers to comment on and analyze current issues. Yet the class characteristics of the guests on such programs are also heavily skewed toward professionals. On prestigious public affairs programs, politicians and professionals have long dominated the guest lists (Croteau and Hoynes 1994). Representatives of organizations speaking on behalf of working people are almost nonexistent on such programs. Public television in general is skewed toward professional sources, usually leaving the public out of the picture (Croteau, Hoynes, and Carragee 1996).

Finally, there is often a racial dimension to class images. The term *working class* often conjures up images of whites, even though people of color are disproportionately working class. Barbara Ehrenreich (1995) notes, "The most intractable stereotype is of the working class (which is, in imagination, only White) as a collection of reactionaries and bigots—reflected, for example, in the use of the terms 'hard hat' or 'redneck' as class slurs" (p. 41). She also observes, "It is possible for a middle-class person today to read the papers, watch television, even go to college, without suspecting that America has any inhabitants other than white-collar people—and, of course, the annoyingly persistent 'black underclass'" (p. 40).

That last phrase is important. In the media, the "poor" tend to be equated with blacks—even though only about 23 percent of people living below the poverty line in the United States are black; about two-thirds of poor people are white; and 43 percent are white non-Hispanic (U.S. Census Bureau 2017b). One study of the major news magazines and the three major networks (Gilens 1996) examined images used to accompany stories about poverty. It found that 62 percent of poor people pictured in newsmagazines and 65 percent of those on television were black. Such gross misrepresentation of class and race can easily contribute to misperceptions on the part of the public. Indeed, polls have shown that Americans—of all races—tend to vastly overestimate the percentage of poor people who are black.

Advertising

Unrepresentative images of class are perhaps most obvious in advertising, which excludes poor people and significantly underrepresents working-class people. Instead, ads featuring comfortable, middle-class and affluent lives fill magazines, films, and television commercials. Much as white people and men are the "norm" against which racial/ethnic minorities and women are contrasted, the affluent middle class is "unmarked" in advertising, serving as the default norm. In addition, class status can trump gender or race, as when an affluent woman or person of color is compared favorably to a working class white man (Callier 2014). On the other hand, when courting working-class consumers in jeans and beer commercials, for example, more affluent men can be portrayed as vaguely effeminate or European, in contrast to "real," hyper-masculine, American men portrayed as holding blue-collar jobs, working on cars, driving trucks, watching sports, and buying the brand's products (McAllister and Kumanyia 2013).

Although such class comparisons have been relatively subtle in the past, McAllister and Aupperle (2017) examined "post-recession" advertising—after the 2007–2012 economic downturn—in the United States and found unusually explicit class comparisons in ads by Buick, Allstate, DirecTV, and other major advertisers. In what they call "class shaming" strategies, these advertisers presented the affluent as victims of an incompetent working class and ridiculed service workers. They presented working-class people consistently as losers and incompetents who did not use the company's brand, whereas smart affluent people did. One Cadillac ad—later lauded on conservative talk radio shows—preached a blend of nationalism and self-reliance as the character in the ad spoke directly to the camera while walking through his opulent house. Ridiculing Europeans who "stroll home . . . stop by the café . . . [and] take August off" the character celebrated Americans, "Because we're crazy driven, hard-working believers. . . . It's pretty simple. You work hard. You create your own luck," he says as he gets in his expensive Cadillac car (pp. 148–9). The latter line echoes the often-heard claim that people are solely responsible for their own fate; structural barriers have no place in producing class inequality.

Sometimes these ads used what McAllister and Aupperle refer to as "working-classface"—analogous to the blackface of minstrel shows—that featured well-known actors engaging in exaggerated class shaming disguised with humor. For example, a series of DirecTV commercials compared various "bad" and "good" versions of actor Rob Lowe, in which the "bad" version had cable whereas the "good" version had DirecTV's satellite service. The good Rob Lowe was always well-groomed, fashionably dressed, and shown in a pristine home. The inferior versions of the Lowe character were marked with exaggerated, stereotypical, working-class attributes—bushy mustache, slicked-back hair, white T-shirt, oversized gold jewelry, and accompanied by poorly dressed and tattooed women showing excess cleavage. The authors conclude that such ads "have implications for how people understand the importance of structural inequalities versus individual explanations for impoverishment and privilege. . . . If it is easy to purchase your way to avoid 'being like this me,' then why don't the poor simply make better consumer decisions?" (p. 153).

Explaining Class Images: "Some People Are More Valuable Than Others"

As we have seen, media portrayals of class are skewed toward the more affluent, neglecting or negatively portraying working-class and poor people The production perspective on media, discussed in Part III, is helpful in alerting us to the various interlocking social forces that are likely responsible for this situation. Class underlies the media industry in a distinctive way, connecting advertisers, producers, and audiences.

First, most media are commercial enterprises supported by advertising dollars. So the first place to look for an explanation of class content is the preferences of advertisers. The for-profit, advertiser-driven nature of all commercial media means that advertisers are keenly interested in the economic status of media consumers. They want to reach people with enough disposable income to buy their products and services, regardless of whether those people are male or female; black, white, Asian, or Latino. You can guess which class a media product reaches by examining the ads that accompany it. Everybody has to buy toothpaste and breakfast cereal, but when a program or publication features ads for jewelry, expensive cars, and investment services, you know it is aimed at an affluent audience.

Second, media producers need advertisers, so they are sensitive to what may attract advertisers or keep them away. They usually attract advertisers by delivering solidly middle-class consumers. The search for such consumers can sometimes take on strange dimensions. For example, to improve the demographic profile (in terms of average household income) of their readership, some newspapers expanded their content aimed at more affluent households, such as "Style" sections with articles that highlight upscale fashion, culture, and restaurants. In addition, some papers made it difficult for poor people to buy their product by limiting the paper's distribution in poor neighborhoods while raising the price of the paper in these areas and reducing it in wealthier areas! In the 1990s, the *Los Angeles Times*, for example, raised its daily sales price in poorer inner-city neighborhoods from 35 cents to 50 cents. At the same time, it reduced the price to 25 cents in affluent surrounding counties (Cole 1995). Newspaper publishers are not the only ones who recognize that affluent people are more important for the media industry than poor or working-class people. In the 1970s, ABC issued a profile of its viewing audience for advertisers, highlighting its desirable demographics. The network titled the profile "Some People Are More Valuable Than Others" (Wilson et al. 2013: 25).

More commonly, media producers accommodate advertisers by simply avoiding content that might offend advertisers. On television, advertisers prefer programs featuring characters who could conceivably be using their products. The show, therefore, serves as a "complementary context" for the ads. As Butsch (2018) notes,

> This requires dramas built around affluent characters for whom consuming is not problematic. Thus, affluent characters predominate, and occupational groups with higher levels of consumer expenditure are overrepresented. Even in a working-class domestic sitcom, is unusual for financial strain to be a regular theme of a show. (p. 446)

The writers and other personnel who create such programs, too, are aware of the need to avoid controversy. Routinely working with severe time constraints, they often resort to tried and tested formulas and draw upon "the small closed community of those engaged in television production" (p. 448): a world that is distinctly middle class.

Third, audiences have a role to play in what determines the fate of media content. Many of the programs depicting working-class characters, for example, are notable both because they are rare and because they were highly popular. Popular programs on television are more likely to succeed. However, that can be overstated; advertisers ultimately trump viewers. Sometimes lower-rated shows that reach a desirable demographic will survive, whereas higher-rated programs that reach a less-desirable audience will be cancelled. That was the case with the long-running *Murder She Wrote*, which was cancelled despite good ratings because it did not appeal to the coveted 18–49 demographic most advertisers prefer. The show's writers took a parting shot at the industry by titling the program's last episode "Death by Demographics."

Sociologist Diana Kendall (2011) reminds us that class stereotypes in news and entertainment media can play a vital role in our collective understanding of inequality. Media images and narratives that represent the poor as the "other"—as genuinely different from mainstream citizens—and those that "play on the idea that the clothing, manners, and speech patterns of the working class are not as good as those of the middle or upper classes" (p. 3) help sustain a view that the middle and upper classes are superior and deserving of their wealth and privilege. At the same time, such representations reveal little about the increasing inequality in American society and do little to illuminate the complexity of the contemporary stratification system.

SEXUAL ORIENTATION: OUT OF THE CLOSET AND INTO THE MEDIA

The LGBT community is another group in society that historically has been underrepresented and distorted in media coverage. For decades, the community been either ignored or ridiculed in nearly all media accounts. Like the movements for racial equality, women's rights, and organized labor, the LGBT movement both developed alternative media and worked for more positive portrayals in the mainstream media. It has had a dramatic impact on U.S. society, changing social norms and laws, and thereby serving as a catalyst for dramatically changing media content. (See Figure 7.6 for highlights.)

Reviewing the literature on the topic, Fejes and Petrich (1993) argue that, until the early 1930s, film portrayals of homosexuals were used either as "comic devices," as "a form of erotic titillation," or "to depict deviance, perversion and decadence" (p. 397). From the mid-1930s to the early 1960s, more conservative norms reigned in Hollywood, and producers severely restricted and censored images of gays and lesbians. When they reemerged in the 1960s, lesbian and gay images were usually quite negative in tone. Fejes and Petrich note that, during this period, "homosexuality was portrayed at best as unhappiness, sickness, or marginality and at worst perversion and an evil to be destroyed" (p. 398). They cite one review of all the films made between 1961 and 1976 that featured a major homosexual character. Of the 32 such films that appeared in this period, LGBT characters are killed in 18, commit suicide in 13, and in the one remaining film, a gay man lives—but only after being castrated.

The portrayal of gays and lesbians in mainstream films has improved markedly since then—there was no place to go but up. Over time, the number of realistic and positive portrayals slowly increased. For example, *Brokeback Mountain* (2005), about two modern cowboys struggling with their sexuality, and *Milk* (2008), the bio-pic of Harvey Milk starring Sean Penn as the first gay man to be elected to public office in California, were two mainstream films that dealt sensitively with issues of homosexuality. Since then many such films have appeared, including *The Kids Are All Right* (2010) *Carol* (2015), *Moonlight* (2016), and *Call Me By Your Name* (2017). Transgender portraits have appeared as well, with *Boys Don't Cry* (1999) and *Transamerica* (2005) marking major Hollywood successes. Although Hollywood was catching up, independent films by lesbians and gays long provided a broader range of images of the LGBT community.

Television has followed much the same route as Hollywood. From comic drag queens to threatening villains, television routinely disparaged homosexuals. In a 1967 CBS documentary the host, Mike Wallace, concluded, "The average homosexual, if there be such, is promiscuous. He's not interested in, nor capable of a lasting relationship like that of a heterosexual marriage"—a claim that now seems especially ironic given the successful push to legally recognize same-sex marriage (Fejes and Petrich 1993: 400). As the gay and lesbian movement gained strength in the 1970s and 1980s, it more actively sought fairer television portrayals of homosexuals. A 1974 episode of the medical drama *Marcus Welby* featured a gay child molester and suggested that homosexuality was a treatable disease.

FIGURE 7.6 ■ Out of the Closet... A Select Timeline of Milestones in LGBT Portrayals in Film and Television

1970　The fictionalized biographical film, *The Christine Jorgensen Story*, is released about real-life transsexual Christine Jorgensen.

1971　On CBS's *All in the Family*, Archie Bunker learns his macho drinking buddy, Steve, is gay. While viewers may have suspected that characters on earlier programs were gay, this is the first clear identification of a gay character on a television sitcom.

1972　ABC's *The Corner Bar*, a short-lived sitcom, features television's first major recurring gay character, a flamboyant set designer named Peter Panama.

1972　ABC's *That Certain Summer* is the first television movie to deal sympathetically with homosexuality.

1977　ABC's *Soap* premiers. A madcap parody of daytime soap operas features Billy Crystal in the recurring role of a gay man.

1983　ABC's *All My Children* features the first gay story line on a daytime soap opera.

1984　After being rejected by the networks, *Brothers* airs on cable's Showtime channel, featuring both homosexual and heterosexual characters discussing sexuality, homophobia, and AIDS.

1985　NBC's *An Early Frost* is the first major movie to deal with AIDS.

1988　ABC's *Roseanne* premieres. Eventually, the title character has a lesbian buddy, a mother with a girlfriend, gay employers, and, in one episode, is kissed by a lesbian in a gay bar.

1989　On ABC's *thirtysomething*, two male characters are shown in bed after having spent the night together. Though they do not touch on camera, advertisers pull $1 million worth of commercials, and the episode is not shown again during the summer rerun season.

1990　CBS's comedy *Northern Exposure* premiers, featuring two recurring gay male characters who run a bed and breakfast and have a wedding ceremony in one episode. In another episode, the show's fictional town of Cicely, Alaska, is revealed to have been founded by 19th-century lesbian pioneers.

1991　*Angels in America*, a two-part play by Tony Kushner about gay life and AIDS, opens, winning the Pulitzer Prize for Drama and Tony Award for best play. HBO converts it into an award-winning miniseries in 2003.

1993　Tom Hanks portrays a gay man with AIDS in *Philadelphia*. Bruce Springsteen writes the movie's title song.

1994　On MTV's *Real World: San Francisco*, a male couple exchanges rings shortly before one of the men dies of AIDS-related complications.

1994　PBS airs the U.K.–produced miniseries drama, *Tales of the City*, set in '70s San Francisco featuring portrayals of gay and lesbian relationships.

1996　On the sitcom *Friends*, Ross' ex-wife marries her lesbian lover in a ceremony officiated by Candace Gingrich, the sister of conservative Republican Congressman Newt Gingrich.

1997　Ellen DeGeneres comes out, as does her character on the ABC sitcom *Ellen*, creating the first gay title character on network television.

1997　ABC's *Relativity* features TV's first full lesbian kiss.

1998　*Will and Grace* premieres, featuring a gay lawyer as one of the title characters.

1999　The film drama *Boys Don't Cry* is released, based on the real-life story of a transsexual man who was raped and murdered by his friends when they discovered his secret.

(Continued)

FIGURE 7.6   ■   (Continued)

2000	Showtime's *Queer as Folk* premieres as the first program whose main characters are gay and includes first graphic depictions of gay sex on TV.
2003	Gay parents become more common. On HBO's *The Wire* a gay detective, Kima Greggs, adopts a child with her partner. A major character on the hit medical drama *E.R.*, Dr. Kerry Weaver, comes out and raises a son with her female partner, a firefighter.
2003	Bravo's *Queer Eye for the Straight Guy* premieres, joining the increasingly popular "reality" TV genre.
2004	Showtime's *The L Word* is the first to focus on a group of lesbian, bisexual, and transgender characters.
2005	*Brokeback Mountain* is released and wins several Oscars. It is a romantic drama about two male cowboys—both married to women—who develop a sexual and emotional relationship.
2005	*Transamerica* is released with a transgender woman as the lead character.
2005	LOGO TV—owned by Viacom—premiers as the first cable channel devoted to LGBT programming.
2007	*Dirty Sexy Money* premieres on ABC, featuring broadcast television's first recurring transgender character.
2007	Soap opera *As the World Turns* airs first-ever kiss between two men on daytime TV.
2008	Sean Penn portrays gay-rights activist Harvey Milk in the film *Milk* and wins an Academy Award.
2009	ABC's *Modern Family* premiers, featuring a committed gay couple who go on to adopt a daughter. President Barack Obama says it's his family's favorite TV program.
2013	Netflix's *Orange Is the New Black*, set in a women's correctional facility, features a diverse cast, including transgender and lesbian characters.
2014	Amazon's *Transparent* focuses on a transgender woman who physically transitions late in life.
2016	*Moonlight*, a film about a young black man coming to terms with his sexuality, becomes the first LGBT film to win an Academy Award for Best Picture.
2017	The *Power Rangers* reboot features a lesbian Yellow Power Ranger, Trini, becoming the first superhero movie with a gay protagonist.

Sources: Compiled by authors from Jacobs (2013), Sparta (2002), Thompson (2013), and media accounts.

Understandably, the program angered gay activists, who responded by organizing media watch efforts that challenged the negative media portrayals of gays and lesbians. Because of such efforts, gay and lesbian characters began to appear on prime-time programs. Such programs, though, almost always framed these images as a "heterosexual view of homosexuality. Dramatic programming portrayed homosexuality as a problem disrupting heterosexuals' lives and expectations" (Fejes and Petrich 1993:401). In the 1980s and 1990s, gay and lesbian characters began appearing in more serious and realistic portrayals, especially in roles highlighting the issue of AIDS. This time, it was conservative and religious fundamentalist groups who organized to challenge the media images. They objected to the positive portrayals of lesbians and gays and organized boycotts against advertisers on such programs.

A milestone was reached in 1997 when the lead character of the situation comedy *Ellen*—and the actress who played her, Ellen DeGeneres—"came out" in a highly publicized and anticipated episode. To commemorate television's first openly gay lead character, the Gay and Lesbian Alliance Against Defamation (GLAAD) sponsored "Coming Out with Ellen" benefits, and the Human Rights Campaign developed a party kit for the thousands of hosts celebrating the event across the country (Rosenfeld 1997).

Lesbian and gay characters have since become much more prominent on television, especially on cable. *Queer as Folk* (2000–2005) aired on Showtime and was the first series to focus on gay characters, including their sexuality. *The L Word* (2004–2009), also on Showtime, was the first series to focus on the lives of lesbian, bisexual, and transgender people. David Fisher of the HBO series *Six Feet Under* (2001–2005) is considered to be among the first complex gay male characters on television. His marriage to a police officer in a 2005 episode was the first ever gay wedding depicted in an American television series.

Since then, television has become dramatically more inclusive. GLAAD (2018) reports inclusion of the following in the 2017–2018 season:

- 58 LGBTQ regular characters on scripted primetime broadcast programs (6.4% of all characters)

- 103 LGBTQ regular characters on scripted prime-time cable programs

- 51 LGBTQ regular characters on first-run series from streaming services

This represents a vast increase from just a few years ago. In fact, the numbers have become so substantial that GLAAD can now track diversity issues *within* the universe of LGBTQ characters. For example, gay men make up the largest percent of LGBTQ characters on broadcast (47%), and cable (42%), whereas lesbians (36%) are the largest segment on streaming programs. As GLAAD's president Sara Kate Ellis noted,

> The LGBTQ characters who make it to TV screens tend to be white gay men, who outnumber all other parts of our community in representation on screen. In actuality, the population of the U.S. counts more women than men, and bisexual people make up the majority of the LGBTQ community. (GLAAD 2018: 3)

She called for more queer people of color, and stories of lesbians and bisexual women, among others, to better represent the diversity within the LGBTQ community.

News coverage of lesbians and gays has also changed over the years. Rarely mentioned before the 1960s, homosexuality entered the news as a result of gay and lesbian activism (Gross 2001). The AIDS epidemic in the 1980s prodded the news media to address issues related to the gay community more directly. In the 21st century, debates about lesbians and gays serving in the military and gay marriage have been front-page stories. The move toward more positive coverage of lesbians and gays has taken place primarily in larger metropolitan areas with large, active, and visible gay and lesbian organizations. Smaller, more conservative communities have often lagged behind in their coverage of gay and lesbian issues.

Over two decades ago, Fejes and Petrich (1993) noted that change in mass media images of gays and lesbians did not occur spontaneously. Such changes "were not brought about by more enlightened social attitudes. Rather, the activism of gays and lesbians in

confronting and challenging negative stereotypes played a decisive role in the change"
(p. 412). The same has hed true in the ensuing years. Nardi (1997) observed that changing images are also partially the result of "an increase in the production of media by
gays and lesbians themselves, such as the lesbian and gay film festivals regularly held in
many major cities, gay newspapers and magazines that increasingly attract mainstream
advertisers, and gay public access television" (p. 438). These important points apply to
all the groups we have examined. Women's organizations and civil rights groups, as well
as lesbian and gay organizations, were significant social factors, in the form of collective
human agency, in influencing the media industry to change the nature of media content.
Labor unions and other organizations representing working-class and poor people have
not had the same impact on media coverage of their constituents.

CONCLUSION

Entertainment and news media do not reflect the diversity of the real world. However,
by its lack of diversity, media content does reflect the inequality that exists in the
social world—and in the media industry. But that inequality is not static, and significant strides have been made in improving the inclusiveness of media representations.
Underrepresentation is often still a reality that should not be overlooked. But the progress
made—often generated by the actions of advocates—should not be ignored either.

Discussion Questions

1. Should media strive to be "realistic" in
    their portrayal of diversity in the social
    world? Why or why not? Are there different
    circumstances when it is more or less
    important to be "realistic"?

2. Do you think that college students are
    portrayed realistically in the mass media?
    Why or why not? If there is a gap between
    media image and reality, how do you account
    for this difference?

3. Explain why middle- and upper-middle-class
    people are vastly overrepresented in mass
    media content.

4. How do you explain the significant
    improvement in the portrayal of the LGBT
    community in mainstream media?

5. Some might argue that in our era of media
    abundance, social inequality and media
    representation are no longer a concern
    because specialized niche content is available
    for everyone. Do you agree? Why or why not?

USERS

Building on our previous discussions of technology, industry, and content, Part V rounds out our sociological analysis of media by focusing on users. Users are people like us: the nonprofessionals who consume, share, and sometimes create media content. Chapter 8 highlights the active role users play in the media process. As audience members, they interpret the media content they read, listen to, and watch. As creators, they use digital tools to make their own content to share with others. Chapter 9 considers media influence: both how individual users might be affected by media and, more broadly, how media may be helping transform the social and political world in which users live.

PART V

iStock.com/PeopleImages

8

AUDIENCES AND CREATORS

As we saw in Chapter 4, media users can exert political influence on media organizations and the agencies that regulate them. This chapter focuses on users' other roles as active audiences and content creators. Although the language to describe our relationship to rapidly changing media is likely to be in flux for some time (remember the "information superhighway," "cyberspace," and "surfing the web"?), we have adopted the simple term "user" to describe contemporary media activity. User has the advantage of being open-ended, so it can include both our roles as audience members and our various roles on the internet. "User" also implies active roles in both interpreting existing media content and creating our own content.

Most of our time is spent as audience members—watching, reading, and listening to content created by others. Understanding how audiences make meaning from the various media content they use was an interest of researchers long before the digital era (Sullivan 2013). The internet, though, changed how people use media, enabling them to comment on, share, and create media content more easily than ever before. Consequently, these activities, too, have become part of what media scholars study to get a better understanding of users. This chapter begins with studies of media audiences and then considers some issues related to internet use and user-generated content.

THE ACTIVE AUDIENCE: BALANCING AGENCY AND STRUCTURE

From the earliest days of broadcast radio, scholars were interested in the potential influence of media content on the people exposed to it, a topic we explore in the next chapter. Much of that early work, though, treated people as passive recipients of media messages that were transmitted by the dominant groups in society. A variety of analyses suggested that various behaviors and attitudes among audience members were shaped by structural forces beyond their control, including the economic structure of the media industry (Murdock and Golding 1973), the political structure of the capitalist state (Althusser 1971), and even the psychic structure of the human mind (Lacan 1977). In such views, people were often indoctrinated by media in ways that were so thorough that they did not even realize they were being dominated.

As we emphasized in Part III, economic and political forces certainly shape the media industry and the content it produces. And, as we explored in Chapter 6, media content is often ideological in the sense that it consistently promotes certain messages over others. But focusing exclusively on such forces downplays the active role of living, breathing audience members, stripping people of human agency. (The situation is similar to the views of technological determinists, discussed in Chapter 2, who see technology "causing" things, without adequately taking into account the role of people actively creating, deploying, and using technology.)

To address such limitations, a variety of researchers began paying more attention to audiences. Two streams of research became especially influential. First, the "uses and gratifications" approach focused on two basic issues: (1) *What* are people doing with media, and (2) *why* are they using media? This orientation recognized that media users could play an active role in choosing what media they were exposed to (known as "selective exposure") and that they often did so to meet particular needs (which gave some of this work a psychological orientation). As we'll see in the next chapter, such work showed that variations in media use among different audiences meant there was no single media "effect" (Rubin 2009; Ruggiero 2000). This approach has proven to be useful as researchers seek to understand internet usage, documenting a baseline of understanding about what users are doing online and their motivations for doing so (Sundar and Limperos 2013).

A second approach, critical cultural studies, focused on how people interpret and make meaning out of the media content they use. This orientation, too, saw audiences as playing an active role in the media process. In particular, researchers emphasized that media content does not necessarily have a single meaning, that people actively interpret such content in variable ways, and that those variable interpretations are often connected with social position (Storey 2015). Such work, too, has been helpful in understanding internet use; it reminds us to ground our understanding of the internet in the daily lives of real users and to attend to the variations that exist in this usage (Bakardjieva 2005).

We draw upon both of these traditions in this chapter because they help paint a more nuanced picture of how the media process works, balancing structural constraints with human agency.

Polysemy: Media's Multiple Meanings

In the field of cultural studies, scholars use the term *polysemy* to describe the notion that multiple meanings can coexist in media content, or "texts." Part of the reason media are polysemic is that media texts contain an "excess" of meaning within them (Fiske 1986). Many of the components of a television program, for example, will fit together into one relatively consistent interpretation that likely reflects the intended meaning of its creators. But lots of bits and pieces around the edges of the program do not quite fit, and the dominant interpretation cannot completely contain them. Thus texts are structured in ways that make it possible for people to "read against the grain."

For example, imagine a film in which soldiers brutally and indiscriminately kill a group of defenseless noncombatants. Although most people would likely find this scene horrific, it is likely to contain the seeds of alternate interpretations, suggesting, for example, the necessity of war, the commitment of soldiers, or the evil of our enemies. Perhaps the victims did not speak the same language as the soldiers, or the soldiers expressed fear or confusion, or earlier scenes showed enemy soldiers disguised as noncombatants, or the battle is proclaimed a victory later in the film. Any of these circumstances can be the key to different readings of even an apparently straightforward text. In this way, media content of all sorts contains elements that can be used to construct different—and sometimes contradictory—meanings.

There is plenty of anecdotal evidence of this. For example, the hit comedy show *M*A*S*H* aired on CBS for 11 years from 1972 to 1983. As it chronicled the trials and tribulations of a military surgical unit during the Korean War, it presented a thinly veiled critique of the Vietnam War through antiauthoritarian and antiwar humor. The show's original writer, Larry Gelbart, intended to convey the message that war is futile. However, he left the program after four years because he feared that the show's long-term success had unintentionally routinized the characters' fatalistic acceptance of war, an interpretation he had never intended. Other interpretations existed, too. One of the series's main actors, Mike Farrell, recounted that he received some letters saying things such as "Boy, you guys make war look like fun" and "After watching your show I've decided I'm going to sign up." Farrell commented, "I've written back and said, 'I don't quite understand how you can watch our show and come to that conclusion'." But Farrell reported that he "also got a wonderful letter from a kid who said that he had intended to be a professional soldier, and after watching our show over the years he had seen that that's not what he wants to do, and as a matter of fact he's decided to become a priest" (in Gitlin 2000: 217). Such experiences illustrate polysemy: the ability of a media text to contain multiple meanings.

Because polysemic texts are "open" to interpretation, they can be enjoyed by a broad range of people. Thus polysemy can be a highly desirable content feature for mass-market media, where producers are competing for the attention of audiences and the most successful media often have components that appeal to different audience segments. Creators are aware of this and often intentionally make room for multiple interpretations of their work. Take, for example, the pioneering HBO drama series *The Sopranos*. The show revolved around Italian-American mob boss Tony Soprano and his effort to manage his family and private life as well as his criminal activity and the extended family around it. Tony Soprano is clearly an antihero; he kills and exploits, yet the audience is called to identify with him and must—at some level—find him likable (Carroll 2004). Many of the characters in *The Sopranos* were portrayed as morally ambiguous; the entire series is built on contrasting meanings and spurs contradictory feelings in the audience—and this is one of the keys to its success. As its creator David Chase explained, "We all have the freedom to let the audience figure out what's going on rather than telling them what's going on" (quoted in Lavery 2006: 5).

Interpretive Constraint: Encoding/Decoding and Social Structure

Polysemy does not mean that texts are wide open to be interpreted in a limitless number of ways. Nor does it mean that audiences have the ultimate power in their interactions with media because they can make the media texts mean whatever they like. Such a view would replace one oversimplified perspective that is all structure and no agency (meaning is given), with an equally problematic one that is all agency and no structure (meaning is entirely open). Instead, it's useful to remember that there are a variety of constraints on possible interpretations.

First, although they may embrace ambiguity, media producers typically have some "preferred reading" for their work—the primary meaning they wish audiences to take away. Stuart Hall ([1973] 1980) introduced the language of "encoding" and "decoding" to understand this process. He argued that authors encode their work with meaning—either consciously or subconsciously—by using broad cultural references and conventions of a particular medium. Film, for example, uses lighting, music, camera angles and editing to suggest a particular understanding to the viewer. A subject filmed from a high camera angle is likely to appear small and vulnerable; a camera angle pointing upward suggests the subject holds a dominant position of power. A big part of the art of filmmaking is learning to master such visual codes and to subtly use them to advance a preferred reading.

For audiences, "decoding" is the process of using implicit knowledge of both medium-specific and broader cultural codes to interpret the meaning of a media text. For example, when they hear a bit of ominous music as a film character is first introduced, viewers know they should understand that character as bad or dangerous. That's a medium-specific code with which we are all familiar. In fact, because we are all connected in various ways to our media-saturated culture, much of our medium-specific competence is so taken for granted that we do not even think about it.

Broader cultural codes matter, too. Some meanings are easier to construct because they draw on widely shared cultural values and sets of assumptions about the way the world works. These codes build on taken-for-granted assumptions that do not have to be articulated. News outlets do not have to explain to U.S. audiences that what the president does is newsworthy. Films and television programs do not have to explain the dynamics that underlie relationships between parents and children or the rich and the poor. By using familiar codes and cultural understandings, media producers can steer the audience to a preferred reading. Other interpretations are possible, but they will be more difficult to arrive at because they challenge common assumptions or depend on the use of alternative informational resources. As a result, although meaning is constructed by audiences and alternatives are possible, one interpretation is likely to be most common because it fits with the underlying values of the dominant culture.

Second, audiences' interpretations of media content are influenced—although not determined—by their social locations. An older person who doesn't follow pop music may not appreciate a stand-up comic's joke that references a current pop star. In a wide variety of ways, our ages, occupations, marital and parental status, races, genders, neighborhoods, educational backgrounds, and the like help structure our daily lives and influence both how we use media and what kinds of interpretive frameworks we bring to our media experiences.

To understand the media process, therefore, we need to be mindful of how meaning is constructed by socially located audiences under specific historical circumstances. This involves a balanced consideration of agency—audiences constructing meaning from polysemic texts—and structure—the patterns of interpretation and the social locations that shape them. Meanings are not produced automatically; they are created by the interaction between the media content and the user who is situated in a particular social location.

DECODING MEANINGS AND SOCIAL POSITION

Active audiences interpret media in diverse ways even though media content often promotes certain messages over others. Several classic studies explored this apparent contradiction by highlighting the role of social structure.

Class and Nationwide News

It is tempting to believe that people are simply free to construct their own interpretations of media because this individualist position assigns great power to each of us. However, David Morley (1980) found that social position influences interpretation, not by determining it but by providing resources used to decode media messages.

Morley studied the British television "magazine" program *Nationwide* by analyzing the "preferred" or "dominant" meaning of the program's messages and then interviewing groups of viewers from different social backgrounds about how they understood the program. He found a tendency for people from different socioeconomic classes to interpret the meaning of the television program in different ways. For example, bank managers read the preferred meaning when decoding *Nationwide* coverage of economic issues. In fact, Morley argues that the *Nationwide* framework was a perfect fit with the commonsense views of the bank managers. They saw so little controversy in the presentation of the economy that they focused their attention on the program's style rather than its content. On the other hand, the group of trade unionists Morley interviewed saw the economic coverage as entirely favoring management, whereas younger management trainees saw it as favoring the unions. Morley reports that these distinctions between the interpretations of the bank managers, management trainees, and trade unionists were rather sharp, providing "the clearest examples of the way in which the 'meaning' of a programme or 'message' depends upon the interpretive code which the audience brings to the decoding situation" (Morley 1992: 112).

Students from different social classes who were part of the study also derived different meanings from the items in *Nationwide*. Groups of middle-class students criticized the program for failing to include enough detail in its coverage of issues. They viewed it as a trivial program, lacking the seriousness that would make an informational program worthwhile. In contrast, the mainly black, working-class students suggested that the program was too detailed and, ultimately, boring because it lacked the entertainment value that makes television worthwhile. In short, the groups of students from different classes also approached *Nationwide* with distinct interpretive frameworks—one group focused on information, the other on entertainment—and thus viewed the program in dramatically different ways.

Social class, Morley concludes, does not *determine* how people interpret media messages. Instead, social class—and we would add age, race, ethnicity, gender, and other central markers of identity—plays a key role in providing us with cultural "tools" for decoding. Often, these are discursive tools, giving people a language and framework for understanding the world. For example, to arrive at a critical interpretation of *Nationwide*'s messages about the economy—what Morley calls an "oppositional" reading, the trade union activists drew upon the language of union politics with which they were familiar—"a new model, outside the terms of reference provided by the programme" (Morley 1992: 117). We can easily imagine oppositional readings of media content among other groups with sufficient discursive resources. For example, a feminist perspective might provide some women with the tools to make oppositional readings of the images of women in popular magazines and films.

Our social positions provide the frames through which we view the world, making some things visible and others more difficult to see. As a result, the meanings we assign to different media products will ultimately be related to social position. Audiences are still active in this view; they still have to do the decoding work, and access to particular tools does not guarantee a particular interpretation. But the same cultural tools are not available to everyone. Our social positions provide us with differential access to an array of cultural tools, which we use to construct meaning in more or less patterned ways. The result is a model of humans as active agents constrained by specific structural conditions.

Gender, Class, and Television

Andrea Press's (1991) study, *Women Watching Television*, is another well-known study that focused on the relationship between social structure and audience interpretation. Press interviewed middle-class and working-class women, focusing on their backgrounds, their attitudes toward gender issues, and their television viewing histories and preferences.

Press suggested that working- and middle-class women used different sets of criteria for evaluating programs and identifying with television characters. The first difference is in assessing the degree of "realism" of television programs. Working-class women tended to place a high value on images they believed to be realistic, whereas middle-class women did not expect television to be realistic. Working-class women were likely to view televised depictions of middle-class life as realistic, especially in comparison to what they saw as the "unreal" (and uncommon) depictions of working-class life. By focusing on realism and believing that television images of middle-class households are realistic, working-class women devalued their own class position because they didn't measure up to the media images. As Press puts it, "Working-class women are particularly vulnerable to television's presentation of the material accouterments of middle-class life as the definition of what is normal in society" (p. 138).

Middle-class women were much less likely to think about whether the programs were realistic as, for the most part, they assumed (and accepted) that they were not. Middle-class women, though, were much more receptive to depictions of women on television than their working-class counterparts. Working-class women were consistently critical of the image of both the independent working woman and the stereotypically sexy woman—two stock images for television characters—in large part because they perceived them to be unrealistic, bearing little resemblance to their sense of what it means to be a woman in American society. Middle-class women, however, were much more likely to focus on the positive nature of these images, either defending such televised characters or identifying with them. The result is that middle-class women's interpretations of televised images of women were part of their own definitions of womanhood, whereas working-class women showed a tendency to resist these interpretations.

We can use Press's (1991) research to suggest a broader speculative connection among social class, the media industry, content, and audience interpretation—all elements of our media/society model. Because of their lived experience, working-class women knew that most television programs presented a distorted, unrealistic picture of working-class life in general and working-class women in particular. However, without extensive lived experience of middle-class life, working-class women were more likely to accept the media's portrayal of the middle class as plausibly realistic. Middle-class women, on the other hand, were more likely to have a background similar to that of middle-class media producers, including having a shared and taken-for-granted understanding of class. Middle-class women, therefore, largely ignored questions of class and found the media's depiction of women's roles as "normal" because the images more closely reflected their own middle-class perspective. Again, social position and meaning making are connected albeit in complex and indirect ways.

Race, News, and Meaning Making

Darnell Hunt (1997) examined the ways that differently "raced" groups interpreted television news coverage of the 1992 Los Angeles riots. The riots erupted after the announcement of the not guilty verdict for the police officers who had severely beaten black motorist Rodney King in an incident that was captured on videotape and aired repeatedly on television news. Hunt noted that attitudes about the riots differed dramatically by race. Much like the subsequent racial divide in views about the O. J. Simpson murder trial, public opinion surveys showed that black and white Americans had very different understandings of the roots, significance, and consequences of the events in Los Angeles in April 1992.

In an effort to make sense of the relationship between media power and audience power, Hunt showed a 17-minute news report from the first night of the riots to 15 groups from the Los Angeles area, equally divided among white, African-American, and Latino groups, and asked each group to discuss what they would say to a 12-year-old child about what they just saw. Hunt's analysis of these group discussions showed that responses to this news segment did not vary much by gender or class but that there were significant racial differences in how viewers interpreted the news.

Hunt (1997) found that black viewers were much more likely than either Latino or white viewers to use solidarity (we, us, our) or distance (they, them, their) pronouns in the group discussion. As black viewers discussed the news coverage of the riots, they identified themselves and the larger issues in racial terms, something that was absent in the white groups' discussions and far less common in the Latino discussions. In addition, the African-American and Latino groups were more visibly active than the white groups as they watched the news segment. Whereas the Latino and especially the black groups talked, laughed, and were generally animated during the screening of the news, the white groups were quiet and motionless as they watched. The ongoing talk among the black viewers was not idle banter but was full of commentary about the news and its credibility. In fact, Hunt found that the black viewers "seemed predisposed to questioning many of the assumptions embedded" (p. 143) in the news coverage, challenging both the accuracy of and the terminology used in the newscast. In contrast, Hunt argued that the white viewers were much more comfortable with the way the newscast covered the events.

Hunt (1997) argued that the viewers in his study constructed "negotiated" readings of the news, with different groups bringing different resources to their decoding. Black viewers were far more likely to decode the news in ways that suggested an alternative or oppositional interpretation of the riots, whereas the white and Latino viewers were likely to interpret the news in line with the text's preferred meaning. Hunt suggested that this racial difference in decoding media was, in large part, the result of differences in social networks and the sense of group solidarity among the different groups. In this particular case, the discursive resources associated with racial identity shaped both how viewers watched the news and how they decoded the news text. At the same time, differential interpretations helped reaffirm a sense of racial identity among viewers. Such "raced ways of seeing," as Hunt termed them, both shape and are constituted by the social process of decoding.

Resistance and Feminist Identity

Another type of media interpretation is one that produces resistance. Feminist scholars have explored the ways women respond to and resist media images. In her discussion of the relationship between media images of dancing and the activity itself, Angela McRobbie (1984) argues that teenage girls construct interpretations of dance films, such as the classic *Flashdance*, in ways that oppose the dominant meaning of the film. Rather than reading the film as a story about a woman who marries her boss's son, using her sexuality to please men in the process of becoming a successful dancer, the girls in

McRobbie's study decoded the film in ways that highlighted their own autonomy and sexuality. Dancing, in this interpretation, is not about pleasing or displaying one's body for men; it is about enjoying one's own body and is an expression of sexuality. This reading opposes the dominant interpretation of female sexuality by asserting a sexual identity that does not require the approval of men. The girls drew on their own experiences of dancing in clubs to reinterpret *Flashdance* in ways that supported their own identities as strong, independent, and sexual females.

Teenage fans of performers such as Madonna and Cyndi Lauper, according to Lisa Lewis (1990), engaged in a similar kind of interpretive resistance. Video performances that built on apparently traditional images of female sexuality and male pleasure—and styles of dress that drew on the same images—were interpreted by teenage fans as expressions of their own desires. For female teenage fans, the sexuality of these videos—which differed dramatically from the traditional MTV video—was a sign of female power because women were the subjects, not the objects. Female fans who imitated the style of these female performers, rather than adorning themselves for men, were asserting their demands for fame, power, and control without giving up their identity as girls. This was the core of their interpretation of the music video texts—texts routinely dismissed in the broader culture as negative portrayals of women.

What connection do these examples have to resistance? Both suggest that there is a relationship between oppositional forms of decoding and social action. These oppositional decodings are part of the construction of a subcultural identity that embodies a resistance to traditional norms and roles. The female fans, in the case of MTV, were principal players in the struggle over music video images—their demands on the music industry helped open the door for female musicians. Also, in both cases, the oppositional decoding is not free-floating; it is part of the collective activities of audiences in specific social settings. Still, the media industry has shown a remarkable capacity for finding ways to package resistance as a new style. In *The Conquest of Cool*, Thomas Frank (1997) shows how the advertising industry has co-opted a rebellious youth culture, developing new marketing campaigns that build on the discourse of rebellion and liberation to promote new forms of "hip consumerism."

Ultimately, the key question about the possibility of resistance concerns the social consequences. How are these interpretations linked to social action? We have seen three examples that provide a clear analysis of the relationships among oppositional decoding, human activity, cultural tools, and social setting. Such examples suggest that oppositional decoding and resistance are useful concepts, but they need to be used with care (Condit 1989). Instead of admiring the almost unlimited capability of people to resist domination, we need to take the notion of resistance seriously by looking at the conditions under which concrete audiences engage in such resistance and what consequences follow.

International Readings of American Television

Different readings of media content can be seen across cultures internationally, too. American television programs have long been popular in other countries. But because meanings are multiple and are constructed by socially located audiences, what do American television programs actually mean to viewers outside the United States who have little or no direct experience with the country? Rather than assume that American television images simply indoctrinate global viewers or argue that international audiences easily adapt these foreign images to their own social situations, some scholars have explored the complex ways in which active audiences make use of images that often are heavily laden with ideological messages.

Liebes and Katz's (1993) classic study focused on the 1980s television program *Dallas*, which was popular with audiences in dozens of countries. This evening drama—which returned in 2012, with some of the original cast members, on TNT—chronicled the lives of a wealthy Texas oil family named Ewing and its lead character/villain J. R. Ewing. The program followed family members through ups and downs, with a regular focus on secret love affairs, backroom business deals, and an almost constant tension between loyalty and betrayal. What was the underlying message in the program?

Liebes and Katz (1993) compared the "decodings" of six different ethnic groups from three different countries: Americans from Los Angeles, Japanese, and four different communities in Israel—recent Russian immigrants, Moroccan Jews, Arab citizens of Israel, and kibbutz members. The study was based on several focus group discussions within each ethnic group; groups of friends watched the program together at one viewer's home and participated in a guided discussion about the program on its completion. In each focus group, viewers were asked to "retell" the story of the just-completed program as if they were explaining it to a friend who had missed the episode. The different ethnic communities used very different storytelling approaches. Both Arabs and Moroccan Jews were most likely to retell the episode on a scene-by-scene basis, often in great detail. The Americans and kibbutzniks were more likely to focus on the characters instead of the plotline. And the Russians explained the message of the program instead of either the action or the characters. Of course, not all members of each ethnic group fit neatly into a box, with all using the same interpretive strategy, but the interpretive patterns were very clear.

Liebes and Katz (1993) suggest that the distinct strategies can be explained by the cultural position of the different groups. Arabs and Moroccan Jews are the most "traditional" groups in the study, and their linear storytelling draws connections between their own cultures and the perceived reality of the lives of the extended family living in Dallas. Russians, on the other hand, draw on their skill at reading between the lines for the underlying message, a skill that was well developed in the former Soviet Union where government propaganda efforts were commonplace. And the American and kibbutznik groups build on their cultures' interest in psychology and group dynamics to explore the attitudes and actions of the characters. In each case, the retelling approach is anchored in underlying cultural dynamics that provide the different audiences with culturally specific resources.

The distinctive retellings of the program indicate that, whereas the different ethnic groups may have watched the same program, they did not see the same thing. For example, the Americans were playful and detached in their reading of the program, whereas the Arabs were emotionally engaged, asserting their opposition to the program's values. As a result, the Arabs were most likely to read the meaning of the program as "Americans are immoral," whereas the Americans were most likely to assert that the programs meant little beyond entertainment. Ultimately, the broad depiction of family relations—their triumphs and tragedies—made *Dallas* widely popular, even if people used different cultural resources to interpret what these images said about people, society, or the United States.

Although it was an international hit, *Dallas* was not popular everywhere. In Japan, where *Dallas* was a bust, viewers made more "critical" statements about the program than any other ethnic group and made very few comments that connected *Dallas* to their own lives. This might help explain why *Dallas* never caught on in Japan; viewers were never able to really engage with the program. Instead, *Dallas* was perceived as full of inconsistencies that the Japanese could not accept—inconsistencies with the genre of the evening drama, with the viewers' perceptions of American society, with their sense of their own society, and even with their view of the characters' motivations. Although its openness to diverse interpretations might help explain why the program was popular in so many different countries, in a Japanese cultural context, *Dallas* evidently had very little to offer viewers.

Making Meaning Online: Second Screens

Traditional interpretive communities in the broadcast era were structured by in-person social relations. Book clubs met to discuss a common reading. Families negotiated what program to watch in the living room, debating its merits along the way. Friends went to the movies and discussed the film's meaning on the way home. Users today have more autonomy about what and with whom they experience media content. Media users are more likely to "meet" online to discuss media content than they are to see each other in person. Facebook groups, online forums, and other venues provide the opportunity for users to collectively develop an understanding of media content. Although there are debates about these communities due to the technical limitations of online environments, Feenberg and Bakardjieva (2004) saw users' participation in virtual communities as opening possibilities for collective meaning making and mobilization around interests and issues that may not be directly political but are important to people's self-realization and well-being. This makes the internet a potential site for developing citizens, not just consumers.

Twitter appears to be an especially popular platform for meaning making online. *The Boys on the Bus* (Crouse 1973) was an influential book about how reporters covered the 1972 presidential election, documenting how journalists negotiated a more or less common understanding of what happening on the campaign trail. Rachel Reis Mourão (2014) invoked this predecessor in her work, "The Boys on the Timeline," about Twitter use by political reporters. Mourão's study of the Tweets of 430 political journalists during the 2012 presidential campaign suggests that, as with the face-to-face process from 40 years earlier, reporters used the online platform to help come to some common understanding of what was occurring and to develop narratives to tell the story. In this way, reporters online constituted a distinct interpretive community, whose interactions on Twitter might be especially important because they informed the political reporting that was shared through mainstream media outlets with a broader general audience.

One of the best-known types of online meaning making has been through the use of the "second screen," where users watching television employ an additional digital "screen" (e.g., mobile phone, tablet) to access Twitter and other internet platforms to discuss what they are seeing on TV in real time. Often by promoting hashtags, popular television programs generate a steady stream of Twitter traffic (Highland, Harrington, and Bruns 2013). In doing so, audience members create and contribute to a real-time, user-generated media landscape that exists alongside, and in response to, traditional mass circulation television. This second screen experience has become increasingly common (McClelland 2012), as a growing segment of television viewers engage in media activity that extends well beyond the boundaries of traditional audience.

Although now mediated through Twitter and other platforms, the process of meaning making is quite similar to that found in traditional audience studies: Users (as audience members) watch, read, or listen to media content, share their reactions, and discuss with others. (Because these reactions usually are shared with others online, this action edges into content creation, which we discuss later in the chapter.) For example, when using second screens with political programming such as news broadcasts and candidate debates, users were found to be looking for more information and wanting to discuss what they were viewing (Gil de Zúñiga, Garcia-Perdomo, and McGregor 2015). Taking part in these discussions was a good predictor of other online political participation. Using a second screen seemed to make news more meaningful and relevant for users, translating into more political engagement and participation.

In some ways, online meaning making opens new doors to expanding the interpretive community to include people well beyond one's immediate environment. However, by no longer having to argue with your brother about the value of a movie you just watched together, you are also free to find a much narrower niche of like-minded individuals with whom to discuss and react to media. As we will see in the next chapter, this fragmentation of audiences into narrow niches can be both empowering—by finding like-minded individuals to affirm one's basic interests and orientations—and distorting—by limiting exposure to different, challenging views.

The second screen phenomenon highlights the ways the audience experience is shifting in the internet era. Audiences may be distracted by their second screen, and they may be even more involved with other users than they are with the program they are ostensibly watching. At the same time, we should not neglect the significance of that "first screen," the media content that engages audience interest and provokes users to post their own comments and content. As scholars continue to study the various forms of media audience activity, it will be helpful to examine specific everyday media practices, paying careful attention to the ways new media users are similar to, and different from, traditional media audiences.

Social Position Online: Black Twitter

A famous 1992 *New Yorker* cartoon featured a pair of dogs at a desktop computer, with one saying to the other, "On the internet nobody knows you're a dog." The cartoon signaled the growing mainstream public awareness of the internet in its early years and suggested that one of its defining characteristics might be the ability to transcend one's "real" identity. In this newly emerging—and then largely text-based—online world, perhaps gender, race, age, nationality—or even species!—wouldn't matter.

Although the ability to fabricate online identities is a feature of some internet use, real-world social identities have proven to be remarkably resilient online. Race is a good example, although similar observations could be made about gender, sexuality, ethnicity, and other social identities. Jenkins (2002) noted that, when early enthusiasts attempted to portray the internet as color-blind, "what they really meant was they desperately wanted a place where they didn't have to think about, look at or talk about racial differences." So rather than overcome race, what tended to happen was that everyone online was assumed to be white unless they stated otherwise. Jenkins noted, "Such missteps were usually not the product of overt racism. Rather, they reflected the white participants' obliviousness about operating in a multiracial context." Now, in a more fully developed online environment, he wrote, we "need to give up any lingering fantasies of a color-blind Web and focus on building a space where we recognize, discuss and celebrate racial and cultural diversity" (Jenkins 2002).

People of color long ago took up the challenge of race-conscious community building online. Rather than ignore race, these users found spaces on the internet to construct and affirm racial identity in a collective context (Byrne 2008; Everett 2008; Nakamura and Chow-White 2012). Racism and hatred exist online, as we will explore in the next chapter, but online spaces populated predominantly by people of color serve as a positive source of support and affirmation. For example, Steele (2018: 123) notes that "bloggers and their communities create spaces that serve different purposes for the African American community, including preservation of culture, public resistance, and strengthening of group institutions." Racialized online communities often involve articulation of symbolic boundaries, defining inclusion and exclusion, as well as the expression of resistance based on experienced injustices (Hughey 2008). Expressions of racial injustice, for example, rarely appear on the Facebook walls of whites but are common on the Facebook walls of people of color, communicating a sense of group membership and race consciousness (Grasmuck, Martin, and Zhao 2009).

Building on a "uses and gratifications" framework, Lee-Won, White, and Potock (2017) surveyed 323 black Twitter users to gauge their motivations for using the platform. They found that much of the online activity could be traced back to personal experiences of discrimination. More specifically, their analysis shows that experiences of discrimination resulted in higher group identification; that such identification was associated with "racial agency"—"the desire and willingness to take actions that could generate positive changes in one's racial community" (p. 7); and, finally, that racial agency was associated with increased Twitter use for seeking information, expressing opinions, and social networking.

So-called Black Twitter—the online community created by African-American users of the micro-blogging service—is one of the best-known racialized spaces online. African Americans have used Twitter at higher rates than their white counterparts, both in terms of number of users and, especially, the frequency of use (Smith 2014; Murthy, Gross, and Pensavalle 2015). Similar to the oppositional interpretive communities discovered in traditional audience studies, Graham and Smith (2016) contend that Black Twitter is an arena of "networked counterpublic" where subordinated or marginalized groups form to develop and share oppositional discourses. Such spaces promote a race consciousness that "encourages pride in blackness and stimulates communal responsibility among all people of color for one another and for the purpose of challenging implicit and explicit racial bias" (Lee 2017, p. 7).

Black Twitter is often used to directly challenge perceived biases in mainstream media stories. Lee (2017) found that Black Twitter use operated as a "digital homespace" for (1) redefinition, (2) enforcing counter-narratives and testimonials, and (3) organizing and building communities. First, users redefined mainstream media content. For example, in the wake of the media's use of unflattering, stereotypical pictures of victims of police violence, Twitter users adopted the "blacktag" #IfTheyGunnedMeDown, rhetorically asking, "What picture from my social media account would the news use to portray me if I were gunned down?" Users adopting the hashtag posted a photo of themselves that might be construed negatively, juxtaposed with a photo that was more typical of their daily life. One pair of photos showed a young black man with friends flashing hand signs that might be mistaken as gang related (they were actually black fraternity signs), alongside of a photo of the same man in his cap and gown at college graduation ceremonies. The lesson was clear: By choosing to highlight unflattering photos, the news media was feeding into reductive, stereotypical narratives about "dangerous" black youth. Second, Black Twitter users developed counter-narratives by dissecting media and police accounts for inconsistences while sharing supporting information and anecdotal experiences. Third, users developed constructive responses by organizing and supporting community-based political campaigns, rallies, protests, and other efforts. Often, online solidarity became fuel for hashtag activism and street-level political organizing, as with the #Ferguson and #BlackLivesMatter campaigns (Bonilla and Ros 2015; Kuo 2016).

Online spaces, then, can serve to nurture collective identities while offering the ability to construct and share critiques of mainstream media as well as engage in political action both online and on the street.

THE PLEASURES OF MEDIA: CELEBRITY GAMES

As scholars took the role of audiences seriously, they also explored the reasons why people use media. One answer was simple: fun. The media world is, in large part, a world of entertainment. We spend a large portion of our lives having fun and seeking pleasure from the media. Media scholars historically tended to be suspicious of the pleasures of media. On one hand, media research through the 1970s paid almost exclusive attention to "serious" forms of media, particularly news. On the other hand, pleasure itself was seen as the problem: Media entertained people as a means of distracting them from the more important arenas in life. After all, how could people be responsible citizens or challenge the social order if they were busy each evening watching *The Bachelor* or posting to Facebook?

Instead of dismissing fun or assuming that it makes people content with the status quo, some work examined the specific sources of media pleasure and the conditions under which people derive fun from media. Feminists, in particular, focused their attention on the realm of pleasure, arguing that the pleasures associated with mass media could be liberating for women (Walters 1995). Feminist media scholar Ien Ang (1985), in a now classic study of *Dallas*, pointed to fantasy as the key to explaining the pleasures of media, noting that fantasy allows us to imagine that we are different, that social problems can be solved, or that we can live in a utopia. International studies had similar findings. For example, Kim (2005) found that young Korean women reflect on their own experiences while considering the worlds they see depicted on global television, which "opens up a rare space in which Korean women can make sense of their life conditions in highly critical ways" (p. 460). And Espiritu (2011) found that young women in the Philippines enjoyed Korean television dramas, which they defined as more "refined and wholesome" than locally produced programs or those imported from the United States and Mexico. Espiritu argues that the women's critique of U.S. television and their expressions of a preference for Korean television can be seen as "an act of resistance to the American cultural hegemony in the Philippines" (p. 369). In a variety of ways, then, the meanings of media pleasures cannot be perceived simply by analyzing a media text; media audiences can incorporate media into complex fantasies that can make daily life much more enjoyable.

One source of popular media fun is celebrities (Turner 2013). How can we explain the national (and international) fascination with the personal lives of actors, musicians, and other media personalities? Serious scholars might be inclined to dismiss the celebrity world as meaningless trivia or, worse yet, to sound an alarm about the dangerous distraction that captivates the public. Joshua Gamson (1994), though, suggested that celebrity watching is a complex act and that audiences use a range of interpretive strategies in these mass-mediated interactions with the celebrity world. Some audiences essentially believe what they see, take the celebrities at face value, and focus on their great gifts or talents. Others see celebrity as an artificial creation and enjoy the challenge of seeing behind the images, unmasking these celebrity "fictions." Other audiences are what Gamson called the "game players," who neither embrace the reality of celebrity nor see it as simple artifice but who adopt a playful attitude toward the celebrity world.

This playfulness revolves around two kinds of activities: gossip and detective work. For some, the fun of celebrity comes from the game of gossip. In this game, it does not matter whether celebrities are authentic people or manufactured creations or whether they deserve their fame or not. The fun lies in the playing of the game, and the game is sharing information about celebrity lives. This game of gossip is fun because the truth of each comment is irrelevant; friends can laugh about the bizarre or enjoy evaluating celebrity relationships with the knowledge that there are no consequences.

Other game players focus their energy on detecting the truth about celebrities. This game is animated by the ever-present question of what is real in this world of images, even though the game players are not certain whether they can ever detect the reality. As a result, the fun lies in the collective detective work, not in any final determination of truth or reality. The game itself is the source of pleasure, as players scrutinize celebrity appearances and entertainment magazines, sharing their knowledge with one another as they peel away the never-ending layers of the proverbial onion. Each performance or news item adds to the story, and the detective game continues. The pleasure comes with the speculation, the moments of "aha," and the search for additional information—which the celebrity system produces almost endlessly.

Ultimately, the world of celebrity is a place where the real and the unreal intermingle and where the boundaries between the two are blurred. Game-playing audiences know that the game is located in a "semifictional" world, which makes it both fun and free. Moreover, the pleasure of these games comes from the very triviality of the celebrities themselves. According to Gamson (1994),

> it is the fact that the game-playing celebrity watchers don't really care about the celebrities—contrary to the stereotypical image of the fan who cares so much and so deeply—that makes the games possible and enjoyable. . . . [Celebrities]

literally have no power of any kind over audiences. If they did, the "freedom" of the games would be dampened. What matters to celebrity-watching play is that celebrities do not matter. (p. 184)

We see that mass-mediated pleasure can come from a recognition by audiences of media's trivial nature, which makes them perfect sites for fun and games.

THE SOCIAL CONTEXT OF MEDIA USE

In addition to interpreting media content, active audiences make significant choices in how and why they use media. This shifts our focus to the act of media use itself.

Romance Novels and the Act of Reading

One of the most influential studies of media audiences is Janice Radway's (1991) classic book, *Reading the Romance*, which challenged many assumptions about "lowbrow" mass media. In part because they are seen as the exclusive domain of women, romance novels are widely denigrated and culturally devalued. Moreover, the romance genre is associated with traditional, heterosexist visions of society: the damsel in distress, the woman who is incomplete without her heroic man, even the woman who finds love with the man who has sexually assaulted her. But instead of assuming that her interpretation of the texts revealed their "true" meaning, Radway compared her analysis of romance novels with the interpretations of a group of white, middle-class women who regularly read them. Her findings suggested that readers are active, but they are also responding to their fundamental social situations.

One of Radway's principal findings was that, when she asked about why they read romance novels, women focused on the *act of reading* instead of on the content of the stories. These readers, who did not work outside of the home but were busy fulfilling their full-time roles as wives and mothers, suggested that the activity itself was meaningful as an escape from the demands of their daily lives. In essence, reading romance novels gave women time to themselves, peace and quiet, and a break from the emotional work of nurturing others. It provided what Radway calls a "free space," away from the social world that the women occupied.

The lives of Radway's romance readers were tightly circumscribed by traditional cultural norms that specified what it meant to be a good wife and mother. Although the women largely accepted these norms, their own emotional needs were not satisfied by their daily existence, precisely because of cultural restrictions on the activity of women. Reading romance novels, then, was a way for women to refuse, if only temporarily, to accept these norms by allowing them to focus on themselves instead of others. This protest was both subtle and partial; it was not outright rebellion against the wife/mother role, but instead, romance reading provided vicarious pleasures that helped satisfy needs not met by these highly circumscribed roles.

But why romance novels in particular? Radway argued that the romance novel allowed the women to "escape" from the constraints of their social existence by taking time each day to enter the fairy-tale world of the romance heroine who has all of her emotional needs satisfied. The polysemy of romance novels did not allow Radway's readers to

Although romance novels are often derided as sexist fluff, a classic study of white middle-class women who read them found that the act of reading can be a way women assert their independence, by providing an escape from the demands of daily life. At the same time, the romantic content offers a way for these women to experience the kind of nurturance they seek in their own lives.

interpret any romance novel in a way that would meet their needs. Instead, women made rigid distinctions between novels they liked and those they disliked. They actively sought out books that allowed them to hold onto the hope that men can satisfy women's needs, that the heroine and hero will live happily ever after, and that the woman's commitment to the relationship will prevail over the traditionally male commitment to public achievement. Reading romance novels, therefore, was both a literal escape, through the act of reading, and a figurative escape, through the fantasy of the romantic plots.

Watching Television with the Family

David Morley (1986) adopted Radway's focus on the act of media use in *Family Television*. The study explored the domestic context of television viewing and showed how television use is embedded within the social relations of the household. The social practice of watching television—often in a collective setting—is, like the act of reading a romance novel, central to what its text means to audiences.

According to Morley (1986), gender is one of the keys to understanding how people experience television in the relatively traditional British families he studied. Because of gender roles within the family, adult men and women watched television very differently. Men were either very attentive when they watched or they didn't watch at all. Women, on the other hand, saw television viewing as a social act that was accompanied by conversation and other household activities. For women, just sitting down to watch television without doing anything else seemed like a waste of time.

Because it is so widely viewed, television is the subject of much small talk. When we talk about television or other forms of media with our friends and families, we engage in a kind of collective interpretive activity. We recount what happened, why it happened, what it means, and what is likely to happen next. All of this is part of a process by which we construct meanings for television programs—or movies, songs, blog posts, and so on. But here, too, women and men differ. According to Morley (1986), whereas women regularly talked about television, men rarely admitted to doing so, either because they did not talk with friends about television or were unwilling to admit that they engage in a behavior they define as feminine.

Interaction with media and discussions about media products are important parts of the process of meaning making. And meanings are generated in social settings by active audiences. As Turner and Tay (2009:2) note, "Television's family audience in the living room has now dispersed—into the kitchen, into the den, study or computer room, into the home theatre, into the bedroom and, finally, out of the home altogether: into the street and onto their mobiles." Still, even as the settings change, the basic point of Morley's work remains relevant. Radway and others adopted the term *interpretive community* to suggest both the social structural forces at work—our membership in communities—and the forces of human agency—the act of interpretation. When we think about audiences, then, we need to remember that the meanings people make of apparently omnipresent media products are connected to experiences and social structures outside the world of media. Media are, in essence, part of our lives and must be understood in the context of the relationships that constitute our lives. As those relationships change, so too will our connections with media.

iStock.com/Fertnig

THE LIMITS OF INTERPRETATION

Television viewing can be a family affair partially mediated by social position. Women and men view television differently. Men tend to watch attentively, whereas women are more likely to engage in casual conversation while they watch or simultaneously carry out household tasks.

As we have seen, the power to define social reality is not something that is simply imposed on unwitting audiences by media producers. The meanings of media messages cannot be reduced to the "encoded," "preferred," "dominant," or even most common reading of a particular media text. Audiences, drawing on specific sets of cultural resources and located in specific social settings, actively interpret media products. The distribution of social and cultural power remains significant, for it structures the discursive resources at our command and the social contexts in which we use media. But this power is not absolute or uncontested. If media messages circulate versions of a "dominant" ideology, these messages are only the raw materials of meaning; they require construction and are subject to revision.

This understanding led some scholars to investigate the possibility that some audiences interpret media texts in an "oppositional" way or engage in a kind of interpretive "resistance." Such audiences, like the teenage girls who were fans of Madonna (discussed earlier in this chapter), "resist" the imposition of preferred meanings, actively reinterpreting media messages in contrary, even subversive, ways. In his study of television, John Fiske (1987) even argued that the act of interpretive resistance itself produces pleasure. In this view, the fun of media use and the "popularity" of popular culture are the result of assertions of independence by audiences; the media allow audiences a kind of freedom to understand the world on their own terms. Resistance is fun, we might say, because it empowers those who do not wield power in their daily lives.

The argument for the almost endless possibilities of resistance is based on faith in the power of citizens to think and behave as active subjects rather than passive objects of history. However, such faith and optimism, although admirable, do not adequately explain the relationship between active audiences and a powerful culture industry, nor do they provide the basis for understanding the possibilities for and conditions conducive to actual resistance. As a result, from the very beginning some critics saw the focus on active audiences and interpretive resistance as involving "invisible fictions" (Hartley 1987) conjured up by the researcher or "pointless populism" (Seaman 1992) that overestimated the autonomy of users and underestimated the power of media. They argued that it can be difficult to ascertain what exactly is "resistant" or "oppositional" about how audiences interpret media. Also, they pointed out that even though some subgroups do not accept the dominant meaning of some media content, that doesn't preclude others from being influenced quite differently by the same content, giving it power in society. Active audiences, such critics noted, fit neatly with a conservative view of consumer pluralism where everyone is free to interpret and use media as they wish and there is no need to worry about concentrated media power or the ideological messages that dominate mainstream content. Although some versions of this criticism can be overly simplistic, they do raise a useful caution against assuming media interpretation is loaded with oppositional readings.

Still, some of these criticisms badly overstated the case. As Livingstone (2015) notes,

> to challenge the authority of text analysts is not to deny the importance of texts. To recognize local processes of meaning making is not to deny the political-economic power of major media conglomerates. To assert that media influence is contingent is not to deny its existence. And to research the shaping role of diverse lifeworlds is not to deny the social structures that, through a complex dynamic, strongly shape those lifeworlds. (p. 442)

As we have seen, Morley's (1980) study of *Nationwide* and Radway's (1991) study of romance readers certainly suggest that audiences have the capacity to produce meanings that are at least partially oppositional. But even here, the resistant possibilities of such readings are limited. Hunt (1997), though, concluded his study of news about the Los Angeles riots by suggesting that viewer opposition to the assumptions embedded in the news can be seen "either as constituting meaningful acts of resistance in their own right, or contributing to a consciousness necessary for meaningful social action at some later point in time" (p. 162). Perhaps real resistance is best shown through such "meaningful social action," not merely through the making of alternative interpretations.

FROM ACTIVE AUDIENCE TO RESISTANT ACTORS

Active audiences sometimes go beyond merely interpreting the dominant media message to creating responses that are examples of cultural resistance.

Interpretive Resistance and Feminist Politics

Linda Steiner's (1988) study of the "No Comment" feature of the original *Ms.* magazine provides a good example of oppositional decoding among a community of readers. *Ms.* was a glossy feminist monthly founded in 1972 and subsequently reincarnated in 1990 as a less slick, advertising-free publication that is now issued quarterly. As such, it represents a type of alternative media, presenting views and analysis often at odds with mainstream media messages. This was done literally in its "No Comment" feature in each edition, which was a compilation of reader-submitted items—mostly advertisements—that were offered as evidence of sexism in American society. The submissions came from a wide range of sources, including large and small newspapers, magazines, catalogs, and billboards.

"No Comment" was a space where readers of *Ms.* could identify images from mainstream media and "expose" their underlying sexism. One common set of images depicted women as the property of men; an insurance ad, for example, suggested that wives were "possessions," and a news article identified a female politician simply by citing her husband's name. Other themes included images that dismissed feminism, advertising that blatantly exploited women's bodies, images that implied that women enjoy sexual violence, and items that trivialized women's accomplishments.

Ms. readers likely either gasped in outrage or had a good laugh, or perhaps both, when they read the items in "No Comment." But what does this have to do with resistance? Steiner (1988) argues that the point of "No Comment" was precisely for the community of feminists around *Ms.* to collectively resist media messages that reinforced a sexist image of the world. The items were put on display in "No Comment" and decoded in ways that opposed their dominant meaning precisely so that the traditional definitions of what it means to be a woman could be resisted by *Ms.* readers. As *Ms.* is a feminist publication, readers of "No Comment" drew on a set of cultural tools that likely would lead to a widely shared oppositional reading of the images as "sexist." This action was a kind of resistance that helped create a feminist group identity opposing the traditional norms and roles that were the underpinnings of the media images being exposed.

These decodings were both public and collective. When readers submitted items to the "No Comment" section as a way of sharing their oppositional decodings with like-minded feminists, they helped build a shared meaning system that could serve as a basis for social solidarity within the feminist community. In so doing, they drew on and helped reproduce a feminist discourse that served as a key resource for such oppositional readings. In turn, the magazine served as a site where meaning making became a more explicitly political act; its slogan is "More than a magazine; a movement" (msmagazine.com).

Culture Jamming

Perhaps the most obvious example of media resistance is culture jamming, "a range of tactics used to critique, subvert, and otherwise 'jam' the workings of consumer culture" (DeLaure and Fink 2017: 6). The main strategy employed by culture jammers is known as "pranking" (Harold 2004). Typical pranks include sabotage and appropriation of company symbols and products to communicate a different message than originally intended by the producer.

Most culture jammers are relatively unknown activists who work in their local communities. Canadian-based Adbusters (adbusters.org) is a network of such activists who engage with the creation of "subvertizements" (ads mimicking mainstream brands) and "uncommercials" (subversive TV and radio spots) (Liacas 2005). A few culture jammers, however, have become well-known. For example, Banksy is the name used by an anonymous graffiti artist whose satirical works have achieved international fame. Andy Bichlbaum and Mike Bonanno, a.k.a. the Yes Men (theyesmen.org), use parody to expose deception perpetrated by multinational corporations, governments, and transnational organizations. For example, the Yes Men created a spoof of the World Trade Organization's (WTO) website, which looked so real that they received invitations to address various groups on behalf of the WTO, where they offered stinging critiques of international economic

Courtesy of Ji Lee

One of the ways Korean-born, New York-based artist Ji Lee engaged in culture jamming is by placing red clown nose stickers on pretentious advertising. Often mocking mainstream media products, such as action movies and sexist ads, the humorous clown noses gently invite the viewer to think of the ad image—and the product it is selling—in a critical way.

institutions. The 2009 documentary *The Yes Men Fix the World* chronicles the group's culture-jamming activities. One media scholar (Strauss 2011) suggests that the film can be an effective tool for teaching public relations students about corporate social responsibility and professional ethics. Just as important, Strauss argues that the film—and culture jamming, more generally—may offer students and teachers a sense of possibility:

> The "Yes Men" movie's final segment invokes the power of individual and collective action and encourages the watcher to do as the Yes Men do: identify injustice in the world, point it out to others, and work to remedy it. In this way, it can be a valuable motivator for students who may have become jaded or feel powerless to address the problems and injustice in society. Perhaps just as importantly, it can also have a similar effect on the instructor by rejuvenating the belief that our chosen profession, and the students we teach, can make a positive impact on our world. (Strauss 2011: 547)

With culture jamming and the alternative feminist press, we have moved from media users as audience members to users as content creators in their own right. The remainder of this chapter continues this focus.

CONTENT CREATION AND DISTRIBUTION

Before the internet, nearly all users were limited to being audience members. They may have been active in interpreting mass-produced content and they may have discussed and criticized media with friends and family, but creating and widely distributing original content was typically beyond their reach. But for more than a generation now, the internet, digitization, convergence, more affordable hardware, and easy-to-use platforms have put the creation of media content within the reach of ordinary users. Users can create and share social media and blog posts, photos, videos, music, and so on. Furthermore, the internet blurs earlier media distinctions by delivering interpersonal communication and mass communication in the same medium. In short, users can be active audience members *and* use the internet for a variety of activities, including creating and distributing original content.

As Blank (2013) argues,

> Even though mass media continue to exist in the sense of a small number of large organizations producing large-circulation and large-audience publications, they have irretrievably lost the dominance that they enjoyed since the beginning of mass-circulation newspapers over 150 years ago. (p. 591)

In this landscape, as Livingstone (2015) points out, the audience was said to be "everywhere and nowhere" (Bird, 2003), evolving into "the people formerly known as the audience" (Rosen, 2006), or just plain "dead" (Jermyn and Holmes, 2006). Media scholars sometimes adopted awkward terms like "prod-user" to describe the shifting nature of the people formerly known as the audience (Bruns 2008; Bruns and Schmidt 2011). In some cases, scholars began examining this new internet-centric world by starting afresh with subdisciplines such as "internet studies" (Dutton 2014) or "digital sociology" (Daniels, Gregory, MacMillan Cottom 2016).

However, as the dust has begun to settle on a generation of internet users, we are beginning to better understand the scope—and limitation—of the changes that have occurred. As we have emphasized throughout this book, the internet's innovations have been significant and profound—and extend well beyond the realm of media studies—but they also have more in common with what came before than many people realize. Nowhere is this more evident than in the area of "audience studies." Traditional studies of the audience, as we have seen, helpfully showed that audiences are active in using media, that they interpret and use media in varying ways, and that this variation is often grounded in their social location. It turns out that all of these lessons are applicable to the world of internet users as well. As we will see, people use the internet in vastly different ways and those differences are often linked to social position.

The subfield that examines internet use in daily life has been especially helpful in normalizing internet use and connecting its analysis to earlier work. Bakardjieva (2011) notes that researchers in this area are interested in (1) how the internet is used by ordinary people in the context of their larger lives, (2) how the social and cultural environment affects internet use, and (3) how internet use is related to other practices and relations of daily life. As she puts it, "to insist on talking about the Internet in everyday life is to deny the medium its extraordinary status, to see it as ordinary, but in no case as unimportant" (p. 59).

The internet has resulted in new forms of online participation and, sometimes, new media content from nonprofessional users. Here, we consider a few insights researchers have gleaned from these developments.

Participatory Culture

Users live in a different media environment today than they did just a few decades ago. Focusing on the changes in television, Michael Curtin (2009) used the term "matrix media" to describe the media landscape enabled by the internet. This complex environment varies across differing local and national conditions but is universally characterized by (1) interactive exchanges among users, (2) multiple sites of productivity, and (3) a diverse range of tools available for interpretation and use. Importantly, Curtin notes that although changes were enabled by technology, it is users themselves who made them happen. Recent developments, he notes, "are spurred by the changing behaviors of audiences that now navigate a growing universe of entertainment, information and interactivity." The resulting matrix media "thrive in an environment where distinctions between production and consumption blur" (p. 19).

Henry Jenkins (2006) focused precisely on this blurring between production and consumption, calling our digital era a period of "participatory culture" that contrasts with the period of audience spectatorship. "Rather than talking about media producers and consumers as occupying separate roles, we might now see them as participants who interact with each other according to a new set of rules that none of us fully understands." He cautions, though, that "[n]ot all participants are created equal. Corporations—and even individuals within corporate media—still exert greater power than any individual consumer or even the aggregate of consumers. And some consumers have greater abilities to participate in this emerging culture than others" (p. 3). Still, the ability for users— "consumers" in Jenkins' terms—to create and share content is distinctly important.

Jenkins (2009) characterizes participatory culture as one:

1. With relatively low barriers to artistic expression and civic engagement

2. With strong support for creating and sharing one's creations with others

3. With some type of informal mentorship whereby what is known by the most experienced is passed along to novices

4. Where members believe that their contributions matter

5. Where members feel some degree of social connection with one another (at the least they care what other people think about what they have created). (p. 7)

This ideal participatory culture is what internet enthusiasts hope for. (Some scholars caution, though, that searching for participation produces a bias in favor of observable activity, underemphasizing important dynamics of nonparticipation and negative or destructive participation [Lutz and Hoffmann 2017].) Journalism scholar Jay Rosen (2006) wrote,

> The people formerly known as the audience are those who were on the receiving end of a media system that ran one way, in a broadcasting pattern, with high entry fees and a few firms competing to speak very loudly while the rest of the population listened in isolation from one another— and who today are not in a situation like that at all.

He optimistically writes, "You don't own the eyeballs. You don't own the press, which is now divided into pro and amateur zones. You don't control production on the new platform, which isn't one-way. There's a new balance of power between you and us." Just how much the balance of power has shifted remains to be seen, but scholars have been examining this new media landscape enabled by the internet.

Participation Online

The ideal of participatory culture is tempered by the reality of uneven online participation. Large online communities and social networks typically have a relatively small number of people who generate most of the content and many more lurkers who look but don't contribute. This phenomenon is sometimes referred to as *participation inequality*, and two popular informal rules of thumb emerged to describe it. The 1% Rule says that, for every person who creates content, there are 99 who do not (Arthur 2006). A variation, the 90–9–1 Principle, says that participation typically breaks down into 90 percent of users who are lurkers, 9 percent who occasionally provide content, and 1 percent who account for most contributions (Nielsen 2006). These are obviously inexact rules of thumb, rates of participation vary from site to site, and participation may change over time. However, the general idea of participation inequality has been confirmed, both anecdotally and through a variety of measurements of participation rates on specific websites (Arthur 2006; McConnell 2006; Wu 2010).

The 1% Rule and 90–9–1 Principle were developed during the internet's earlier years and are geared toward single websites. But what about internet use more broadly? Perhaps a person reads Wikipedia entries without contributing, but she is active in an online forum on her favorite hobby; in one context, she is a lurker, whereas in another, she is a contributor. The media marketing research firm Forrester Research (Bernoff and Anderson 2010) surveys adults to assess their degree of internet participation and has developed overlapping categories of users to describe various roles, ranked from most to least active:

1. **Creators** make content that is consumed by others, such as writing blogs and uploading videos, music, and text.

2. **Conversationalists** share their opinions with consumers, companies, and others, for example, through social-networking sites or Twitter.

3. **Critics** respond to the content of others by posting reviews, commenting on blog entries, or editing wiki articles.

4. **Collectors** organize content for themselves or others, using Really Simple Syndication (RSS) feeds, tags, and voting mechanisms such as Digg.

5. **Joiners** maintain profiles on social-networking sites.

6. **Spectators** consume content generated by others.

7. **Inactives** neither create nor consume new media content.

Table 8.1 provides an example of the data Forrester collects on these categories.

Two issues stand out from this basic data. First, perhaps not surprisingly, the most common role played by those who use the internet is that of spectator, just as it was with traditional mass media. Some people are simply not interested in being content creators. Creating any substantial content is time-consuming and still requires a level of technological literacy that is not universally shared. As a result, even online, most people, most of the time, will be audience members, spectators consuming the creations of others. For example, the 2015 Common Sense Media "census" of U.S. youth found that teens spend more than 5 hours per day, on average, with digital media, but only 3 percent of that time is spent creating their own media through activities such as making digital music or art, writing, and making videos (Common Sense Media 2015).

Second, internet use varies by region, even when data is limited to a few wealthy societies. Japan has about half the rates of "conversationalists" and "joiners," for example, than does the United States or European Union. This suggests that participation and content

TABLE 8.1   ■   Social Media Participation Types, 2011 (in Percent)

According to some industry estimates, about a quarter of internet users in the United States, European Unions, and Japan are "creators" who produce some type of original content that others see.

	United States	European Union	Japan
Creators	24	23	25
Conversationalists	36	26	18
Critics	36	33	24
Collectors	23	22	15
Joiners	68	50	29
Spectators	73	69	72
Inactives	14	21	24

Source: Forrester Research, Inc., n.d.

creation varies by cultural context. Cultural forces shape the user experience so that, for example, compared to most Western countries, Turks are much more likely to use social media to follow others for learning and social interaction without creating original content to share (Kurtulus, Özkan, and Öztürk 2015). As we will see in our final chapter, the continued globalization of internet access has only highlighted the importance of understanding media use in its specific cultural context.

Media scholars, too, have created many different typologies to describe the dimensions of internet use, for example, grouping users by how often they used the internet, the range of activities they engaged in, the reason why they went online, and their attitudes toward their online activities, among others. (See Blank and Groselj [2014] for a review of typologies.) In one example, using data from nearly 1,500 British internet users, Blank and Groselj (2014) found that the more than 40 types of internet activities could be grouped into 10 categories with participation rates as follows:

E-mail	93.5%
Information seeking	85.7%
Classic mass media	78.3%
Socializing	61.2%
Commerce	59.8%
School and work	48.1%
Entertainment	46.3%
Blogging	30.1%
Production (creative content)	23.4%
Vice (gambling, porn)	20.9%

E-mail is the most common use of the internet and socializing is fourth, both inter-personal forms of communication. Meanwhile, consuming content—whether looking for information or using traditional mass media sites—remains among the most popular uses of the internet. The list is a good reminder that the internet is often used to get daily tasks done, such as shopping or schoolwork. The percentage of users producing new cre-ative content and blogging were a minority, similar to the numbers for "creators" in the Forrester research.

Slicing the data in a different way, Blank (2013) concluded that there are three basic categories of internet activities. Three-quarters of users (75%) engaged in social and entertainment activities (using a social networking sties and uploading pictures, videos, and music); one-third (34%) produced skilled content (writing blog posts, maintaining a personal website, and posting other creative content); and about one in eight (13%) used the internet for civic purposes, such as using e-mail for political contact or posting a comment on a political issue.

Who Are the Content Creators?

In the early days of the internet, considerable focus was given to the issue of the "digital divide"—the inequality that existed in simple access to the internet (van Dijk 2006, 2017). Such a divide is still very real, for example, between nations in the global con-text and between the old and young within western societies (Friemel 2014). However, as internet access expanded to include a growing and increasingly diverse population of users, it became obvious that access did not necessarily translate into participa-tion. As the digital divide closed somewhat, a "participation gap" (Jenkins 2009) or "second-level digital divide" (Hargittai 2001) came into sharper focus. Research began to explore (1) what are the various ways people use the internet, (2) what motivates this usage, and (3) who creates content?

Although methodologies and analyses vary, sometimes producing contradictory results, there do seem to be some general trends in these studies (Blank 2013; Hargittai and Walejko 2008; Schradie 2011). All agree that, to varying degrees, social position is associated with differing levels of internet participation and content creation, although there are differences about which social characteristics are most significant and what types of participation are most affected. Perhaps not surprisingly, age appears to matter quite a bit; younger users are typically found to produce more content than older users. This may be related to the fact that young people are "digital natives," born into a world where the internet is a taken-for-granted part of life (Palfrey and Gasser 2008). However, variation can occur even over a small range of years; Hargittai and Walejko (2008) find younger college students, for example, produce more content than older students.

Class seems to have the most significant effect on who creates. Income and, especially, education—as indicators of class position—are key to the creation divide; people with high school education create less than those with college degrees. For college students, the level of parental education is a good predictor of how likely someone is to be a cre-ator. Schradie (2011) found, for example, that bloggers are more than 1.5 times likely to have a college than a high school degree; and compared to those with a high school education, college graduates are twice as likely to post photos and three times as likely to write an online review or comment to a newsgroup. Part of that difference is due to the original digital divide; those with higher incomes are more likely to have consistent and high-quality internet access at home and work, making it easier to participate online. However, part of the difference, Schradie argues, is because of the differing cultural tools associated with class; users with more education tend to find ways to use the internet that enhances their lives, giving them more incentive to participate and produce content. Education is also associated with some skills, such as writing, that are important for some kinds of content creation.

Other factors may matter but apparently less so. Results regarding gender differences, for example, so far have been inconsistent. It does appear that women are less likely than men to post content online, but the gap disappears as women get more internet experience. Schradie (2011) found that race and ethnicity have smaller and more ambiguous impact. Blank (2013) found that being employed reduced the likelihood that people produced political content, whereas having a college degree rather dramatically increased the likelihood of doing so; college students, therefore, were among the most politically active online.

Why Create?

Beyond estimating the type and extent of online participation, researchers have examined the motivations for producing user-generated content. Often this has been done within particular communities of users ranging from women bloggers (Chen 2015) and Wikipedia contributors (Rafaeli and Ariel 2008) to widely read political commentators (Ekdale, Namkoong, Fung, and Perlmutter 2010), and young adults (Vainikka and Herkman 2013), among many others (Bechmann and Lomborg 2012; Fullwood, Nicholls, and Makichi 2014; Livingstone 2013; Macek 2013; Matikainen 2015; van Dijck 2011).

Not surprisingly, given our understanding of active audiences, motivations vary both by the type of content being created (e.g., expressive or informational, constructive or confrontational) and by the type of user involved (e.g., regular or intermittent user, anonymous or identifiable). But these studies point to three interrelated motivations that are especially important for nonprofessionals:

- **Self-expression/identity formation.** Users create content for its own sake as an opportunity to express themselves and use their talents and skills. In the process, they help construct or solidify a sense of identity: an independent, creative self.

- **Interaction/community building.** The process of self-expression and identity formation usually takes place in the context of a community. Belonging to the community involves interacting (not just lurking) and typically comes with perceived, although often unstated, social obligations such as supporting other members. Getting positive feedback from community members is a highly motivating event, whereas disparaging or inappropriate feedback can undermine motivation.

- **Sharing.** Community membership helps motivate users to create new content because of the social expectation that new content will be shared with others. Sharing can be done to learn from feedback, get positive attention, gain popularity by entertaining or informing others, and establish one's role in the group.

There are many methodological hurdles to overcome in getting a clear picture of internet users and their motivations. Still, studies have begun to clarify the nature of internet use today. As technology evolves, as a larger percentage of the population grows up immersed in a digital world, and as our data improve, we will need to revise our understanding accordingly. But for the time being, it appears that the internet has had a major impact on media use, that ordinary users who are significant creators remain a minority, but that this minority has a considerable impact on internet life.

Media Fans

One particularly active subset of internet creators consists of those who identify as fans of a particular genre, text, or author. Scholars have explored the activities and experiences of a wide range of media fans and the practices of "fandom," developing a specialized subfield within media scholarship of fan studies (Gray, Sandvoss, and Harrington 2017; Jenkins 2012). Fandom existed before the internet, but online forums and websites have made it much easier for fans to build community by creating and sharing content (Booth 2010).

Fan studies emerged in the 1990s as a challenge to the popular stereotype of the fan as a "fanatic," an eccentric or extremist whose obsession makes them different from most media audiences. Rather than dismiss fans for their avid interest, fan studies scholarship has explored the various forms of fan activity.

First, fans are undoubtedly active interpreters of media, using their accumulated knowledge as an interpretive resource. In fact, learning extensive background information is a defining feature of the fan experience—and the depth of knowledge and intensity of commitment is part of what differentiates fans from casual audiences. Fans learn about the nuances of plot development, character traits, narrative techniques, or loose ends from a prequel. Fans use their knowledge to help them make sense of a plot twist, a new sound, or the return of a familiar character. Participating in this interpretive activity, the process of decoding is often a source of pleasure for media fans and is often a central part of what makes media fandom fun.

Second, fandom is a social activity. Many fans are active participants in online fan communities, which typically offer fans regular opportunities to share their media interests with like-minded others and sometimes offer opportunities to get together face-to-face. They can share information about their favorite books, TV programs, artists, or film genres, debating the meaning of recent developments and building collective interpretations of the media texts. Fan communities offer a variety of ways for fans to connect, from online discussion forums and Facebook pages to fan newsletters and annual conferences. For example, SoapOperaFan.com hosts online discussion forums dedicated to each of the major daytime soaps. Mockingjay.net is a fan site devoted to news related to the *Hunger Games* books and movies. Harry Potter enthusiasts can attend any number of conventions hosted by organizations such as The Leaky Cauldron and The Group That Shall Not Be Named. For many fans, some kind of ongoing interaction with other fans is the core activity of the media fan experience.

Third, some fans become activists, participating in collective action aimed at promoting, saving, or changing a particular media form or text. Fans are typically connected through shared participation in fan communities. As a result, fans are often already orga-nized and are ready to mobilize in the face of a perceived injustice. Fans have organized campaigns to save television programs slated for cancellation, including an unsuccessful 1999 fan effort to continue the 35-year run of the daytime soap opera *Another World* (Scardaville 2005) and the 2012 campaign that brought the NBC comedy *Community* back for another season. Fans of Nickelodeon's cartoon *Avatar: The Last Airbender* organized a 2009 campaign demanding that the film adaptation include Asian actors. Although these fan-activists failed and the film was made with white actors, the cam-paign continued as an ongoing effort to promote the casting of Asian Americans and other underrepresented groups in Hollywood films (Lopez 2011). Sometimes fans par-ticipate in activist efforts that have no specific connection to their media interests; for example, Lady Gaga mobilized her fan community in support of marriage equality for gay and lesbian couples.

Fourth, fans have long been producers of original media content. In the predigital era, fans produced and distributed their own, often photocopied, publications—dubbed fan-zines, or just zines—that were full of fan commentary about a specific media form. Many of the most popular zines focused on music, with a rich variety of early zines focused on punk rock in the 1970s and 1980s. Fans of *Star Trek*, one of the first organized fan communities, were pioneers in the development of fan fiction—stories written by fans that extended the story lines of the television programs, often imagining new experiences and challenges for the major characters. Fan fiction has become increasingly popular, with online platforms making it easier to produce and distribute fan-authored stories. The website fanfiction.net archives fan fiction associated with anime, movies, comics, television shows, and other media, with a vast library of tens of thousands of stories. Fan-produced media offer dedicated fans an opportunity to express themselves, hone their skills, and build media-based connections with similarly interested fans.

Fandom is one example of how user-generated content and communities interact online with traditional, professionally produced media content.

Users as Gatekeepers and Distributors

One of the defining differences between the traditional broadcast model of mass media and today's internet environment is that the role of professional "gatekeepers" has been diminished, if not entirely eliminated. For example, when space and time constraints limited the amount of news that could be reported in a daily newspaper or evening news broadcast, one of the central tasks of editors was to act as a "gatekeeper," choosing which news and views would pass through to readers and viewers. Radio disc jockeys played a similar role with music; television programmers did the same with entertainment programming and so on. With the internet, though, such space and time limitations have vanished, effectively ending the age of gatekeeping in a traditional sense. Users can self-publish books, sidestepping editors; musicians can share their music on SoundCloud, bypassing record companies; budding film directors can upload and share their creations via YouTube or Vimeo.

However, in a sea of media content, users can be overwhelmed by the vast range of options, resulting in "choice fatigue" (Ellis 2000: 171). Consequently, a different sort of "gatekeeping" process has necessarily arisen, one in which users play an active role in bringing attention to some content while helping ensure other content languishes in obscurity. (Platform-based algorithms also play a key role here, something we explore in the next chapter.) In some cases, users play a role in critiquing media content so that it is less likely to be seen by others. Conversely, users can play a central role in distributing content that is often referred to as "viral media." Jenkins, Ford, and Green (2013), though, criticize the "viral" metaphor because it suggests a passive audience subject to infection or contamination by outside influences. In reality, they argue, it is the active participation of users that helps promote what they call "spreadable media."

How this happens varies by media type. For example, reviewing and recommending movies and TV shows is no longer the exclusive domain of professional reviewers. Sites like Rotten Tomatoes enable users to rate and review films and television programs alongside the aggregated reviews of published critics (Faughnder 2017). In the same way that sites like Yelp help people choose a restaurant, Rotten Tomatoes is regularly consulted by nearly half of moviegoers age 25 to 44. Industry insiders say its ratings can make or break a movie at the box office. The site has been credited with both fueling the success of hits and hastening the death of poorly received films. The inclusion of user reviews and ratings alongside those of professional critics sometimes reveals significant gaps in popular and professional tastes. Audiences loved films like *War Room* (2015) and *The Accountant* (2016), which received poor reviews from critics. Conversely, critics generally liked films such as *Berberian Sound Studio* (2013) and *Willow Creek* (2014), which were panned by audiences. Internet platforms like Rotten Tomatoes enable the views of users to be quickly shared, right alongside more traditional professional critics, thereby changing the gatekeeping process.

Gatekeeping was originally associated with news professionals (White 1950), and here too, its form has been altered by user participation. Professional journalists highlight some stories more than others on their websites through more prominent placement or eye-catching graphics. But ordinary media users now also influence which news receives attention. Jane Singer (2014) explored this new dynamic—what she calls "secondary gatekeeping"—in her two-month study of content on 138 U.S. newspaper websites, chosen to be diverse in terms of geography, size, and other characteristics. She found that all papers offered their online users the opportunity to be involved in some form of gatekeeping.

One type of gatekeeping was the monitoring of fellow users; most sites (76%) asked readers to report abusive comments or recommend comments to other users (59%). Singer observes, "In assigning users the responsibility of identifying potentially problematic comments from other users, news organizations have opened the door to sharing with their audiences the role of gatekeeper over the ethical standards of what they publish" (p. 67).

A second and perhaps more significant type of gatekeeping involved de facto user feedback on published stories. Users' activities on most sites (82%) were tracked and automatically converted into a list of clickable stories identified as "most popular," "most read," or "most viewed." Typically, such lists were prominently displayed on newspapers' sites, as Singer notes, "allocating valuable online real estate to a realm of news judgment that journalists previously have not only controlled but also fiercely protected" (p. 68). Such metrics are closely followed in newsrooms to better understand user interests and inform decisions on future stories.

Third, users were able to promote the wider circulation of news stories, fulfilling a traditional gatekeeping role of deciding what stories merit dissemination. Nearly all papers offered users the ability to distribute the site's content via e-mail (97%) or through "share" buttons for Reddit, Facebook, Twitter, and other social media (94%).

Such features on news sites are so commonplace that they are easily taken for granted. But as Singer argues, they mark a significant change in journalism. "Through the implementation of these and other sophisticated automated tools, journalists have relinquished control over what formerly was an exclusive right to identify and communicate to audiences which stories were the day's 'best'" (p. 68). She continues,

> journalists who long have defined themselves largely as society's gatekeepers now find the role is broadly shared with members of an increasingly active audience. Users are choosing news not only for their own consumption but also for the consumption of others, including those within their personal circle of acquaintances and those who are part of an undifferentiated online public. This shift toward "user-generated visibility" suggests a new way of looking at one of the oldest conceptualizations of the journalist's role in our society. (p. 68)

Newspapers in the 18th century were relatively expensive, and a single copy was typically read by multiple users. Some publishers at the time developed the convention of leaving the fourth page blank, so readers could add commentary for the benefit of subsequent readers (Hermida 2011). Ever since then, newspaper and other media outlets have sought feedback from users. But the internet has enabled users to play a much more active role in either promoting content by recommending or sharing it or criticizing content by writing a negative review. Book, film, and music reviews on Amazon, for example, help guide users to their purchases. Because of the internet, reviews and recommendations are potentially seen by other users well beyond their immediate social circles, in effect constituting a form of meaningful content creation in its own right.

CONCLUSION

The central contribution of user research lies in its highlighting of individual and collective forms of human agency. The active audience tradition brought real people into focus in media research by exploring the interactions among people, their social positions, and the media texts they interpreted. Studies of internet users have expanded this focus by considering how users participate online, sometimes creating their own original content.

Although users are active, their activity is still subject to a variety of structural constraints. The media messages themselves matter—even if they can have multiple meanings—because they make some interpretations more likely than others. The cultural tools that users bring to interpreting and creating media are not uniform; different people from different social locations will not have the same resources at their command. By ordering the distribution of cultural tools, social structure serves as a constraint on meaning making and media creation.

Users are active, then, but they are not fully autonomous; a sociology of the media needs to be sensitive to both user agency and structural constraints. Users are also not necessarily immune to the influence of media. Understanding how media potentially influence individual users and society as a whole is the issue we explore in the next chapter.

Discussion Questions

1. How, if at all, do you consider yourself as "active" when you watch television, listen to music, read a book, or browse the web? Are the forms of activity different for different types of media?

2. Do you think social context influences your experience of movie viewing? Why or why not? Consider the similarities and differences in watching a film in a theater, the classroom, on a television screen in a family living room, and on a laptop with headphones.

3. What resources are necessary for individuals to decode media in an oppositional way? Do you think you have ever interpreted media in ways that challenged the preferred reading? Why or why not?

4. Do you create and share original content on the internet? If you do, why do you do it? Do your motivations seem to fit with research described in this chapter? If you don't, why not? What do your answers suggest about the nature of online media creation?

The Washington Post / Contributor / Getty Images

9

MEDIA INFLUENCE

As we saw in Part III, economic forces, as well as some legal and informal political pressures, are constraints on the media industry. As we saw in the previous chapter, users actively interpret media content, sometimes challenging the preferred reading its creators intended. These dynamics highlight forces that limit media influence. However, media *do* affect society in a variety of ways, and this chapter examines some of these influences. We begin by considering some key ideas from "media effects" theory and research, which often focuses on how media exposure might affect individuals. Then we look at broader media influence on social institutions—sometimes called "mediatization"—by considering the example of politics. Finally, we note some of the influences that the internet and social media may be having on society. Together, these approaches suggest media's wide-ranging influence in contemporary life.

LEARNING FROM MEDIA EFFECTS RESEARCH

When members of USA Archery—a group that promotes the sport—were asked about archery role models in a 2016 survey, they were just as likely to mention fictional characters as real-life archers. Nearly half (48.5%) of the female respondents under 18 said the character Katniss Everdeen from *The Hunger Games* movies had "a lot" or "some" influence on their decision to take up archery; more than one third (36.4%) said they were influenced by the Princess Merida character from the Disney animated movie *Brave*. After both films were released in 2012, there was an 86 percent spike in U.S. archery participation over the next two years, with women's participation more than doubling during that time (Geena Davis Institute on Gender in Media 2016).

So how are we to understand this simple example? Did media "cause" people to become archers? Obviously not, otherwise how would we explain the vast majority of people who saw the films but didn't pick up a bow? But the timing of the dramatic increase in archery participation, especially among girls and women, is striking and unlikely to be coincidental, especially because participants themselves cite these films as key influences.

Welcome to the complicated, often ambiguous world of media effects where nearly everyone knows *something* is going on but where it is notoriously difficult to pinpoint exactly why, how, to what degree, and on whom media may be having an influence. Usually, of course, the concern is not with taking up archery but with things like public opinion, violence, substance abuse, voting behavior, hate-group radicalization, and consumerism. (Negative behaviors tend to get much more attention than the positive influences of media.) In such cases, there is often popular suspicion that media effects are strong and immediate. But decades of media research scholarship suggests more complex and subtle influences.

Summaries of the evolution of media effects research often suggest a pendulum: Early theories saw media as having a direct and immediate impact; the next wave of work swung to the opposite extreme, theorizing "limited effects;" finally, recent work has swung back partially, highlighting long-term influences. Although simple and easy to follow, this story is misleading. In reality, there were no wild pendulum swings in the research. For example, this typical summary usually attributes to early work a "hypodermic" or "silver bullet" claim that media could inject a message directly into the "bloodstream" of the public. In fact, later scholars applied such metaphors to early work when seeking to discredit it (Lubken 2008; Pooley 2006; Sproule, 1989). Even the best-known popular example of dramatic media influence—the widespread panic caused by Orson Welles's 1938 radio broadcast of H. G. Wells's novel *War of the Worlds*—turns out to be largely a myth in part fueled by newspapers trying to undermine the new medium to which they were losing advertisers (Campbell 2010; Pooley and Socolow 2013). So early impressions of media influence both in the research and in the public mind were not as extreme as is sometimes portrayed. The supposed opposite swing in research was also not so extreme, containing within it evidence of different types of influence.

The simple "pendulum" narrative is attractive because it tells a neat story of the forward progress of research findings. In reality, dozens of different and sometimes conflicting theories have long coexisted, looking at very different aspects of media and at differing types of effects. Temporary change or lasting influence? Immediate impact or long-term effects?

Influencing what people think or how they behave? Persuading change or reinforcing existing beliefs? Direct impact or indirect influence? These and many other variables characterize this area of research. Making sense of this diversity can be difficult. One review (Bryant and Miron 2004) whittles things down to 26 key theories that were frequently cited in the literature; another (Neuman and Guggenheim 2011) organizes 29 theories into six clusters.

We don't want to impose an order on this body of research that isn't there. A complete review of media effects work is far beyond the scope of this chapter. (See, e.g., Bryant, Thompson, and Finklea 2012; Perse 2008; Potter 2012; Sparks 2015.) Instead, for our purposes, we only want to flag some examples of important concepts and findings that have emerged from this work. We group these ideas into two simple categories: (1) theories and research that suggest mitigating factors reduce media influence and (2) work that highlights various sorts of media influence. These two strains of thought have coexisted from the earliest media research, and they will always be present because they represent both sides of the structure/agency dynamic that is a central part of the media process.

EARLY WORKS: ESTABLISHING THE AGENDA

Even though they were often speculative in nature, early works about media effects were influential in helping establish the agenda for later research. They signaled that the growing world of media was a significant development worthy of serious attention.

The Press and Democracy

Some of the earliest concern with media effects involved the news media's role in democratic life and the ability of media to influence what people thought. Sociologists and other scholars were writing about this at least as far back as the mid-1800s, long before the existence of communications or media studies departments (Hardt 2001). Karl Marx (1818–1883)—himself a sometime journalist and newspaper columnist—wrote about the importance of press freedom for democracy. Ferdinand Toennies (1855–1936) was concerned about communication and public opinion more generally in a rapidly changing urban society. Max Weber (1864–1920), another sometime political journalist who even helped launch a daily newspaper, understood the news media as an important vehicle for spreading ideas that could become influential and as central to the process of political decision making. In the early 20th century, U.S. sociologist Charles Horton Cooley (1864–1929) noted that modern communication enabled information to travel fast and far and wrote of the newspaper as "indispensable to the organization of the public mind" (1909: 83). In the wake of government propaganda efforts to shape public opinion during World War I, journalist Walter Lippmann (1889–1974) wrote critically of the "mass" public's reliance on stereotypes to understand the world and wrote approvingly of the role of media in the "manufacture of consent" when done in the public interest (1920: 173).

The importance of such works was that they signaled the growing significance of the news media in societies that were rapidly urbanizing. As we will see, in the wake of such work, early researchers were very interested in the role media played in democratic life, perhaps helping form public opinion or even sway voters.

Entertainment and Children

Beginning in 1929, a team of 18 social scientists conducted 13 studies over a four-year period examining film content, audience composition, and the possible influence of movies. These Payne Fund Studies—named after the private foundation that financed the work—were among the first empirical work to examine possible media effects. In one study, University of Chicago sociologist Herbert Blumer (1900–1987) tried to understand how movies might be influencing children and adolescents. Given the novelty of the subject at the time, this was an "exploratory" effort, and Blumer (1933) acknowledged that because of the "intangible character" of the topic, "[t]he customary methods of study used in social and psychological science have not seemed to be of much promise" (p. xi). Instead, his team relied on people self-reporting their media experiences, collecting more than 1,800 essays from college students, high school students, office employees, and factory workers, along with surveys of 1,200 grade-school children and in-depth interviews with more than 130 college and high school students.

The study's findings suggested the existence of considerable media influence. Children imitated movies in their play; adolescents learned how to impress their love interests copying techniques from movie roles. Movies were the source of fear in some children and sorrow and passion in some adults. People of all ages learned from movies; they took what they saw as meaningful, and they formed some understandings about the world based on those images. "We have called attention," Blumer (1933) concluded,

> to the way in which motion pictures may furnish people with ideas as to how they should act, notions of their rights and privileges, and conceptions of what they would like to enjoy. We have indicated, finally, how motion pictures may implant attitudes. (p. 194)

With his social-psychological orientation, Blumer placed these findings in the context of children and adolescents learning about the world around them and developing a sense of self. Sometimes that meant children were just playing as they imitated characters from movies. Sometimes, especially with adolescents, movies were a source of inspiration, copying behaviors they found attractive and promising. Either way, Blumer concluded that movies were a "genuine educational institution" (p. 196), and because "they often present the extremes as if they were the norm" (p. 197), they may conflict with other sources of education, such as the family, schools, and religious institutions.

Blumer (1933) argued that movies' power came from their artistic form. He suggested that movies draw people in and generate "emotional agitation" that leaves the viewer "malleable to the touch of what is shown. Ordinary self-control is lost. Impulses and feeling are aroused, and the individual develops a readiness to certain forms of action which are foreign in some degree to his ordinary conduct" (p. 198). For most people, this state was temporary (as with crying during a sad film), but "as our cases have shown, occasionally it may be quite abiding" (p. 198). Blumer noted variation in these effects, appearing most significant, for example, in those with less education and in those from, in essence, low-income areas where family life was often less stable.

Blumer's methodology was problematic, especially in how it asked leading questions about the influence of movies (Petersen 2013). But, for its day, the research was rather sophisticated: a large-scale multi-method study that considered real-world media practices, included comparisons by social location, and contained appropriate nuances and qualifications. The mainstream media simplified and played up the study's findings, sometimes fearfully suggesting that movies could be the source of children's behavior problems. The study itself, though, was more tentative, leaving the door open for movies being either a good or a bad influence, and fully acknowledging that movies do not affect all people similarly. The work's long-term significance lay in moving beyond news media and taking seriously the potential influence of media content that was "just" entertainment.

Mass Society and Media Influence

Blumer's study of movies had some similarities to a line of thinking that was suspicious of the ordinary "masses" of people. In 1896, Gustave Le Bon had warned of "emotional contagion" in his book *The Crowd: A Study of the Popular Mind*. Perfectly rational individuals, Le Bon cautioned, could get caught up in crowd behaviors and take part in actions they otherwise would never consider. Such thinking was not far removed from Blumer's idea that movies could overcome people's self-control and leave them "malleable to the touch of what is shown." One of the reasons that people in crowds or at the movies were suspected of being open to outside influence was that modern life had undermined the stability of traditional communities, leaving many people rootless and vulnerable in a "mass society."

Concern over the use of propaganda in World War I was only exacerbated when it was used to an even greater extent by all sides in the Second World War. The United States and its allies deployed the tools of radio broadcasts and moviemaking in selling the war effort, but it was the propaganda efforts of Nazi Germany and the Soviet Union that most concerned American observers after the war. Mass society theory of this period was a broad current of sociological thought that included the suggestion that media influence could be dramatic (Kornhauser 1959; Reisman 1953). Although it existed in various forms, at the core of the theory was the argument that then-contemporary society was characterized by growing homogenization of the population, a decline in interpersonal and group relations, and a weakening of more traditional personal bonds. The traditional extended family was giving way to smaller (and, later, fragmented) nuclear families whose members spent less time with one another because of work and school. Strong religious ties gave way to more perfunctory religious, or even secular, identities. An urban "melting pot" culture discouraged ethnic group identity. Cohesive neighborhoods and community participation declined with the rise of dispersed and isolated suburbs. Work in large bureaucratic organizations became more alienating.

Although mass society theorists saw trends toward isolation and depersonalization in postwar America, they also noticed the continued rise in media, especially television. They argued that these media played a crucial role in uniting (and homogenizing) a disparate and atomized population. Stripped of significant personal ties, the mass population was especially susceptible to the influence of media messages. The language of mass society was perhaps best suited to totalitarian regimes. However, the notion of an alienated public tuned into media to gain some semblance of collective identity fit well with popular concerns about media influence.

Collectively, these early works established much of the agenda for media effects research that has followed. They opened the door for understanding the media as an influential force in society while also adding caveats that later researchers would build upon to suggest limits to this influence.

MITIGATING MEDIA EFFECTS

By the middle of the 20th century, almost everyone recognized the significance of media, and researchers gave closer attention to its role in society. This work was occurring in an environment where there was popular concern about the influences of media on traditional values as well as the impact of political propaganda on the democratic process.

Limited Effects and the Two-Step Flow of Influence

"Limited effects"—and sometimes the more extreme "minimal effects"—is the umbrella term that came to be used for various arguments suggesting the media's influence was lessened by intervening social and psychological factors. Just as with the earlier "hypodermic" model, later critics popularized the terms "limited effects" and "minimal effects" rather than the theorists to whom they are applied.

Limited effects theory is most closely associated with Columbia University sociologist Paul Lazarsfeld and his colleagues, who produced several studies that developed the perspective (Lazarsfeld, Berelson, and Gaudet 1944; Katz and Lazarsfeld 1955; Klapper 1960). The best-known work, *The People's Choice* (1944), used a panel format—where particular respondents are contacted multiple times during a set period of time—to study if and how information influenced Erie County, Ohio, voters during the 1940 presidential election. The study found media's influence—radio and newspapers at the time—was far less significant than many people assumed; media messages rarely changed voters' minds about candidates. Instead, for most people, media messages reinforced existing beliefs.

This study and later work argued that the media's influence was limited for a variety of reasons, including what scholars sometimes refer to as the three "selectives." Many people do not pay attention to news (selective exposure), making them unlikely to be affected by media content. Those who are exposed to it tend to already have strong political beliefs, tend to interpret media content in ways that support their already-existing perceptions (selective understanding), and are more likely to recall information consistent with their views (selective remembering). These "selectives," coupled with other social dynamics, helped explain why media influence was so limited. In the preface to the second edition of *The People's Choice* (Lazarsfeld, Berelson, and Gaudet 1948: xx) the authors noted, "the individual preserves his security by sealing himself off from propaganda which threatens his attitudes," and "he finds those attitudes reinforced in his contacts with other members of his group. Because of their common group membership, they will share similar attitudes and will exhibit similar selective tendencies." (As we will see, scholars presented a similar analysis a half century later when the internet enabled people to choose their personal networks and news sources, potentially reinforcing preexisting ideas.)

Whatever effect the media *did* have, *The People's Choice* authors argued, was primarily achieved through a "two-step flow of influence" involving local opinion leaders. "Opinion leaders"—who made up about 20 percent of the study's participants—were people who reported that they had either tried to convince someone of a political idea or had been asked a political question by someone else. Although they were overrepresented among men and the middle class, as opposed to women and the working class, the researchers noted that opinion leaders were scattered throughout all segments of society. Lazarsfeld and his colleagues thought "opinion leaders" straddled the worlds of media and interpersonal communication; they paid closer attention than most to the news, and they discussed politics with others. Accordingly, they played the central role in the two-step flow of influence. The media transmitted information to opinion leaders, and in turn, these leaders could influence those with whom they had personal contact.

The findings of the limited effects tradition were reassuring for anyone anxious about the power of media to promote propaganda. (And as we will see, the idea of limited effects resurfaced in work on the internet's possible influence.) In fact *The People's Choice* ends on an explicitly optimistic note:

> In a way, the outcome of the election in Erie County is the best evidence for the success of face-to-face contacts. . . . In the last analysis, more than anything else people can move other people. From an ethical point of view this is a hopeful aspect in the serious social problem of propaganda. The side which has the more enthusiastic supporters and which can mobilize grass-root support in an expert way has a great chance of success. (Lazarsfeld et al. 1948: 157–158)

In the end, the study suggested, democracy was safe in the hands of ordinary Americans who were perfectly capable of resisting the effects of any media influence.

However, there were problems with the limited effects claims. For one thing, they focused narrowly on short-term behaviors that political campaigners and marketers (who financed some of the studies) were interested in, namely, voting and buying. By doing so, they underestimated other sorts of influences, some of which were evident in the studies' own findings. To be fair, though, one of the defining publications of the perspective warned the reader against going "overboard in blindly minimizing the effects and potentialities of mass communications" (Klapper 1960: 252). For example, limited effects studies found that media reinforced existing ideas, a notion that didn't interest marketers and political campaigners who wanted to change people's minds but that spoke to the ideological power of media to reinforce mainstream values (as we discuss later in "Cultivation Theory"), while excluding unpopular ideas (discussed in "The "Spiral of Silence"). Second, the two-step process suggested that media could be very effective at spreading ideas throughout society, even to people who had not been exposed to the original messages. This has become an important insight again as the internet enables the spread of information—and misinformation—though social contacts rather than through mainstream media. Still, despite its shortcomings, the limited effects model gave more weight to the ability of the reader to select, screen, and judge media information, an orientation that was taken up in a very different way by active audience studies.

Active Audiences

Chapter 8 explored many aspects of active audiences, so we mention this approach in passing here only to put it in its historical context. The active audience tradition emphasized that people could interpret media content in multiple ways and that the social location of users was often important in affecting how they understood media messages. By recognizing the agency of users, this tradition suggested that mitigating characteristics of users diluted media's power. Researchers found that people's class, race, gender, and other social characteristics were associated with how they tended to interpret, understand, and react to media content. Active audience work also flagged the importance of social context in affecting how people used and understood media.

HIGHLIGHTING MEDIA INFLUENCE

Critics of the "limited effects" approach (Gitlin 1978) argued that it had missed a wide range of important media influences, normalizing the growing power of the media industries. They tried to expand the scope of media research to consider broader issues of production, power, and influence. In Part III, we explored some of those ideas from the production perspective. In Chapter 6 we considered some of the ideological implications of media influence. Here we review some examples of media effects research and theory that highlight the many ways that media influence matters (Scheufele and Tewksbury 2006).

Agenda Setting and Framing

In a classic phrasing of the "agenda-setting" role of the media, Bernard Cohen (1963) argued that the media "may not be successful in telling people what to think, but it is stunningly successful in telling its readers what to think about" (p. 13). This ability to direct people's attention toward certain issues highlighted the important role that journalists play in selecting and shaping the news.

One investigation that empirically examined Cohen's claim studied media and undecided voters in the 1968 presidential election (McCombs and Shaw 1972, 1977). It found a remarkable similarity between the media's issue focus and the issue agenda of undecided voters. Although this finding showed a correlation between the media's agenda and the agenda of voters, the study's design did not allow for determining a causal relationship.

Funkhouser (1973) tackled the issue by looking at three sources of data: (1) public opinion polls regarding the most important issues facing the nation, (2) media coverage in the nation's top three weekly newsmagazines, and (3) statistical indicators measuring the "reality" of key issue areas. Confirming earlier findings, Funkhouser found substantial correlation between public opinion and media coverage. More important, he found that neither public opinion nor media coverage correlated well with statistical indicators of the "real" world. For example, media coverage and public concern regarding the Vietnam War peaked *before* the greatest number of U.S. troops were sent there. Media coverage and public concern about unrest on college campuses and in urban areas also peaked *before* the period in which the greatest number of campus demonstrations and urban riots took place. This suggested that the media's coverage of issues affected public opinion more than the issues' objective prominence in the "real" world. It also showed that media coverage did not necessarily reflect real-world trends.

A variety of studies, including experimental work, have continued to confirm a causal relationship between media coverage and the issue agenda of the audience. Iyengar and Kinder (2010), for example, showed test participants different videotapes of edited television news broadcasts. The different versions of the broadcasts were the same, with one exception. The researchers added stories to the tapes so that some participants saw pieces on either the environment, national defense, or inflation. Tests before and after viewing showed that participants were more likely to choose as important those issues the researchers had highlighted in each of the doctored broadcasts. Researchers found some agenda-setting effects after the viewing of only a single broadcast. However, most effects took place only after participants had watched several of the altered newscasts, suggesting a cumulative effect of media exposure.

Framing: Second-Level Agenda Setting

If agenda setting is about *what* news is covered, framing is about *how* that coverage is constructed (D'Angelo and Kuypers 2010; Iyengar 1991; Johnson-Cartee 2005). With roots in the work of sociologist Erving Goffman (1974), a frame refers to the context into which the media places facts. Framing theory suggests that how the media organizes and presents information influences how people are likely to understand the story. Thus, some scholars refer to framing as second-level agenda setting (McCombs 2014). The media's organization of a story can involve everything from verbal or visual clues to the inclusion/exclusion of facts and the order in which journalists tell the story.

Frames organize information and help make it intelligible. For example, journalists might frame a bus driver's strike as a massive inconvenience for commuters. On the other hand, they might frame that same event as a desperate attempt by underpaid and disrespected workers to finally be heard. Both stories might be factually accurate, but the choices made about which information to highlight will likely encourage the viewer to understand the story in a particular way. Participants in news events are constantly trying to influence the frame in which the media presents stories. Union opponents would likely want the media to highlight the inconvenience frame for the story; labor proponents would want poor pay and working conditions to be the center of attention.

Gamson (1992), along with Druckman and Nelson (2003), have shown that frames vary in their effectiveness. Gamson examined how regular working people in his focus group study constructed meaning by combining media-based information with popular wisdom and experiential knowledge. His study treated the media as a tool or resource that people can use, to varying degrees, to help them make sense of current events. Such studies suggest framing effects may be most pronounced when individuals have no direct contact with an issue and thus are dependent on the media for information.

New Agenda-Setting Players in the Internet Era

Although the basic agenda-setting function of the media is well established, it is neither simple nor complete (McCombs 2014). In the digital age, professional journalism is no longer the undisputed source for agenda setting. As we saw in the previous chapter, users now play a role in the process of promoting and distributing media content, eroding the media's exclusive ability to set the agenda via its gatekeeping function. Political bloggers have become significant agenda-setting actors, too; they and professional journalists influence each other's agendas (Wallsten 2007).

The biggest change in traditional agenda setting comes from social media. For example, Neuman, Guggenheim, Jang, and Bae (2014) examined the relationship between online discussion (via Twitter, blogs, discussion forums, and message boards) and mainstream news outlets (including local newspaper and broadcast websites, national broadcast, and print media) on 29 political issues. Their massive data analysis clearly showed that online discussions did not follow lock-step mainstream media the way traditional agenda setting would predict. Instead, each arena operated with some independence: Social media discussed social issues (e.g., birth control, same-sex marriage) and public order issues (e.g., guns and drugs) more than the news media; news media outlets focused more on economics (especially policy) and the process of governing. Overall, social media discussions were just as likely to *precede* news media coverage as they were to follow it, and in half the cases there was an interlocking cycle of mutual and reciprocal causation to the coverage.

Such analyses suggest that social media has affected the balance of power somewhat. It has opened up a new era of interdependence between traditional media outlets and social media users, replacing an older version of one-way agenda setting. The players here are not equally powerful; professional media still control the largest platforms for public discourse. However, the sheer scale and pervasiveness of social media mean its cumulative impact can be influential.

The Spiral of Silence

If agenda setting noted the media's ability to highlight certain topics, "spiral of silence" theory drew attention to the ideas that were left out of public discourse (Donsbach, Salmon, and Tsfati 2014). Experimental studies have long suggested that people tend to conform to group expectations (Asch 1952, 1955), and political researchers have long known of the "bandwagon effect," where people adopt positions or support candidates because they are perceived to be popular (Dizney and Roskens 1962). Spiral of silence theory elaborated on these themes.

Spiral of silence theory came from Elisabeth Noelle-Neumann (1916–2010), a conservative German public opinion researcher. Once affiliated with Nazi organizations during World War II, Noelle-Neumann sometimes wrote anti-Semitic material for Nazi publications about the supposed Jewish control of the media, although she later denied ever personally being a Nazi (Bogart 1991; *New York Times* 1991; Noelle-Neumann 1991). Her history is relevant because she experienced the dramatic changes that occurred upon the defeat of Nazi Germany. Racist views that had been dominant under the Nazis became marginalized in the postwar era. It is from this environment that Noelle-Neumann (1974, 1993) developed the idea that those who held minority views were likely to remain silent when they believed that others disagreed. This allows dominant views to advance uncontested and gives people who hold those views the incorrect impression that everyone agrees with them.

More formally, one comprehensive review of spiral of silence theory and research summarized the five key dynamics of this process (Scheufele and Moy 2000):

1. Societies require some degree of agreement about basic values and goals and exert social pressure on individuals to agree, including an implicit threat of isolation for those who do not.

2. As individuals develop their own opinions, they fear social isolation and seek to conform to what they see as the prevailing views in their community.

3. People monitor their environment, paying careful attention to the opinions of others as they try to decipher the most common opinions and future opinion trends.

4. People are likely to express their opinions when they believe their views are popular or rising in popularity. However, when they believe their views are unpopular or declining in popularity, they are likely to be guarded and remain silent.

5. "The tendency of the one to speak up and the other to be silent starts off a spiraling process which increasingly establishes one opinion as the prevailing one" (Noelle-Neuman 1974).

The spiral of silence narrows public discussion by squeezing out minority views and overstating the degree of political consensus. The media play an important role in this process because people often look to media for indications of which views are currently popular. If they do not see their perspectives reflected there, they are likely to believe that their views are marginal, making it more likely they will be quiet. This is not necessarily a bad thing because it can effectively keep in check views that are widely seen as dangerous or abhorrent, such as racist or misogynistic attitudes.

The unexpected 2016 election of Donald Trump triggered renewed interest in spiral of silence ideas as popular commentators suggested it might help explain why polls often underestimated support for Trump and why, in the wake of his election, far right supporters felt emboldened to express racist and anti-Semitic views that had previously been marginalized (Mecking 2017; Whiteley 2016). Trump supporters, and conservatives more generally, have been vehement critics of the mainstream media, often accusing it of generating "fake news," having a "liberal bias," being "politically correct," and largely ignoring their views. As spiral of silence theory suggests, Trump's election may have animated some who had previously been silent because they had not seen their views included in the mainstream media.

The ideas received renewed attention, as well, because of attempts to shape the discourse found on social media. In particular, whereas early studies suggested that Twitter and other platforms could be useful for social movement mobilization, other studies have shown that autocratic leaders have adjusted and found ways to use social media to discourage dissent; an effort sometimes called "computational propaganda" (Woolley and Howard 2017). For example, Spaiser and her colleagues (2017) looked at protests against Russian president Vladimir Putin in 2011–2012, finding that both anti- and pro-Putin Twitter users tried to influence the political discourse around the protests. At first, anti-Putin messages dominated Twitter, but then a small core of very active users successfully flooded Twitter with pro-Putin messages, shifting the balance decisively in Putin's favor. The researchers could not determine if real supporters, hired "trolls," or fake Twitter "bots" primarily generated these messages. (A Twitter bot is software that controls a fake Twitter account, making it look like a real person by tweeting, retweeting, "liking," "following," and even sending direct messages to other users.) Either way, the content had its effect. They note,

> With the political discourse on Twitter beginning to noticeably shift in favor of the Putin supporters, oppositionally minded people on Twitter may have started to slide into a so-called "spiral of silence." . . . They perceived their political view to be in a shrinking minority, finding insufficient resonance in the discourse on Twitter, and gradually stopped [speaking] up. (p. 148)

Another study (Hampton et al. 2014) examined the willingness of people to discuss the controversial case of Edward Snowden, the National Security Agency (NSA) employee who leaked information regarding widespread government surveillance of Americans' e-mail and phone records. The case was chosen precisely because public opinion about the surveillance program was deeply divided. Consistent with the themes of the spiral of silence, the survey found that "[i]n both personal settings and online settings, people were more willing to share their views if they thought their audience agreed with them." Social media did not change these dynamics; people who thought their Facebook network would agree with their views were about twice as likely to join a discussiion about the case. In fact, users were more reticient to share their ideas online than they were in face-to-face situations; about twice as many were willing to talk about the case in person compared to online.

More broadly, as we will explore, the internet offers many available sources of information (including blatantly inaccurate information) and venues for discussion with like-minded individuals. It may be that people who had previously felt isolated—trapped in the spiral of silence Noelle-Neumann describes—are now more likely to be emboldened by seeing others who share their views. For those unjustly marginalized in the past, this can be a blessing, but insofar as it may also inspire others who hold hateful or violent views, it poses a challenge for society.

Learning from Media

Because they communicate messages, all media can be educational, and a variety of learning theory approaches have considered how and what is being learned. Much of this work has focused on children and their use of television. The range of effects examined in such work is enormuos and includes educational impact (e.g., learning and becoming school ready), emotional effects (e.g., triggering fear in young children), phsycial aggression, racial and gender stereotyping, empathy development, associations with obesity, and developing healthy body image (Mares and Kretz 2015). In the internet era, new concerns such as cyberbulling among kids (Chen, Ho, and Lwin 2017) and the effects of pornography (Gunter 2014) have been studied. Here we want to focus on the basic learning theory that underlies much of this research.

The basic idea that children can adopt behaviors they have learned from media dates back at least to Blumer's (1933) consideration of the impact that movies might be having on children and adolescents. Such thinking became more formalized, though, with the work of psychologist Albert Bandura, Dorothea Ross, and Sheila A. Ross (1961) (see also Bandura 1977, 1986). Bandura argued that children learn behaviors from their social environment, what he termed "observational learning." Children see various "models"—parents, friends, characters on televeision, and so on—some of whom they may imitate. The response that imitative behavior receives from others—positive or negative—acts to reinforce learning, and consequently, the child may decide to either discard or adopt the behavior long term. The child also learns when observing the consequences of another person's behavior, known as "vicarous reinforcement." A movie character treated as a hero after violently vanquishing a foe, for example, might be seen by a child as a role model to imitate because the behavior was positively received. Of course, children have many—and often competing—models to observe, but those with characteristics that the child would like to have are the ones they are most likely to identify with. Identification involves adopting mutiple behaviors associated with the model and internalizing them as the child's own. The implications for media are clear: The models put forward in media content may have real consequences for some children. But the effects of such content are variable, depending on the child's social context and psychological condition.

One example of learning from media involves what children learn from advertising. Living in a capitalist society means that children are bombarded from an early age with advertising and commericials intended to help sell products. Considerable evidence exists that such marketing to children can have long-term negative effects (Kasser and Linn 2016). These include promoting a highly materialistic value orientation, unhealthy eating habits, negative body image issues that contribute to eating disorders, increases in violence and aggression, and the adoption of risky lifestyles, including unhealthful eating habits, cigarette use, and alcohol abuse.

More broadly, a variety of effects research has examined how people of all ages learn from the media to which they are exposed. Although there are a range of results, some seem especially well supported. Considerable evidence exists, for example, that heavy exposure to violent media contributes to more aggressive behavior, desensitizes users from the effects of violence, and increases the likelihood of users seeing themselves as living in a hostile, "mean world." That latter effect is part of long-term exposure to media, the focus of cultivation theory.

Cultivation Theory

Cultivation theory considers the long-term effects of television viewing on how people see and understand the social world. It is based on the Cultural Indicators Project launched in the late 1960s by George Gerbner and his associates (Gerbner et al. 2002; Morgan and Shanahan 2014; Morgan, Shanahan, and Signorielli 2012). They argue that television's effects come from prolonged and extensive exposure to its contents in general rather than from any particular program or genre. After controlling for social demographic features, long-term heavy viewers of television content tend to see the real world as more closely resembling television depictions than do light viewers.

Television content—meticulously catalogued over decades in this ongoing project—presents a distorted image of the world. However, for heavy viewers over the long term, this image becomes "real;" heavy viewers internalize many of the distorted views of the social and political world presented by television (such as those discussed in Chapter 7).

For example, compared to the real world, television programs drastically underrepresent older people (who are not usually a major target of advertisers), and heavy viewers tend to underestimate similarly the number of older people in society. Television portrays crime and violence much more frequently than it occurs in real life, and these television portrayals seem to influence heavy viewers in this area as well. Heavy viewers are more likely than moderate or light viewers to believe that most people cannot be trusted and that most people are selfishly looking out for themselves, what Gerbner calls a "mean world syndrome" (Gerbner, Gross, Morgan, and Signorielli 1984; Gerbner, Mowlana, and Nordenstreng 1993).

The impact of television cultivation on political belief seems to be in a conservative direction (Gerbner et al. 1982, 1984). A journalistic pose of an "objective" balancing of views seems to encourage heavy viewers to avoid calling themselves either "conservatives" or "liberals." However, self-described "moderates" who are heavy television viewers actually hold beliefs that are closer to those of conservatives than to those of liberals on a whole range of social issues, such as race, abortion, and LGBT rights. On economic issues, heavy viewers are more likely than moderate or light viewers to adopt the conservative call for lower taxes, but they are also more likely to support a populist call for more social services. In society more broadly, television has played a homogenizing role for otherwise heterogeneous populations. Immersion in television culture produces a "mainstreaming" effect, whereby heavy viewing mutes differences based on cultural, social, and political characteristics. The outlooks and values portrayed on television come to be the dominant culture of mainstream society.

Scholars conducted most of these studies in the era of limited television content, viewed on the major national broadcast networks. The long-term effects of media abundance and the fragmentation of audiences across different platforms will not be known for some time.

MEDIATIZATION

Consider two examples:

- Because the internet has enabled people to easily search for online health information, physicians often see patients who have already consulted "Doctor Google" before visiting their office. Research suggests that this has enabled patients to play a more active role in a shared decision-making process with their doctor, resulting in improved patient compliance with medical instructions and improved health-care outcomes (Osei-Firmpong, Wilson, and Lemke 2018).

- The popularity of crime scene dramas on television led to talk of the "CSI Effect"—named after the popular *CSI* television series and its spin-offs. The claim for the CSI Effect was that jurors who watched such programs had unrealistic expectations for real-life courtroom proceedings and were less likely to convict defendants without the presence of forensic evidence. Subsequent research cast doubt on whether such an effect ever existed, but it did find that some attorneys were *anticipating* the effect and therefore requesting unnecessary forensic tests as a way to surmount it. This spike in test requests has created backlogs in crime labs, negatively affecting the criminal justice system (Alldredge 2015).

In these examples, different spheres of social life have been influenced by the media but in ways that go well beyond anything considered by traditional "media effects" research. Instead, these are small examples of how society has now integrated media throughout everyday life, affecting social interactions and altering aspects of daily living. Collectively, some sociologists and media scholars refer to such changes as the *mediatization* of society. (Some scholars use the spelling "mediatisation" and others have used "mediation" to mean something very similar.) In this section, we examine the concept of mediatization and explore its impact on one social institution: the world of politics.

The Concept of Mediatization

Compared to other work on media's influence, mediatization is a shift in focus, stepping back and considering media dynamics on a much larger scale than other theories typically have. At its simplest level, mediatization "refers to a social change process in which media have become increasingly influential in and deeply integrated into different spheres of society" (Strömbäck and Esser 2014a: 244). In the mediatization perspective, the media industry still exists as a distinct entity, but media have integrated themselves into other areas of social life. Consequently, "social institutions and cultural processes have changed character, function and structure in response to the omnipresence of media" (Hjarvard 2008: 106). By suggesting a very broad look at the interaction between media and other aspects of social life, mediatization extends beyond the boundaries of what most "media studies" have addressed. Hepp, Hjarvard, and Lundby (2015) even suggest that "[m]edi-atization is . . . an attempt to build a theoretical framework that will allow us to discuss the influences of media and communications in other social and cultural domains with researchers from other disciplines" (p. 316).

Mediatization is not an alternative to other effects theories; instead, Schulz (2004: 90) notes that it "both transcends and includes media effects." For example, work on the mediatization of politics has incorporated insights from agenda setting, framing, and other theories (Esser and Strömbäck 2014). In addition, mediatization shares with medium theory (discussed in Chapter 2) an interest in how media penetrates daily life through the variety of ways users adopt and adapt it (Bird 2003; Couldry 2012). Indeed, sociologists Nick Couldry and Andreas Hepp (2017) argue for the need to rethink the character of the entire social world "starting out from the principle that the social is constructed from, and through, technologically mediated processes and infrastructures of communication, that is, through what we have come to call 'media'" (p. 1).

Hjarvard (2008), summarizing the work of Krotz (2007), notes that we can think of mediatization as an ongoing meta-level social process on a par with the growth of individualization or globalization. Like those other processes, mediatization is not a single thing; it evolves over time and manifests itself differently in different social and cultural contexts. In this sense, mediatization has been occurring since the rise of media itself. However, most observers argue that mediatization has accelerated since the latter part of the 20th century, particularly in modern, highly industrialized, and predominantly Western societies. As media continue to expand globally, the dynamics already experienced in those societies will likely spread to other nations, taking on local variations along the way.

Mediatization has its critics (e.g., Deacon and Stanyer 2014) who point out that it is underdeveloped as a theory and who argue that it overemphasizes the role of media in social life. Even its proponents acknowledge that "empirical work firmly rooted in the mediatization concept is still relatively scarce" (Hepp et al. 2015: 315) and that "thus far mediatization has the character of a theoretical perspective or framework rather than a proper theory" (Strömbäck and Esser 2014b: 244). Still, we have found this framework—and the language it offers—to be helpful in thinking about media and society. Although we adopted it long before we were familiar with the term "mediatization," the title of this book, *Media/Society*, suggests the integration of media and the broader social world that is part of mediatization's focus. Even our model of "Media and the Social World" from Chapter 1 is potentially compatible with mediatization, showing how the media industry is both a separate entity and embedded within the larger social world.

The Mediatization of Society and Media Logic

The changes mediatization scholars seek to document and understand reverberate throughout society. Examples include the ones we've mentioned previously from the worlds of health care and criminal justice, but we can find others almost anywhere. For example, in earlier eras specific physical places tended to ground and limit social life. Education took place in schools, places of worship centered religious activity, politics happened in and around government buildings, and artists presented their work on stages, in galleries, and in museums. Mediatization has contributed to the "virtualization of social institutions" (Hjarvard 2008: 129), enabling all of these activities to be experienced through the media. Music is a good example. As we explored in Chapter 2, music was once exclusively a live, in-person experience. When people began to use media to transmit sound, early radio musical broadcasts were simply attempts to reproduce that live concert experience. Over time, though, recorded music developed in its own right, and the live concert was no longer the basis for most recordings. Now, users experienced music at home through recordings, and audiences increasingly expected musicians at live performances to reproduce what they had recorded; the existence of recording media changed the live face-to-face experience (Auslander 1999; Katz 2010).

Such examples are all around us: smartphones with internet access in schools, religious services broadcast on television, online shopping, and more. Education, religion, the economy, and, as we saw earlier, health care and the criminal justice system are all among the social institutions that the media and digital communications have affected. Winfried Schulz (2004) groups the changes in communication and interaction brought about by mediatization into four key categories:

1. Media extend the ability of humans to communicate across both time and space.

2. Media replace some forms of face-to-face interactions, as with online banking.

3. Media infiltrate and coexist with everyday communication, as with checking your cell phone while talking with a friend or "talking around" a television program while watching with others.

4. "Media logic" encourages people to adjust their attitudes and behaviors.

This last point regarding "media logic" needs some explanation.

"Media logic" refers to the various needs associated with the production processes for a particular medium. Altheide and Snow (1979, 1991) write that media—and the genres of content within them—have a "format" (related to the idea of conventions) that establishes rules and codes for defining, selecting, and presenting media content.

> Format consists, in part, of how material is organized, the style in which it is presented, the focus or emphasis on particular characteristics of behavior, and the grammar of media communication. Format becomes a framework or a perspective that is used to present as well as interpret phenomena. (Altheide and Snow 1979: 10)

Part of media's power to affect society comes from the adjustments people make when interacting with media, adapting their actions to anticipate the "media logic." In this way, media logic is a feature of mediatization that connects media production to media effects. A simple example of media logic in politics is politicians adjusting how they speak to emphasize sound bites—short statements that will meet journalists' need for pithy quotes that are easy to insert in a news story. Politicians are well aware that such quotes often oversimplify issues terribly, but they are also aware that journalists are likely to ignore lengthier, more nuanced statements because they won't fit easily into a story's expected format. As a result, they are pressured to conform to the media logic if they want their views to be included in a story. That, too, is a type of media effect.

There is no single "media logic," although there are commonalities across media forms. Each medium and type of content has distinctive attributes. For example, the internet has introduced a distinctive "network logic" that appears to have influenced political participation by encouraging movements such as the Occupy Wall Street, Black Lives Matter, and Me Too campaigns to network online, with little identifiable, centralized leadership (Bennett and Segerberg 2013). As we will see, social media has its own "social media logic" that results from its unique characteristics.

THE MEDIATIZATION OF POLITICS

Scholars first applied the idea of mediatization to changes in the political sphere. In 1986, Swedish media researcher Kent Asp referred to the mediatization of political life as the process whereby "a political system to a high degree is influenced by and adjusted to the demands of the mass media in their coverage of politics" (translated in Hjarvard 2008: 106).

Esser and Strömbäck (2014) note that "the mediatization of politics may be defined as a long-term process through which the importance of the media and their spill-over effects of political processes, institutions, organizations and actors have increased" (p. 6). Each of the definition's elements is important: (1) Mediatization is "a long-term process," not a single development; (2) regardless of variation, the key feature is the increasing importance and influence of media; (3) mediatization influences all aspects of political life, including actors and institutions; (4) some of media's influence is indirect, involving "spill-over effects."

Building on decades of work before them, Strömbäck and Esser have done the most to delineate the elements of the mediatization of politics (Esser and Strömbäck 2014; Strömbäck 2008; Strömbäck and Esser 2014a, 2014b). They see a continuum between the original "political logic" that once reigned in politics and the pressures from "media logic" that subsequently emerged. With "political logic," the needs of the political system are primary, shaping the process of political communication. Participating actors see media companies as having an informal public service duty to help make democracy work, and the primary concern is the need to have an informed citizenry, as interpreted by political actors and institutions. With "media logic," the media's needs take precedence, shaping how political communication takes place, how the media cover it, and how citizens understand it. The participating actors see media companies as strictly commercial enterprises, and the need to have content that people find interesting and that is commercially viable becomes the primary concern. (This distinction is similar to our discussion of the public sphere model versus the market model of media [Croteau and Hoynes 2006].)

There is a rich tradition of scholarship that has addressed the influence of media in political life, long before the terms "media logic" or "mediatization" were in use. We turn now to some of those ideas.

The Politics of Image

The influence of media on social institutions is perhaps most obvious in the world of politics in part because candidates organize electoral campaigns around media and then use media to help govern. Those who wish to communicate broadly on political matters must consider the news media's underlying "media logic" (Altheid and Snow 1979). Strömbäck and Esser (2014b) argue this news media logic contains three dimensions: professionalism (the sort of issues regarding norms and professional practice raised in Chapter 5), commercialism (the economic pressures discussed in Chapter 3 as they relate to influencing news production), and media technology (the manner in which the unique features of media technology limit or enable producers, discussed in Chapter 2). Politicians and other political actors must anticipate how the media are likely to cover an issue and construct their message in such a way as to be effective within the pre-existing confines of media logic. In this way, media logic has an effect on political communication before it even happens. As we will see, though, the technological evolution of the internet has enabled some political functions to bypass traditional media.

Political Actors

At its simplest level, we see the importance of media in the fact that a comfortable, camera-friendly style and appearance greatly enhance a candidate's chance of success. All major campaigns have media "handlers," consultants who coach candidates on improving their appearance in the media and who handle media inquiries.

The first Kennedy–Nixon debate of 1960 has come to symbolize the influence of television on politics. Looking fit, tanned, and confident, the underdog Kennedy was seen as having defeated the underweight, pale, and sweaty Nixon, still recovering from a recent hospitalization. The event raised the importance of appearances in political campaigns.

The infamous 1960 presidential debate between John Kennedy and Richard Nixon has become the iconic example representing the importance of appearance in politics. In that televised debate, Nixon declined to wear the heavy makeup that aides recommended. On camera, he appeared haggard and in need of a shave, whereas a layer of television makeup supported Kennedy's youthful and vibrant appearance. The significance of this difference in appearance became apparent after the debate. A slim majority of those who heard the debate on the radio thought Nixon had won, whereas an equally slim majority of those who watched the debate on television gave the edge to Kennedy. In later years, there has been considerable discussion about the validity of the polls on which this story rests, but political operatives had already learned the lesson: Appearance matters. After this dramatic event, the fear of not performing well in televised debates so intimidated presidential hopefuls that it was 16 years before presidential candidates would agree to another televised debate.

Charismatic individuals who have experience in dealing with the media are at a decided advantage in the world of politics. A number of celebrities have used their media skills, status, and experience to pursue political careers. As a developer, Donald Trump made a career of courting media coverage and cultivating his image long before he became a politician. His later years on prime-time reality television are widely thought to be a significant reason for his political success (Nussbaum 2017). Ronald Reagan's reputation as the "great communicator" was surely in part the result of the training he received as actor, radio personality, and ad salesman. His oratorical skills were largely limited to scripted events. He was notorious for misstating facts and for rambling, sometimes incoherently, when faced with spontaneous speaking situations. On occasion, he even confused his movie roles with real-life experiences. The ability of his staff to maintain the president's polished public image was central to his success. After the first two years of poor showings in the polls, high public popularity marked the Reagan presidency—even though polls showed most Americans disagreed with many of Reagan's key policy positions. Some took this result to be the ultimate triumph of image over substance. As Reagan's own chief of staff, Donald Regan (1988), admitted,

> Every moment of every public appearance was scheduled, every word was scripted, every place where Reagan was expected to stand was chalked with toe marks. The President was always being prepared for a performance, and this had the inevitable effect of preserving him from confrontation and the genuine interplay of opinion, question, and argument that form the basis of decision. (p. 248)

Every presidential election since then has continued to highlight the importance of being telegenic in contemporary politics and the value of carefully staging appearances for media coverage. The affable politicking of Bill Clinton, the folksy charm of George W. Bush, the charismatic speech making of Barack Obama, and the pugnacious style of Donald Trump each, in their own way, played well in the media, serving up images, soundbites, and Tweets that the news media could easily use. In contrast, to varying degrees, the losing candidates from those years—Bob Dole, John Kerry, John McCain, Mitt Romney, and Hillary Clinton—were all awkward on camera.

Being comfortable in the media spotlight has helped many media celebrities to successfully pursue political careers: Jack Kemp, Bill Bradley, Fred Thompson, Jesse Ventura, Arnold Schwarzenegger, Sarah Palin, Al Franken, to name just a few, were all in the media spotlight before becoming politicians. In fact, politicians with media connections are commonplace. Among the members of Congress in 2017–2018 were these:

- 21 public relations or communications professionals (three in the Senate, 18 in the House)

- Seven radio talk show hosts (one Senate, six House)

- Seven radio or television broadcasters, managers, or owners (two Senate, five House)

- Eight reporters or journalists (one Senate, seven House)

- Two speechwriters in the House

- One public television producer in the House

- One newspapers publisher in the House

- One documentary filmmaker in the Senate (Manning 2018)

The media-related skills needed for those jobs translate well into politics.

Setting the Stage

The significance of media images goes well beyond the specific characteristics of the candidate to include the more general visual context in which a candidate appears. In this regard, too, observers often point to Ronald Reagan's campaign and presidency as a benchmark for the masterful use of visuals to enhance a candidate's image. Both during the campaign and after the election victory, the Reagan team showed remarkable skill at manipulating media coverage by providing television with an irresistible visual to support the "line of the day"—the message the White House wanted the media to emphasize in that day's reporting. In this way, they could direct media coverage—at least in visual terms—by making it efficient for the news media to use the visual settings they had orchestrated. The administration even coordinated the 1986 U.S. bombing of Libya to coincide with the start of the evening news (Kellner 1990). Michael Deaver, the Reagan White House media specialist, later pointed out that he and his staff found television reporters quite "manageable" because he gave "the nightly news good theater, a good visual every evening, and pretty much did their job for them" (*Nightline* 1989). Ever since then, every administration has followed suit in trying to stage visuals to direct the media's attention to the intended theme of the day or week.

Political operatives stage various types of media events, including speeches, "spontaneous events" (which, as the name ironically suggests, are supposed to look spur of the moment), state visits, foreign trips, and arts or culture-related events. Such events allow candidates or elected officials to control the agenda, construct favorable political images providing audiences with visual cues, help authenticate a leader's image, "tell a story" and thus dramatize policy, and give the audience an emotional experience by using powerful symbols such as the flag or military personnel (Schill 2009). The effect of media events, however, is cumulative: A single event rarely produces a decisive shift in public perception, but a series of events is more likely to have impact (Scott, Nardulli, and Shaw 2002).

For example, the careful construction of photo opportunities has become a routine part of presidential politics. Most of the pictures we see of the president are likely to have been scripted ahead of time by collaborative "advance teams" of reporters and political aides who scout out the best angles for photo opportunities at upcoming events. Using stand-ins for the president and his entourage, these advance teams often stage practice photos that they later distribute to the media. These photos, along with notes about the camera lenses likely to produce the best results, are then used by photojournalists in planning their coverage of the "real" event.

Postmodernist theorists, especially Baudrillard (1983), have argued that the rising importance of images signaled a new kind of "reality." In postmodern society, they argue, the image has come to replace the "real" as a new form of "hyperreality." As a result, the public is often unable to distinguish between image and reality. The practical application of postmodernist theory to the political world suggests that substantive policy debates will continue to take a backseat to polished, telegenic candidates and scripted photo opportunities.

The Decline of Political Parties

Entman (1989) notes a central dilemma in media and politics: "to become sophisticated citizens Americans would need high-quality, independent journalism; but news organizations, to stay in business while producing such journalism, would need an audience of sophisticated citizens" (p. 10). In such a scenario, the media cannot be the primary connection of citizens to politics; the commercial interests that drive a media logic, favoring image over substance, will not allow it. The problem has been compounded by the fact that political parties—once a key source of citizen information—have failed as well.

As the media became more important in political campaigns, political party organizations became less important (Negrine 2008; Negrine, Mancini, Holtz-Bacha, and Papathanassopoulos 2007). In American politics, political parties used to maintain a grassroots organization that contacted voters, educated them about candidates, and encouraged them to vote. This system resulted in an intricate infrastructure of party workers, often organized down to the urban "block captain." For the most part, such organizational structures have ceased to exist. Now, media serve as the primary avenue for information about candidates and individual campaigns using internet platforms to try to reach voters. Also in decline are a range of other "mediating institutions" (Greider 1992)—especially labor unions—that used to serve as structures to organize and mobilize groups of ordinary citizens. These institutions once served as links between the public and the political process on an ongoing basis, not only during election campaigns.

Now that media serve as the vehicles for conveying political messages and mobilizing voters, candidates spend the vast bulk of campaign finances on producing and airing campaign commercials and developing their internet infrastructure (Louw 2010). Rather than being active participants in dialogues about issues and candidates, citizens are an audience for televised debates, political commercials, and online advertising that sell the latest candidate. Public service campaigns to encourage voting do nothing to create any lasting political structure. Instead, such endeavors promote voting as an individual act devoid of any long-term political commitment, likely contributing to civic disengagement and political apathy (Norris 2000).

However, this can be a windfall for media. In the midst of the 2016 presidential election, the CEO of CBS, Leslie Moonves, had a moment of candor about his network's relationship to the campaign. "It may not be good for America, but it's damn good for CBS," he said. The candidates were spending heavily on television advertising, although as Moonves noted, "Most of the ads are not about issues." Still, from a business perspective, "The money's rolling in and this is fun," he noted. "I've never seen anything like this, and this going to be a very good year for us. Sorry. It's a terrible thing to say. But, bring it on, Donald [Trump]. Keep going" (Bond 2016).

The decline of party structures has been accompanied by a decline in party allegiance. In the 1940s, when researchers conducted early studies of voters, the most important determinant of a person's vote was party affiliation, followed by group allegiance, perception of the candidate's personality, and consideration of issues. After more than a half century of media coverage, the order of importance has changed. Now, in presidential campaigns, the candidate's personality is of greatest importance to voters, followed by the issues, party membership, and group membership (Bartels 2002; Graber 2009; Prysby and Holian 2008).

Entman observes, "America lacks the effective political parties or other mechanisms to mobilize the participation of the average person in politics" (p. 9). Parties are therefore dependent on media to reach voters, whereas voters are dependent on media to get information, an interdependence that leaves media in an influential position (Dalton 2014). In both cases, the media's power and influence have been extended.

Communication Professionals and "Post-Truth" Politics

To achieve their political objectives, politicians employ media-savvy professionals who use political marketing techniques to mold and steer public opinion (Louw 2010). Today's communications professionals have two distinct, although overlapping, arenas of work. The first involves accommodating and trying to influence traditional news coverage. The second involves using the internet to target and mobilize voters directly. In both cases, media have heavily influenced the political process.

Working with the News Media

"Spin" is a form of propaganda that involves the creation and diffusion of a specific interpretation of an event, a campaign, or a policy, with the aim of creating consensus and public support. Public relations experts who employ such news management tactics are sometimes called "spin doctors," even by the reporters they are trying to manipulate. The importance of public relations consultants in politics is partly a consequence of the central role of television in daily life, even in the internet era (Louw 2010). Television plays to the advantage of politicians because it can easily provoke emotional responses and can be useful in building public indignation or generating enthusiastic support.

Spin is effective because of the symbiotic relationship among public relations teams, politicians, and journalists. Spin doctors need the news media to disseminate stories that serve their clients' agendas, and journalists need access to powerful politicians to effectively report on government. As a result, journalists are vulnerable to well-crafted spin. However, because reporters do not like to be openly manipulated by public relations professionals, there is often tension between spin doctors and journalists.

Spin tactics include leaking stories to journalists and providing them with selective "off-the-record" information, scripting speeches in a way that makes sound editing and quote retrieval easy, orchestrating strategic photo opportunities, as well as organizing smear campaigns against opponents and planting stories on the internet, for example, by posting videos on YouTube (Louw 2010). By deploying these techniques, spin doctors seek to set the agenda for the media and their audiences by defining what's important and offering easily digestible interpretations of events.

Spin, however, does not always work. In some cases, spin can backfire and become a problem for politicians and public relations handlers. In a political world where a candidate's image is a valuable currency, the appearance of deception, dishonesty, or incompetence can be very damaging. One of the most famous spin failures in modern politics occurred in 2003, when President George W. Bush took the cockpit of a Navy jet to theatrically land on the aircraft carrier Abraham Lincoln returning from the war in Iraq. Standing in front of a large "Mission Accomplished" banner, the president announced the end of combat operations in Iraq. The event, carefully staged by the Bush team, dominated the newscasts. *Washington Post* media critic Tom Shales (2003), described the event as a "patriotic spectacular, with the ship and its crew serving as crucial backdrops for Bush's remarks, something to cheer the viewing nation and to make Bush look dramatically commander in chief." However, the powerful—but premature—"mission accomplished" image came to haunt Bush as the war and the bloody occupation of Iraq dragged on past the end of his presidency.

Using the Internet

Political professionals quickly saw the potential of the internet and incorporated it into their electoral strategies. By producing and distributing their own content, campaigns control their messages and bypass journalists to communicate directly to the public. Famously using Twitter to do so, Donald Trump made explicit the tactic of bypassing—and bashing—journalists, telling a FOX interviewer, "I think that maybe I wouldn't be here if it wasn't for Twitter, because I get such a fake press, such a dishonest press" (CNN 2017).

Campaigns first used the internet extensively during the 1996 election to post press releases and position papers online and to respond quickly to developing stories. In 2004, campaign professionals started to take more full advantage of the two-way communication potential of the internet to engage supporters. Democrat Howard Dean's campaign pioneered the use of the internet as a way to parlay many small contributions into substantial fund-raising. Some of the staff from that campaign led a similar effort for Obama's 2008 campaign and pushed internet use further. Obama's campaign team posted more than 1,800 videos on YouTube, perhaps most notably a celebrity-studded "Yes We Can" music video by Will.i.am. Thanks to the campaign's interactive site, each supporter could create her or his own network, organize events, and even phone undecided voters in his or her neighborhood, thereby taking on many of the functions that political parties used to serve. By 2012, the Obama campaign was using state-of-the-art techniques that one analysis noted made Obama's "much-heralded 2008 social media juggernaut—which raised half billion dollars and revolutionized politics—look like cavemen with stone tablets" (Romano 2012).

For example, if you Googled the phrase "immigration reform" during the 2012 campaign, an ad from the Obama campaign would likely have accompanied your results because the campaign was courting supporters of immigration reform. Clicking on that ad to visit the Obama site would have loaded cookies onto your computer that not only tracked what you viewed on the campaign website but also your movements across the web to see where you shop and what other interests you have—a technique often used by commercial advertisers. If you opened your Facebook page, the campaign could gather more information on your circle of friends and your "likes," among other things. On a subsequent visit to the Obama website, the campaign's software would highlight content customized to your expanded data profile, including your interest in immigration reform. If you supplied the campaign with your e-mail address, the campaign would also make pitches for financial contributions by highlighting the issue it knew you were already interested in, customized to your likely demographic based on the data it gathered on you. It would also likely encourage you to join with other voters in your area to help with the campaign.

The 2016 Trump campaign copied and expanded these sorts of tactics, taking them to new levels. A digital team of more than 100 staffers—from programmers and data scientists to media buyers and copywriters—worked to target a detailed database of millions of likely voters. They hired Cambridge Analytica, a commercial data-science company that says it has about 5,000 data points on every single American and uses these to produce psychological profiles of likely voters (Laposky 2017b). The campaign used Facebook's customizable advertising services to target people who had particular characteristics with tailored ads and messages. For example, because data suggested young voters and African Americans were unlikely to support Trump, the campaign might send them messages disparaging Hillary Clinton in an effort to discourage turnout. People more likely to be receptive to Trump received other messages trying to incite or inspire action. Software generated customized messages based on the users' demographic characteristics and online data trails. The results were staggering. As one journalist reported, Trump's digital director recounted that in a single day, the campaign "sprayed ads at Facebook users that led to 100,000 different webpages, each micro-targeted at a different segment of voters" (Mims 2016).

In the process of using such tactics, the Trump campaign transformed political communications, relying heavily on social media to circulate messages. The campaign could not only bypass traditional journalists, but it could also have supporters—rather than the campaign—delivering messages that went viral to people in their social networks. By coming from friends and family, these messages took on an air of authenticity and credibility. In reality, they were often the product of the campaign's spin operations and were full of misinformation, such as the idea that Pope Francis had endorsed Trump. Although politics have long included disinformation, when the Trump campaign and right-wing European populist movements gained momentum using such big-data techniques, some observers called 2016 the dawning of the "era of post-truth politics" (Freeland 2016), and the *Oxford English Dictionary* even named "post-truth" its 2016 word of the year (Oxford Dictionaries 2016).

Russian agents joined in on the creation and spread of misinformation supporting the Trump campaign (Intelligence Community Assessment 2017). The post-election revelations of Russian interference and the misuse of Facebook data contributed to the 2018 bankruptcy and closure of Cambridge Analytica (Romm and Timberg 2018). It also played a key role in the special counsel's investigation (ongoing as of this writing) into possible collusion between the Trump campaign and Russian agents (Bump 2018).

With traditional journalism marginalized, political parties debilitated, elections interfered with by foreign agents, and social media loaded with misinformation, some scholars even began to ask "Can democracy survive the internet?" (Persily 2017). After the election, misinformation and distortions became a hallmark of the Trump administration (Kellner 2018), and journalists were left simply cataloging the ever-growing number of outright lies coming from the White House (Leonhardt and Thompson 2017). Trump was even able to flip on its head media criticism charging his campaign and its supporters with spreading false information; he famously dismissed any criticism of his actions as "fake news," supposedly perpetrated by biased journalists.

Social Movements

In the absence of effective or responsive political parties, social movements offer an avenue for citizen participation in politics. The media have also influenced these efforts.

Social movements are groups of citizens who have banded together to promote a social or political cause. Keeping in mind the idea of media logic, we can think of the relationship between media and social movements as a transaction between two complex systems, each trying to accomplish a particular goal. Movements ask the media to communicate their messages to the public, while the media look to movements as one potential source of "news." However, the media hold the upper hand in their relationship with social movements. Movements usually need the mass media to widely publicize their activities. Such coverage helps social movements mobilize support, achieve validation as a significant political player, and expand the scope of conflict to attract potential allies or mediators. The media, on the other hand, have many alternatives to social movements as news sources (Gamson and Wolfsfeld 1993).

The task that faces social movements, therefore, is twofold. First, they must convince media gatekeepers that they are worthy of coverage; that is, they represent an interesting story angle or are significant "players" in the issues at hand. This task involves the direct issue of media access. Social movement activists often find that they need to conform to media expectations to gain this access. As the author of a media handbook for activists colorfully puts it, "An effective media strategy requires—at least to some extent—a willingness to cater to the often warped priorities and short attention span of the news media"

(Salzman 1998: 3). Small grassroots organizations that do not achieve what the media consider "player" status may even have to resort to dramatic actions, such as demonstrations and protests, to attract the media's attention.

Second, social movements must work to influence the nature of the media coverage they receive. This task involves the struggle over framing messages (Gamson and Modigliani 1989; Gitlin 1980; Snow et al. 1986; Snow, Vliegenthart, and Corrigall-Brown 2007; Tuchman 1978). Gaining access to media coverage by staging dramatic actions can be counterproductive for a movement if the media use a discrediting frame in their coverage. Discrediting techniques used by the media include downplaying content in favor of emphasizing the spectacle of an event, painting demonstrators as deviant and unrepresentative of the population, granting comparable coverage and thus "false balance" to a tiny number of counterdemonstrators, and undercounting the attendance at demonstrations (Parenti 1986). For example, the Occupy movement that began in 2011 successfully brought national attention to the neglected issue of economic inequality. However, over time, the tactic that attracted media attention—long-term encampments on Wall Street and other locations—was not only difficult to maintain but was used by critics to suggest that the protesters did not represent average Americans.

As with electoral politics, the media's desire for succinct sound bites and interesting visuals has a significant impact on social movement efforts. Mass media will usually ignore movements that are unable to accommodate journalists' needs. Although pandering to media desires for dramatic visuals risks undermining the effective communication of a movement's message, proactive planning is a necessity if movements are to do all they can to develop favorable media coverage (Ryan 1991). Grassroots citizens' organizations with few resources for public relations and media strategizing are at a distinct disadvantage when they face off against well-funded government agencies, corporations, and other organizations, especially when these movements are challenging mainstream norms.

The hurdles social movements face when they attempt to cultivate positive media attention from the mainstream media have often led to their use of "alternative" or "independent" media to promote their messages (Downing 2001, 2011; Langlois and Dubois 2005). For example, in the late 19th and early 20th centuries, the labor movement produced a diverse array of labor newspapers, often catering to different immigrant groups (Hoerder and Harzig 1987; Pizzigati and Solowey 1992). In the politically vibrant environment of 1960s social activism, a thriving "underground" press emerged, made up of local newspapers and even alternative wire services reflecting the views and concerns of political activists and countercultural participants (Armstrong 1981). In the 1970s and 1980s, the do-it-yourself politics and sensibility of the punk and hard-core scenes resulted in a wide variety of "zines" that combined political and cultural analysis and commentary.

Today, the internet serves as the "printing press" of many social movement organizations, providing information and analysis that are rarely found in mainstream media. Thanks in part to the increased availability of affordable media-making tools and software, social movement media projects have dramatically expanded their production capacity. Movement organizations have used the internet and social media extensively to post information and videos, promote their causes, and solicit new members (Kahn and Kellner 2004). Social media has also enabled the rapid sharing of information among movement participants, and various hashtag-activism campaigns have drawn the attention of mainstream media outlets, expanding the reach of their messages.

Citizen Alienation

Citizens in democracy need adequate information to take appropriate political action, and the media can be a source of such information. A well-functioning free press can be an invaluable tool for holding those in power accountable. That is why the media are such an important element of the democratic process and why the First Amendment protects a "free press." However, if the news media become merely commercial enterprises scrambling for the attention of consumers rather than a resource that serves citizens, the results can be corrosive to democracy. One of the great questions facing news organizations is how mainstream news outlets can remain economically viable without losing their public service function in an era when users expect news to be available online for free. At best, paywalls and benevolent benefactors seem to be stopgap measures.

In the meantime, critics find news coverage of politics to be deficient in a number of ways. News accounts of elections emphasize personal stories, personalities, and pre-planned campaign events and are less likely to explain the background and implications of substantive issues and policy debates (Graber and Dunaway 2018). Too often, critics contend, the media are less interested in where candidates stand on the issues than in their electability as measured by polls. For example, one study of the early months of the presidential primary campaign in 2007 found that news coverage focused on the horse race far more than any other topic, with "strategy and polls" accounting for half of all the coverage. Although this study found that horse race coverage was the dominant framework in all sectors of the news media—newspapers, network and cable television, commercial and public radio, the internet—coverage of strategy and polls was highest at the online news outlets (PEJ 2007).

Entman (1989) argues that media have distorted the political process by turning elections into a horse race and governing into a strategic chess match. Cappella and Jamieson (1997) argue that this focus on the "game" of politics—running campaigns and maneuvering to govern—rather than the substance of issues, policies, and their consequences helps drive a "spiral of cynicism" the erodes public trust and fuels disengagement from politics (Goldfarb 1991; Robinson 1976; Rosen 1993). This sort of coverage has an effect on political actors as well. D'Angelo and Esser (2014) note the prevalence of "metacoverage" in U.S. presidential campaigns. The news media spend a considerable amount of time explaining and analyzing the media strategies of the campaigns. This media about media, in turn, can influence campaign media strategies moving forward, creating an endless loop of influence.

In the end, cynicism permeates media coverage as well. Too often, critics argue (Rosen 1993: 9), the media suggest that

> yet another president is a bumbling clown, that government is a hopeless
> mess, that politics repays no serious effort to attend to it. Mindlessly, the press
> contributes to these perceptions and then stands back to survey the damage as if
> it were some naturally occurring disaster.

The Internet's Uncertain Political Future

By definition, the mediatization of politics has meant the growing influence of media. As we have seen, this influence ranges from an impact on political elites—politicians and campaign operatives—to the institutional structure of political parties. It has affected how social movements attempt to communicate their messages, and perhaps most important, it has fanned the flames of growing citizen alienation and cynicism.

The internet has contributed to the most recent wave of change—one we are still riding to an uncertain destination. Early enthusiasts suggested that the internet was a unique opportunity to help revive our ailing democracy, but more recently, we have also seen how powerful forces can use its technology to further corrode democracy. Clearly, new technologies, by themselves, are not the solution. Barnett's (1997) early observation remains accurate: "The real challenge—to change the dominant political culture from one of alienation, cynicism and detachment to one of concerned involvement—cannot be left simply to new communicative devices" (p. 213).

There is no doubt that the internet is enabling new forms of political expression and organizing. However, society—and those in power—have heard only a few of these new voices. Hindman (2009) highlights the important distinction between speaking and being heard. Hindman's analysis of millions of web pages on a half dozen political topics shows that very few of the new voices speaking are being heard because their sites attract very few readers and are not linked by other sites. Instead, Hindman finds that online audiences are actually *more* concentrated at a few major sites than audiences for traditional media. He points out that "despite—or rather because of—the enormity of the content available online, citizens seem to cluster strongly around the top few information sources in a given category" (p. 18). This clustering creates a hierarchy that is

> structural, woven in to the hyperlinks that make up the web; it is economic, in the dominance of companies like Google, Yahoo! and Microsoft; and it is social, in the small group of white, highly educated, male professionals who are vastly overrepresented in online opinion. (pp. 18–19)

Still, as the internet matures and a "hybrid media system" (Chadwick 2017) emerges that interlaces old and new, we have seen examples of different ways to be heard (Gainous and Wagner 2014). In some cases, so-called hashtag activism has enabled isolated voices to coalesce, attracting attention to neglected issues. #Ferguson and #BlackLivesMatter help put a spotlight on police shootings and structural racism. #MeToo highlighted sexual harassment as a widespread social problem. #NeverAgain became the rallying call for students threatened by gun violence. Importantly, such efforts attracted coverage from traditional media outlets, vastly amplifying their messages. Such activism will never replace traditional political organizing, but it has a useful role to play (Tufecki 2017).

Various studies have reached similar conclusions about social media use, political knowledge, and political participation (Bode 2016; Wolfsfeld, Yarchi and Samuel-Azran 2016). First, following political news in traditional media outlets increases learning about politics and current affairs, but doing so on social media generally does not, regardless of previous level of political interest or knowledge. Following news on social media appears to be mostly a supplement to, not a replacement for, traditional media. Whereas social media exposes users incidentally to political information, offering the *opportunity* for learning, little or no actual learning about politics appears to come from social media use; those who take advantage of it are already relatively well informed. However, social media use is associated with higher levels of political participation, both online and offline.

As one study concluded, "There is absolutely no support for the notion of 'slacktivism.' The citizens in this study who used the social media to keep up with political affairs were more likely to leave their house and participate" (Wolfsfeld et al. 2016: 2109).

The truth is that we do not know if or how citizens will revive our ailing democracy. We are even less certain what role—for good or ill—the internet may play in this process. The issue is a rapidly moving target, and the full effect of new technologies may not be seen for some time as young people adopt new media use habits, digital technologies evolve, and regulators respond (Chadwick 2006, 2017; Shah, Kwak, and Holbert 2001). In the meantime, these technologies are influencing social life and raising a variety of pressing issues.

DIGITAL DILEMMAS: ONLINE MEDIA INFLUENCE

The "Triple Revolution" (Rainie and Wellman 2012) of the expanding internet, mobile communications, and social networks has reverberated throughout everyday life. For most people, it has been a positive occurrence. To mark the 25th anniversary of the development of the World Wide Web—the software on which most internet traffic operates—the Pew Research Center (2014b) surveyed Americans on their use of the internet and their opinion of its impact. Overall, 76 percent of users saw the internet's impact as good thing for society as a whole, and a whopping 90 percent said it had been a good thing for them personally. In addition to being important for job-related reasons, two-thirds (67%) of respondents said the internet had strengthened their relationships with family and friends. More than two-thirds (70%) said they had been treated kindly or generously by others online, compared to just 25% who said they had been treated unkindly or been attacked online. The internet has become such a part of daily life that nearly half (46%) said it would be hard or nearly impossible to give it up.

However, as the internet matures, many scholars and ordinary citizens have raised questions about its influence on society. In this section, we sample a few of these emerging dilemmas, focusing on social media and its unintended consequences.

Social Media Logic and Algorithmic Power

One of the most popular elements of the internet is social media platforms such as Facebook, Instagram, and Twitter (see Figure 9.1). Such sites blend elements of interpersonal digital communication with traditional media forms, enabling users to create, share, and respond to content. Van Dijck and Peoll (2013) identify four key elements of "social media logic"—the strategies, mechanisms, and economies that are the foundation for social media platforms: programmability, popularity, connectivity, and datafication. We can trace the influence of social media back to one or more of these features.

- **Programmability** is "the ability of a social media platform to trigger and steer users' creative or communicative contributions, while users, through their interaction with these coded environments, may in turn influence the flow of communication and information activated by such a platform" (p. 5). The technological element of programmability includes the computer code,

FIGURE 9.1 ■ Social Media Platforms Globally

The reach of social media platforms is enormous, dominated by Facebook products and Google's YouTube. In the wake of the abuse of such platforms, many observers have called for new regulations on how they operate.

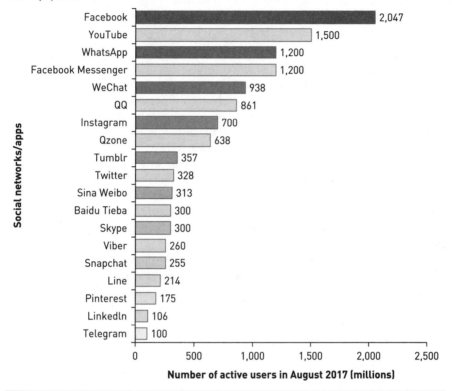

Number of active users in August 2017 (millions)

Source: Statista (2017).

algorithms, and interfaces associated with each platform. The user element includes the choices people make and the feedback they provide while using these platforms.

- **Popularity** also involves technological elements (e.g., algorithms) and user actions. Each platform offers mechanisms for quantifying and boosting the popularity of people, topics, and things. Social media encourage users to reach out and engage others, bringing more traffic to the sites. "Likes," "followers," "retweets," and similar mechanisms all quantify popularity and encourage it further.

- **Connectivity** involves linking people to each other as well as connecting people to content and, crucially, connecting advertisers to people. Depending on the platform, these can involve friends lists, channel subscriptions, or "following" playlists of other users. Advertisers can then target users in part based on the choices they make with these connections.

- **Datafication** involves the quantification of every aspect of digital activity, including which content users view and for how long; which connections people make; and which materials elicit a response. It includes all the "profile" data, photos, and other content a user voluntarily posts. It also includes passive meta-data such as time stamps and GPS locations generated by smartphones. Harvesting such "big data" troves for the use of advertisers is the economic lifeblood of social media platforms.

Because of the underlying logic of social media, these platforms are not "neutral"; they help steer users to certain types of action. They are also a key mechanism by which corporations track users. Journalist John Lanchester (2017) points out, "even more than it is in the advertising business, Facebook is in the surveillance business. Facebook, in fact, is the biggest surveillance-based enterprise in the history of mankind. It knows far, far more about you than the most intrusive government has ever known about its citizens."

Algorithms are a key component of social media logic. Algorithms are simply software code programmed to accomplish various tasks without human intervention. Programmers write guiding rules for how the algorithm should operate, and then without further intervention, they apply the algorithm to vast quantities of data, searching, sorting, recommending, and so on. Sometimes the results can be unintentionally alarming.

For example, Facebook ads can be used for racist purposes. Facebook's automated system to purchase advertising relies on algorithms that identify the interests of users based on what they read, share, and write on the platform as well as what these activities imply about the user. The result of this automated process is tens of thousands of potential ad buy categories that enable advertisers to target their message specifically to users who show interest in what they have to offer. Much of this is benign; posting a selfie from a rap concert you attended might get you tagged as a music lover from a particular location who would be receptive to ads about new music releases or upcoming concerts in your area. However, once created, the system operates largely without human involvement, which leaves it open to bias and abuse. To prove the point, journalists succeeded in taking out ads on Facebook that targeted people that Facebook's algorithms identified as being interested in topics such as "Jew hater" and "How to burn Jews." Facebook approved the ads within 15 minutes (Angwin, Varner, and Tobin 2017). Google similarly allows advertisers to target people based on what they type in their search bars. The result is that they accepted ads created to target people based on racist searches such as "Black people ruin everything" and "Jewish parasite" (Kantrowitz 2017). Conversely, journalists also showed that Facebook's ad system could be used to prevent housing ads from being shown to racial minorities, a probable violation of fair housing laws, which prohibit discrimination in housing advertising (Angwin and Parris 2016). In both cases, after journalists contacted Facebook, the company said it amended its procedures to prevent such actions in the future.

Because the computations that occur as algorithms churn through big data are massive and involve so many different variables, creators often don't exactly know how they work or what they will produce, giving algorithms a degree of autonomy. Because algorithms are usually proprietary, people outside the companies that use them cannot tell how they are written, cloaking them in a degree of secrecy. Because users are often unaware of—or do not think about—algorithms, they have a considerable degree of power (Beer 2009; Pasquale 2015; Turow 2006).

Algorithms produce all sorts of outcomes we regularly see, including Facebook news feeds, Google search results and map routes, "you might like" suggestions about music or movies, and "people you might know" prompts, among countless others. Often these can be convenient, alerting you to a band, new product, or person that might interest you. However, as we will see, algorithms are also a central element of some of the biggest digital dilemmas. They are not a technology issue so much as a social and political issue, asking us to think about how we want our digital media to operate.

The Crisis in Journalism

Internet-based companies have used technology to disrupt existing industries, under-mining the financial foundation for traditional journalism (Franklin 2011; Jones 2009; McChesney and Pickard 2011; Meyer 2009). Subscriptions that had once funded news-paper journalism plummeted as users flocked to "free" online content. Print advertising, which had made up the bulk of revenue for news organizations, also fled to the internet; Craigslist and eBay replaced the newspaper classified ads, whereas Google, Facebook, and online ad brokers replaced display ads. As users and advertisers moved online, publishers decided they had to follow.

Stand-alone news websites offered free online content, reinforcing the expectation that news should be available without cost. Some introduced pay walls to try to recap-ture some lost revenue. In the hope of finding greater readership, "distributed content" became common, where publications allowed their content to appear on Facebook and other platforms. Unfortunately, of the people who find a news story from social media, about two-thirds remember the social media site where they found it, but fewer than half remember which news outlet originally published it (Kalogeropoulos and Newman 2017). Still, publishers competed to create content that met the format and content pref-erences of those platforms. When Facebook research showed users engaged with video presentations more than text, the call for news outlets to "pivot to video" followed. In one example, *The Washington Post*, best known for its sober political coverage, began creating scripted funny videos as a way to attract more users via distributed content (Bilton 2017).

That is a change from how news organizations have operated in the past. At legacy news sites—whether the printed newspaper or online website—news organizations offer the user a package of content. Users might skim the headlines, check out the sports, and delve deep into a feature article—all from a single news outlet. That means the editorial staff at the outlets produces a well-rounded package of information and news, along with lighter lifestyle and entertainment stories. With distributed content, though, each story—or video—must stand on its own. Users graze across many different outlets with-out ever leaving the Facebook or Apple News platform where they first see the content. They may not click on that serious *Post* story on health care reform, but they might watch a funny video. When the financial success of news outlets comes increasingly to rely on the "success" of clicks on individual articles, the dynamics of journalism change. Fed with the metrics that measure every move of a reader online, editors cannot help but be influenced by the likely popularity of a story when making decisions about what is worth assigning or writing about and what is not.

Rather than bypass gatekeepers, as some had predicted, the internet has merely created a new category of gatekeepers. As one journalism study (Bell and Owen 2017) of the situation put it, "There is a rapid takeover of traditional publishers' roles by companies including Facebook, Snapchat, Google, and Twitter. . . . These companies have evolved beyond their role as distribution channels, and now control what audiences see and who gets paid for their attention, and even what format and type of journalism flourishes" (p. 9). Meanwhile, as we saw in Chapter 3, print journalism jobs continued to plummet, newspapers closed, and the rise in internet-based journalism employment did not come close to keeping up with job losses elsewhere. Cuts hit local and state news organizations especially hard, often leaving city halls and statehouses with minimal coverage or none at all.

Some scholars have tried to strike a more positive tone, arguing that other developments offset the economic and technological challenges that news organizations have faced (Alexander, Breese, and Luengo 2016). For example, a generation of quality journalists has taken up the new tools of digital journalism, More important, they claim, in the face of economic and technological trials, journalism has produced a robust defense of its goals and purpose in our culture, even if the traditional mechanisms to deliver that journalism are less viable. In a digital world, assisting citizens' involvement in democratic life and holding those in power accountable continue to be journalism's reason for being. However, developments online are making those tasks more difficult than ever to achieve.

Information Distortions: Misinformation and Echo Chambers

Forty-seven minutes after news appeared about a high school mass shooting in Parkland, Florida, in 2018, right-wing posters on an anonymous chat board known for racist and anti-Semitic content were already plotting how to respond. They decided to try to influence public perception of the event by spreading the lie that the students interviewed afterward were "crisis actors"—performers pretending to be students—and that the event was a "false flag"—staged to generate support for gun restrictions. Right-wing activists have used this tactic on other occasions, including after the Sandy Hook, Connecticut, and Aurora, Colorado, shootings. Over the next few hours, they scoured the students' social media feeds looking for anything they could use against them. They created memes ridiculing the students and questioning their truthfulness. They darkened photos of the shooter so he would not appear so white. Before the end of the day, right-wing conspiracy radio host Alex Jones was raising the possibility of a "false flag" on his *Infowars* program. After posters found out that one student was the son of an FBI agent, they promoted this as "evidence" that the event was part of a larger FBI-run anti-Trump campaign. The Tweets and memes circulated rapidly through social networks, with Donald Trump Jr. even "liking" a tweet about the supposed anti-Trump campaign. As these fallacies circulated, people outraged by the offensive claims criticized them, inadvertently helping spread them across the internet. Within the week, the number one "Trending" video on YouTube labeled the FBI agent's son a fake "actor." One regular poster in another right-wing forum put it this way the day after the Parkland attack, "There's a war going on outside . . . and it is only partially being fought with guns. The real weapon is information and the attack is on the mind" (Timberg and Harwell 2018; Yglesias 2018).

The ability of a small number of anonymous users to influence the national discussion of major issues speaks to the power of social media. The decentralized internet offered the promise of democratic participation and a "participatory culture" (Jenkins 2009) without the gatekeepers that controlled traditional media. Ironically, highly centralized, corporate-owned social platforms emerged to display user work, host discussions, and facilitate networking. Some of this was beneficial: Charitable causes could crowdsource funding for their projects. Activists could use Twitter to help organize against repressive regimes. Citizens could start Facebook groups to help address community concerns. Amateurs could share their creative talents on YouTube and post instructional do-it-yourself videos on an incredible range of topics. Reddit users could find a treasure trove of information in sub-forums on countless topics.

https://www.vox.com/policy-and-politics/2018/2/22/17036018/parkland-conspiracy-theories

Right-wing memes like this one falsely suggest that tragic mass shootings were actually staged by liberals and populated by "crisis actors" playing the roles of victims. Such messages try to sow seeds of doubt about the authenticity of news, encourage divisiveness, and undermine any calls for gun legislation.

However, in bypassing traditional news media gatekeepers, information—and misinformation—could travel quickly and unimpeded across social networks because of how social media platforms work (Cacciatore, Scheufele, and Iyengar 2016). First, to serve the needs of advertisers, social media sites use their algorithms to divide users into tiny niche groups and steer users toward the same kind of content for which they have already shown a preference. Second, amid an abundance of varied content, users may select only information consistent with their views. Third, users can also interact only with like-minded individuals in self-selected online social networks. The result can be "echo chambers" (Sunstein 2002) or "filter bubbles" (Pariser 2011), where users are never exposed to alternative views but have their existing views constantly reinforced. If users "like" stories or videos taking one side or another on a social or political issue, the algorithms will feed them similar stories and downplay opposing views. If users "follow" active Twitter accounts or "subscribe" to YouTube channels that share political content with which they agree, they will be exposed to a steady stream of reinforcing messages. Over time, Facebook news feeds, Twitter streams, YouTube recommendations, and other sources can all amplify a single point of view.

Sometimes the promotion of fake news is not for political purposes. People can make money by attracting viewers who are sold to advertisers. One news story traced a stream of largely fabricated pro-Trump stories to a website created by a 22-year-old computer science student in Georgia, one of Russia's former republics. The student said he'd tried to promote Hillary Clinton at first, but his site did not get many views. He switched to fabricating clickbait stories that promoted Donald Trump with headlines such as "Oh My God! Trump to Release Secret Document That Will Destroy Obama!" As a result, his traffic—and revenues—soared. "For me, this is all about income," he said (Higgins, McIntire, and Dance 2016).

One way to look at this development is as the digital version of the "limited effects" model (Bennet and Iyengar 2008, 2010). From this perspective, social media's influence on political communication is limited because users are self-selecting what they are exposed to and algorithms are just serving up content that reinforces existing attitudes and beliefs. Such arguments, though, are subject to similar critiques made about the earlier limited effects work: They overemphasize the importance of changing people's minds and underestimate the significance of reinforcing existing beliefs. In contrast, some studies suggest that a "high-choice ideologically diverse media environment" coupled with exposure to negative political ads increases polarization (Lau et al. 2017). Moreover, some scholars suggest it is precisely this ability to cater information to existing beliefs that has made the internet and, especially, social media a powerful element in the current era of political partisanship (Sunstein 2002). That is because companies like Facebook make money by expanding the number of users it has, keeping them engaged on the site and selling their attention to advertisers. Algorithms that identify content with which users are engaged may well end up promoting content that is inflammatory, shocking, outrageous, or controversial (Tufekci 2018). Inflaming passions promotes engagement; discussing calmly usually does not.

Addressing the problem of automated homogeneity is not easy. When Facebook used human curators to choose featured stories for its "Trending" sidebar, it ran straight into controversy. An anonymous employee claimed that the curators were systematically suppressing conservative news stories (Nunez 2016), and conservative activists went into action. Breitbart, the far-right website, scoured the social media accounts of the employees, finding liberal content they offered up as evidence of pervasive anti-right bias. Although an internal investigation "found no evidence that this report is true" (Zuckerberg 2016), Facebook capitulated, firing the team, retooling the feature, and holding a much-publicized meeting between Mark Zuckerberg and high-profile conservatives to assuage their concerns. In the end, Facebook returned to relying on algorithms for the feature.

The consequences of such developments vary. At its mildest, people may just get a distorted picture of reality, not taking into account opposing views. However, once misinformation and outright lies attacking other people enter the information network, the potential negative consequences escalate. At least some of the partisan gridlock of recent years is very likely attributable to this "juiced-up" information environment that delivers a constant stream of highly provocative, highly selective, and often misleading or false messages. At its worst, such efforts can be an attack on the legitimacy of democracy itself.

Computational Propaganda: Trolls and Twitter Bots

Facebook's own published research shows that the social media platform can influence voter registration and turnout (Bond et al. 2012; Jones et al. 2016). In a randomized, controlled experiment involving 61 million Facebook users during the 2012 election cycle, the company tweaked the news feeds of some of them and increased voter turnout by more than 340,000, a potentially significant number. In 2016, voter registration spiked when Facebook temporarily placed a simple reminder encouraging people to register to vote (Chokshi 2016). These examples are a reminder of the potential power of social media—and the potential for abuse.

So far, Russian interference in the 2016 U.S. presidential election is the most prominent—but certainly not the only—example of computational propaganda, "the use of algorithms, automation, and human curation to purposefully distribute misleading information over social media networks" (Woolley and Howard 2017: 6). Although the impact it had on voter turnout or voter preference is unclear, election inference was aimed at helping Donald Trump win the presidency. The various U.S. intelligence agencies investigated this interference, and the declassified summary of the joint Intelligence Community Assessment (2017) concluded:

We assess Russian President Vladimir Putin ordered an influence campaign in 2016 aimed at the US presidential election. Russia's goals were to undermine public faith in the US democratic process, denigrate Secretary Clinton, and harm her electability and potential presidency. We further assess Putin and the Russian Government developed a clear preference for President-elect Trump. . . . We also assess Putin and the Russian Government aspired to help President-elect Trump's election chances when possible by discrediting Secretary Clinton and publicly contrasting her unfavorably to him. (p. ii)

From this assessment and media accounts (Dewey 2016; Parkinson 2016; Reed 2016), we know that Russian operatives bought ads to spread false information, created fake Facebook groups and Twitter accounts to rile up the electorate and spread disinformation, and even organized both sides of competing protests to stir up discord. For example, a Russian effort created a "Heart of Texas" Facebook group that eventually had 225,000 followers and a corresponding Twitter account. The group organized a series of anti-Clinton and anti-immigrant rallies in Texas just days before the election. Many similar efforts took place, including one that created an anti-Muslim rally in Idaho promoted as "Citizens Before Refugees" (Bertrand 2017). In Michigan, one of the key battleground states, junk news spread by social media was shared just as widely as legitimate professional news in the days leading up to the election (Howard, et al. 2017). At this writing, the FBI's investigation into Russian meddling in the election is continuing, but we already know a considerable amount about using media in such efforts in the United States and elsewhere.

One overview of the current state of knowledge about computational propaganda comes from an Oxford University project carried out by an international team of 12 researchers (Woolley and Howard 2017). The researchers examined case studies of computational propaganda in nine countries, including the United States, Brazil, the Ukraine, Russia, and China. They interviewed 65 leading experts in the topic; identified large social networks on Facebook, Twitter, and Weibo (the Chinese micro-blogging site that is like a mix of Twitter and Facebook); and analyzed tens of millions of posts on seven different social media platforms during periods of intensified propaganda efforts around elections and political crises. These social media accounts are important because, as the researchers note, in some countries "companies, such as Facebook, are effectively monopoly platforms for public life" and are "the primary media over which young people develop their political identities" (p. 2).

The researchers found widespread computational propaganda that employed different tactics and took on different characteristics in different settings. In authoritarian countries, "social media platforms are a primary means of social control," and some platforms are controlled or effectively dominated by government and disinformation campaigns aimed at their own citizens. For example, nearly half of Twitter activity in Russia is managed by highly automated government-connected accounts. In democracies, advocates or outside forces can use social media platforms to try to manipulate broad public opinion or to target specific segments of the population. In such cases, large numbers of fake accounts are set up and managed to give the appearance of widespread public support or opposition to an issue or candidate. (Fake accounts are a broader problem for Facebook and Google. They charged advertisers by the number of clicks on their ads, but it is well-known that a significant percentage of these clicks are produced by bots using fake accounts. The industry publication *AdWeek* estimates that one out of six dollars in online advertising is spent for fraudulent clicks [Lanchester 2017].)

The researchers note that "[t]he most powerful forms of computational propaganda involve both algorithmic distribution and human curation—bots and trolls working together" (p. 5). They point out that social media bots used for political manipulation "are also effective tools for strengthening online propaganda and hate campaigns. One person, or a small group of people, can use an army of political bots on Twitter to give the illusion of large-scale consensus" (p. 6).

Right-wing organizations and causes are the source of most misinformation in the United States (Howard et al. 2017). During the 2016 presidential election, a network of Trump supporters on Twitter shared the greatest variety of junk news sources and circulated more junk news items than all other groups put together; extreme-right groups did the same on Facebook.

Hate and Censorship

On May 18, 2015, at 11:38 a.m., President Barack Obama posted his first Tweet from the newly opened @potus Twitter account. Presidential tweeting was a novelty then, and his friendly first greeting was, "Hello, Twitter! It's Barack. Really!" It took only 10 minutes for the racial epithets to start; at 11:48 someone replied "get cancer nigger" (Badash, 2015). New technologies have enabled old racism to flourish—the latest media content filled with racist overtones and imagery include Tweets (Cisneros and Nakayama 2015), viral videos (Gray 2015), memes (Yoon 2016), and even search engine results (Noble 2018)—and racist hatred permeates the web (Jakubowicz et al. 2017).

Racism—and hatred more broadly—seems to thrive online. At home, a broad variety of hate groups uses the internet to recruit, organize, and spread lies. Globally, terrorist groups do the same. These groups used to rely on mainstream media to publicize their cause. As Barnett and Reynolds (2009) note, acts of terrorism were primarily efforts to attract "the attention of the news media, the public, and the government. As coverage of September 11 showed, media are delivering the terrorist's message in nearly every conceivable way" (p. 3). Some critics argue that mainstream news media often indirectly assist terrorists in publicizing both their grievances and their capabilities. However, in recent years, terrorists have relied more heavily on their own media. The internet affords global terrorist groups and their supporters opportunities to communicate through both social media sites like YouTube and their own websites, which include discussion groups, videos, political articles, instruction manuals, and leaders' speeches (Seib and Janbek 2011). They also can use the internet for encrypted communications.

In the wake of Russian interference with the 2016 presidential election that used these platforms, public concern grew, and elected officials began considering possible regulation if the companies did not address the most egregious issues. Now on alert, the corporations that owned the platforms began stepping in to try to identify and prevent "fake news" and hate sites. Google's head lawyer announced new steps to combat terrorism content on its YouTube platform, including hiring more humans to staff their "Trusted Flagger" program. It also would devote "more engineering resources to apply our most advanced machine learning research to train new 'content classifiers' to help us more quickly identify and remove extremist and terrorism-related content;" in other words, it would tweak their algorithms (Walker 2017). Twitter (2017), too, announced that it had shut down nearly 300,000 accounts for "promoting terrorism." Less than 1 percent of those were at the request of governments; Twitter itself was acting as the censor, preempting any need for government intervention. In 2017, when alt-right demonstrators in Charlottesville, VA, sparked violence, including the killing of a counter-demonstrator, Facebook moved to shut down a variety of accounts associated with the movement, including "Right Wing Death Squad" and "White Nationalists United." The day before, it had already shut down "Unite the Right," the page used to organize the rally (Herrman 2017). When he testified before Congressional committees in 2018, Facebook CEO Mark Zuckerberg acknowledged that it was "inevitable that there will need to be some regulation" (Kang and Roose 2018).

All of these events exposed the contradiction of having public discourse on a privately owned social media site. Who decides what views warrant attention or banishment? In civic life—in the public sphere—the First Amendment guarantees freedom of speech against attempts at government control. However, in the private world of Google and Facebook, the First Amendment does not apply. Private corporations judge the limits of speech. Whether and how governments should regulate such sites—either to compel them to do more to eliminate extremist hate content or to insist they abide by free speech standards—will be a continuing concern in the coming years. As Dhar (2017) argues, "We cannot trust digital platforms with self-policing . . . since it is in conflict with their primary goal of maximizing shareholder value." Furthermore, he warns,

> There are no easy answers, but turning a blind eye to this new Internet phenomenon will continue to expose us to considerable peril in the future. The U.S. government and our regulators need to understand how digital platforms can be weaponized and misused against its citizens, and equally importantly, against democracy itself. (p. 728)

Managing Our Social Selves

Some of the very people who have designed social media's best-known and most compulsive features have since denounced their negative influence. Jason Rosenstein, the Facebook engineer who designed the "like" button says, "It is very common for humans to develop things with the best of intentions and for them to have unintended, negative consequences." He now goes to great extremes to avoid addictive aspects of the internet and says, "One reason I think it is particularly important for us to talk about this now is that we may be the last generation that can remember life before." Tristan Harris, a former Google employee turned public critic agrees, warning, "All of our minds can be hijacked. Our choices are not as free as we think they are" (Lewis 2017).

Given the larger political, social, and economic implications of internet platforms, it is easy to overlook their potential impact on ordinary users. However, there is a growing body of social-psychological research examining how social media use may affect users. The underlying social media logic drives these influences, too.

A "network effect" is said to exist when the value of a product or service increases the more people use it. Social media are certainly an example of this. For users, the benefits of a particular platform increase when other people they know also use it. For companies that own the platforms—and for advertisers using them to target potential customers— their economic value increases with more people joining and staying active. From a social media company's perspective, the goal is always to attract more users and to keep existing users online as long as possible to sell their attention to advertisers. Achieving these goals involves promoting engagement—participation and involvement.

To promote engagement, social media encourages self-disclosure and the erasure of the line between public and private identity. Internet users are well-trained to accept such loss of privacy; we routinely "accept" privacy policies that we do not read. (One study estimated that if average internet users read every privacy and data use policy they encountered on the internet, they'd be spending about 40 minutes a day doing so—244 hours in a year [McDonald and Cranor 2008].) Upon signing up for an account, sites usually prompt users to create a profile, making some of their information public. These profiles often encourage people to define themselves through products they consume: favorite movies, music, books, and the like.

Next, social media urge self-promotion: telling people your thoughts, what you are doing, where you are going, what you are consuming (Curran et al. 2016). By creating content—posts, pictures, links, and so on—in the context of a social media platform, that content is instantly commodified and used to attract more eyeballs to sell to advertisers. Anyone using a social media site like Facebook, Twitter, or Reddit is, in a sense, working for those companies for free because their activities help engage others and thereby add value to the company.

However, the specifics of the content users produce do not really matter; it is the resulting engagement from others that is valuable. Miller (2008) notes, for example,

Wikimedia Commons

Selfies are not new, as this image from roughly 1900 shows. However, today's selfies are often published online, blurring the boundary between private and public.

In the drift from blogging, to social networking, to microblogging we see a shift from dialogue and communication between actors in a network, where the point of the network was to facilitate an exchange of substantive content, to a situation where the maintenance of a network itself has become the primary focus. (in Curran et al. 2016: 158)

That focus is highlighted by tracking the number of "followers" or "friends" each user has. These numbers help cultivate a sense of micro-celebrity and, for some people, can be a compelling measure of popularity. Carefully grooming a public image of oneself to maximize that popularity becomes a common feature of social media. The reciprocal nature of this process—following those who follow you, retweeting others in the hope they will retweet you, and so on—helps to promote engagement. Algorithms, too, provide an endless feedback loop aimed at boosting engagement; platforms use data produced by past user activities to generate real-time predictive analytics that suggest more people, content, or topics the user might find of interest. This can make social media use compelling.

The social connections that are made and maintained purely through social media—with no interaction in the physical word—are more likely to be connections of convenience with little or no commitment (Curran et al. 2016). In the physical world, social contacts are often unavoidable, as with family members, coworkers, neighbors, and classmates. They require social skills to manage, and the inability to do so carries consequences. Online, social contacts are much less demanding; users can quickly resolve any significant inconvenience by blocking or "unfollowing" the person. The situation is reminiscent of sociologist Zymunt Bauman's often-quoted observation about contemporary life—what he called "liquid modernity": "In a liquid modern life there are no permanent bonds, and any that we take up for a time must be tied loosely so that they can be untied again, as quickly and as effortlessly as possible, when circumstances change" (Gera 2017). Social media seems designed for just such a situation.

Research suggests that social media and internet use can be a mixed bag for users, depending on social factors they bring to the experience. One meta-analysis of research finds that the experience of users is often a good one, from which individuals can find similar people, get positive social support from interacting with them, and develop a sense of community and satisfaction. An enhanced sense of social support, in turn, can lead to a higher quality of life (Oh, Ozkaya, and Larose 2014).

Another meta-review of existing social psychological research suggests that the motivation for using Facebook is a combination of two basic factors: (1) the need for belonging to a group to enhance a sense of self-worth and (2) the need to present oneself to others (Nadkarni and Hofmann 2012). As a result of these factors, people cultivate their online persona to present their "best" side to others, much as we do in daily face-to-face interactions. This is not a fiction; users present a fairly accurate picture of their personality through their online activities (although they tend to enhance their level of emotional stability), and their offline personality traits carry over into the online world. For example, Facebook users who are extroverted offline tend to have more online "friends" than introverts. However, online presentations of self are often what users perceive to be socially desirable identities that they aspire to have offline but that they have not yet been able accomplish.

Negative psychological consequences may arise when some individuals confuse these idealized online personas with a fully accurate reality. A variety of research suggests that comparing oneself against idealized online personas can leave users envious, dissatisfied, and focused on the negative shortcomings of their own lives (Appel, Berlach, and Crusius 2016). For example, one study of college-age students found that negatively comparing oneself with others in the context of social media placed the individuals at risk for rumination—repetitively focusing on one's distress—that can lead to depressive symptoms (Feinstein et al. 2013). Another longitudinal study similarly found that using Facebook was negatively associated with well-being. An increase in clicking on "likes," links, or status updates on Facebook was associated with a decrease in self-reported mental health (Shakya and Christakis 2017).

Facebook's own published research shows that emotions expressed by Facebook users can influence the emotions of other users, a process called "emotional contagion" (Kramer, Guillory, and Hancock 2014). By doctoring the content of some news feeds, the researchers were able to show that when they reduced positive expressions in the feed, people posted fewer positive messages in turn. When they reduced negative expressions in the feed, a similar reduction in negative posts followed. (Unease about the ethics of a study manipulating people's emotions prompted the article to be published with an accompanying "Editorial Expression of Concern.")

Although the public often interprets a correlation between social media use and depression as likely a causal one, the opposite might be true. One study attempting to disentangle preexisting psychological traits from the impact of Facebook use suggests that people who are already depressed may use social media as a sort of digital diary: an outlet for expressing themselves without necessarily having a specific audience in mind. For some, doing so may serve as a safety valve to cope with negative thoughts. Alternatively, some users may be trying to use Facebook to build social connections to help combat their depressive symptoms (Scherr and Brunet 2017). In both cases, social media use might be useful for people already experiencing depressive symptoms.

In rarer cases, some analysts argue that people with certain preexisting psychological conditions can become addicted to internet use just as they can to gambling. Components of such "addiction" include preoccupation with internet use; repeated unsuccessful attempts to reduce use; disturbances in mood when attempting to reduce use; greater use than anticipated or desired; lying about the extent of use; and overuse to the point of jeopardizing employment, education, or relationships (Christakis 2010). However, such arguments are an indictment of the *abuse* of internet use, not its use per se, in the same way that alcohol abuse does not suggest that its moderate use is necessarily negative.

CONCLUSION

We have sketched out just a few of the many ways that media can influence the social world and have noted some of the ways that social scientists have tried to understand those influences. Media have surely transformed the way most people live in contemporary society. Developing an understanding of how they might be influence us is the least we can do in trying to exploit the advantages of media while minimizing their negative effects.

Discussion Questions

1. What are the key arguments of each of the following theoretical models? Which seem more plausible to you? Why?

    a. Limited effects

    b. Agenda setting

    c. The spiral of silence

    d. Cultivation theory

2. What is mediatization? How does this concept differ from other media effects theories?

3. What do you think might be done to combat the negative effects of the mediatization of politics?

4. What "digital dilemma" do you think is the most important one facing us today? Why?

5. Is there an apparent media influence NOT covered in this chapter that you think is especially important? If so, explain.

AFTERWORD

10

GLOBALIZATION AND
THE FUTURE OF MEDIA

In the mid-1960s, Canadian cultural scholar Marshall McLuhan (1964) wrote that, with the rise of electronic media, "we have extended our central nervous system itself in a global embrace" (p. 19). McLuhan believed that the growth of electronic media marked a new phase in human history. For the first time, physical distance was no longer a barrier, and instantaneous mass communication across the globe was possible. The result was that McLuhan popularized the notion of the "global village," in which the people of the world would be brought closer together as they made their voices heard. Such an information environment, according to McLuhan, "compels commitment and participation.

We have become irrevocably involved with, and responsible for, each other" (McLuhan and Fiore 1967: 24). McLuhan wrote before the internet existed. However, later internet enthusiasts echoed McLuhan's vision when they saw this new medium as a way to promote global understanding and peace.

In the years since McLuhan wrote, the media have moved steadily toward becoming truly global in nature. All major media corporations have an international presence, distributing their content worldwide. For example, 21st Century Fox (2017: 9) touts that its "global video brands—FOX, National Geographic, FOX News, FOX Sports, FX, Star India, Hulu and Sky . . . connect over 1 billion subscribers in approximately 50 languages in more than 170 countries." Millions of viewers worldwide see major sporting events; some part of the television coverage of the 2016 Rio Olympic Games was seen by an estimated 3.6 billion people, or nearly half the world's population (Baker 2016). Google (2018c) has offices in over 50 countries; Twitter (2018) is available in 34 languages. Facebook (2018a) has 2.1 billion active monthly users and 1.4 billion active users every day. The internet is a global phenomenon, with more than 4.2 billion people online by 2018—more than half of the world's population (Internet World Stats 2018).

However, the consequences of increasingly global media have not been as straightforward or as simple as McLuhan hoped. In fact, ambiguity and contradiction mark the trends in media globalization (Lule 2017). Some developments produce positive changes of the sort McLuhan envisioned; others seem cause for alarm. Either way, whatever future direction the media take, it will have a global facet. Understanding some of the basic global dimensions of media, therefore, is important in considering the future of all media.

This chapter explores the nature and potential consequences of media globalization. We have already addressed some global dimensions of media in earlier chapters. It is impossible to separate globalization from the issues with which we have been concerned. However, this chapter allows us to do two things. First, we discuss media globalization as a distinct social force that both contributes to social change and is influenced by global changes. Second, we reintegrate concepts that in earlier sections of this book we separated for analytic purposes. In the real world, technology, ownership and production, regulation, content and ideology, and users are all inextricably intertwined. We had to separate these and other concepts to discuss them coherently. In this final chapter, though, we move freely from one topic to another in a more integrated manner that more closely resembles the real—and complex—world of media.

WHAT IS GLOBALIZATION?

In broad terms, globalization involves a number of ongoing interrelated processes, including the internationalization of finance and trade, the development of international organizations such as the World Bank, the increased circulation of people, the growth of transnational nongovernmental organizations (NGOs) such as Oxfam and Amnesty International, and the diffusion of digital technologies. The idea of "global media" is tightly linked to these larger globalization processes.

In relation to the media, we can think of globalization as having two central components. The first relates to the changing role of geography and physical distance. As we discussed in Chapter 2, with electronic media, users can carry out instantaneous communication over great distances. Globalization carries this phenomenon to its global limits, enabling almost real-time communications around the world. Such electronic communication has been a feature of globalization at the same time as it has facilitated other forms of globalization, such as international finance and manufacturing, which would be impossible without international communication networks.

The second dimension of globalization involves the content of this communication. With electronic media and mobile devices, information and the ideas, images, and sounds of different cultures are potentially available to vast networks of people outside the culture from which the message originated. In this sense, culture becomes more accessible to larger numbers of people, with both potentially positive outcomes and potentially negative consequences, as we will see.

Crossing Limits of Time and Space

When humans began orbiting the Earth, photographs taken from space allowed people for the first time to see the planet in a single image—a tiny blue ball amid the vast darkness of space. Perhaps nothing better captures the symbolism of globalization than these now well-known pictures. In the click of a camera's shutter, the vast expanses of the Earth, which had taken humankind centuries to explore and map, suddenly seemed small and fragile. A single photographic image captured the great distance between the plains of Africa and the plains of the American Midwest, suggesting that perhaps the distance was not so great after all.

The ability to capture the entire globe in a single image was symbolic of the move toward globalization in many arenas. Space, in the form of physical distance, has come to have less practical significance. Physical transportation to all corners of the globe is easier than ever, making immigration, international travel, and the transportation of goods commonplace. When people do move, electronic communications often enable them to stay in touch with those at home. Travelers, immigrants, and even sometimes refugees can contact friends and family via the internet or a cell phone; they can listen to online radio stations and watch satellite television broadcasts in their native languages. By making a Skype call, typing an e-mail message, or communicating via a microblogging platform, travelers can dissolve the distance between the sender and receiver of a message. In some cases, electronic communication can make the need for physical travel obsolete: Many meetings, for example, happen by video link, and some companies rely on employees working remotely from around the world.

Although such communication has reduced the significance of space, it has also overcome the barrier of time. Communication happens almost instantaneously, meaning that we are often plugged into the media world 24/7. Feeling a habitual need to check our texts, e-mails, or social networking pages is a symptom of the accelerated rate at which communication takes place. Such communications can be useful and fun; they can also be overwhelming and stressful. The speed and ease with which media content can be produced, coupled with the speed and ease with which we can access information, also means that our biggest task is often sifting through it all to find what is useful to us.

Crossing Cultural Boundaries

Globalization is not just about the technological innovations used to communicate over long distances. In addition, and perhaps more important, it also refers to the exchange and intermingling of cultures from different parts of the globe. The globalization of media, especially, refers to the content—the cultural products—available globally. The United Nations Conference on Trade and Development (UNCTAD) identified five trends that have facilitated the expansion of global creative industries: (1) the deregulation of national cultural and media policy; (2) increasing global incomes that allow more spending on media and cultural products; (3) technological change and digitalization; (4) the global rise of service industries; and (5) the expansion of international trade (UNCTAD 2004: 5). Together, these developments have made it easier to cross cultural boundaries.

Music is a helpful example that illustrates the globalization of media. Music is one of the easiest media products to travel globally because its language is universal. Print media may be international to a degree, but the barriers of language and literacy limit their reach. Producers must translate print media to cross cultural boundaries, and a significant literate audience must be available to receive the product. Visual media, such as television and movies, are more accessible because an audience does not have to be literate to enjoy them. Usually, though, these media have dialogue that producers must subtitle or dub in the local language. Music, however, can sell across national and cultural borders even when the lyrics are in a foreign tongue that is not understood. The music, not the lyrics, generates sales.

The globalization of music has resulted in at least three developments. First, music that would not normally have traveled beyond a particular culture is now more readily available to different cultures. Physical recordings, especially CDs, are available worldwide. Local radio stations air such recordings, enabling listeners to hear music from around the world. For those with internet access, downloads and streaming make a wider variety of music available than ever before.

A second development has been the exchange of musical elements among different cultures. For example, in traditional African cultures where music performances were part of communal events, multiple drummers would each play a single drum, bringing together different drum sounds while allowing mobility for dance. Western jazz and rock drummers, who did not need to be mobile, adapted this technique by assembling a collection of different drums in a drum kit. On the other hand, contemporary Afro-pop often integrates the electric guitars of Western rock and roll with melodies and rhythms of more traditional African music. In both of these cases, artists have incorporated and adapted components of one culture within the context of another. We might say that global media has compressed the cultural distance between them.

Globalization of music has also resulted in a third development, a hybrid form of music that incorporates many different cultures in its new, unique sound. By using a wide variety of instruments and incorporating melodic and rhythmic sensibilities from many cultures, musicians produce new music that is not clearly identifiable with any single culture, thus it sometimes goes by the name "world music." Critics disagree as to whether this sort of synthesis represents a positive integration of different cultures or the "melting" of distinct cultures into a more homogeneous blend. Whatever the verdict, the resulting sounds reflect the globalization of culture in yet another way.

As we will see, one of the major issues surrounding the globalization of media is how, and on what terms, culture travels.

The Promise and Reality of Media Globalization

In McLuhan's (1964) vision of the "global village," media offer an electronic soapbox from which differing voices may speak. This multiplicity of voices, in turn, extends the range of publicly available knowledge about many different areas and aspects of the world. Finally, the airing of voices and knowledge can promote greater understanding among different nations and cultures.

There is no doubt that today's new media technologies facilitate much greater communication and enable the sharing of cultural products as never before. However, major hurdles prevent McLuhan's notion of a global village from becoming reality. People in a global forum are easily lost in the cacophony of voices competing for attention. Power is still in the hands of a small number of major media conglomerates that heavily influence the choice of which voices people will hear. In addition, the world's stark economic inequalities mean that, even if it is available, much of the world's population does not have access to media content. Once again, we see that social factors override technological capabilities.

Curran et al. (2016: 7–11) elaborate, reminding us that the "impact of the internet does not follow a trajectory dictated solely by its technology, but is filtered through the structures and processes of society" (p. 7). They argue that the internet—and by extension other media—has not met the optimistic hopes of early enthusiasts because of seven key constraints:

1. **The world is unequal,** and the digital divide—the gap between those who have internet access and those who do not—reflects the vast economic inequalities that exist.

2. **Language divides the world.** Because most people speak only one language, the internet is segregated by language.

3. **Language is a medium of power.** As a result, those who speak English, for example, can reach a much larger population on the internet (see Table 10.1). Those who speak lesser-known languages are effectively shut off from broad internet communications.

4. **People have differing degrees of cultural capital.** Those with education, good writing skills, and relevant expertise can join in with online discussions; those without such cultural capital are marginalized.

5. **Conflicting values, beliefs, and interests divide the world.** These conflicting values spill over onto the internet, where repressive governments try to control communication and hate groups and extremists of all stripes thrive.

6. **Nationalist cultures limit internationalism on the internet.** Whether it is the national focus of television networks or the closed nature of the Chinese internet, largely cut off from the rest of the world, national interests and cultures tend to trump efforts at globalism online.

7. **Authoritarian governments can manage the internet.** The growing effectiveness of authoritarian regimes in controlling their nation's internet access and content has tempered early hopes for an open, unrestrained internet that could help promote democratic forces.

Because of such constraints, the promise of the global village remains largely unfulfilled.

Some might argue that the growth of global media has led to a series of developments that may be more a cause for concern than a source of hope. As we have seen, the globalization of media has included the rise of centralized media conglomerates of unprecedented size and influence. Commercial interests, rather than educational concerns or altruistic motives, have usually fueled this globalization of media. In addition, ironically, the segmentation of the internet into "echo chambers" and "filter bubbles" means that often people remain isolated amid this vast communication network. In short, the dream of a global village in which equals share information and culture to promote greater understanding does not describe the reality of most of today's global media. Although media globalization continues to offer some promise, we must also be aware of the social impact of these enticing developments. We explore below four key areas of concern related to media globalization: ownership, content, regulation, and user access.

TABLE 10.1 ■ Most Common Languages on the Internet, 2018

Half of all websites are written in English, making it the dominant language online. Despite technology that connects us, language is still an important barrier contributing to a segregated internet. People who know only English cannot understand half of internet sites; people who know only one language other than English cannot understand the vast majority of the internet.

1. English	51.8%
2. Russian	6.6%
3. German	5.8%
4. Spanish	5.1%
5. Japanese	4.9%
6. French	4.1%
7. Portuguese	2.7%
8. Italian	2.5%
9. Chinese (all)	2.0%
10. Polish	1.7%
11. Turkish	1.3%
12. Dutch, Flemish	1.3%
13. Korean	0.9%
14. Czech	0.9%
15. Arabic	0.6%

Source: W3Techs (2018).

THE GLOBAL MEDIA INDUSTRY

The first area we explore is that of ownership. As we saw in Part III, we must understand ownership and control of production to understand the overall nature of media.

Global Products, Centralized Ownership

As of early 2018, the most streamed song ever and the most watched video ever on YouTube was "Despacito" by Puerto Rican artist Luis Fonsi, featuring Daddy Yankee, and cowritten by Panamanian singer–songwriter Erika Ender. The song had been streamed more than a billion times on Spotify and viewed an astounding 5 billion times on YouTube alone—numbers that continue to increase. The song features a catchy pop-reggaeton dance beat, and the video adds a sexy model, sun-kissed Puerto Rican locales, and beautiful cinematography. However, it was an unlikely hit; "Despacito" was the first Spanish-language song to reach #1 on the U.S. pop charts since the novelty dance song "Macarena" 20 years earlier.

One way to understand the song's unlikely crossover success is to tout the democratic power of internet streaming to overcome cultural boundaries and respond to popular taste. However, the song's massive success is also due to something more banal: corporate promotion in a global marketplace. The Spanish-language song was recorded as part of an ongoing effort to reach the growing Latino market by the Latin music division of Universal Music Group (UMG), itself a division of the Vivendi media conglomerate. "We're actively pursuing new sounds and music that can travel globally and that respect and enhance Latin culture," said the president of UMG's Republic Group, which headed the massive effort promoting "Despacito" to mainstream radio and media (Cobo 2017).

The song was a hit in Latin America and reached the top of YouTube's global music chart and Spotify's Global Top 50, but it generated little interest in the United States until pop icon and fellow-UMG artist Justin Bieber recorded a remix with an English verse. Tapping into the pop icon's global brand, the record label quickly issued and promoted the remix, putting both the original song and Bieber's version on the international charts. The head of UMG noted that "[b]ringing in Justin Bieber meant that we could take something that was well on its way, and really take it to heights that would have been perceived as unimaginable when the song was written" (Savage 2017). (Such cross-promotion is not without its pitfalls, though. Bieber angered Latin music fans when he performed the song live without knowing the Spanish lyrics, inserting words like "burrito" and "Doritos" instead [Bacle 2017].)

Using "synergy"—taking one company asset to promote another to the benefit of both—is just one type of promotional strategy that media conglomerates use. The global reach of media conglomerates enables a vast arsenal of promotion strategies, sometimes tailored to local markets. To pick just one example, in India, UMG promotion included a contest (and Twitter hashtag) called #DespacitoMovement. Fans were invited to submit videos of themselves dancing to the song, creating free social media promotion for the song as fans shared their videos online. A winner of the contest was chosen, and famed Indian choreographer Shiamak Davar directed and choreographed her in an Indian version of the song's video. The contest results and ensuing video were heavily promoted in the Indian press, creating yet another layer of advertising for the song (Radio and Music 2017). As the song's momentum increased globally, the record label could use its success to garner even more attention. The label promoted stories about the song's record-setting streaming numbers, helping give the song even wider exposure in mainstream media.

The global success of "Despacito" embodies some of the key elements of global media today: a hybrid mash-up of cultures shared across the globe but owned and promoted by a Western media conglomerate. In this respect, the song is not unique. Apple Music has some 45 million songs available for streaming. Apple's iTunes Store categorizes its songs into nearly 50 major genres with dozens more subgenres, ranging from Classical Opera to Death Metal, from Korean Hip-Hop to Traditional Bluegrass, and from Indonesian Religious music to Electronic Dubstep. This cornucopia of diversity, however, makes it easy to over-look an underlying reality: As we saw in Chapter 3, just three conglomerates—Universal Music Group, Sony Music Entertainment, and Warner Music Group—dominate the popular music industry, accounting for more than two-thirds of all music sales worldwide.

More broadly, a handful of large media corporations produce most of the media content available in the global marketplace. A few movie studios dominate the world's box offices. In 2017, just four studios combined to take in almost two-thirds of gross worldwide revenue: Buena Vista (Disney) 21.8%, Warner Bros. (Time Warner) 18.4%, Universal (Comcast) 13.8%, and 20th Century Fox 12%.

Television production has also developed a global dimension, often with centralized ownership. For example, the long-running reality television show *Big Brother* has been produced in more than 50 countries worldwide, including Serbia, India, the Philippines, Nigeria, and Ecuador. The show is modified slightly to fit local tastes, but a single company owns the program's many versions. Other formats that have been exported worldwide include *Who Wants to Be a Millionaire?*, *American Idol*, and *Dancing with the Stars*. Western companies dominate other forms of television too. The Monte Carlo Television Festival (2018) gives an award each year to the television series with the largest global audience in three categories. As is usually the case, the 2017 winners were U.S. productions: *The Big Bang Theory* (comedy), *NCIS* (drama), and *The Bold and the Beautiful* (telenovelas and soap opera).

Marginon / Alamy Stock Photo

The Walt Disney Company is one of the largest media conglomerates in the world, with more than 195,000 employees and $55 billion in 2017 revenues generated from across the globe.

Music, movies, and reality television illustrate that although the distribution of media products has spread out across the globe, the ownership and control of media production are largely centralized in a few large conglomerates usually composed of dozens, if not hundreds, of different companies. Consumers, seeing a wide variety of company names on the products they buy, may not realize that these different brands are often divisions of the same multinational corporation with production and distribution facilities dispersed in many different countries.

Traditional Media: Disney Worldwide

A brief look at one of the major traditional media companies will illustrate the vast expanse of these corporations. In Chapter 3, we saw that Disney was a sprawling conglomerate with dozens of companies involved in various types of media in the United States. Figure 10.1 takes a closer look at some of Disney's international properties. The extensive reach of this one company includes holdings in broadcast television, cable television, film production, interactive media, and publishing, along with some online media properties and, of course, its media-themed resorts. (At this writing, Disney is awaiting approval for the purchase of 21st Century Fox, which would dramatically expand its international holdings.)

The example of Disney illustrates that, whereas the tentacles of global corporations extend to all sectors of the media and to all corners of the globe, the control of the

---

FIGURE 10.1   ■   Walt Disney Company, Select International Holdings, 2017

In addition to its well-known U.S. properties (see Chapter 3), Walt Disney has operations in more than 40 countries and territories, with holdings in various media.

Television

- ESPN—which owns 19 television channels outside of the United States (primarily in Latin America) that reach 61 countries and territories in four languages (English, Spanish, Portuguese, and French). ESPN.com and the ESPN app are available worldwide in three languages.

- Disney Channel, Disney Junior, Disney XD—more than 100 Disney-branded television channels are broadcast in 34 languages and 162 countries/territories.

- A&E (50% ownership)—programming is available in more than 200 countries and territories, including A+E Networks Latin America, A+E Networks UK, A+E Networks Asia, A+E Networks India, A+E Networks Germany, and A+E Networks Italy.

- Hungama—Indian cable channel targeted at kids.

- UTV/Bindass—Indian cable entertainment and music channels targeted at teens.

- CTV (30% ownership)—which owns channels in Canada, including The Sports Networks (TSN) 1–5, Le Réseau des Sports (RDS), RDS2, RDS Info, ESPN Classic Canada, Discovery Canada, and Animal Planet Canada.

- Seven TV (partial ownership)—free over-the-air Disney Channel in Russia.

- Disney Television (Germany), Inc., including RTL Disney TV (50% ownership), RTL II channel, Germany, and Kividoo—children's SVOD service, ATV2 channel, Austria, RTL 2 Austria

- Walt Disney Television International Japan.

- UTV Software Communications—Indian multimedia conglomerate.

Movies

- 29.9% of all global box office revenue in 2017 (Walt Disney Pictures, Buena Vista, Pixar, Marvel, Lucasfilm, and Touchstone).

- The Walt Disney Company Latin America, including Miravista Films, The Walt Disney Company Argentina, and Patagonik Film Group.

- Walt Disney Studios Japan.

Music

- Disney Music Group—produces, publishes, sells, and licenses music worldwide.

Publishing

- Creates, distributes, licenses, and publishes a variety of products in multiple countries and languages, including children's books, comic books, graphic novel collections, learning products, and storytelling apps.

- Disney Publishing Worldwide Japan.

Subscription Services

- Disney Cinemagic and Disney Cinema, available in Europe.

Radio

- Radio Disney—available in Latin America.

Consumer Products and Interactive Media

- Licenses literary properties to various manufacturers, game developers, publishers, and retailers throughout the world.

- Sells merchandise through retail stores, internet shopping sites, and wholesalers; 87 Disney stores in Europe, 55 stores in Japan, and two stores in China.

- Sells games through app distributors, online, and through consumers' in-game purchases.

- Charges tuition at 27 English language learning centers in China (Disney English).

- Disney Interactive Group Japan.

Parks and Resorts

- Disneyland Paris.

- Hong Kong Disneyland Resort (47% ownership).

- Shanghai Disney Resort (43% ownership).

- Tokyo Disney Resort.

Sources: Walt Disney Company (2017); BoxOfficeMojo (2018); media accounts.

corporate conglomerates remains centralized in wealthy, developed nations. Globalization of the media clearly does not extend to ownership, which has not yet gone beyond a few prosperous nations. Western media corporations dominate the flow of media products around the world (Artz 2015; Hamm and Smandych 2005; Miller et al. 2008).

The significance of centralized ownership and control is that decision making related to the purpose and content of the media, as well as the benefits that accrue from owning what are often highly profitable ventures, remains firmly in the hands of a few major corporations based in the wealthiest nations.

The New Global Media Giants: Google and Facebook

The promise of the internet was that it could be a decentralized network of voices side-stepping the traditional big media gatekeepers. As we have seen, some of that certainly has occurred, as millions of people worldwide create, comment on, and share media content. However, as we have also seen, new media giants have emerged—especially Google and Facebook—whose platforms have captured a vastly disproportionate share of internet advertising revenue and whose algorithms quietly shape the online experiences of billions of users worldwide, becoming the new gatekeepers.

A full one-third of all digital advertising revenue worldwide goes to one company: Google (technically, its parent company, Alphabet) (Statista 2018b). That is because Google sites account for more than 85 percent of all online searches worldwide (Statista 2018c). In fact, 12 of the world's top 40 websites in terms of traffic are Google search sites focused on different national markets (see Table 10.2). This gives Google an amazing amount of influence over internet traffic flow because users rarely explore beyond the first page or two of search results.

TABLE 10.2 ■ Google Search Sites and Global Rankings, 2018		

Although Americans use the familiar Google.com site, people in other countries use other Google search sites whose algorithms tailor results by country. Such Google sites account for 12 of the top 40 websites worldwide.

Rank	Site	Country Focus
1.	Google.com	United States
8.	Google.co.in	India
17.	Google.co.jp	Japan
23.	Google.de	Germany
24.	Google.co.uk	United Kingdom
25.	Google.com.br	Brazil
27.	Google.fr	France
29.	Google.ru	Russia
33.	Google.it	Italy
35.	Google.es	Spain
38.	Google.com.hk	Hong Kong
39.	Google.com.mx	Mexico

Source: Alexa (2018).

While Google's U.S. search site is the most heavily trafficked in the world, its YouTube video platform is the world's second most popular website (see Table 10.3). Originally a platform for user-generated content, YouTube has evolved into a hybrid site featuring material from traditional media companies alongside amateur videos. YouTube is also

TABLE 10.3   ■   World's Most Visited Websites, 2018

The world's top websites provide a snapshot of internet dynamics. U.S. commercial sites dominate the list, but the presence of Chinese equivalents speaks to the way language fragments the internet—and to how the Chinese government restricts access to outside web services. Four of the top 10 sites—YouTube Facebook, Wikipedia, and Reddit—rely mostly on user-generated content. Only Wikipedia is nonprofit.

Rank	Website	Type	Country	Parent Company
1.	Google.com	Search	United States	Alphabet
2.	YouTube.com	Video	United States	Alphabet
3.	Facebook.com	Social	United States	Facebook
4.	Baidu.com	Search	China	Baidu
5.	Wikipedia.org	Reference	United States	Wikipedia Foundation
6.	Reddit.com	Social	United States	Advance Publications
7.	Yahoo.com	News	United States	Verizon
8.	Google.co.in	Search	United States	Alphabet
9.	QQ.com (WeChat)	Integrated Apps	China	Tencent Holdings
10.	Amazon.com	Shopping	United States	Amazon

Source: Alexa (2018).

Note: There are competing ways to rank the world's top websites, producing somewhat different results. One commonly cited list, used here, is produced by Alexa (an Amazon-owned company), whose rankings are based on a combination of average daily visitors and number of page views.

the world's most popular source of on-demand music streaming, accounting for almost half (46%) of all such streaming (IFPI 2017b). That is more than Spotify, Apple Music, Tidal, Deezer, and Napster combined. In 2017, Google built upon its powerful YouTube user base to enter the television live-streaming market with its launch of YouTube TV.

The reason Chinese sites appear on the list of the world's most popular websites is only partially due to the large size of China's population. It mostly results from the fact that China bans Facebook, Google, and other Western sites through filters popularly known as "The Great Firewall." The Chinese sites are essentially Chinese parallels to Google (Baidu.com), Facebook (RenRen.com), YouTube (YouKu.com), Twitter (Weibo .com), and Amazon (Taobao.com). WeChat (QQ.com) is a type of integrated app that combines features Westerners associate with Google, Facebook, Skype, Twitter, Tinder, Instagram, Amazon, Uber, and more. China would like its citizens to experience the internet through these government-friendly, state-approved apps. The data they provide on users' activities online and off are invaluable for state surveillance (Mozur, Scott, and Isaac 2017).

Whereas Google owns the world's top two websites, Facebook has the third. (Facebook also owns Instagram, ranked number 15 on the world's most visited sites.) The pace of Facebook's growth has been astronomical. In 2007, it had 58 million monthly users, with $153 million in annual revenue, and was operating at a *loss* of $138 million. By 2017, it had more than 2.1 billion monthly users, $40.6 billion in revenue, and earned $15.9 billion in profits (Statista 2018a). In early 2018, the amount of time U.S. and Canadian users spent on the site declined for the first time ever, possibly signaling trouble ahead, but Facebook remains, far and away, the leading social media site (Wagner and Molla 2018).

Growth for companies like Facebook has plateaued now that most people who have internet access and want to use their services already do so. However, as of 2017, nearly half of the world's population still had no internet access, and major differences in access speed sometimes limit how users can use the internet. In 2017, the world average for broadband connection speed was about 7.7 megabits per second (Mbps) but it ranged from Nigeria's slow average of 1.5 Mbps to South Korea's speedy average of 28.6 Mbps— 19 times faster (Broadband Commission on Sustainable Development 2017). As we noted in Chapter 3, Facebook runs projects to make its social media platform more widely available in developing countries, thus potentially expanding their user base. Facebook's nonprofit Open Compute Project, assists in developing open-source hardware needed to run the internet, and the company has launched satellites and worked to develop solar-powered unmanned aircraft that relay the internet to remote areas that otherwise have no access (Facebook 2018b). However, its best-known program in this area is Free Basics, which offers limited basic services—including Facebook—free without data charges (Free Basics 2018).

Free Basics is, in effect, a "walled garden" that gives users free access to a limited number of services (without data charges) but denies access to other parts of the internet. Facebook believes that, if users get a taste of the internet for free, they will be willing to pay for greater access. The Free Basics program has been highly controversial because critics argue it is a clear violation of net neutrality principles that insist ISPs treat all internet content equally. Critics also charge Facebook with bringing new "digital colonialism" to the world's developing countries. In India, for example, the Telecom Regulatory Authority of India banned Free Basics after a public outcry fueled a nationwide "Save the Internet" campaign supporting net neutrality (Anastácio 2016; Bhatia 2016; Shahin 2017).

The problems with Free Basics are more widespread. Global Voices, a citizen and media activist group promoting internet freedom, issued a study of Free Basics in Colombia, Ghana, Kenya, Mexico, Pakistan, and the Philippines. They found that, in addition to violating net neutrality, Free Basics failed to serve the linguistic needs of local populations, featured limited local content but steered users toward U.S. companies, and harvested huge amounts of data about its users. In short, they found Free Basics served the goals of the corporation promoting it more than the needs of the people who it was supposedly helping. By 2018, Facebook shut down Free Basics in select countries where criticism had been most vocal.

Facebook's size has other troubling ramifications. Since 2012, more than 50 countries have passed laws to better control how their citizens use the internet. Often, those control efforts involve Facebook. In Vietnam, for example, Facebook agreed to delete posts that the government said made inaccurate statements about government officials. In Israel, Facebook has worked with the government to identify content that it said should be censored. Germany sued Facebook over its refusal to let users use a pseudonym for privacy purposes. France sued Facebook over its censorship of a nude painting posted by an art teacher. Brazil blocked Facebook's WhatsApp messaging application. Burundi blocked access to virtually all social media, including Facebook, Instagram, and Twitter (Mozur et al. 2017). Such actions are likely only the beginning, as nations move to try to control the internet.

As Unwin (2013) cautions,

> The internet has been shown to contribute to economic growth through expanding access to information, increasing the pace of interactions and providing demand for raw materials needed for the internet's infrastructure equipment. However, there is little evidence that the internet growth has spurred equality, or, on balance, contributed to an expansion of freedom. (p. 543)

INTERPRETING GLOBAL MEDIA CONTENT

Regardless of who owns or distributes it, global media content has stirred ongoing debate. We note three frameworks that interpret global media in different ways: cultural imperialism, culture clash, and cultural hybridity. We briefly take up each of these arguments, along with their limitations.

Cultural Imperialism and Its Limits

The cultural imperialism thesis argued that media products of the West, especially of the United States, so dominate the rest of the world that they amount to a form of cultural imperialism. Early articulations of this position predated the internet and emphasized the role of television. These were an important antidote to ethnocentric and sometimes racist thinking about the superiority of American culture (Boyd-Barrett 1977; Schiller 1971).

The history of colonialism was the background for the cultural imperialism thesis. Western societies had long dominated large swaths of the globe, enriching themselves by extracting natural resources through either military conquest or economic domination. The result was often a relationship of dependency in which colonial powers undercut local industry and development, leaving colonies to rely upon the economic investment and expertise of wealthier colonial powers. In addition, colonial powers often sought to impose their culture on the local population, for example, leading to the spread of English and Christianity around much of the globe.

The cultural imperialism thesis saw similar colonial dynamics in the activities of multinational media corporations. U.S. media companies had a head start with well-developed and well-financed infrastructures producing high-quality film and television programming. Most nations simply did not have the resources to develop the infrastructure necessary to produce the high production values associated with expensive media products. Western media companies could add to their profits without incurring additional production costs by exporting content already created for the domestic market. When a for-profit market model drives media-related decision making, as it does in many nations, it generally makes good short-term business sense to import cheap U.S.-made cultural products. In the long run, the cheap prices offered by U.S. media companies to rerun American television programs and movies undermined the potential development of local media industries. In this way, U.S. companies maintained ownership and control over media content, while other nations became dependent on the United States for cultural production. In addition to economic domination, critics were deeply concerned about the cultural impact of this flood of Western media, believing it contributed to a decline in traditional local values. For example, U.S. media tended to promote individualism and consumerism, which often conflicted with the traditional values in the nations where such products were seen. The impact on local cultures, critics contended, could be devastating (Hamm and Smandych 2005; Mattelart 1979; Schiller 1992).

The flood of Western media around the globe is undeniable, and at the time the cultural imperialism thesis was developed, the imbalance was even greater than today. The cultural imperialism approach usefully put a spotlight on the power of Western media conglomerates. However, a simple cultural imperialism argument has several limitations (Elasmar and Bennett 2003; Tomlinson 1991, 2003).

First, the cultural imperialism thesis often does not distinguish among different types of media. U.S. products clearly dominate some capital-intensive media sectors, most notably the movie industry. On average, a U.S. feature film costs well over $100 million to make, not including the marketing budget, which can be as much or more than the production costs (Verrier 2009). The biggest budget films can cost several times that amount. For example, the blockbuster *Avatar* cost about $310 million to produce and $150 million to advertise (Barnes 2009). The biggest hit television programs, too, are extravagantly expensive; some episodes of *Game of Thrones* cost $15 million each to make (Ryan and Littleton 2017). This is far more than most non–U.S. production studios can afford. However, in the range of media products, such high-ticket items are the exception. Print has always been local because it is affordable to create, relies on local languages, is based on local issues, and is expensive to export. For other media, such as most television and music, local indigenous content has grown, and regional export centers have developed (Laing 1986). The cultural imperialism thesis, therefore, paints with too broad a brush.

Second, and relatedly, the cultural imperialism thesis underestimates the role played by local media. Locally produced media content, finely attuned to local cultures, tends to be enormously popular. Digital technologies have lowered the cost of producing such content in recent years. Thus, local producers have successfully competed in some cases with the global media conglomerates by providing localized alternatives that differentiate themselves from homogenized international media fare. This is true even in the most expensive types of media: film and television. For example, a 25-year longitudinal study of South Korean television found that the proportion of imported programming that aired was reduced by about half, to less than 8 percent (Lee 2007). The Korean film industry, too, has expanded dramatically in recent years. The percentage of films that Korean audiences watched that were Korean-made more than doubled between 1996, when it was 23.1 percent, and 2004, when it reached 54.2 percent (Flew 2007). Film production in China and Nigeria has also expanded dramatically in recent years. However, the biggest example of a vibrant film industry outside of the West is not new at all. "Bollywood," the section of the Indian film industry specializing in Hindi-language films, is based in Mumbai and dates back to the silent film era of the early 20th century. (The name comes from a fusion of Bombay—Mumbai's former name—and Hollywood.) Bollywood specializes in musicals, romantic feature films, and melodramas and produces many more films than Hollywood does each year. These films are generally low budget but are popular in India (Bose 2006). Bollywood films make up more than 40 percent of the Indian market; regional films make up another 50 percent, and international films are less than 10 percent (Deloitte 2016). Therefore, although they may not be as well funded as their international counterparts, there are often local alternatives to imported Western fare. Indeed, some signs suggest that the tide of U.S. imports may have reached its peak as local media industries compete more effectively for national markets.

Third, the simple cultural imperialism thesis fails to recognize the ideological diversity within media products. For example, Gray (2007) notes that the assumption that U.S. media exports invariably promote a chauvinistic U.S. worldview is too simple. His study points out that one of the most successful U.S. cultural exports, the long-running animated series *The Simpsons*, is often a highly critical parody of American culture and capitalist values. As such, it is part of a long tradition of U.S. television shows—popular both at home and abroad—that have shown the United States as unequal and often dysfunctional. Therefore, even if media corporations export U.S. products widely and foreign users consume them enthusiastically, there are competing messages within these popular media products.

Fourth, the cultural imperialism thesis generally assumes a passive audience being influenced by foreign media. This fails to adequately take into account the role of "active audiences" discussed in Chapter 8. The meaning a particular product holds for local audiences may vary widely because of local cultural values (Butcher 2003; Liebes and Katz 1993; Sreberny-Mohammadi 1997; Strelitz 2003). Thus, we cannot assume that foreign audiences interpret U.S. media products in any single way. In fact, the circulation of U.S.–produced global media products does not seem to be creating any singular Americanized consciousness, as some had feared. Nor is it creating any singular enlightened "global consciousness," as some had hoped. In considering the power of global media, we need to be cautious about the belief that exposure to media products fundamentally changes people.

In the end, the cultural imperialism framework usefully highlighted the power of wealthy Western countries and the unequal flow of cultural goods. However, it overestimated the influence of such media content and underestimated the capacity of local media industries and the resiliency of local cultures.

Global Culture Clash?

Rather than seeing a one-way flow of culture from the West as dominating other countries, another approach to understanding global media sees a deep, long-lasting clash between irreconcilable views of the world. Proponents of a "clash of civilizations" argued that Western values are under assault from, especially, Islamic forces (Huntington 1996). Such arguments were widely criticized as simplistic and ahistorical (Skidmore, 1998; Pieterse 1996). They lumped together disparate cultures into single "civilizations" and made sweeping generalizations that do not hold up to scrutiny, but they proved to be popular, especially after the 9/11 attacks.

One variation of this culture clash thesis came from Benjamin Barber (1995) in his now-classic book *Jihad vs. McWorld*. In it, he paints a picture of a global cultural conflict between the forces of secular transnational consumer capitalism ("McWorld") that connects the world and the movements of religious and ethnic tribal fundamentalism ("Jihad") that divides it. He argues that these forces are starkly contradictory, but oddly, each fuels the other. "Jihad" is a declaration of resistance against the homogenizing and secular forces of transnational capitalism. However, it offers no vision of what is possible in a modern, globalized world. Instead, parochial hatred that threatens to undermine the nation-state characterizes "Jihad." In contrast, "McWorld" feeds the popular desire to reach beyond the confines of local, often religious, norms and constraints, but it reduces individuals to consumers, and it, too, threatens the democratic institutions of the nation-state by insisting on global trade in a universal marketplace.

This approach is a useful reminder that cultural values are often deep-seated and are unlikely to be immediately transformed by the import of foreign cultural products. Indeed, such imports may stir a backlash. However, this bipolar vision oversimplifies much more complicated realities and does little to help us understand the world of global media.

Hybrid Culture

A third framework for understanding global media content sees neither cultural domination nor an intractable cultural clash. Instead, it views contemporary culture as being an amalgamation of differing influences, sometimes referred to as cultural hybridity (Kraidy 2005; Pieterse 2004). (This is not to be confused with the idea of "hybrid media systems," which refers to the convergence of media *technologies* rather than cultures.) Although writers use the term in a variety of ways, cultural hybridity usually highlights the fluidity of culture over time. Globalization has merely accelerated a cultural hybridization process that has always taken place.

For example, while recognizing the heavy presence of U.S.–imported media content, observers of the Latin-American context have long highlighted the attachment to locally produced material. They prefer to speak about "asymmetrical interdependence" rather than cultural imperialism or cultural clashes, acknowledging that the presence of U.S. media in local markets is not linear but blended with some forms of localization of national broadcasting systems (Straubhaar 1991). In Brazil, Flew (2007) sees "a combination of selective incorporation of international best practice and a restless search to develop programme types that tapped into local cultural desires and dynamics, such as the *telenovela*"—a television soap opera miniseries (p. 121).

Meanwhile, in the area of pop music, other cultures have long influenced Western artists. Musicians such as Paul Simon, David Byrne (formerly of Talking Heads), and Sting (formerly of The Police) are among the best-known mainstream artists who incorporated African and South American sounds and musicians into their work decades ago. Observers have sometimes criticized the process of Western musicians drawing on indigenous cultures as being exploitative because it represents the raiding of local culture for the profit of Western artists and record conglomerates. However, others argue that the increased exposure of indigenous music has led to a greater appreciation of it by a wide variety of audiences. In fact, "world music" has grown in popularity to become a recognizable music category that represents both music produced in particular parts of the world and an amalgam of varied instruments and rhythms resulting in a distinctive "global" sound ungrounded in any single cultural tradition.

The meeting of Western and international music can be complicated. For example, various elements of South African "township jive," *mbaqanga*, *kwela*, and Zulu choral music dominated the sound on Paul Simon's now-classic Grammy-winning album

Graceland. Simon's interest in South African popular music was sparked in part by the fact that the sound reminded him of 1950s American rock and roll. In fact, American rock music and other African-American musical styles of the 1950s and 1960s were distributed in South Africa (Garofalo 1992). Thus, local cultures had absorbed the infusion of 1950s American rock and roll and had produced new sounds that, in turn, were the inspiration for popular American music in the 1980s and 1990s. Since then, a wide variety of musicians have created hybrid music, assembling sounds from different cultures. A simple model of cultural imperialism cannot account for the complicated interconnections that have become world music.

One reason hybridization occurs is because local cultures are resilient. Media corporations know that there are limits to the appeal of Western—and, in particular, U.S.—culture in other nations. In response to changing circumstances, many multinational corporations have become more sophisticated in addressing local markets in foreign countries. Most media conglomerates have adopted some variation of a two-pronged approach to selling cultural products. The first prong of the strategy is the promotion and distribution of Western artists as global superstars. For example, global music stars such as Beyoncé and Drake are able to sell albums regardless of linguistic differences. The second prong of the corporate strategy is to accommodate local cultures. For example, although it has struggled in recent years, MTV (2018) still promotes itself as "the world's premiere youth entertainment brand. With a global reach of more than a half-billion households." It achieved this status by exporting its U.S. model while creating dozens of "localized" versions, including MTV Africa, MTV Asia, MTV Australia, MTV Brasil, MTV Europe, MTV Latin America, and MTV Russia. These channels feature a mixture of international and local musical artists.

The resilience of local cultures has also led Western media companies to invest in indigenous talent, which they can then package and sell to local or regional markets, if not a global market. Japan's Hikaru Utada, Russia's Valeriya, China's Wei Wei, Ghana's Samini, and a host of other artists sell millions of recordings in their regions but are almost unknown in the United States. This approach, of course, is itself a double-edged sword. Even as major media conglomerates acknowledge the importance of local cultural tastes, they may be undermining local media companies by moving into local media markets. Sometimes, this means being in outright competition with local companies, creating a David-and-Goliath scenario. In other cases, this movement has taken the form of joint ventures in the coproduction of cultural products such as television programs and movies.

The irony is that the corporate drive for profit—the very force that has fueled fears of cultural imperialism—has also forced companies to pay attention to local cultures and customs, even if only superficially. Companies have realized that locally customized media products often sell better than standardized global products.

One consequence of "local adaptation" has been that, in some parts of the world, the resistance to foreign culture has waned. Although, as the "culture clash" theorists remind us, extremists decry the invasion of Western secular culture, the most recent wave of television and other cultural products abroad has not met with the kind of opposition that marked earlier influxes of foreign culture. In an era when global corporations are careful to tailor at least superficially their products to local cultural tastes, the flow of Western goods abroad now occurs with less resistance.

MTV.com

The familiar MTV logo heads the MTV Vietnam web page, where English and Vietnamese language and music sit side by side. Western media companies have often tailored their product to local audience taste preferences.

Hybridity is an acknowledgment of contemporary reality. The media's facilitation of global communication has had an effect. Artists draw upon a wide palette of influences from across the globe. Often the resulting creations are, indeed, hybrids. However, hybridity refers primarily to the nature of the resulting cultural product. Who owns and controls those products? Who has the power to promote and share this culture? Does this process dilute the distinctive elements of local cultures? If we are to understand global media better, considerations of power, production, and control—the issues that the cultural imperialism thesis focused on—need to be part of the equation.

REGULATING GLOBAL MEDIA

Who governs McLuhan's global village? We saw in Chapter 4 that regulation constitutes a major social force influencing the media. However, whereas national governments usually create and enforce regulations, by definition, global media cross these boundaries (Sreberny 2005), posing regulatory challenges for national governments (Calabrese 1999; Price 2002).

In particular, three structural changes weakened the capacity of national governments to regulate the media. First, national governments and international organizations feel pressure from global media conglomerates and transnational private capital. For example, the International Chamber of Commerce is very vocal in promoting corporate interests and advocating against any regulation (Flew 2007). Second, global "free trade" agreements circumvent the influence and control of national governments insofar as they set many of the rules and standards governments and companies are obliged to follow (Chakravartty and Sarikakis 2006). For example, the World Trade Organization's Trade Related Aspects of Intellectual Property Rights (TRIPS) regulates the rights of performers, broadcasters, and music producers, superseding national rules (Ó Siochrú and Girard 2002). Third, the borderless nature of the internet makes it difficult to constrain with national regulations (Goldsmith and Wu 2008).

Still, as we will see, a variety of efforts have tried to shape the nature of global media development, including democratizing internet governance and protecting the viability of distinctive local cultures. The earliest such effort focused on the "information flow" of news, which is where we begin.

The Politics of Information Flow

One arena for regulating the shape of global media is international forums. The formal political concern with media globalization dates back at least as far as 1925. In that year, the League of Nations—the precursor to the United Nations—created a committee charged with determining methods of contributing towards the organization of peace, especially: (a) by ensuring the more rapid and less costly transmission of Press news with a view to reducing risks of international misunderstanding; (b) And by discussing all technical problems the settlement of which would be conducive to the tranquillisation of public opinion. (in Gerbner et al. 1993: 183)

The League of Nations, therefore, endorsed the dissemination of information worldwide through the media as a tool for promoting peace and understanding. This approach continued in later years.

A quarter century later, the uses of propaganda during World War II prompted more concern about the distribution of information in the media. The United States used the forum of the United Nations to promote a policy that allowed for the international collection, sale, and distribution of information worldwide. The Final Act of the 1948 UN Conference on Freedom of Information argued, "freedom of information is a fundamental right of the people, and it is the touchstone of all the freedoms to which the United Nations is dedicated without which world peace cannot well be preserved." The act further stipulated that, to be valid, freedom of information depended on "the availability to the people of a diversity of sources of news and opinion," and it condemned the use of "propaganda either designed or likely to provoke or encourage any threat" to peace (in Gerbner et al. 1993: 179, 181).

Although the idea that information should flow freely across national boundaries sounds benign to Western ears, many developing countries came to understand it as privileging the "First World's" market-driven perspective of information flow. The First World—that is, wealthy, developed countries—and developing nations had very different levels of infrastructure development and capital resources. As a result, the operating reality of "free" international information flow was that major news organizations from developed nations dominated the collection and dissemination of information. It was as if everyone had been invited to contribute to a multicultural mural, but only some people were equipped with paint and brushes. Those with advantages in resources were able to express their visions, whereas a lack of resources effectively silenced others.

Western wire services such as the Associated Press (AP) and United Press International (UPI) in the United States and Reuters in the United Kingdom dominated the news accounts that traveled around the globe. They collected information and wrote news stories from what has been described as "a limited perspective reflecting the economic and cultural interests of the industrialized nations" (MacBride and Roach 1993: 6). This criticism extended to entertainment media as well as to the use of newer technologies, such as satellites—and later the internet—to transmit directly news and entertainment.

Developing nations, which did not have the private investment needed to support major commercial media, looked to their governments to nurture media that served public, rather than private, needs. These public needs covered a vast and varied territory, including the dissemination of basic information on public health, agricultural practices, and child education, as well as more generalized access to news information to advance a democratic society.

To many Westerners, the involvement of government in the organization and production of media immediately raised the specter of censorship and state domination, which in some cases did occur. However, in many developing nations, government involvement with local media represented the only way to ensure the existence of an alternative to Western media conglomerates. In addition, many developing nations did not want the "free flow" of information from the West simply to flood them. Instead, they wanted a free and more balanced flow of information. The intervention of government was needed to regulate the vast quantity of information flowing from more developed nations, an action that Westerners found antithetical to the idea of a "free" information flow.

In this context, the call by poorer nations for a "New World Information and Communication Order" (NWICO) was taken up by the United Nations Educational Scientific and Cultural Organization (UNESCO). While reaffirming the right of journalists to "have freedom to report and the fullest possible access to information," a 1978 UNESCO declaration on the media also suggested that media contribute to peace and understanding "by giving expression to oppressed people who struggle against colonialism, neo-colonialism, foreign occupation and all forms of racial discrimination and oppression and who are unable to make their voices heard within their own territories" (in Gerbner et al. 1993: 176). The declaration suggested a need to hear those voices that had not been included in the established media—a position that threatened the status quo.

In 1980, UNESCO appointed an International Commission for the Study of Communication Problems, chaired by Irish Nobel laureate Seán MacBride. The commission's task was to analyze communication in modern societies and propose policies to further human development through communication. The MacBride Commission's (1980) report, titled "Many Voices, One World," identified the "right to communicate" as a basic human right. The commission also criticized proponents of a simple "free flow" of information, arguing that critical acceptance of this doctrine reinforced Western cultural domination in developing countries.

Developing nations saw their efforts as an attempt to balance the scales of information production and distribution that had always been tipped sharply in favor of wealthier Western nations. Some in the West saw such efforts as a form of censorship that threatened their freedom to interpret the world and to communicate their interpretation globally. Western nations, threatened by the NWICO proposals, responded with a powerful campaign aimed at discrediting the idea of a new information and communication order—and UNESCO. The United States and the UK—the two countries most responsible for the export of Western news—announced their resignation from UNESCO at the end of 1983. The campaign was successful, stalling any progress for NWICO and paralyzing the work of UNESCO. NGOs advanced the NWICO debate by starting to organize independently of the UN and national governments. Progressive media professionals and academics formed the MacBride Roundtable, an advocacy group that met annually, bringing new actors into the discussion. However, there was little progress. In the 1990s, the United Nations and UNESCO backed away from the promotion of NWICO. In 1997, the UK rejoined UNESCO; in 2003, the United States followed.

The NWICO case illustrates how difficult it is to influence the nature of global media, especially when some players have much more power in the discussions. The challenges recurred with the rise of the internet.

Internet Governance

Unwin (2013: 542) reminds us, "The Internet did not just happen. It was shaped and developed explicitly by the commercial interests largely of US capital." Although in its early years the internet quickly expanded beyond its U.S. roots to become an international network, the United States retained vastly disproportionate influence in setting the basic standards for the internet's operations. They did this, in part, by controlling the Internet Corporation for Assigned Names and Numbers (ICANN), which was widely criticized for its lack of transparency and accountability and for its proximity to the U.S. Department of Commerce (DeNardis 2013; Mueller 2002, 2010).

Founded in 1998, ICANN (2018) oversees a number of technical issues keeping the internet secure, stable, and interoperable. It is best known for maintaining the Internet Assigned Numbers Authority (IANA)—the database of unique internet addresses—and for creating top-level domain names (e.g., .com, .info, .mil), country-specific domains (e.g., .ae for United Arab Emirates, .jp for Japan, and .mx for Mexico) as well as domains using Arabic, Chinese, and other language-specific characters. ICANN's work may seem esoteric to outsiders, but it provoked intense debates among experts and analysts from different countries who resented the unequal role the United States played in influencing it. Finally, in 2016, the U.S. government relinquished oversight of ICANN, making it an independent nonprofit with a governing board whose members are elected from various stakeholder communities, including government, the communities of technical and telecommunications experts, industry, and internet users. Board members must include representation from the worlds' major regions (Asia/Pacific, Africa, Europe, Latin America/Caribbean, and North America). Although concerns about transparency and accountability continue, the move toward more independence was widely applauded (Finley 2016).

Debates about the nature of internet governance became part of the United Nations World Summit on the Information Society (WSIS) in Geneva (2003) and Tunis (2005) that brought together government representatives and the private sector to discuss, among other things, partnerships to help overcome the global digital divide. Given this focus, some NGOs that were interested in human rights issues and the democratization of information felt their concerns were marginalized (Unwin 2013). The Association for Progressive Communications, for example, played an important role in making sure discussions were about more than simply expanding internet access. As their mission statement notes,

> we help grassroots groups use the technology to develop their communities and further their rights, and we work to make sure that government policies related to information and communication serve the best interests of the general population, especially people living in the global South. (Association for Progressive Communications 2018)

The debates at these summits about how the internet should be governed not only contributed to ICANN's removal from U.S. oversight, but it also led to the creation of the Internet Governance Forum (IGF), an international forum for policy dialogue.

The inaugural meeting of the IGF took place in 2006 and has been occurring in a different country each year ever since. The forum is not a governing body; it has no decision-making authority. Its purpose is simply to facilitate discussions among a diverse set of stakeholders from government, private-sector, NGO, and technical communities. These discussions have addressed a wide range of issues, including capacity building in developing countries, internet security, human rights and free expression, and access and diversity issues. The IGF often makes recommendations to the appropriate governing bodies for suggested change (Internet Governance Forum 2018).

Internet governance underlies the smooth functioning of the entire internet, and nation-states will continue to have a role to play in its governance (Goldsmith and Wu 2008). As issues continue to arise with security and free expression, as well as technical developments, these governing and advisory bodies will continue to play an important role in the future of the internet.

Preserving Diversity

There is no denying that American television, films, and music are ubiquitous in most societies across the globe, even in wealthy nations (UNESCO 2017). One analysis found that in 2012–2013 U.S. films made up six of the top 10 movies across 51 countries, including eight of the top 10 films in Latin America (UNESCO 2015: 129). In recent years, U.S. productions have made up just under two-thirds of the European film market as a whole. In contrast, European films account for less than 10 percent of the North American film market (European Audiovisual Observatory 2016). European-produced programming is virtually nonexistent on American television outside of BBC productions on public television. If American media products dominate the developed countries of Europe—with their relative affluence and rich media tradition—you can just imagine the role U.S. media play in poorer countries that do not have substantial film or television production industries. UNESCO (2010) notes that the dominant trends in global media and culture are "the top-down flow of content from economically and socially powerful groups to less privileged and disadvantaged groups; from the more developed countries and media houses to the less developed countries and networks," resulting in "radically changing concepts of identity and the social bonds within communities and cultures, often at the cost of local cultural expression" (pp. 1–2). In the wake of such imbalances, the idea of cultures losing their distinctive elements is perhaps what critics fear most. If films, television, and music become globally mass-produced and homogenized—like so many standardized McDonald's restaurants strewn across the international cultural landscape—then the world as a whole loses.

As it did with the "free flow" of information debate, the United States has long opposed any measures that might restrict the flow of cultural goods across national borders. For example, in opposing cultural regulations during the 1993 negotiations for the General Agreement on Trades and Tariffs (GATT), then-president of the MPAA, Jack Valenti, said, "Culture is like chewing-gum, a product like any other." Other countries, though, disagreed. France's then-president François Mitterrand responded, "The mind's creations are no mere commodities and can't be treated as such" (Poirier 2013). European negotiators made clear their intention to exempt cultural products from the overall push for more free trade.

This notion of "cultural exception" became a rallying cry for those wanting to resist the flood of American movies and television programs into Europe and elsewhere. A decade later when opponents of the "cultural exception" idea reemerged ahead of the 2013

U.S.–European Union trade talks, the backlash was immediate and intense. Leading figures in the European film industry launched a petition arguing that "The Cultural Exception Is Non-negotiable!" and that cultural and creative goods should continue to be exempted from any free trade agreement (Petition of European Filmmakers 2013). The petition received more than 5,000 signatures from European directors, writers, technicians and producers. Some of the biggest names in Hollywood expressed their support, too. Director Steven Spielberg argued that "[t]he cultural exception is the best way to defend diversity in film-making." German director Wim Wenders told the European Parliament in a letter, "Culture is not merchandise; you can't put it in the same category as cars, lamps, or screws and bolts" (France 24 2013). Parliament agreed, passing a resolution that kept cultural goods out of the trade negotiations.

Over time, "cultural exception" has evolved into a broad call for protecting cultural diversity. Most important, in 2005, UNESCO adopted the Convention on the Protection and Promotion of the Diversity of Cultural Expressions. (The vote was 148–2, with only the United States and Israel opposing.) The convention aims to protect and promote cultural diversity, creating "the conditions for cultures to flourish and to freely interact in a mutually beneficial manner," encouraging dialogue among cultures, and promoting respect for the diversity of cultures (UNESCO 2005).

Although support has been international, the concrete attempts to preserve cultural diversity have taken place at the national level. As we discussed earlier, foreign media imports sometimes swamp local cultures for two key reasons: (1) a lack of local infrastructure to support locally produced media and (2) the widespread availability of cheap imported media that are irresistible to for-profit media outlets. Some national regulations aimed at preserving diversity try to alter these economic realities either by subsidizing local media production, creating publicly funded media outlets, or taxing the import of foreign media content. Another strategy is to set basic content quotas for locally produced media. Some countries use a mix of these strategies.

For example, the European Union sets a baseline for European cultural content for its member states, but a number of countries extend this requirement with national quotas. The European Union has stipulated that 51 percent of all broadcast programming must be produced within the European Union (Little 2008). In France, though, television stations must air at least 40 percent French-produced content, while taxes on television channels, internet providers, box office proceeds, and more go to subsidize French filmmakers (Buchsbaum 2017). Because of such efforts, France has a higher percentage of domestic film and television programming than other European countries. Meanwhile, in Italy, 60 percent of film and television fiction content must be European made, including 20 percent from Italy (Middleton 2017).

Other countries have their own content requirements (Office of the United States Trade Representative 2017). In Brazil, a 2011 law requires pay-TV stations to show at least three and a half hours of Brazilian-made content each day, leading to a boom in the television and film industries there (Acioli 2017). In Argentina, 60 percent of private broadcast television programming must be local. In Malaysia, 80 percent of broadcast television content must be locally produced; similarly, 60 percent of radio programming must be local. South Africa mandates that its over-the-air television broadcast station carries 45 percent South African content; 60 percent of the music played on radio stations must be South African (National Association of Broadcasters 2018). In Canada, "CanCon" laws

Transformers is advertised to audiences in China. Despite the massive growth in the number of movie theaters there, China limits the number of foreign films that can be shown to just 34 per year.

initiated in the 1960s now require that 55 percent of the material aired by private Canadian broadcasters be produced, all or in part, in Canada or by Canadians.

In a case that's more outright protectionism, China has taken a direct approach to supporting its national film industry. It allows the import of just 34 foreign films each year. To evade this restriction, Hollywood studios have had to find Chinese partners to coproduce movies, exempting them from the import limit. These partnerships enable Chinese producers to learn the skills of successful movie production. In recent years, the Chinese film industry has grown dramatically and is poised to become the world's largest movie producer. China's massive audience for films now gets the attention of Hollywood studios, who increasingly add Chinese actors and plot elements to attract those audiences. It was no accident that the Chinese Space Agency saved the day in *The Martian*, that the Chinese Communist Party stands up to invading aliens in *Transformers: Age of Extinction* (partially set in Hong Kong), and that *Rogue One: A Star Wars Story* prominently features two Chinese actors (Beech 2017).

The internet and video-on-demand streaming services have posed new challenges for local content. Netflix is the giant in this field, offering streaming services while greatly ramping up its original content creation. Netflix has pioneered the use of data analytics to create its programming. It uses algorithms to parse its massive database of viewer habits as a way to increase the chance of success for its own productions. Critics contend the result is blandly derivative work that simply copies what has already been successful rather than breaking new creative ground. The European Union moved to require video-on-demand streaming services such as Netflix to devote 30 percent of their available catalog to European content. Other countries have initiated similar requirements, although Netflix has consistently fought content restrictions. In 2017, for example, Netflix streamed content to nearly 8 million Australians without employing a single person in the country. Its television broadcast competitors there face local-content requirements, but Netflix did not. Australia moved toward blocking that loophole, extending cultural content requirements to streaming services. In Canada, Netflix moved to preempt such a requirement by pledging to invest $500 million in local Canadian productions over five years (Kostaki 2017; McDuling 2018).

As these examples suggest, even in a world where the internet crosses national boundaries, national regulations still matter.

GLOBAL MEDIA USERS: LIMITS OF THE "GLOBAL VILLAGE"

If the world's major media conglomerates are all from North America, Europe, and Japan—wealthy, industrial nations—can we call such a fundamentally unequal media system truly "global"? McLuhan's (1964) "global village" suggested an even playing field occupied by equally influential actors. That image certainly does not describe the state of media production.

One could argue, however, that the essence of "global media" is consumption rather than production. What makes media global, you might say, is that users around the world can access it. Indeed, the expansion of the internet has been dramatic. By 2018, more than 4.2 billion people were using the internet, and there were 3.2 billion active social media users; 52 percent of internet traffic was through smartphones (We Are Social 2018.)

However, inequality reigns here as well. Media are not equally accessible around the world. Globally, patterns of media consumption follow the same pattern as economic inequality. The richer nations, which disproportionately own and produce media, disproportionately use media. The egalitarian image of a "global village" once again obscures reality.

We can see this most easily with the gap in access to information and communication technologies between the wealthy and poor regions of the world, known as the "global digital divide." Despite rhetoric to the contrary, the staggering degree of economic inequality that exists globally shapes the extent of media use. With all the talk of global media and instantaneous communication, it is easy to forget that the basic struggle for survival still marks daily life for significant segments of the Earth's population. Almost half the world's population has no access to the internet.

Figure 10.2 shows the massively skewed distribution of internet access around the world. Although almost nine out of 10 people in North America are internet users, barely one out of 10 people in middle Africa has access to the internet.

FIGURE 10.2 ■ Internet Users as Percent of Regional Population, 2018

The world's economic inequalities are reflected in the widely diverging rates of internet access. Nearly half the world's population is not online.

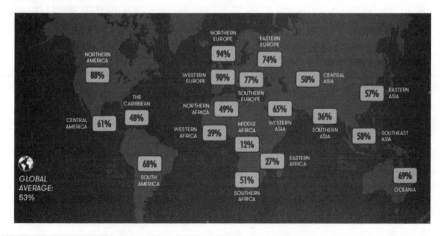

Source: We Are Social (2018).

Such vast disparities indicate that we cannot analyze the use of media in any uniform global manner. Only the middle- and upper-class segments of many countries are able to afford regular access to global media products. Writing about South America, one early commentator noted, "In a continent where so many are still poor, the mass culture tends to accentuate differences. . . . It makes a student in Buenos Aires much closer to a counterpart in New York than to someone in a poor province 300 miles away" (Escobar and Swardson 1995: 1, A18). The people in many poorer nations who tune into the global media are the relative elites of those nations.

We can also see the digital divide—and the difficulty in bridging it—in the case of the affordable laptop. In 2002, MIT professor Nicholas Negroponte launched a campaign called "One Laptop Per Child," with the aim of providing schoolchildren in developing countries with their own specially designed $100 laptop. However, the program directors' faith in technology and the device's top-down design overlooked the social dimension of technological adoption. The people in poor countries struggling with basic subsistence issues often had little use for laptops. The campaign abandoned its original design for the computers to be powered by hand cranks, making them usable in areas without electricity, because it proved to be unfeasible. Instead, people in developing countries found cell phones to be much more useful for both internet access and personal communications. Despite its noble intentions, the laptop program proved to be controversial and, in the eyes of many observers, a failure (Nussbaum 2007; Rawsthorn 2009). Faith that technology designed by Westerners and brought to the developing world would help change the dynamics of global inequality proved naïve. The enormous disparities between wealthy and poor nations were too big to bridge with just laptops.

Finally, the digital divide also is relevant to understanding the misperceptions about the impact of social media on pro-democracy movements in recent years, especially in the Middle East and northern Africa. In 2009, demonstrators protesting a disputed presidential election in Tehran, Iran, posted regular updates on Twitter for outside observers. The U.S. State Department even asked Twitter to delay scheduled maintenance to avoid disrupting communication among activists. A few years later, social media also played a role in the various Arab Spring protests, including the Egyptian revolution (Howard and Hussain 2013; Saleh 2012). Demonstrators used the internet to help organize their protests and to send video of their actions to the outside world, but the protests were also organized through existing traditional networks and organizations, especially labor unions (Lee and Weinthal 2011). In fact, the impact and significance of social media should not be overstated. For example, although the Iranian demonstrations were widely touted in Western media as the "Twitter revolution," later analysis suggested that most of the Twitter chatter originated from outside Iran, and the messages that originated from within the country were largely aimed at outside audiences, not local citizens (Esfandiari 2010). Those messages frequently perpetuated wild, unsubstantiated rumors that often confused the situation. Within Iran, such high-tech communications played a much less significant role than old-fashioned word of mouth. Western observers seemed to overlook the fact that Twitter did not support Farsi, the language most used in Iran. As Mehdi Yahyanejad, the Los Angeles manager of a Farsi-language news site, commented at the time: "Twitter's impact inside Iran is zero. . . . Here [in the United States], there is lots of buzz, but once you look . . . you see most of it are Americans tweeting among themselves" (Musgrove 2009). Such observations suggest that we need to be cautious when assessing the role of these new media in political life.

As these examples suggest, the global digital divide manifests itself in a variety of ways. McLuhan's global village is far from our current reality.

THE UBIQUITY OF CHANGE AND THE FUTURE OF MEDIA

Change is one of the great constants of human history. The discipline of sociology emerged, in large measure, in response to the political, economic, and intellectual changes that marked 19th-century Europe. Social thinkers of the day were trying to make sense of the revolutionary changes that were taking place around them, as modern industrial societies replaced traditional agrarian societies. Industrialization, diverse urban populations, and cities supplanted the agrarian, homogenous populations of rural life. The price paid for this dramatic transformation included poverty, urban slums, exploitative child labor practices, dangerous and underpaid work, and a host of other social problems.

In the 21st century, the expansion of digital communications has marked a new revolution in social life with its own price to be paid. Unwin (2013) cautions that the internet has had

> dehumanizing and alienating effects. Just as factory production in the nineteenth century made humans appendages of machines, so too in the twenty-first century has the Internet made people ever more the appendages of computers. In so doing, users are becoming further alienated from the physical world of nature and creativity; and ever more constrained by those who design the virtual realities of which we are a part. (p. 549)

The technological changes that will come through the remainder of this century are likely to be as profound as those that marked the dawning of industrialization. For example, in the short term:

- Expanded options for streaming will continue to change how we experience television, music, and movies, making the internet more central than ever to the media landscape.

- Augmented and virtual reality technologies will likely take on broader significance as their development advances and media producers and users increasingly adopt it.

- The "internet of things" is likely to expand as "smart homes" become more common. A part of this web of technology will be new ways to filter our access to information, news, and entertainment through increasingly sophisticated interactive digital "assistants" (Bardot 2017; Marconi and Siegman 2017).

- Wearable technology is likely to expand, making, as one observer put it, the internet like electricity—less visible and intrusive but more deeply embedded in people's lives (Pew Research Center 2014a; Rainie 2017).

More important, though, are the social developments that may or may not influence the evolution of media and communications:

- Language, nationality, and political perspective will continue to fragment the internet.

- Authoritarian governments are likely to continue their crackdown on domestic internet use and to use the internet as a weapon abroad (Mueller 2017).

- The regulation of online tech companies may emerge as one response to issues of cybersecurity and foreign meddling in elections. However, will such efforts make a difference? And what will be the costs in terms of free speech, privacy, and concerns regarding surveillance?

- The internet will likely be the battlefield for a future international conflict, as nation-states launch digital attacks on critical infrastructure now integrated into the internet. How will governments respond? What will this mean for the future of open internet access? For surveillance and security?

- Encryption technologies will continue to enable both privacy and the anonymous sharing of information online as well as facilitate a wide array of illicit activity on the dark web from the sale of illegal drugs, weapons, and stolen credit card numbers to human trafficking, child pornography, and terrorism. Here too, will governments eventually seek to intervene more forcefully in this arena? What form will this intervention take, and how will this affect other users?

- Journalism's financial crisis will continue. The repression of journalists is likely to continue, and the fight against misinformation online will expand.

- New forms of propaganda will likely proliferate and circulate online, making it increasingly difficult for citizens to evaluate competing truth claims.

- Media companies, advertisers, and governments are likely to use increasingly intrusive practices of surveillance to collect more and more data on our behaviors, beliefs, and social connections.

These are just a few of the more obvious issues we are likely to face. However, the direction taken by future media will depend on the decisions made by members of society. Nothing is inevitable about the march of media technology or the social developments that surround it. Perhaps you have a role to play in helping steer the future direction and uses of media and technology.

Our argument for a sociological analysis of media began in Chapter 1 with a sketch of a model for approaching the study of media and the social world. We have tried to show that understanding the media involves understanding a series of social relationships. By now, it should be clear that looking only at media content—the most common way to talk about "the media"—provides us with an incomplete picture of the media and their significance for society. Instead, we must be alert to the relationships that exist within our model, relationships that involve technology, the media industry, media content, active audiences and users, and the social world beyond the media. Even in the years to come, regardless of the changes that occur, understanding the media will mean understanding these social relations in all their complexity.

Discussion Questions

1. Marshall McLuhan envisioned an electronic "global village" in which people would become "irrevocably involved with, and responsible for, each other." In what ways has McLuhan's vision proven to be correct? In what ways was he wrong?

2. Why is it so difficult for developing nations to compete with media products produced in wealthier developed countries?

3. Do you think "cultural imperialism" remains a threat? Why or why not?

4. What are some of the ways that countries have responded to the influx of foreign media products in their attempt to protect local culture?

5. What do you think will be the most significant change in media during your lifetime? Explain.

REFERENCES

Abbate, Janet. 1999. *Inventing the Internet*. Cambridge, MA: MIT Press.

Acioli, Renata. 2017. "In Brazil, Film and TV Law Fosters Industry Boom." *Sparksheet* (http://sparksheet .com/in-brazil-film-and-tv-law-fosters-industry-boom/).

Ackerman, Seth. 2001. "The Most Biased Name in News: Fox News Channel's Extraordinary Right-Wing Tilt." *Extra!* July/August. Retrieved March 7, 2011 (http://www.fair.org/index.php?page=1067).

Aday, Sean. 2010. "Chasing the Bad News: An Analysis of 2005 Iraq and Afghanistan War Coverage on NBC and Fox News Channel." *Journal of Communication* 60 (1): 144–164.

Aday, Sean, Steven Livingston, and Maeve Hebert. 2005. "Embedding the Truth: A Cross-cultural Analysis of Objectivity and Television Coverage of the Iraq War." *Harvard International Journal of Press/Politics* 10 (1): 3–21.

Ahlkvist, Jarl A. and Robert Faulkner. 2002. "Will This Record Work for Us?: Managing Music Formats in Commercial Radio." *Qualitative Sociology* 25 (2): 189–215.

Alba, Davey. 2017. "Facebook's Officially a Media Company: Time to Act Like One." *Wired*, March 6 (https://www.wired.com/2017/03/facebooks-officially-media-company-time-act-like-one/).

Alexa. 2018. "Top Sites." (https://www.alexa.com/topsites).

Alexander, Jeffrey C., Elizabeth Butler Breese, and María Luengo, eds. 2016. *The Crisis of Journalism Reconsidered*. New York, NY: Cambridge University Press.

Alldredge, John. 2015. "The 'CSI Effect' and Its Potential Impact on Juror Decisions." *Themis: Research Journal of Justice Studies and Forensic Science* 3 (1): 6 (http://scholarworks.sjsu.edu/themis/vol3/iss1/6).

Allen-Robertson, James. 2015. "The Materiality of Digital Media: The Hard Disk Drive, Phonograph, Magnetic Tape and Optical Media in Technical Close-up." *New Media & Society* 19 (3): 455–470.

Altheide, David L., and Robert P. Snow. 1979. *Media Logic*. Thousand Oaks, CA: Sage.

Altheide, David L., and Robert P. Snow. 1991. *Media Worlds in the Postjournalism Era*. New York, NY: Aldine de Gruyter.

Althusser, Louis. 1971. *Lenin and Philosophy*. London: New Left Books.

Anand, Bharat N., Kyle Barnett, and Elizabeth Carpenter. 2004. *Random House Case Study*. Boston, MA: Harvard Business School.

Anastácio, Kimberly. 2016. "A View from the Cheap Seats: Internet and Colonialism." GigaNet: Global Internet Governance Academic Network, Annual Symposium 2016 (https://ssrn.com/abstract=2909369).

Andrews, Kenneth T., and Neal Caren. 2010. "Making the News: Movement Organizations, Media Attention, and the Public Agenda." *American Sociological Review* 75 (6): 841–866.

Ang, Ien. 1985. *Watching Dallas*. London, UK: Methuen.

Angwin, Julia, and Terry Parris Jr. 2016. "Facebook Lets Advertisers Exclude Users by Race." *ProPublica*. October 28 (https://www.propublica.org/article/facebook-lets-advertisers-exclude-users-by-race).

Angwin, Julia, Madeleine Varner, and Ariana Tobin. 2017. "Facebook Enabled Advertisers to Reach

'Jew Haters.'" *ProPublica*. September 14 (https://www.propublica.org/article/facebook-enabled-advertisers-to-reach-jew-haters).

Appel, Helmut, Alexander L. Gerlach, and Jan Crusius. 2016. "The Interplay between Facebook Use, Social Comparison, Envy, and Depression." *Current Opinion in Psychology* 9: 44–49.

Armstrong, David. 1981. *A Trumpet to Arms*. Boston, MA: South End Press.

Arthur, Charles. 2006. "What Is the 1% Rule?" *The Guardian*. July 20. Retrieved December 8, 2010 (http://www.guardian.co.uk/technology/2006/jul/20/guardianweeklytechnologysection2).

Artz, Lee. 2015. *Global Entertainment Media: A Critical Introduction*. Malden, MA: John Wiley & Sons.

Asch, Solomon E. 1952. *Social Psychology*. Englewood Cliffs, NJ: Prentice Hall.

———. 1955. "Opinions and Social Pressures." *Scientific American* 193 (5): 31–35.

Askin, Noah, and Michael Mauskapf. 2017. "What Makes Popular Culture Popular? Product Features and Optimal Differentiation in Music." *American Sociological Review* 82 (5): 910–944.

ASNE (American Society of News Editors). 2017. "The ASNE Newsroom Diversity Survey" (http://asne.org/diversity-survey-2017)

Association for Progressive Communication. 2018. "About APC" (https://www.apc.org/en/about).

Atton, Chris, and James F. Hamilton. 2008. *Alternative Journalism*. London, UK: Sage.

Aufderheide, Patricia. 1990. "After the Fairness Doctrine: Controversial Broadcast Programming and the Public Interest." *Journal of Communication* 40 (3): 47–72.

———. 1999. *Communications Policy and the Public Interest: The Telecommunications Act of 1996*. New York, NY: Guilford Press.

Auletta, Ken. 1991. *Three Blind Mice: How the TV Networks Lost Their Way*. New York: Random House.

———. 2001. *World War 3.0: Microsoft and Its Enemies*. New York: Random House.

Auslander, Philip. 1999. *Liveness: Performance in a Mediatized Culture*. New York, NY: Routledge.

Bacle, Ariana. 2017. "Justin Bieber Doesn't Know the Spanish Lyrics to 'Despacito.' " *Entertainment Weekly*. May 25 (http://ew.com/music/2017/05/25/justin-bieber-doesnt-know-despacito-spanish-lyrics/).

Badash, David. 2015. "'Hello N*gger': Conservatives Welcome President Obama to Twitter." *New Civil Rights Movement* (http://www.thenewcivilrightsmovement.com/davidbadash/1_hello_n_gger_conservatives_welcome_president_obama_to_twitter).

Bagdikian, Ben. 2004. *The New Media Monopoly*. Boston, MA: Beacon Press.

Bailey, Sarah, Pulliam. 2018. "How the Mom Internet Became a Spotless, Sponsored Void." *Washington Post*, January 26 (https://www.washingtonpost.com/outlook/how-the-mom-internet-became-a-spotless-sponsored-void/2018/01/26/072b46ac-01d6-11e8-bb03-722769454f82_story.html?utm_term=.4e06cab658ea).

Bakardjieva, Maria. 2005. *Internet Society: The Internet in Everyday Life*. Thousand Oaks, CA: Sage.

———. 2011. "The Internet in Everyday Life: Exploring the Tenets and Contributions of Diverse Approaches." Pp. 59–82 in Mia Consalvo and Charles Ess, eds. *The Handbook of Internet Studies*. Blackwell Publishing.

Baker, C. Edwin. 1994. *Advertising and a Democratic Press*. Princeton, NJ: Princeton University Press.

Baker, Liana B. 2016. "Half the World Watching Games, Opening Ceremony Ratings Flat: IOC." Reuters. August 17 (https://uk.reuters.com/article/us-olympics-rio-ioc-broadcast/half-the-world-watching-games-opening-ceremony-ratings-flat-ioc-idUKKCN10S1ZX).

Baldasty, Gerald J. 1992. *The Commercialization of News in the Nineteenth Century*. Madison, WI: University of Wisconsin Press.

Bandura, Albert. 1977. *Social Learning Theory*. Englewood Cliffs, NJ: Prentice Hall.

———. 1986. *Social Foundations of Thought and Action: A Social Cognitive Theory*. Upper Saddle River, NJ: / Prentice Hall, Inc.

Bandura, Albert. Dorothea Ross, and Sheila A. Ross. 1961. "Transmission of Aggression through the Imitation of Aggressive Models." *Journal of Abnormal and Social Psychology* 63 (3): 575–582.

Barber, Benjamin R. 1995. *Jihad vs. McWorld*. New York, NY: Ballantine Books.

Bardot, Trushar. 2017. "The Future of News Is Humans Talking to Machines." *NiemanLab*. September 18 (http://www.niemanlab.org/2017/09/the-future-of-news-is-humans-talking-to-machines/).

Barnard, Stephen R. 2016. "'Tweet or Be Sacked': Twitter and the New Elements of Journalistic Practice". *Journalism* 17 (2): 190–207.

Barnes, Brookes. 2009. "Avatar Is No. 1 but without a Record." *New York Times*. December 20. Retrieved December 9, 2010 (http://www.nytimes.com/2009/12/21/movies/21box.html).

Barnett, Brooke, and Amy Reynolds. 2009. *Terrorism and the Press*. New York: Peter Lang.

Barnett, Steven. 1997. "New Media, Old Problems: New Technology and the Political Process." *European Journal of Communication*. 12 (2): 193–218.

Bartels, Larry. 2002. "The Impact of Candidate Traits in American Presidential Elections." Pp. 44–69 in *Leaders' Personalities and the Outcomes of Democratic Elections*, edited by Anthony King. New York: Oxford University Press.

Battani, Marshall. 1999. "Organizational Fields, Cultural Fields, and Art Worlds: The Early Effort to Make Photographs and Make Photographers in the Nineteenth Century." *Media, Culture, and Society* 21 (5): 601–626.

Bauder, David, Lynn Elber, and Frazier Moore. 2015. "TV Networks Make Unequal Progress toward On-screen Diversity." Associated Press. January 21 (https://www.apnews.com/a86e495dbe714a1e849d3d72d5d8d0ff).

Baudrillard, Jean. 1983. *Simulations*. New York: Semiotext(e).

———. 1988. *Selected Writings*. Mark Poster, ed. Stanford, CA: Stanford University Press.

Bechmann, Anja, and Stine Lomborg. 2012. "Mapping Actor Roles in Social Media: Different Perspectives on Value Creation in Theories of User Participation." *New Media & Society* 15 (5): 765–781

Becker, Howard S. 1982. *Art Worlds*. Berkeley, CA: University of California Press.

Beech, Hannah. 2017. "How China Is Remaking the Global Film Industry." *TIME*. January 26 (http://time.com/4649913/china-remaking-global-film-industry/).

Beer, David. 2009. "Power through the Algorithm? Participatory Web Cultures and the Technological Unconsciousness." *New Media & Society* 11 (6): 985–1002.

Bell, Emily, and Taylor Owen. 2017. "The Platform Press: How Silicon Valley Reengineered Journalism." Columbia Journalism School, Tow Center for Digital Journalism (http://towcenter.org/wp-content/uploads/2017/04/The_Platform_Press_Tow_Report_2017.pdf).

Bennett, W. Lance. 2009. *News: The Politics of Illusion*. 8th ed. New York: Longman.

Bennett, W. Lance, and Shanto Iyengar. 2008. "A New Era of Minimal Effects? The Changing Foundations of Political Communication." *Journal of Communication* 58: 707–731.

———. 2010. "The Shifting Foundations of Political Communication: Responding to a Defense of the Media Effects Paradigm." *Journal of Communication* 60: 35–39.

Bennett, W. Lance, and David Paletz, eds. 1994. *Taken by Storm: The Media, Public Opinion, and U.S. Foreign Policy in the Gulf War*. Chicago, IL: University of Chicago Press.

Bennett, W. Lance, and Alexandra Segerberg. 2013. *The Logic of Connective Action: Digital Media and the Personalization of Contentious Politics*. New York, NY: Cambridge University Press.

Berelson, Bernard. 1952. *Content Analysis in Communication Research*. New York, NY: Free Press.

Berger, Peter L., and Thomas Luckmann. 1966. *The Social Construction of Reality*. New York, NY: Doubleday.

Bernoff, Josh, and Jacqueline Anderson. 2010. "Social Technographics Defined." Forrester. Retrieved

December 8, 2010 (http://www.forrester.com/empo wered/ladder2010).

Bertrand, Natashia. 2017. "Shuttered Facebook Group that Organized Anti-Clinton, Anti-immigrant Rallies across Texas Was Linked to Russia." *Business Insider*. September 13 (http://www.businessinsider.com/face book-group-russia-texas-anti-immigrant-ral lies-2017-9).

Bhatia, Rahul. 2016. "The Inside Story of Facebook's Biggest Setback." *The Guardian*. May 12 (https:// www.theguardian.com/technology/2016/may/12/ facebook-free-basics-india-zuckerberg).

Bielby, William T., and Denise D. Bielby. 1994. "All Hits Are Flukes: Institutionalized Decision Making and the Rhetoric of Network Prime-Time Program Development." *American Journal of Sociology* 99: 1287–1313.

———. 2003. "Controlling Prime-time: Organizational Concentration and Network Television Programming Strategies." *Journal of Broadcasting & Electronic Media* 47: 573–596.

Bijker, Wiebe E., Thomas P. Hughes, and Trevor Pinch. 2012. *The Social Construction of Technological Systems*. Cambridge, MA: MIT Press.

Bilton, Ricardo. 2017. "With Scripted Comedy Videos, The *Washington Post* Wants to Provide 'New Entry Points to the News.'" NiemanLab. September 14 (http://www.niemanlab.org/2017/09/with-scripted-comedy-videos-the-washington-post-wants-to-pro vide-new-entry-points-to-the-news/).

Bird, S. Elizabeth. 2003. *The Audience in Everyday Life: Living in a Media World*. New York: Routledge.

Birkinbine, Benjamin, Rodrigo Gomez, and Janet Wasko, eds. 2017. *Global Media Giants*. New York: Routledge.

Black Lives Matter. 2018. "Black Lives Matter." (https:// blacklivesmatter.com/).

Blank, Grant. 2013. "Who Creates Content?" *Information, Communication & Society* 16 (4): 590–612.

Blank, Grant, and Darja Groselj. 2014. "Dimensions of Internet Use: Amount, Variety, and Types." *Information, Communication & Society* 17 (4): 417–435.

Blondheim, Menahem. 1994. *News over the Wires: The Telegraph and the Flow of Public Information in America 1844–1897*. Cambridge, MA: Harvard University Press.

Blum, Andrew. 2012. *Tubes: A Journey to the Center of the Internet*. New York, NY: HarperCollins.

Blumer, Herbert. 1933. *Movies and Conduct*. New York, NY: Macmillan.

Boczkowski, Pablo. 2004. *Digitizing the News: Innovation in Online Newspapers*. Cambridge, MA: MIT Press.

———. 2009. "Technology, Monitoring and Imitation in Contemporary News Work." *Communication, Culture & Critique* 2 (1): 39–58.

———. 2010. *News at Work: Imitation in an Age of Information Abundance*. Chicago, IL: University of Chicago Press.

Bode, Leticia. 2016. "Political News in the News Feed: Learning Politics from Social Media." *Mass Communication and Society*. 19: 24–48.

Bogart, Leo. 1991. "The Pollster & the Nazis." *Commentary*. August 1 (https://www.commentary magazine.com/articles/the-pollster-the-nazis/).

Bogle, Donald. 2016. *Toms, Coons, Mulattoes, Mammies, and Bucks: An Interpretive History of Blacks in American Film*. New York, NY: Bloomsbury Academic.

Bolter, Jay David, and Richard Grusin. 2000. *Remediation: Understanding New Media*. Cambridge, MA: MIT Press.

Bond, Paul. 2016. "Leslie Moonves on Donald Trump: 'It May Not Be Good for America, but It's Damn Good for CBS.'" *The Hollywood Reporter*. February 29 (hollywoodreporter.com/news/leslie-moonves-donald-trump-may-871464).

Bond, Robert M., Christopher J. Fariss, Jason J. Jones, Adam D. I. Kramer, Cameron Marlow, Jaime E. Settle, and James H. Fowler. 2012. "A 61-million-person experiment in social influence and political mobiliza-tion." *Nature* 489: 295–298.

Bonilla, Yarimar, and Jonathan Ros. 2015. "#Ferguson: Digital Protest, Hashtag Ethnography, and the Racial Politics of Social Media in the United States." *American Ethnologist* 42: 4–17.

Bonilla-Silva, Eduardo. 2014. *Racism without Racists: Color-blind Racism and the Persistence of Racial Inequality in America*. Landham, MD: Rowman & Littlefield.

Boorstin, Daniel. 1961. *The Image*. New York: Atheneum.

Booth, Paul. 2010. *Digital Fandom: New Media Studies*. New York, NY: Lang.

Bose, Derek. 2006. *Brand Bollywood: A New Global Entertainment Order*. Thousand Oaks, CA: Sage.

Bowker. 2016. "Report from Bowker Shows Continuing Growth in Self-Publishing." September 7 (http://www.bowker.com/news/2016/Report-from-Bowker-Shows-Continuing-Growth-in-Self-Publishing.html).

Box Office Mojo. 2018. "Studio Market Share." (http://www.boxofficemojo.com/studio/?view=compa ny&view2=yearly&yr=2017&p=.htm)

Boyd-Barrett, Oliver. 1977. "Media Imperialism: Towards an International Framework for an Analysis of Media Systems." Pp. 116–135 in *Mass Communication and Society*, edited by James Curran, Michael Gurevitch and Janet Woollacott. London, UK: Edward Arnold.

Braid, Mary. 2004. "Page Three Girls—The Naked Truth." *BBC News Online*. September 14. Retrieved November 29, 2010 (http://news.bbc.co.uk/2/hi/uk_news/magazine/3651850.stm).

Branch, Taylor. 1988. *Parting the Waters: America in the King Years 1954–1963*. New York: Simon & Schuster.

Brand, Stewart. 1968. "The Purpose of the Whole Earth Catalog." *Whole Earth Catalog*. Fall (http://www.wholeearth.com/issue/1010/article/196/the.pur pose.of.the.whole.earth.catalog).

Brigs, Asa, and Peter Burke. 2009. *A Social History of the Media: From Gutenberg to the Internet*. Malden, MA: Polity Press.

Brill's Content. 1998. "Dan Rather on Fear, Money, and the News." October: 116–121.

Brimeyer, Ted, Eric O. Silva, and R. Jolene Byrne. 2016. "What Do Unions Do? Media Framing of the Two-Faces of Labor." *Journal of Labor and Society* 19: 517–532.

Broadband Commission for Sustainable Development. 2017. "The State of Broadband: Broadband catalyzing sustainable development." UNESCO. September (https://www.itu.int/dms_pub/itu-s/opb/pol/S-POL-BROADBAND.18-2017-PDF-E.pdf).

Brodkin, Jon. 2016. "Pay-for-Play: Verizon Wireless Selling Data Cap Exemptions to Content Providers." *ARS Technica*. January 19 (https://arstechnica.com/information-technology/2016/01/verizon-wireless-selling-data-cap-exemptions-to-content-providers/).

Bruns, Axel. 2008. *Blogs, Wikipedia, Second Life, and Beyond: From Production to Produsage*. New York: Peter Lang.

Bruns, Axel, and Jan-Hinrik Schmidt. 2011. "Produsage: A Closer Look at Continuing Developments." *New Review of Hypermedia and Multimedia* 17 (1): 3–7.

Bryant, Jennings, and Dorina Miron. 2004. "Theory and Research in Mass Communication." *Journal of Communication* 54 (4), 662–704.

Bryant, Jennings, Susan Thompson, and Bruce W. Finklea. 2012. *Fundamentals of Media Effects*. Long Grove, IL: Waveland Press.

Buchsbaum, Jonathan. 2017. *Exception Taken: How France Has Defied Hollywood's New World Order*. New York, NY: Columbia University Press.

Buckingham, David. 1993. *Reading Audiences: Young People and the Media*. New York, NY: Manchester University Press.

Bump, Philip. 2017. "Trump Reportedly Wants to Cut Cultural Programs That Make Up 0.02 Percent of Federal Spending." *Washington Post*. January 19 (https://www.washingtonpost.com/news/the-fix/wp/2017/01/19/trump-reportedly-wants-to-cut-cultural-programs-that-make-up-0-02-percent-of-federal-spending).

———. 2018. "A (So Far) Complete Timeline of the Investigation into Trump and Russia." *The Washington Post*. April 24 (https://www.washingtonpost.com/news/politics/wp/2018/02/05/a-so-far-complete-timeline-of-the-investigation-into-trump-and-russia).

Bureau of Labor Statistics. 2017. "Newspaper Publishers Lose over Half Their Employment from January 2001 to September 2016." U.S. Department of Labor. *The Economics Daily.* August 3 (https://www .bls.gov/opub/ted/2017/newspaper-publishers-lose- over-half-their-employment-from-january-2001-to- september-2016.htm).

———. 2018. "Union Members Summary." U.S. Department of Labor (https://www.bls.gov/news .release/union2.nr0.htm).

Butcher, Melissa. 2003. *Transnational Television, Cultural Identity and Change: When STAR Came to India.* Thousand Oaks, CA: Sage.

Butsch, Richard. 2003. "A Half Century of Class and Gender in American TV Domestic Sitcoms." *Cercle.* 8: 16–34.

———. 2005. "Five Decades and Three Hundred Sitcoms About Class and Gender." Pp. 111–135 in *Thinking Outside the Box: A Contemporary Television Genre Reader*, edited by Gary R. Edgerton and Brian G. Rose. Lexington, KY: University Press of Kentucky.

———. 2018. "Why Television Sitcoms Kept Re-creating Male Working-Class Buffoons for Decades." Pp. 442– 450 in Gail Dines, Jean M. Humez, Bill Yousman, and Lori Bindig Yousman, eds. 2018. *Gender, Race, and Class in Media.* Thousand Oaks, CA: Sage.

Byrne, Dara N. 2008. "Public Discourse, Community Concerns, and Civic Engagement: Exploring Black Social Networking Traditions on Blackplanet.com." *Journal of Computer-Mediated Communication* 13 (1): 319–340.

Cacciatore, Michael A., Dietram A. Scheufele, and Shanto Iyengar. 2016. "The End of Framing as We Know It . . . and the Future of Media Effects." *Mass Communication and Society* 19 (1): 7–23.

Calabrese, Andrew. 1999. "Communication and the End of Sovereignty?" *Info: Journal of Policy, Regulation and Strategy for Telecommunications, Information and Media* 1 (4): 313–326.

Callier, Patrick. 2014. "Class as a Semiotic Resource in Consumer Advertising: Markedness, Heteroglossia, and Commodity Temporalities." *Discourse & Society* 25 (5), 581–599.

Campbell, Christopher P., Kim M. LeDuff, Cheryl D. Jenkins, and Rockell A. Brown, eds. 2012. *Race and News: Critical Perspectives.* New York, NY: Routledge

Campbell, W. Joseph. 2010. "Fright beyond Measure? The Myth of the War of the Worlds." Pp. 26–44 in *Getting it Wrong: Ten of the Greatest Misreported Stories in American Journalism.* Berkeley, CA: University of California Press.

Cantor, Murial G. 1990. "Prime-time Fathers: A Study in Continuity and Change." *Critical Studies in Mass Communication* 7: 275–285.

Cappella, Joseph N., and Kathleen Hall Jamieson. 1997. *Spiral of Cynicism: The Press and the Public Good.* New York: Oxford University Press.

Carney, Nikita. 2016. "All Lives Matter, but So Does Race: Black Lives Matter and the Evolving Role of Social Media." *Humanity & Society* 40 (2): 180–199.

Carr, David. 2014. Barely Keeping up in TV's New Golden Age. *New York Times.* March 10, p. B1.

Carroll, Noël. 2004. "Sympathy for the Devil." Pp. 121– 136 in *The Sopranos and Philosophy*, edited by Richard Greene and Peter Vernezze. LaSalle, IL: Open Court.

Carvin, Andy. 2013. *Distant Witness.* New York: CUNY Journalism Press.

Castells, Manuel. 2001. *The Internet Galaxy. Reflections on the Internet, Business, and Society.* New York: Oxford University Press.

Center for American Progress and the Free Press. 2007. "The Structural Imbalance of Political Talk Radio." (https://cdn.americanprogress.org/wp-con tent/uploads/issues/2007/06/pdf/talk_radio.pdf)

Center for Responsive Politics. 2018. Various data- bases at OpenSecrets.org.

Chadwick, Andrew. 2006. *Internet Politics: States, Citizens, and New Communication Technologies.* New York: Oxford University Press.

———. 2017. *The Hybrid Media System: Politics and Power.* New York, NY: Oxford University Press.

Chakravartty, Paula, and Katharine Sarikakis. 2006. *Media Policy and Globalization.* Edinburgh, UK: Edinburgh University Press.

Chen, Gina M. 2015. "Why Do Women Bloggers Use Social Media? Recreation and Information Motivations Outweigh Engagement Motivations." *New Media & Society* 17 (1): 24–40.

Chen, Liang, Shirley S. Ho, and May O. Lwin. 2017. "A Meta-analysis of Factors Predicting Cyberbullying Perpetration and Victimization: From the Social Cognitive and Media Effects Approach." *New Media & Society* 19 (8): 1194–1213.

Cheney, Richard. 1992. "Media Conduct in the Persian Gulf War: Report to Congress." Washington, DC: Department of Defense, Public Affairs Office.

Childress, Clayton. 2017. *Under the Cover.* Princeton, NJ: Princeton University Press.

Chin, Christina B., Meera E. Deo, Faustina M. DuCros, Jenny Jong-Hwa Lee, Noriko Milman, and Nancy Wang Yuen. 2017. "Tokens on the Small Screen: Asian Americans and Pacific Islanders in Prime Time and Streaming Television." (https://www.aapisontv.com/uploads/3/8/1/3/38136681/aapisontv.2017.pdf).

Chiuy, Yvonne. 1995. "FTC Settles Car Ad Boycott Case." *Washington Post.* August 2, p. F3.

Chmielewski, Dawn C., and Rebecca Keegan. 2011. "Merchandise Sales Drive Pixar's 'Cars' Franchise." *Los Angeles Times.* June 21. Accessed July 8, 2013 (http://articles.latimes.com/2011/jun/21/business/la-fi-ct-cars2-20110621).

Chokshi, Niraj. 2016. "Facebook Helped Drive a Voter Registration Surge, Election Officials Say." *New York Times.* October 12 (https://www.nytimes.com/2016/10/13/us/politics/facebook-helped-drive-a-voter-registration-surge-election-officials-say.html).

Christakis, Dimitri A. 2010. "Internet Addiction: A 21st Century Epidemic?" *BMC Medicine* 8: 61.

Chung, Philip W. 2007. "The 25 Most Notorious Yellow Face Film Performances." *AsianWeek.* November, 28. Retrieved August 7, 2013 (http://www.asianweek.com/2007/11/28/the-25-most-infamous-yellow-face-film-performances-part-1/).

CIRP (Consumer Intelligence Research Partners). 2017. "Amazon Echo Dominates US, with 75% of Users." (http://files.constantcontact.com/150f9af2201/92e32c6b-80ad-46ee-a11e-467eaa9f6b75.pdf).

Cisneros, J. David, and Thomas K. Nakayama. 2015. "New Media, Old Racisms: Twitter, Miss America, and Cultural Logics of Race." *Journal of International and Intercultural Communication* 8 (2): 108–127.

Clark, Charles S. 1991. "The Obscenity Debate." *CQ Researcher.* 1: 971–991.

Clifford, Stephanie. 2010. "Before Hiring Actors, Filmmakers Cast Products." *New York Times.* April 5, p. A1.

CNN. 2016. "Facebook CEO: 'We're a Technology Company. We're Not a Media Company.'" (http://money.cnn.com/video/technology/2016/08/29/facebook-ceo-were-a-technology-company-were-not-a-media-company-.cnnmoney/index.html).

———. 2017. "Transcript: Inside Politics." March 16 (http://transcripts.cnn.com/TRANSCRIPTS/1703/16/ip.02.html).

Cobo, Leila. 2017. "The Success of 'Despacito' Has Labels Looking to Latin." Billboard. June 15 (http://www.billboard.com/articles/news/magazine-feature/7832991/despacito-success-record-labels-looking-latin).

Cohen, Bernard. 1963. *The Press and Foreign Policy.* Princeton, NJ: Princeton University Press.

Cohen, Patricia. 2018. "We All Have a Stake in the Stock Market, Right? Guess Again." *The New York Times.* February 8 (https://www.nytimes.com/2018/02/08/business/economy/stocks-economy.html?hp&action=click&pgtype=Homepage&clickSource=story-heading&module=first-column-region&region=top-news&WT.nav=top-news).

Coldewey, Devin. 2017. "Commission Impossible: How and Why the FCC Created Net Neutrality." *TechCrunch.* May 30 (https://techcrunch.com/2017/05/30/commission-impossible-how-and-why-the-fcc-created-net-neutrality/).

Cole, Williams. 1995. "Readers for Sale! What Newspapers Tell Advertisers about Their Audience." *Extra!.* 8 (3): 6–7.

Colhoun, Damaris. 2015. "BuzzFeed's Censorship Problem." *Columbia Journalism Review.* April 16 (https://www.cjr.org/analysis/buzzfeed_censorship_problem.php).

Commission on Freedom of the Press. 1947. *A Free and Responsible Press*. Chicago, IL: University of Chicago (https://archive.org/details/freeandrespon sib029216mbp).

Committee to Protect Journalists. 2017. "Record Number of Journalists Jailed as Turkey, China, Egypt Pay Scant Price for Repression." December 13 (https://cpj.org/reports/2017/12/journalists-prison-jail-record-number-turkey-china-egypt.php).

Common Sense Media. 2015. *The Common Sense Census: Media Use by Tweens and Teens* (https://www.commonsensemedia.org/research/the-common-sense-census-media-use-by-tweens-and-teens).

Concave. 2017. "Top 10 Brands in 2016 Movies." February 24 (http://concavebt.com/top-10-brands-2016-movies/).

Condit, Celeste M. 1989. "The Rhetorical Limits of Polysemy." *Critical Studies in Mass Communication* 6 (2): 103–122.

Constine, Josh. 2016. "Zuckerberg Implies Facebook Is a Media Company, Just 'Not a Traditional Media Company.'" *TechCrunch*. December 21 (https://techcrunch.com/2016/12/21/fbonc/).

Cooky, Cheryl, and Michael Messner. 2018. *No Slam Dunk: Gender, Sport and the Unevenness of Social Change*. Rutgers, NJ: Rutgers University Press.

Cooky, Cheryl, Michael A. Messner, and Michela Musto. 2015. "It's Dude Time!": A Quarter Century of Excluding Women's Sports in Televised News and Highlight Shows." *Communication & Sport* 3: 261–287.

Cooley, Charles Horton. 1909. *Social Organization: A Study of the Larger Mind*. Charles Scribner's Sons.

Coontz, Stephanie. 2016. *The Way We Never Were: American Families and the Nostalgia Trap*. New York, NY: Basic Books.

Corporation for Public Broadcasting. 2018. "CPB Financial Information." (http://cpb.org/aboutcpb/financials).

Cortell, Andrew P., Robert M. Eisinger, and Scott L. Althaus. 2009. "Why Embed? Explaining the Bush Administration's Decision to Embed Reporters in the 2003 Invasion of Iraq." *American Behavioral Scientist* 52 (5): 657–677.

Coser, Lewis A., Charles Kadushin, and Walter W. Powell. 1982. *Books: The Culture and Commerce of Publishing*. New York: Basic Books.

Cottle, Simon. 2007. "Ethnography and News Production: New(s) Developments in the Field." *Sociology Compass* 1 (1), 1–16.

Couldry, Nick. 2012. *Media, Society, World: Social Theory and Digital Media Practice*. Malden, MA: Polity Press.

Couldry, Nick, and Andreas Hepp. 2017. *The Social Construction of Mediated Reality*. Malden, MA: Polity Press.

Cowan, Tyler. 2000. *What Price Fame?* Cambridge, MA: Harvard University Press.

Crane, Diana. 1992. *The Production of Culture*. Newbury Park, CA: Sage.

Crawford, Alan Pell. 1993. "Finis to Fin-Syn." *Mediaweek*. April 12, p. 15.

Creative Commons. 2018. "About the Licenses." (http://creativecommons.org/about/licenses).

Cripps, Thomas. 1993. "Film." Pp. 131–185 in *Split Image: African Americans in the Mass Media*, 2nd ed., edited by Jannette L. Dates and William Barlow. Washington, DC: Howard University Press.

Cronauer, Adrian. 1994. "The Fairness Doctrine: A Solution in Search of a Problem." *Federal Communications Law Journal* 47 (1): 51–77.

Croteau, David, and William Hoynes. 1994. *By Invitation Only: How the Media Limit Political Debate*. Monroe, ME: Common Courage Press.

———. 2006. *The Business of Media: Corporate Media and the Public Interest*. 2nd ed. Thousand Oaks, CA: Pine Forge/Sage.

———. 2019. *Experience Sociology*. New York, NY: McGraw-Hill.

Croteau, David, William Hoynes, and Kevin M. Carragee. 1996. "The Political Diversity of Public Television: Polysemy, the Public Sphere, and the Conservative Critique of PBS." *Journalism and Mass Communication Monographs* 157: 1–55.

Crouse, Timothy. 1973. *The Boys on the Bus*. New York, NY: Ballantine Books.

Crowell, Colin. 2017. "Our Approach to Bots & Misinformation." Twitter. June 14 (https://blog.twitter.com/official/en_us/topics/company/2017/Our-Approach-Bots-Misinformation.html).

Crowley, David, and Paul Heyer. 1991. *Communication in History*. New York: Longman.

Curran, James. 1977. "Capitalism and Control of the Press, 1800–1975." Pp. 195–230 in *Mass Communication and Society*, edited by James Curran, Michael Gurevitch, and Janet Woollacott. London, UK: Edward Arnold.

———. 2011. *Media and Democracy*. New York, NY: Routledge.

Curran, James, Natalie Fenton, and Des Freedman. 2016. *Misunderstanding the Internet*. New York, NY: Routledge.

Curtin, Michael. 2009. "Matrix Media." Pp. 13–19 in Graeme Turner and Jinna Tay, eds. *Television Studies after TV: Understanding Television in the Post-Broadcast Era*. New York, NY: Routledge.

Dalton, Russell J. 2014. *Citizen Politics: Public Opinion and Political Parties in Advanced Industrial Democracies*. Thousand Oaks, CA: Sage.

D'Angelo, Paul, and Frank Esser. 2014. "Metacoverage and Mediatization in US Presidential Elections: A Theoretical Model and Qualitative Case Study." *Journalism Practice* 8 (3): 295–310.

D'Angelo, Paul, and Jim A. Kuypers, eds. 2010. *Doing News Framing Analysis: Empirical and Theoretical Perspectives*. New York, NY: Routledge.

Daniels, Jessie, Karen Gregory, and Tressie McMillan Cottom, eds. 2016. *Digital Sociologies*. Bristol, UK: Policy Press.

Dano, Mike. 2017. How Verizon, AT&T, T-Mobile, Sprint and More Stacked Up in Q2 2017. *FierceWireless*. August 8 (https://www.fiercewireless.com/wireless/how-verizon-at-t-t-mobile-sprint-and-more-stacked-up-q2-2017-top-7-carriers).

Dargis, Manohla. 2017. "Review: In 'Get Out,' Guess Who's Coming to Dinner? (Bad Idea!)." *The New York Times*. February 23 (https://www.nytimes.com/2017/02/23/movies/get-out-review-jordan-peele.html?rref=collection%2Fcollection%2Fmovie-guide).

Dates, Jannette L. 1993. "Commercial Television." Pp. 267–327 in *Split Image: African Americans in the Mass Media*, 2nd ed., edited by Jannette L. Dates and William Barlow. Washington, DC: Howard University Press.

Dates, Jannette L., and William Barlow, eds. 1993. *Split Image: African Americans in the Mass Media*. 2nd ed. Washington, DC: Howard University Press.

Dávila, Arlene, and Yeidy M. Rivero, eds. 2014. *Contemporary Latina/o Media: Production, Circulation, Politics*. New York, NY: New York University Press.

Dawson, Jan. 2017. "Pay TV Providers Are Weathering the Loss of Cord-Cutting Subscribers." *Variety*. May 11 (http://variety.com/2017/voices/columns/pay-tv-cord-cutting-subscribers-1202421426/).

De Lissovoy, Noah, Venkat Ramaprasad, Stacia Cedillo, and Courtney B. Cook. 2016. "Scripted Fantasies and Innovative Orientalisms: Media, Youth, and Ideology in the Age of the 'War on Terror.'" *Cultural Studies Critical Methodologies* 17 (6): 442–456. doi: https://doi.org/10.1177/1532708616673653

Deacon, David, and James Stanyer. 2014. "Mediatization: Key Concept or Conceptual Bandwagon?" *Media, Culture & Society* 36 (7): 1032–1044.

Deery, June. 2015. *Reality TV*. Malden, MA: Polity Press.

DeLaure, Marilyn, and Moritz Fink. 2017. "Introduction." Pp. 1–35 in DeLaure, Marilyn, Moritz Fink, and Mark Dery, eds. 2017. *Culture Jamming: Activism and the Art of Cultural Resistance*. New York, NY: New York University Press.

Deloitte. 2016. "Indywood: The Indian Film Industry." (https://www2.deloitte.com/content/dam/Deloitte/in/Documents/technology-media-telecommunications/in-tmt-indywood-film-festival-noexp.pdf).

Democracynow.org. 2018. "About Democracy Now!" (https://www.democracynow.org/about).

Dempsey, John, and Josef Adalian. 2007. "'Office,' 'Earl' Land at TBS." *Variety*. June 21. Retrieved November 29, 2010 (http://www.variety.com/article/VR1117967376?refCatId=14).

Denardis, Laura. 2013. "The Emerging Field of Internet Governance." Pp. 555–575 in *The Oxford Handbook of Internet Studies*, edited by William H. Dutton. New York, NY: Oxford University Press.

Denton, Robert, ed. 1993. *The Media and the Persian Gulf War.* Westport, CT: Praeger.

Derks, Daantje, Arjan E. R. Bos, and Jasper von Grumbkow. 2008. "Emoticons and Online Message Interpretation." *Social Science Computer Review* 26 (3): 379–388.

Deuze, Mark. 2007. *Media Work.* Malden, MA: Polity Press.

Dewey, C. 2016. "Facebook Fake-News Writer: 'I Think Donald Trump is in the White House Because of Me.'" *The Washington Post.* November 17 (https://www.washingtonpost.com/news/theintersect/wp/2016/11/17/facebook-fake-news-writer-i-think-donald-trump-isin-the-white-house-because-of-me/).

Dhar, Vasant. 2017. "Should We Regulate Digital Platforms?" *Big Data* 5 (4): 277–278.

Dill, Karen E., Douglas A. Gentile, William A. Richter, and Jody C. Dill. 2005. "Violence, Sex, Race, and Age in Popular Video Games: A Content Analysis." Pp. 115–130 in *Psychology of Women Book Series. Featuring Females: Feminist Analyses of Media*, edited by E. Cole & J. H. Daniel. Washington, DC: American Psychological Association.

Dines, Gail. 2010. *Pornland: How Porn Has Hijacked Our Sexuality.* Boston, MA: Beacon Press.

Dines, Gail, Jean M. Humez, Bill Yousman, and Lori Bindig Yousman, eds. 2018. *Gender, Race, and Class in Media.* Thousand Oaks, CA: Sage

Dixon, Travis L. 2015. "Good Guys Are Still Always in White? Positive Change and Continued Misrepresentation of Race and Crime on Local Television News." *Communication Research* 44 (6): 775–792.

Dizney, Henry F., and Ronald W. Roskens. 1962. "An Investigation of the 'Bandwagon Effect' in a College Straw Election." *The Journal of Educational Sociology* 36 (3): 108–114.

Djankov, Simeon, Caralee McLiesch, Tatiana Nenova, and Andrei Shleifer. 2003. "Who Owns the Media?" *Journal of Law and Economics* 46(October): 341–381.

Donders, Karen. 2011. *Public Service Media and Policy in Europe.* New York: Palgrave McMillan.

Donsbach, Wolfgang, Charles T. Salmon, and Yariv Tsfati. 2014. *The Spiral of Silence: New Perspectives on Communication and Public Opinion.* New York, NY: Routledge.

Douglas, Susan J. 1987. *Inventing American Broadcasting, 1899–1922.* Baltimore, MD: Johns Hopkins University Press.

Douglas, Susan, and Meredith W. Michaels. 2004. *The Mommy Myth: The Idealization of Motherhood and How It Has Undermined Women.* New York: Free Press.

Dowd, Timothy J. 2004. "Concentration and Diversity Revisited: Production Logics and the U.S. Mainstream Recording Market, 1940 to 1990." *Social Forces* 82 (4): 1411–1455.

Downing, John D. H. 2001. *Radical Media: Rebellious Communication and Social Movements.* Thousand Oaks, CA: Sage.

———. 2011. *Encyclopedia of Social Movement Media.* Thousand Oaks, CA: Sage.

Doyle, Gillian. 2002. *Media Ownership: The Economics and Politics of Convergence and Concentration in the UK and European Media.* London, UK: Sage.

Druckman, James N., and Kjersten R. Nelson. 2003. "Framing and Deliberation: How Citizens' Conversations Limit Elite Influence." *American Journal of Political Science* 47 (4): 729–744.

Dutton, William H. 2014. *The Oxford Handbook of Internet Studies.* Oxford, UK: Oxford University Press.

The Economist. 2001. "Fit to Run Italy?" Retrieved April 14, 2011 (http://www.economist.com/node/593654?story_id=593654).

Edelstein, David. 2017. "The Dark Tower Is Not *That* Terrible . . . But It Does Feel Like a Copy of a Copy of a Copy." *Vulture.* August 4 (http://www.vulture.com/2017/08/the-dark-tower-is-not-that-terrible-but-is-perfunctory.html).

Ehrenreich, Barbara. 1995. "The Silenced Majority." Pp. 40–43 in *Gender, Race, and Class in Media*, edited by Gail Dines and Jean M. Humez. Thousand Oaks, CA: Sage.

Eisenstein, Elizabeth. 1968. "Some Conjectures about the Impact of Printing on Western Society and Thought." *Journal of Modern History* 40 (1): 1–56.

———. 1979. *The Printing Press as an Agent of Change.* Cambridge, UK: Cambridge University Press.

Ekdale, Brian, Kang Namkoong, Timothy K.F. Fung, and David D. Perlmutter. 2010. "Why Blog? (Then and Now): Exploring the Motivations for Blogging by American Political Bloggers." *New Media & Society* 12 (2): 217–234.

Elasmar, Michael G., and Kathryn Bennett. 2003. "The Cultural Imperialism Paradigm Revisited: Origin and Evolution." Pp. 1–16 in *The Impact of International Television*, edited by Michael G. Elasmar. New York, NY: Routledge.

Electronic Frontier Foundation. 2018. "Section 230 of the Communications Decency Act." (https://www.eff.org/issues/cda230).

Ellis, John. 2000. *Seeing Things: Television in the Age of Uncertainty.* New York, NY: I. B. Taurus.

eMarketer. 2017. "Google and Facebook Tighten Grip on US Digital Ad Market." September 21 (https://www.emarketer.com/Article/Google-Facebook-Tighten-Grip-on-US-Digital-Ad-Market/1016494).

Entman, Robert. 1989. *Democracy without Citizens.* New York: Oxford University Press.

———. 1992. "Blacks in the News: Television, Modern Racism, and Cultural Change." *Journalism Quarterly* 69: 341–361.

Entman, Robert, and Andrew Rojecki. 2000. *The Black Image in the White Mind.* Chicago, IL: University of Chicago Press.

Epstein, Edward J. 1973. *News from Nowhere.* New York: Vintage.

Eschner, Kat. 2017. "John Philip Sousa Feared 'The Menace of Mechanical Music.'" *Smithsonian Magazine* (https://www.smithsonianmag.com/smart-news/john-philip-sousa-feared-menace-mechanical-music-180967063).

Escobar, Gabriel, and Anne Swardson. 1995. "From Language to Literature, a New Guiding Lite." *Washington Post.* September 5, pp. 1, A18.

Esfandiari, Golnaz. 2010. "The Twitter Devolution." *Foreign Policy.* June 10. Retrieved November 30, 2010 (http://www.foreignpolicy.com/articles/2010/06/07/the_twitter_revolution_that_wasnt).

Espiritu, Belinda Flores. 2011. "Transnational Audience Reception as a Theater of Struggle: Young Filipino Women's Reception of Korean Television Dramas." *Asian Journal of Communication* 21 (4): 355–372.

Esser, Frank, and Jesper Strömbäck, eds. 2014. *Mediatization of Politics.* Palgrave Macmillan, London.

European Audiovisual Observatory. 2016. "Focus: World Film Market Trends." (https://rm.coe.int/0900001680783d9c).

European Commission. 2010. "Microsoft Case." Accessed February 16, 2011 (http://ec.europa.eu/competition/sectors/ICT/microsoft/index.html).

———. 2014. "Factsheet on the 'Right to be forgotten' Ruling." (http://ec.europa.eu/justice/data-protection/files/factsheets/factsheet_data_protection_en.pdf)

———. 2017. "Security Union: Commission Steps Up Efforts to Tackle Illegal Content Online." September 28 (http://europa.eu/rapid/press-release_IP-17-3493_en.htm).

European Union. 2016. "Regulation 2016/679 of the European Parliament and of the Council." (https://eur-lex.europa.eu/legal-content/EN/TXT/?uri=celex%3A32016R0679).

———. 2017. "The Audio Visual Media Services Directive." June 27 (http://www.europarl.europa.eu/RegData/etudes/BRIE/2016/583859/EPRS_BRI%282016%29583859_EN.pdf).

Everett, Anna. 2008. "Introduction." Pp. 1–14 in *Learning Race and Ethnicity: Youth and Digital Media*, edited by Anna Everett. Cambridge, MA: The MIT Press.

Ewen, Stuart. 1976. *Captains of Consciousness.* New York: McGraw-Hill.

Facebook. 2018a. "Facebook Reports Fourth Quarter and Full Year 2017 Results." (https://investor.fb.com/investor-news/press-release-details/2018/Facebook-Reports-Fourth-Quarter-and-Full-Year-2017-Results/default.aspx).

———. 2018b. "Open Compute Project." (http://www.opencompute.org/).

Faughnder, Ryan. 2017. "How Rotten Tomatoes Became Hollywood's Most Influential—and Feared—Website." *Los Angeles Times*. July 21 (http://www.latimes.com/business/hollywood/la-fi-ct-rotten-tomatoes-20170721-htmlstory.html).

FCC (Federal Communications Commission). 1998. "FCC Explores Idea of Creating Low Power FM Radio Service for Local Communities." Retrieved December 23, 1998 (www.fcc.gov/mmb/prd/lpfm).

———. 2004. "Report to the Congress on the Low Power FM Interference Testing Program." Retrieved February 16, 2011 (http://fjallfoss.fcc.gov/edocs_public/attachmatch/DOC-244128A1.pdf).

———. 2013. "Broadcast Station Totals as of March 31, 2013." (http://www.fcc.gov/document/broadcast-station-totals-march-31-2013).

———. 2017. "FCC Broadcast Ownership Rules." (https://www.fcc.gov/consumers/guides/fccs-review-broadcast-ownership-rules).

———. 2018a. "Obscenity, Indecency & Profanity—FAQ." (https://www.fcc.gov/reports-research/guides/obscenity-indecency-profanity-faq).

———. 2018b. "Policy Review of Mobile Broadband Operators' Sponsored Data Offerings for Zero-Rated Content and Service." (http://transition.fcc.gov/Daily_Releases/Daily_Business/2017/db0111/DOC-342982A1.pdf).

Feenberg, Andrew, and Maria Bakardjieva. 2004. "Consumers or Citizens? The Online Community Debate." Pp. 1–30 in *Community in the Digital Age: Philosophy and Practice*, edited by Andrew Feenberg and Darin Barney. Lanham, MD: Rowan & Littlefield.

Feinstein, Brian A., Rachel Hershenberg, Vickie Bhatia, Jessica A. Latack, Nathalie Meuwly, and Joanne Davila. 2013. "Negative Social Comparison on Facebook and Depressive Symptoms: Rumination as a Mechanism." *Psychology of Popular Media Culture* 2 (3): 161–170.

Fejes, Fred. 1992. "Masculinity as Fact: A Review of Empirical Mass Communication Research on Masculinity." Pp. 9–22 in *Men, Masculinity, and the Media*, edited by Steve Craig. Newbury Park, CA: Sage.

Fejes, Fred, and Kevin Petrich. 1993. "Invisibility, Homophobia and Heterosexism: Lesbians, Gays and the Media." *Critical Studies in Mass Communication* 20: 396–422.

Feldman, Dana. 2016. "Netflix Has Slashed Its Library By More Than 50% Since 2012." *Forbes*. October 3 (https://www.forbes.com/sites/danafeldman/2016/10/03/netflix-has-slashed-its-library-by-more-than-50-since-2012/#4fc34701750a).

Finley, Klint. 2016. "The Internet Finally Belongs to Everyone." *Wired*. October 3 (https://www.wired.com/2016/10/internet-finally-belongs-everyone/).

Fischer, Claude. 1992. *America's Calling*. Berkeley, CA: University of California Press.

Fischer, Sara. 2017. "Gut Check: 'The Duopoly Has THAT Much Control.'" Axios Media Trends. August 29 (https://www.axios.com/newsletters/axios-media-trends-f9a3c7f5-9d7b-429d-b295-6f9f8e4f6a90.html).

Fishman, Mark. 1980. *Manufacturing the News*. Austin, TX: University of Texas Press.

Fiske, John. 1986. "Television: Polysemy and Popularity." *Critical Studies in Mass Communication*. 3: 391–408.

———. 1987. *Television Culture*. London, UK: Routledge Kegan Paul.

Flegenheimer, Matt, and Michael M. Grynbaum. 2018. "Trump Hands Out 'Fake News Awards,' sans the Red Carpet." *New York Times*. January 17 (https://www.nytimes.com/2018/01/17/business/media/fake-news-awards.html).

Flew, Terry. 2007. *Understanding Global Media*. New York: Palgrave.

Flint, Joe. 1993. "Networks Win, Hollywood Winces as Fin-Syn Barriers Fall." *Broadcasting & Cable*. November 22, pp. 6, 16.

Forbes. 2018. "Michael Bloomberg." (https://www.forbes.com/profile/michael-bloomberg/).

Forrester Research. n.d. "What's the Social Technographics Profile of Your Customers?" Retrieved

April 14, 2011 (http://www.forrester.com/empowered/tool_consumer.html).

Fowler, Mark S., and Daniel L. Brenner. 1982. "A Marketplace Approach to Broadcast Regulation." *Texas Law Review* 60: 207–257.

Fox, Mark A. 2006. "Market Power in Music Retailing: The Case of Wal-Mart." *Popular Music and Society* 28 (4): 501–519.

France 24. 2013. "Film World Leaps to Defence of French 'Cultural Exception.'" June 14. Retrieved July 24, 2013 (http://www.france24.com/en/20130614-french-cultural-exception-spielberg-weinstein-berenice-bejo-cannes-france).

Frank, Thomas. 1997. *The Conquest of Cool.* Chicago, IL: University of Chicago Press.

Franklin, Bob, ed. 2011. *The Future of Journalism: Developments and Debates.* New York, NY: Routledge.

Free Basics. 2018. "Connecting the World." (https://info.internet.org/en/).

Free Press. 2018. "Net Neutrality: What You Need to Know Now. "Save the Internet (https://www.savetheinternet.com/net-neutrality-what-you-need-know-now).

Freedman, Des. 2008. *The Politics of Media Policy.* Malden, MA: Polity Press.

Freedom House. 2004. *Freedom of the Press 2004: A Global Survey of Media Independence.* Lanham, MD: Rowman & Littlefield.

Freeland, Jonathan. 2016. "Post-truth Politicians Such as Donald Trump and Boris Johnson Are No Joke." *The Guardian.* May 13 (https://www.theguardian.com/commentisfree/2016/may/13/boris-johnson-donald-trump-post-truth-politician).

Freeman, Michael. 1994a. "A Last Gasp for Fin-Syn?" *Mediaweek.* November 28, p. 5.

———. 1994b. "Producers Fight for Fin-Syn." *Mediaweek.* December 5, pp. 10, 12.

Friemel, Thomas N. 2014. "The Digital Divide Has Grown Old: Determinants of a Digital Divide among Seniors." *New Media & Society* 18 (2): 313–331.

Frith, Simon. 1981. *Sound Effects.* New York: Pantheon.

Fritsch-El Alaoui, Khadija. 2009/2010. "Teaching the Meter of the Impossible in a Classroom: On Liberal Hollywood's Mission Impossible." *Transformations* 20 (2): 129–137.

FTC (Federal Trade Commission). 2000. "Marketing Violent Entertainment to Children." Retrieved July 19, 2001 (www.ftc.gov/reports/violence/vioreport.pdf).

Fuller, Linda. 1995. "Hollywood Holding Us Hostage: Or, Why Are Terrorists in the Movies Middle Easterners?" Pp. 187–198 in *The U.S. Media and the Middle East: Image and Perception*, edited by Yahya R. Kamalipour. Westport, CT: Greenwood Press.

Fullwood, Chris, Wendy Nicholls, and Rumbidzai Makichi. 2014. "We've Got Something for Everyone: How Individual Differences Predict Different Blogging Motivations." *New Media & Society* 17 (9): 1583–1600.

Funkhouser, G. Ray. 1973. "The Issues of the Sixties: An Exploratory Study in the Dynamics of Public Opinion." *Public Opinion Quarterly* 66: 942–948, 959.

Gainous, Jason, and Kevin M. Wagner. 2014. *Tweeting to Power: The Social Media Revolution in American Politics.* New York, NY: Oxford University Press.

Gamson, Joshua. 1994. *Claims to Fame.* Berkeley, CA: University of California Press.

———. 1998. *Freaks Talk Back: Tabloid Talk Shows and Sexual Nonconformity.* Chicago, IL: University of Chicago Press.

Gamson, William. 1992. *Talking Politics.* New York: Cambridge University Press.

Gamson, William, David Croteau, William Hoynes, and Theodore Sasson. 1992. "Media Images and the Social Construction of Reality." *Annual Review of Sociology* 18: 373–393.

Gamson, William, and Andre Modigliani. 1989. "Media Discourse and Public Opinion on Nuclear Power." *American Journal of Sociology* 95: 1–37.

Gamson, William, and Gadi Wolfsfeld. 1993. "Movements and Media as Interacting Systems." *Annals of the American Academy of Political and Social Science* 528 (July): 114–125.

Gans, Herbert. 2004. *Deciding What's News*, 25th anniversary ed. Chicago, IL: Northwestern University Press.

Garofalo, Reebee, ed. 1992. *Rockin' the Boat: Mass Music and Mass Movements*. Boston, MA: South End.

Gates, Bill. 1996. "Content Is King." Posted by Heath Evans on *Medium*, January 29, 2017 (https://medium.com/@HeathEvans/content-is-king-essay-by-bill-gates-1996-df74552f80d9).

Geena Davis Institute on Gender in Media. 2016. *Hitting the Bullseye: Reel Girl Archers Inspire Real Girl Archers*. Los Angeles, CA: Mount Saint Mary's University (https://seejane.org/wp-content/uploads/hitting-the-bullseye-reel-girl-archers-inspire-real-girl-archers-full.pdf).

Gentile, Douglas A. 2009. "The Rating Systems for Media Products." Pp. 527–551 in *Handbooks in Communication and Media*, edited by Sandra L. Calvert and Barbara J. Wilson. Oxford, UK: Blackwell Publishing.

Gentile, Douglas A. and John P. Murray. 2014. "Media Violence and Public Policy." Pp. 413–432 in *Media Violence and Children*, edited by Douglas A. Gentile. Santa Barbara, CA: Praeger.

Gera, Vanessa. 2017. "Zygmunt Bauman, Sociologist Who Wrote Identity in the Modern World, Dies at 91." *Washington Post*. January 9 (https://www.washingtonpost.com/world/zygmunt-bauman-sociologist-who-wrote-identity-in-the-modern-world-dies-at-91/2017/01/09/ba6f821e-d6b2-11e6-b8b2-cb5164beba6b_story.html).

Gerbner, George, Larry Gross, Michael Morgan, and Nancy Signorielli. 1982. "Charting the Mainstream: Television's Contributions to Political Orientations." *Journal of Communication* 32 (2): 100–127.

———. 1984. "Political Correlates of Television Viewing." *Public Opinion Quarterly* 48 (1): 283–300.

Gerbner, George, Larry Gross, Michael Morgan, Nancy Signorielli, and James Shanahan. 2002. "Growing Up with Television: Cultivation Processes." Pp. 43–68 in *Media Effects: Advances in Theory and Research*, edited by Jennings Bryant and Dolf Zillmann. Mahwah, NJ: Lawrence Earlbaum Associates.

Gerbner, George, Hamid Mowlana, and Kaarle Nordenstreng, eds. 1993. *The Global Media Debate: Its Rise, Fall, and Renewal*. Norwood, NJ: Ablex.

Gianatasio, David. 2013. "Hunkvertising: The Objectification of Men in Advertising." *Adweek*. October 7 (http://www.adweek.com/brand-marketing/hunkvertising-objectification-men-advertising-152925/).

Gil de Zúñiga, Homero, Victor Garcia-Perdomo, and Shannon C. McGregor. 2015. "What Is Second Screening? Exploring Motivations of Second Screen Use and Its Effect on Online Political Participation." *Journal of Communication* 65 (5): 793–815.

Gilens, Martin. 1996. "Race and Poverty in America: Public Misperceptions and the American News Media." *Public Opinion Quarterly* 60 (4): 515–541.

Gillespie, Tarleton, Pablo J. Boczkowski, and Kirsten A. Foot. 2014. "Introduction." Pp. 1–18 in *Media Technologies: Essays on Communication, Materiality, and Society*, edited by Tarleton Gillespie, Pablo J. Boczkowski, and Kirsten A. Foot. Cambridge, MA: MIT Press

Ginsborg, Paul. 2005. *Silvio Berlusconi: Television, Power and Patrimony*. London, UK: Verso.

Gitlin, Todd. 1978. "Media Sociology: The Dominant Paradigm." *Theory and Society* 6(2): 205–253.

———. 1980. *The Whole World Is Watching: Mass Media in the Making and Unmaking of the New Left*. Berkeley, CA: University of California.

———. 2000. *Inside Prime Time*. Berkeley, CA: University of California Press.

Giuffrida, Angela. 2017. "Silvio Berlusconi Takes Public Office Ban to Human Rights Court." *The Guardian*, November 22 (https://www.theguardian.com/world/2017/nov/22/silvio-berlusconi-appeal-against-public-office-ban-reaches-echr).

GLAAD (Gay & Lesbian Alliance Against Defamation). 2018. "Where We Are on TV: '17–'18." (https://www.glaad.org/whereweareontv17).

Glascock, Jack. 2001. "Gender Roles on Prime-Time Network Television: Demographics and Behaviors." *Journal of Broadcasting & Electronic Media* 45 (4): 656–669.

Glaser, April. 2017. "Political Ads on Facebook Now Need to Say Who Paid for Them." *Slate*. December 18 (http://www.slate.com/blogs/future_tense/2017/12/18/political_ads_on_facebook_now_need_to_say_who_paid_for_them.html).

GMMP (Global Media Monitoring Project). 2010. *Who Makes the News?* World Association for Christian Communication. Retrieved November 6, 2010 (http://www.whomakesthenews.org/gmmp-2010-reports.html).

———. 2015. *Who Makes the News.* World Association of Christian Communication (http://whomakesthenews.org/gmmp-2015).

Goffman, Erving. 1974. *Frame Analysis.* New York, NY: Harper & Row.

Goldfarb, Jeffrey. 1991. *The Cynical Society.* Chicago, IL: University of Chicago Press.

Goldsmith, Jack, and Tim Wu. 2008. *Who Controls the Internet?* New York, NY: Oxford University Press.

Gonzalez, Juan, and Joseph Torres. 2011. *News for All the People: The Epic Story of Race and the American Media.* Brooklyn, NY: Verso.

Goodman, Amy, with David Goodman. 2004. *The Exception to the Rulers.* New York, NY: Hyperion.

Google. 2018a. "Google Fiber." (https://fiber.google.com/about/).

———. 2018b. "Google Station." (https://station.google.com/).

———. 2018c. "Our Offices." (https://www.google.com/about/locations).

———. 2018d. "Project Fi." (https://fi.google.com/about/).

———. 2018e. "Project Loon." (https://x.company/loon/).

Gordon, Janey. 2008. "Community Radio, Funding and Ethics. The UK and Australian Models." Pp. 59–79 in *Notions of Community. A Collection of Community Media Debates and Dilemmas*, edited by Janey Gordon. New York: Peter Lang.

Gottfried, Jeffrey, and Elisa Shearer. 2016. *News Use across Social Media Platforms 2016.* Pew Research Center (http://assets.pewresearch.org/wp-content/uploads/sites/13/2016/05/PJ_2016.05.26_social-media-and-news_FINAL-1.pdf).

Graber, Doris A. 2009. *Mass Media and American Politics.* 8th ed. Washington, DC: Congressional Quarterly Press.

Graber, Doris A., and Johanna Dunaway. 2018. *Mass Media and American Politics.* Thousand Oaks, CA: Sage.

Graham, Roderick, and Shawn Smith. 2016. "The Content of Our #Characters: Black Twitter as Counterpublic." *Sociology of Race and Ethnicity* 2 (4): 433–449.

Gramsci, Antonio. 1928/1971. *Selections from the Prison Notebooks.* New York, NY: International Publishers.

Grasmuck, Sherri, Jason Martin, and Shanyang Zhao. 2009. "Ethno-racial Identity Displays on Facebook." *Journal of Computer-mediated Communication* 15 (1): 158–188.

Graves, Lucia. 2017. "This Is Sinclair, 'The Most Dangerous U.S. Company You've Never Heard of.'" *The Guardian.* August 17 (https://www.theguardian.com/media/2017/aug/17/sinclair-news-media-fox-trump-white-house-circa-breitbart-news).

Gray, Herman. 1989. "Television, Black Americans, and the American Dream." *Critical Studies in Mass Communication* 16 (6): 376–386.

———. 2004. *Watching Race: Television and the Struggle for Blackness.* Minneapolis: University of Minnesota Press.

———. 2015. "The Feel of Life: Resonance, Race, and Representation." *International Journal of Communication* 9: 1108–1119.

Gray, Jonathan. 2007. "Imagining America: *The Simpsons* Go Global." *Popular Communication* 5 (2): 129–148.

Gray, Jonathan, Cornel Sandvoss, and C. Lee Harrington, eds. 2017. *Fandom: Identities and Communities in a Mediated World.* New York, NY: New York University.

Greco, Albert N., Clara E. Rodriguez, and Robert M. Wharton. 2007. *The Culture and Commerce of Publishing in the 21st Century.* Stanford, CA: Stanford University Press.

Greenberg, Bradley S., and Jeffrey E. Brand. 1994. "Minorities and the Mass Media: 1970s to 1990s." Pp. 273–314 in *Media Effects: Advances in Theory and Research*, edited by Jennings Bryant and Dolf Zillman. Hillsdale, NJ: Lawrence Erlbaum.

Greenberg, Bradley S., and Tracy R. Worrell. 2007. "New Faces on Television: A 12-Season Replication." *The Howard Journal of Communications* 18: 277–290.

Gregory, Julia. 2017. "Press Association Wins Google Grant to Run News Service Written by Computers." *The Guardian*. July 6 (https://www.theguardian.com/technology/2017/jul/06/press-association-wins-google-grant-to-run-news-service-written-by-computers).

Greider, William. 1992. *Who Will Tell the People: The Betrayal of American Democracy*. New York, NY: Simon & Schuster.

Griffith, Erin. 2017. "Memo to Facebook: How to Tell if You're a Media Company." *Wired*. October 12 (https://www.wired.com/story/memo-to-facebook-how-to-tell-if-youre-a-media-company/).

Gross, Larry. 2001. *Up from Invisibility*. New York, NY: Columbia University Press.

Gross, Terry. 2018. "After 16 Years, Afghanistan War Is 'at Best a Grinding Stalemate,' Journalist Says." *Fresh Air*. National Public Radio. February 6 (https://www.npr.org/2018/02/06/583625482/after-16-years-afghanistan-war-is-at-best-a-grinding-stalemate-journalist-says).

Grynbaum, Michael M. 2017. "Trump Calls the News Media the 'Enemy of the American People.'" *New York Times*. February 17 (https://www.nytimes.com/2017/02/17/business/trump-calls-the-news-media-the-enemy-of-the-people.html).

Grynbaum, Michael M. 2018. "Trump Renews Pledge to 'Take a Strong Look' at Libel Laws." *New York Times*. January 10 (https://www.nytimes.com/2018/01/10/business/media/trump-libel-laws.html).

Guardian, The. 2010. "WikiLeaks Embassy Cables: The Key Points at a Glance." November 29 (https://www.theguardian.com/world/2010/nov/29/wikileaks-embassy-cables-key-points).

Gunter, Barrie. 2014. "Pornography and Sexualization." Pp. 172–196 in *Media and the Sexualization of Childhood*. New York, NY: Routledge.

Hafner, Katie, and Matthew Lyon. 1996. *Where Wizards Stay Up Late: The Origins of the Internet*. New York, NY: Simon & Schuster.

Hall, Stuart. 1973/1980. "Encoding/Decoding." Pp. 128–38 in *Culture, Media, Language: Working Papers in Cultural Studies, 1972–79*, edited by Centre for Contemporary Cultural Studies. London, UK: Hutchinson.

———. 1997. "The Work of Representation." Pp. 13–74 in *Representation: Cultural Representations and Signifying Practices*, edited by Stuart Hall. Thousand Oaks, CA: Sage.

———. 1982. "The Rediscovery of 'Ideology': Return of the Repressed in Media Studies." Pp. 56–90 in *Culture, Society, and the Media*, edited by Michael Gurevitch, Tony Bennett, James Curran, and Janet Woollacott. London, UK: Routledge Kegan Paul.

Hall, Stuart, Jessica Evans, and Sean Nixon, eds. 2013. *Representation: Cultural Representations and Signifying Practices*. London: Sage.

Hamm, Bernd, and Russell Smandych, eds. 2005. *Cultural Imperialism*. Toronto, ON: University of Toronto Press.

Hampton, Keith N., Lee Rainie, Weixu L, Maria Dwyer, Inyoung Shin, and Kristen Purcell. 2014. "Social Media and the 'Spiral of Silence.'" Washington, DC: Pew Research Center (http://www.pewinternet.org/2014/08/26/social-media-and-the-spiral-of-silence/).

Hardt, Hanno. 2001. *Social Theories of the Press: Constituents of Communication Research, 1840s to 1920s*. Lanham, MD: Rowman & Littlefield.

Hargittai, Eszter. 2001. "Second-Level Digital Divide: Mapping Differences in People's Online Skills." (arXiv preprint cs/0109068).

Hargittai, Eszter, and Gina Walejko. 2008. "The Participation Divide: Content Creation and Sharing in the Digital Age." *Information, Communication & Society* 11 (2): 239–256.

Harold, Christine. 2004. "Pranking Rhetoric: Culture Jamming as Media Activism." *Critical Studies in Media Communication* 21 (3): 189–211.

Hartley, John. 1987. "Invisible Fictions: Television Audiences, Paedocracy, Pleasure." *Textual Practice* 1 (2): 121–138.

Hartman, Andrew. 2015. *A War for the Soul of America: A History of the Culture Wars*. Chicago: University of Chicago Press.

Hepp, Andreas, Stig Hjarvard, and Knut Lundby. 2015. "Mediatization: Theorizing the Interplay between Media, Culture and Society." *Media, Culture & Society* 37 (2) 314–324.

Herman, Edward, and Noam Chomsky. 2002. *Manufacturing Consent: The Political Economy of Mass Media*. New York, NY: Pantheon.

Hermida, Alfred. 2011. "Mechanisms of Participation: How Audience Options Shape the Conversation." Pp. 13–33 in *Participatory Journalism: Guarding Open Gates at Online Newspapers*, edited by Singer Jane B., Hermida A, Domingo D., et al. Malden, MA: Wiley-Blackwell.

Herrman, John. 2017. "How Hate Groups Forced Online Platforms to Reveal Their True Nature." *New York Times Magazine*. August 21 (https://www.nytimes.com/2017/08/21/magazine/how-hate-groups-forced-online-platforms-to-reveal-their-true-nature.html).

Hibberd, Matthew. 2008. *The Media in Italy: Press, Cinema and Broadcasting from Unification to Digital*. New York, NY: Open University Press.

Hickey, Neil. 1995. "Revolution in Cyberia." *Columbia Journalism Review*. July/August, pp. 40–47.

Higgins, Andrew, Mike McIntire, and Gabriel J.X. Dance. 2016. "Inside a Fake News Sausage Factory: 'This Is All about Income.'" *New York Times*. November 25 (https://www.nytimes.com/2016/11/25/world/europe/fake-news-donald-trump-hillary-clinton-georgia.html).

Highland, Tim, Stephen Harrington, and Axel Bruns. 2013. "Twitter as a Technology or Audiencing and Fandom: The #Eurovision Phenomenon." *Information, Communication & Society* 16 (3): 315–339.

Hillis, Ken, Michael Petit, and Kylie Jarrett. 2012. *Google and the Culture of Search*. New York, NY: Routledge.

Hills, Jill. 1991. *The Democracy Gap: The Politics of Information and Communication Technologies in the United States and Europe*. New York, NY: Greenwood.

Hindman, Elizabeth Blanks, and Ryan J. Thomas. 2016. "When Old and New Media Collide: The Case of WikiLeaks." *New Media & Society* 16 (4): 541–558.

Hindman, Matthew. 2009. *The Myth of Digital Democracy*. Princeton, NJ: Princeton University Press.

Hintz, Arne. 2011. "Dimensions of Policy Change: Mapping Community Media Policy in Latin America." *Canadian Journal of Communication* 36: 147–159.

Hirsch, Mario, and Vibeke G. Petersen. 1992. "Regulation of Media at the European Level." Pp. 42–56 in *Dynamics of Media Politics: Broadcast and Electronic Media in Western Europe*, edited by Kareen Siune and Wolfgang Truetzschler. London, UK: Sage.

Hitland, Paul, Kenneth Olmstead, and Skye Toor. 2017. "Public Comments to the Federal Communications Commission about Net Neutrality Contain Many Inaccuracies and Duplicates." Pew Research Center. October 29 (http://www.pewinternet.org/2017/11/29/public-comments-to-the-federal-communications-commission-about-net-neutrality-contain-many-inaccuracies-and-duplicates/).

Hjarvard, Stig. 2008. "The Mediatization of Society." *Nordicom Review* 29 (2): 105–132.

Ho, Karen K. 2017. "Diversity in Newsrooms Has Been Bad for Decades and It Probably Won't Get Better: Study." *Columbia Journalism Review*. August 16 (https://www.cjr.org/business_of_news/diversity-newsrooms-asne-study.php).

Hoerder, Dirk, and Christiane Harzig. 1987. *The Immigrant Labor Press in North America, 1840s–1970s*. Westport, CT: Greenwood Press.

Hoggart, Riahcard. 1957/2017. *The Uses of Literacy*. New York, NY: Routledge.

Holsti, Ole R. 1969. *Content Analysis for the Social Sciences and Humanities*. Reading, MA: Addison-Wesley.

Hout, Michael. 2007. "How Class Works in Popular Conception: Most Americans Identify with the Class Their Income, Occupation, and Education Implies for Them." Survey Research Center. *University of California, Berkeley* (http://ucdata.berkeley.edu/rsfcensus/papers/Hout-ClassIDJan07.pdf).

Howard, Philip N., Gillian Bolsover, Bence Kollanyi, Samantha Bradshaw, and Lisa-Maria Neudert. 2017.

"Junk News and Bots during the U.S. Election: What Were Michigan Voters Sharing over Twitter?" Data Memo 2017.1. Oxford, UK: Project on Computational Propaganda (http://comprop.oii.ox.ac.uk/research/working-papers/junk-news-and-bots-during-the-u-s-election-what-were-michigan-voters-sharing-over-twitter/).

Howard, Philip, and Muzammi Hussain. 2013. *Democracy's Fourth Wave? Digital Media and the Arab Spring*. New York: Oxford University Press.

Hoynes, William. 1994. *Public Television for Sale: Media, the Market, and the Public Sphere*. Boulder, CO: Westview.

Hughes, Thomas. 1983. *Networks of Power: Electrification in Western Society, 1880–1930*. Baltimore, MD: Johns Hopkins University Press.

Hughey, Matthew W. 2008. "Virtual (Br)others and (Re)sisters: Authentic Black Fraternity and Sorority Identity on the Internet." *Journal of Contemporary Ethnography* 37 (5): 528–560.

Hunt, Darnell M. 1997. *Screening the Los Angeles "Riots": Race, Seeing and Resistance*. New York: Cambridge University Press.

———. 2013. "Writers Guild of America—West 2013 Staff Briefing." Retrieved July 19, 2013 (http://www.wga.org/uploadedFiles/who_we_are/tvstaffing brief2013.pdf).

———. 2016. "The 2016 Hollywood Writers Report: Renaissance in Reverse?" Writers Guild of America, West (http://www.wga.org/uploadedFiles/who_we_are/HWR16.pdf).

Hunter, James Davison. 1991. *Culture Wars*. New York: Basic Books.

Hunter, James Davison, and Alan Wolfe. 2006. *Is There a Culture War?* Washington, DC: Brookings Institution Press.

Huntington, Samuel. 1996. *The Clash of Civilizations and the Remaking of World Order*. New York, NY: Touchstone.

Husseini, Sam. 1994. "NBC Brings Good Things to GE." *Extra!*. November/December, p. 13.

IBISWorld. 2017. Television Production in the US: Market Research Report. July (https://www.ibisworld.com/industry-trends/market-research-reports/information/motion-picture-sound-recording-industries/television-production.html).

ICAAN (Internet Corporation for Assigned Names and Numbers). 2018. "Beginner's Guides." (https://www.icann.org/resources/pages/beginners-guides-2012-03-06-en).

IFPI (International Federation of the Phonographic Industry). 2017a. "Connecting with Music." (http://www.ifpi.org/downloads/Music-Consumer-Insight-Report-2017.pdf).

———. 2017b. "Global Statistics." (http://www.ifpi.org/global-statistics.php).

iHeartMedia. 2018 (http://iheartmedia.com/iheart media/index).

Indymedia.org. 2018. About Indymedia (https://www.indymedia.org/or/static/about.shtml).

Ingram, Matthew. 2017. "Google and Facebook Account for Nearly All Growth in Digital Ads." *Fortune*, April 26 (http://fortune.com/2017/04/26/google-facebook-digital-ads/).

Intelligence Community Assessment. 2017. "Assessing Russian Activities and Intentions in Recent US Elections." January 6 (https://www.dni.gov/files/documents/ICA_2017_01.pdf).

Internet Governance Forum. 2018. "About the IGF." (https://www.intgovforum.org/multilingual/tags/about).

Internet World Stats. 2018. "Internet Usage Statistics (https://www.internetworldstats.com/stats.htm).

Isaac, Mike. 2018. "Facebook Overhauls News Feed to Focus on What Friends and Family Share." *New York Times*. January 11 (https://www.nytimes.com/2018/01/11/technology/facebook-news-feed.html).

Iyengar, Shanto. 1991. *Is Anyone Responsible? How Television Frames Political Issues*. Chicago, IL: University of Chicago Press.

Iyengar, Shanto, and Donald R. Kinder. 2010. *News That Matters: Television and American Opinion*. Updated ed. Chicago, IL: University of Chicago Press.

Jackson, Janine. 2014. "14th Annual Fear and Favor Review." FAIR. February (https://fair.org/extra/14th-annual-fear-and-favor-review/).

Jackson, Linda A., and Kelly S. Ervin. 1991. "The Frequency and Portrayal of Black Families in Fashion Advertisement." *Journal of Black Psychology* 18 (1): 67–70.

Jacobs, Matthew. 2013. "LGBT Milestones in Pop Culture: The Watershed Moments That Got Us Where We Are Today." *Huffington Post*. Retrieved July 20, 2013 (http://www.huffingtonpost.com/2013/06/13/lgbt-milestones-in-pop-culture_n_3429832.html).

Jakubowicz, Andrew, et al. 2017. *Cyber Racism and Community Resilience: Strategies for Combating Online Race Hate*. New York: Springer.

Jeffords, Susan. 1989. *The Remasculinization of America*. Bloomington, IN: Indiana University Press.

Jeffords, Susan, and Lauren Rabinovitz, eds. 1994. *Seeing through the Media: The Persian Gulf War*. New Brunswick, NJ: Rutgers University Press.

Jenkins, Henry. 2002. "Cyberspace and Race." *Technology Review* (http://www.technologyreview.com/web/12797/).

———. 2006. *Convergence Culture: Where Old and New Media Collide*. New York, NY: New York University Press.

———. 2009. *Confronting the Challenges of Participatory Culture: Media Education for the 21st Century*. Cambridge, MA: MIT Press.

———. 2012. *Textual Poachers: Television Fans and Participatory Culture*, 2nd ed. New York: Routledge.

Jenkins, Henry, Sam Ford, and Joshua Green. 2013. *Spreadable Media*. New York, NY: New York University Press.

Jermyn, Deborah, and Su Holmes. 2006. "The Audience Is Dead: Long Live the Audience! Interactivity, 'Telephilia' and the Contemporary Television Audience." *Critical Ideas in Television Studies* 1 (1), 49–57.

Jessell, Harry A. 1993. "Networks Victorious in Fin-Syn Fight." *Broadcasting and Cable*. April 5, pp. 7, 10.

Jordan, Tim. 2008. *Hacking*. Malden, MA: Polity Press.

Johnson, Austin H. 2016. Transnormativity: A New Concept and Its Validation through Documentary Film about Transgender Men. *Sociological Inquiry* 86 (4): 465–491.

Johnson, Kirk. 2018. "As Low-Power Local Radio Rises, Tiny Voices Become a Collective Shout." *New York Times*. January 6 (https://www.nytimes.com/2018/01/06/us/low-power-radio.html).

Johnson-Cartee, Karen S. 2005. *News Narratives and News Framing*. Lanham, MD: Rowman and Littlefield.

Jones, Alex. 2009. *Losing the News: The Future of the News That Feeds Democracy*. New York, NY: Oxford University Press, 2009.

Jones, Jason J., Robert M. Bond, Eytan Bakshy, Dean Eckles, and James H. Fowler. 2016. "Social Influence and Political Mobilization: Further Evidence from a Randomized Experiment in the 2012 U.S. Presidential Election." *PLoS ONE* 12 (4): e0173851.

Josey, Christopher L., Ryan J. Hurley, Veronica Hefner, and Travis L. Dixon. 2009. "Online News and Race: A Content Analysis of the Portrayal of Stereotypes in a New Media Environment." Pp. 135–142 in *Race/Gender/Media: Considering Diversity across Audiences, Content, and Producers*, edited by Rebecca Ann Lind. New York, NY: Pearson.

Jost, Kenneth. 1994a. "The Future of Television." *CQ Researcher*. 4: 1131–1148.

Kahle, Shannon, Nan Yu, and Erin Whiteside. 2007. "Another Disaster: An Examination of Portrayals of Race in Hurricane Katrina Coverage." *Visual Communication Quarterly* 14 (Spring): 75–89.

Kahn, Frank J., ed. 1978. *Documents of American Broadcasting*. 3rd ed. Englewood Cliffs, NJ: Prentice Hall.

Kahn, Richard, and Douglas Kellner. 2004. "New Media and Internet Activism: From the 'Battle of Seattle' to Blogging." *New Media & Society* 6 (1): 87–95.

Kalogeropoulos, Antonis, and Nic Newman. 2017. "'I Saw the News on Facebook': Brand Attribution When

Accessing News from Distributed Environments." University of Oxford: Reuters Institute for the Study of Journalism (http://reutersinstitute.politics.ox.ac.uk/sites/default/files/2017-07/Brand%20attributions%20report.pdf).

Kane, John V., and Benjamin J. Newman. 2017. "Organized Labor as the New Undeserving Rich?: Mass Media, Class-based Anti-union Rhetoric and Public Support for Unions in the United States." *British Journal of Political Science* 1: 30. doi:10.1017/S000712341700014X.

Kang, Cecilia, and Kevin Roose. 2018. "Zuckerberg Faces Hostile Congress as Calls for Regulation Mount." *The New York Times.* April 11 (https://www.nytimes.com/2018/04/11/business/zuckerberg-facebook-congress.html).

Kantrowitz, Alex. 2017. "Google Allowed Advertisers to Target 'Jewish Parasite,' 'Black People Ruin Everything.'" *BuzzFeed.* September 15 (https://www.buzzfeed.com/alexkantrowitz/google-allowed-advertisers-to-target-jewish-parasite-black).

Karr, Alphonse. 1849. *Les Guêpes.* Paris: Michael Levy Frères (https://archive.org/details/lesgupes06karruoft).

Karr, Tim. 2010. "Obama FCC Caves on Net Neutrality—Tuesday Betrayal Assured." The Blog (Huffington Post) (https://www.huffingtonpost.com/timothy-karr/obama-fcc-caves-on-net-ne_b_799435.html).

———. 2017. "Net Neutrality Violations: A Brief History." *Free Press* (https://www.freepress.net/blog/2017/04/25/net-neutrality-violations-brief-history).

Kasser, Tim, and Susan Linn. 2016. "Growing Up under Corporate Capitalism: The Problem of Marketing to Children, with Suggestions for Policy Solutions." *Social Issues and Policy Review* 10 (1): 122–150.

Kastrenakes, Jacob. 2017. "EU Says It'll Pass Online Hate Speech Laws if Facebook, Google, and Others Don't Crack Down." *The Verge.* September 28 (https://www.theverge.com/2017/9/28/16380526/eu-hate-speech-laws-google-facebook-twitter).

Katz, Elihu, and Paul Lazarsfeld. 1955. *Personal Influence.* New Brunswick, NJ: Transaction.

Katz, Mark. 2010. *Capturing Sound: How Technology Changed Music.* Berkeley, CA: University of California Press.

———. 2012. "Sound Recording: Introduction." Pp. 11–28 in *Music, Sound, and Technology in America: A Documentary History of Early Phonograph, Cinema, and Radio,* edited by Timothy D. Taylor, Mark Katz, and Tony Grajeda. Durham, NC: Duke University Press.

Kelley, Robin D. G. 1994. *Race Rebels.* New York: Free Press.

Kellner, Douglas. 1990. *Television and the Crisis of Democracy.* Boulder, CO: Westview.

———. 2018. "Donald Trump and the Politics of Lying." Pp. 89–100 in *Post-Truth, Fake News,* edited by Michael Peters, Sharon Rider, Mats Hyvönen, Tina Besley. Springer.

Kendall, Diana. 2011. *Framing Class: Media Representation of Wealth and Poverty in America.* Lanham, MD: Rowman & Littlefield.

Keohane, Joe. 2017. "What News-Writing Bots Mean for the Future of Journalism. *Wired.*" February 16 (https://www.wired.com/2017/02/robots-wrote-this-story/).

Kian, Edward M., Michael Mondello, and John Vincent. 2009. "ESPN—The Women's Sports Network? A Content Analysis of Internet Coverage of March Madness." *Journal of Broadcasting & Electronic Media* 53 (3): 477–495.

Kim, Youna. 2005. "Experiencing Globalization: Global TV, Reflexivity and the Lives of Young People." *International Journal of Cultural Studies.* 8 (4): 445–463.

King, Claire Sisco. 2010. "The Man Inside: Trauma, Gender, and the Nation in *The Brave One.*" *Critical Studies in Media Communication* 27 (2): 111–130.

Kirst, Seamus. 2016. "#OscarsSoWhite: A 10-point Plan for Change by the Hashtag's Creator." *The Guardian.* February 25 (https://www.theguardian.com/film/2016/feb/25/oscarssowhite-10-point-plan-hashtag-academy-awards-april-reign).

Klapper, Joseph. 1960. *The Effects of Mass Communication.* Glencoe, IL: Free Press.

Klein, Hugh, and Kenneth S. Shiffman. 2009. "Underrepresentation and Symbolic Annihilation of Socially Disenfranchised Groups ('Out Groups') in Animated Cartoons." *The Howard Journal of Communications* 20: 55–72.

Klinenberg, Eric. 2005. "Convergence: News Production in a Digital Age." *Annals of the American Academy of Political and Social Science* 597(January): 48–64.

———. 2007. *Fighting for Air: The Battle to Control America's Media*. New York: Metropolitan Books.

Koblin, John. 2017. "Netflix Says It Will Spend up to $8 Billion on Content Next Year." *New York Times*. October 16 (https://www.nytimes.com/2017/10/16/business/media/netflix-earnings.html).

Kohut, Andrew. 2000. "Self Censorship: Counting the Ways." *Columbia Journalism Review*. May/June, p. 42.

Kornhauser, William. 1959. *The Politics of Mass Society*. New York: Free Press.

Kosar, Kevin R. 2012. "Congressional Oversight of Agency Public Communications: Implications of Agency New Media Use." *Washington, DC: Congressional Research Service* (http://www.fas.org/sgp/crs/misc/R42406.pdf).

Kostaki, Irene. 2017. "EU Ministers Agree to Raise 'Netflix Quota' to 30%." *New Europe*. May 23 (https://www.neweurope.eu/article/eu-council-raises-eu-content-netflix-quota-30/).

Kovach, Steve. 2017. "Facebook and the Rest of Big Tech Are Now Big Media, and It's Time We Start Treating Them That Way." *Business Insider*. October 14 (http://www.businessinsider.com/facebook-and-google-are-now-media-companies-2017-10).

Kovarik, Bill. 2016. *Revolutions in Communications: Media History from Gutenberg to the Digital Age*. New York, NY: Bloomsbury Academic.

Kraidy, Marwan M. 2005. *Hybridity, or the Cultural Logic of Globalization*. Philadelphia, PA: Temple University Press.

Kramer, Adam DI, Jamie E. Guillory, and Jeffrey T. Hancock. 2014. "Experimental Evidence of Massive-Scale Emotional Contagion through Social Networks." *Proceedings of the National Academy of Sciences* 111 (24): 8788–8790.

Krotz, Friedrich. 2007. *Mediatisierung: Fallstudien zum Wandel von Kommunikation*. [Mediatization: Case Studies on the Transformation of Communication.] Wiesbaden: VS Verlag für Socialwissenschaften.

Krugman, Dean M., and Leonard N. Reid. 1980. "The 'Public Interest' as Defined by FCC Policy Makers." *Journal of Broadcasting* 24: 311–323.

Kunz, William M. 2009. "Prime-Time Television Program Ownership in a Post-Fin/Syn World." *Journal of Broadcasting & Electronic Media* 53 (4): 636–651.

Kuo, Rachel. 2016. "Racial Justice Activist Hashtags: Counterpublics and Discourse Circulation." *New Media & Society* 20 (2): 495—514.

Kurtulus, Sema, Erdem Özkan, and Selen Öztürk. 2015. "How Do Social Media Users in Turkey Differ in Terms of Their Use Habits and Preferences?" *International Journal of Business and Information* 10 (3): 337–364.

Labaton, Stephen. 2000. "F. C. C. Heads for Showdown with Congress over Radio Plan." *New York Times*. March 26, p. C1.

Lacan, Jacques. 1977. *Écrits: A Selection*. New York, NY: Norton.

Laing, David. 1986. "The Music Industry and the 'Cultural Imperialism' Thesis." *Popular Music and Society* 8: 331–41.

Lanchester, John. 2017. "You Are the Product." *London Review of Books* 39 (16): 3–10.

Langlois, Andrea, and Frédéric Dubois, eds. 2005. *Autonomous Media: Activating Resistance & Dissent*. Montréal, QB: Cumulus Press.

Lanier, Jaron. 2013. *Who Owns the Future?* New York, NY: Simon & Schuster.

Laposky, Issie. 2017a. "How Bots Broke The FCC's Public Comment System." *Wired*. November 28 (https://www.wired.com/story/bots-broke-fcc-public-comment-system/).

———. 2017b. "What Did Cambridge Analytica Really Do for Trump's Campaign?" *Wired*. October 26 (https://www.wired.com/story/what-did-cambridge-analytica-really-do-for-trumps-campaign/).

Lau, Richard R., David J. Andersen, Tessa M. Ditonto, Mona S. Kleinberg, and David P. Redlawsk. 2017. "Effect of Media Environment Diversity and Advertising Tone on Information Search, Selective Exposure, and Affective Polarization." *Political Behavior* 39 (1): 231–255.

Lauzen, Martha M. 2018. "The Celluloid Ceiling: Behind-the-Scenes Employment of Women on the Top 100, 250, and 500 Films of 2017." San Diego State University: Center for the Study of Women in Television & Film (http://womenintvfilm.sdsu.edu/wp-content/uploads/2018/01/2017_Celluloid_Ceiling_Report.pdf).

Lauzen, Martha M., and David M. Dozier. 2005. "Recognition and Respect Revisited: Portrayals of Age and Gender in Prime-Time Television." *Mass Communication and Society* 8 (3): 241–256.

Lauzen, Martha M., David M. Dozier, and Nora Horan. 2008. "Constructing Gender Stereotypes through Social Roles in Prime-Time Television." *Journal of Broadcasting & Electronic Media* 52 (2): 200–214.

Lavery, David. 2006. "Introduction: Can This Be the End of Tony Soprano?" Pp. 1–14 in *Reading the Sopranos: Hit TV from HBO*, edited by David Lavery. London, UK: I.B. Tauris.

Lazarsfeld, Paul, Bernard Berelson, and Hazel Gaudet. 1944. *The People's Choice*. New York, NY: Duell, Sloan & Pearce.

———. 1948. *The People's Choice: How the Voter Makes up His Mind in a Presidential Campaign*. New York: Columbia University Press.

Le Bon, Gustave. 1896. *The Crowd: A Study of the Popular Mind*. New York, NY: The MacMillan Co.

Lecompte, Celeste. 2015. "Automation in the Newsroom." *Nieman Reports* 69 (3): 32–45.

Lee, Eric, and Benjamin Weinthal. 2011. "Trade unions: The Revolutionary Social Network at Play in Egypt and Tunisia." *Guardian*. February 10. Retrieved February 24, 2011 (http://www.guardian.co.uk/commentisfree/2011/feb/10/trade-unions-egypt-tunisia).

Lee, Latoya A. 2017. "Black Twitter: A Response to Bias in Mainstream Media." *Social Sciences* 6 (1): 26.

Lee, Sangoak. 2007. "A Longitudinal Analysis of Foreign Program Imports on South Korean Television, 1978–2002: A Case of Rising Indigenous Capacity in Program Supply." *Journal of Broadcasting & Electronic Media* 51 (1): 172–187.

Lee-Won, Roselyn J., Tiffany N. White, and Bridget Potocki. 2017. "The Black Catalyst to Tweet: The Role of Discrimination Experience, Group Identification, and Racial Agency in Black Americans' Instrumental Use of Twitter." *Information, Communication & Society* 21 (8): 1–19.

Leonhardt, David, and Stuart Thompson. 2017. "Trump's Lies." December 17. *New York Times* (https://www.nytimes.com/interactive/2017/06/23/opinion/trumps-lies.html).

Lessig, Lawrence. 2005. *Free Culture: The Nature and Future of Creativity*. New York: Penguin.

Leveson Inquiry, The. 2012. "An Inquiry into the Culture, Practices, and Ethics of the Press: Executive Summary." November. London: The Stationary Office.

Levin, Gary. 2017a. "Nielsen Reveals: Who's Watching What on Netflix." *USA Today*. October 18 (https://www.usatoday.com/story/life/tv/2017/10/18/nielsen-reveals-whos-watching-what-netflix/773447001/).

———. 2017b. "Who's Watching What: TV Shows Ranked by Racial and Ethnic groups." *USA Today*. June 27 (https://www.usatoday.com/story/life/tv/2017/06/27/whos-watching-what-tv-shows-ranked-racial-and-ethnic-groups/103199848/).

Levine, Elana. 2001. "Toward a Paradigm for Media Production Research: Behind the Scenes at *General Hospital*." *Critical Studies in Media Communication* 18 (1): 66–82.

Levy, Steven. 2010. *Hackers: Heroes of the Computer Revolution*, 25th anniversary ed. Cambridge, MA: O'Reilly.

Lewis, Lisa. 1990. *Gender Politics and MTV*. Philadelphia, PA: Temple University Press.

Lewis, Paul. 2017. "'Our Minds Can Be Hijacked': The Tech Insiders Who Fear a Smartphone Dystopia." *The Guardian*. October 6 (https://www.theguardian.com/technology/2017/oct/05/smartphone-addiction-silicon-valley-dystopia?CMP=share_btn_tw).

Liacas, Tom. 2005. "101 Tricks to Play with the Mainstream: Culture Jamming as Subversive Recreation." Pp. 61–74 in *Autonomous Media: Activating Resistance and Dissent*, edited by Andrea Langlois and Frédréric Dubois. Montréal, QB: Cumulus Press.

Licklider, J.C.R. 1960. "Man-Computer Symbiosis." Pp. 73–82 in *The New Media Reader*, edited by Noah Wardrip-Fruin and Nick Montfort (2003). Cambridge, MA: MIT Press.

Licklider, J.C.R., and Robert W. Taylor. 1968. "The Computer as a Communication Device." Pp. 21–41 in "In Memoriam: J. C. R. Licklider 1915–1990," edited by Robert W. Taylor. Digital Systems Research Center (http://memex.org/licklider.pdf).

Liebes, Tamar, and Elihu Katz. 1993. *The Export of Meaning*. Cambridge, MA: Polity.

Lievrouw, Leah A. 2011. *Alternative and Activist New Media*. Malden, MA: Polity.

———. 2014. "Materiality and Media in Communication and Technology Studies: An Unfinished Project." Pp. 21–51 in *Media Technologies: Essays on Communication, Materiality, and Society*, edited by Tarleton Gillespie, Pablo J. Boczkowski, and Kirsten A. Foot. Cambridge, MA: MIT Press.

Lievrouw, Leah A., and Sonia Livingstone, eds. 2006. *Handbook of New Media. Social Shaping and Social Consequences of ICTs*. London, UK: Sage.

Lind, Rebecca Ann. 2017. *Race and Gender in Electronic Media*. New York, NY: Routledge.

Lind, Rebecca, and James A. Danowski. 1998. "The Representation of Arabs in U.S. Electronic Media." Pp. 157–168 in *Cultural Diversity and the U.S. Media*, edited by Yahya R. Kamalipour and Theresa Carilli. Albany, NY: SUNY Press.

Lippmann, Walter. 1922. *Public Opinion*. New York, NY: Harcourt Brace and Company.

Lister, Martin, Jon Dovey, Seth Giddings, Iain Grant, and Kieran Kelly. 2009. *New Media: A Critical Introduction*. 2nd ed. New York, NY: Routledge.

Little, Vance. 2008. "Audiovisual Media Services Directive: Europe's Modernization of Broadcast Services Regulations." *Journal of Law, Technology & Policy* 1: 223–236.

Livingstone, Sonia. 2013. "The Participation Paradigm in Audience Research." *The Communication Review* 16 (1–2): 21–30.

———. 2015. "Active Audiences? The Debate Progresses But Is Far from Resolved." *Communication Theory* 25: 439–446.

Loeb, Laura. 2015. "The Celebrity Talk Show: Norms and Practices." *Discourse, Context, and Media* 10: 27–35.

Long, Elizabeth. 1985. *The American Dream and the Popular Novel*. Boston, MA: Routledge Kegan Paul.

Longley, Lawrence, Herbert Terry, and Erwin Krasnow. 1983. "Citizen Groups in Broadcast Regulatory Policy-Making." *Policy Studies Journal* 12: 258–270.

Lopes, Paul D. 1992. "Innovation and Diversity in the Popular Music Industry, 1969 to 1990." *American Sociological Review* 57: 56–71.

Lopez, Lori Kido. 2011. "Fan Activists and the Politics of Race in *The Last Airbender*." *International Journal of Cultural Studies* 15 (5): 431–445.

Louw, Eric P. 2010. *The Media and the Political Process*. 2nd ed. Thousand Oaks, CA: Sage.

Lovink, Geert. 2013. "A World Beyond Facebook: Introduction to the Unlike Us Reader." Pp. 9–16 in *Unlike Us Reader: Social Media Monopolies and Their Alternatives*, edited by Geert Lovink and Miriam Rasch, eds. Amsterdam: Institute of Network Cultures.

Lubet, Alex. 2017. "Playing It Safe: A Brief History of Lip-Synching." *The Conversation*. January 11 (https://theconversation.com/playing-it-safe-a-brief-history-of-lip-syncing-70888).

Lubken, Deborah. 2008. "Remembering the Straw Man: The Travels and Adventures of Hypodermic." Pp. 19–42 in *The History of Media and Communication Research*, edited by David W. Park & Jefferson Pooley. New York, NY: Peter Lang Publishing.

Lule, Jack. 2017. *Globalization and Media: Global Village of Babel*. Lanham, MD: Rowman & Littlefield.

Luther, Catherine A., Carolyn Ringer Lepre, and Naeemah Clark. 2018. *Diversity in U.S. Mass Media*. Malden, MA: John Wiley & Sons.

Lutz, Christoph, and Christian Pieter Hoffmann. 2017. "The Dark Side of Online Participation: Exploring Non-, Passive and Negative Participation." *Information, Communication & Society* 20 (6): 876–897.

MacBride Commission. 1980. *Many Voices, One World: Towards a New, More Just, and More Efficient World Information and Communication Order.* London, UK: Kogan Page. Retrieved December 9, 2010 (http://unesdoc.unesco.org/images/0004/000400/040066eb.pdf).

MacBride, Sean, and Colleen Roach. 1993. "The New International Information Order." Pp. 3–11 in *The Global Media Debate: Its Rise, Fall, and Renewal*, edited by George Gerbner, Hamid Mowlana, and Kaarle Nordenstreng. Norwood, NJ: Ablex.

Macek, Jakub. 2013. "More Than a Desire for Text: Online Participation and the Social Curation of Content." *Convergence* 19 (3): 295–302.

MacKenzie, Donald, and Judy Wajcman, eds. 1999. *The Social Shaping of Technology.* Philadelphia, PA: Open University Press.

Madrigal, Alexis C., and Adrienne Lafrance. 2014. "Net Neutrality: A Guide to (and History of) a Contested Idea." *Atlantic*. April 25 (https://www.theatlantic.com/technology/archive/2014/04/the-best-writing-on-net-neutrality/361237/).

Maheshwari, Sapna. 2017. "Different Ads, Different Ethnicities, Same Car." *New York Times*. October 12 (https://www.nytimes.com/interactive/2017/10/12/business/media/toyota-camry-ads-different-ethnicities.html).

Majoribanks, Tim. 2000. *News Corporations, Technology, and the Workplace.* Cambridge, UK: Cambridge University Press.

Manning, Jennifer E. 2018. "Membership of the 115th Congress: A Profile." Washington, DC: Congressional Research Service (https://www.senate.gov/CRSpubs/b8f6293e-c235-40fd-b895-6474d0f8e809.pdf).

Marchetti, Gina. 1989. "Action-Adventure as Ideology." Pp. 182–197 in *Cultural Politics in Contemporary America*, edited by Ian H. Angus and Sut Jhally. New York, NY: Routledge Kegan Paul.

Marconi, Francesco, Alex Siegman, and Machine Journalist. 2017. "The Future of Augmented Journalism." *AP Insights* (https://insights.ap.org/uploads/images/ap_insights_the_future_of_augmented_journalism.pdf).

Mares, Marie-Louise, and Valerie Kretz. 2015. "Media Effects on Children." Pp. 35–41 in *International Encyclopedia of the Social & Behavioral Sciences*, 2nd ed., Vol. 15. New York, NY: Elsevier.

Martin, Christopher. 2003. *Framed! Labor and the Corporate Media.* Ithaca, NY: ILR Press.

Mastro, Dana E., and Elizabeth Behm-Morawitz. 2005. "Latino Representation on Primetime Television." *Journalism & Mass Communication Quarterly* 82 (1): 110–130.

Matikainen, Janne. 2015. "Motivations for Content Generation in Social Media." *Participations: Journal of Audience & Reception Studies* 12 (1): 41–58.

Mattelart, Armand. 1979. *Multinational Corporations and the Control of Culture.* Atlantic Highlands, NJ: Humanities Press.

———. 2003. *The Information Society.* Thousand Oaks, CA: Sage.

Matwick, Kelsi, and Keri Matwick. 2015. "Inquiry in Television Cooking Shows." *Discourse & Communication* 9 (3): 313–330.

McAdam, Doug. 1982. *Political Process and the Development of Black Insurgency, 1930–1970.* Chicago, IL: University of Chicago Press.

McAllister, Matthew P., and Anna Aupperle. 2017. "Class Shaming in Post-Recession U.S. Advertising." *Journal of Communication Inquiry* 41 (2): 140–156.

McAllister, Matthew. P., and Kumanyika, Chenjerai. 2013. "'Brut Slaps . . . and Twins': Hypercommercialized Sports Media and the Intensification of Gender Ideology." Pp. 237–251 in *The Routledge Companion to Advertising and Promotional Culture*, edited by Matthew P. McAllister and Emily West. New York, NY: Routledge.

McChesney, Robert W. 1994. *Telecommunications, Mass Media, and Democracy.* New York, NY: Oxford University Press.

———. 1999. *Rich Media, Poor Democracy: Communications Politics in Dubious Times.* Urbana, IL: University of Illinois Press.

———. 2004. *The Problem of the Media: U.S. Communication Politics in the Twenty-First Century*. New York, NY: Monthly Review Press.

———. 2007. *Communication Revolution*. New York, NY: The New Press.

———. 2008. *The Political Economy of Media*. New York, NY: Monthly Review Press.

McChesney, Robert W., and Victor Pickard, eds. 2011. *Will the Last Reporter Please Turn out the Lights: The Collapse of Journalism and What Can Be Done to Fix It*. New York, NY: The New Press.

McClelland, Stephen. 2012. "Social Networks and the Second Screen." *Intermedia* 40 (3): 16–21.

McCombs, Maxwell E. 2014. *Setting the Agenda: The Mass Media and Public Opinion*. 2nd ed. Cambridge, UK: Polity.

McCombs, Maxwell, and Donald L. Shaw. 1972. "The Agenda-Setting Function of the Mass Media." *Public Opinion Quarterly* 36: 176–187.

———. 1977. *The Emergence of American Political Issues: The Agenda-Setting Function of the Press*. St. Paul, MN: West.

McConahay, John B. 1986. "Modern Racism, Ambivalence, and the Modern Racism Scale." Pp. 91–125 in *Prejudice, Discrimination, and Racism*, edited by John F. Dovidio and Samuel L. Gaertner. Orlando, FL: Academic Press.

McConnell, Ben. 2006. "The 1% Rule: Charting Citizen Participation." *Church of the Customer Blog*. Retrieved December 8, 2010 (http://customerevangelists.type pad.com/blog/2006/05/charting_wiki_p.html).

McCracken, Ellen. 1993. *Decoding Women's Magazines*. New York, NY: St. Martin's.

McDermott, Terry. 2010. "Dumb Like a Fox." *Columbia Journalism Review* 48 (6): 26–32.

McDonald, Aleecia M., and Lorrie Faith Cranor. 2008. "The Cost of Reading Privacy Policies." *I/S: A Journal of Law and Policy for the Information Society* 4 (3): 540–565.

McDuling, John. 2018. "Australia Loves Netflix. But Does Netflix Love Australia?" *Sydney Morning Herald*.

March 9 (https://www.smh.com.au/business/compa nies/the-relentless-rise-of-netflix-will-come-at-a-cost-20180308-p4z3cm.html).

McIlroy, Thad. 2016. "What the Big 5's Financial Reports Reveal about the State of Traditional Book Publishing." *BookBusiness*. August 5 (http://www .bookbusinessmag.com/post/big-5-financial-re ports-reveal-state-traditional-book-publishing/).

McLaughlin, Margaret L., Kerry K. Osborne, and Christine B. Smith. 1995. "Standards of Conduct on Usenet." Pp. 90–111 in *Cybersociety*, edited by Steven G. Jones. Thousand Oaks, CA: Sage.

McLeod, Kembrew. 2010. "How to Make a Documentary about Sampling—Legally." *The Atlantic Monthly*. March 31 (http://www.theatlantic.com/entertainment/ archive/2010/03/how-to-make-a-documentary-about-sampling-legally/38189/).

McLuhan, Marshall. 1962. *The Gutenberg Galaxy*. Toronto, ON: University of Toronto Press.

———. 1964. *Understanding Media: the Extensions of Man*. New York, NY: McGraw Hill.

McLuhan, Marshall, and Quentin Fiore. 1967. *The Medium Is the Message: An Inventory of Effects*. New York, NY: Bantam.

McNamara, Mary. 2010. "Television Review: 'The Bridge' on CBS." *The Los Angeles Times*. July 10. Retrieved November 8, 2010 (http://articles.latimes.com/2010/ jul/10/entertainment/la-et-thebridge-20100710).

McQuail, Denis, and Sven Windahl. 1993. *Communications Models for the Study of Mass Communication*. New York, NY: Longman.

McQuail, Denis, Rosario de Mateo, and Helena Tapper. 1992. "A Framework for Analysis of Media Change in Europe in the 1990s. Pp. 8–25 in *Dynamics of Media Politics: Broadcast and Electronic Media in Western Europe*, edited by Kareen Siune and Wolfgang Truetzschler. London, UK: Sage.

McRobbie, Angela. 1984. "Dance and Social Fantasy." Pp. 130–161 in *Gender and Generation*, edited by Angela McRobbie and Mica Nava. London, UK: Macmillan.

Mecking, Olga. 2017. "This Scientific Theory Explains Why People Keep Quiet on Things That Matter." *The*

Week. April 4 (http://theweek.com/articles/685976/scientific-theory-explains-why-people-keep-quiet-things-that-matter).

Media Action Network for Asian Americans (MANAA). 2018. "A Memo from MANAA to Hollywood: Asian Stereotypes." (http://manaa.org/?page_id=543).

Melican, Debra Burns, and Travis L. Dixon. 2008. "News on the Net: Credibility, Selective Exposure, and Racial Prejudice." *Communication Research* 35 (2): 151–168.

MEO. 2018. "Internet + Mobile." (https://www.meo.pt/internet/internet-movel/telemovel/pacotes-com-telemovel).

Messner, Marcus, and Marcia Watson DiStaso. 2008. "The Source Cycle: How Traditional Media and Weblogs Use Each Other as Sources." *Journalism Studies* 9 (3): 447–463.

Messner, Michael A., and Cheryl Cooky. 2010. *Gender in Televised Sports: News and Highlights Shows, 1989–2009*. Los Angeles, CA: Center for Feminist Research, University of Southern California.

Messner, Michael, Margaret Carlisle Duncan, and Kerry Jensen. 1993. "Separating the Men from the Girls: The Gendered Language of Televised Sports." *Gender & Society* 7 (1): 121–137.

Meyer, Philip. 2009. *The Vanishing Newspaper: Saving Journalism in the Information Age*. University of Missouri Press.

Meyrowitz, Joshua. 1985. *No Sense of Place*. New York: Oxford University Press.

Mickle, Tripp. 2017. Apple Readies $1 Billion War Chest for Hollywood Programming. *The Wall Street Journal*, August 16 (https://www.wsj.com/articles/apple-readies-1-billion-war-chest-for-hollywood-programming-1502874004?tesla=y&mod=e2tw).

Middleton, Rich. 2017. "Italy Readies Local Content Quotas." C21Media (http://www.c21media.net/italy-readies-local-content-quotas/).

MIDIA Research. 2017. "Amazon Music: The Dark Horse Comes out of the Shadows." October 20 (https://www.midiaresearch.com/blog/amazon-music-the-dark-horse-comes-out-of-the-shadows/).

Milan, Stefania, and Arne Hintz. 2010. "Media Activists and Communication Policy Processes." Pp. 317–319 in *Encyclopedia of Social Movement Media*, edited by John Downing. Thousand Oaks, CA: Sage.

Miller, Laura Jean. 2006. *Reluctant Capitalists: Bookselling and the Culture of Consumption*. Chicago, IL: University of Chicago Press.

Miller, Toby, Nitin Govil, John McMurria, Ting Wang, and Richard Maxwell. 2008. *Global Hollywood 2*. London, UK: British Film Institute.

Miller, V. 2008. "New Media, Networking, and Phatic Culture." *Convergence* 14 (4): 387–400.

Milliot, Jim. 2016. "BEA 2016: E-book Sales Fell 13% in 2015, Nielsen Reports." *Publishers Weekly*. May 12 (https://www.publishersweekly.com/pw/by-topic/industry-news/bea/article/70350-bea-2016-e-book-sales-fell-13-in-2015-nielsen-reports.html).

Mims, Christopher. 2016. "How Facebook Is Dominating the 2016 Election; Social Network's Vast Reach and Micro-targeting Tools Are Manna for Political Advertisers." *Wall Street Journal*. October 2 (https://www.wsj.com/articles/how-facebook-is-dominating-the-2016-election-1475429365).

MIT Technology Review. 2002–2017. "Ten Breakthrough Technologies." Various years (https://www.technologyreview.com/lists/technologies/2017/).

Monte Carlo Television Festival. 2018. "Palmarès des Nymphes d'Or." (http://www.tvfestival.com/600-).

Morgan, Marcyliena, and Dionne Bennett. 2011. "Hip-Hop & the Global Imprint of a Black Cultural Form." *Daedalus* 140 (2):176–196.

Morgan, Michael, and James Shanahan. 2014. "Effects and Cultivation." Pp. 356–365 in *The SAGE Handbook of Television Studies*, edited by Manuel Alvarado, Milly Buonanno, Herman Gray, and Toby Miller. Thousand Oaks, CA: Sage.

Morgan, Michael, James Shanahan, and Nancy Signorielli, eds. 2012. *Living with Television Now*. New York, NY: Peter Lang.

Morley, David. 1980. *The Nationwide Audience*. London, UK: British Film Institute.

———. 1986. *Family Television*. London, UK: Comedia.

———. 1992. *Television, Audiences, and Cultural Studies*. London, UK: Routledge Kegan Paul.

Morozov, Evgeny. 2011. *The Net Delusion: The Dark Side of Internet Freedom*. New York, NY: Public Affairs.

———. 2013. *To Save Everything, Click Here: The Folly of Technological Solutionism*. New York, NY: Public Affairs.

Morris, Aldon. 1984. *The Origins of the Civil Rights Movement*. New York, NY: Free Press.

Moses, Lucia. 2017. "*The Washington Post*'s Robot Reporter Has Published 850 Articles in the Past Year." *Digiday*. September 14 (https://digiday.com/media/washington-posts-robot-reporter-published-500-articles-last-year/).

MotherJones.com. 2018. "What Is Mother Jones?" (https://www.motherjones.com/about/#01).

Motion Picture Association of America. 2018. "Guide to Ratings." (https://www.filmratings.com/RatingsGuide).

Mourão, Rachel Reis. 2014. "The Boys on the Timeline: Political Journalists' Use of Twitter for Building Interpretive Communities." *Journalism* 16 (8):1107–1123.

Mowlana, Hamid, George Gerbner, and Herbert Schiller, eds. 1992. *Triumph of the Image: The Media's War in the Persian Gulf*. Boulder, CO: Westview.

Mozur, Paul, Mark Scott, and Mike Isaac. 2017. "Facebook Faces a New World as Officials Rein In a Wild Web." *New York Times*. September 17 (https://www.nytimes.com/2017/09/17/technology/facebook-government-regulations.html).

MTV. 2018. "MTV Press." (http://www.mtvpress.com/networks/mtv).

Mueller, Milton. 1981. "Interview with Mark S. Fowler." *Reason*. November: 32–35 (https://reason.com/archives/1981/11/01/interview-with-mark-fowler/print).

———. 2002. *Ruling the Roost: Internet Governance and the Taming of Cyberspace*. Cambridge, MA: MIT Press.

———. 2010. *Networks and States: The Global Politics of Internet Governance*. Cambridge, MA: MIT Press.

———. 2017. *Will the Internet Fragment? Sovereignty, Globalization and Cyberspace*. Malden, MA: Polity Press.

Murdock, Graham, and Peter Golding. 1973. "For a Political Economy of Mass Communications." *Socialist Register* 10: 205–234.

Murray, Noel. 2017. "TV's Callous Neglect of Working-class America." *The Week* (http://theweek.com/articles/671974/tvs-callous-neglect-workingclass-america).

Murthy, Dhiraj, Alexander Gross, and Alexander Pensavalle. 2015. "Urban Social Media Demographics: An Exploration of Twitter Use in Major American Cities." *Journal of Computer-Mediated Communication* 21 (1): 33–49.

Museum of Failure. 2018. "About: Over One Hundred Failed Products and Services from around the World" (http://failuremuseum.com/about/).

Musgrove, Mike. 2009. "Twitter Is a Player in Iran's Drama." *Washington Post*. June 17. Retrieved November 30, 2010 (http://www.washingtonpost.com/wp-dyn/content/article/2009/06/16/AR2009061603391.html).

Music Business Worldwide. 2017. "Global Market Shares 2016." February 26 (https://www.musicbusinessworldwide.com/global-market-shares-2016-sony-and-warner-gain-on-universal-as-indies-rule/).

Musto, Michela, Cheryl Cooky, and Michael A. Messner. 2017. "'From Fizzle to Sizzle!' Televised Sports News and the Production of Gender-Bland Sexism." *Gender & Society* 31 (5): 573–596.

Nacos, Brigitte L., and Oscar Torres-Reyna. 2007. *Fueling Our Fears: Stereotyping, Media Coverage, and Public Opinion of Muslim Americans*. Lanham, MD: Rowman & Littlefield.

Nadkarni, Ashwini, and Stefan Hofmann. 2012. "Why Do People Use Facebook?" *Personality and Individual Differences* 52 (3): 243–249.

Nakamura, Lisa. 2009. "Don't Hate the Player, Hate the Game: The Racialization of Labor in *World of Warcraft*." *Critical Studies in Media Communication* 26 (2): 128–144.

Nakamura, Lisa, and Peter A. Chow-White 2012. *Race after the Internet*. New York, NY: Routledge.

Nardi, Peter. 1997. "Changing Gay and Lesbian Images in the Media." Pp. 427–442 in *Overcoming Heterosexism and Homophobia: Strategies That Work*, edited by James T. Sears and Walter Williams. New York, NY: Columbia University Press.

National Association of Broadcasters. 2018. "Broadcasting in South Africa." (http://www.nab.org.za/content/page/broadcast-industry).

National Center for Health Statistics. 2017. "Wireless Substitution: Early Release of Estimates from the National Health Interview Survey, July-December 2016." (https://www.cdc.gov/nchs/data/nhis/earlyrelease/wireless201705.pdf).

National Public Radio. 2018. "Public Radio Finances" (npr.org/about-npr/178660742/public-radio-finances).

National Science Foundation. 1992. "The NSFNET Backbone Services Acceptable Use Policy." (https://www.livinginternet.com/doc/merit.edu/acceptable_use_policy.htm).

Naughton, John. 2000. *A Brief History of the Future: From Radio Days to Internet Years in a Lifetime*. Woodstock, NY: Overlook Press.

Negrine, Ralph. 2008. *The Transformation of Political Communication: Continuities and Changes in Media and Politics*. New York, NY: Palgrave MacMillan.

Negrine, Ralph, Paolo Mancini, Christina Holtz-Bacha, and Stylianos Papathanassopoulos, eds. 2007. *The Professionalisation of Political Communication*. Bristol, TN: Intellect.

Nesbitt, Jim. 1998. "Radio Pirates Feel the Heat." *Cleveland Plain Dealer*. July 19, p. 1D.

Neuendorf, Karen. 2017. *The Content Analysis Guidebook*. Thousand Oaks, CA: Sage.

Neuman, W. Russell, and Lauren Guggenheim. 2011. "The Evolution of Media Effects Theory: A Six-Stage Model of Cumulative Research." *Communication Theory* 21:169–196.

Neuman, W. Russell, Lauren Guggenheim, S. Mo Jang, and Soo Young Bae. 2014. "The Dynamics of Public Attention: Agenda-setting Theory Meets Big Data." *Journal of Communication* 64 (2): 193–214.

New York Times. 1991. "Professor Is Criticized for Anti-Semitic Past." November 27 (http://www.nytimes.com/1991/11/28/us/professor-is-criticized-for-anti-semitic-past.html).

Nicas, Jack. 2018. "Facebook to Require Verified Identities for Future Political Ads." *New York Times*. April 6 (https://www.nytimes.com/2018/04/06/business/facebook-verification-ads.html).

Nielsen. 2017a. "Command Your Buzz: Understanding How Owned Strategies Drive Impact." May 2 (http://www.nielsensocial.com/command-your-buzz-understanding-how-owned-strategies-drive-impact/).

———. 2017b. "Over 92% of All Adult Viewing in the U.S. Is Done on the TV Screen. Insights." May 25 http:// (www.nielsen.com/us/en/insights/news/2017/over-92-percent-of-all-adult-viewing-in-the-us-is-done-on-the-tv-screen.html).

———. 2017c. "Screen Time Dollar Signs." (http://www.nielsen.com/us/en/insights/news/2017/screen-time-dollar-signs.html).

———. 2017e. "The Nielsen Total Audience Report, Q1 2017." (http://www.nielsen.com/content/dam/corporate/us/en/reports-downloads/2017-reports/total-audience-report-q1-2017.pdf).

———. 2017f. "TV Season in Review: The Top Social Moments of the 2016–17 Season." June 7 (http://www.nielsen.com/us/en/insights/news/2017/tv-season-in-review-the-top-social-moments-of-the-2016-17-season.html).

Nielsen, Jakob. 2006. "Participation Inequality: Encouraging More Users to Contribute." Online Retrieved December 8, 2010 (http://www.useit.com/alertbox/participation_inequality.html).

Nightline. 1989. ABC News. September 27.

Noam, Eli M., ed. 2009. *Media Ownership and Concentration in America*. New York, NY: Oxford University Press.

———. 2016. *Who Owns the World's Media?* New York, NY: Oxford University Press.

Noble, Safiya Umoja. 2018. *Algorithms of Oppression: How Search Engines Reinforce Racism*. New York, NY: New York University Press.

Noble, Safiya Umoja, and Brendesha M. Tynes, eds. 2016. *The Intersectional Internet: Race, Sex, Class, and Culture Online*. New York, NY: Peter Lang Publishing.

Noelle-Neumann, Elisabeth. 1974. "The Spiral of Silence: A Theory of Public Opinion." *Journal of Communication* 24 (2): 43–51.

———. 1991. "Accused Professor Was Not a Nazi." *New York Times*. December 14 (http://www.nytimes.com/1991/12/14/opinion/l-accused-professor-was-not-a-nazi-257591.html).

———. 1993. *The Spiral of Silence*. Chicago, IL: University of Chicago Press.

Norris, Pippa. 2000. *A Virtuous Circle: Political Communications in Post-Industrial Societies*. New York, NY: Cambridge University Press.

Nunez, Michael. 2016. "Former Facebook Workers: We Routinely Suppressed Conservative News." *Gizmodo*. May 9 (https://gizmodo.com/former-facebook-workers-we-routinely-suppressed-conser-1775461006).

Nussbaum, Bruce. 2007. "It's Time to Call One Laptop per Child a Failure." *Business Week*. September 24. Retrieved December 9, 2010 (http://www.businessweek.com/innovate/NussbaumOnDesign/archives/2007/09/its_time_to_call_one_laptop_per_child_a_failure.html).

Nussbaum, Emily. 2017. "The TV that Created Donald Trump." *The New Yorker*. July 31 (https://www.newyorker.com/magazine/2017/07/31/the-tv-that-created-donald-trump).

Ó Siochrú, Seán, and Bruce Girard. 2002. *Global Media Governance*. Lanham, MD: Rowman & Littlefield.

O'Barr, William. 1994. *Culture and the Ad*. Boulder, CO: Westview.

Office of the United States Trade Representative. 2017. "2017 National Trade Estimate Report on Foreign Trade Barriers." (https://ustr.gov/sites/default/files/files/reports/2017/NTE/2017%20NTE.pdf).

Oh, Hyun Jung, 2014. "How Does Online Social Networking Enhance Life Satisfaction?" *Computers in Human Behavior* 30: 69–78.

Elif Ozkaya, and Robert Larose. / The Relationships among Online Supportive Interaction, Affect, Perceived Social Support, Sense of Community, and Life Satisfaction." / doi: http://dx.doi.org/10.1016/j.chb.2013.07.053

Olson, David R. 1994. *The World on Paper: The Conceptual and Cognitive Implications of Writing and Reading*. New York, NY: Cambridge University Press.

Osei-Frimpong, Kofi, Alan Wilson, and Fred Lemke. 2018. "Patient Co-creation Activities in Healthcare Service Delivery at the Micro Level: The Influence of Online Access to Healthcare Information." *Technological Forecasting and Social Change* 126: 14–27.

Oxford Dictionaries. 2016. "Word of the Year 2016 Is . . ." (https://en.oxforddictionaries.com/word-of-the-year/word-of-the-year-2016).

Palfrey, John, and Urs Gasser. 2008. *Born Digital: Understanding the First Generation of Digital Natives*. New York, NY: Basic Books.

Panday, Jyoti. 2017. "An Over-the-top Approach to Internet Regulation in Developing Countries." Electronic Frontier Foundation (https://www.eff.org/deeplinks/2017/10/over-top-approach-internet-regulation-developing-countries).

Parenti, Michael. 1986. *Inventing Reality: The Politics of the Mass Media*. New York, NY: St. Martin's.

Pariser, Eli. 2011. *The Filter Bubble: How the New Personalized Web Is Changing What We Read and How We Think*. New York, NY: Penguin.

Parkinson, H. J. 2016. "Click and Elect: How Fake News Helped Donald Trump Win a Real Election." *The Guardian*. November 14 (https://www.theguardian.com/commentisfree/2016/nov/14/fake-news-donald-trump-election-alt-right-social-media-tech-companies).

Pasquale, Frank. 2015. *The Black Box Society: The Secret Algorithms That Control Money and Information*. Cambridge, MA: Harvard.

Pautz, Michelle. 2002. "The Decline in Average Weekly Cinema Attendance: 1930–2000." *Issues in Political Economy.* Vol. 11 (http://blogs.elon.edu/ipe/issues/volume-11-july-2002/).

Pecquerie, Bernard. 2018. "AI Is the New Horizon for News." *Medium.* January 5 (https://medium.com/global-editors-network/ai-is-the-new-horizon-for-news-22b5abb752e6).

Pehlke, Timothy Allen, Charles B. Hennon, Marie Radina, and Katherine A. Kuvalanka. 2009. "Does Father Still Know Best? An Inductive Thematic Analysis of Popular TV Sitcoms." *Fathering: A Journal of Theory, Research, and Practice about Men as Fathers* 7 (2): 114–139. doi:10.3149/fth.0702.114

PEJ (Project for Excellence in Journalism). 2007. "The Invisible Primary—Invisible No Longer: A First Look at Coverage of the 2008 Presidential Campaign." October 29. Retrieved November 11, 2010 (http://www.journalism.org/node/8187).

———. 2009. "Covering the Great Recession: How the Media Have Depicted the Economic Crisis during Obama's Presidency." Retrieved November 29, 2010 (http://www.journalism.org/sites/journalism.org/files/Covering%20the%20Great%20Recession.pdf).

Perlberg, Steven, and Deepa Seetharaman. 2016. "Facebook Signs Deals with Media Companies, Celebrities for Facebook Live." *Wall Street Journal.* June 22 (https://www.wsj.com/articles/facebook-signs-deals-with-media-companies-celebrities-for-facebook-live-1466533472).

Perse, Elizabeth M. 2008. *Media Effects and Society.* Mahwah, NJ: Lawrence Erlbaum.

Persily, Nathaniel. 2017. "Can Democracy Survive the Internet?" *Journal of Democracy* 28 (2): 63–76.

Petersen, Christina. 2013. "The Crowd Mind: The Archival Legacy of the Payne Fund Studies' Movies and Conduct (1933)." *Mediascape.* University of California Los Angeles School of Film, Television, and Digital Media (http://www.tft.ucla.edu/mediascape/Winter2013_CrowdMind.html).

Peterson, Richard A., and N. Anand. 2004. "The Production of Culture Perspective." *Annual Review of Sociology* 30: 311–334.

Peterson, Richard A., and David G. Berger. 1975. "Cycles in Symbol Production: The Case of Popular Music." *American Sociological Review* 40: 158–173.

Peterson, Robin T. 2007. "Consumer Magazine Advertisement Portrayal of Models by Race in the US: An Assessment." *Journal of Marketing Communications* 13 (3): 199–211.

Petition of European Filmmakers. 2013. "The Cultural Exception Is Non-negotiable!" (https://12826.lapetition.be/).

Pew Research Center. 2014a. "The Internet of Things Will Thrive by 2025." (http://www.pewinternet.org/2014/05/14/internet-of-things/).

Pew Research Center. 2014b. "The Web at 25." (http://www.pewinternet.org/2014/02/27/the-web-at-25-in-the-u-s/).

Pew Research Center. 2015. "Teens, Social Media & Technology Overview, 2015." (http://assets.pewresearch.org/wp-content/uploads/sites/14/2015/04/PI_TeensandTech_Update2015_0409151.pdf).

Pew Research Center. 2016. *State of the News Media 2016.* June 15 (http://assets.pewresearch.org/wp-content/uploads/sites/13/2016/06/30143308/state-of-the-news-media-report-2016-final.pdf).

Pew Research Center. 2017a. "Internet/Broadband Fact Sheet." (http://www.pewinternet.org/fact-sheet/internet-broadband/).

———. 2017b. "Mobile Fact Sheet." (http://www.pewinternet.org/fact-sheet/mobile/).

———. 2017c. "News Useacross Social Media Platforms." September 6 (http://www.journalism.org/2017/09/07/news-use-across-social-media-platforms-2017/).

Philips, Angela. 2010. "Old Sources: New Bottles." Pp. 87–101 in *New Media, Old News: Journalism and Democracy in the Digital Age*, edited by Natalie Fenton. Thousand Oaks, CA: Sage.

Pickard, Victor. 2015. *America's Battle for Media Democracy: The Triumph of Corporate Libertarianism and the Future of Media Reform.* New York, NY: Cambridge University Press.

Pierson, David. 2017. "Why Facebook, Twitter and Google Are Suddenly Taking Russian Meddling Very Seriously." *Los Angeles Times*. October 31 (http://www.latimes.com/business/la-fi-tn-tech-hearings-20171031-story.html).

Pieterse, Jan Nederveen N. 1996. "Globalisation and Culture: Three Paradigms." *Economic and Political Weekly* 31 (23): 1389–1393.

———. 2004. *Globalization and Culture: Global Mélange*. Lanham, MD: Rowman and Littlefield.

Pinch, Trevor. 2008. "Technology and Institutions: Living in a Material World." *Theory and Society* 37 (5): 461.

Pizzigati, Sam, and Fred J. Solowey. 1992. *The New Labor Press*. Ithaca, NY: ILR/Cornell University Press.

Poirier, Agnès. 2013. "Why France Is Gearing up for a Culture War with the United States." *The Guardian*. June 7 (https://www.theguardian.com/commentisfree/2013/jun/07/france-culture-war-united-states).

Pooley, Jefferson. 2006. "Fifteen Pages That Shook the Field: *Personal Influence*, Edward Shils, and the Remembered History of Mass Communication Research." *Annals of the American Academy of Political and Social Science* 608 (1): 130–156.

Pooley, Jefferson, and Michael J. Socolow. 2013. "The Myth of the War of the Worlds Panic." *Slate*. October 28 (http://www.slate.com/articles/arts/history/2013/10/orson_welles_war_of_the_worlds_panic_myth_the_infamous_radio_broadcast_did.html).

Porter, Rick. 2016. "Failure Factor." TV by the Numbers. June 1 (http://tvbythenumbers.zap2it.com/more-tv-news/failure-factor-how-bad-was-the-2015-16-tv-season-for-new-shows/).

———. 2018a. "College Football Playoff Semifinal Dominate the Cable Top 25 for Jan. 1–7." TV by the Numbers. January 10 (http://tvbythenumbers.zap2it.com/weekly-ratings/cable-top-25-for-jan-1-7-2018/).

———. 2018b. "NFL Playoffs, Golden Globes Carry NBC to No. 1." TV by the Numbers. January 9 (http://tvbythenumbers.zap2it.com/weekly-ratings/week-15-broadcast-top-25-and-network-rankings-jan-1-7-2018/).

Postman, Neil. 1985. *Amusing Ourselves to Death*. New York, NY: Penguin.

Potter, W. James. 2012. *Media Effects*. Thousand Oaks, CA: Sage.

Powell, Walter W. 1985. *Getting into Print*. Chicago, IL: University of Chicago Press.

Powers, Matthew. 2011. "What's New in the Sociology of News?: Connecting Current Journalism Research to Classic Newsroom Studies." Paper presented at the International Communication Association. Boston, MA.

Pred, Allan R. 1973. *Urban Growth and the Circulation of Information*. Cambridge, MA: Harvard University Press.

Press, Andrea. 1991. *Women Watching Television*. Philadelphia, PA: University of Pennsylvania Press.

Price, Monroe. 2002. *New Role of the State in Media and Sovereignty*. Cambridge, MA: MIT

Prindle, David F. 1993. *Risky Business*. Boulder, CO: Westview.

Prysby, Charles, and David Holian. 2008. "Who Votes on the Basis of the Candidate's Personality? Vote Choice in U.S. Presidential Elections, 1992–2004." Paper presented at the Annual Meeting of the American Political Science Association, Boston, MA, August 28.

Public Broadcasting System. 2018. "Financial Reports." (http://www.pbs.org/about/about-pbs/financials/).

Public Knowledge. 2018. "Net Neutrality." (https://www.publicknowledge.org/issues/net-neutrality).

Puette, William J. 1992. *Through Jaundiced Eyes: How the Media View Organized Labor*. Ithaca, NY: ILR Press.

Quick, Rebecca. 1998. "U.S. to Unveil Policy on Issuing Internet Names." *Wall Street Journal*. June 4, p. B4.

Radio and Music. 2017. "Universal Music Launches 'Despacito' Dance Video; Luis Fonsi Loves It." (http://www.radioandmusic.com/entertainment/editorial/news/170803-universal-music-launches-despacito-dance).

Radway, Janice A. 1991. *Reading the Romance: Women, Patriarchy, and Popular Literature*. 2nd ed. Chapel Hill, NC: University of North Carolina Press.

Rafaeli, Sheizaf, and Yaron Ariel. 2008. "Online Motivational Factors: Incentives for Participation and Contribution in Wikipedia." Pp. 243–267 in *Psychological Aspects of Cyberspace: Theory, Research, and Applications*, edited by Azy Barak, ed. Cambridge, UK: Cambridge University Press.

Rainie, Lee. 2017. "The Internet of Things Is the Next Digital Evolution—What Will It Mean?" Pew Charitable Trusts (http://trend.pewtrusts.org/en/archive/sum mer-2017/the-internet-of-things-is-the-next-digital-evolution-what-will-it-mean).

Rainie, Lee, and Barry Wellman. 2012. *Networked: The New Social Operating System*. Cambridge, MA: The MIT Press.

Rawsthorn, Alice. 2009. "Nonprofit Laptops: A Dream Not Yet Over." *New York Times*. November 8. Retrieved December 9, 2010 (http://www.nytimes .com/2009/11/09/arts/09iht-design9.html?ref=nicholas_ negroponte).

Ray, Rashawn, Melissa Brown, and Wendy Laybourn. 2017. "The Evolution of #BlackLivesMatter on Twitter: Social Movements, Big Data, and Race." *Ethnic and Racial Studies* 40 (11): 1795–1796. (See various articles in this special issue.)

Reardon, Marguerite. 2015. "Net Neutrality: How We Got from There to Here." CNET. February 24 (https:// www.cnet.com/news/net-neutrality-from-there-to-here/).

Redden, Joanna, and Tamara Witschge. 2010. "A New News Order? Online News Content Examined." Pp. 171–186 in *New Media, Old News*, edited by Natalie Fenton. Thousand Oaks, CA: Sage.

Reed, M. 2016. "Donald Trump Won Because of Facebook." *New York Magazine*. November (http:// nymag.com/selectall/2016/11/donaldtrump-won-be cause-of-facebook.html).

Regan, Donald. 1988. *For the Record*. New York: Harcourt Brace.

Reisman, David. 1953. *The Lonely Crowd*. Garden City, NY: Doubleday.

Rendall, Steve, and Tara Broughel. 2003. "Amplifying Officials, Squelching Dissent." *Extra!* May/June.

Retrieved November 1, 2010 (http://www.fair.org/ index.php?page=1145).

Renner, Nausicaa. 2017. "As AI Enters Newsrooms, Journalists Have Urgent Responsibility." *Columbia Journalism Review*. June 16 (https://www.cjr.org/ tow_center/artificial-intelligence-newsrooms .php).

Rennie, Ellie. 2006. *Community Media: A Global Introduction*. Lanham, MD: Rowman & Littlefield.

Reporters Without Borders. 2013. "World Press Freedom Index: 2013." (http://en.rsf.org/press-free dom-index-2013,1054.html).

———. 2017. "The World Press Freedom Index: 2017." (https://rsf.org/en/2017-press-freedom-index-ev er-darker-world-map).

Rhodes, Jane. 1993. "The Visibility of Race and Media History." *Critical Studies in Mass Communication* 20: 184–190.

RIAA (Recording Industry Association of America). 2017. "2016 RIAA Shipment & Revenue Statistics." (https://www.riaa.com/reports/news-notes-2016-riaa-shipment-revenue-statistics)/.

———. 2018. "Parental Advisory Label." (https://www .riaa.com/resources-learning/parental-advisory-label/).

Roberts, Jeff John. 2017. "How to Regulate Facebook Like a Broadcaster." *Fortune*. September 25. (http:// fortune.com/2017/09/25/facebook-broadcaster/).

Robertson, John W. 2010. "The Last Days of Free Market Hegemony? UK TV News Coverage of Economic Issues in Spring 2008." *Media, Culture & Society* 32: 517–529.

Robinson, Michael J. 1976. "Public Affairs Television and the Growth of Political Malaise: The Case of the 'Selling of the Pentagon.'" *American Political Science Review* 70: 409–432.

Robinson, MJ. 2017. *Television on Demand*. New York, NY: Bloomsbury Academic.

Robinson, Nick. 2016. "Militarism and Opposition in the Living Room: The Case of Military Videogames." *Critical Studies on Security* 4 (3): 255–275.

Robinson, Tom, Mark Callister, Brad Clark, and James Phillips. 2009. "Violence, Sexuality, and Gender Stereotyping: A Content Analysis of Official Video Game Web Sites." *Web Journal of Mass Communication Research* 13 (June): 1–17.

Rodman, Gilbert B., ed. 2014. *The Race and Media Reader.* New York, NY: Routledge.

Rogers, Everett. 1986. *Communication Technology.* New York: Free Press.

Rohlinger, Deana A. 2002. "Eroticizing Men: Cultural Influences on Advertising and Male Objectification." *Sex roles* 46(3–4): 61–74.

Romano, Lois. 2012. "Obama's Data Advantage." *Politico.* Retrieved January 8, 2013 (http://www.politico.com/news/stories/0612/77213.html)

Romm, Tony, and Craig Timberg. 2018. "Cambridge Analytica Shuts Down Amid Scandal over Use of Facebook Data." *The Washington Post.* May 2 (https://www.washingtonpost.com/news/the-switch/wp/2018/05/02/cambridge-analytica-shuts-down-amid-scandal-over-use-of-facebook-data).

Roose, Kevin, and Cecilia Kang. 2018. "Mark Zuckerberg Testifies on Facebook Before Skeptical Lawmakers." *Washington Post.* April 10 (https://www.nytimes.com/2018/04/10/us/politics/zuckerberg-facebook-senate-hearing.html).

Rose, Tricia. 1994. *Black Noise.* Hanover, NH: Wesleyan University Press.

Rosen, Jay. 1993. "Who Won the Week? The Political Press and the Evacuation of Meaning." *Tikkun* 8 (4): 7–10, 94.

———. 2006. "The People Formerly Known as the Audience." *Pressthink.* June 27 (http://archive.pressthink.org/2006/06/27/ppl_frmr.html).

Rosenblum, Barbara. 1978. *Photographers at Work.* New York: Holmes & Meier.

Rosenfeld, Megan. 1997. "The 'Ellen' Coming Out Club." *Washington Post.* April 24, p. B1.

Rowell, Alex. 2017. "What Everyone Should Know about America's Diverse Working Class." Center for American Progress (https://www.americanprogressaction.org/issues/economy/reports/2017/12/11/169303/everyone-know-americas-diverse-working-class/).

Rubin, Alan M. 2009. "Uses-and-Gratification Perspective on Media Effects." Pp. 165–184 in *Media Effects: Advances in Theory and Research,* edited by Jennings Bryant and Mary Beth Oliver. New York: Routledge.

Ruddick, Graham. 2017. "UK Government Considers Classifying Google and Facebook as Publishers." *The Guardian.* October 11 (https://www.theguardian.com/technology/2017/oct/11/government-considers-classifying-google-facebook-publishers).

Ruggiero, Thomas E. 2000. "Uses and Gratifications Theory In The 21st Century." *Mass Communication & Society* 3: 3–37.

Russell, Karl. 2017. "Bill O'Reilly's Show Lost More Than Half Its Advertisers in a Week." *The New York Times.* April 11 (https://www.nytimes.com/interactive/2017/04/11/business/oreilly-advertisers.html).

Ryan, Charlotte. 1991. *Prime Time Activism.* Boston, MA: South End Press.

Ryan, Maureen, and Cynthia Littleton. 2017. "TV Series Budgets Hit the Breaking Point as Costs Skyrocket in Peak TV Era." *Variety.* September 26 (http://variety.com/2017/tv/news/tv-series-budgets-costs-rising-peak-tv-1202570158/).

Sachdev, Ameet. 2010. "FTC Cracks Down on Fake Online Endorsements." *Chicago Tribune.* October 11. Retrieved November 29, 2010 (http://articles.chicagotribune.com/2010-10-11/business/ct-biz-1011-web-reviews—20101011_1_ftc-cracks-endorsements-mary-engle).

Saleh, Nivien. 2012. "Egypt's Digital Activism and the Dictator's Dilemma: An Evaluation." *Telecommunications Policy* 36 (6): 476–483.

Salganik, Matthew J., Peter S. Dodds, and Duncan J. Watts. 2006. "Experimental Study of Inequality and Unpredictability in an Artificial Cultural Market." *Science* 311: 854–856.

Salzman, Jason. 1998. *Making the News: A Guide for Nonprofits and Activists.* Boulder, CO: Westview.

Sands, Darren. 2017. "What Happened to Black Lives Matter?" *BuzzFeed.* June 21 (https://www

.buzzfeed.com/darrensands/what-happened-to-black-lives-matter).

Sandvine. 2016. "2016 Global Internet Phenomena." (https://www.sandvine.com/hubfs/downloads/archive/2016-global-internet-phenomena-report-latin-america-and-north-america.pdf).

Sarikakis, Katharine, and Daya K. Thussu, eds. 2006. *Ideologies of the Internet.* Cresskill, NJ: Hampton Press.

Savage, Mark. 2017. "'Despacito' Breaks Global Streaming Record." BBC News. July 19 (http://www.bbc.com/news/entertainment-arts-40642701).

Scardaville, Melissa C. 2005. "Accidental Activists: Fan Activism in the Soap Opera Community." *American Behavioral Scientist* 48 (7): 881–901.

Scharrer, Erica. 2012. "Television and Gender Roles: Cultivating Conceptions of Self and Other." Pp. 81–99 in *Living with Television Now: Advances in Cultivation Theory and Research*, edited by Michael Morgan, James Shanahan, and Nancy Signorielli. New York, NY: Peter Lang.

Schell, L. A. 1999. *Socially Constructing the Female Athlete: A Monolithic Media Representation of Active Women.* Unpublished doctoral dissertation, Texas Woman's University, Denton. Retrieved overview and excerpt November 4, 2010 (http://www.womenssportsfoundation.org/Content/Articles/Issues/Media-and-Publicity/D/DisEmpowering-Images—Media-Representations-of-Women-in-Sport.aspx).

Scherr, Sebastian, and Antonia Brunet. 2017. "Differential Influences of Depression and Personality Traits on the Use of Facebook." *Social Media + Society* (January–March 2017): 1–14.

Scheufele, Dietram A., and David Tewksbury. 2006. "Framing, Agenda Setting, and Priming: The Evolution of Three Media Effects Models." *Journal of Communication* 57 (1): 9–20.

Scheufele, Dietram A., and Patricia Moy. 2000. "Twenty-five Years of the Spiral of Silence: A Conceptual Review and Empirical Outlook. *International Journal of Public Opinion Research* 12 (1): 3–28.

Schiffer, Michael. 1991. *The Portable Radio in American Life.* Tucson, AZ: University of Arizona Press.

Schill, Dan. 2009. *Stagecraft and Statecraft: Advance and Media Events in Political Communication.* Lanham, MD: Lexington Books.

Schiller, Herbert. 1971. *Mass Communications and American Empire.* Boston, MA: Beacon.

———. 1989. *Culture, Inc.* New York, NY: Oxford University Press.

———. 1992. *Mass Communications and American Empire.* 2nd ed. Boulder, CO: Westview.

Schneider, Michael. 2018. "Peak TV Tally: There Were More Shows Than Ever in 2017, Which Is Why It's Impossible to Keep Up." IndieWire (http://www.indiewire.com/2018/01/how-many-shows-on-tv-2017-fx-john-landgraf-tca-1201913645/)

Scholz, Trebor. 2010. "Market Ideology and the Myths of Web 2.0." *First Monday* 13 (3) March 3. Retrieved December 8, 2010 (http://firstmonday.org/htbin/cgiwrap/bin/ojs/index.php/fm/article/view/2138/1945).

Schradie, Jen. 2011. "The Digital Production Gap: The Digital Divide and Web 2.0 Collide." *Poetics* 39 (2): 145–168.

Schudson, Michael. 1978. *Discovering the News.* New York, NY: Basic Books.

———. 1984. *Advertising: The Uneasy Persuasion.* New York, NY: Basic Books.

———. 2011. *The Sociology of News.* 2nd ed. New York, NY: W.W. Norton.

Schultz, Julianne. 1998. *Reviving the Fourth Estate.* New York, NY: Cambridge University Press.

Schulz, Winfried. 2004. "Reconstructing Mediatization as an Analytical Concept." *European Journal of Communication* 19 (1): 87–101.

Scolari, Carlos A. 2012. "Media Ecology: Exploring the Metaphor to Expand the Theory." *Communication Theory* 22 (2): 204.

Scott, Althaus R., Peter F. Nardulli, and Daron R. Shaw. 2002. "Candidate Appearances in Presidential Elections, 1972–2000." *Political Communication* 19: 49–72.

Seaman, William R. 1992. "Active Audience Theory: Pointless Populism." *Media, Culture & Society* 14 (2): 301–311.

Seggar, John F., Jeffrey K. Hafen, and Helena Hannonen-Gladden. 1981. "Television's Portrayals of Minorities and Women in Drama and Comedy Drama, 1971–80." *Journal of Broadcasting* 25: 277–288.

Seib, Philip, and Dana M. Janbek. 2011. *Global Terrorism and New Media*. New York, NY: Routledge.

Shah, Dhavan V., Nojin Kwak, and R. Lance Holbert. 2001. "'Connecting' and 'Disconnecting' with Civic Life: Patterns of Internet Use and the Production of Social Capital." *Political Communication* 18 (2): 141–162.

Shaheen, Jack G. 2008. *Guilty: Hollywood's Verdict on Arabs after 9/11*. Northampton, MA: Olive Branch Press.

———. 2014. *Reel Bad Arabs: How Hollywood Vilifies a People*. Northampton, MA: Olive Branch Press.

Shahin, Saif, 2017. "Facing up to Facebook: How Digital Activism, Independent Regulation, and Mass Media Foiled a Neoliberal Threat to Net Neutrality." *Information, Communication & Society*. doi: 10.1080/1369 118X.2017.1340494.

Shakya, Holly B., and Nicholas A. Christakis. 2017. "Association of Facebook Use with Compromised Well-Being: A Longitudinal Study. " *American Journal of Epidemiology* 185 (3): 203–211.

Shales, Tom. 1995. "The Fat Cat Broadcast Bonanza." *Washington Post*. June 13, pp. C1, C9.

———. 2003. "Aboard the Lincoln: A White House Spectacular." *Washington Post*. May 2, p. C1.

Shaw, Lucas, and Mark Bergen. 2017. "With 40 New Original Shows, YouTube Targets TV's Breadbasket." *Bloomberg Technology*, May 4 (https://www.bloom berg.com/news/articles/2017-05-04/with-40-new-original-shows-youtube-targets-tv-s-breadbasket).

Shedden, David. 2010. "New Media Timeline, 1969–2010." Poynter Institute. Retrieved November 29, 2010 (poynter .org/content/content_view.asp?id=75953).

Shiver, Jube, Jr. 1998. "Eye on the Sky: FCC Agents Guard the Crowded Airwaves against Pirates and Accidental Interference." *Los Angeles Times*. July 20. Retrieved November 29, 2010 (http://articles.latimes .com/1998/jul/20/business/fi-5408).

Sigal, Leon. 1973. *Reporters and Officials: The Organization and Politics of Newsmaking*. Lexington, MA: Lexington Books.

Signorielli, Nancy. 2009. "Race and Sex in Prime Time." *Mass Communication and Society* 12: 332–352.

Silverstone, Roger, and Eric Hirsch. 1992. *Consuming Technologies: Media and Information in Domestic Spaces*. New York, NY: Routledge.

Simmons, Steven J. 1978. *The Fairness Doctrine and the Media*. Berkeley, CA: University of California Press.

Singer, Jane B. 2014. "User-Generated Visibility: Secondary Gatekeeping in a Shared Media Space." *New Media & Society* 16 (1) 55–73.

Sink, Alexander, and Dana Mastro. 2017. "Depictions of Gender on Primetime Television: A Quantitative Content Analysis." *Mass Communication and Society* 20 (1): 3–22.

Skidmore, David. 1998. "Huntington's Clash Revisited." *Journal of World-Systems Research* 4 (2): 181–188.

Smedley, Audrey, and Brian Smedley. 2012. *Race in North America: Origin and Evolution of a Worldview*. Boulder, CO: Westview Press.

Smith, Aaron. 2014. "African Americans and Technology Use: A Demographic Portrait." Pew Research Center (http://assets.pewresearch.org/wp-content/uploads/sites/14/2014/01/African-Americans-and-Technology-Use.pdf).

Smith, Stacy L., Marc Choueiti, and Katherine Pieper. 2016. "Inclusion or Invisibility? Comprehensive Annenberg Report on Diversity in Entertainment." Annenberg School for Communication, University of Southern California (http://annenberg.usc.edu/sites/default/files/2017/04/07/MDSCI_CARD_Report_FINAL_Exec_Summary.pdf).

———. 2018a. "Inclusion in the Director's Chair? Gender, Race, and Age of Directors across 1,100 Films from 2007–2017." Annenberg School for Communication, University of Southern California (http://assets.uscan nenberg.org/docs/inclusion-in-the-directors-chair-2007-2017.pdf).

———. 2018b. "Inclusion in the Recording Studio? Gender and Race/Ethnicity of Artists, Songwriters, and Producers across 600 Popular Songs from 2012–2017." Annenberg School for Communication, University of Southern California (http://assets.uscannenberg .org/docs/inclusion-in-the-recording-studio.pdf).

Snider, Mike. 2017. Koch Brothers Firm's Investment in 'Time' Raises Questions of Editorial Independence. *USA Today*, November 27 (https://www.usatoday.com/story/money/business/2017/11/27/koch-brothers-investment-time-raises-questions-editorial-independence/896944001/).

Snow, David A., E. Burke Rochford, Jr., Steven K. Worden, and Robert D. Benford. 1986. "Frame Alignment Processes, Micromobilization, and Movement Participation." *American Sociological Review* 51: 464–481.

Snow, David A., Rens Vliegenthart, and Catherine Corrigall-Brown. 2007. "Framing the French Riots: A Comparative Study of Frame Variation. *Social Forces* 86 (2): 385–415.

Solotaroff, Paul. 2015. "Trump Seriously: On the Trail with the GOP's Tough Guy." *Rolling Stone*. September 9 (https://www.rollingstone.com/politics/news/trump-seriously-20150909).

Sousa, John Philip. 1906. "The Menace of Mechanical Music." *Appleton's Magazine* 8: 278–284.

Spaiser, Viktoria, Thomas Chadefaux, Karsten Donnay, Fabian Russmann, and Dirk Helbing. 2017. "Communication Power Struggles on Social Media: A Case Study of the 2011–12 Russian Protests." *Journal of Information Technology & Politics* 14 (2): 132–153.

Spangler, Todd. 2017a. "Netflix Plans to Release 80 Original Films in 2018." *Variety*. October 16 (http://variety.com/2017/digital/news/netflix-80-films-release-2018-ted-sarandos-1202591430/).

Spangler, Todd. 2017b. "YouTube Says It Deleted Over 150,000 Kid Videos Targeted by Sex Predators." *Variety*. November 28 (http://variety.com/2017/digital/news/youtube-deletes-kid-videos-pedophile-comments-1202624410/).

Sparks, Glen G. 2015. *Media Effects Research*. Boston, MA: Cengage.

Sparta, Christine. 2002. "Emergence from the Closet." *USA Today*. March 11 (http://usatoday30.usatoday.com/life/television/2002/2002-03-11-coming-out-timeline.htm?iframe=true&width=80%&height=80%).

Spigel, Lynn. 1992. *Make Room for TV*. Chicago, IL: University of Chicago Press.

Sproule, J. Michael. 1989. "Progressive Propaganda Critics and the Magic Bullet Myth." *Critical Studies in Mass Communication* 6 (3): 225–246.

Spyglass Intelligence. 2017. "Top 12 US Consumer Magazine Publishers: Circulation & Advertising Revenue." (http://www.spyglassintel.com/visualization-of-circulation-revenue-for-the-top-12-us-consumer-magazine-publishers/).

Squires, Catherine. 2009. *African Americans and the Media*. Malden, MA: Polity Press.

Squires, James. 1993. *Read All about It! The Corporate Takeover of America's Newspapers*. New York, NY: Times Books.

Sreberny, Annabelle. 2005. "Contradictions of the Globalizing Moment." *Global Media and Communication* 1: 11–15.

Sreberny-Mohammadi, Annabelle. 1997. "The Many Faces of Imperialism." Pp. 48–68 in *Beyond Cultural Imperialism*, edited by Peter Golding and Phil Harris. Thousand Oaks, CA: Sage.

Starr, Paul. 2004. *The Creation of the Media: Political Origins of Modern Communications*. New York, NY: Basic Books.

Statista. 2017. "How People Spend Time on Social Platforms Globally, in 5 Charts." *Digiday* (https://digiday.com/marketing/people-spend-time-social-platforms-globally-5-charts/).

Statista. 2018a. "Facebook—Statistics & Facts." (https://www.statista.com/topics/751/facebook/).

Statista. 2018b. "Net Digital Ad Revenues of Google as Percentage of Total Digital Advertising Revenues Worldwide from 2016 to 2019." (https://www.statista.com/statistics/193530/market-share-of-net-us-online-ad-revenues-of-google-since-2009/).

Statista. 2018c. "Worldwide Desktop Market Share of Leading Search Engines from January 2010 to October 2017." (https://www.statista.com/statistics/216573/worldwide-market-share-of-search-engines/).

Statt, Nick. 2017. "Alphabet's Project Loon Delivers Internet Service to 100,000 People in Puerto Rico." *The Verge*. November 9 (https://www.theverge.com/2017/11/9/16630494/alphabet-project-loon-puerto-rico-internet-connectivity-update).

Steele, Catherine Knight. 2018. "Black Bloggers and Their Varied Publics: The Everyday Politics of Black Discourse Online." *Television & New Media* 19 (2): 112–127.

Steiner, Linda. 1988. "Oppositional Decoding as an Act of Resistance." *Critical Studies in Mass Communication* 5 (1): 1–15.

Stelter, Brian. 2010. "FCC Is Set to Regulate Net Access." *New York Times*. Retrieved February 16, 2011 (http://www.nytimes.com/2010/12/21/business/media/21fcc.html).

Sterne, Jonathan. 2014. 'What Do We Want?' 'Materiality!' 'When Do We Want It?' 'Now!' Pp. 119–127 in *Media Technologies: Essays on Communication, Materiality and Society*, edited by Tarleton Gillespie, Pablo J. Boczkowski, and Kirsten A. Foot. Cambridge, MA: MIT Press.

Storey, John. 2015. *Cultural Theory and Popular Culture: An Introduction*. New York, NY: Routledge.

Strate, Lance. 2017. "Understanding the Message of Understanding Media." *Atlantic Journal of Communication* 25 (4): 244–254.

Straubhaar, Joseph. 1991. "Beyond Media Imperialism: Asymmetrical Interdependence and Cultural Proximity." *Critical Studies in Mass Communication* 8 (1): 39–59.

Strauss, Jessalynn R. 2011. "Public (Relations) Disturbances and Civil Disobedience: Why I Use 'The Yes Men Fix the World' to Teach Public Relations Ethics." *Public Relations Review* 37: 544–547.

Strelitz, L. 2003. "Where the Global Meets the Local: South African Youth and Their Experience of Global Media." Pp. 234–256 in *Global Media Studies: Ethnographic Perspectives*, edited by Patrick D. Murphy and Marwan M. Kraidy. New York: Routledge.

Strömbäck, Jesper. 2008. "Four Phases of Mediatization: An Analysis of the Mediatization of Politics." *The International Journal of Press/Politics* 13 (3): 228–246.

Strömbäck, Jesper, and Frank Esser. 2014a. "Introduction: Making Sense of the Mediatization of Politics." *Journalism Studies* 15: 3, 243–255.

———. 2014b. "Mediatization of Politics: Towards a Theoretical Framework." Pp. 3–28 in *Mediatization of Politics*, edited by Frank Esser and Jesper Strömbäck. Palgrave Macmillan, London.

Sullivan, Eileen. 2018. "Arizona's G.O.P. Senators Assail Trump for His Attacks on the Press." *New York Times*. January 17 (https://www.nytimes.com/2018/01/17/us/politics/flake-mccain-trump-freedom-of-the-press.html).

Sullivan, John L. 2013. *Media Audiences: Effects, Users, Institutions, Power*. Thousand Oaks, CA: SAGE.

Sullivan, Margaret. 2016. "Call It a 'Crazy Idea,' Facebook, but You Need an Executive Editor." *Washington Post* (https://www.washingtonpost.com/lifestyle/style/call-it-what-you-want-facebook-but-you-need-an-executive-editor/2016/11/20/67aa5320-aaa6-11e6-a31b-4b6397e625d0_story.html).

Sundar, S. Shyam, and Anthony M. Limperos. 2013. "Uses and Grats 2.0: New Gratifications for New Media." *Journal of Broadcasting & Electronic Media* 57 (4): 504–525.

Sunstein, Cass. 2002. *Republic.com*. Princeton, NJ: Princeton University Press.

Tai, Cordelia. 2017. "Diversity Report: The Magazine Covers Have Spoken, 2017 Was Fashion's Most Inclusive Year Yet." *The Fashion Spot*. December 14 (http://www.thefashionspot.com/runway-news/776179-diversity-report-fashion-magazine-covers-2017/).

Tang, Tang, Gregory D. Newton, and Xiaopeng Wang. 2007. "Does Synergy Work? An Examination of Cross-Promotion Effects." *The International Journal on Media Management* 9 (4): 127–134.

Taylor, Ella. 1989. *Prime Time Families*. Berkeley, CA: University of California Press.

Taylor, Phillip M. 1992. *War and the Media: Propaganda and Persuasion in the Gulf War*. New York, NY: St. Martin's.

Thompson, John. 2010. *Merchants of Culture: The Publishing Business in the Twenty-First Century*. New York, NY: Penguin Group.

Thompson, Krissah. 2013. "Yep, We've Come a Long Way." *Washington Post*. March 26, p. C1.

Timberg, Craig, and Drew Harwell. 2018. "We Studied Thousands of Anonymous Posts about the Parkland Attack—and Found a Conspiracy in the Making." *Washington Post*. February 27 (https://

www.washingtonpost.com/business/economy/we-studied-thousands-of-anonymous-posts-about-the-parkland-attack---and-found-a-conspiracy-in-the-making/2018/02/27/04a856be-1b20-11e8-b2d9-08e748f892c0_story.html).

Timberg, Craig, Hamza Shaban, and Elizabeth Dwoskin. 2017. "Fiery Exchanges on Capitol Hill as Lawmakers Scold Facebook, Google and Twitter." *Washington Post.* November 1 (https://www.washingtonpost.com/news/the-switch/wp/2017/11/01/fiery-exchanges-on-capitol-hill-as-lawmakers-scold-facebook-google-and-twitter).

Tomlinson, John. 1991. *Cultural Imperialism: A Critical Introduction.* New York, NY: Continuum.

———. 2003. "Media Imperialism." Pp. 113–134 in *Planet TV: A Global Television Reader*, edited by Lisa Parks and Shanti Kumar. New York, NY: New York University Press.

Townhall.com. 2018. "Townhall.com—the Leading Conservative and Political Opinion Website." (https://townhall.com/aboutus).

Trilling, Damian, Petro Tolochko, and Bjorn Burscher. 2017. "From Newsworthiness to Shareworthiness." *Journalism & Mass Communication Quarterly* 94 (1): 38–60.

Troilo, Jessica. 2017. "Stay Tuned: Portrayals of Fatherhood to Come." *Psychology of Popular Media Culture* 6 (1): 82–94.

Trunomi. 2018. "GDPR Portal." (https://www.eugdpr.org).

Tuchman, Gaye. 1978. *Making News: A Study in the Construction of Reality.* New York, NY: Free Press.

Tufecki, Zeynep. 2017. *Twitter and Tear Gas: The Power and Fragility of Networked Protest.* New Haven, CT: Yale University Press (twitterandteargas.org/downloads/twitter-and-tear-gas-by-zeynep-tufekci.pdf).

———. 2018. "YouTube, the Great Radicalizer." *The New York Times.* March 10 (https://www.nytimes.com/2018/03/10/opinion/sunday/youtube-politics-radical.html).

Tuggle, C.A. 1997. "Differences in Television Sports Reporting of Men's and Women's Athletics: ESPN SportsCenter and CNN Sports Tonight." *Journal of Broadcasting & Electronic Media* 41 (1): 14–24.

Turner, Fred. 2006. *From Counterculture to Cyberculture: Stewart Brand, the Whole Earth Network, and the Rise of Digital Utopianism.* Chicago, IL: University of Chicago Press.

Turner, Graeme. 2010. *Ordinary People and the Media.* Thousand Oaks, CA: Sage.

———. 2013. *Understanding Celebrity.* Thousand Oaks, CA: Sage.

Turow, Joseph. 1997. *Breaking up America: Advertisers and the New Media World.* Chicago, IL: University of Chicago Press.

———. 2006. *Niche Envy: Marketing Discrimination in the Digital Age.* Cambridge, MA: MIT Press.

———. 2011. *The Daily You: How the New Advertising Industry Is Defining Your Identity and Your Worth.* New Haven, CT: Yale University Press.

Twenge, Jean. 2017. *iGen: Why Today's Super-connected Kids Are Growing Up Less Rebellious, More Tolerant, Less Happy—and Completely Unprepared for Adulthood—and What That Means for the Rest of Us.* New York, NY: Artria Books.

20th Century Fox. 2017. "2017 Annual Report." (https://www.21cf.com/investor-relations/annual-reports).

Twitter. 2017. "Twitter Transparency Report." September (transparency.twitter.com).

———. 2018. "Twitter for Websites Supported Languages." (https://dev.twitter.com/web/overview/languages).

UNCTAD (United Nations Conference on Trade and Development). 2004. *Creative Industries and Development.* June 4. Retrieved December 9, 2010 (http://www.unctad.org/Templates/Page.asp?intItemID=5106&lang=1).

UNESCO (United Nations Educational, Scientific and Cultural Organization). 2005. "Convention on the Protection and Promotion of the Diversity of Cultural Expressions 2005." October 20. Retrieved December 9, 2010 (http://portal.unesco.org/en/ev

.php-URL_ID=31038&URL_ DO=DO_ TOPIC&URL_ SECTION=201.html).

———. 2010. "Creative Content: Radio, TV, New Media." Retrieved October 18, 2010 (http://portal.unesco.org/ci/en/ev.php-URL_ID=5459&URL_DO=DO_TOPIC&URL_SECTION=201.html).

———. 2015. "Reshaping Cultural Policies: A Decade Promoting the Diversity of Cultural Expressions for Development." (http://unesdoc.unesco.org/images/0024/002428/242866e.pdf).

———. 2017. "Re Shaping Cultural Policies 2018." (http://unesdoc.unesco.org/images/0026/002605/260592e.pdf).

Unwin, Tim. 2013. "The Internet and Development: A Critical Perspective." Pp. 531–554 in *The Oxford Handbook of Internet Studies*, edited by William H. Dutton. New York, NY: Oxford University Press.

U.S. Census Bureau. 1999. *Statistical Abstract of the United States: 1999*. Table 1440 (https://www2.census.gov/library/publications/1999/compendia/statab/119ed/tables/sec31.pdf).

———. 2012. *Statistical Abstract of the United States: 2012*. Table 1132 (https://www2.census.gov/library/publications/2011/compendia/statab/131ed/2012-statab.pdf).

———. 2014. "Table 10. Projections of the Population by Sex, Hispanic Origin, and Race for the United States: 2015 to 2060 (NP2014-T10)" (https://www.census.gov/data/tables/2014/demo/popproj/2014-summary-tables.html).

———. 2017a. "Educational Attainment in the United States: 2016." (https://www.census.gov/data/tables/2016/demo/education-attainment/cps-detailed-tables.html).

———. 2017b. "Income and Poverty in the United States: 2016." (https://www.census.gov/content/dam/Census/library/publications/2017/demo/P60-259.pdf).

———. 2018. "Quick Facts: United States." (https://www.census.gov/quickfacts/fact/table/US/PST045217).

U.S. Energy Information Administration. 2017. "Average Number of Televisions in U.S. Homes Declining." (https://www.eia.gov/todayinenergy/detail.php?id=30132).

Usher, Nikki. 2014. *Making News at* The New York Times. Ann Arbor: University of Michigan Press.

Vaidhyanathan, Siva. 2011. *The Googlization of Everything*. Berkeley, CA: University of California Press.

Vainikka, Eliisa, and Juha Herkman. 2013. "Generation of Content-Producers? The Reading and Media Production Practices of Young Adults." *Participations: A Journal of Audience and Reception Studies* 10 (2): 118–138.

van Cuilenburg, Jan, and Denis McQuail. 2003. "Media Policy Paradigm Shifts: Towards a New Communications Policy Paradigm." *European Journal of Communication* 18 (2): 181–207.

van de Rijt, Arnout, Eran Shor, Charles Ward, and Steven Skiena. 2013. "Only 15 Minutes? The Social Stratification of Fame in Printed Media." *American Sociological Review* 78 (2): 266–289.

van Dijck, José. 2011. "Users Like You? Theorizing Agency in User-Generated Content." *Media, Culture & Society* 31 (1): 41–58.

———. 2013. *The Culture of Connectivity: A Critical History of Social Media*. New York, NY: Oxford University Press.

van Dijck, José, and Thomas Poell. 2013. "Understanding Social Media Logic." *Media and Communication* 1 (1) 2–14.

van Dijk, Jan. 2006. "Digital Divide Research, Achievements and Shortcomings." *Poetic*, 34: 221–235.

———. 2017. "Digital Divide: Impact of Access." *The International Encyclopedia of Media Effects*. Malden, MA: Wiley-Blackwell.

Verrier, Richard. 2009. "MPAA Stops Disclosing Average Costs of Making and Marketing Movies." *Los Angeles Times*. April 1. Retrieved July 24, 2013 (http://articles.latimes.com/2009/apr/01/business/fi-cotown-mpaa1).

Vincent, James. 2017. "Google Fined a Record €2.4 Billion by the EU for Manipulating Search Results." *The Verge*. June 27 (https://www.theverge.com/2017/6/27/15872354/google-eu-fine-antitrust-shopping).

Vonderau, Patrick. 2017. "The Spotify Effect: Digital Distribution and Financial Growth." *Television & New Media*: 1–17 (https://doi.org/10.1177/1527476417741200).

W3Techs. 2018. "Usage of Content Languages for Websites." February (https://w3techs.com/technologies/overview/content_language/all).

Wagner, Kurt, and Rani Molla. 2018. "Facebook Lost Daily Users for the First Time Ever in the U.S. and Canada." *Recode*. January 31 (https://www.recode.net/2018/1/31/16957122/facebook-daily-active-user-decline-us-canda-q4-earnings-2018).

Walker, Kent. 2017. "Four Steps We're Taking Today to Fight Terrorism Online." (https://blog.google/topics/google-europe/four-steps-were-taking-today-fight-online-terror/).

Wallsten, Kevin. 2007. "Agenda Setting and the Blogosphere: An Analysis of the Relationship between Mainstream Media and Political Blogs." *Review of Policy Research* 24 (6): 567–587.

Walt Disney Company. 2018. "Fiscal Year 2017 Annual Financial Report." (https://thewaltdisneycompany.com/investor-relations/#reports).

Walters, Suzanna D. 1995. *Material Girls*. Berkeley, CA: University of California Press.

We Are Social. 2018. *Global Digital Report* (https://wearesocial.com/sg/blog/2018/01/global-digital-report-2018).

Weedon, Alexis. 2007. "In Real Life: Book Covers in the Internet Bookstore." Pp. 117–127 in *Judging a Book by Its Cover*, edited by Nicole Matthews and Nickianne Moody. Burlington, VT: Ashgate.

Weinberg, Tamir. 2016. "Are Fake Online Reviews Killing Consumer Confidence?" *Marketing Land*. October 21 (https://marketingland.com/fake-online-reviews-killing-consumer-confidence-194239).

White, Armond. 2017. Return of the Get-Whitey Movie. *National Review*. February 24 (http://www.nationalreview.com/article/445206/jordan-peeles-get-out-trite-get-whitey-movie).

White, David Manning. 1950. "The Gatekeeper: A Case Study in the Selection of News." *Journalism Quarterly* 27: 383–390.

Whiteley, Paul. 2016. "Four Reasons Why the Polls Got the U.S. Election Result So Wrong." *Newsweek*. November 14 (http://www.newsweek.com/polls-2016-us-elections-trump-potus-hillary-clinton-520291).

Widdicombe, Lizzie. 2018. "Rate Your Boss". *The New Yorker*. January 22.

Williams, Dmitri, Nicole Martins, Mia Consalvo, and James D. Ivory. 2009. "The Virtual Census: Representations of Gender, Race and Age in Video Games." *New Media & Society* 11 (5): 815–834.

Williams, Raymond. 1974. *Television, Technology, and Cultural Form*. New York: Schocken Books.

Wilson, Clint C., II, Felix Gutierrez, and Lena M. Chao. 2013. *Racism, Sexism, and the Media*. Thousand Oaks, CA: Sage.

Winner, Langdon. 1977. *Autonomous Technology: Technics-out-of-control as a Theme in Political Thought*. Cambridge, MA: MIT Press.

Wolff, Edward N. 2017. "Household Wealth Trends in the United States, 1962 to 2016: Has Middle Class Wealth Recovered?" National Bureau of Economic Research (NBER) Working Paper No. 24085 (http://www.nber.org/papers/w24085).

Wolfsfeld, Gadi, Moran Yarchi, and Tal Samuel-Azran. 2016. "Political Information Repertoires and Political Participation." *New Media & Society* 18 (9): 2096–2115.

Womack, Ytasha. 2013. *Afrofuturism: The World of Black Sci-Fi and Fantasy Culture*. Chicago, IL: Lawrence Hill Books.

Women's Media Center. 2017. "The Status of Women in The U.S. Media 2017." (http://www.womensmediacenter.com/assets/site/reports/the-status-of-women-in-u.s.-media-2017/10c550d19ef9f3688f_mlbres2jd.pdf).

Woolley, Samuel C., and Philip N. Howard. 2017. "Computational Propaganda Worldwide: Executive Summary." Working Paper 2017.11. Oxford, UK: Project on Computational Propaganda (comprop.oii.ox.ac.uk).

Wu, Michael. 2010. "The Economics of 90–9-1: The Gini Coefficient (with Cross-sectional Analyses)." Lithium Lithosphere. Retrieved December 8, 2010 (http://lithosphere.lithium.com/t5/Building-Community-the-Platform/bg-p/MikeW/label-name/90–9-1).

Wu, Paulina. 2015. "Impossible to Regulate?: Social Media, Terrorists, and the Role for the U.N." *Chicago Journal of International Law* 16 (1): 281–311.

Wu, Tim. 2011. *The Master Switch: The Rise and Fall of Information Empires*. New York, NY: Vintage Books.

———. 2016. *The Attention Merchants: The Epic Scramble to Get Inside Our Heads*. New York, NY: Alfred A. Knopf.

———. 2017. "How the FCC's Net Neutrality Plan Breaks with 50 Years of History." *Wired*. December 6 (https://www.wired.com/story/how-the-fccs-net-neutrality-plan-breaks-with-50-years-of-history).

Yglesias, Matthew. 2018. "The Parkland Conspiracy Theories, Explained." *Vox*. February 22 (https://www.vox.com/policy-and-politics/2018/2/22/17036018/parkland-conspiracy-theories).

Yin-Poole, Wesley. 2017. "South Park: The Fractured but Whole's Difficulty Slider Changes the Colour of Your Skin." EuroGamer (http://www.eurogamer.net/articles/2017-09-07-south-park-the-fractured-but-whole-difficulty-slider-changes-the-colour-of-your-skin).

Yoon, InJeong. 2016. "Why Is It Not Just a Joke? Analysis of Internet Memes Associated with Racism and Hidden Ideology of Colorblindness." *Journal of Cultural Research in Art Education* 33: 92.

YouTube. 2018. "How Content ID Works." (https://support.google.com/youtube/answer/2797370?visit_id=1-636521506772611105-1677034236&rd=1).

Zafirau, Stephen. 2008. "Reputation Work in Selling Film and Television: Life in the Hollywood Talent Industry." *Qualitative Sociology* 31 (2): 99–127.

Zarkin, Kimberly A., and Michael J. Zarkin. 2006. *The Federal Communications Commission: Front Line in the Culture and Regulation Wars*. Westport, CT: Greenwood Press.

Zenith. 2017. "The Top 30 Global Media Owners 2107." (https://www.zenithusa.com/top-30-global-media-owners-2017/).

Zuckerberg, Mark. 2016 (https://www.facebook.com/zuck/posts/10102830259184701).

———. 2017. Facebook. September 30 (https://www.facebook.com/zuck/posts/10104074437830721).

———. 2018. Facebook. January 4 (https://www.facebook.com/zuck/posts/10104380170714571).

INDEX

A&E, 73, 350*f*

Abbate, Janet, 54

ABC

See American Broadcasting Corporation (ABC)

ABC Family, 73

Academy Awards, 239, 240

The Accountant, 297

Acioli, Renata, 365

Ackerman, Seth, 87

Acquisition editors, 181–182

Acronyms, 186

Act of reading, 283–284

Action-adventure films, 205–206

Active users, 9, 15, 269–272, 288–289, 306–307, 329*f*, 357

Ad photographers, 176–177, 179–181

Adalian, Josef, 141

Aday, Sean, 87, 136

Adbusters, 287

Adele, 157

Adelson, Sheldon, 88

Admonishment, 186–187

Advanced Research Projects Agency (ARPA), 54

Advertising

advertising-content connection, 98–100, 223–224, 258, 260–261

algorithmic power, 330–331, 338

audience segmentation, 236–237, 259–261

brand integration, 99–100

commercial radio broadcasting, 48

conglomeration impact, 84–85

consumerism, 216–219

contemporary news media, 103–105, 104*f*

European media, 114, 115

Facebook, 81–82, 82*f*

fraudulent/deceptive advertising, 126–127

global media culture, 219–222

Google, 81–82, 82*f*

historical perspective, 217–218

ideological viewpoints, 193, 216–222

impact on children, 312

Internet, 223, 331–332

media platforms, 65–66

new momism, 212–213

news media, 84–85, 98, 103–105, 104*f*, 166

19th century British and American press, 100–102

online advertising, 81

photography, 176–177, 179–181

political campaigns, 321

racial and ethnic diversity, 233

regulatory policies, 126–127

revenue decline, 94–95

secondary discourses, 220–221

self-censorship, 103

social class and position, 259–261

social media platforms, 145, 146

stereotypical portrayals, 194–195

television broadcasts, 50, 65, 81, 92–94, 261

traditional versus digital journalism, 331–332

user tracking, 323, 333

women's magazines, 218–219

AdWeek, 336

Affluent populations, 244, 256, 259–261

African Americans

alternative journalism, 245

civil rights movement, 18–21

early racist images, 238

film industry, 232, 238, 239–240

media content decoding and interpretation, 274–275

modern racism, 239–240, 243–244

newsroom representation, 246

online communities, 280

political marginalization, 241, 243

population percentages, 232, 234, 234*f*, 235

social class and position, 244

stereotypical portrayals, 194–195, 237–238, 241, 243, 244, 259, 281

television programming, 232–233, 234*f*, 236, 237*f*, 244

video game characters, 234–235

See also Race and ethnicity

Afrofuturism, 227

Agency, 13

   See also Social Constructionism; Technological determinism

Agenda-setting players and roles, 307–309

Agents of SHIELD, 76

Ahlkvist, Jarl A., 162

AIDS epidemic, 263f, 264, 265

Ailes, Roger, 87

Airwave access, 7, 47–49, 51, 117, 119, 122, 128

   See also Radio broadcasting

Al Jazeera, 200

Alba, Davey, 80

Alexa, 352t, 353t

Alexander, Jeffrey C., 332

Algorithms

   algorithmic journalism, 169–170

   algorithmic power, 330–331, 333–334, 338

   autonomous technology, 30

Alibaba, 82f

All in the Family, 93, 211, 252, 263f

All Lives Matter, 243

All My Children, 263f

All-American Girl, 233

Alldredge, John, 314

Allen-Robertson, James, 29

Allstate, 259

Alphabet, 352

Alternative journalism, 173–174, 245, 286–287, 325

Alternative media, 89, 149, 245–246

Althaus, Scott L., 136

Altheide, David L., 316

Althusser, Louis, 269

Alt-right demonstrators, 337

Amateur radio operators, 47–48, 50

The Amazing Race, 94

Amazon

   advertising revenue, 82f

   advertising-content connection, 223

   audience share, 94

   book selling, 183

   media platforms, 64

   original programming, 95, 96

   ownership concentrations and changes, 72, 73

   ratings systems, 132

   sexual minorities, 264f

   streaming services, 46, 73, 95

   top websites and global rankings, 353t

   user reviews and feedback, 298

Amazon Echo, 5, 26f

Amazon Prime, 95

Amazon Video, 158

AMC, 95, 237f, 241

America Online, 136–137

America Online (AOL), 41

American Bandstand, 44

American Broadcasting Corporation (ABC)

   audience share, 94

   fin-syn regulations, 140–141

   historical perspective, 50

   ownership concentrations and changes, 73, 79

   racial and ethnic diversity, 237f, 241

   regulatory policies, 111

   sexual minorities, 263f, 264f

   top prime-time programs, 237f

American Idol, 94, 99, 158, 349

American Marconi Company, 47, 49

American press, 102

American rock and roll, 359

American Sniper, 193–194

American Society of News Editors (ASNE), 246, 247

American Telephone and Telegraph (AT&T)

   See AT&T

America's Got Talent, 94, 158, 237f

America's Next Top Model, 93

Amnesty International, 343

Analog media, 58

Anand, Bharat N., 181

Anand, N., 63

Anastácio, Kimberly, 354

Andersen, David J.

   See Lau, Richard R.

Anderson, Jacqueline, 291

Andrews, Kenneth T., 200

Android, 65

Ang, Ien, 281

Angels in America, 263f

Angwin, Julia, 330

The Anna Nicole Show, 156

Another World, 296

Antitrust legislation, 39–41, 41f, 68, 109, 111, 140, 145

Appel, Helmut, 339

Apple, 26f, 56, 72, 96, 139

Apple Homepod, 26f

Apple Music, 42, 64, 96, 349, 353

Apple News, 331

Apple Newton, 59

Apple TV, 4

The Apprentice, 163

Arab Spring protests, 167, 215, 368

Arabs/Arab Americans, 240, 277

Archie's Place, 93, 253

Archway Publishing, 182

Are You the One?, 93

Ariel, Yaron, 294

Armstrong, David, 325

ARPANET, 54, 55, 56

Arthur, Charles, 291

Artificial intelligence (AI) tools, 169–170

Artz, Lee, 351

The Aryan, 238

As the World Turns, 264f

Asch, Solomon E., 309

Asian American Journalists Association, 246

Asian Americans/Pacific Islanders (AAPI)
    alternative journalism, 245
    early racist images, 238, 239, *239*
    film industry, 232
    newsroom representation, 246
    population percentages, 232, 234, 234f, 235, 241
    stereotypical portrayals, 241, 242f
    television programming, 233, 234f, 237f, 241, 242f
    video game characters, 234–235

Askin, Noah, 155

ASNE (American Society of News Editors), 246, 247

Asp, Kent, 316

Associated Press (AP), 38, 111, 171, 361

Association for Progressive Communications, 363

Asymmetrical interdependence, 358

AT&T
    antitrust legislation, 39–41, 41f, 68
    competitive market, 42
    economic dynamics, 79
    historical perspective, 39–42
    infrastructure conduits, 64, 74
    pay-for-play arrangements, 138
    radio broadcasting, 48–49
    television platforms, 73
    unfair competition, 139

AT&T Long Lines, 40

Atie, Rosalie
    See Jakubowicz, Andrew

Atlantic Records, 65

Atton, Chris, 173

Audience fragmentation, 279

Audiences
    active users, 9, 15, 269–272, 288–289, 306–307, 329f, 357
    advertising targeting, 236–237, 259–261
    advertising-content connection, 98–100, 103–105, 223–224, 330
    celebrity-watching play, 282–283
    content creation and distribution, 288–298
    content influences, 230
    content preferences, 229
    family audiences, 284–285
    film ratings systems, 297
    foreign audiences, 357
    international audiences, 276–278
    interpretive resistance, 285–287
    liberal versus conservative viewpoint, 120–121, 128–129, 192
    low-cost programming, 94–95
    media content decoding and interpretation, 271–278, 286–287
    media effects and influence, 306–307, 357
    new momism, 212–213
    news media, 98, 166
    19th century British and American press, 100–102
    online meaning making, 278–279
    owned versus organic activity, 65–66
    personalized journalism, 169–170
    polysemic texts, 270–271, 283–284
    prime-time programming, 140–141, 152–153
    product creation and promotion costs, 155
    radio broadcasts, 46–51
    ratings systems, 130–132, 133f
    reading romance novels, 283–284
    research background, 269–270
    second screen use, 278–279
    size determinations, 93, 95
    television broadcasts, 50–51, 53–54, 93
    See also Ideologies; Users

Audio compact disks (CDs), 26f, 42

Audiocassettes, 40, 42

Aufderheide, Patricia, 122, 123f, 128

Augmented journalism, 170

Auletta, Ken, 84, 145

Aupperle, Anna, 259–260

Aurora, Colorado, mass shooting, 332

Auslander, Philip, 315

Authoritarian governments, 108, 335, 347, 353, 370

Autocratic societies, 108

Automobile advertising, 259–260

Autonomous technology, 30–31

Auto-Tune, 44

Avatar, 62, 356

Avatar: The Last Airbender, 296

Axios, 82*f*

Baby Bells, 41, 41*f*, 42

Baby Boomers, 6*f*

The Bachelor, 65, 281

The Bachelorette, 93

Backstreet Boys, 156

Bacle, Ariana, 348

Badash, David, 336

Bae, Soo Young, 309

Bagdikian, Ben, 67, 86, 90

Bahfen, Nasya

    See Jakubowicz, Andrew

Baidu, 82*f*, 353, 353*t*

Baidu Tieba, 329*f*

Bailey, Sarah Pulliam, 213

Bakardjieva, Maria, 36, 270, 278, 289

Baker, C. Edwin, 105

Baker, Liana B., 343

Bakshy, Eytan

    See Jones, Jason J.

Baldasty, Gerald J., 102

Bandura, Albert, 312

Bandwagon effect, 309

Bandwidth limitations, 51–52

Banksy, 287

Bannon, Steve, 174

Barber, Benjamin R., 357

Bardot, Trushar, 369

Barlow, William, 237–238, 244

Barnard, Stephen R., 167

Barnes, Brookes, 356

Barnett, Brooke, 336

Barnett, Kyle, 181

Barnett, Steven, 327

Barney Miller, 211

Barris, Kenya, 233

Bartels, Larry, 321

Batman vs. Superman: Dawn of Justice, 70

Battani, Marshall, 176

Bauder, David, 233

Baudrillard, Jean, 34, 320

Bauman, Zymunt, 339

Baywatch, 156

The Beatles, 44

Beats/beat reporters, 164–165

Bechmann, Anja, 294

Becker, Howard S., 161–162

Beech, Hannah, 366

Beer, David, 331

Behm-Morawitz, Elizabeth, 233

Belief systems, 191

Bell, Alexander Graham, 39

Bell, Emily, 81, 332

Bell Labs, 40

Bell Telephone Company, 39, 40

Ben Amor, Hamada, 215

Benford, Robert D.

    See Snow, David A.

Bennett, Dionne, 215

Bennett, Kathryn, 356

Bennett, W. Lance, 135, 172, 316, 333

Berberian Sound Studio, 297

Berelson, Bernard, 228, 305

    See also Lazarsfeld, Paul

Bergen, Mark, 81

Berger, David G., 90–91

Berger, Peter L., 35

Berlusconi, Silvio, 86–87

Berners-Lee, Tim, 55

Bernoff, Josh, 291

Berry, Halle, 240

Bertelsmann, 67, 68, 70

Bertrand, Natashia, 335

BET, 53

Bewitched, 210, 254

Beyoncé, 44, 359

Bezos, Jeff, 88

Bhatia, Rahul, 354

Bhatia, Vickie

    See Feinstein, Brian A.

Bichlbaum, Andy, 287

Bieber, Justin, 348

Bielby, Denise D., 140, 159

Bielby, William T., 140, 159

The Big Bang Theory, 93, 237f, 349
Big Brother, 93, 349
Big Five publishers, 70
Big Little Lies, 220
Big Three music companies, 70, 71f
The Biggest Loser, 94
Bijker, Wiebe E., 35
Billboard magazine, 90, 91, 155, 157, 246, 247
Billy Lynn's Long Halftime Walk, 208
Bilton, Ricardo, 331
Bird, S. Elizabeth, 289, 314
Birkinbine, Benjamin, 63
Birth of a Nation, 238
Black Like Me, 239
Black Lives Matter (BLM), 20–21, 243, 281, 316, 327
Black Panther, 76, 227
Black Twitter, 279–281
Black underclass, 244, 259
Blackface, 238
black-ish, 233, 244
Blacks in Gaming, 235
Blank, Grant, 288, 292, 293, 294
Bliuc, Ana-Maria
    See Jakubowicz, Andrew
Block booking deals, 139–140
Blogs/blogging, 57, 167, 213, 280, 293, 338, 344
    See also Content creation and distribution
Blondheim, Menahem, 38
Bloomberg, Michael, 87
Blum, Andrew, 29
Blumer, Herbert, 303, 304, 311
Boczkowski, Pablo J., 28, 166, 167, 168
Bode, Leticia, 327
Bogart, Leo, 309
Bogle, Donald, 232
The Bold and the Beautiful, 349
Bollywood, 356
Bolsover, Gillian
    See Howard, Philip N.
Bolter, Jay David, 58
Bonanno, Mike, 287
Bond, Paul, 321
Bond, Robert M., 334
    See also Jones, Jason J.
Bonilla, Yarimar, 281
Bonilla-Silva, Eduardo, 241
Book publishing
    acquisition editors, 181–182
    booksellers, 183
    editorial decision-making, 180–185
    hit status, 155–156, 159
    mass-market books, 156
    norms and conventions, 162, 183
    ownership concentrations and changes,
        68, 69–70f, 70, 72
    political contributions, 118t
    product creation and promotion costs, 155
    scholarly publishing, 183–185
    self-publishing, 182
    star power, 157–158
    unsolicited manuscripts, 181–182
    user-generated content, 296
    vertical and horizontal integration, 74, 77f
Boorstin, Daniel, 34
Booth, Paul, 295
Bos, Arjan E. R., 186
Bosch, 95
Bose, Derek, 356
Bots, 311, 335–336
Bowker, 182
Box Office Mojo, 351f
Boy bands, 156
Boyd-Barrett, Oliver, 355
Boys Don't Cry, 262, 263f
Boyz II Men, 156
Bradley, Bill, 319
Bradshaw, Samantha
    See Howard, Philip N.
Brady Bunch, 254
Braid, Mary, 85
Branch, Taylor, 18
Brand, Jeffrey E., 233
Brand, Stewart, 222
Brand integration, 99–100
Branded entertainment, 99
Brave, 301
The Brave One, 230
Bravo, 53, 73, 96, 264f
Brazilian media regulations, 365
Breach notification, 145
Breaking Bad, 95
Breese, Elizabeth Butler, 332
Breitbart, Andrew, 174
Breitbart News, 174, 334
Brenner, Daniel L., 112, 113
Brewer, Doug, 117

The Bridge, 257–258

Brigs, Asa, 25

Brill's Content, 85

Brimeyer, Ted, 258

British Broadcasting Corporation (BBC), 36, 114

British press, 100–102

Broadband Commission for Sustainable Development, 354

Broadband Internet connectivity, 4, *4f*, *6f*, *27f*, 354

Broadcast journalism, 157

Broadcast licenses, 117, 119–120, 128, 147

Broadcast media
   racial and ethnic diversity, *236f*
   regulatory policies, 122
   star power, 157

Broadcast news, 85

Broadcast television
   adoption rates, *4f*
   agenda-setting effects, 308
   animated comedies, 253
   audience interpretation, 271–278
   changing American family, 210–212
   competitive markets, 53–54
   connective devices, 3–4
   copies and spin-offs, 93, 156, 160, 211
   cultivation theory, 312–313
   cultural codes, 271–272
   domestic viewing context, 284–285
   family audiences, 284–285
   family-based situation comedies, 229, 233, 249, 252–254
   fan communities, 296
   gender diversity, 247–249
   globalization impact, 343, 349
   hit status, 159–160
   ideological analysis, 193, 208, 210–213
   international perspectives, 276–278, 281–282
   locally produced media content, 356–357, 365
   marketing strategies, 50–51
   new momism, 212–213
   nostalgic programs, 211
   organized labor representations, 257–258
   political coverage, 318, 321–322
   polysemic texts, 270–271
   presidential debates, 318
   prime-time programming, 140–141, 156, 210
   production costs, 356
   racial and ethnic diversity, 232–233, *234f*, *237f*, 241, *242f*, 244, 274–278

reality television, 93–94, 156, 208, 210, 254, 256–257
   sexual minorities, 262, 263–*264f*, 264–265
   star power, 159, 160
   U.S. market share, 364
   women's sports coverage, 249, 250
   work-family programs, 211–212
   See also Cable television

Brodkin, Jon, 138

Brokeback Mountain, 262, *264f*

Brothers, *263f*

Broughel, Tara, 89

Brown, Melissa, 18

Brown, Rockell A., 243

Brunet, Antonia, 340

Bruns, Axel, 278, 289

Bryant, Jennings, 302

Buchsbaum, Jonathan, 365

Buckingham, David, 31

Buena Vista, 349

Buick, 259

Bump, Philip, 120, 324

Bureau of Alcohol, Tobacco, and Firearms (ATF), 127

Bureau of Labor Statistics, 97, *97f*, 257

Burke, Peter, 25

Burscher, Bjorn, 81

Bush, George H. W., 135

Bush, George W., 135, 319, 322

Business
   economic news, 202–203
   international advertising, 221–222
   U.S. press, 102
   See also Advertising; Economics; Media companies

Business ads, 221–222

Butcher, Melissa, 357

Butsch, Richard, 252, 253, 254, 261

Buzzbot, 169

BuzzFeed, 103

Byrne, Dara N., 280

Byrne, David, 358

Byrne, R. Jolene, 258

Cable lines, 64, 66

Cable News Network (CNN), 53

Cable television
   adoption rates, *4f*, *27f*
   audience share, 94

connective devices, 3
gender diversity, 247
historical perspective, 25*f*, 52–54
as news source, 166–167
ownership concentrations and changes, 67, 68, 73, 74
political contributions, 118*t*
racial and ethnic diversity, 236*f*
Cacciatore, Michael A., 333
Cadillac, 260
Calabrese, Andrew, 360
California Adventure Park, 161
Call Me By Your Name, 262
Callier, Patrick, 259
Callister, Mark, 247
Cambridge Analytica, 323, 324
Campbell, Christopher P., 243
Campbell, W. Joseph, 301
Campus demonstrations, 307
Canada
    cable television, 350*f*
    locally produced media content, 366
CanCon laws, 366
Cantor, Murial G., 254
Capitalism, 196–197, 357–358
    See also Consumerism
Cappella, Joseph N., 326
Captain America: Civil War, 70, 99
Caren, Neal, 200
Carey, Mariah, 44
Carney, Nikita, 243
Carol, 262
Carpenter, Elizabeth, 181
Carr, David, 73
Carragee, Kevin M., 259
The Carrie Diaries, 160
Carroll, Noël, 271
Cars, 160–161
Cars 2, 160–161
Cars 3, 160–161
Cartoon Network, 73
Carvin, Andy, 167
Castells, Manuel, 55
Catholic Church, 37
CBS
    See Columbia Broadcasting System (CBS)
CBS Corp., 67–68, 70
Cedillo, Stacia, 205

Celebrities
    audience game-playing, 282–283
    interview conventions, 163
    political careers, 318, 319
    product endorsements, 99
    reality programming, 156
    star power, 156–160
Celebrity Rehab with Dr. Drew, 156
Cell phones, 4–5, 4*f*, 6*f*, 27*f*
    See also Smartphones
Censorship
    film industry, 130–132
    global Internet, 116
    military censorship, 134–136, 153
    online media, 336–337
Center for American Progress and the Free Press, 128
Center for Responsive Politics, 118*t*
Centre for Contemporary Cultural Studies, University of Birmingham, 36
CenturyLink, 41*f*, 42
CERN
    See European Laboratory for Particle Physics (CERN)
Chadefaux, Thomas
    See Spaiser, Viktoria
Chadwick, Andrew, 327, 328
Chakravartty, Paula, 360
Chance, 95
Changing American family, 210–212
Chao, Lena M., 231
    See also Wilson, Clint C., II
Charlie Chan film series, 239
Charter Communications (Spectrum), 64, 68, 74
Chase, David, 271
Cheers, 93, 160
Chen, Gina M., 294
Chen, Liang, 311
Cheney, Richard, 135
Cherokee Phoenix, 245
Chico and the Man, 233
Child Online Protection Act (COPA, 1998), 130
Children's programming, 112, 115, 132, 153–154
Children's Television Act (1990), 153–154
Childress, Clayton, 181
Chin, Christina B., 233, 241
China
    computational propaganda, 335
    film industry, 356, 366

indigenous talent, 359
print media, 25, 26f
social media platforms, 329f, 335
websites, 82f, 353, 353t
Chiuy, Yvonne, 258
Chmielewski, Dawn C., 161
Choice fatigue, 296
Chokshi, Niraj, 334
Chomsky, Noam, 205
Choueiti, Marc, 232, 246
See also Smith, Stacy L.
Chow-White, Peter A., 280
Christakis, Dimitri A., 340
Christakis, Nicholas A., 339
The Christine Jorgensen Story, 263f
Chung, Philip W., 239
Cinemax, 73, 79
CIRP (Consumer Intelligence Research Partners), 5
Cisneros, J. David, 336
Citizen activists, 147, 149, 324–325
See also Public interest advocacy
Citizen alienation, 326
Civil rights movement
Black Lives Matter (BLM), 20–21, 243, 281, 316, 327
film industry, 239
mid-20th century, 18–20
See also Race and ethnicity
Civil War era, 134
Clark, Brad, 247
Clark, Charles S., 129
Clark, Naeemah, 231
Clarkson, Kelly, 158
Clash of civilizations, 357–358
Class shaming advertising strategies, 259–260
Clear Channel Communications, 72
Clear channels, 49
The Cleveland Show, 253
Clickbait, 80, 333
Clifford, Stephanie, 100
Clinton, Bill, 319
Clinton, Hillary, 319, 333, 335
CNBC, 73, 96
CNN, 73, 79, 85, 143, 167, 249, 322
Cobo, Leila, 348
Coercion, 197
Cohen, Bernard, 307
Cohen, Patricia, 202
Coldewey, Devin, 137

Cole, Williams, 261
Colhoun, Damaris, 103
Coll, Steve, 207
Collaborative wikis, 57
Collectors, 291, 292t
College textbook industry, 157–158
Colonialism, 355
Color-blind racism, 241, 251, 279–280
Columbia Broadcasting System (CBS)
audience share, 93, 94
fin-syn regulations, 140–141
historical perspective, 50
ownership concentrations and changes, 73
racial and ethnic diversity, 237f
sexual minorities, 263f
top prime-time programs, 237f
Comcast
advertising revenue, 81
corporate holdings, 96
economic dynamics, 78, 79
film studios, 349
global film industry, 70
infrastructure conduits, 64, 74
net neutrality policy, 137
ownership concentrations and changes,
65, 70, 73, 74
programming and distribution controls, 96
Comedy Central, 67
Commercial logic, 152
Commercial radio, 48
Commercial short message service (SMS), 26f
Commercial television, 35, 53–54, 65
Commission on Freedom of the Press, 111–112
Committee to Protect Journalists, 108–109
Common carriers
historical perspective, 40
regulatory policies, 122, 137–138
Common sense, 198–199
Common Sense Media, 291
Communication professionals
See Public relations professionals
Communications Decency Act (1996), 130, 143
Community, 296
Community Antenna Television (CATV), 52
Community building, 294
Community radio, 49
Compact disks (CDs), 26f, 42
Compuserve, 41

Computational propaganda, 310, 334–336
Computers
    adoption rates, 4–5, 4f
    historical perspective, 25f
    See also Internet
Concave, 99
Condit, Celeste M., 276
Conglomeration and integration
    economic dynamics, 78–79
    historical perspective, 122
    industry impact, 84–85
    key characteristics, 74, 76, 77f
    regulatory policies, 122–124
    self-promotion, 83–84
    Walt Disney Company, 62–63, 68, 75–76f, 78, 96
Congressional powers and responsibilities, 109–110
Connected televisions, 5, 6f
Connective media devices, 3–5, 4f, 6f, 57
Connelly, Karen
    See Jakubowicz, Andrew
Conrad, Frank, 48
Consalvo, Mia, 234
    See also Williams, Dmitri
Consensus, 201
Consent, 197
Constine, Josh, 144
Constitutional protections, 109–110, 121, 124–125
Constructed reality, 17
Consumer Intelligence Research Partners, 5
Consumerism
    advertising messages, 216–217
    culture clash thesis, 357–358
    early 20th century, 217–218
    global media culture, 219–222, 356
    lifestyle messages, 216–220, 223
    women's magazines, 218–219
    youth culture, 276
Contemporary media model, 9–10, 10f, 16–18, 16f
Contemporary news media, 103–105, 104f
Content creation and distribution
    active users, 288–289
    activity categories, 292–293
    creator characteristics, 293–294
    creator motivation, 294–295
    cultural contexts, 292
    fan communities, 295–296
    gatekeepers and distributors, 296–298, 331–332, 333
    participation categories, 291–292, 292t

    participatory culture, 289–290, 332–333
    participatory inequality, 290–291
Content sharing, 294, 295
Controversial programming, 88–89, 93, 152, 210
Convention on the Protection and Promotion of the
        Diversity of Cultural Expressions, 365
Conventions, 162–163
    See also Professional norms and practices
Convergence, 58, 79, 113, 122, 123f
Convergence culture, 161
Conversationalists, 291, 292t
Cook, Courtney B., 205
Cookies, 323
Cooky, Cheryl, 249, 250, 251
    See also Musto, Michela
Cooley, Charles Horton, 302
Coontz, Stephanie, 12
Cooper, Anderson, 157
Cooper, James Fenimore, 238
Copps, Michael, 87
Copyright Act (1790), 125
Copyright laws, 124–126, 126f, 144
Copyright Term Extension Act (1998), 125
The Corner Bar, 263f
Cornwell, Patricia, 156
Corporation for Public Broadcasting (CPB), 120
Corrigall-Brown, Catherine, 325
Cortell, Andrew P., 136
The Cosby Show, 94, 212, 244, 254
Coser, Lewis A., 181, 182
Cosmopolitan, 219, 233
Cotillard, Marion, 158
Cottle, Simon, 163
Couldry, Nick, 314
Council of Europe, 86
Council on American-Islamic Relations (CAIR), 240
Countercultural beliefs and values, 56–57, 131, 222, 325
Cowan, Tyler, 157
Craigslist, 331
Crane, Diana, 63
Cranor, Lorrie Faith, 338
Crawford, Alan Pell, 140
Creative Commons, 126, 126f
Creative Commons licenses, 126, 126f
Creators, 291, 292t
Cripps, Thomas, 232
Critics, 291, 292t
Cronauer, Adrian, 128

Cross-cultural boundaries, 345–346, 348
Cross-media promotions, 78, 84
Cross-ownership, 123–124, 123f
Croteau, David, 11, 35, 63, 110, 198, 202, 259, 317
Crouse, Timothy, 278
Crowdsource funding, 333
Crowell, Colin, 143
Crowley, David, 26f
The Crown, 95
Crusius, Jan, 339
Crystal, Billy, 263f
CSI, 93, 313
CSI Effect, 313–314
CSI: Miami, 93
CSI: New York, 93
CTV, 350f
Cultivation theory, 312–313
Cultural capital, 346
Cultural codes, 271–272
Cultural exception/cultural diversity, 364–365
Cultural hybridity, 345, 358–360
Cultural imperialism, 115, 355–357, 359
Cultural Indictors Project, 312
Cultural leadership, 197, 199
Cultural resistance, 214–215, 239–240, 244, 245–246,
    287–288
Cultural warfare, 193–194
Culture clash thesis, 357–358, 359
Culture jamming, 287–288
Curran, James, xv, 59, 100–101, 338, 339, 346
The Curse of Oak Island, 93
Curtin, Michael, 289
CW Network, 73, 141
Cyber radio stations, 26f
Cyberbullying, 311

Daddy Yankee, 348
The Daily Show, 163
Dallas, 94, 277–278, 281
Dalton, Russell J., 321
Dance, Gabriel J. X., 333
Dances with Wolves, 240
Dancing with the Stars, 94, 349
D'Angelo, Paul, 308, 326
Daniels, Jessie, 289
Dano, Mike, 74
Danowski, James A., 240
Dargis, Manohla, 193

The Dark Tower, 156
Data harvesting, 330
Data protection officers, 145
Data transfer capacity limitations, 139
Dates, Jannette L., 232, 237–238, 244
Davar, Shiamak, 348
Dávila, Arlene, 231
Davila, Joanne
    See Feinstein, Brian A.
Dawson, Jan, 5
Daytime talk shows, 256
De Lissovoy, Noah, 205
de Mateo, Rosario, 114
Deacon, David, 315
Deadliest Catch, 93
Dean, Howard, 322–323
Deaver, Michael, 319–320
Deceptive advertising, 126–127
Decision-making process, 180–185
Deep Space Nine, 227
Deery, June, 256–257
Deezer, 353
The Defiant Ones, 239
DeGeneres, Ellen, 163, 263f, 264–265
DeLaure, Marilyn, 287
#DeleteFacebook campaign, 144
Dell Computers, 99
Deloire, Christophe, 108
Deloitte, 356
Democracy Now!, 173–174
Democracynow.org, 174
Democratic societies
    media regulation, 114–115
    news organizations, 302, 326
    political environment, 108–109
    structure-agency dynamics, 14
Dempsey, John, 141
Denardis, Laura, 363
Denton, Robert, 135
Deo, Meera E.
    See Chin, Christina B.
Department of Agriculture, 127
Depp, Johnny, 157
Depression, 340
Deregulation debate, 110, 112–113, 116, 122–124, 123f, 128
Derks, Daantje, 186
Desktop computers, 4–5, 4f
"Despacito," 348–349

#DespacitoMovement, 348–349

Desperate Housewives, 212

Detective game, 282

Deuze, Mark, 166

Developing nations, 115–116, 361–362, 368

Dewey, C., 335

Dhar, Vasant, 337

Dial-up modems, 40

Die Hard, 205

Digital advertising, 81

Digital audio workstations (DAWs), 44

Digital colonialism, 354

Digital convergence, 58, 79, 113, 122, 123*f*

Digital divide, 293, 346, 367–369

Digital multimedia platforms, 25–26*f*, 27

Digital Subscriber Line (DSL) service, 40, 64

Digital technology
    film industry, 45
    future changes and developments, 369–371
    globalization impact, 343–346
    Internet, 58, 222–224
    lifestyle messages, 223
    music industry, 42–44, 72
    television broadcasts, 50
    traditional versus digital journalism, 331–332
    videos, 26*f*, 46

Digital video disks (DVDs), 26*f*, 46, 158

Digital video recorders (DVRs), 26*f*, 95

Digitization, 58

Dill, Jody C., 234

Dill, Karen E., 234

Dines, Gail, 121, 231

DirecTV, 64, 74, 79, 259, 260

DirecTV Now, 73

Dirty Sexy Money, 264*f*

Discovery Channel, 53

Discrimination, 198

Dish Network, 64, 73, 74

Disney
    See Walt Disney Company

Disney Channel, 156, 350*f*

Disney Channels Worldwide, 73

Disney Interactive Group, 351*f*

Disney Music Group, 351*f*

Disney Publishing, 351*f*

Disney Television, 350*f*

Disneyland resorts, 351*f*

DiStaso, Marcia Watson, 167

Ditonto, Tessa M.
    See Lau, Richard R.

Diversity
    See Inclusiveness and diversity

Divx Disc, 59

Dixon, Travis L., 243, 244
    See also Josey, Christopher L.

Dizney, Henry F., 309

Djankov, Simeon, 115

Do Not Disturb, 160

Dodds, Peter S., 155

Dole, Bob, 319

Domain names, 363

Dominant ideologies, 192–193, 216, 272, 285–286

Donahue, Phil, 256

Donders, Karen, 114

Donnay, Karsten
    See Spaiser, Viktoria

Donsbach, Wolfgang, 309

Dot.com companies, 57

Douglas, Michael, 206

Douglas, Susan J., 46, 47, 212–213

Douglass, Frederick, 245

Dove, 103

Dovey, Jon
    See Lister, Martin

Dowd, Timothy J., 91

Downing, John D. H., 149, 325

Doyle, Gillian, 90, 121

Dozier, David M., 247, 248

Dr. Laura, 213

Drake, 359

Druckman, James N., 308

Dubois, Frédéric, 325

DuCros, Faustina M.
    See Chin, Christina B.

Dumont network, 50

Dunaway, Johanna, 326

Duncan, Margaret Carlisle, 249
    See also Messner, Michael A.

Dunn, Kevin
    See Jakubowicz, Andrew

Dutton, William H., 289

DVD/Blu-Ray players, 4, 4*f*, 6*f*

DVRs, 4, 4*f*, 6*f*

Dwoskin, Elizabeth, 142

Dwyer, Maria
    See Hampton, Keith N.

E!, 96

An Early Frost, 263f

Eastwood, Clint, 208

eBay, 331

E-books, 26f, 183

Echo chambers, 333, 347

Eckles, Dean

   See Jones, Jason J.

Economics

   cultivation theory, 313

   ideological viewpoints, 196–197

   media content decoding and interpretation, 272–273

   news coverage, 202–203, 204f, 272–273

   user inequality, 366–368

   See also Advertising; Media companies; Media

     ownership

Economist, The, 86

Ed Sullivan Show, 53

Edelstein, David, 156

Edison, Thomas, 42

Editorial decision-making, 180–185

Educational level, 293–294

Educational programming, 153–154

Efron, Zac, 156

Egyptian revolution, 167, 368

Ehrenreich, Barbara, 259

Eisenstein, Elizabeth, 33, 37, 109

Eisinger, Robert M., 136

Ekdale, Brian, 294

El Général, 215

El Misisipi, 245

Elasmar, Michael G., 356

Elba, Idris, 156

Elber, Lynn, 233

Electromagnetic frequencies, 46, 47, 117, 119, 122

Electronic books, 72

Electronic dance music (EDM), 44

Electronic Frontier Foundation, 143

Elites versus insiders, 201–202

Elle, 219

Ellen, 263f, 264–265

Ellis, John, 296

Ellis, Sara Kate, 265

E-mail, 292, 293, 344

eMarketer, 81

Embedded reporter program, 135–136, 153

Emojis, 186

Emotional contagion, 339–340

Empire, 65, 233, 237f

Encryption technologies, 336, 370

Ender, Erika, 348

English press, 100–102

Entertainment Software Rating Board, 134

Entman, Robert, 241, 243, 244, 320, 321, 326

Epstein, Edward J., 162, 163

E.R., 264f

Ervin, Kelly S., 233

Eschner, Kat, 43

Escobar, Gabriel, 368

Esfandiari, Golnaz, 368

Espiritu, Belinda Flores, 282

ESPN, 53, 73, 78, 79, 249, 250, 350f

Esser, Frank, 314, 315, 316–317, 326

European Audiovisual Observatory, 364

European Commission, 115, 145, 146

European Federation of Journalists, 86

European film industry, 45, 46, 364–365

European Laboratory for Particle Physics (CERN), 55

European media regulation, 114–115

European Parliament, 86, 365

European Union, 115, 144, 145, 291, 292t, 365, 366

Evans, Jessica, 226

Everett, Anna, 280

Ewen, Stuart, 217, 218

Explainer journalism, 168

Exported entertainment, 219–221

Extreme Makeover, 94

Eye in the Sky, 208

Facebook

   active users, 329f, 343

   advertising revenue, 81–82, 82f, 353

   advertising-content connection, 99, 223, 330

   algorithmic power, 330–331, 333–334, 338

   book publishing, 182

   computational propaganda, 335

   developing nations, 116

   fake news, 142–144

   historical perspective, 26f

   ideological viewpoints, 193, 333

   international presence, 343

   legal challenges, 354

   media content, 80–81

   media dominance, 68, 79–83

   media platforms, 64, 65, 142–144

   net neutrality policy, 137

news content, 143, 146, 167, 331, 332, 334

norms and conventions, 185, 187–188

personalized content delivery, 80

political impact, 334

Russian election interference, 335

self-policing practices, 146, 337

social connections, 338, 339, 340

telecommunications infrastructure, 82–83, 354

tiered access arrangements, 138

top websites and global rankings, 353, 353t

user base, 80, 353–354

user contributions, 298, 333, 338

user tracking, 323, 330, 333

Facebook Live, 80

Facebook Messenger, 329f

Facetime, 138

Face-to-face communication, 15

Fact-based journalism, 171–174

Failures, 156

Fair use laws, 124

Fairness Doctrine (1949), 112, 120, 121, 127–129

Fake news, 108–109, 142–143, 310, 323–324, 333, 336

False consciousness, 196–197

Fame, 156–160

Family audiences, 284–285

Family Guy, 212, 253

Family Matters, 253

Family sitcoms, 210

Family structure, 12

Family-based situation comedies, 229, 233, 249, 252–254

Fan communities, 295–296

Fan fiction, 296

Fantasy film genre, 227

Fanzines, 296

Fariss, Christopher J.

    See Bond, Robert M.

Farmer lines, 39

Farrell, Mike, 270

Father Knows Best, 210, 254

Faughnder, Ryan, 297

Faulkner, Robert, 162

Fax machines, 40

Fear of a Black Planet, 124

Federal Communications Commission (FCC)

    broadcast licenses, 117, 119, 128

    enforcement responsibilities, 154

    Fairness Doctrine (1949), 128

    film ratings systems, 132

functional role, 111–113, 127

historical perspective, 40, 49

indecent programming, 129

lobbying influences, 117

media advocacy organizations, 147, 149

net neutrality policy, 137–138, 149

regulatory policies, 50, 52, 111–113, 117, 122–124, 123f

television broadcast programming, 140–141

Federal Election Commission (FEC), 118t, 145

Federal Radio Commission (FRC), 48, 49

Federal Trade Commission (FTC), 126, 127, 140, 258

Feenberg, Andrew, 278

Feinstein, Brian A., 339

Fejes, Fred, 247, 249, 262, 264, 265–266

Feldman, Dana, 141

Female athletes, 249–250

Female sexuality, 275–276

Feminist perspective

    gender inequality, 249

    interpretive resistance, 275–276, 285–287

    media pleasure and entertainment, 281–282

    oppositional readings, 273, 275–276

Fenton, Natalie, 59

    See also Curran, James

#Ferguson, 281, 327

Fiber-optic communications

    adoption rates, 4f, 27f

    economic dynamics, 79

    economic strategies, 74

    historical perspective, 26f

    as service conduits, 64

    television broadcasts, 3, 4f, 6f

Fictional universes, 63, 161

Fifty Shades of Grey, 182

File sharing, 144

Film Trust, 45, 46, 139

Film/film industry

    advertising-content connection, 99, 100

    block booking deals, 139–140

    censorship and ratings systems, 130–132, 133f

    civil rights movement, 239

    cross-media promotions, 84

    digital technology, 45–46

    early racist stereotypes, 238–239

    encoded meanings, 271–272

    failures, 156

    fantasy film genre, 227

    gender diversity, 247

genre analyses, 205–208
globalization impact, 343, 349
historical perspective, 25f, 27, 45–46
hit status, 155–156, 158
ideological viewpoints, 192–193
impact on children, 303–304, 311–312
influential effects, 303–304, 311–312
locally produced media content, 356–357, 366
media content decoding and interpretation, 275–276
organized labor representations, 257
ownership concentrations and changes, 67, 68, 70
political contributions, 118t
polysemic texts, 270
production costs, 356
racial and ethnic diversity, 192–193, 232, 239–240,
    242f, 245, 246
science fiction film genre, 227
sequels, 156, 160–161
sexual minorities, 262, 263–264f
shifting ideological viewpoints, 191
social influence, 45–46
star power, 157, 159
streaming services, 46
technological characteristics, 30f
U.S. market share, 364
user reviews and ratings, 297
user-generated content, 296
vertical and horizontal integration, 74, 77f, 83–84
See also Walt Disney Company
Filter bubbles, 333, 347
Finding Dory, 70
Fink, Moritz, 287
Finklea, Bruce W., 302
Finley, Klint, 363
Fin-syn (financial interest and syndication) regulations,
    140–141
Fiore, Quentin, 32, 343
Fiorina, Carly, 194
First Amendment (U.S. Constitution), 109, 121, 326, 337
First World nations, 361
Fischer, Claude, 28, 39, 42
Fisher, David, 265
Fishman, Mark, 163, 164, 165
Fiske, John, 270, 285
FiveThirtyEight, 168
Flags of our Fathers, 208
Flaming, 187
Flashdance, 275–276

Flegenheimer, Matt, 108
Flew, Terry, 356, 358, 360
Flickr photo sharing site, 26f
Flint, Joe, 140
The Flintstones, 154, 253
FM radio broadcasting, 49
Focus Features, 70
Fonsi, Luis, 348
Food and Drug Administration (FDA), 126, 127
Foot, Kirsten A., 28
Forbes, 87
Force, use of, 197
Ford, Harrison, 205
Ford, Sam, 297
Foreign audiences, 357
For-profit organizations
    audience and revenue decline, 94–95
    content and distribution controls, 95–96
    news media, 96–98
    prime-time profit pressures, 92–94
    prime-time profits, 92–94
Forrester Research, 291, 292t, 293
Fortune, 88
45-rpm records, 43
Foster, Jodie, 230
The Fosters, 212
Fowler, James H.
    See Bond, Robert M.; Jones, Jason J.
Fowler, Mark S., 112, 113
Fox
    audience share, 94
    conglomeration impact, 85, 96
    economic dynamics, 79
    film studios, 141
    international presence, 343
    ownership concentrations and changes, 68, 73
    programming and distribution controls, 141
    racial and ethnic diversity, 233, 235, 237f
    talent search shows, 158
    top prime-time programs, 237f
Fox, Mark A., 134
Fox Entertainment Group, 70
Fox News, 68, 85, 87, 88, 98, 129, 163, 192, 343
Fox Searchlight, 70
Fox Sports, 343
Foxy Brown, 239
Framing theory, 308
France 24, 365

Frank, Reuven, 124

Frank, Thomas, 276

Franken, Al, 319

Franklin, Bob, 331

Franzen, Benjamin, 124

Frasier, 93, 160

Fraudulent advertising, 126–127

Free Basics, 82, 354

Free Internet services, 223

Free market systems, 110, 112, 115

Free Press, 137

Freedman, Des, 59, 117, 121

   See also Curran, James

Freedom House, 87

Freedom of expression, 108–109

Freedom of information, 361

Freedom of speech, 109, 130, 337

Freedom of the press, 108–109, 121–124, 173, 302, 326

Freedom's Journal, 245

Freeland, Jonathan, 324

Freeman, Michael, 140

French media regulations, 365

Fresh Off the Boat, 233, 241

Friday Night Lights, 212

Friemel, Thomas N., 293

Friends, 93, 233, 263f

Friendster, 26f

Frith, Simon, 159

Fritsch-El Alaoui, Khadija, 207

Fu Manchu, 239

Fuller, Linda, 240

Fullwood, Chris, 294

Fung, Timothy K. F., 294

Funkhouser, G. Ray, 307

Furious 7, 65

FX, 62, 68, 343

Gainous, Jason, 327

Gallagher, Margaret, 195

Game of Thrones, 95, 356

Game-playing audiences, 282–283

Gamson, Joshua, 256, 282–283

Gamson, William, 198, 308, 324, 325

Gans, Herbert, 163, 201

Garcia-Perdomo, Victor, 279

Garofalo, Reebee, 359

Gasser, Urs, 293

Gates, Bill, 78

Gaudet, Hazel, 305

   See also Lazarsfeld, Paul

Gay & Lesbian Alliance Against Defamation (GLAAD), 89, 233, 234f, 247, 265

Gay community

   See LGBTQ community

Geena Davis Institute on Gender in Media, 301

Gelbart, Larry, 270

Gender

   family-based situation comedies, 249, 252–254

   Internet participation and content creation, 294

   interpretive resistance, 275–276, 285–286

   media content decoding and interpretation, 273–274, 275, 286–287

   media representations, 247–249

   nature versus culture, 198

   new momism, 212–213

   rap music, 214

   shifting ideological viewpoints, 191

   stereotypical portrayals, 194–195, 238, 246–251, 247–249

   television programming, 247–249

   television viewing, 284

   women's magazines, 218–219

   women's sports coverage, 249–251

   See also Race and ethnicity

Gender bland sexism, 251

General Agreement on Trades and Tariffs (GATT), 364

General Data Protection Regulation (GDPR), 144

General Electric, 48, 84

Generation X, 6f

Generation Z, 6f

Genre analyses

   film industry, 205–208

   television programming, 208, 209f, 210–213

Gentile, Douglas A., 130, 234

The George Lopez Show, 253

Gera, Vanessa, 339

Gerbner, George, 135, 312, 313, 361, 362

Gerlach, Alexander R., 339

Geronimo, 240

Get Out, 192–193, 245

Ghostbusters, 99

Gianatasio, David, 248

Giddings, Seth

   See Lister, Martin

Gil de Zúñiga, Homero, 279

Gilens, Martin, 259

Gillespie, Tarleton, 28

Gilmore Girls, 212
Ginsborg, Paul, 114
Girard, Bruce, 360
Gitlin, Todd, 92, 93, 152, 271, 307, 325
Giuffrida, Angela, 87
GLAAD (Gay & Lesbian Alliance Against Defamation), 89, 233, 234f, 247, 265
Glamour, 219, 233
Glascock, Jack, 247
Glaser, April, 145
Glassdoor, 186, 187
Global Editors Network, 170
Global media industry
    advertising messages, 219–222
    centralized ownership and production control, 348–349
    cultural exception/cultural diversity, 364–365
    cultural hybridity, 345, 358–360
    cultural imperialism, 115, 355–357, 359
    culture clash thesis, 357–358, 359
    digital divide, 367–369
    economic inequality, 366–368
    foreign audiences, 357
    future changes and developments, 369–371
    indigenous media industries, 115, 356
    information flow, 360–362
    Internet governance, 363–364
    locally produced media content, 356–357, 358, 365–366
    media content, 219–221, 349, 355–360
    most visited websites, 353t
    occurrences and users, 342–343
    promotion strategies, 348–349
    regulatory policies, 360–366
    U.S. market share, 364
    user base, 366–369, 367f
    Western imports, 355–359
    See also Google; Walt Disney Company
Global Media Monitoring Project (GMMP), 195
Global village, 342, 346, 366–369
Global Voices, 354
Globalization
    basic concepts, 343–347
    challenges and constraints, 346–347
    cross-cultural boundaries, 345–346, 348
    information environment, 342–343
    instantaneous communication, 342, 344
    key components, 343–344
    promotion strategies, 348–349
    temporospatial limits, 344

Gloria, 93
Gmail, 138
Goebbels, Joseph, 49
Goffman, Erving, 308
Gold Rush, 94
The Golden Hills' News, 245
Goldfarb, Jeffrey, 326
Golding, Peter, 269
Goldsmith, Jack, 360, 364
Gomez, Rodrigo, 63
Gone with the Wind, 238
Gonzalez, Juan, 244–245
Good Times, 93, 211, 253
Goodman, Amy, 136
Goodman, David, 136
Google
    advertising revenue, 81–82, 82f, 352
    advertising-content connection, 99, 223, 330
    algorithmic power, 330, 331
    computational propaganda, 335
    fake news, 142–143
    international presence, 343
    Internet traffic flow, 352
    legal challenges, 145
    media content, 80–81
    media dominance, 68, 79–83
    media platforms, 64, 65, 142–143
    net neutrality policy, 137
    news content, 143, 332
    norms and conventions, 185
    personalized content delivery, 80
    popularity, 352
    regulatory policies, 145
    search sites and global rankings, 352t
    telecommunications infrastructure, 82–83
    top websites and global rankings, 353t
    user base, 80
    user tracking, 330
    See also YouTube
Google Chromecast, 4
Google Fiber internet service, 83
Google Glass, 17, 26f, 59
Google Home, 5, 26f
Google News, 80
Google Play, 132
Google Station, 83
Gordon, Janey, 49
Gore, Al, 56, 134

Gore, Tipper, 134

Gossip game, 282

Gottfried, Jeffrey, 143

Govil, Nitin
    See Miller, Toby

Graber, Doris A., 321, 326

Grace under Fire, 212

Graceland, 359

Graham, Roderick, 280

#GrammysSoMale, 235, 248*f*

Gramophones
    See Phonographs; Sound recordings

Gramsci, Antonio, 197, 198–199

Grand Upright Music Ltd. v. Warner Bros. Records Inc.
    (1991), 124

Grant, Iain
    See Lister, Martin

Grasmuck, Sherri, 280

Grassroots organizations, 324–325

Graves, Lucia, 87

Gray, Herman, 244, 336

Gray, James, 158

Gray, Jonathan, 295, 357

The Greaser's Revenge, 238

The Great Firewall, 353

Greco, Albert N., 182

Green, Joshua, 297

Greenberg, Bradley S., 233, 247

Gregory, Julia, 169

Gregory, Karen, 289

Greider, William, 320–321

Griffith, D. W., 59, 238

Griffith, Erin, 80

Groselj, Darja, 292

Gross, Alexander, 280

Gross, Larry, 265, 313
    See also Gerbner, George

Gross, Terry, 207

Grossman, Lawrence, 84

The Group That Shall Not Be Named, 295

Grusin, Richard, 58

Grynbaum, Michael M., 108, 109

Guardian, The, 136, 168

Guardians of the Galaxy 2, 76

Guess Who's Coming to Dinner, 239

Guggenheim, Lauren, 302, 309

Guillory, Jaime E., 339

Gunter, Barrie, 311

Gutenberg, Johannes, 32, 36

Gutierrez, Felix, 231
    See also Wilson, Clint C., II

Hachette Book Group, 70

Hackers, 55

Hafen, Jeffrey K., 233

Hafner, Katie, 54

Hall, Stuart, 36, 199, 226, 271

Hamilton, James F., 173

Hamm, Bernd, 351, 356

Hampton, Keith N., 311

Hancock, Jeffrey T., 339

Handmaid's Tale, 73, 95

Hanks, Tom, 157, 263*f*

Hannonen-Gladden, Helena, 233

Happy Days, 211

Hardt, Hanno, 302

Hargittai, Eszter, 293

Harington, C. Lee, 295

Harold, Christine, 287

Harper Collins, 68, 70

Harrington, Stephen, 278

Harris, Tristan, 337

Hartley, John, 285

Hartman, Andrew, 193

Harwell, Drew, 332

Harzig, Christiane, 325

Hashtag activism, 327

Hate groups, 336

The Have and Have-Nots, 237*f*

Hayes, Rutherford B., 38

Hays, William, 131

Hays Code, 131

HBO (Home Box Office)
    drama series, 95
    economic dynamics, 79
    historical perspective, 53
    ownership concentrations and changes, 72, 73
    racial and ethnic diversity, 241
    sexual minorities, 263*f*, 264*f*
    subscriber fees, 53

Hearst, 72

Heavy television viewers, 312–313

Hebert, Maeve, 136

Hefner, Veronica
    See Josey, Christopher L.

Hegemony, 197–200, 203, 213, 215–216

Helbing, Dirk
　See Spaiser, Viktoria
Heliograf, 169–170
Helsingborg, Sweden, 59
Hennon, Charles B., 254
Hepp, Andreas, 314, 315
Herkman, Juha, 294
Herman, Edward, 205
Hermida, Alfred, 298
Herrman, John, 337
Hershenberg, Rachel
　See Feinstein, Brian A.
Heyer, Paul, 26f
Hibberd, Matthew, 114
Hickey, Neil, 117
Higgins, Andrew, 333
High Performance Computing and Communication Act
　(1991), 56
Highland, Tim, 278
High-speed coaxial cable lines, 66
High-speed internet connections, 74, 79
Hillis, Ken, xv
Hills, Jill, 114
Hindman, Elizabeth Blanks, 136
Hindman, Matthew, 327
Hintz, Arne, 49, 149
Hip consumerism, 276
Hip-hop culture, 215
Hirsch, Eric, 36
Hirsch, Mario, 115
Hispanic Americans
　alternative journalism, 245
　early racist images, 238, 239
　film industry, 232
　media content decoding and interpretation, 275
　newsroom representation, 246
　population percentages, 232, 234, 234f, 235
　television programming, 233, 234f, 237f
　video game characters, 234–235
History Channel, 73, 93
Hitland, Paul, 149
Hjarvard, Stig, 314, 315, 316
　See also Hepp, Andreas
Ho, Karen K., 246
Ho, Shirley S., 311
Hoerder, Dirk, 325
Hoffmann, Christian Pieter, 290

Hofmann, Stefan, 339
Hoggart, Riahcard, 36
Holbert, R. Lance, 328
Holian, David, 321
Hollywood agents, 162
Hollywood movie industry, 45, 131, 139–140
Hollywood Writers Report, 246, 247
Holmes, Su, 289
Holsti, Ole R., 228
Holt, Lester, 157
Holtz-Bacha, Christina, 320
Home broadband access, 4, 4f, 27f
Homeland, 95
Homicide, 93
Homogeneous media products, 38, 53, 90–91
Homosexuality
　See LGBTQ community
The Honeymooners, 252
Hoover, Herbert, 48
Horan, Nora, 247
Horizontal integration, 74, 76, 77f, 83–84
Horse race coverage, 326
House of Cards, 93, 141
Hout, Michael, 252
How I Met Your Mother, 93
How to Get Away With Murder, 237f, 249
Howard, Philip N., 310, 334, 335, 336, 368
Hoynes, William, 11, 35, 63, 110, 198, 202, 259, 317
Huey, John, 87–88
Hughes, Langston, 245
Hughes, Thomas P., 30–31, 35
Hughey, Matthew W., 280
Hulu
　audience share, 94
　historical perspective, 26f
　hit films, 158
　international presence, 343
　media platforms, 64
　original programming, 95, 96
　ownership concentrations and changes, 63, 72, 79
　ratings systems, 132
　streaming services, 46, 73, 95, 141
Human agency, 13
　See also Social Constructionism; Technological
　　determinism
Human Rights Campaign, 265
Humez, Jean M., 231

Hungama, 350*f*

Hunger Games, 160, 295, 301

Hunt, Darnell M., 246, 247, 274–275, 286

Hunter, James Davison, 193

Huntington, Samuel, 357

Hurley, Ryan J.

   See Josey, Christopher L.

Hurricane Katrina, 243

The Hurt Locker, 207

Hussain, Muzammi, 368

Husseini, Sam, 84

Hutchins Commission, 111–112

Hybrid culture thesis, 358–360

Hybrid music, 345, 358–359

Hyperreality, 34, 320

I Dream of Jeannie, 210

IAC, 82*f*

IBISWorld, 72

iBooks, 72

ICAAN (Internet Corporation for Assigned Names and
   Numbers), 363

iCloud, 138

Identity formation, 294

Ideologies

   advertising messages, 193, 216–219

   analytical challenges, 204–205

   basic concepts, 191–192

   consumerism, 217–219

   cultural contradictions and battles, 192–194, 285–286

   dominant ideologies, 192–193, 216, 285–286

   economic news, 202–203, 204*f*, 272–273

   elites versus insiders, 201–202

   film genre analyses, 205–208

   hegemony, 197–200, 203, 213, 215–216

   Internet, 222–224

   Marxism, 191, 196–197

   media representations, 199–200

   news media, 201–203

   rap music, 213–216

   social norms and values, 194–195

   television programming, 208, 209*f*, 210–213

   theoretical perspective, 196–200

IFPI (International Federation of the Phonographic
   Industry), 42, 353

#IfTheyGunnedMeDown, 281

iHeartMedia, 72

I'm No Angel, 130

Imagery

   See Photography; Television

iMessage, 138

Imitated products, 153, 155–156

The Immigrant, 158

In the Heat of the Night, 239

Inactives, 291, 292*t*

Inclusiveness and diversity, 231, 232–235

Indecent material, 129–130

Independent filmmakers, 45, 46, 139–140

Independent record companies, 90–91

Independent telephone companies, 39–40

India

   cable television, 350*f*

   film industry, 356

   music contests, 348–349

   regulatory policies, 116

Indiana Jones and the Temple of Doom, 206

Indiana Jones films, 205

Indigenous media industries, 115, 356

Indigenous talent, 359

Indymedia.org, 174

Information distortions, 324, 332–334

Information flow, 360–362

Information seeking, 292, 293

Information superhighway, 56

Infowars, 332

In-game advertising, 99

Ingram, Matthew, 81

Innis, Harold, 32

Insiders

   See Elites versus insiders

Instagram, 26*f*, 65, 138, 329*f*, 353

Instantaneous communication, 342, 344

Intellectual property rights, 125

   See also Copyright laws

Intelligence Community Assessment, 324, 334–335

Interactive journalism, 168

International advertising, 219–221

International audiences, 276–278, 281–282

International Chamber of Commerce, 360

International Commission for the Study of
   Communication Problems, 362

International Federation of the Phonographic Industry
   (IFPI), 42

International music, 345, 358–359

Internet
    access and connection speed, 354
    active users, 9, 15, 288–289, 357
    activity categories, 292–293
    addictive effects, 337–340
    advertising messages, 223, 331–332
    agenda-setting players, 308–309
    authoritarian governments, 370
    censorship, 116
    challenges and constraints, 346–347
    common languages, 347t
    communication models, 8–9, 10f
    connective devices, 4–5, 4f, 57
    content creation and distribution, 288–298
    data transfer capacity limitations, 139
    developing nations, 116
    digital technology, 58
    economic growth, 355
    fraudulent/deceptive advertising, 127
    future changes and developments, 369–371
    globalization impact, 342–343
    governance, 363–364
    hate groups, 336
    historical perspective, 25f, 41, 54–57
    ideological viewpoints, 222–224
    impact survey, 328
    infrastructure characteristics, 57–59
    locally produced media content, 366
    marketing strategies, 57
    materiality theory, 29–30
    matrix media, 289
    military applications, 54, 55
    motherhood, 213
    net neutrality, 136–139, 149, 354
    as news source, 166–167
    norms and conventions, 185–188
    ownership concentrations and changes, 74
    packet switching technology, 54–55, 55f
    participation categories, 291–292, 292t
    participatory culture, 332–333
    political campaigns, 323
    political contributions, 118t
    political coverage, 321–324
    political participation, 326–328
    privatization, 56
    pro-democracy movements, 368
    psychological factors, 339–340
    public relations professionals, 322–324
    racial and ethnic diversity, 279–281
    regulatory policies, 56, 58, 115, 122, 137–138, 144–146, 149, 337, 360
    sexually explicit materials, 129–130
    social influence, 57, 59
    social movements, 325
    technological characteristics, 30f
    terrorist groups, 336
    traditional versus digital journalism, 331–332
    unfair competition, 139
    user base, 367, 367f
    user demographics, 6f
    user privacy protections, 144–145
    user tracking, 323, 330, 333
    See also Facebook; Google; Social media
Internet Assigned Numbers Authority (IANA), 363
Internet Corporation for Assigned Names and Numbers (ICANN), 363
Internet Governance Forum (IGF), 363–364
Internet of Things (IoT), 5, 57, 369
Internet service providers (ISPs), 41, 122, 136–139
Internet Society, 56
Internet World Stats, 343
Interpersonal communication, 7–8, 9, 58
Interpretive communities, 284–285
Interpretive resistance, 275–276, 285–287
Invasive marketing, xvii
iPads, 26f
iPhones, 139
Iranian protests, 368–369
Iraq War, 89, 135–136, 153, 208, 322
Isaac, Mike, 146, 353
    See also Mozur, Paul
Islam, 357
Islamic State of Iraq and Syria (ISIS), 207
Israeli television viewers, 277
Italian media, 86–87
iTunes Store, 95, 132, 349
Ivory, James D., 234
    See also Williams, Dmitri
Iyengar, Shanto, 308, 333

Jackson, Janine, 103
Jackson, Linda A., 233
Jackson, Samuel L., 157, 240
Jacobs, Matthew, 264f
Jakubowicz, Andrew, 336
Jamieson, Kathleen Hall, 326
Janbek, Dana M., 336
Jang, S. Mo, 309

Japan
    Internet participation categories, 291, 292*t*
    television content decoding and interpretation, 277, 278
Jarhead, 208
Jarrett, Kylie, xv
Jason Bourne, 99
The Jeffersons, 93, 211
Jeffords, Susan, 135, 206–207
Jenkins, Cheryl D., 243
Jenkins, Henry, xv, 161, 279–280, 289–290, 293, 295,
    297, 333
Jensen, Kerry, 249
    See also Messner, Michael A.
Jermyn, Deborah, 289
Jessell, Harry A., 140
The Jetsons, 154
Jihad, 357–358
Joey, 93
Johnson, Austin H., 199–200
Johnson, Dwayne (The Rock), 156
Johnson, Kirk, 120
Johnson administration, 128
Johnson-Cartee, Karen S., 308
Joiners, 291, 292*t*
Jonas Brothers, 156
Jones, Alex, 331, 332
Jones, Jason J., 334
    See also Bond, Robert M.
Joplin, Janis, 215
Jordan, Tim, 55
Jorgensen, Christine, 263*f*
Josey, Christopher L., 244
Jost, Kenneth, 26*f*
Journalistic routines, 164–166
Journalistic transparency, 170
Joy, 160
Junk news, 335
    See also Russian election interference

Kadushin, Charles, 181
    See also Coser, Lewis A.
Kahle, Shannon, 243
Kahn, Frank J., 128
Kahn, Richard, 55, 325
Kalogeropoulos, Antonis, 331
Kane, John V., 258
Kang, Cecilia, 144, 337
Kantrowitz, Alex, 330
Karloff, Boris, *239*

Karr, Alphonse, xv
Karr, Tim, 137, 139
Kasser, Tim, 312
Kastrenakes, Jacob, 146
Katz, Elihu, 277, 305, 357
Katz, Mark, 43, 315
Keegan, Rebecca, 161
Kelley, Robin D. G., 214
Kellner, Douglas, 55, 319, 324, 325
Kelly, Kieran
    See Lister, Martin
Kelly, Megyn, 157
Kemp, Jack, 319
Kendall, Diana, 252, 261
Kennard, William E., 119
Kennedy, John F., 318
Kennedy administration, 128
Keohane, Joe, 169
Kerry, John, 319
Khalifa, Wiz, 65
Kian, Edward M., 250
Kibbutznik groups, 277
The Kids Are All Right, 262
Kim, Youna, 281–282
Kinder, Donald R., 308
King, Claire Sisco, 230
King, Rodney, 274
King, Stephen, 156
King of Queens, 253
King of the Hill, 253
Kingsbury Commitment (1913), 39–40
Kirst, Seamus, 240
Kjellberg, Felix Arvid Ulf, 66
Klapper, Joseph, 305, 306
Klein, Hugh, 247
Kleinberg, Mona S.
    See Lau, Richard R.
Klinenberg, Eric, 166, 167
Koblin, John, 141
Koch, Charles and David, 87–88
Kohut, Andrew, 103
Kollanyi, Bence
    See Howard, Philip N.
Korean media industry, 356
Korean War, 270
Korean women, 281–282
Kornhauser, William, 304
Kosar, Kevin R., 127
Kostaki, Irene, 366

Kovach, Steve, 143

Kovarik, Bill, 25

Kraidy, Marwan M., 358

Kramer, Adam D. I., 339
   See also Bond, Robert M.

Krasnow, Erwin, 147

Kretz, Valerie, 311

Krotz, Friedrich, 314

Krugman, Dean M., 112

Ku Klux Klan, 238

Kumanyika, Chenjerai, 259

Kunz, William M., 141

Kuo, Rachel, 281

Kurtulus, Sema, 292

Kushner, Tony, 263*f*

Kuvalanka, Katherine A., 254

Kuypers, Jim A., 308

Kwak, Nojin, 328

The L Word, 88, 264*f*, 265

L.A. Law, 233

Labaton, Stephen, 119

Labor unions, 257–258, 273

Lacan, Jacques, 269

Lady Gaga, 296

Lafrance, Adrienne, 137

Laing, David, 356

Lamar, Kendrick, 245

Lanchester, John, 330, 336

Landlines, 5

Langlois, Andrea, 325

Lanier, Jaron, 223

Laposky, Issie, 149, 323

Laptop computers, 4–5, 4*f*, 57, 368

Larose, Robert, 339

Las Vegas Review-Journal, 88

Latack, Jessica A.
   See Feinstein, Brian A.

Late Night with Seth Meyers, 163

Late-night comedy news programs, 163

Latino/Latina Americans
   alternative journalism, 245
   early racist images, 238, 239
   film industry, 232
   media content decoding and interpretation, 275
   newsroom representation, 246
   population percentages, 232, 234, 234*f*, 235
   television programming, 233, 234*f*, 237*f*
   video game characters, 234–235

Lau, Richard R., 334

Lauper, Cyndi, 276

Lauzen, Martha M., 247, 248

Lavery, David, 271

Law and Order, 93

Lawrence, Jennifer, 160

Laybourn, Wendy, 18

Lazarsfeld, Paul, 305, 306

Le Bon, Gustave, 304

League of Nations, 360–361

The Leaky Cauldron, 295

Lear, Norman, 211

Learning theory, 311–312

Leave It to Beaver, 210, 254

Lecompte, Celeste, 170

LeDuff, Kim M., 243

Lee, Eric, 368

Lee, Jenny Jong-Hwa
   See Chin, Christina B.

Lee, Latoya A., 280

Lee, Sangoak, 356

Lee-Won, Roselyn J., 280

Legion of Decency, 131

Lemke, Fred, 313

Lennon, John, 215

Leonhardt, David, 324

Lepre, Carolyn Ringer, 231

Lesbian community
   See LGBTQ community

Lessig, Lawrence, 126

Letters from Iwo Jima, 208

The Leveson Inquiry, 85

Levin, Gary, 236, 237*f*

Levine, Elana, 195

Levy, Steven, 55

Lewis, Lisa, 276

Lewis, Paul, 337

LGBTQ community
   media representations, 199–200, 262, 263–264*f*,
     264–266
   nature versus culture, 198
   prime-time programming, 88–89

Liacas, Tom, 287

Liberal versus conservative viewpoint, 120–121,
   128–129, 192, 201, 313, 334

Licklider, J. C. R., 54–55

Liebes, Tamar, 277, 357

Lievrouw, Leah A., 28, 29, 149, 173, 200

Life, 111

Lifestyle messages, 216–220, 223
Lifetime Television, 73
Limited effects theory, 305–306, 333–334
Limperos, Anthony M., 269
Lind, Rebecca Ann, 231, 240, 244
Line, 329f
LinkedIn, 82f, 329f
Linn, Susan, 312
Lionsgate, 70
Lippmann, Walter, 302
Lip-synching, 44
Liquid modernity, 339
Lister, Martin, 58
Literary agents, 181, 182
Little, Vance, 365
Little Big Man, 240
Littleton, Cynthia, 356
Live music performances, 43–44
Livingston, Steven, 136
Livingstone, Sonia, 28, 286, 289, 294
Local Community Radio Act (2011), 119
Locally produced media content, 356–357, 358, 365
Loeb, Laura, 163
Logic of safety, 93
LOGO TV, 264f
Lomborg, Stine, 294
Long, Elizabeth, 205
Long-distance communication, 38–42, 47, 48–49,
    52–53
Longley, Lawrence, 147
Long-playing (LP) records, 42, 43
Lopes, Paul D., 91
Lopez, Lori Kido, 296
Los Angeles riots (1992), 274–275, 286
Los Angeles Times, 64, 170, 257, 261
Loss of privacy, 338
Lou Grant, 93
Louw, Eric P., 88, 321, 322
Love & Hip Hop Atlanta, 237f
Lovink, Geert, xv
Low-cost programming, 94–95
Lowe, Rob, 260
Low-power radio campaign, 117, 119–120, 149
Lubet, Alex, 44
Lubken, Deborah, 301
Luce, Henry, 111
Luckmann, Thomas, 35
Luengo, Maria, 332
Lule, Jack, 343

Lumière, Auguste and Louis, 45
Lundby, Knut, 314
    See also Hepp, Andreas
Luther, Catherine A., 231
Luther, Martin, 37
Lutz, Christoph, 290
Lwin, May O., 311
Lyon, Matthew, 54

M*A*S*H, 94, 211, 270–271
MacBride, Seán, 361, 362
MacBride Commission, 362
MacBride Roundtable, 362
Macek, Jakub, 294
Machine Journalist, 170
Machine-to-machine (M2M) communication, 5
Machinima, 66
MacIntosh computers, 56
MacKenzie, Donald, 35
Macmillan, 70
Mad Men, 95
Madam Secretary, 249
Maddow, Rachel, 163
Madonna, 44, 276, 285
Madrigal, Alexis C., 137
Magazines
    advertising-content connection, 100
    alternative feminist press, 286–287
    ideological viewpoints, 213
    media content decoding and interpretation, 286–287
    motherhood, 213
    norms and conventions, 162
    oppositional readings, 286–287
    ownership concentrations and changes, 68, 72
    political contributions, 118t
    racial and ethnic diversity, 233
    women's magazines, 218–219
Magnetic tape recordings, 40, 42
Maheshwari, Sapna, 236
Mainframe computers, 56
Majoribanks, Tim, 166
Makichi, Rumbidzai, 294
Mancini, Paolo, 320
Manning, Chelsea/Bradley, 136
Manning, Jennifer E., 319
Manuscripts
    See Book publishing; Print media
Many-to-many communication, 58
Marchetti, Gina, 205, 206

Marconi, Francesco, 170, 369
Marconi, Guglielmo, 47
Marconi Company, 47, 49
Marcus Welby, 262
Mares, Marie-Louise, 311
Marginalized populations, 310–311
Marketing Evaluations, Inc., 156
Marlow, Cameron
    See Bond, Robert M.
Married to Jonas, 156
Married with Children, 212, 253
The Martian, 366
Martin, Christopher, 257
Martin, Jason, 280
Martins, Nicole, 234
    See also Williams, Dmitri
Marvel Cinematic Universe, 63, 76, 161
Marvel's The Defenders, 93
Marx, Karl, 302
Marxism, 191, 196–197
The Mary Tyler Moore Show, 93, 211
Masculine films, 206–207
The Mask of Fu Manchu, 239
Mason, Gail
    See Jakubowicz, Andrew
Mass communication, 7–8, 9, 58
Mass shootings, 332
Mass society theory, 304–305
Mass-market books, 156
Master of None, 241
Mastro, Dana E., 233, 248, 249
Materiality theory, 29–30, 30f
Matikainen, Janne, 294
Matrix media, 289
Mattelart, Armand, 222, 356
Matwick, Kelsi, 205
Matwick, Keri, 205
Maude, 93, 211
Mauskapf, Michael, 155
Maxwell, Richard
    See Miller, Toby
McAdam, Doug, 18
McAllister, Matthew P., 259–260
McCain, John, 319
McChesney, Robert W., xv, 46, 56, 89, 98, 166, 331
McClelland, Stephen, 279
McCombs, Maxwell, 307, 308
McConahay, John B., 241

McConaughey, Matthew, 156
McConnell, Ben, 291
McCracken, Ellen, 218, 219
McDaniel, Hattie, 238
McDermott, Terry, 87
McDonald, Aleecia M., 338
McDuling, John, 366
McGregor, Shannon C., 279
McIlroy, Thad, 72
McIntire, Mike, 333
McLaughlin, Margaret L., 186, 187
McLeod, Kembrew, 124
McLiesch, Caralee, 115
McLuhan, Marshall, 32–33, 56, 342–343, 346, 367
McMillan Cottom, Tressie, 289
McMurria, John
    See Miller, Toby
McNamara, Mary, 257
McQuail, Denis, 7, 111, 114
McRobbie, Angela, 275–276
McWorld thesis, 357–358
Me Too movement, 316, 327
Mean world syndrome, 312, 313
Mecking, Olga, 310
Media Action Network for Asian Americans (MANAA), 242f
Media advocacy organizations, 147, 148f, 149
Media companies
    advertising dynamics, 98–105, 104f
    audience and revenue decline, 94, 95
    conglomeration and integration, 74, 75–76f, 76, 78–79, 83–85, 122–124, 123f
    content and distribution controls, 95–96
    content diversity, 90–92
    controversial programming, 88–89, 93, 152, 210
    cross-media versus single-source promotions, 78, 84
    cultural imperialism, 355–357, 359
    economic dynamics, 78–79, 95–96
    for-profit organizations, 92–98
    key tasks, 64–67
    low-cost programming, 94–95
    ownership concentrations and changes, 67–68, 70, 72–74, 85–92, 122–124, 123f
    political influence, 85–89, 107–117, 118t, 119–132, 134–136, 153–154
    prime-time profit pressures, 92–94
    private ownership, 86–87
    product creation and promotion costs, 155

regulatory policies, 109–117, 118t, 119–132, 123f, 126f, 133f, 134–146, 153–154
self-promotion, 83–84
See also Facebook; Google
Media content
active users, 269–272
advertising accuracy, 126–127
advertising-content connection, 98–100, 223–224, 258, 330
audience fragmentation, 279
audience influences, 230
audience interpretation, 271–278, 286–287
audience preferences, 229
Black Lives Matter (BLM), 20–21
censorship, 130–132, 134–136, 153
child-centered content example, 227–230
civil rights movement, 18–20
communication models, 9–10, 10f, 16, 16f
conglomeration impact, 84–85
consumerism, 216–219
content diversity, 90–92
creation and distribution, 288–298
cultural contradictions and battles, 192–194
cultural ideologies, 193–194, 285–286
cultural resistance, 214–215, 239–240, 244, 245–246
culture jamming, 287–288
domestic viewing context, 284–285
economic dynamics, 78–79, 95–96
economic news, 202–203, 204f, 272–273
elites versus insiders, 201–202
encoded meanings, 271–278
Fairness Doctrine (1949), 127–129
film genre analyses, 205–208
gatekeepers and distributors, 296–298, 331–332, 333
gender stereotypes, 246–251
global media culture, 219–221, 349, 355–360
international audiences, 276–278, 281–282
interpretive resistance, 275–276, 285–287
liberal versus conservative viewpoint, 120–121, 192, 201
locally produced media content, 356–357, 358, 365
modern racism, 239–241, 243–244
multiple meanings, 270–271, 276–278
obscene materials, 129–130
online meaning making, 278–279
oppositional readings, 273, 275–276, 285–286
organized labor representations, 257–258
owned versus organic activity, 65–66

personalized content delivery, 80
platforms, 65–66
pleasure and entertainment, 281–283
polysemic texts, 270–271, 283–284
producer intent, 229
product creation and promotion costs, 155
race and ethnicity, 192–193, 231–246
rap music, 213–216
ratings systems, 130–132
"real" world representations, 225–228, 274
reality television, 254, 256–257
regulatory policies, 118t, 126–132, 133f, 134–136
second screen use, 278–279
as self-enclosed text, 230
self-regulation, 130–132, 153
sexual minorities, 262, 263–264f, 264–266
shareworthy content, 81
significance analyses, 228–230
social class and position, 251–262
social context, 283–285
social media platforms, 80–81
social norms and values, 194–195, 229
sports coverage, 249–251
stereotypical portrayals, 194–195
structure-agency dynamics, 15–16, 271–272
tabloid talk shows, 254, 256–257
television programming, 208, 209f, 210–213
white-controlled production, 244–246, 247
zero-rated content, 138
See also Ideologies; Race and ethnicity; Social inequality
Media ecology
See Medium theory
Media effects and influence
active audiences, 306–307, 357
agenda-setting role, 307–309
cultivation theory, 312–313
democratic principles, 302
early research, 302–305
entertainment and children, 303–304
film industry, 303–304, 311–312
foreign audiences, 357
framing theory, 308
learning impacts, 311–312
limited effects theory, 305–306, 333–334
mass society, 304–305
mediatization, 313–328
mitigation efforts, 305–306

online media influence, 328–340
research background, 301–307
spiral of silence theory, 309–311
structure-agency dynamics, 12–16, 162, 271–272
Media giants, 67–68, 78–83, 352
See also Facebook; Google
Media globalization
basic concepts, 343–347
centralized ownership and production control,
348–349
challenges and constraints, 346–347
cross-cultural boundaries, 345–346, 348
cultural exception/cultural diversity, 364–365
cultural hybridity, 345, 358–360
cultural imperialism, 115, 355–357, 359
culture clash thesis, 357–358, 359
digital divide, 367–369
economic inequality, 366–368
foreign audiences, 357
future changes and developments, 369–371
indigenous media industries, 115, 356
information flow, 360–362
instantaneous communication, 342, 344
Internet governance, 363–364
key components, 343–344
locally produced media content, 356–357, 358,
365–366
media content, 219–221, 349, 355–360
most visited websites, 353t
occurrences and users, 342–343
promotion strategies, 348–349
regulatory policies, 360–366
temporospatial limits, 344
U.S. market share, 364
user base, 366–369, 367f
Western imports, 355–359
See also Google; Walt Disney Company
Media industry
advertising dynamics, 98–105, 104f
audience and revenue decline, 94, 95
Black Lives Matter (BLM), 20–21
civil rights movement, 18–20
communication models, 9–10, 10f, 16, 16f
compliance strategies, 153
conglomeration and integration, 74, 75–76f, 76,
78–79, 83–85, 122–124, 123f
content and distribution controls, 95–96
content diversity, 90–92

controversial programming, 88–89, 93, 152, 210
cross-media versus single-source promotions, 78, 84
decision-making practices, 152–161
economic dynamics, 62–63, 78–79, 95–96, 152–153
economic inequality, 366–368
editorial decision-making, 180–185
exported entertainment, 219–221
fin-syn regulations, 140–141
for-profit organizations, 92–98
globalization impact, 342–343
hit status, 155–156, 158–160
ignoring behaviors, 154
imitated products, 153, 155–156
interpretation/reinterpretation strategies, 153–154
key tasks, 64–67
legal challenges, 154
low-cost programming, 94–95
mergers, 62–63, 65, 68
norms and conventions, 162–163, 185–188
objectivity, 170–174
occupational roles, 175–176
organizational characteristics, 161–185
ownership concentrations and changes, 67–68, 70,
72–74, 85–92, 122–124, 123f
photography, 176–177, 179–180
political influence, 85–89, 107–117, 118t, 119–132,
134–136, 153–154
preemption strategies, 153
prime-time profit pressures, 92–94
private ownership, 86–87
product creation and promotion costs, 155
production-oriented perspective, 63–64
"real" world representations, 225–228, 274
regulatory policies, 109–117, 118t, 119–132, 123f,
126f, 133f, 134–146, 153–154
self-censorship, 130–132, 134, 337
self-promotion, 83–84
sequels and spin-offs, 93, 156, 160–161
star power, 156–160
structure-agency dynamics, 13–16, 152–153
technological innovations, 167, 169–170
uncertainty considerations, 159–161
U.S. market share, 364
Western imports, 355–359
See also Facebook; Global media industry; Google;
Ideologies; News media; News production;
Social inequality
Media logic, 316, 317

Media outlets, 118*t*, 121–126, 123*f*, 126*f*
  See also Cable television; Streaming services
Media ownership
  advertising dynamics, 98–105, 104*f*
  audience and revenue decline, 94, 95
  concentrations and changes, 67–68, 70, 72–74, 85–92,
    122–124, 123*f*
  conglomeration and integration, 74, 75–76*f*, 76,
    78–79, 83–85, 122–124, 123*f*
  content and distribution controls, 95–96
  content diversity, 90–92
  controversial programming, 88–89, 93, 152, 210
  cross-media versus single-source promotions, 78, 84
  economic dynamics, 78–79, 95–96
  for-profit organizations, 92–98
  global media industry, 348–349
  low-cost programming, 94–95
  political influence, 85–89, 107–117, 118*t*, 119–132,
    134–136, 153–154
  prime-time profit pressures, 92–94
  private ownership, 86–87
  regulatory policies, 118*t*, 121–126, 123*f*, 126*f*,
    153–154
  self-promotion, 83–84
  See also Facebook; Google
Media personnel
  content significance, 229
  news production, 163
  norms and conventions, 162–163
  occupational roles, 175–176
  photographers, 176–177, 179–180
  structure-agency dynamics, 14–15, 162
Media pluralism, 90
Media representations
  See Media content
Media sharing, 46
Media technology
  adoption rates, 4*f*, 27*f*
  autonomous technology, 30–31
  Black Lives Matter (BLM), 20–21
  civil rights movement, 18–20
  communication models, 9–10, 10*f*, 16, 16*f*
  historical perspective, 25, 25–26*f*, 27, 36–44, 59–60, 121
  materiality theory, 29–30, 30*f*
  medium theory, 31–35
  news media, 167
  potential impact, 31–35
  social constructionism, 17, 28, 35–36

  technological determinism, 28–29, 32–36
  technological momentum, 30–31
Media/mass media
  active users, 9, 15, 269–272, 288–289, 357
  adoption rates, 4*f*
  analytical challenges, 204–205
  civil rights movement, 18–21
  communication models, 7–10, 7*f*, 8*f*, 10*f*, 16–18, 16*f*
  content creation and distribution, 288–298
  economic and political constraints, 152–154
  globalization impact, 342–343
  military press restrictions, 134–136, 153
  norms and conventions, 162–163, 185–188
  pervasiveness and significance, 3–7, 6*f*
  political influence, 85–89
  polysemic texts, 270–271, 283–284
  push-pull interactions, 12–16, 18, 31, 63–64
  sexual minorities, 262, 263–264*f*, 264–266
  social influence, 31–35
  social movements, 324–325
  social norms and values, 194–195, 229
  sociological perspective, 10–16, 63–64
  star power, 156–160
  structural constraint-human agency dynamics,
    12–16, 152–153
  technological characteristics, 29, 30*f*
  user demographics, 6*f*
  See also Advertising; Global media industry;
    Ideologies; Race and ethnicity; Social inequality
Mediatization
  basic concepts, 314–315
  citizen alienation, 326
  media logic, 316, 317
  political systems, 316–328
  social movements, 324–325
  social world impacts, 315–316
Medium theory, 31–35
Melican, Debra Burns, 244
MEO, 138
Meredith Corp., 72
Meredith Corporation, 87
Messner, Marcus, 167
Messner, Michael A., 249, 250, 251
  See also Musto, Michela
Meuwly, Nathalie
  See Feinstein, Brian A.
Meyer, Philip, 331
Meyrowitz, Joshua, 32

Miami Vice, 233

Michaels, Meredith W., 212–213

Mickey Mouse Protection Act (1998), 125

Mickle, Tripp, 96

Microblogging services, 27f, 187, 338, 344

Microbroadcasters, 119–120

Microcomputers, 25f

Microprocessors, 25f

Microsoft, 82f, 100, 145

Microwave towers, 52, 53

Mid-20th century civil rights movement, 18–20

The Middle, 253

Middle-class populations
    advertising targeting, 259–261
    family-based situation comedies, 252–254
    marketing strategies, 50–52
    media content decoding and interpretation, 273–274
    media representations, 252
    news media, 258
    reading romance novels, 283–284

Middleton, Rich, 365

MIDIA Research, 72

Midnight Cowboy, 132

Milan, Stefania, 149

Military censorship, 134–136, 153

Military/war films, 205, 206–208

Milk, 262, 264f

Milk, Harvey, 262, 264f

Millennials, 6f

Miller, Laura Jean, 183

Miller, Toby, 351

Miller, V., 338

Milliot, Jim, 183

Milman, Noriko
    See Chin, Christina B.

MILNET, 55

Mims, Christopher, 323

The Mindy Project, 233

Minimal effects theory, 305–306

Minority populations
    See Race and ethnicity

Minstrel shows, 238

Miron, Dorina, 302

Misinformation, 119, 143, 170, 306, 324, 332–334, 370

Missing in Action, 206

Mission Impossible, 205

MIT Technology Review, 26f

Mitterrand, François, 364

Mockingjay.net, 295

Modern Family, 62, 99–100, 212, 220, 264f

Modern racism, 239–241, 243–244

Modigliani, Andre, 325

Molla, Rani, 354

Mom, 213

Momism, 212–213

Mommy blogs, 213

Mondello, Michael, 250

Monopolies
    cable television, 53–54
    film industry, 45
    Hollywood studio system, 131, 139–140
    regulatory policies, 111, 122–124
    telephone industry, 39–42, 41f

Monte Carlo Television Festival, 349

Moonlight, 262, 264f

Moonves, Leslie, 321

Moore, Frazier, 233

Morgan, Marcyliena, 215

Morgan, Michael, 312, 313
    See also Gerbner, George

Morley, David, 272, 273, 284, 286

Moroccan Jews, 277

Morozov, Evgeny, 222, 223

Morris, Aldon, 18

Moses, Lucia, 169

Mother!, 160

Mother Jones, 173

Motherhood, 212–213

MotherJones.com, 173

Motion Picture Association of America (MPAA), 131, 132, 133f, 364

Motion Picture Producers and Distributors of America (MPDA), 131

Motion pictures
    advertising-content connection, 99
    censorship and ratings systems, 130–132, 133f
    digital technology, 45–46
    encoded meanings, 271–272
    failures, 156
    fantasy film genre, 227
    gender diversity, 247
    genre analyses, 205–208
    globalization impact, 343, 349
    historical perspective, 25f, 27, 45–46
    hit status, 155–156, 158
    impact on children, 303–304, 311–312

influential effects, 303–304, 311–312

locally produced media content, 356–357, 366

media content decoding and interpretation, 275–276

organized labor representations, 257

ownership concentrations and changes, 67, 68, 70

political contributions, 118t

polysemic texts, 270

production costs, 356

racial and ethnic diversity, 192–193, 232, 239–240, 242f, 245, 246

science fiction film genre, 227

sexual minorities, 262, 263–264f

shifting ideological viewpoints, 191

social influence, 45–46

star power, 157, 159

technological characteristics, 30f

U.S. market share, 364

user reviews and ratings, 297

user-generated content, 296

Mourão, Rachel Reis, 278

Movie censorship and ratings systems, 130–132, 133f

Movie theaters, 99, 131–132, 139–140

Mowlana, Hamid, 135, 313

Moy, Patricia, 309

Mozur, Paul, 353, 354

MP3 players, 26f, 42

Ms. magazine, 286–287

MSNBC, 73, 85, 96, 129

MTV, 53, 67, 263f, 359

Mueller, Milton, 112, 363, 370

Multimedia streaming devices, 4, 4f, 6f, 26f

    See also Streaming services

Murder She Wrote, 261

Murdoch, Rupert, 68, 85, 87

Murdock, Graham, 269

Murray, John P., 130

Murray, Noel, 254

Murthy, Dhiraj, 280

Museum of Failure, 59

Musgrove, Mike, 369

Music Business Worldwide, 70, 91

Music industry

    commercialization, 215–216

    content creation and promotion costs, 155

    content diversity, 90–91

    copyright and intellectual property, 124–125

    cross-cultural boundaries, 345, 348–349

    cultural hybridity, 345, 358–359

    digital music, 42–44, 72

    gender diversity, 247, 248f

    hit status, 159

    homogeneous media products, 90–91

    imitated products, 156

    indigenous talent, 359

    locally produced media content, 365–366

    open versus closed systems, 91

    ownership concentrations and changes, 70, 71f, 72, 91–92

    parental warning labels, 132, 134

    political contributions, 118t

    promotion strategies, 348–349

    rap music, 213–216

    sound recordings, 30f, 42

    star power, 157

    streaming services, 72, 348, 352–353

    U.S. market share, 364

    user-generated content, 296

    vertical and horizontal integration, 74, 77f

    video technology, 65

    See also Walt Disney Company

Musto, Michela, 249, 250, 251

Nacos, Brigitte L., 240

Nadkarni, Ashwini, 339

Nakamura, Lisa, 234, 280

Nakayama, Thomas K., 336

Namkoong, Kang, 294

Napster, 144, 353

Narcos, 73, 95

Nardi, Peter, 266

Nardulli, Peter F., 320

National Association of Black Journalists, 246

National Association of Broadcasters (NAB), 119, 132, 149, 366

National Association of Hispanic Journalists, 246

National Association of Realtors (NAR), 100

National Broadcasting Corporation (NBC)

    audience share, 94

    conglomeration impact, 84

    fin-syn regulations, 140–141

    historical perspective, 49, 50

    ownership concentrations and changes, 73

    programming and distribution controls, 96

    racial and ethnic diversity, 237f

    regulatory policies, 111

    sexual minorities, 263f

talent search shows, 158
top prime-time programs, 237f
National Cable Television Association (NCTA), 132
National Center for Health Statistics, 5, 27f
National Collegiate Athletic Association (NCAA), 250
National Geographic network, 62, 343
National Public Radio (NPR), 119, 120
National Science Foundation (NSF), 55, 56
National Security Agency (NSA), 311
Nationalist cultures, 346
Nationwide, 272–273, 286
Native American Journalists Association, 246
Native Americans
    alternative journalism, 245
    early racist images, 238
    newsroom representation, 246
    stereotypical portrayals, 238, 240
    video game characters, 234–235
Nature versus culture, 198–200
Naughton, John, 54
Nazi Germany, 49, 304, 309
Nazi propaganda, 49, 304
NBC
    See National Broadcasting Corporation (NBC)
NBC News, 84
NBC Universal, 72, 79
NC-17 rated films, 132
NCIS, 93, 94, 210, 237f, 349
NCIS: Los Angeles, 93
Negrine, Ralph, 320
Negroponte, Nicholas, 368
Nelson, Kjersten R., 308
Nenova, Tatiana, 115
Nesbitt, Jim, 117
Net neutrality, 122, 136–139, 149, 354
Netflix
    audience share, 93, 94
    historical perspective, 26f
    hit films, 158
    media platforms, 64
    original programming, 72, 95, 96, 141, 366
    racial and ethnic diversity, 241
    ratings systems, 132
    sexual minorities, 264f
    streaming services, 46, 73, 95, 141–142, 366
    subscriber fees, 96
    tiered access arrangements, 139
    vertical integration, 83, 141–142

Netiquette, 186
Network effect, 337
Network television broadcasting
    advertising dynamics, 99–100, 103–105, 104f
    agenda-setting effects, 308
    animated comedies, 253
    audience and revenue decline, 94, 95
    audience interpretation, 271–278
    changing American family, 210–212
    competitive markets, 53–54
    copies and spin-offs, 93, 156, 160, 211
    cultivation theory, 312–313
    cultural codes, 271–272
    domestic viewing context, 284–285
    family audiences, 284–285
    family-based situation comedies, 229, 233, 249,
        252–254
    fan communities, 296
    gender diversity, 247–249
    globalization impact, 343, 349
    historical perspective, 25f
    hit status, 159–160
    ideological analysis, 193, 208, 210–213
    international perspectives, 276–278, 281–282
    locally produced media content, 356–357, 365
    new momism, 212–213
    nostalgic programs, 211
    organized labor representations, 257–258
    political coverage, 318, 321–322
    polysemic texts, 270–271
    presidential debates, 318
    prime-time profit pressures, 92–94
    prime-time programming, 140–141, 152–153, 156,
        210
    production costs, 356
    racial and ethnic diversity, 232–233, 234f, 237f, 241,
        242f, 244, 274–278
    reality programming, 93–94, 156
    reality television, 93–94, 156, 208, 210, 254, 256–257
    regulatory policies, 140–141
    sexual minorities, 262, 263–264f, 264–265
    star power, 159
    U.S. market share, 364
    women's sports coverage, 249, 250
    work-family programs, 211–212
    See also Cable television
Neudert, Lisa-Marie
    See Howard, Philip N.

Neuendorf, Karen, 228
Neuman, W. Russell, 302, 309
#NeverAgain, 327
New Edition, 156
New Kids on the Block, 156
New Line, 70
New momism, 212–213
New versus old media, 10, 27
New World Information and Communication Order
    (NWICO), 362
New York Post, 68
New York Times, 105, 108, 135, 167, 168, 171, 177
New Yorker, 279
Newman, Benjamin A., 258
Newman, Nic, 331
News Corp., 68, 70, 85
News Corporation, 67, 68, 87
News media
    advertising dynamics, 103–105, 104f, 166, 331
    alternative journalism, 173–174, 245, 325
    audience and revenue maximization, 98, 166
    conglomeration impact, 84–85
    democratic principles, 302, 326
    diversified sourcing, 166–167
    economic coverage, 202–203, 204f, 272–273
    elites versus insiders, 201–202
    expanded volume, 166–167
    fake news, 108–109, 142–143, 310, 323–324
    gatekeepers and distributors, 297–298, 331–332, 333
    gender diversity, 247
    horse race coverage, 326
    ideological constructs, 201–203
    ideological viewpoints, 193, 333
    influential effects, 302
    interactive journalism, 168
    media coverage and public opinion, 307–308
    modern racism, 241, 243, 244
    norms and conventions, 162–163
    objectivity, 170–174
    oppositional readings, 273
    organized labor representations, 257
    political coverage, 318–324, 326
    political influence, 85–89
    presentation and engagement, 168–169
    profit pressures and cost-cutting efforts, 96–98
    public relations professionals, 321–324
    racial and ethnic diversity, 246, 274–275
    second screen use, 279
    sexual minorities, 265
    social class and position, 258–259, 272–273
    social media platforms, 80–81, 143, 146, 331–332, 333
    social movements, 324–325
    speed and homogenization, 167–168
    star power, 157
    stereotypical portrayals, 195
    technological innovations, 167, 169–170
    traditional versus digital journalism, 331–332
    user contributions, 297–298
News of the World, 85
News production
    alternative journalism, 173–174, 245, 325
    diversified sourcing, 166–167
    economic pressures, 166
    expanded volume, 166–167
    interactive journalism, 168
    journalistic routines, 164–166
    news gathering processes, 164–166
    newsroom automation, 169–170
    newsworthiness, 163–164, 167, 172–173
    norms and conventions, 162–163
    objectivity, 170–174
    presentation and engagement, 168–169
    racial and ethnic diversity, 246
    speed and homogenization, 167–168
    structure-agency dynamics, 163
    technological innovations, 167, 169–170
    traditional versus digital journalism, 331–332
NewsHour, 105
Newspapers
    advertising dynamics, 104, 166, 261, 331
    alternative journalism, 325
    conglomeration impact, 85
    controversial content, 102
    democratic principles, 302
    employment changes, 97, 97f
    gatekeepers and distributors, 297–298
    gender diversity, 247
    historical perspective, 25f
    ideological viewpoints, 193
    19th century British and American press, 100–102
    ownership concentrations and changes, 68
    political contributions, 118t
    profit pressures and cost-cutting efforts, 96–98
    racial and ethnic diversity, 245, 246
    stereotypical portrayals, 195
    user contributions, 297–298

Newsworthiness, 163–164, 167, 172–173

Newton, Gregory D., 78

Nicas, Jack, 146

Nicholls, Wendy, 294

Nickelodeon, 67

Nielsen, 3, 4, 4f, 5, 6f, 65, 95, 115

Nielsen, Jakob, 291

The Nigger, 238

Nightline, 320

19th century advertising, 100–102

90-9-1 Principle, 291

Nintendo, 234

Nixon, Richard M., 318

Nixon, Sean, 226

Nixon administration, 52, 128

"No Comment" feature, 286–287

Noah, Trevor, 163

Noam, Eli M., 79, 121

Noble, Safiya Umoja, 244, 336

Noelle-Neumann, Elisabeth, 309, 310, 311

Nongovernmental organizations (NGOs), 343, 362, 363

Nordenstreng, Kaarle, 313

Norms

    See Professional norms and practices

Norris, Chuck, 206, 207

Norris, Pippa, 321

North American film market, 364

Northern Exposure, 263f

Nostalgic programs, 211

NSFNET, 55, 56

NSYNC, 156

Nunez, Michael, 334

Nussbaum, Bruce, 368

Nussbaum, Emily, 318

NYPD Blue, 93

Ó Siochrú, Seán, 360

Obama, Barack, 135, 264f, 319, 323, 336

O'Barr, William, 220, 221

Objectivity

    alternative journalism, 173–174

    basic concepts, 170–171

    origins, 171–172

    political consequences, 173

    routine journalistic practices, 172–173

Oboler, Andre

    See Jakubowicz, Andrew

Obscene materials, 129–130

Occupational roles, 175–176

Occupy Wall Street movement, 316, 325

O'Connell, Jerry, 160

Oculus Rift, 26f

Odd Mom Out, 213

The Office, 141, 160

Office of the United States Trade Representative, 365

Official news sources, 166

Oh, Hyun Jung, 339

Old versus new media, 10, 27

Oligopolies, 91, 92, 140, 223

Olmstead, Kenneth, 149

Olson, David R., 25

On-demand television, 95, 158

1% Rule, 290–291

One-to-many communication, 7–8, 9, 58

One-to-one communication, 7–8, 9

Online advertising, 81

Online alternative media, 89

Online booksellers, 183

Online discussions, 309

Online meaning making, 278–279

Online media, 95, 236f, 244

Online media influence

    addictive effects, 337–340

    censorship, 336–337

    computational propaganda, 334–336

    hate groups, 336–337

    information distortions, 324, 332–334

    self-management concerns, 337–340

    social media platforms, 328–331, 329f, 333–334, 336–337

    traditional versus digital journalism, 331–332

Online news media, 85, 98, 246, 247, 331–332

Ono, Yoko, 215

Open Compute Project, 82, 354

Open Internet Order, 137–138

Oral traditions, 37

Orange Is the New Black, 264f

O'Reilly, Bill, 104

The O'Reilly Factor, 104, 104f

Organized labor, 257–258, 273

The Original, Aboriginal, Erratic, Operatic, Semi-Civilized and Demi-Savage Extravaganza of Pocahontas, 238

Osborne, Kerry K., 186

    See also McLaughlin, Margaret L.

The Osbournes, 156

#OscarsSoWhite, 235, 240

Osei-Frimpong, Kofi, 313

Otherness, 221, 261

Over-the-air (OTA) broadcast media
    See Radio broadcasting; Television

Over-the-top (OTT) services, 116

Owen, Taylor, 81, 332

OWN, 237f

Owned versus organic activity, 65–66

Oxfam, 343

Oxford Dictionaries, 324

Oxygen, 73, 96

Özkan, Erdem, 292

Ozkaya, Elif, 339

Öztürk, Selen, 292

Ozzie and Harriet, 210

Pacific Islanders
    See Asian Americans/Pacific Islanders (AAPI); Race
        and ethnicity

Paletz, David, 135

Palfrey, John, 293

Palin, Sarah, 319

Panday, Jyoti, 116

Pandora, 42, 64, 82f, 138

Papathanassopoulos, Stylianos, 320

Paradies, Yin
    See Jakubowicz, Andrew

Paramount Pictures, 67, 70, 139–140

Paramount Vantage, 70

Parental advisory labels, 132, 134

Parenti, Michael, 325

Parents, 213

Parents' Music Resource Center (PMRC), 134

Pariser, Eli, 333

Parkinson, H. J., 335

Parkland, Florida, mass shooting, 332

Parris, Terry, Jr., 330

Partial paywalls, 98

Participation categories, 291–293, 292t

Participatory culture, 289–290, 332–333

Participatory inequality, 290–291

Partisan journalism, 173–174

Party of Five, 241

Pasquale, Frank, 331

Patterson, James, 156

Pautz, Michelle, 45

Pay-for-play arrangements, 138

Payne Fund Studies, 303

Paywalls, 98

Pecquerie, Bernard, 170

Peele, Jordan, 193, 245

Peer-to-peer (P2P) platforms, 144

Pehlke, Timothy A., 254

PEJ (Project for Excellence in Journalism), 203, 204f, 326

Penguin Random House, 68, 69–70f, 70

Penn, Sean, 262, 264f

Pensavalle, Alexander, 280

Pentagon Papers, 135

Pentagon terrorist attack, 135

People, 68, 72

People of color
    See Race and ethnicity

The People's Choice (Lazarsfeld, Berelson, and Gaudet),
    305–306

Periscope, 139

Perlberg, Steven, 80

Perlmutter, David D., 294

Perse, Elizabeth M., 302

Persian Gulf War, 135, 153, 207

Persily, Nathaniel, 324

Personal communication, 7–8

Personal computers, 56

Personalized content delivery, 80

Personalized journalism, 169–170

Petersen, Christina, 303

Petersen, Vibeke G., 115

Peterson, Richard A., 63, 90–91

Peterson, Robin T., 233

Petit, Michael, xv

Petition of European Filmmakers, 365

Petrich, Kevin, 262, 264, 265–266

Pew Research Center, 4, 4f, 5, 27f, 80, 97, 103, 328, 370

PewDiePie, 66

Philadelphia, 263f

Philippines, 282

Philips, Angela, 167–168

Phillips, James, 247

Phoenix, Joaquin, 158

Phone-hacking scandal, 85

Phonographs, 25f, 27, 42

Photography
    historical perspective, 25f, 27, 176
    occupational role, 176–177, 179–180
    organizational and professional norms, 177, 179–180
    presidential politics, 320, 322
    professional socialization, 177, 179–180
    social influence, 34, 320

Photojournalists, 176–177, 179
Phyllis, 93
Pickard, Victor, 103, 111, 112, 331
Pieper, Katherine, 232, 246
    See also Smith, Stacy L.
Pierson, David, 142
Pieterse, Jan Nederveen N., 357, 358
Pimp My Ride, 256
Pinch, Trevor, 29, 36
Pinterest, 329*f*
    tiered access arrangements, 138
Pipes
    economic dynamics, 78–79
    Facebook, 82–83
    functional role, 64, 66–67
    Google, 82–83
    ownership concentrations and changes, 73–74
    political contributions, 118*t*
Piracy, 44, 117, 119
Pixar Animation, 160
Pizzigati, Sam, 325
Platforms
    characteristics and functional role, 64, 143–144
    connectivity, 329
    content and distribution controls, 95–96, 288–298
    datafication, 330
    economic dynamics, 78–79
    fake news, 142–143
    film ratings systems, 297
    ownership concentrations and changes, 72–73
    political contributions, 118*t*
    popularity, 329
    programmability, 328–329
    social media logic, 328–330
    subscriber fees, 95, 96
    user content and delivery, 65–66
    vertical and horizontal integration, 83–84
    See also Social media
Playstation, 234
Podcasts, 26*f*
Poell, Thomas, 328
Poirier, Agnès, 364
Poitier, Sidney, 239
Political ads, 145, 146
Politics/political influence
    agenda-setting effects, 308–309
    authoritarian governments, 108, 335, 347, 353, 370
    bots and trolls, 336
    campaign tactics, 321, 323–324
    celebrities, 318, 319
    citizen alienation, 326
    cultivation theory, 312–313
    democratic societies, 108, 114–115
    elites versus insiders, 201–202
    horse race coverage, 326
    ideological viewpoints, 193–194
    image and communication considerations, 317–324
    informal social and economic pressure, 147, 149
    information flow, 360–362
    Internet use, 321–324, 326–328
    low-power radio campaign, 117, 119–120, 149
    media advocacy organizations, 147, 148*f*, 149
    media content, 193–194
    media coverage, 318–324, 326
    media-savvy professionals, 321–324
    mediatization effects, 316–328
    19th century British and American press, 100–102
    photo opportunities, 320, 322
    political party decline, 320–321
    regulatory policies, 109–117, 118*t*, 119–132, 123*f*, 126*f*, 133*f*, 134–146, 153–154
    second screen use, 279
    social media platforms, 333–334
    social movements, 18–21, 324–325
    spiral of silence theory, 309–311
    two-step flow of influence theory, 305–306
    user involvement, 144–145
    user self-selection, 333–334
    user tracking, 323–324
Polysemy, 270–271, 283–284
Pooley, Jefferson, 301
Poor populations, 105, 244, 245, 256–261, 368
Pop music industry, 44, 90–92, 155, 358–359
Pope, Cassadee, 158
Pornography, 129–130, 132, 311
Porter, Rick, 92, 93
Postman, Neil, 33–34
Postmodern theory, 34, 320
"Post-truth" politics, 324
Potocki, Bridget, 280
Potter, Harry, 295
Potter, W. James, 302
Povich, Maury, 256
Powell, Walter W., 181, 183, 184
    See also Coser, Lewis A.
Power and ideology, 196–200, 214–215

Power Rangers, 264f
Powers, Matthew, 163, 166
Pranking, 287
Pred, Allan R., 37f
Presidential debates, 318
Presley, Elvis, 53
Press, Andrea, 273–274
Press Association, 169
Press Freedom Index, 108
Press pool system, 135, 153
Price, Monroe, 360
Prime-time profits, 92–94
Prime-time programming
    animated comedies, 253
    controversial programming, 210
    economic dynamics, 152–153
    fin-syn regulations, 140–141
    gender diversity, 247–249
    racial and ethnic diversity, 232–233, 234f, 237f, 241,
        242f, 244
    sexual minorities, 264–265
    star power, 156
Prindle, David F., 159
Print media
    advertising-content connection, 100–102
    alternative feminist press, 286–287
    civil rights movement, 20
    conglomeration impact, 85
    constitutional protections, 121
    cross-cultural boundaries, 345
    democratic principles, 302
    distribution limitations, 37–38, 37f
    historical perspective, 25, 25f, 27, 36–38
    ideological viewpoints, 193, 213
    media content decoding and interpretation, 286–287
    norms and conventions, 162
    oppositional readings, 286–287
    ownership concentrations and changes, 68, 72
    political contributions, 118t
    racial and ethnic diversity, 233, 237–238
    regulatory policies, 122
    social influence, 32, 33–34, 37
    technological characteristics, 30f
    traditional versus digital journalism, 331–332
    user-generated content, 296
    women's magazines, 218–219
Privacy policies, 338
Privacy rights, 144–145

Private media ownership, 86–87
Pro-democracy movements, 167, 215, 368–369
Product endorsements, 99, 127, 221
Products
    advertising-content connection, 98–100, 223–224,
        258, 330
    conglomeration impact, 84–85
    content and distribution controls, 95–96
    content creation, 64–65
    content creation and promotion costs, 155
    content diversity, 90–92
    economic dynamics, 78–79
    foreign audiences, 357
    functional role, 64
    global media culture, 216–220, 355–357
    hegemony, 197–200, 203, 213, 215–216
    hit status, 155–156, 158–160
    imitated products, 153, 155–156
    low-cost programming, 94–95
    ownership concentrations and changes, 68, 69–70f,
        70, 71f, 72, 85–92
    political contributions, 118t
    rap music, 213–216
    sequels and spin-offs, 93, 156, 160–161, 211
Professional norms and practices
    book publishing, 162, 183
    Internet, 185–188
    key journalistic practices, 172
    news media, 162–163
    objectivity, 170–174
    occupational roles, 176
    photography, 177, 179–180
    print media, 162, 183
    radio broadcasting, 162
    television, 163
Professional socialization, 175–177, 179–185
The Profit, 94
Project Fi, 83
Project for Excellence in Journalism (PEJ),
        203, 204f, 326
Project Loon, 82–83
Project Runway, 94
Prometheus Radio Project, 147, 149
Prometheus Radio Project v. FCC (2004), 149
Propaganda
    campaign tactics, 321–322
    computational propaganda, 310, 334–336
    future trends, 370

state-owned media, 86, 108
wartime propaganda efforts, 171, 304, 361
Protestant Reformation, 37
Prysby, Charles, 321
Pseudo-events, 34
Public access television programming, 52–53
Public affairs programs, 259
Public broadcasting services, 114, 120, 121, 259
Public Broadcasting System (PBS), 120, 263*f*
Public domain, 125–126
Public Enemy, 124
Public interest advocacy, 110, 112, 116, 128–129,
    137–138, 147, 149
Public Knowledge, 137
Public opinion polls, 307
Public relations professionals, 171–172, 321–324
Publishing industry
    See Book publishing
Puette, William J., 257
Purcell, Kristen
    See Hampton, Keith N.
Push-pull interactions, 12–16, 18, 31, 63–64
Putin, Vladimir, 310–311, 335

Q Scores, 156–157
QQ, 329*f*, 353, 353*t*
Quakebot, 170
Queer as Folk, 264f, 265
Queer Eye for the Straight Guy, 264f
Quick, Rebecca, 56
Qzone, 329*f*

Rabinovitz, Lauren, 135
Race and ethnicity
    action-adventure film genre, 206
    advertising representations, 233
    alternative journalism, 245
    cultural resistance, 214–215, 239–240, 244,
        245–246
    early racist images, 238–239
    family-based situation comedies, 233
    film industry, 192–193, 232, 239–240, 242*f*, 245, 246
    inclusiveness and diversity, 231, 232–237
    Internet participation and content creation, 294
    key production-related issues, 231–232
    media content, 192–193, 231–246
    media content decoding and interpretation,
        274–275, 277–278

media representations, 231, 232–233, 237–241,
    243–244
    modern racism, 239–241, 243–244
    nature versus culture, 198
    Nazi Germany, 309
    news media, 245, 246, 274–275
    online identities and communities, 279–281
    population percentages, 232, 234, 234*f*, 235, 241
    production control, 231–232
    racial hatred, 336
    rap music, 213–216
    shifting ideological viewpoints, 191, 212
    social class and position, 244
    stereotypical portrayals, 194–195, 231, 232–233,
        237–241, 242*f*, 243–246, 281
    television programming, 232–233, 234*f*, 237*f*, 241
    white-controlled production, 244–246
    See also Gender
Racial agency, 280
Racism
    See Civil rights movement; Race and ethnicity
Radical press, 101–102
Radina, M. Elise, 254
Radio Act (1912), 47
Radio and Music, 349
Radio broadcasting
    adoption rates, 4*f*, 27*f*
    advertising, 48
    broadcast licenses, 117, 119–120, 147
    competition, 47–49, 50
    gender diversity, 247
    historical perspective, 25–26*f*, 27, 46–49
    locally produced media content, 365–366
    low-power radio campaign, 117, 119–120, 149
    military applications, 47
    musical diversity, 90–91
    norms and conventions, 162
    ownership concentrations and changes, 72, 122, 123*f*
    political contributions, 118*t*
    prevalence, 3, 6*f*
    regulatory policies, 122
    social influence, 46–49
    stereotypical portrayals, 195
    technological characteristics, 30*f*
    user-generated content, 296
Radio Corporation of America (RCA), 48–49, 50
Radio Disney, 351*f*
Radio programmers, 162

Radiotelegraphy, 47

Radiotelephony, 47

Radway, Janice A., 283–284, 286

Rafaeli, Sheizaf, 294

Raiders of the Lost Ark, 205

Rainie, Lee, xv, 328, 370

  See also Hampton, Keith N.

Ramaprasad, Venkat, 205

Rambo, 205, 206

Rap music, 213–216

Rather, Dan, 85

Rating systems, 297

Ratings systems, 130–132

Rational thought, 33

Rawsthorn, Alice, 368

Ray, Rashawn, 18

Ray Ban sunglasses, 99

Ray Donovan, 95

Reading, 283–284

Reagan, Ronald, 112, 128, 206, 318, 319

The Real World, 93

"Real" world representations, 225–228, 274

  See also Social inequality

Real World: San Francisco, 263f

Reality

  ideological viewpoints, 191

  media representations, 199–200, 225–228, 274

  objective journalism, 172–173

  social constructionism, 17, 28, 35–36

  visual imagery, 34, 320

Reality television, 93–94, 156, 208, 210, 254, 256–257

Reardon, Marguerite, 137

Recording Industry Association of America (RIAA), 72, 132

Recording technology

  See Sound recordings

Redbook, 219

Redden, Joanna, xv

Reddit, 298, 333, 338, 353t

Redlawsk, David P.

  See Lau, Richard R.

Reed, M., 335

Regan, Donald, 318

Regulatory policy

  antitrust legislation, 39–41, 41f, 68, 109, 111, 140, 145

  cable television, 52

  campaign contributions, 117, 118t

  citizen participation, 117

  copyright and intellectual property, 124–126, 126f

  developing nations, 115–116

  fraudulent/deceptive advertising, 126–127

  global media industry, 360–366

  historical perspective, 109–113

  international perspective, 113–116

  Internet, 56, 58, 115, 122, 137–138, 144–146, 337, 360

  liberal versus conservative viewpoint, 120–121, 128–129

  lobbying influences, 117, 118t

  low-power radio campaign, 117, 119–120, 149

  media access and distribution, 136–146

  media content, 118t, 126–132, 133f, 134–136

  media ownership, 118t, 121–126, 123f, 126f, 153–154

  net neutrality, 122, 136–139, 149, 354

  political influence, 109–117, 118t, 119–132, 123f, 126f, 133f, 134–136, 153–154

  radio broadcasts, 47

  regulation versus deregulation debate, 110, 112–113, 116, 122–124, 123f, 128

  social media platforms, 142–146, 336–337

  television broadcasts, 50, 140–141

  vertical integration, 139–142

  Western democratic societies, 114–115

  See also Federal Communications Commission (FCC)

Reid, Leonard N., 112

Reisman, David, 304

Relativity, 263f

Rendall, Steve, 89

Renner, Nausicaa, 170

Rennie, Ellie, 49

Reporters And Data And Robots (RADAR), 169

Reporters Without Borders, 108

Repressive governments, 108–109

Republic Group, 348

Return-to-Vietnam film genre, 206–207

Reuters, 361

Reynolds, Amy, 336

Rhoda, 93

Rhodes, Jane, 245

RIAA (Recording Industry Association of America), 72, 132

Rice, Anne, 156

Rice, Thomas Dartmouth, 238

Richter, William A., 234

Ride Along 2, 99

Right to access, 144

Right to be forgotten, 144–145

Right-wing activists, 332, 336, 337

Rio Olympic Games (2016), 343
Rivero, Yeidy M., 231
Roach, Colleen, 361
Roberts, Jeff John, xv
Roberts, Nora, 156
Robertson, John W., 203
Robeson, Paul, 245
Robinson, Michael J., 326
Robinson, MJ, xv
Robinson, Nick, 205
Robinson, Tom, 247
Robot journalism, 169–170
Rochford, E. Burke, Jr.
    See Snow, David A.
Rodman, Gilbert B., 231
Rodriguez, Clara E., 182
Rogers, Everett, 26f
Rogue One: A Star Wars Story, 70, 366
Rohlinger, Deana A., 248
Rojecki, Andrew, 243
Roku, 4, 26f
Rolling Stone, 194
Romance novels, 283–284
Romancing the Stone, 205
Romano, Lois, 323
Romm, Tony, 324
Romney, Mitt, 319
Roose, Kevin, 144, 337
Ros, Jonathan, 281
Rose, Tricia, 213, 214, 215
Roseanne, 253, 263f
Rosen, Jay, 289, 290, 326
Rosenblum, Barbara, 177, 180
Rosenfeld, Megan, 265
Rosenstein, Jason, 337
Roskens, Ronald W., 309
Ross, Dorothea, 312
Ross, Sheila A., 312
Rotten Tomatoes, 297
Rounds, 165
Rowell, Alex, 252
R-rated films, 132
Rubin, Alan M., 269
Ruddick, Graham, 80
Ruggiero, Thomas E., 269
Rules of Engagement, 240
Rush Hour, 205
Russell, Karl, 104

Russian election interference, xv, 113, 142, 144, 145,
    146, 324, 334–335
Russian immigrants, 277
Russmann, Fabian
    See Spaiser, Viktoria
Ryan, Charlotte, 199, 200, 325
Ryan, Maureen, 356

Sachdev, Ameet, 127
Saleh, Nivien, 368
Salganik, Matthew J., 155
Salmon, Charles T., 309
Salzman, Jason, 325
Samini, 359
Samuel-Azran, Tal, 327
    See also Wolfsfeld, Gadi
San Jose Mercury News, 258
Sands, Darren, 21
Sandvine, 96
Sandvoss, Cornel, 295
Sandy Hook, Connecticut, mass shooting, 332
Sanford and Son, 211
Sarikakis, Katharine, 223, 360
Sasson, Theodore, 198
Satellite television
    adoption rates, 4f, 27f
    connective devices, 3
    economic dynamics, 79
    historical perspective, 26f, 53
    ownership concentrations and changes, 74
    political contributions, 118t
Satellite-based digital radio services, 26f
Savage, Mark, 348
Scandal, 233, 249
Scardaville, Melissa C., 296
Scharrer, Erica, 247
Schell, L. A., 249
Scherr, Sebastian, 340
Scheufele, Dietram A., 307, 309, 333
Schiffer, Michael, 46
Schill, Dan, 320
Schiller, Herbert, 89, 135, 220, 355, 356
Schmidt, Jan-Hinrik, 289
Schneider, Michael, 236, 236f
Scholarly publishing, 183–185
Scholz, Trebor, 57
Schradie, Jen, 293–294
Schudson, Michael, 168, 171–172, 217

Schultz, Julianne, 88
Schulz, Winfried, 314, 315
Schwarzenegger, Arnold, 319
Science fiction film genre, 227
Scientific thought, 33
Scolari, Carlos A., 32
Scott, Althaus R., 320
Scott, Mark, 353
    See also Mozur, Paul
Scott, Willard, 84
Seaman, William R., 285
Second Life, 57
Second screens, 278–279
Secondary gatekeeping, 297
Second-level agenda setting, 308
"See You Again" (Khalifa), 65
Seetharaman, Deepa, 80
Segerberg, Alexandra, 316
Seggar, John F., 233
Segregation
    See Civil rights movement
Seib, Philip, 336
Seinfeld, 233
Selective deregulation, 116
Self-censorship, 103, 132, 134, 337
Self-enclosed text, 230
Self-expression, 294
Self-promotion, 83–84
Self-publishing, 182
September 11, 2001, terrorist attacks, 135, 207, 240, 336
Sequels, 156, 160–161
Service & Technology Academic Resource Team
    (START), 100
Service slowdowns, 138, 139
Settle, Jaime E.
    See Bond, Robert M.
78-rpm records, 42, 43
Sex and the City, 160
Sexism, 198, 249–250, 251, 286–287
Sexual harassment, 104, 104f
Sexual identity, 196, 200
Sexual minorities, 262, 263–264f, 264–266
Sexuality, 131, 198, 214, 218, 242f, 275–276
Sexually explicit material, 115, 129–130, 132
Shaban, Hamza, 142
Shaft, 239
Shah, Dhavan V., 328
Shaheen, Jack G., 240

Shahin, Saif, 354
Shakya, Holly B., 339
Shales, Tom, 124, 322
Shanahan, James, 312
    See also Gerbner, George
Shareworthy content, 81
Sharing content, 294, 295
Shark Tank, 94
Shaw, Daron R., 320
Shaw, Donald L., 307
Shaw, Lucas, 81
Shearer, Elisa, 143
Shedden, David, 26f
Sherman Anti-Trust Act (1890), 140
Shiffman, Kenneth S., 247
Shin, Inyoung
    See Hampton, Keith N.
Shiver, Jube, Jr., 117
Shleifer, Andrei, 115
Shor, Eran, 157
Showtime, 53, 72, 88, 95, 264f, 265
Sicardi, Arabelle, 103
The Siege, 240
Siegman, Alex, 170, 369
Sigal, Leon, 163
Signorielli, Nancy, 233, 247, 312, 313
    See also Gerbner, George
Silva, Eric O., 258
Silverstone, Roger, 36
Simmons, Russel, 246
Simmons, Steven J., 128
Simon, Paul, 358–359
Simon & Schuster, 70, 182
Simpson, O. J., 274
The Simpsons, 62, 94, 212, 253, 357
Sina, 82f
Sina Weibo, 329f, 335
Sinclair Broadcast Group, 87, 88, 154
Singer, Jane B., 297–298
Single-source promotions, 78
Sink, Alexander, 248, 249
Six Feet Under, 265
Skidmore, David, 357
Skiena, Steven, 157
Sky, 343
Skype, 26f, 116, 138, 139, 329f, 344
Slang, 186
Sling, 26f, 73

Smandych, Russell, 351, 356

Smart speakers, 5, 26f

Smartphones
  accessibility, 57
  adoption rates, 4–5, 4f
  developing nations, 116
  historical perspective, 26f
  mediatization effects, 315
  user demographics, 6f
  video technology, 46

Smedley, Audrey, 231

Smedley, Brian, 231

Smith, Aaron, 280

Smith, Bessie, 245

Smith, Christine B., 186
    See also McLaughlin, Margaret L.

Smith, Shawn, 280

Smith, Stacy L., 232, 233, 246, 247, 248f

Snapchat, 26f, 82f, 138, 187, 329f, 332

Snider, Mike, 88

Snow, David A., 325

Snow, Robert P., 316

Snowden, Edward, 311

So You Think You Can Dance, 158

Soap, 263f

Soap operas, 52, 295, 358

SOAPnet Network, 73

SoapOperaFan.com, 295

Social class and position
  advertising targeting, 259–261
  family-based situation comedies, 233, 249, 252–254
  ideological viewpoints, 196–197
  Internet participation and content creation, 293–294
  media content, 251–262
  media content decoding and interpretation, 271–275
  news media, 258–259, 272–273
  organized labor representations, 257–258
  public affairs programs, 259
  racial and ethnic diversity, 244
  "real" world representations, 225–228, 274
  reality television, 254, 256–257
  social inequality, 244, 251–262
  tabloid talk shows, 254, 256–257

Social constructionism, 17, 28, 35–36

Social constructs, 198

Social Content Ratings, 65

Social inequality
  gender stereotypes, 246–251
  racial and ethnic diversity, 192–193, 231–246

"real" world representations, 225–228, 274

sexual orientation, 262, 263–264f, 264–266

social class and position, 244, 251–262

Social media
  active users, 329f
  activity categories, 292–293
  addictive effects, 337–340
  agenda-setting effects, 309
  algorithmic power, 330–331, 333–334, 338
  authoritarian governments, 335, 353
  Black Lives Matter (BLM), 20–21
  book publishing, 182
  bots and trolls, 336
  campaign tactics, 323–324
  computational propaganda, 310
  copyright enforcement, 144
  economic and political impact, xv
  fake accounts, 335–336
  hate groups, 336
  ideological viewpoints, 193, 333
  international presence, 343
  media platforms, 65–66, 142–146
  news content, 80–81, 143, 146, 167, 331–332
  norms and conventions, 185–188
  owned versus organic activity, 65–66
  participation categories, 291–292, 292t
  political activism, 327–328
  political communication, 333–334
  pro-democracy movements, 368
  psychological factors, 339–340
  regulatory policies, 142–146, 336–337
  Russian election interference, 334–335
  self-censorship, 337
  self-disclosure and self-promotion, 338
  self-management concerns, 337–340
  self-policing practices, 146
  social connections, 338–340
  social media logic, 328–330
  social movements, 325
  user base, 367
  user contributions, 298
  user privacy protections, 144–145
  user self-selection, 333
  user tracking, 330
  user-generated content, 143, 328–330, 333, 338

Social movements, 18–21, 324–325

Social networks, 57

Social norms, 194–195, 229, 276

Social order, 201, 206

Social structures
  interpretive communities, 284–285
  media content decoding and interpretation, 271–275
  structure-agency dynamics, 12–14, 271–272
Social world
  civil rights movement, 19–20
  contemporary media models, 9–10, 10f, 16–18, 16f
  future changes and developments, 370
  media representations, 225–228, 274
  mediatization effects, 315–316
Socialization, 175–177, 179–185
Socializing, 292, 293
Socioeconomic status
  See Social class and position
Socolow, Michael J., 301
Sohu, 82f
Solitary listening, 43
Solotaroff, Paul, 194
Solowey, Fred J., 325
Sony Betamax, 59
Sony Music Entertainment, 70, 71f, 349
Sony Pictures Classics, 70
Sony Pictures Entertainment, 70
The Sopranos, 271
Soul Train, 44
Sound recordings
  content diversity, 90–91
  historical perspective, 25f, 27, 42–44
  ownership concentrations and changes, 70, 71f, 72,
    91–92
  political contributions, 118t
  social influence, 43–44
  streaming services, 72
  technological characteristics, 30f
  See also Music industry
SoundCloud, 138, 216, 296
Sousa, John Philip, 43
South Africa
  locally produced media content, 365–366
  popular music, 358–359
Soviet Union, 304
Spaiser, Viktoria, 310–311
Spangler, Todd, 141, 146
Sparks, Glen G., 302
Sparta, Christine, 264f
Spears, Britney, 44
Spectators, 291, 292t
Spectrum
  See Charter Communications (Spectrum)

Speed, 205, 206
Spielberg, Steven, 365
Spigel, Lynn, 50, 52
Spin tactics/spin doctors, 171, 321–324
Spin-offs, 93, 156, 160, 211
Spiral of silence theory, 309–311
Sports Center, 249, 250
Sports coverage, 249–250
Sports Illustrated, 68, 72
Sports Tonight, 249
Spotify, 42, 64, 72, 138, 348, 353
Spreadable media, 297
Springer, Jerry, 256
Springsteen, Bruce, 263f
Sproule, J. Michael, 301
Sputnik, 54
The Spy (Cooper), 238
Spyglass Intelligence, 72
Squires, Catherine, 231
Squires, James, 85
Sreberny, Annabelle, 360
Sreberny-Mohammadi, Annabelle, 357
Staged events, 34, 320, 322
Stallone, Sylvester, 206, 207
Standalone news websites, 331
Standard phone jacks, 40
Standardized communication protocols, 55
Standards of conduct, 186–188
  See also Professional norms and practices
Stanyer, James, 315
Star, 237f
Star India, 343
Star Trek, 227, 296
Star Trek: Discovery, 227
Star Wars film franchise, 63, 161
Stardom, 156–160
Starkman, Dean, 167
Starr, Paul, 45, 114
State-owned media, 86, 108, 114–116
Statista, 329f, 352, 353
Statt, Nick, 83
Steele, Catherine Knight, 280
Steiner, Linda, 286, 287
Stelter, Brian, 137
Stereotypes
  gender roles, 194–195, 238, 246–251
  organized labor representations, 257
  race and ethnicity, 194–195, 231, 232–233, 237–241,
    242f, 243–246, 281

reality television, 256

sexual minorities, 262, 264–266

shifting ideological viewpoints, 191

white-controlled production, 244–246, 247

working-class populations, 253–254, 256–257, 259–261

Sterne, Jonathan, 29

Sting, 358

Stock market/stock ownership, 202–203, 204f, 258

Stop-Loss, 208

Storey, John, 270

Stowe, Harriet Beecher, 238

Strate, Lance, 32

Straubhaar, Joseph, 358

Strauss, Jessalynn R., 288

Stravinsky, Igor, 43

Streaming services

audience share, 93, 94

audio recordings, 42–44

developing nations, 116

film entertainment, 46

gender diversity, 247

locally produced media content, 366

music industry, 72, 348, 352–353

ownership concentrations and changes, 72, 73

pay-for-play arrangements, 138

racial and ethnic diversity, 236f

ratings systems, 132

social media platforms, 80

subscriber fees, 85, 96

television entertainment, 54, 72, 73, 93, 95

tiered access arrangements, 138

vertical integration, 141–142

video entertainment, 46, 54, 72, 73, 95, 138

voice-activated smart speakers, 5

Strelitz, L., 357

Strömbäck, Jesper, 314, 315, 316–317

Structural racism, 20

Structure-agency dynamics, 12–16, 162, 271–272

Studio recordings, 43–44

Subscription services

historical perspective, 27f

music industry, 42

news media, 98

original programming, 81, 141

streaming services, 85, 96

telecommunications, 74

Walt Disney Company, 351f

Suddenly Susan, 241

Sullivan, Eileen, 108

Sullivan, John L., 269

Sullivan, Margaret, 143

Sully, 99

The Sun, 85

Sundar, S. Shyam, 269

Sunstein, Cass, 333, 334

Surveillance practices, 353, 370

Survivor, 94

Survivor: Heroes vs. Healers vs. Hustlers, 94

Survivor: Pulau Tiga, 94

Sutherland, Kiefer, 160

Swardson, Anne, 368

Syfy, 96

Synergy, 83

Syriana, 207

Tablets, 4, 4f, 6f, 26f, 57

Tabloid news, 85

Tabloid talk shows, 254, 256–257

Tai, Cordelia, 233

Talent search shows, 158

Tales of the City, 263f

Talk radio

Black Lives Matter (BLM), 21

motherhood, 213

programming diversity, 128–129

Talk shows, 163, 194, 208, 254, 256–257

Tang, Tang, 78

Tapper, Helena, 114

Taxi, 211

Taylor, Ella, 210, 211–212

Taylor, Phillip M., 135

Taylor, Robert W., 54–55

TBS, 73

Technological determinism, 28–29, 32–36

Technological momentum, 30–31

Technological solutionism, 222

Technology

See Digital technology

Techno-redemptive ideology, 222

Techno-utopianism, 56–57

Telecom Regulatory Authority of India, 354

Telecommunications

developing nations, 116

Facebook, 82–83, 354

Google, 82–83

political contributions, 118*t*

regulatory policies, 122

Telecommunications Act (1996), 122, 123*f*, 124, 130, 132

Telegram, 329*f*

Telegraph

historical perspective, 25*f*, 27, 38

social influence, 33–34

Teleguide, 59

Telemundo, 73, 96

Telenovelas, 358

Telephones

adoption rates, 27*f*

historical perspective, 25*f*, 27, 39–42, 41*f*

political contributions, 118*t*

See also Smartphones

Television

adoption rates, 4*f*, 27*f*

advertising, 50, 65, 81, 92–94

advertising dynamics, 99–100, 103–105, 104*f*

advertising-content connection, 261

agenda-setting effects, 308

animated comedies, 253

audience interpretation, 271–278

audience segmentation, 236–237, 237*f*

audience share, 93, 94

broadcast licenses, 147

changing American family, 210–212

competitive markets, 53–54

conglomeration impact, 84–85

connective devices, 3–4, 4*f*

controversial programming, 88–89, 93, 152, 210

copies and spin-offs, 93, 156, 160, 211

cultivation theory, 312–313

cultural codes, 271–272

digital technology, 50

domestic viewing context, 284–285

family audiences, 284–285

family-based situation comedies, 229, 233, 249, 252–254

fan communities, 296

fin-syn regulations, 140–141

gender diversity, 247–249

globalization impact, 343, 349

historical perspective, 25–26*f*, 27, 50–54

hit status, 159–160

ideological analysis, 193, 208, 210–213

imitated products, 153, 155–156

international perspectives, 276–278, 281–282

locally produced media content, 356–357, 365

marketing strategies, 50–51

media-focused programming, 208, 209*f*

new momism, 212–213

norms and conventions, 163

nostalgic programs, 211

online meaning making, 278–279

organized labor representations, 257–258

ownership concentrations and changes, 67, 68, 72, 73, 122, 123*f*

political contributions, 118*t*

political coverage, 318, 321–322

polysemic texts, 270–271

presidential debates, 318

prevalence, 3–4, 6*f*, 50

prime-time programming, 140–141, 152–153, 156, 210

production costs, 356

programming practices, 50–53, 72, 73, 92–94

racial and ethnic diversity, 232–233, 234*f*, 236, 237*f*, 241, 242*f*, 244, 274–278

ratings systems, 132

reality programming, 93–94, 156

reality television, 93–94, 156, 208, 210, 254, 256–257

regulatory policies, 50, 140–141

second screen use, 278–279

sexual minorities, 262, 263–264*f*, 264–265

shifting ideological viewpoints, 191

social influence, 32–35, 50–54

star power, 157, 159, 160

stereotypical portrayals, 194–195

streaming services, 54, 72, 73, 93, 95

technological characteristics, 30*f*

U.S. market share, 364

user demographics, 6*f*

vertical integration, 140–141

women's sports coverage, 249, 250

work-family programs, 211–212

See also Cable television

Temporospatial limits, 344

Tencent, 82*f*

Terrorist attacks, 135, 207, 240

Terrorist groups, 336

Terry, Herbert, 147

Tesla, Nikola, 59

Tewksbury, David, 307

Textbook publishers, 157–158

Texting, 26*f*

Thank You for Your Service, 208

That Certain Summer, 263f

Thatcher, Margaret, 87

The Economist, 86

The Night Of, 241

theyesmen.org, 287

Thirty Mile Zone, 165

thirtysomething,, 263f

This Is Us, 212, 237f

Thomas, Ryan J., 136

Thompson, Fred, 319

Thompson, John, 182

Thompson, Krissah, 264f

Thompson, Stuart, 324

Thompson, Susan, 302

Three Kings, 207

Throttling, 138, 139

Thussu, Daya K., 223

The Tick, 73

Tidal, 353

Tiered access arrangements, 138

Timberg, Craig, 142, 324, 332

Time, 68, 72, 88, 111

Time, Inc., 68, 72, 87

Time Warner

   conglomeration and integration, 66

   economic dynamics, 79

   film studios, 349

   global film industry, 70

   mergers, 136–137

   news coverage, 165

   ownership concentrations and changes, 66, 67, 68,
      70, 72, 73

TMZ, 165

TNT, 73

To Kill a Mockingbird, 239

Tobin, Ariana, 330

Today Show, 52

Toennies, Ferdinand, 302

Tolochko, Petro, 81

Tomlinson, John, 356

Toor, Skye, 149

Top Chef, 94

Top Gun, 205, 207

Toronto School, 32

Torres, Joseph, 244–245

Torres-Reyna, Oscar, 240

The Tortellis, 93

Totalitarian governments, 108

Townhall.com, 174

Trade Related Aspects of Intellectual Property Rights
   (TRIPS), 360

Trade unions, 273

Traditional mass media, 7–8, 8f, 65–66, 79, 350

   See also Media/mass media; Television

Traditional racism, 241

Traditional versus digital journalism, 331–332

Transamerica, 262, 264f

Transformers: Age of Extinction, 366

Transgender individuals, 199–200

   See also LGBTQ community

Transmission Control Protocol/Internet Protocol (TCP/
   IP), 55

Transnational consumer capitalism, 357–358, 360

Transnational nongovernmental organizations
   (NGOs), 343

Transnormative ideology, 200

Transparent, 95, 264f

Transportation Department, 127

Trash TV

   See Tabloid talk shows

Travel ads, 221

Treasury Department, 127

Tribune Company, 154

Trilling, Damian, 81

Triopoly, 82f

Triple Revolution, xv, 328

Troilo, Jessica, 254

Trolls, 310, 336

Trump, Donald

   campaign tactics, 323–324

   clickbait stories, 333

   election interference, 334–335

   fake news, 109, 310, 333, 336

   Internet use, 322

   journalistic attacks, 109, 154, 322

   media image, 318

   nationalistic rhetoric, 108–109

   net neutrality policy, 138

   presidential actions, 202

   presidential campaign, 87, 163, 174, 194, 323–324

   working-class voters, 251, 254, 310

   See also Russian election interference

Trump, Donald, Jr., 332

Trunomi, 144

truTV, 73

Tsfati, Yariv, 309

Tuchman, Gaye, 163, 164, 325
Tufecki, Zeynep, 21, 327, 334
Tuggle, C. A., 249
Tumblr, 329f
TuneIn, 138
Tunisia, 167, 215
Turner, Fred, 56
Turner, Graeme, xv, 282
Turner, Ted, 53
Turner Classic Movies, 73
Turow, Joseph, xv, 237, 331
TV-Stove, 51
Twenge, Jean, xv
20th Century Fox, 62, 68, 70, 141, 349
21st Century Fox, 62, 68, 72, 343
24, 160
24-hour cable news, 167
21 Jump Street, 156
Twitter
    advertising revenue, 82f
    Black Lives Matter (BLM), 20
    Black Twitter, 279–281
    book publishing, 182
    computational propaganda, 310–311, 335
    fake news, 142–143
    historical perspective, 26f
    ideological viewpoints, 193, 333
    international presence, 343
    media advocacy organizations, 149
    media platforms, 142–143
    news content, 143, 146, 167, 332
    norms and conventions, 185, 187
    online meaning making, 278–279
    owned versus organic activity, 65
    as political communication, 322, 333
    pro-democracy movements, 167, 368–369
    racial hatred, 336
    Russian election interference, 335
    self-censorship, 337
    streaming services, 80
    terrorist groups, 336–337
    tiered access arrangements, 138
    user contributions, 298, 333, 338
Twitter bots, 311, 334–336
Two and a Half Men, 212
2 Broke Girls, 93
Two-step flow of influence, 305–306
Tynes, Brendesha M., 244

Ugly Betty, 160
UN Conference on Freedom of Information, 361
UN Convention on the Protection and Promotion of the
    Diversity of Cultural Expressions, 365
Uncle Tom's Cabin (Stowe), 238
Uncommon Valor, 206
UNCTAD (United Nations Conference on Trade and
    Development), 345
Underground press, 325
Underwood, Carrie, 158
UNESCO (United Nations Educational, Scientific, and
    Cultural Organization), 362, 364, 365
Unilateral reporters, 136
Union organizations, 257–258, 273
United Church of Christ, 147
United Nations, 361, 362
United Nations Conference on Trade and Development
    (UNCTAD), 345
United Nations Educational, Scientific, and Cultural
    Organization (UNESCO), 362, 364, 365
United Nations World Summit on the Information
    Society (WSIS), 363
United Press International (UPI), 361
Universal Music Group (UMG), 70, 71f, 348
Universal Pictures, 65, 70, 96, 349
Universal Television, 96, 141
Unlicensed radio broadcasting, 117, 119–120
Unsolicited manuscripts, 181–182
Unwin, Tim, 355, 363, 369
U.S. Census Bureau, 27f, 227, 232, 234f, 252, 259
U.S. Constitution, 109–110
U.S. Department of Agriculture, 127
U.S. Department of Commerce, 363
U.S. Department of the Treasury, 127
U.S. Department of Transportation, 127
U.S. Energy Information Administration, 27f
U.S. press, 102
U.S. State Department, 368
USA Network, 73, 96
User-generated content
    creator characteristics, 293–294
    fan communities, 295–296
    motivational factors, 294–295
    news media, 167, 168
    participation categories, 291–293, 292t
    social media platforms, 143–144, 328–330,
        333, 338
    technological innovations, 46

Users
  active users, 9, 15, 269–272, 288–289, 306–307,
      329f, 357
  advertising-content connection, 98–100, 223–224, 330
  Black Lives Matter (BLM), 20–21
  celebrity-watching play, 282–283
  civil rights movement, 18–20
  communication models, 10f, 16f, 17
  content creation and distribution, 288–298
  demographic makeup, 6f
  family audiences, 284–285
  fan communities, 295–296
  film ratings systems, 297
  film technology, 45–46
  as gatekeepers and distributors, 296–298
  gatekeepers and distributors, 297
  global media industry, 366–369
  international audiences, 276–278
  Internet service providers (ISPs), 137–138
  interpretive resistance, 285–287
  media content decoding and interpretation, 271–278,
      286–287
  media platforms, 65–66
  norms and conventions, 185–188
  online meaning making, 278–279
  owned versus organic activity, 65–66
  personalized content delivery, 80
  political influence, 144–145
  polysemic texts, 270–271, 283–284
  privacy protections, 144–145
  reading romance novels, 283–284
  research background, 269–270
  second screen use, 278–279
  social constructionism, 35–36
  social media platforms, 80, 143–144
  standards of conduct, 186–188
  structure-agency dynamics, 15–16, 271–272
  tracking practices, 323–324, 330
  See also Internet
Usher, Nikki, 167, 168
Utada, Hikaru, 359
UTV/Bindass, 350f

Vaidhyanathan, Siva, 185
Vainikka, Eliisa, 294
Valenti, Jack, 364
Valeriya, 359
Values and belief systems, 191
van Cuilenburg, Jan, 111

van de Rijt, Arnout, 157
van Dijck, José, xv, 294, 328
van Dijk, Jan, 293
Vanity Fair, 177
Variable boundaries, 8–9
Variety shows, 52
Varner, Madeleine, 330
V-chips, 132
Ventura, Jesse, 319
Verizon
  advertising revenue, 82f
  competitive market, 42
  conglomeration and integration, 68
  economic dynamics, 78
  infrastructure conduits, 64, 74
  net neutrality policy, 137
  pay-for-play arrangements, 138
  regulatory policies, 41f
Verrier, Richard, 356
Vertical integration, 74, 77f, 83–84, 139–142
VH1, 156, 237f
Viacom, 67, 70
Viber, 329f
Vice Media, 73
Video game consoles, 4, 4f, 6f, 25f
Video games
  gender diversity, 247
  in-game advertising, 99
  racial and ethnic diversity, 234–235
  ratings systems, 134
  self-censorship, 132
Video streaming services, 5
  See also Streaming services
Videocassette recorders (VCRs), 25f, 46
Video-on-demand, 366
Videos
  digital technology, 26f, 46
  music industry, 65
  streaming services, 46, 54, 72, 73, 95, 138
Vietnam syndrome, 206–207
Vietnam War, 134–135, 206, 270, 307
Vimeo, 46, 296
Vincent, James, 145
Vincent, John, 250
Viral media, 297
Virtual behavior, 186–188
Virtual game worlds, 57
Virtual reality services, 26f
Virtual worlds, 57

Visual imagery
    See Photography; Television
Viva Valdez, 233
Vivendi media conglomerate, 348
Vliegenthart, Rens, 325
Vogue, 219, 233
The Voice, 94, 158
Voice-activated smart speakers, 5, *26f*
von Grumbkow, Jasper, 186
Vonderau, Patrick, xv
Voter registration, 334
Vox, 168
Voyager, 227

W3Techs, *347t*
Wagner, Kevin M., 327
Wagner, Kurt, 354
Wajcman, Judy, 35
Walejko, Gina, 293
Walker, Kent, 336
The Walking Dead, 65, *237f*, 241
Wall Street Journal, 68, 87, 105
Wallace, Mike, 262
Wallsten, Kevin, 309
Walmart, 134
Walt Disney Company
    conglomeration and integration, 62–63, 68, 76,
        78, 96
    consumer products, *351f*
    corporate holdings, *75–76f*, *350–351f*
    cross-media promotions, 78
    economic dynamics, 79
    film studios, 349, *350–351f*
    international presence, 350, *350–351f*
    media dominance, 64, 67
    ownership concentrations and changes, 67, 72, 73
    product portfolios, 70
    programming and distribution controls, 96, 141, 350
    publishing holdings, *351f*
    streaming services, 141
    subscription services, *351f*
    television channels, *350f*
    theme parks, 161, *351f*
Walt Disney Studios, 70, *350–351f*
Walters, Suzanna D., 281
Wang, Ting
    See Miller, Toby
Wang, Xiaopeng, 78
War films, 205, 206–208

"War of the Worlds" radio broadcast, 301
War Room, 297
Ward, Charles, 157
Warner Bros., 70, 73, 79, 141, 349
Warner Music Group, 70, *71f*, 349
Washington, Denzel, 240
Washington Post, 88, 105, 135, 167, 169, 322, 331
Wasko, Janet, 63
Watchdog groups, 235
Watts, Duncan J., 155
We Are Social, 367, *367f*
Weapons of mass destruction (WMD), 89, 207
Wearable technology, 57, 370
Weather Channel, 53, 96
Web 2.0, 57
Webb, Rebecca, 120
Weber, Max, 302
Websites, 185–188, *353t*
WeChat, *329f*
Weedon, Alexis, 183
The Weekly Standard, 87
Wei Wei, 359
Weibo, *329f*, 335, 353
Weinberg, Tamir, 127
Weinstein Company, 158
Weinthal, Benjamin, 368
Weixu, L.
    See Hampton, Keith N.
Welch, Jack, 84
Wellman, Barry, xv, 328
Wells, H. G., 301
Wenders, Wim, 365
West, Mae, 130
Western Electric, 40
Western imports, 355–359
Western Union, 38, 39, 121
Western wire services, 361
Westinghouse, 48
Westworld, 95, 210
Wharton, Robert M., 182
WhatsApp, 65, 138, *329f*, 354
White, Armond, 193
White, David Manning, 163, 297
White, Tiffany N., 280
White supremacy, 238
Whiteley, Paul, 310
Whiteness, 231
Whiteside, Erin, 243
Whittle Communications, 100

Who Wants to Be a Millionaire?, 94, 349
Whole Earth Catalog, 56, 222
Wibbitz, 169
Widdicombe, Lizzie, 186
WikiLeaks, 136
Wikipedia, 57, 353*t*
Will and Grace, 263*f*
Will.i.am, 323
Williams, Dmitri, 234, 235
Williams, Raymond, 31, 36
Willis, Bruce, 206
Willow Creek, 297
Wilson, Alan, 313
Wilson, Clint C., II, 231, 233, 238, 240, 245, 261
Wilson, Woodrow, 238
Windahl, Sven, 7
Winfrey, Oprah, 246
Winner, Langdon, 30, 31
The Wire, 264*f*
Wire services, 38
    See also Telegraph
Wireless technology, 47, 64, 116
    See also Radio broadcasting
Witschge, Tamara, xv
Wolfe, Alan, 193
Wolff, Edward N., 202, 258
Wolfsfeld, Gadi, 324, 327, 328
Womack, Ytasha, 227
Women
    Internet participation and content creation, 294
    interpretive resistance, 275–276, 285–286
    media content decoding and interpretation, 273–274, 286–287
    media representations, 247–249
    middle-class marketing strategies, 50–52
    reading romance novels, 283–284
    sports coverage, 249–251
    television viewing, 284
    See also Gender
Women's magazines, 218–219
Women's Media Center, 247
Wonder Years, 212, 254
The Wooing and Wedding of a Coon, 238
Woolley, Samuel C., 310, 334, 335
Worden, Steven K.
    See Snow, David A.
Wordsmith, 169
Work routines, 164–166

Work-family programs, 211–212
Working class population, 196–197, 251–254, 256–261, 273–274
Working Mother, 213
Working-class press, 101–102
World Bank, 343
World music, 345, 358–359
World of Dance, 237*f*
World of Warcraft, 57
World Trade Center terrorist attacks, 135, 207, 240
World Trade Organization (WTO), 287–288, 360
World War I
    European film industry, 45
    newsreel propaganda, 31
    radio broadcast restrictions, 47
    wartime propaganda efforts, 171, 304
World War II
    military press restrictions, 134
    newsreel propaganda, 31
    regulatory policies, 111, 114
    war films, 207–208
    wartime propaganda efforts, 304, 361
World Wide Web, 55–56, 328
Worldview, 191
    See also Ideologies
Worrell, Tracy R., 247
Written text
    See Print media
Wu, Michael, 291
Wu, Paulina, xv
Wu, Tim, 35, 38, 39, 40, 41, 45, 46, 48, 49, 50, 52, 53, 59–60, 80, 130, 131, 137, 139, 360, 364

Xbox, 234
XM radio, 26*f*
X-Men, 62, 63, 160
X-Men Apocalypse, 99
X-rated films, 132

Yahoo, 68, 82*f*, 353*t*
Yahyanejad, Mehdi, 368–369
Yarchi, Moran, 327
    See also Wolfsfeld, Gadi
The Yellow Menace, 238
Yelp, 82*f*, 297
Yes Men, 287–288
The Yes Men Fix the World, 288
Yglesias, Matthew, 332

Yin-Poole, Wesley, 235
Yoon, InJeong, 336
Yousman, Bill, 231
Yousman, Lori Bindig, 231
YouTube
    active users, 329f
    audience share, 94
    copyright enforcement, 144
    fake news, 142–143
    historical perspective, 26f
    ideological viewpoints, 193, 333
    media content, 80–81
    media platforms, 64, 65, 142–143
    misinformation dissemination, 332
    music distribution, 216, 348, 352–353
    political campaigns, 323
    political spin tactics, 322
    popularity, 352
    rap music, 215
    self-policing practices, 146
    technological innovations, 46, 57
    television and video entertainment, 95
    terrorist groups, 336
    tiered access arrangements, 139
    top websites and global rankings, 353t
    user-generated content, 46, 296, 333
YouTube Red, 81, 96
Yu, Nan, 243
Yuen, Nancy Wang
    See Chin, Christina B.

Zafirau, Stephen, 162
Zarkin, Kimberly A., 111
Zarkin, Michael J., 111
Zenith, 81
Zero-rated content, 138
Zhao, Shanyang, 280
Zines, 296, 325
Zuckerberg, Mark, 142, 143, 144, 334, 337
Zulu choral music, 358

ABOUT THE AUTHORS

 **David Croteau** is an Associate Professor Emeritus in the Sociology Department at Virginia Commonwealth University (VCU). He has also worked in VCU's Academic Learning Transformation Lab (ALT Lab), helping faculty incorporate new technologies into their teaching. He is the author of *Politics and the Class Divide: Working People and the Middle-Class Left.*

 **William Hoynes** is Professor of Sociology and former Director of the Media Studies Program at Vassar College in Poughkeepsie, New York, where he teaches courses on media, culture, and social theory. He is the author of *Public Television for Sale: Media, the Market, and the Public Sphere.*

Croteau and Hoynes are the coauthors of *Experience Sociology, The Business of Media: Corporate Media and the Public Interest,* and *By Invitation Only: How the Media Limit Political Debate.*